146
148
156
158
216
220
165
168
224
227
176
184
230
232
194
234
364
289
322
367
292
324
325
366
302
327
328
368
374

HOUSING DESIGN

HOUSING DESIGN
A MANUAL

BERNARD LEUPEN & HARALD MOOIJ

With contributions by:
Rudy Uytenhaak
Birgit Jürgenhake
Robert Nottrot
John Zondag

NAi Publishers

FOREWORD FOR THE FIRST DUTCH EDITION [2008]

Housing is not only a major part of the construction that takes place in the Netherlands, but also a major architectural challenge here. Dutch housing enjoys a fine reputation worldwide because of its high architectural quality and the numerous new design solutions architects have come up with over the last hundred years. Perhaps more than anywhere else in the world, housing in this country represents a challenge for designers. There is room for innovation and experimentation, which also offers young designers opportunities to build up their own practice. Indeed housing design is an important element of the architecture programme at the Faculty of Architecture of the Delft University of Technology. The Housing Design Chair aims to record the rich housing tradition of the Netherlands, hand it down and develop it further. Our chair programme, for instance, has conducted a great deal of research into design outlooks and housing concepts from the recent past. Studies into the work and ideas of Adolf Loos and Le Corbusier, the Russian Constructivists, Scharoun, Bakema, Alison and Peter Smithson, Team X and others have led to wonderful exhibitions and publications. Current design issues are also addressed in research and teaching, of course.

Publications such as *Frame and Generic Space* (Bernard Leupen's thesis research) and *Time-based Architecture* (Leupen, Van Zwol, Heijne) focus on aspects of the dwelling's flexibility and adaptability. This year [2008] will see the publication of an analytical report on the Vinex suburban districts in the *Vinex Atlas* and a design research project into density, *Cities Full of Space* (Rudy Uytenhaak). *Het woongebouw* (The Residential Building, by Jasper van Zwol), a book about significant residential buildings of the last century, will also soon be published, as well as the first issue of *DASH* (Delft Architectural Studies on Housing), a new series of publications on current design issues in housing.

What was missing until now was a 'handbook' more focused on the practice of design. *Housing Design* fulfils a long-cherished intention to produce a book that examines the design of housing in all its aspects. The knowledge and experience of the Chair of Housing Design were brought together and systematized in this in a clear way, in order to appeal to a broad audience of users: students and architects, but developers and clients as well. In this way we hope to provide impetus for a renewal of housing design in this country.

A major challenge awaits. Of all planned new construction project, over half are intended for areas that have until now remained unbuilt. Increasing densities and mobility in these areas call for a reassessment of the dwelling types that have been used hitherto. The other, steadily growing part of the challenge will have to be met through the renovation of existing residential areas. Adding, densifying and improving within an existing context form a huge challenge in terms of quality as well as quantity. These too call for new solutions that will make the existing residential areas more sustainable and give dwellings a longer lifespan.

Innovation begins with the knowledge of what is already there. The wealth of the principles already developed deserves to be studied again and again. Comparing and analysing solutions helps in selecting the right design principles for the new challenge. This book aims to provide a basis for this. It is based on the work of many. Bernard Leupen and Harald Mooij have collected all this and brought it all together with tireless dedication into an inspirational and clear handbook. The publisher's unconditional support proved a major motivation. Finally thanks are owed to BAM Vastgoed, for their indispensable and substantial financial contribution.

The knowledge gathered and developed in this book represents a significant part of the body of knowledge in the field of housing design as it has been developed or collected, for the most part, in the Netherlands. We consider the international dissemination of this knowledge, certainly at a time when more than half of the world's population resides in urban areas, to be of crucial importance. We hope to stimulate the international exchange of this knowledge so that debates taking place elsewhere may also be reflected in the debate in this country. In this we include both the dissemination and exchange of ideas in architecture practices abroad and in the Netherlands as well as the debate in knowledge centres and academic institutions.
We are confident that *Housing Design* will earn a place alongside such internationally renowned books as Federike Schneider's *Floor Plan Atlas* and Roger Sherwood's *Modern Housing Prototypes*. The strength of our book lies mainly in the extensive theoretical exposition of the typologies used, as well as on the breadth of themes addressed in this publication.

We wish you much reading enjoyment, and even more important, design enjoyment!

Dick van Gameren
Chair of Housing Design
Architecture Department of the Faculty of Architecture
Delft University of Technology

FOREWORD FOR THE SECOND, REVISED ENGLISH-LANGUAGE EDITION
FOREWORD FOR THE SECOND, REVISED EDITION, NOW TRANSLATED INTO ENGLISH

The highly successful publication of the first version of *Het ontwerpen van woningen* (in Dutch) has encouraged us to produce a second version , both revised and more extensive, this time accompanied by an English translation, *Housing Design*. Authors Bernard Leupen and Harald Mooij were ready and willing to compile this second, revised edition with great enthusiasm. The information collected and developed in this book represents a significant portion of the body of knowledge in the domain of housing design as developed or collected for the most part in the Netherlands. We consider a worldwide dissemination of this knowledge to be of major importance, cetainly in an age in which more than half the world's population is living in urban areas. With this book we hope to stimulate the international exchange of this knowledge and know-how, so that debate taking place elsewhere can also be reflected in the debate in the Netherlands. By this we mean dissemination and exchange of ideas in architecture practices here and abroad as well as debate in knowledge centres and academic institutions.
We feel that Housing Design is set to find a significant place alongside internationally renowned books such as Federike Schneider's *Floor Plan Atlas* and Roger Sherwood's *Modern Housing Prototypes*. The strength of our book lies primarily in the extensive theoretical foundation provided for the typologies used, as well as the broad range of themes presented in this volume.

Dick van Gameren
Chair of Housing Design
Architecture Department of the Faculty of Architecture
Delft University of Technology

INTRODUCTION

Housing design seems a simple task: everyone has lived in a home and so has at least the benefit of that first-hand experience. In practice as in teaching, however, the 100 m^2 of the average dwelling prove a challenging puzzle to solve, time and time again. The challenge becomes even more complex when multiple dwellings are stacked and linked to form residential buildings, especially when different types of dwellings are combined within a single building. Design becomes still more complicated when additional programmes are added, such as work space, retail premises, parking or leisure facilities. Finally, a residential building exists not in a vacuum, but as part of an urban network, a context. All in all, these are more than enough reasons to compile a book on housing design.

The scope of *Housing Design* extends beyond design-specific problems. It is meant to be a broadly applicable book about the design of dwellings–a handbook, as its subtitle indicates. This lends the book a certain ambition: to be a book you keep on hand as you design, prepare and develop new housing projects. As a handbook, this publication can be read in a variety of ways: you can read it like a textbook, from start to finish; you can navigate it using the matrices and pictograms; or you can leaf through it until an inspiring project catches your attention.
To ensure that the book can be read in all these different ways, we have given it a clearly defined structure. To make it broadly applicable, we have endeavoured to address the subject from as broad a perspective as possible. Eight chapters deal, each in turn, with dwelling as a phenomenon, with typology, with spatial development, with dwelling tectonics and materials and finally with the context in which dwellings are designed.
The first two chapters are descriptive in nature. The first examines what the dwelling is, in a physical as well as a philosophical sense. In order to understand what *a dwelling* is, as a place, we need to figure out what *dwelling* is, as something we do. Dwellings and the phenomenon of dwelling are concepts everyone knows, and everyone has an image in mind of what they are, yet they remain difficult to define. In order to better understand these concepts, we look at their evolution and transformation: dwelling in a changing society and dwelling and modernity are the main themes here.
The 'Typology' chapter deals with dwelling typology. This chapter sets out the framework for the chapters that follow. The concept of type used in this chapter is based on typology as an instrument of design. This concept of type encompasses such notions as the adaptation, combination and transformation of types. The two typologies explicated in this chapter (typology according to spatial configuration and typology according to material configuration)

form the backbone of the four following chapters. Typology according to spatial configuration is elaborated in the chapters 'Dwellings', 'Residential Building' and 'Urban Ensemble', while typology according to material configuration is elaborated in the 'Tectonics' chapter.
The 'Dwellings' chapter describes the spatial organization of the dwelling in relation to activity and place. The chapter then describes the configuration of the dwelling systematically, based on its width, depth and height. From this point on the chapters are project-oriented. A series of attractive examples from the Netherlands and abroad, most of them recent, guide the reader through the issues associated with housing design.
Complexity increases in the 'Residential Building' chapter, through the horizontal linking and vertical stacking of dwellings and the configuration of the residential building up to and including the dwelling access (the system in multistorey residential buildings needed to get from the communal entrance to the private front door).
In the 'Urban Ensemble' chapter, the configuration of the urban ensemble is described in relation to residential buildings and dwelling types. The assembling of separate dwellings or residential buildings into a greater urban whole has produced a range of identifiable types of morphological configuration. Using examples, the qualities of these various types are demonstrated, as a basis for new uses in future projects.
The 'Tectonics' chapter opens with a general introduction and explains why a book on housing design needs to include tectonics. The chapter is then divided into four sections dealing with the 'layers' that make up a building: 'Load-Bearing Structure', 'Skin', 'Scenery' and 'Service Elements'. These sections are again organized according to projects.
The penultimate chapter of the book deals with context and is in two parts. The first part describes ways of looking at a context. Concise instructions provide the reader with the tools to analyse, for instance, the morphology of an existing section of a city. The second half of the chapter reprises the rhythm of the book's project-oriented organization. In this section the focus is on the project. Here too the chapter examines a series of interesting projects from the Netherlands and abroad, each time placing the emphasis on the following question: What exactly was the challenge, in terms of the urban design preconditions the architect initially had to satisfy?
The book concludes with a chapter entitled 'The Design Process', which brings together many aspects from the previous chapters. This is achieved through the description of the design processes of three projects. This description is generously illustrated with original design sketches.

In order to make a distinction between the reading sections and the project discussions, we have used two different fonts. The reading texts are distinguished from the project descriptions through the use of a different colour. To help the reader navigate through the book, the sections in the various chapters open, where relevant, with an overview of the typology upon which each particular section is based. In many instances the typology is represented in a matrix. The types to be differentiated are indicated by pictograms. These pictograms then feature in the margins of the projects discussed. To distinguish them from other graphic elements, the pictograms are set in a different colour.

We would like to take this opportunity to thank the many people who contributed to the content of this book, in the first and second editions or in other ways. First there are the colleagues who have given us the benefit of their knowledge in the form of texts and comments. Rudy Uytenhaak, for instance, in his role as housing design practice professor, challenged us with his texts on tectonics, context and beauty. Robert Nottrot and John Zondag helped lay the foundations for the 'Dwellings' chapter, while Birgit Jürgenhake shared her knowledge of façades and the relationships between inside and outside; Vincent Ligtelijn made suggestions on the phenomenon of *place* in the work of Aldo van Eyck; finally, Cecile Calis assisted us in providing necessary structural details.
Dick van Gameren, as holder of the Chair of Housing Design at Delft University of Technology, stimulated us with his critiques and supported us at crucial moments. We obtained a great deal of illustration material from various architecture practices and institutions, whom we wish to thank for their cooperation. We also wish to thank our student assistants, Mohamad Sedighi and Alexander van Zweeden, who took care of the numerous analytical drawings with unflagging energy. No book is possible without a publisher and designer. A good working relationship with them is of the greatest importance. We therefore wish to thank Marcel Witvoet of NAi Publishers and designers Joost Grootens and Tine van Wel of Studio Joost Grootens.

Bernard Leupen, Harald Mooij

DWELLING

Cities and memory
In vain, great-hearted Kublai, shall I attempt to describe Zaira, city of high bastions. I could tell you how many steps make up the streets rising like stairways, and the degree of the arcades' curves, and what kind of zinc scales cover the roofs; but I already know this would be the same as telling you nothing. The city does not consist of this, but of relationships between the measurements of its space and the events of its past: the height of a lamppost and the distance from the ground of a hanged usurper's swaying feet; the line strung from the lamppost to the railing opposite and the festoons that decorate the course of the queen's nuptial procession; the height of that railing and the leap of the adulterer who climbed over it at dawn; the tilt of a guttering and a cat's progress along it as he slips into the same window; the firing range of a gunboat which has suddenly appeared beyond the cape and the bomb that destroys the guttering; the rips in the fish net and the three old men seated on the dock mending nets and telling each other for the hundredth time the story of the gunboat of the usurper, who some say was the queen's illegitimate son, abandoned in his swaddling clothes there on the dock.
As this wave from memories flows in, the city soaks it up like a sponge and expands. A description of Zaira as it is today should contain all Zaira's past. The city, however, does not tell its past, but contains it like the lines of a hand, written in the corners of the streets, the gratings of the windows, the banisters of the steps, the antennae of the lightning rods, the poles of the flags, every segment marked in turn with scratches, indentations, scrolls.
From: Italo Calvino, *The invisible cities* (1972)

On the surface, housing design seems a straightforward task. After all, society has a virtually constant need for new homes. Households are ever increasing in number and dilapidated dwellings need to be replaced by new homes that meet today's requirements. What's more, everyone knows instinctively what a dwelling is, simply because it is an indispensable part of every human life. We are born in a home; it's where we learn to walk and talk; it's where we grow up. We visit our friends' homes; we come home after outside activities. We move into at least one dwelling after leaving our parents' home and we may raise children of our own there. Even people who have no home–whether temporarily or for extended periods–know precisely what we mean when we say 'a dwelling'.

Yet there is wide variety in what the thought of 'a dwelling' conjures up to different people. Ask an Eskimo and a South African what a home is, and they might both answer in the same terms and yet be describing very different structures. Conversely, the same dwelling may have an entirely different meaning to someone who works at home or has a family as opposed to someone who only occasionally sleeps there. Our idea of a dwelling is defined by our individual frame of reference. We know the homes in which we have lived and the way we lived in them; we know the dwellings we have visited or those we have seen during our travels. And our notions about *dwelling*–something we do–and *dwellings*–places–are also influenced by the images and narratives we absorb from history, literature, paintings, film, photographs and exhibitions.

We know, for example, that nomadic peoples occupy their dwellings for a succession of short periods; some in vast structures they leave behind when they move on to find new housing somewhere else, others in lightweight tent structures they take with them and set up elsewhere. We know that the *log hogans* of the Navajos in Arizona contain a single, circular space, in which every spot has a specific ceremonial significance. The dwellings in Morocco's kasbahs cannot be considered separately from the dwellings that surround them, from the proximity of the souk and the mosque with which they form a unit. Among the Dogon in Mali, loam houses form a configuration of places and small volumes that bear symbolic parallels to the human body. And in Western countries a 'drive-in' dwelling offers its occupants optimal privacy as well as an anonymous connection between the home and the outside world. Different worlds with different cultural backgrounds, which have resulted in different expectations in terms of the organization of housing. Yet these are all dwellings. [→ 01-06]

Once we design housing and become conscious of the many variations in its significance and interpretation, the first question we need to address is just what a dwelling is. What is it that makes a dwelling a dwelling?

One dictionary definition of a dwelling is 'a house, or part of a house, in which one lives'. This definition carries an important implication:

01

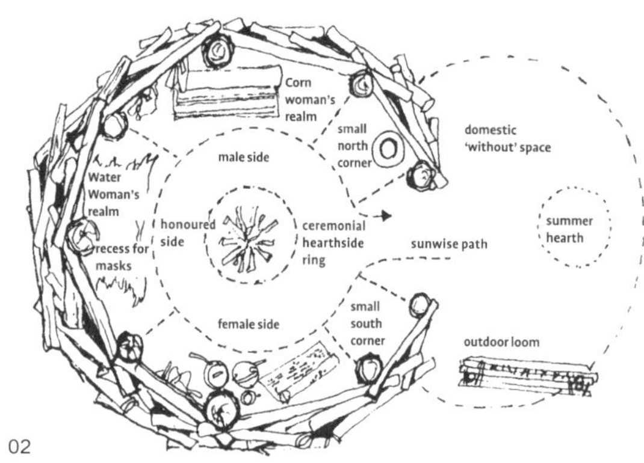
Corn
woman's
realm
small
north
corner
domestic
'without' space
male side
Water
Woman's
realm
honoured
side
ceremonial
hearthside
ring
summer
hearth
sunwise path
recess for
masks
female side
small
south
corner
outdoor loom
02

03

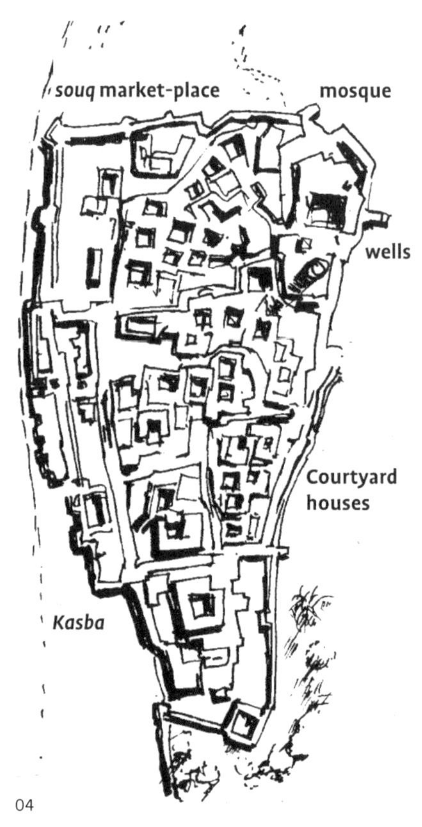
souq market-place
mosque
wells
Courtyard
houses
Kasba
04

05

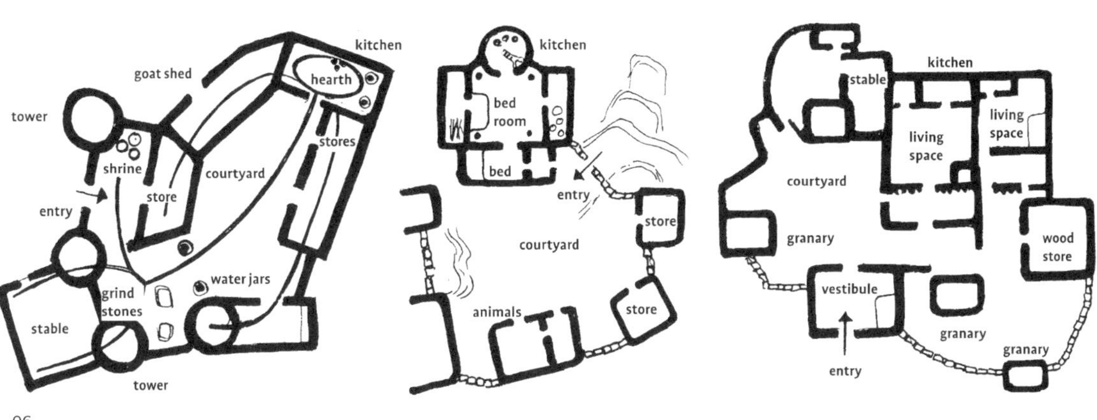

06

01 Nomad dwelling. While temporary and limited in size, the tent structure meets the housing needs of its occupants.
02, 03 Plan and interior of a *log hogan*
04 Plan of a Moroccan kasbah
05, 06 Dogon dwellings in Mali. Aerial photo and plans.

not only is the dwelling distinct from other places – where one does *not* live – but the reverse is also true: a place, a house, only becomes a dwelling once it is lived in. Occupants, not designers, make the house a dwelling, a home, simply by living – dwelling – there. How do they do that? What happens to turn a place, a space, a tent or a house into a home? In other words, what does it mean to dwell?

DWELLING AND PROTECTION

Around 1100, a Flemish monk in an English monastery scribbled a sentence on the cover of a manuscript, probably just to try out his quill: '*Hebban olla vogala nestas hagunnan hinase hic enda thu wat unbidan we nu.*'[1] Nine hundred years later, these words taken from an old Dutch love song are considered the romantic wellspring of Dutch literature. Even today the Dutch still use the expression 'building a nest' in the sense of starting a family and setting up a home for that purpose.

1 Literal translation: 'All the birds have started nests except me and you, what are we waiting for.'

Birds build a nest; rabbits dig a warren, foxes a den. They are not constantly doing this, nor do they remain in the shelter they construct all their lives. The instinct to withdraw to a sheltered abode is directly linked to the birth and raising of offspring. Adult animals are sufficiently armed against the deprivations and dangers of the outside world, but their dwelling provides protection in periods of vulnerability. Once the young are strong enough to face the dangers on their own, both they and their parents abandon the family nest.

Humans are far less equipped than animals to face the deprivations and dangers of their immediate surroundings. Additional shelter is a necessity not just to raise children in safety but for everyday self-preservation. We seek this in the first place in clothing, and secondly in a larger envelope closed off from the outside world. We initially did this in holes in the ground and in caves, but as technology advanced, we moved on to structures – built by ourselves or by others – increasingly better suited to our needs.

One of the first things a dwelling does, therefore, is create a division between a controllable world inside and an uncertain world outside. As we spend more time in it, this inner world becomes larger; we attach greater importance to it; the dwelling becomes not just a shelter but a place of residence. Its space is adapted and arranged to serve this residence: the inner world acquires more and more significance. Shutting out the outside world makes it possible to create our own living environment – a self-made habitat whose occupants can shape their own lives as they see fit.

The more consciously and explicitly they do this, the more 'lived in' the home becomes. In that sense the phenomenon of dwelling might be seen as a form of the art of living:

Some dwellers simply understand the art of dwelling better than others.

For dwelling is an art, at least if we use the term in the sense Aristotle gives it. It is an operation in which the goal coincides with its performance, as in dance or theatre. And as the dancer reveals himself in the dance, in spite of the fact that he knows his actions are bound by a choreography, so is the dweller himself explicitly present in his movements, even as his self-expression is tempered by the form in which his movement is contained.[2]

Self-expression, made possible by self-chosen separation, is tempered by this separation. Equally, the limits of self-actualization are defined by the size and shape of the envelope. Protection against the outside world is also a constraint on the individual domain – the freedom found in the personal world also a limitation on that freedom.

Indeed this can make a dwelling seem oppressive and give its occupants a sense more of confinement than of comfort. In that respect, it is remarkable how many conceptions of ideal, desirable or even paradisiacal states depict humans without clothing or shelter and in harmony with nature, living among the beasts with no protection of any kind. These seem to suggest that we would be truly happy only if that protection we so cherish were unnecessary. [→ 07]

From inside the dwelling, the boundary with the outside world can now be approached and crossed from the other side, in search of contact, pleasure, work or adventure. The protective envelope becomes a point of departure towards the freedoms of the world outside. The ease with which the interaction between the private world inside and the desired elements outside can be achieved determines to a large extent the occupants' enjoyment of their home and their potential for self-actualization.

DWELLING AND IDENTITY

This actualization of an individual identity, according to the German philosopher Martin Heidegger, is the true essence of dwelling. Based on ontology (the 'study of being') Heidegger attempted to decipher the meaning and the nature of being and of things, investigating the origin of linguistic concepts along the way. In his essay 'Building Dwelling Thinking'[3] he traces the meaning of the German word *bauen*, 'to build', back to its etymological root, the High German word *buan*, which also means 'to dwell'. In their original meaning, building and dwelling prove to be inextricably linked to each other: building is related to dwelling; dwelling implies building.

And Heidegger goes further: even the conjugations *ich bin*, 'I am', and *du bist*, 'you are', of the German verb *sein*, 'to be', can be traced back to the same root word, *buan*.[4] In this, based on its root meaning, he imparts dwelling with an existential dimension as well: people *are* because they dwell, unified in the ancient word for building;

2
H. Hoeks, 'Wonen als grensverkeer', in: E. Wils, *Wonen in Indië* (The Hague: Tong Tong Foundation, 2001).

3
Martin Heidegger, 'Bauen Wohnen Denken' (1951), transl. Albert Hofstadter, in: *Poetry, Language, Thought* (New York: Harper & Row, 1971), 143–161.

4
Other words in various North European languages show a kinship with this High German ancestor: in Norwegian the word for 'to build' is *bygge*, a building is a *bygnig* and a *by* is a city. At the start of the twentieth century, Russian artists Vladimir Tatlin and Alexander Rodchenko championed new forms of domesticity under the slogan '*novyi byt*', see H. Heynen and G. Baydar, *Negotiating Domesticity: Spatial Productions of Gender in Modern Architecture* (London/New York: Routledge, 2005). Heidegger himself makes a link with 'neighbour' (*Nachbar*), 'he who dwells nearby', so that the word implies a certain solidarity, living together in the same 'neighbourhood' (*Nachbarschaft*).

07

07 Hieronymus Bosch, *The Garden of Earthly Delights*, 1480–1490

dwelling and building are a form of self-realization (*Darstellung*) that shapes earthly existence (*Dasein*).

Furthermore, *buan* here connects the meaning of building, in the sense of putting up edifices, with cultivating the land, fencing in and taking care of things that grow. It was only later that these two meanings diverged, so that the sense of dwelling vanished from the definition of building we know today. It is this loss of meaning that Heidegger observes in the ways twentieth-century civilization dwells and builds.

The essence of building, he argues, is to let dwell; to build means to bring forth places on earth where people dwell. This applies to the building of houses but also of bridges, squares and other non-residential structures; they all belong to the domain of dwelling, or as Heidegger puts it:

Building and thinking are, each in its own way, inescapable for dwelling. The two, however, are also insufficient for dwelling so long as each busies itself with its own affairs in separation instead of listening to one another. They are able to listen if both – building and thinking – belong to dwelling, if they remain within their limits and realize that the one as much as the other comes from the workshop of long experience and incessant practice.[5]

Although the period Heidegger was writing in (an era of reconstruction in the aftermath of the Second World War) was marked by severe housing shortages, he identifies the real housing problem by observing that 'mortals ever search anew for the nature of dwelling, that they must ever learn to dwell'.[6] And, he says: 'Only if we are capable of dwelling, only then can we build.'[7]

5
Heidegger, 'Bauen Wohnen Denken', op. cit. (note 3), 160–161.

6
Ibid., 161.

7
Ibid., 160.

DWELLING AND THE HOUSING ENVIRONMENT

We live in a dwelling, but not just there. We also live in a street, in a village or in a city, in the woods, in the countryside, in the mountains or by the sea; in a province, a country, on a continent and on earth; in a suburb or a city centre, near the ring road, next to a shopping centre and close to friends. Dwelling takes place as part of a greater whole, in an environment that defines the experience of dwelling at varying levels. While *the dwelling* – the place – effects a separation between inside and outside, *dwelling* – the phenomenon – takes place on both sides of this line of separation. How you get from home to work, where you do your shopping, where you go out and where you meet up with friends – all of this is part of dwelling in the larger sense. Dwelling is implicitly contained in a social context, in a human society.

Indeed, the way dwelling is shaped, as well as the relationships between dwelling and other social activities, is significantly linked to culture. Local weather conditions, patterns of social behaviour,

For my parents, that house with its weird bays and its windows scarcely bigger than shooting slits must have been a dream come true. They were the first occupants, the cement was not dry in the mortar courses when they followed their simple furniture up the stairs. It was not the new street that was important to them, not the neighbourhood and certainly not the neighbours, who were all new and strangers to each other, but who from day one were busy saying hello, arranging meetings, paying visits, telling stories, doing mutual favours, organizing their lives to make them congenial and cheerful and worthwhile. As far as they could, my parents withdrew from all social intercourse. It wasn't people, it was the house itself from which they expected security and happiness, the roof, the ceiling, the walls, bricks and mortar.
I'm quite sure they entered it that first time with the firm intention of becoming one with every cranny and skirting board, so that it would not only socially, but biologically impossible ever to tear them away. For them it was an advantage that the house was dark and poky, because its function was to be as little as possible like the rest of the world.
Our neighbourhood had been planned in the Depression by the city's strong men, patriarchs with a social conscience who saw it as their sacred duty to give the population four walls and a roof over their heads. But only in theory did they recognize people's right to accommodation according to their own requirements and taste. Or else they would have given us residents light, space and big windows instead of subjecting us to a geometrically pure street plan, a succession of squares, shops, bathhouses and doorways which one could traverse in only one direction and a house design that was so compelling that not so much as a chair, let alone a table or a settee, could be placed in a spot which the power-that-be considered socially irresponsible.
The streets were distinguished solely by the house fronts. Some undulated and finished up in sharp right angles, others started out straight but converged in series of round tower, crowned with battlements, as if the Middle Ages had paid a flying visit. The bricks had been laid in the strangest shapes to create a fascinating pattern of lines and shapes, not for the benefit of the individual houses or their residents, but as a constituent part and embellishment of the whole, the street, the neighbourhood aesthetics. Roof tiles, window frames, gutters, staircases, even the house numbers seemed intended in the first instance as ornaments. They were not ours and never would be; we were simply allowed to live behind them.[1]

[1] H.M van den Brink, *On the Water*, translated by P. Vincent (New York: Grove Press, 2001), 8–10.

traditions, religion and economic interests determine to a large degree which activities take place on either side of the boundary between inside and outside. These do not vary simply from country to country: even the same city will contain a great variety of highly divergent housing environments, from quiet residential neighbourhoods with parks and a school to busy traffic arteries lined with apartment blocks, shops and other facilities. Different parts of the city can also display significant differences in standards of living: luxury developments or stately urban districts on the one hand and impoverished areas or slums on the other.

These differing housing environments were built at different times, according to different notions about the needs of residents and the organization of activities in the city – and sometimes without any specific notions at all. Ultimately, however, what all of these housing environments share is an interaction between the world their residents create for themselves and activities elsewhere in the city. Indeed the quality of a housing environment, to a significant degree, lies in the access it provides to the facilities its residents require.

DWELLING AND SOCIAL CHANGE

Changes in the social organization of our activities are often directly related to the use of the home and its significance for dwelling. The industrialization of Europe in the nineteenth century, for instance, brought with it major changes to the daily lives of the middle class. Prior to this, the home, which consisted of only a few rooms in spite of often large families, was often also the place where its occupants plied their trade. It was usually a scene of hustle and bustle and it afforded little privacy, if any.[8]

The advent of industry changed all this. For the first time, a division between home and workplace was created on a mass scale: the man was out of the house during the day, in the public world, while the woman kept the home and took care of the children. After work the man would go home, that is to say to a place he did not share with the public world. This division had major implications for the meaning of the home in nineteenth-century society. This traditional idea is the reason, for instance, that late into the twentieth century the home was still regarded as the woman's domain, a place that was homely, soothing and private, in contrast with the public, 'manly' outside world. These opposing connotations had not been nearly so marked prior to industrialization, and yet afterwards it would be a very long time before women were accepted into the 'public' sphere, or men could carry out home decoration or housekeeping work with any degree of respect.[9]

In the rise of the increasingly well-to-do middle class during the nineteenth century, Walter Benjamin sees the emergence – for the

8
W. Rybczynski, *Home: A Short History of an Idea* (London: Penguin Books, 1986), 28.

9
Heynen and Baydar, *Negotiating Domesticity*, op. cit. (note 4), 11.

08

08 H.H. Richardson, Glessner House, 1885–1887, Chicago, library

first time in history–of the private individual, who creates his private world at home in contrast to his public life outside it [←08]:

The private individual, who in the office has to deal with realities, needs the domestic interior to sustain him in his illusions . . . In the interior, he brings together remote locales and memories of the past. His living room is a box in the theatre of the world . . . The interior is not just the universe of the private individual; it is also his étui.[10]

10
Walter Benjamin, *The Arcades Project* [*Das Passagen-werk*], transl. Howard Eiland and Kevin McLaughlin (Cambridge, MA: Belknap Press of Harvard University Press, 1999), 19–20.

Benjamin sees in the endeavours of the nineteenth-century bourgeois a yearning for a deeper meaning of dwelling, in which home and occupant are entirely attuned to each other:

The original form of all dwelling is existence not in the house but in the shell. The shell bears the impression of its occupant. In the most extreme instance, the dwelling becomes a shell. The nineteenth century, like no other century, was addicted to dwelling. It conceived the residence as receptacle for the person, and it encased him with all his appurtenances so deeply in the dwelling's interior that one might be reminded of the inside of a compass case, where the instrument with all its accessories lies imbedded in deep, usually violet folds of velvet.[11]

11
Ibid., 220.

THE RISE OF MASS HOUSING CONSTRUCTION

When Benjamin wrote this, the nineteenth century had been over for some time. The rise of industry in the nineteenth century had had a very dramatic impact not just on the individual's perception of the home but also on the city and on housing. Industrialization led to a mass migration of people in search of work in the city. The great agricultural crisis in Europe around 1880 accelerated this process of urbanization. The poor housing conditions of the new working class in the emerging industrial cities was initially only the purview of city planners and engineers involved in sewer management and the supply of drinking water. A few exceptions aside, it was only at the start of the twentieth century that architects would begin to take an interest in the construction of working-class housing. We can find famed projects from this era in places like Vienna (Karl Ehn's Karl-Marx-Hof) and the Spaarndammerbuurt in Amsterdam ('Het Schip' by Michel de Klerk).

In the 1930s, working-class housing construction moved to the top of the political agenda. In various European countries, progressive architects joined forces to produce optimal designs. Inspired by the great leaps achieved by the exact sciences as well as by the successes of mass production and the time-and-motion studies on which it was based, housing design became a science. Moscow, Berlin, Frankfurt, Rotterdam, Amsterdam, Paris: in all these places, as well as others, studies were carried out, designs produced and buildings constructed according to the new principles of modernism and functionalism.

Djerzinski had lived on the rue Frémicourt for ten years, during which he had grown accustomed to the quiet. In 1993 he had felt the need for a companion, something to welcome him home in the evening. He settled on a white canary. A fearful animal, it sang in the mornings though it never seemed happy. Could a canary be happy? Happiness is an intense, all-consuming feeling of joyous fulfillment akin to inebriation, rapture or ecstasy. The first time he took the canary out of its cage, the frightened creature shit on the sofa before flying back to the bars, desperate to find a way back in. He tried again a month later. This time the poor bird fell from an open window. Barely remembering to flutter its wings, it landed on a balcony five floors below on the building opposite. All Michel could do was wait for the woman who lived there to come home, and fervently hope that she didn't have a cat. It turned out that she was an editor at Vingt Ans and worked late; she lived alone. She didn't have a cat.

Michel recovered the bird after dark; it was trembling with cold and fear, huddled against the concrete wall. He occasionally saw the woman again when he took out the garbage. She would nod in greeting, and he would nod back. Something good had come of the accident–he had met one of his neighbors.

From his window he could see a dozen buildings–some three hundred apartments. When he came home in the evening, the canary would whistle and chirp for five or ten minutes. Michel would feed the bird and change the gravel in its cage. Tonight, however, silence greeted him. He crossed the room to the cage. The canary was dead, its cold white body lying on the gravel.

He ate a Monoprix TV dinner–monkfish in parsley sauce, from their Gourmet line–washed down with a mediocre Valdepeñas. After some hesitation, he put the bird's body into a plastic bag, which he topped off with a beer bottle, and dumped in the trash chute. What was he supposed to do–say mass?

He didn't know what was at the end of the chute. The opening was narrow (though large enough to take the canary). He dreamed that the chute opened onto vast garbage cans filled with old coffee filters, ravioli in tomato sauce and mangled genitalia. Huge worms, as big as the canary and armed with terrible beaks, would attack the body, tear off its feet, rip out its intestines, burst its eyeballs. He woke up trembling; it was only one o'clock. He swallowed three Xanax. So ended his first night of freedom.

From: Michel Houellebecq, *The Elementary Particles* (1998)

Their architects came together to form the Congrès Internationaux d'Architecture Moderne, CIAM for short.

TRENDS AND DEVELOPMENTS

The consolidation of housing construction as part of the modernization of society brought its own problems. New developments succeeded one another closely and at an ever-increasing pace, influencing modes of living and thinking about dwelling throughout the course of the twentieth century. These developments continue to this day, all focused on the organization of activities on both sides of the dividing line between inside and outside.
First there was an observable evolution in the course of which dwelling seemed to turn inward. Connecting homes to a central supply of drinking water meant people no longer had to walk to a collective pump to get water. The evacuation of waste water through the sewers made communal toilets obsolete. Once every home was connected to the gas mains and the coal stove had been replaced by gas fires or central heating, people stopped relying on the coalman. Going to the public baths also became a thing of the past once showering at home became an option. Cables now deliver individual electricity, radio, television, telephone and Internet, maintaining contact with the outside world from inside the home.[12]
Yet the outside world has penetrated the home at the same time. The use of all these services can be measured, so that suppliers garner information about their customers' habits. Advertising and commerce come right into the home to tell people what they should buy or how they should live. In this context, in fact, it has been said that the private sphere has been colonized.
In addition, activities that used to take place inside the home have been shifted outside. We have already touched on the relocation of the workplace outside the home–just for men in the nineteenth century, but later more and more women would be working outside the home. The home has become a place for domestic chores and togetherness, after work is completed elsewhere. Schools and other educational institutions have also become increasingly generalized, so that children and young adults spend increasing periods of time out of the house. Another trend has been the relocation of activities as a result of the expansion of health care. The sick are increasingly cared for outside the home, partly because there are fewer people at home to take care of them. For the same reason, the care of elderly members of the family has been delegated to nursing homes. Birth and death also occur less and less in the home, so that the home is losing significance as a domain for all-encompassing dwelling and living. An additional trend has been the steady decrease in population density. The number of one- and two-person households grew exponentially during the

12
Willem Koerse discusses these changes and their impact on dwelling in the Netherlands in greater detail in his essay 'Over wonen, woning en privacy', in: *Architectuur als decor. Filosoferen over de gebouwde omgeving* (Amsterdam: Thoth, 1992).

second half of the twentieth century. Thanks to the rise in the standard of living, one or two people now live in dwellings that not so long ago housed entire families with seven or more children, including grandparents and other relatives in need. The square footage of housing per person has increased dramatically.
As a result, for a growing number of people, the dwelling has gradually ceased to be the place where we come home to a family setting: in it we find at most one person, or no one at all. The dwelling has become less a 'home' and more a place of transit, like the other places we pass through over the course of a day. The 'multipurpose trip' has become the norm: people no longer go home first after each activity. This has served to undermine the connection with our own place of residence: people have become less oriented towards social cohesion in and around the home. The more educated we are, the more time we spend with colleagues and friends in other parts of the city rather than with our immediate neighbours, in regard to whom we most jealously cherish our privacy.
At the same time, young one- and two-person households display a strong affinity towards venues 'in town': pubs, restaurants, theatres, cinemas. People are often out of the house even at night. In such households, dwelling has been relocated even more to the world outside, to the other side of the divide created by the home. Dwelling in fact seems to take place more and more independently of the dwelling itself.
This has made a dwelling and a housing environment increasingly interchangeable for these households. The dwelling as a ready-made object serves as a temporary abode for an outer-directed existence, and in that sense becomes almost akin to a hotel room in which we stay for a given period of time. When external circumstances or changing requirements make the abode less suitable, we abandon it just as casually for another readymade dwelling somewhere else. The freedom that this independence from the dwelling affords has gone hand in hand with a certain loss of the 'sense of home'. When dwelling is spread across many places outside the home, it is impossible to find dwelling unified as a whole in any single place. 'Homeless' dwelling also implies a certain restlessness, a vagabond search that seems most prevalent among young two-income couples.[13]
A more recent trend has been the rise in work at home. A growing number of self-employed professionals, and the ways technology has made it possible to stay in touch with the world from home, have brought the workplace back into the home. A different kind of workplace, in a different home, in a different age and with a different occupant.
At the same time there has been a recent increase in new housing demand for older one- and two-person households. Longer life expectancies, higher standards of living and an aging population have meant a rise in the number of active older people willing to

13
Koerse, 'Over wonen, woning en privacy', op. cit. (note 12), 22.

change homes. Immigration has also increased diversity in the number of different dwelling cultures. Dwelling patterns from South America, Africa, the Middle East and Asia are adjusting in their own ways to housing built in the Netherlands. It seems only a matter of time before these imported customs lead to new housing built specifically to accommodate their dwelling requirements.

An important point to make is that the trends and tendencies outlined here have not taken place separately or in sequence, but diffusely and simultaneously. 'Homeless' dwelling exists alongside the timeless family home, working at home simultaneously with almost never being home because of work somewhere else. The list is not complete: new occasions and possibilities for change are emerging all the time. Dwelling is subject to a continuous process of evolution, even as a number of constants remain applicable.

DWELLING AND MODERNITY

According to Hilde Heynen, the sense of homelessness described above is a defining aspect of modernity as it has been conceived since the early twentieth century. Modernity alludes to the experience of living in a society driven by development and change, a society no longer dominated by a generally accepted tradition. New developments offer exciting possibilities and perspectives, but because the world changes so fast as to undermine all certainties and established values, the result is confusion, and the individual finds it difficult to feel at home anywhere. To Heynen, modernity is also 'marked by a moment of ambivalence: the appetite for progress, growth and emancipation on the one hand, melancholy about and nostalgia for what is being irretrievably lost on the other'.[14] Or as Marshall Berman puts it:

To be modern is to find ourselves in an environment that promises us adventure, power, joy, growth, transformation of ourselves and the world and, at the same time, that threatens to destroy everything we have, everything we know, everything we are.[15]

Uncertainty and discontinuity are necessary conditions for change, progress and the subversion of the stuffy conventions of the past. And while the home stands for security and domesticity, Heynen argues, the perception of modernity is by definition not homelike. Modernity and 'feeling at home' are by nature polar opposites. It is therefore no surprise that the writers, artists and architects of the Modern Movement, in the early twentieth century, focused so much of their energy on 'subverting' this idea of dwelling. [→ 09-10] The bourgeois, nineteenth-century notion of the home as a lined case for its occupant, as a depository of personal possessions in darkly upholstered rooms, was consequently swept aside to make way for radically new forms of dwelling, associated with new forms of freedom:

For it is the hallmark of this epoch that dwelling in the old sense of the

14
Heynen and Baydar, *Negotiating Domesticity*, op. cit. (note 4), 1.

15
Marshall Berman, *All That Is Solid Melts Into Air: The Experience of Modernity* (New York: Penguin Books, 1982), 15.

09

10

11

09, 10 B. Taut, reforming a middle-class living room, 1923
11 L. Mies van der Rohe, Glashochhaus, 1919–1921, maquette

word, where security had priority, has had its day. Giedion, Mendelsohn, Le Corbusier turned the abiding places of man into a transit area for every conceivable kind of energy and for waves of light and air. The time that is coming will be dominated by transparency.[16] [← 11]
New designs succeeded one another at breakneck speed, inspired by new production methods, new materials, new domestic products and new ideas about new ways of living. A new home meant an entirely new lifestyle, which was often designed by the architect in the form of a fully furnished interior. Periodicals were launched to disseminate the new ideas among the public at large. In the Netherlands, the Stichting Goed Wonen (Good Living Foundation), in an effort to raise the tone of working-class homes, published an eponymous magazine that, using photos of noteworthy contemporary homes, aimed to teach its readers how they should – and especially how they should not – be decorating and using their homes. Anything that reeked of the nineteenth-century bourgeois dwelling was dismissed as old-fashioned and dull.

But there were other voices. As early as 1910 Adolf Loos had railed against the craze for innovation among artists and architects of the Vienna Secession, who aimed to help mankind out of its supposed misery by imposing new modes of dwelling. In his now famous words, Loos distinguished architecture from the arts and championed the occupant's comfort:

The house has to please everyone, contrary to the work of art which does not. The work is a private matter for the artist. The house is not. The work of art is brought into the world without there being a need for it. The house satisfies a requirement. The work of art is responsible to none; the house is responsible to everyone. The work of art wants to draw people out of their state of comfort. The house has to serve comfort. The work of art is revolutionary; the house is conservative. The work of art shows people new directions and thinks of the future. The house thinks of the present. Man loves everything that satisfies his comfort. He hates everything that wants to draw him out of his acquired and secured position and that disturbs him. Thus he loves the house and hates art.[17]

Whereas the Modern Movement and modernist architecture are now identified with a specific period in the early twentieth century, this is not at all true of the idea of modernity. Modernity stands for an orientation towards the future that will be different from the present as well as from the past.

16 Walter Benjamin, 'Die Wiederkehr des Flaneurs', quoted in Hilde Heynen, *Architecture and Modernity: A Critique* (Cambridge, MA: MIT Press, 1999), 114–115.

17 Adolf Loos, 'Architecture' (1910), quoted in Roberto Schezen, Kenneth Frampton and Joseph Rosa, *Adolf Loos: Architecture 1903–1932* (New York: Monacelli Press, 1996).

DESIGNING DWELLINGS

What does all this mean for the designer? We know that it is the occupant who makes the house a home by dwelling in it. The architect merely designs the envelope within which this dwelling takes place.

Just what happens in there is largely unpredictable, or at the very least impossible to define with any precision. Who the occupants will be, how long they will stay and the degree to which they situate the spheres of dwelling and work within the home is usually not known in advance.

We also know that to build brings forth places in which to dwell. The designer anticipates these places, and therefore has to form an idea of what kind of places these are to be. These places are where the occupants will later demonstrate their art of living, within the constraints placed upon them by the envelope.

The architect creates places in which to dwell but also sets constraints upon this. The completed design offers opportunities for the emergence of certain forms of dwelling and hinders others. Every wall, floor, opening and measurement of space plays a role in defining – intentionally or not – the possibilities inherent within the home. Architects are outlining these possibilities as they create their design, with every line they add to their drawings. The freedom of potential habitation, to a significant degree, is already circumscribed in a dwelling's floor plan and cross sections. So architects have to consider very carefully which forms of habitation they want to accommodate in their design, and which forms they exclude in the process. It is within this crucible that their first choices are forged. Whether they aim to radically reform the home, as the modernists did in the early twentieth century, to design a dwelling as a straitjacket for a precisely defined pattern of daily use or to plunk a standardized dwelling inside a publicly subsidized housing block, each of these examples generates possibilities and constraints for different forms of habitation.

The number of rooms within the dwelling, their dimensions, orientation and position relative to one another, the opportunities for contact with the outside world; the modes of access, how the transition between inside and outside is mediated; the dwelling's orientation in relation to other dwellings and its immediate surroundings, the way in which the new edifice shapes and responds to its context – architects provide answers to all of these questions as they develop and shape their design. But all of the answers put together do not automatically lead to the final form. However extensive the designers' knowledge of dwelling and however definite their opinions, there are always many different ways of shaping the substance of dwelling. How then do architects organize their design?

From the Renaissance until the end of the nineteenth century, such choices were regulated by the prevailing style. More than simply the external appearance and the kind of decorations, a style largely defined the total composition of the edifice. The style was based on an architectural system,[18] a clear set of rules dictating the proper dimensions, proportions, rhythm, organization of the space, structural system and use of materials.

Around 1900 these underlying rules and systems began to be called

18
The term 'architectural system' was introduced in Emil Kaufmann's *Architecture in the Age of Reason* (Cambridge, MA: Harvard University Press, 1955).

into question from all directions. Victor Horta challenged symmetry; Adolf Loos opened the assault on ornamentation; Le Corbusier developed new rules of composition; Gerrit Rietveld and Ludwig Mies van der Rohe broke open the organization of space. Gradually a new architecture emerged, characterized by the absence of a coherent and generally accepted architectural system. Every design now seems to be searching for its own identity, based on its own set of rules.[19]

In essence, these underlying design rules are developed as one-offs for each design. A coherent whole can now be achieved by deriving the various design choices from one guiding main idea, to which all other decisions are subordinated. This main idea, the foundation of the design, we call the *concept*. The development of a concept is the first step towards shaping and organizing the design:

A concept need not yet reach a verdict about the form of the final design; its primary purpose is to make statements about the idea, the character and the direction of the solutions. The concept expresses the basic idea behind a design; it provides direction for the design choices and simultaneously excludes variants; in a manner of speaking, it organizes the design choices.[20]

A concept is the representation of an idea. In principle this can be expressed in many different ways, in a blueprint, a diagram, a picture or a story. It can be based on the programme to be designed, a reaction to the context, an idea about the users, the expected significance of the building or a metaphor. It can be an abstract idea or closely linked to a form to be designed. But the concept remains the basic rationale, the idea – it is not literally the form itself. Other choices are based on the concept. How strong the concept is, how much it can be elaborated and whether design choices support the concept determine to what extent the concept permeates the building and gives it its identity.

The chapters that follow deal with the separate facets of housing design: from the set of typological tools with which design choices can be identified and implemented, through a selection of different forms of dwellings, residential buildings and urban configurations, structural principles and material applications, to the identification of the existing context and the brief formulated within it. None of these sections, however, is intended as a prescription for how a designer on a new project should design a good building, good dwellings or a good housing environment. Each new project requires a new vision from the designer, who needs to be able to turn ideas about dwelling into strong principles in order to arrive at a clear concept, so that the design can be further modelled and developed into a positive contribution to an ever-changing housing environment. Within this context, dwellings still need to be designed, developed and built, over and over again. It should be evident that the construction of this housing is not so much a technical challenge as a cultural one.

19
Bernard Leupen, 'Concept and Type', in: T.M. de Jong and D.J.M. van der Voordt (eds.), *Ways to Study and Research Urban Architectural and Technical Design* (Delft: Delft University Press, 2002), 109.

20
Bernard Leupen et al., *Design and Analysis* (Rotterdam: 010 Publishers, 1997), 13.

TYPOLOGY

However original architects may be, they are bound to fall back on previously used ideas and principles – whether they like to or not. We cannot keep reinventing the wheel. Different possibilities have been put forward by others; different combinations have been tried and tested. Housing designers can draw and build on a wealth of information. They have an immense and varied housing output – worldwide – at their disposal.
It can be argued that building on existing knowledge closes our eyes to new possibilities. Sometimes new inventions are made or new territory explored as a result of a lack of knowledge combined with an open-minded approach. However, this observation does not warrant the proposition: spread no knowledge and you will discover so much more. The great, innovative architects, from Palladio to Jean Nouvel and from Berlage to Koolhaas, all share(d) an unrivalled knowledge of the history of architecture and the architectural output of their time.
To draw on this knowledge and capitalize on this experience, this knowledge must be systematized. This systematization of widely used solutions is based on types. The subject area of classifying, naming and schematizing the design of buildings or parts of buildings is known as typology. What does typology mean and how does the concept of type differ from other architectural classifications? How can an architect put typology to use to arrive at a better design? These are the questions that this chapter seeks to answer. To get a better understanding of the concept of type, a brief historical retrospective is necessary. Because the meaningful use of types and typology is often coupled with the modification and transformation of types, this chapter will also look at the concept of transformation. With the help of a few case studies, the second part of the chapter will show how types can be used in the design process.

SYSTEMATIZATION

How is knowledge systematized? In everyday parlance, we use all kinds of classifications, whether we are talking about cars (saloon, convertible, van), bikes (city bike, mountain bike, racing bike) or pans (wok, casserole, grill pan). These terms all stand for collections that share certain principles, objectives, forms or functions, even though the objects within these collections can vary considerably. Likewise we have different words for different kinds of houses. An estate agent, for example, might talk about a canalside house or a converted farmhouse.[1] However, the different types of cars, bikes, pans or houses that we talk of do not make up a typology in the scientific sense of the word.
A scientific classification is based on very specific characteristics; the different categories are, in principle, exclusive. Well-known

1 The Dutch property website Funda (http://www.funda.nl/) features categories that are used in everyday parlance, but that are not always easy to define.

examples include the classification of the world of plants by the likes of Carl Linnaeus (1707–1778) and the periodic table of elements devised by Dmitri Ivanovich Mendeleev (1834–1907). In both classifications the subject has been subdivided into categories according to certain principles. Mendeleev created categories of chemical elements on the basis of their atomic weight (more specifically on the basis of the number of protons in the element's nucleus), while Linnaeus categorized plants on the grounds of formal attributes such as the position of the petals and the number of stamens [→ 01]. The categories in both systems are exclusive: a certain chemical element or a particular plant only fits a single category. Mendeleev and Linnaeus classified reality as they knew it at the time to arrive at a better understanding of it.

Of course buildings can be classified on a scientific basis as well. Depending on the purpose, such a classification or typology[2] of buildings can be described in different ways. Again, it will have to be made on the basis of specific characteristics and should, where possible, include mutually exclusive categories. How a typology of buildings is put together will depend on the purpose of the typology. Indeed, it is important to remember that a typology is an intellectual construct with a specific purpose; reality can be classified in an infinite number of ways. Estate agents, for example, will classify homes according to customers' expectations of both the home and its surroundings. Location and income play a key role in this. Architects, on the other hand, will favour a classification that says something about different design principles, allowing them to weigh up their design choices.

This brings us to an important point, because there is a significant difference between a typology used by an estate agent, a property investor or a resident and that used by an architect. Whereas for the first group the typology is merely an instrument with which to classify buildings, for the architect and others who are actively involved in the design process, a building typology is a design tool. How does this exclusive concept of typology differ from other building typologies? In the first place, the designer will need a typology that can be used to generate potential design decisions. This means that a designer's classification will be structured along design principles. In contrast to what it meant to Mendeleev and Linnaeus, the concept of type as discussed in this chapter does not only serve to classify and understand present reality. Above all, it plays a role in the design process, in the creation of new types and combinations of types. French architecture theorist Philippe Panerai speaks of a generative typology,[3] which he defines as the description of the reproducible system of related design tools and design choices. Depending on the situation and the programme, a new design can be generated on the basis of a type in this sense of the word. Such a type is 'solidified experience' and can be stored in the proverbial

2
Both classification and typology are systems of organization. Typology refers primarily to tangible things such as the world of plants or technical objects, whereas classification is a broader concept that can also be applied to abstract phenomena. The Universal Decimal Code (UDC) is a case in point; this classification is commonly used in libraries to organize subjects ranging from philosophy to technology.

3
Philippe Panerai, 'Typologieën: een middel tot inzicht in de logica van ruimtelijke patronen', *Wonen-TA/BK*, no. 2 (1981), translated and introduced by Francis Strauven, 11. Originally published as 'Typologies', *Les Cahiers de la recherche architecturale*, no. 4 (December 1979).

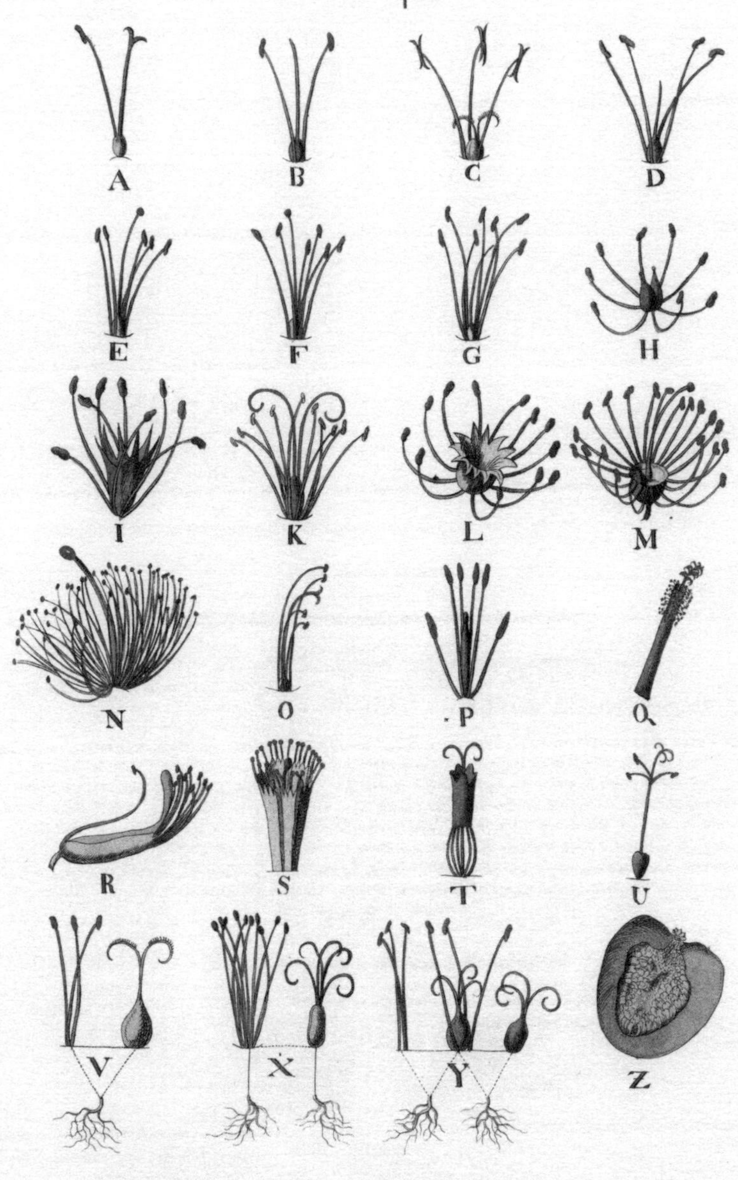

01

01 Page from C. Linnaeus's catalogue of the botanical world

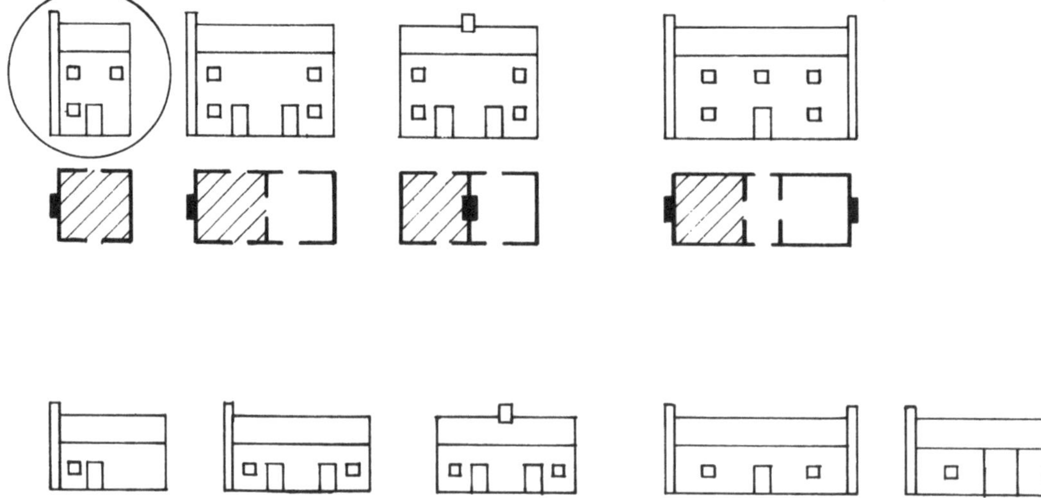

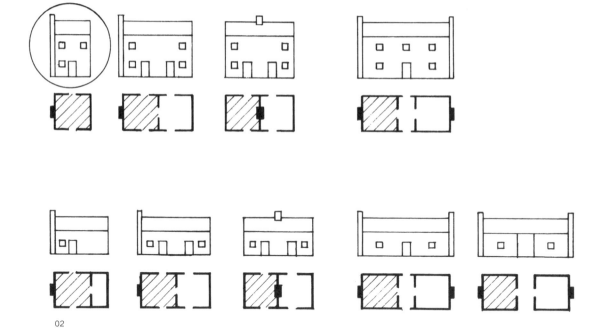

02

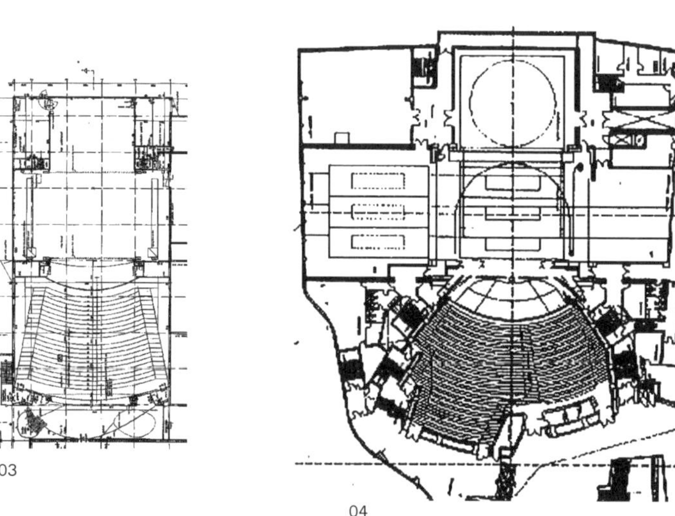

03

04

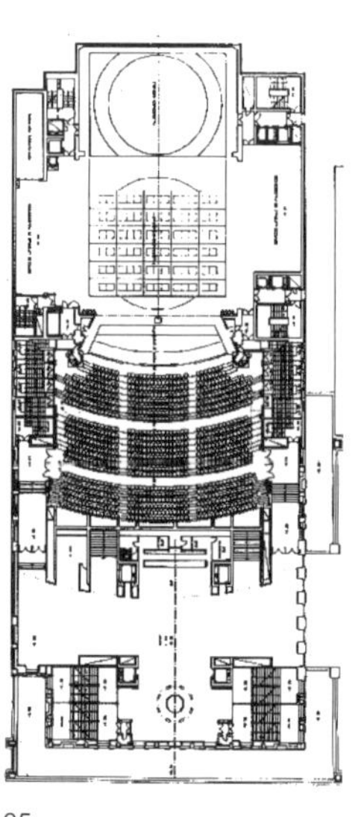

05

02 S. Holl, Stack houses
03 R. Koolhaas/OMA, Dance Theatre, 1987, The Hague, floor plan
04 A. Aalto, Stadttheater, 1988, Essen, floor plan
05 A. Rossi, Teatro Carlo Felice, 1991, Genoa, floor plan

'memory suitcase', transported and unpacked again. A type can be regarded as a carrier of design experiences with a similar problem, the genes of a design solution.[4]

Depending on experience and study, designers will have a series of examples in their heads. American architect Steven Holl gives us an impression in *Rural and Urban House Types in North America*, from which a page has been reproduced here.[5] [← 02] But few architects display their sources of inspiration quite so openly. What we do know is that many renowned architects have an in-depth knowledge of architecture history and are extremely well-informed about their colleagues' work. How this theoretical knowledge ultimately leads to a design is difficult to ascertain, since this is often an unconscious process for highly experienced architects.

4
Bernard Leupen et al., *Design and Analysis* (Rotterdam: 010 Publishers, 1997), 132.

5
Steven Holl, *Rural and Urban House Types in North America, Pamphlet Architecture 9* (New York: William Stout & Pamphlet Architecture Press, 1982).

THE ORIGINS OF THE CONCEPT OF TYPE

The concept of type used here can be traced back to the ideas about typology developed by the French architecture theorist Antoine Chrysostome Quatremère de Quincy (1755–1849) and the Italian architecture historian Giulio Carlo Argan (1909–1992). The term type comes from the Greek 'typos' and is so broad that it can be used to describe many subtle distinctions and variations of the same idea, such as the concepts of model, mould, imprint, template and relief. From the eighteenth century onwards, type is used as a theoretical tool for the classification of terms, as in Linnaeus's celebrated classification of plants.[6]

It is with this meaning that the concept enters into the architecture discourse. In the *Encyclopédie méthodique, Architecture* (1788), architecture theorist Quatremère de Quincy defines the concept of type as follows:

The word type is also used synonymously with the word 'model', although there is between the two a difference that is easy enough to understand. The word 'type' presents less the image of a thing to copy or imitate completely, than the idea of an element which ought itself to serve as a rule for the model.[7]

In Quatremère de Quincy's definition, the type is defined as 'more or less vague'. On the basis of the type 'each (artist) can conceive works of art that may have no resemblance'.[8] According to the Italian art historian Argan, who revived interest in Quatremère de Quincy's text in the 1960s, it is the *internal form structure* that unites works that are based on a similar type. According to Argan, a more comprehensive analysis of this internal form structure will reveal the similarities between the two objects. But what is this internal form structure? What is it that fundamentally links two seemingly different buildings?

6
Carl Linnaeus, *Classes Plantarum* (Leiden: 1739).

7
For more background information, see also Francis Strauven, 'Typologieën', op. cit. (note 3), 6–9, and Antoine Chrysostome Quatremère de Quincy, 'Type' (1825), in: K. Michael Hays (ed.), *The Oppositions Reader: Selected Readings from A Journal for Ideas and Criticism in Architecture 1973–1984* (Cambridge, MA and London: MIT Press, 1998), 617–620.

8
Antoine Chrysostome Quatremère de Quincy, *Encyclopédie méthodique: Architecture*, Vol. III (Paris: 1788), 544.

The Type: A Case Study of Three Theatres

As argued before, we know from experience that certain forms, diagrams or models are more useful than others. In the case of repetition or narrowly defined programmes (housing, theatres, prisons, etcetera), especially, we often see the same recurring principles. To describe the role of type in the design process, we will take a detour to theatre design. Why theatre design in a book about housing design? The nice thing about theatres is that the number of theatre types is limited, making it relatively easy to pinpoint where the influence of type and where the influence of a particular architectural view comes into play. Besides, it is often the client who will stipulate a particular type of theatre and, as the following suggests, theatre makers rather than architects develop theatre types.

We have images of three theatres to illustrate this: the Danstheater (1987) in The Hague by Rem Koolhaas/OMA, the Stadttheater Essen (1988) by Alvar Aalto and the Teatro Carlo Felice (1991) in Genoa, designed by Aldo Rossi. Despite their very distinctive architectural styles, these theatres do have something in common. On closer inspection the structures of the three buildings show two similarities. First of all, in all three cases the stage and the auditorium are connected through a so-called *proscenium arch*. Seated in the auditorium, viewers watch the stage via this arch, which can be closed off with a curtain. Unlike the classical Greek theatre, the audience watches the stage as if it were a diorama. A second similarity can be found in the structure of the house, the auditorium. Although all three look different, in each the audience is seated on a rising slope. The auditorium has a so-called shell-shaped floor, guaranteeing all spectators a good view of the stage. [← 03-05]

The Concept of Type Operates between Word and Diagram

A theatre with a good view of the stage may seem obvious, but until Gottfried Semper drew up his design for the Festspielhaus in Bayreuth (1872), a large part of the audience, especially those from the upper echelons of society, would traditionally be seated in boxes. These boxes are situated on horseshoe-shaped balconies around an auditorium with a flat floor and positioned so that it is easier to see one's fellow spectators than the stage. In the eighteenth and nineteenth centuries, people went to the theatre to see and be seen; what was happening on the stage was of secondary importance. The Scala in Milan – a famous proscenium theatre – is a case in point. The plan clearly shows the boxes arranged in a horseshoe shape. When Richard Wagner commissioned Gottfried Semper to design a theatre, he made it clear that it had to be a theatre that prioritized the performance of his operas. Every single spectator had to have

06

07

06 G. Semper, Festspielhaus (Festival Theatre), 1872, Bayreuth
07 R. Koolhaas/OMA, Dance Theatre, The Hague. One of the shell-shaped halls: same type, different architecture

the best possible view of the stage. To achieve this, Semper broke with a long-standing tradition and designed an auditorium with a shell-shaped floor. In a way Semper's auditorium can be seen as a proscenium stage with an element from the classical Greek theatre. Since then, the shell-shaped auditorium has become a commonly used type, as the theatres designed by Koolhaas, Aalto and Rossi testify.

The concept of type can also be applied to the corresponding spatial organization – or the internal form structure, as Argan calls it. The three theatres under discussion have two types in common: the proscenium arch and the shell-shaped or Bayreuth auditorium, named after the German town that is home to Semper's design. The similarities between these three theatres can be captured in a diagram depicting the internal form structure of the shared principles. Such a diagram is known as a typological diagram: a representation of the type. But please note: the diagram is not the actual type. The concept of the type is positioned between the diagram and the word, in this case between the diagram representing the configuration and the words 'shell-shaped theatre' and 'proscenium arch'. [← 06–07; → 08–09]

This may seem mere word play: type, internal form structure, etcetera. Apparently the concept of type revolves around a similarity between buildings on the basis of their structure, that is to say, on the basis of the interrelationship between the dominant elements in a design. Going back to housing design: there is a dwelling type with two bays. Many single-family houses are based on this type, with the house subdivided into a narrow and a wide bay. The wide bay contains the larger rooms (living room, dining room), while the narrow bay contains the circulation areas (corridor, staircase) and service areas (kitchen, toilet). The term bay refers to a structural unity. The structure of a house consists of two load-bearing walls with another wall in between to ensure that the span is not too wide. This so-called intermediate support divides the house into two bays. In principle this type says something about the relationship between the rooms and between the load-bearing walls.[→ 10a–b]

This raises the question of what the concept of type, as outlined in the paragraphs above, refers to: an entire building or house, the arrangement of buildings in the urban design scheme, elements of the building, the linking of rooms or a particular kind of structure? In principle the concept covers them all; there can be types of a reproducible system of related design choices or a generative typology at all levels. Although the design-related concept of type is, in principle, separate from function (the concept is first and foremost based on the internal form structure of designs), there is a typology that is particularly relevant to the area of housing. After all, many housing blocks, like theatres, have specific structures.

TYPOLOGICAL LEVELS

An important aspect of typology-based design is the interrelationship of the design decisions. The concept of typological level plays a central role in this. A typological level can be seen as a level of scale on which the design decisions constitute a coherent system of choices. Argan, for example, identified three typological levels with which to analyse the buildings of his era:[9]

—the overall building configuration;
—the major structural elements;
—the decorative elements.

The last, the decorative elements, may strike us as slightly old-fashioned, but we must bear in mind that Argan was first and foremost an art historian. The concept of decorative elements could be translated into contemporary parlance as dividing and finishing elements or skin and scenery.[10]

Thanks to Argan's definition of typological levels, we can look at these levels both individually and in relation to one another, which makes typology not just a classification system, but also a tool with which to analyse buildings. It means that buildings no longer just represent a type; they can be unravelled into different components, each of which refers to a particular type. Thanks to their specific articulation in a certain building these components together form a specific building.

If we cast our minds back to the three theatres, we could say that the three are similar at the level of the overall building configuration: they all conform to the type of the proscenium arch with shell-shaped auditorium. However, they vary considerably at the major structural level (Genoa is mainly stacked brick, while Essen is a hybrid structure of reinforced concrete and steel and The Hague predominantly steel with a concrete base). At the third level, the decorative elements, the three theatres are also rather different. There is little resemblance in their architectural expression and detailing.

Following Argan, we can also identify typological levels in residential buildings. But having found Argan's three levels not entirely adequate, we have developed them further in this book. Argan's first level, the overall building configuration, immediately presents us with complications. The complexity of the residential building has prompted us to add an extra level. The residential building is made up of *independent housing units*, such as flats and maisonettes. A particular horizontal sequence or perhaps vertical stack of independent housing units together make up the building. In the case of a stack, there are additional elements that provide access to the stacked dwelling, such as staircases, corridors, galleries and lifts and that link the communal front door to the dwelling door. We use the term *dwelling access* for this set of elements.

9
Giulio Carlo Argan, 'On the Typology of Architecture', *Architectural Design* (December 1963). Published in Dutch as 'Het concept van architectonische typologie. Architectuur-fragmenten', in: H. Engle and F. Claessens (eds.), *Wat is architectuur?*, transl. L. van Duin (Delft: Publicatiebureau Faculteit der Bouwkunde, 1991), 65–70.

10
Bernard Leupen, 'Concept and Type', in: T.M. de Jong and D.J.M. van der Voordt (eds.), *Ways to Study and Research Urban, Architectural and Technical Design* (Delft: Delft University Press, 2002), 31–32.

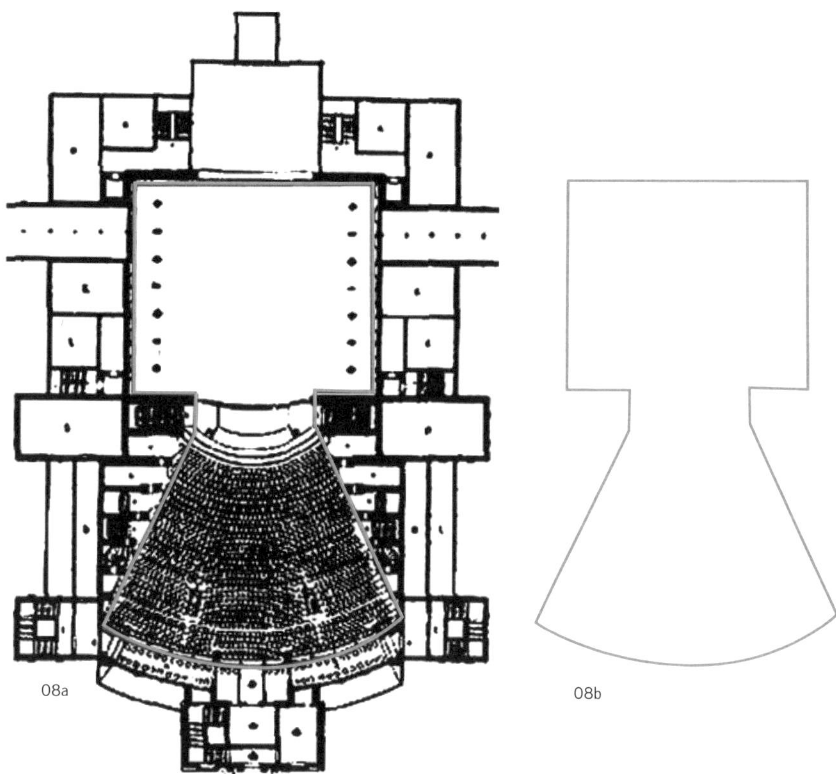

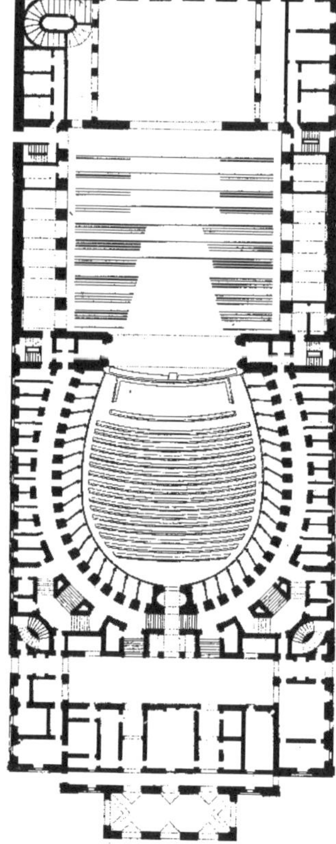

08a G. Semper, Festspielhaus, Bayreuth, floor plan with typological scheme
08b Typological scheme of the shell-shaped hall with proscenium stage
09 Floor plan of the Scala, 1778, Milan, an example of an eighteenth-century theatre
10a Two-bay dwelling
10b Two-bay dwelling with upstairs and downstairs flat

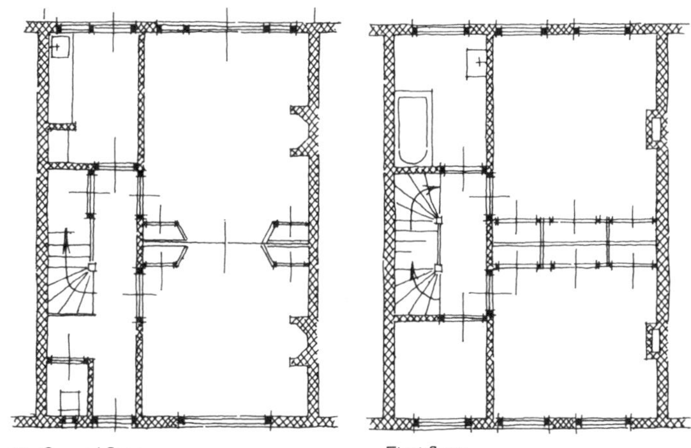

10a Ground floor

First floor

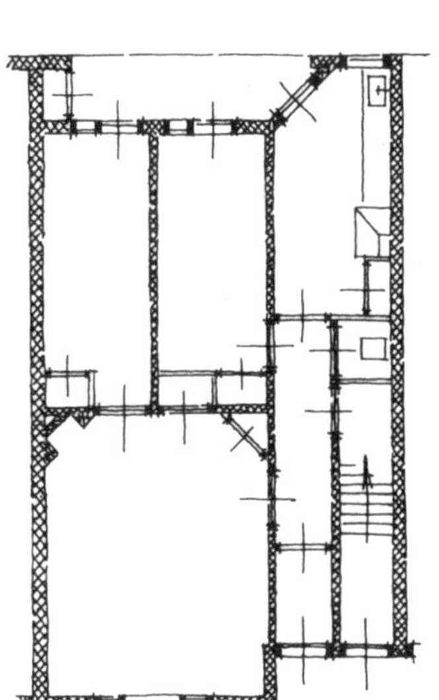

10b Downstairs flat

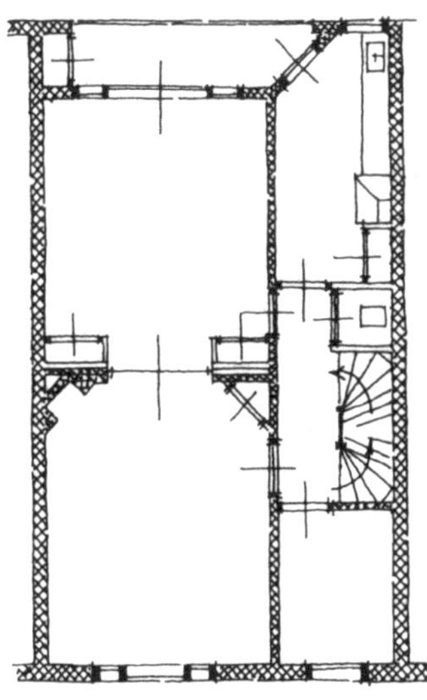

Upstairs flat

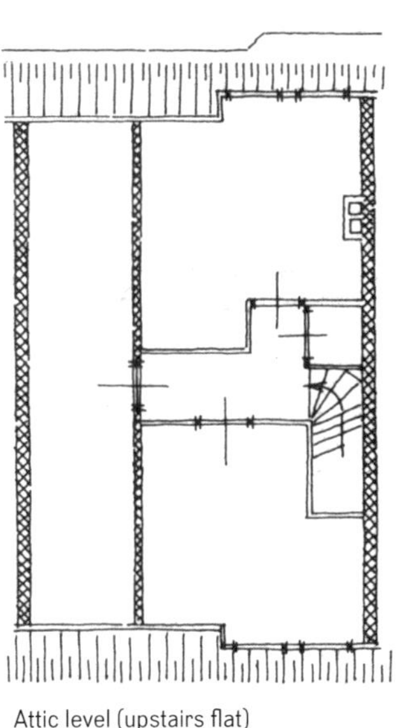

Attic level (upstairs flat)

We can draw up a typology of both the independent housing unit and the dwelling access. Although these typologies are closely related, we will initially look at them separately under the headings: 'Spatial Organization of the Dwelling', 'Linking and Stacking' and 'Dwelling Access'. Finally, the linking or stacking of the independent units in combination with a certain kind of access also results in a particular building shape, the *building form*: row, slab, 'mat', tower, and so forth.
We have added another level for the large-scale residential building in relation to the urban ensemble. Preceding Argan's first level, we have identified the level of the *configuration of the urban ensemble*. This is the level that covers the way buildings are grouped within the urban ensemble: are the blocks parallel, do the buildings form a perimeter block or a superblock, etcetera.
Our classification retains Argan's second level, the major structural elements, as the *load-bearing structure*. It covers columns, beams, load-bearing walls, trusses and structural floors. The structure transfers the building load down to the foundation.
Argan's third level, that is the decorative elements, can be subdivided into:
—*Skin* (façade, underside and roof). The skin separates inside and outside, while at the same time presenting the building to the outside world.
—*Scenery* of the space (cladding, inner doors and walls, the finishing of floors, walls and ceilings). The scenery defines the visual and tactile properties of the rooms.
—*Service elements* (pipes and ducts, devices and other facilities). The service elements control the supply and drainage of water, energy, fresh air and include the devices and dedicated rooms associated with these tasks.

A diagram of Argan's levels for the residential building and development as we understand them in this book looks like this:

Argan	Housing Design	
	Ch 5 Urban Ensemble	
1st level: The overall building configuration	Ch 4 Residential Building	Spatial Organization of the Dwelling
		Dwelling Access
	Ch 3 Dwellings	
2nd level: The major structural elements	Ch 6a Structure	
3rd level: The decorative elements	Ch 6b Skin Ch 6c Scenery Ch 6d Service Elements	

In the following chapters, the concept of Argan's typological levels is looked at in greater detail for stacked housing. In the first three chapters, the emphasis is on layout type at the level of the dwelling, the building and the urban ensemble. The next chapter covers the typology of the structural elements. Needless to say, these typologies are interrelated. For example, a structure with load-bearing walls determines the layout of the rooms inside. That we have nevertheless opted for this division can be justified by the belief that typological classifications must also function as an analytical tool. To analyse the relationship between rooms and the overall structure, we must first be able to label each separate component. In the final two chapters, where this line of reasoning is developed in more detail, the relationship is given the attention it deserves in a number of analyses.

THE APPLICATION OF A TYPE

Existing types are rarely applied without some adjustment. As a rule, the type will undergo modification during the design process. Following Argan, we can identify two phases in the metamorphosis from type to design: the *formation* of the type, and the moment of *form specification*. During the actual design process these two phases will overlap.[11]

11
Argan, 'On the Typology of Architecture', op. cit. (note 9), 69.

The Formation of the Type

During the first phase, the formation of the type, the typological diagram – the result of a process of reduction – will undergo a number of modifications. If the modification of a typological diagram results in a new variant of the existing type, we speak of the adjustment of the type. Forms of adjustment include rotations, shifts, the introduction of differences in level and mirroring. In the case of structural changes to the type we speak of the transformation (remodelling) of the existing type to a new type. Each of the individual typological levels of the design can go through this phase several times. One can imagine that years or even centuries of adjustment after adjustment or transformation after transformation can result in series of slowly evolving types. In the case of such family trees we speak of *typological series*. Each one of these series contains a wealth of experience and tradition. [→ 11]

The Moment of Form Specification

During the second phase, the moment of form specification, the modified diagram is exposed on all typological levels to an architectural idiom chosen by the designer. The type is 'dressed' and given architectural expression. Insertion into an architectural system[12] results in the definitive composition and formal elaboration. It gives the design its distinctive features. The typological analyses below illustrate the application and transformation of a dwelling type.

12
For the concept of 'architectural system', see Leupen et al., *Design and Analysis*, op. cit. (note 4), 27.

Case Study: The Transformation of the Access Staircase

The entrance with stairs is a type of access commonly used in the twentieth century for stacked dwellings of up to four floors. The modification of the entrance and stairs access in the Schöne Aussicht project by Herman Hertzberger in the Dönche neighbourhood in Kassel (1980–1982) is extraordinary. Hertzberger has transformed the entrance from the usual front steps and access landing into a meeting place between the homes. Although the homes themselves have not undergone a fundamental change, the transformation of the entrance has a distinct influence on the quality of the layout. We can identify a number of steps in the transformation process in Kassel. The most fundamental change that the entrance has undergone is the opening up of the foyer area through the rotation of the two adjacent homes. This step moves the kitchen to the front and allows the creation of a spacious balcony with a good aspect at the corner. Because it now has a front aspect, the kitchen can have a window. Hertzberger makes this a corner window overlooking the stairwell, thereby creating a form of social monitoring of otherwise anonymous entrance stairs.

The stairs are made even more visible and incorporated into the residents' daily lives via another modification. Hertzberger increases the size of the landings and fits them with sandboxes. A common

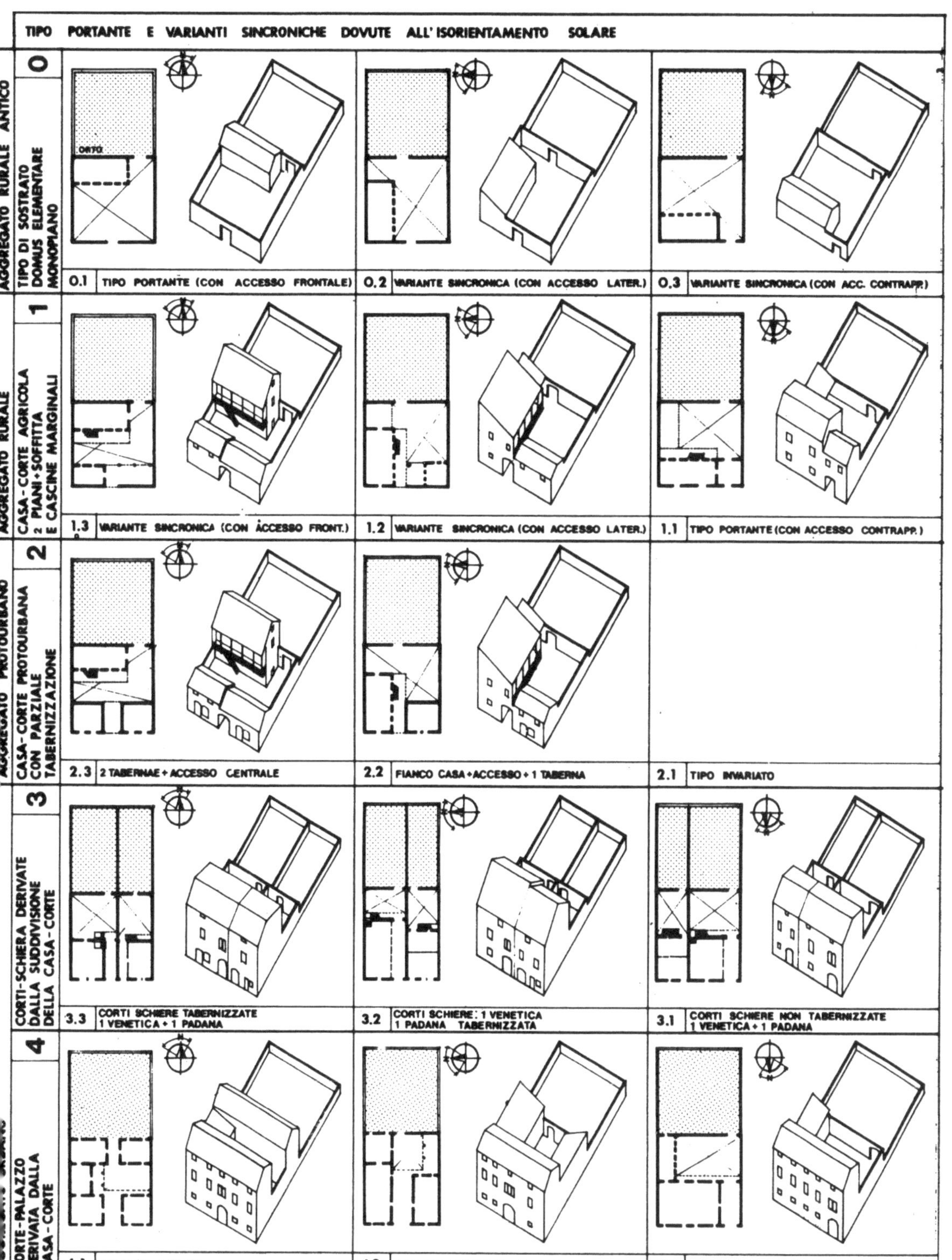
TIPO PORTANTE E VARIANTI SINCRONICHE DOVUTE ALL' ISORIENTAMENTO SOLARE
AGGREGATO RURALE ANTICO
0
TIPO DI SOSTRATO DOMUS ELEMENTARE MONOPIANO
ORTO
0.1 TIPO PORTANTE (CON ACCESSO FRONTALE)
0.2 VARIANTE SINCRONICA (CON ACCESSO LATER.)
0.3 VARIANTE SINCRONICA (CON ACC. CONTRAPP.)
AGGREGATO RURALE
1
CASA-CORTE AGRICOLA 2 PIANI + SOFFITTA E CASCINE MARGINALI
1.3 VARIANTE SINCRONICA (CON ACCESSO FRONT.)
1.2 VARIANTE SINCRONICA (CON ACCESSO LATER.)
1.1 TIPO PORTANTE (CON ACCESSO CONTRAPP.)
AGGREGATO PROTOURBANO
2
CASA-CORTE PROTOURBANA CON PARZIALE TABERNIZZAZIONE
2.3 2 TABERNAE + ACCESSO CENTRALE
2.2 FIANCO CASA + ACCESSO + 1 TABERNA
2.1 TIPO INVARIATO
3
CORTI-SCHIERA DERIVATE DALLA SUDDIVISIONE DELLA CASA-CORTE
3.3 CORTI SCHIERE TABERNIZZATE 1 VENETICA + 1 PADANA
3.2 CORTI SCHIERE: 1 VENETICA 1 PADANA TABERNIZZATA
3.1 CORTI SCHIERE NON TABERNIZZATE 1 VENETICA + 1 PADANA
4
CORTE-PALAZZO DERIVATA DALLA CASA-CORTE
4.1 ACCESSO ASSIALE
4.2 ACCESSO CENTRALE NON ASSIALE
4.3 ACCESSO PERIFERICO

11

11 Typological series, transformation of the *Domus elementare*

12a

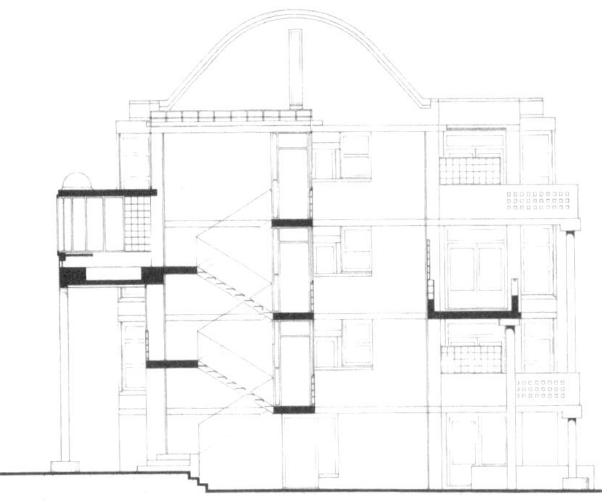

12b

12c

12 H. Hertsberger, Schöne Aussicht housing, 1982, Kassel-Dönche

a Staircase access zone with balcony
b Section and floor plan
c Transformation of the entrance access to the access as implemented in the Schöne Aussicht project

criticism of stacked housing is that the residents of the upper floors have little or no contact with children playing at street level. By situating the play area (the sandbox) only a short distance from the homes and by providing sightlines from the kitchen, Hertzberger enables the parents to have contact with their children. Finally, by opening up the entrance area, enhancing the landings with a sandbox and large patios, Hertzberger manages to give architectural expression to the entire access area and to make it a special entrance. The monumental columns supporting the balconies increase the impact of this entrance. [← 12a–c]

Case Study: The Combination of Two Dwelling Types
New dwelling types can be developed by combining two existing types. The Panorama houses (1994) in Huizen by Neutelings Riedijk Architecten are a case in point.
The initial plan was to create a development consisting of single-family row housing. The houses would be marketed as owner-occupied dwellings on private lots. However, the architects' interpretation of the special location led to the development of a new type, which can be seen as a combination of the single-family row house and the single-level apartment or flat. This kind of modification appears virtually confined to Dutch housing and has its origins in housing competitions during the 1980s, such as the one for flexible housing on the Kruisplein in Rotterdam.[13]
The idea behind the dwelling type developed by Neutelings Riedijk is as follows: the houses are aligned north-south. Because the best view (a lake called Gooimeer) is to the north of the houses, residents will follow the direction of the light when they look out of the window at the view. To make the most of this view, a width of 6 m was not enough. A house developed width-wise would be ideal.
[→ 13a–e]
A cross between a single-family row house and a flat was the solution. This solution came about by interlinking sets of two dwellings each and produced a living room with a width of 12 m. The home with its entrance on the left has a sun room on the ground floor; the living room is situated across the full width of the first floor, while there is space for a bedroom on the second floor. The other home (entered from the right) has a sun room and bedroom on the ground floor and first floor respectively, while the large living room occupies the full width of the second floor. A carport is situated between the two dwellings, while the communal garden at the rear of the properties has been subdivided. Some living rooms have a balcony.
The disadvantage of this intertwining of two homes is that the living rooms do not border the garden, which is a standard feature of a row house. A second disadvantage is that the homes are no longer on residents' own land. Because the dwellings interlock, ownership

13
W. Patijn et al., *Prijsvraag Jongerenhuisvesting Kruisplein* (Rotterdam: DROS Volkshuisvesting, 1982).

13a

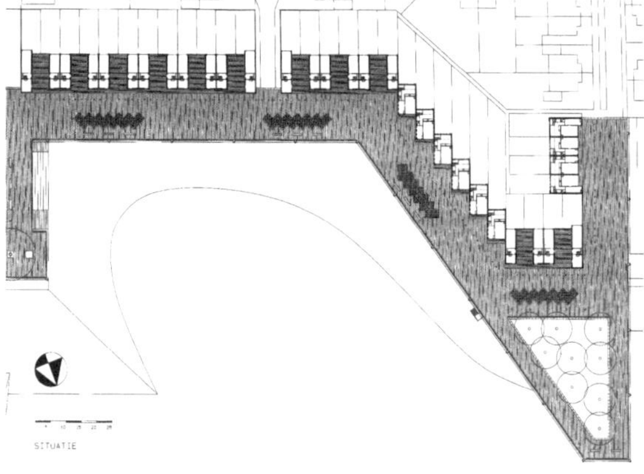

13b

13c

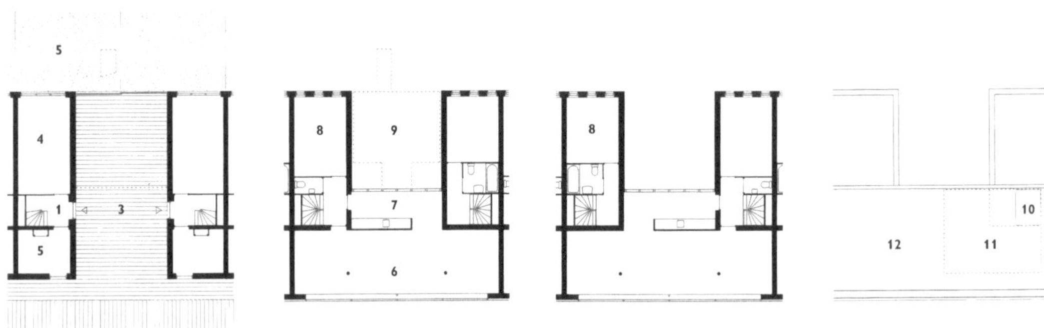

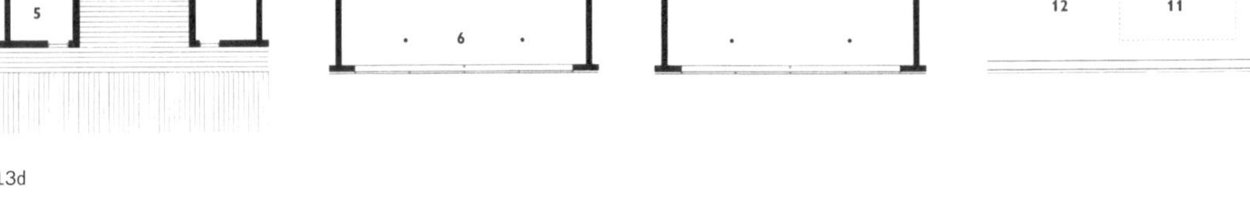

13d

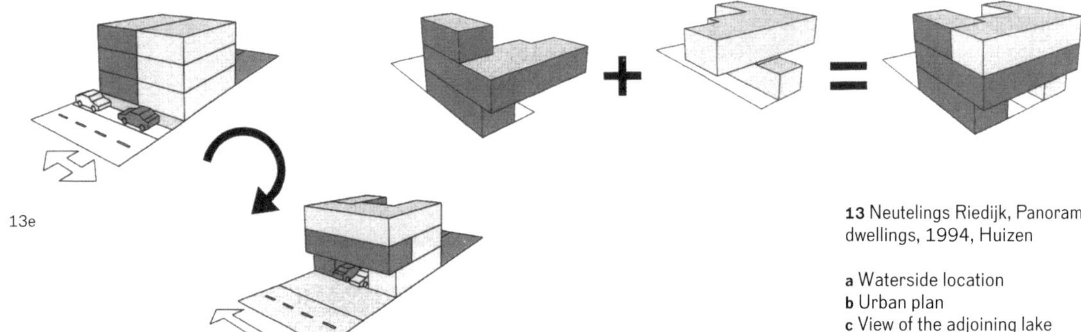

13e

13 Neutelings Riedijk, Panorama dwellings, 1994, Huizen

a Waterside location
b Urban plan
c View of the adjoining lake
d Floor plans
e Typological transformations

of the land is shared. This requires a homeowners' association for every pair of homes, so that residents can look after their interests, such as the shared foundation and roof. Although this is an undesirable situation for privately owned properties, it did not put off buyers because of the benefits offered by the new type.

Case Study: The Combination of Two Types of Structure
There are two basic types of structure (see also Chapter 6, 'Tectonics'): structures with load-bearing walls and structures with columns (comparable to Le Corbusier's Dom-ino skeleton). [→ 14a–b] House builders tend to prefer load-bearing walls because of their fire resistance and soundproofing qualities. On the other hand, a skeleton offers more freedom in the configuration of the rooms. A good example of an inventive combination of these two basic types can be found in Liesbeth van der Pol's housing design in the Dapperbuurt neighbourhood in Amsterdam (1992), a redevelopment project. The commission from housing association Lieven De Key stipulated 49 affordable homes for the street's original residents, which meant that the budget was limited. To cater to the future residents' diverse households and lifestyles the homes were given a transformable living space.
The structure, which goes a long way towards creating the necessary freedom, is quite special. Van der Pol used a concrete construction with load-bearing walls, which she alternated with supporting yokes of columns and beams. In the large central transformable space, Van der Pol defiantly placed the structure in full view. Although the structure introduces few functional constraints, its form is quite emphatic. In fact, its presence is further emphasized by the oblique position of the yoke, which appears to exclaim: Look at me, I'm responsible for the transformability! [→ 15a–c, see also p. 116]
The structure responsible for the transformable living space can be seen as an unusual combination of the two aforementioned basic types: the (Dom-ino) skeleton and the structure with load-bearing walls. Van der Pol used the load-bearing wall as a dividing wall, which also provides the necessary fire resistance and soundproofing between the dwellings. But because the additional support in the middle of the house to reduce the span does not have to meet these requirements, Van der Pol chose a different type of structure here in her quest for more freedom: the skeleton. Both structural types can be combined without too much difficulty. The oblique position of the columns and beam, as described above, is simply an architectural gesture and does not have a structural role.

Whereas there is considerable cohesion between the design decisions on the same typological level of a plan, the situation is much more complex when it comes to decisions at different typological levels. The relationship between the different levels of a design is an interesting

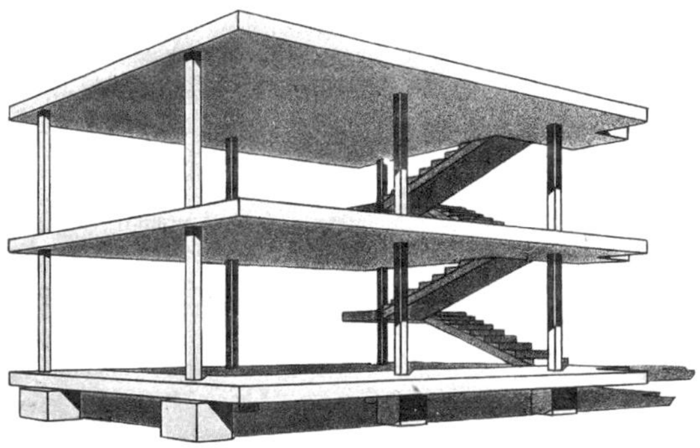

14a

14b

14a Le Corbusier, Dom-ino skeleton, 1914
14b Le Corbusier, Villa Savoy
1929, Poissy, interior

subject. For example, the designer of a large residential building can opt for a façade composition in which the small-scale individual units present themselves to the outside world as the constituent parts of the whole. It is equally conceivable to have a façade that emphasizes the large scale of the overall building and in which the homes are no longer recognizable as individual units. Nonetheless, the two different façades can hide one and the same dwelling type. How autonomous or interdependent are different typological levels in relation to one another? This is not just a question of personal opinion, but a question of use, technical possibilities and convention. The next few chapters will look more closely at design on each individual level before moving on to the relationships between the various levels.

The concept of type elaborated in this chapter is applied in the rest of this book. The typological transformation is also explained using several examples. In the next four chapters, we will examine the spatial and material organization of the housing construction project in greater depth. The categories used in this examination represent an implementation of the theoretical framework established in this chapter. The two typologies developed in this chapter–typology according to spatial configuration and typology according to material configuration–form the backbone of the following chapters. Spatial configuration typology is elaborated in the chapters 'Dwellings', 'Residential Building' and 'Urban Ensemble' and material configuration typology is elaborated in the chapter 'Tectonics'.

flexibiliteit

karakteristiek

15a

15b

15c

15 L. van der Pol (Dok architecten)
Pieter Vlamingstraat, 1992,
Amsterdam

a principle floor plan
b conceptual model of the open floor plan
c interior with obliquely positioned columns and joist

DWELLINGS

If dwelling, as our first chapter contends, consists of the myriad activities we engage in every day in and around the home as well as between the home and the workplace, pub and theatre, school and beach – in short everything that makes us feel 'at home' in a place, in a village or a city – then the spaces of dwelling can also be found on all these levels of scale. The organization of dwelling space in fact does encompass all of these levels. We organize our home floor plan, but we also connect the front door with the street, think about where to park our bicycle or car, how we get past the neighbours or whether the neighbours are walking past our windows, whether we want to live close to street level or prefer a panoramic view of the city. But we also think about whether the new building fits in with the existing urban structure, whether it is higher or lower, positioned more forward or set further back – all of which has an impact on the number of dwellings that fit inside it and how large these can or should be.

In the consideration of dwelling space and places, these levels of scale are often intertwined; they are inextricably linked in a complex entanglement of interests. Changes on one level have immediate implications for others. During the design process, therefore, all the levels will continually intertwine, in a constant search for improvement to the whole.

An actual project will often begin on the scale level of the city: there is a site that can be built upon; a programme is drawn up; the designer is asked to bring the two together into a building. Sometimes designers will start from an 'ideal' dwelling floor plan and attempt to fit this within the parameters the city block affords them, but even here the scale level is higher than that of a precise adaptation within the dwelling itself. Knowledge and experience enable designers to estimate the implications of given dimensions and orientation for the quality of the organization of internal space.

In a book that seeks to draw attention to the organization of our dwelling spaces at all levels, we presume no such insider knowledge. In order to make the ultimate decisions at the scale level of the building understandable, we first need to look at the organization of the space down to the square metre. From a didactic standpoint, we have therefore opted for a progression from small to large, from the organization of places and spaces to an organization of dwellings in a residential building and finally to the organization of residential buildings as part of the city. This chapter deals with the organization of places and spaces within the individual dwelling, in other words the configuration of the dwelling or housing unit.

ACTIVITY, PLACE AND SPACE

Dwelling consists of human activities that take place inside as well as outside, in the spaces of dwellings, the spaces of residential buildings, the spaces of the street and neighbourhood, and the spaces of the city and its broader environs. Within this, a dwelling creates conditions for everyday rituals that occupy a place in and around the home throughout the seasons. Designing a dwelling means considering how these activities can be given appropriate places, in proper relation to one another, within a suitable envelope and with easy access.

The spatial organization of dwelling therefore consists of organizing the various places in which these activities occur, and defining the spaces in which they can best unfold. Conversely, this means that in order to design the spaces of a dwelling so that they provide sufficient room for us to carry out our activities in comfort, we must first define which activities can be carried out in which place, how they relate to one another, how much comfort is desirable or possible in this regard and what demands they place on the spaces needed for the purpose.

The first chapter of this book already highlighted how the distribution of activities into various spaces not only differs from one country and one culture to the next, but can change rapidly within a country or culture, sometimes in a span of no more than five or ten years. Moreover, these differences and changes exist continuously, simultaneously and in parallel to one another within the same society. It is therefore vitally imperative, in every new project, to consider who we are designing for, and which possibilities are being included and excluded in the dwelling.

From Activity to Spatial Design

The number of different activities we carry out inside a dwelling is virtually endless: coming in, hanging up our coats, reading a book, listening to music, doing the dishes, watching television, brushing our teeth, eating breakfast, washing our hands, throwing away rubbish, getting dressed, and so on. Making an inventory of these activities every single time would be virtually impossible and highly time-consuming. Furthermore it is not always useful to design daily life in such detail, when individual versions of it can differ so widely. Behavioural scientists identify connections in our daily activities; they distinguish patterns of collection and division that form a representation of a given mode of living or lifestyle. Charting these patterns and recording their changes is an interesting and extensive area of study, but for the practice of design it often takes us too far afield.

Designers are better served by a simplified representation based on the use of space. For instance, in an easy chair you can sit, have a cup of coffee, watch television or read the newspaper–what matters to the designer is the chair itself, the room it takes and its distance from the table, the coffeemaker or the television. The designer thinks primarily in terms of basic activities like sitting, eating, cooking, washing and sleeping, and subordinates other activities to these. Occupants, finally, first identify in the dwelling the spaces that accommodate their activities: living room, kitchen, bedroom, study, formal reception room, bathroom, vestibule. They see the result of the design process, the crystallized spatial system, and make use of the spaces as these allow them to do so.

During the design process, however, such an approach would be too limiting. It is by no means certain that every separate basic activity requires a separate space: perhaps a less standard space is required, or the use of different spaces may be interchangeable. Designing a dwelling begins with situating the places where the activities of dwelling can take place. These are the places within the dwelling where daily occupations can best be accommodated. To a significant degree, it is the design of these places, their dimensions, position and relation to one another as well as to light, views, air and space, that give a dwelling its quality. [→ 01]

Between Ideal and Reality

If we design without any limitations on budget or space, we are able to assign every conceivable activity a place of its own, each refined to our heart's content in an ideal location. Yet even with unlimited freedom you can only allocate space once: choices have to be made, for instance between the quality of a large space in which many activities come together and that of various smaller spaces that may or may not be interconnected.

Besides intended use, spatial and aesthetic requirements play an important role: think of the perception, for instance, of pleasing spatial proportions, of spatial sequences, of contrasts great and small, high and low, angles of light and shadow, sheltered enclosures and open views. As a designer you have numerous means at your disposal to provide a fascinating and meaningful envelope for dwelling. The dwelling can become the spatial representation of a dwelling ideal. History is filled with inspiring examples of residential houses created in this way.

The majority of housing construction, however, takes place within spatial, financial and political constraints. When every dwelling requirement cannot be granted unlimited fulfilment, a designer also has to choose: which places merit precedence, getting more space or a better position, at the expense of others, which have to do with less. These choices determine the various possibilities of habitation, the character of the dwelling, its quality.

It is then possible to further define the way the dwelling is to be used and experienced. Places are kept together or separated from

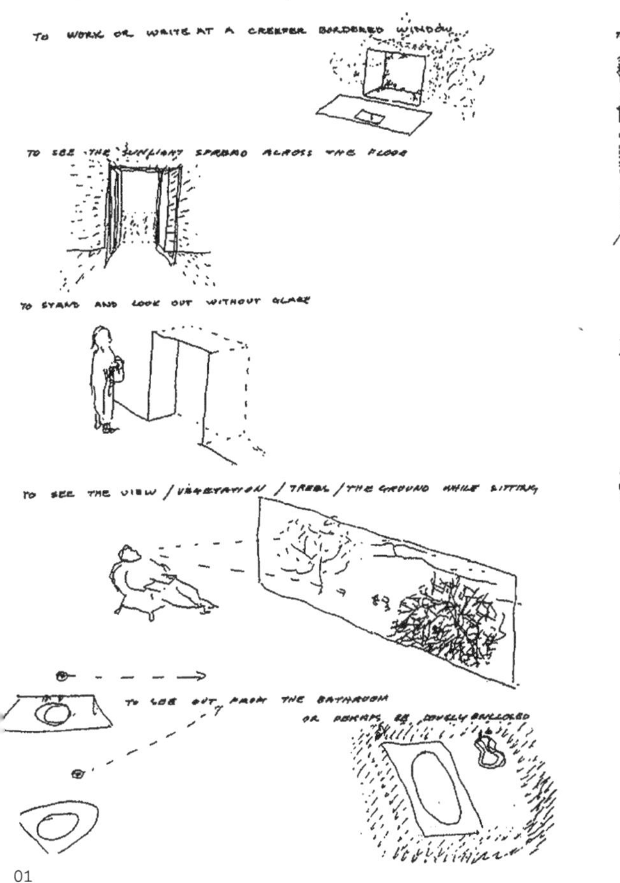

01

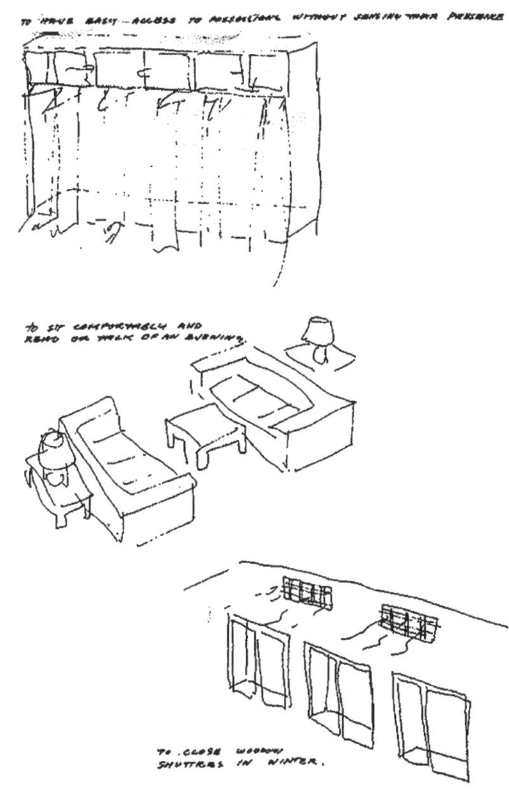

01 Sketches by A. and P. Smithson illustrating how a carefully designed (sheltered) space can accommodate the small pleasures of life

one another by walls, floors, objects and differences in elevation, linked to one another by openings, doors, windows and stairs, supplied with (sun-)light, views and fresh air and connected to services. Ultimately, the spaces of the dwelling derive their form, dimensions and meaning in part from the material that envelops them, its colour and its texture.

Basic Activities of Dwelling

While dwelling features highly specific characteristics that differ among countries, cultures and occupants, there are also discernible similarities. For one, the dwelling seems, regardless of the era, level of development and geographic location, to be the locus of operation for a number of dwelling-specific activities. Analyses of the use of dwellings in various cultures show that a number of recurring activities occupy, virtually always and everywhere, a place in and around the home.

In his book *Japanese Houses: Patterns for Living*, Kiyoyuki Nishihara contrasts dwelling in the Western world with the traditional Japanese home.[1] Whereas in the Western home spaces are often named after their use (living room, bedroom, bathroom, kitchen, and so forth), spaces in the Japanese home have names that reflect their relationship to one another: *zashiki* (main room), *naka-no-ma* (middle room), *tsugi-no-ma* (the room next to the big room). This describes the spatial system of the house without locking down what the spaces are for. Nishihara argues that whereas the Western concept usually features single-function spaces, spaces in the Japanese home are used in much more diversified ways. [→ 02-03]

Remarkably, however, activities that take place within the home as a whole are placed on the same footing through a certain degree of abstraction. Following Nishihara's example, we divide these general, basic activities into the categories gathering, sleeping, cooking, eating, washing and working. In a place of 'gathering', many activities can occur: sitting, watching television, reading the newspaper, etcetera; however, it is also the place to gather, which requires sufficient space. 'Washing' includes sub-activities like cleaning the body, clothing and dishes, as well as using the toilet.

The ways these activities are carried out, what sub-activities comprise them, what utensils they require, their locus of operation inside or outside the home, the space(s) they require and their relationship to one another are all aspects that may differ significantly from one dwelling to another. Yet in all of them we recognize the same basic activities. The use of these six activities enables us to compare the use of dwellings in various cultures.

1 Kiyoyuki Nishihara, *Japanese Houses: Patterns for Living* (Tokyo: Japan Publications, 1968).

Programme, Function and Dimensions

Further analysis reveals another generally shared feature. For the last 4,000 years, dwellings all over the world have included a place

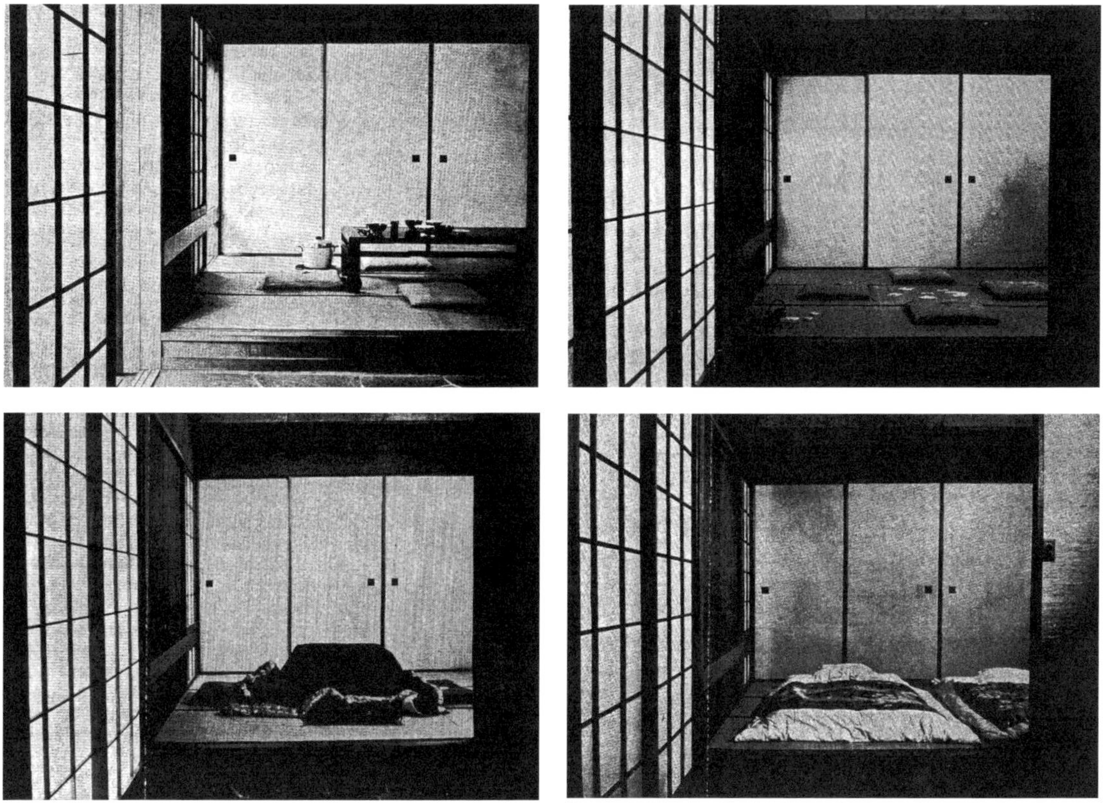

02

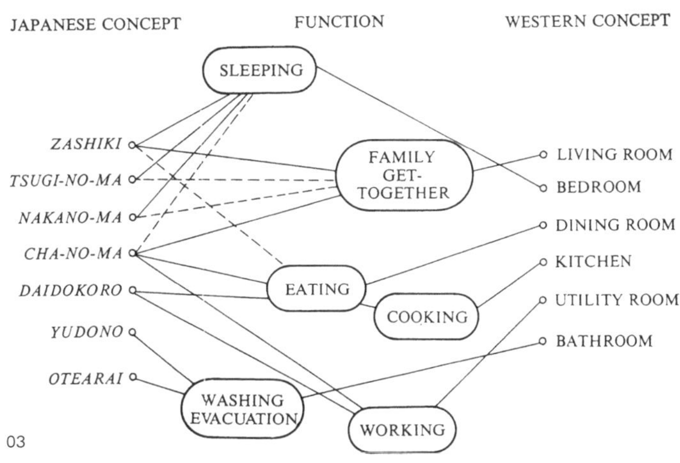

03

02 Differing uses of the same room over the course of a winter day: breakfast, use during the day, gathering of family in the evening and sleeping

03 Comparison between the functional approach to spaces in the Western world and in Japan

measuring about 4 m across the diagonal in which people can gather. [← 04] Only in single-occupancy dwellings or temporary accommodations like hotels is such a place missing from the individual housing unit; these spaces are then often found on a separate level, for instance the lobby of the hotel or the common room in a university residence hall. New-build housing is also likely to include a place about 4 m across the diagonal for the activity of gathering.[2]

2 Bernard Leupen, 'Polyvalence, a concept for the sustainable dwelling', *Nordsk architekturforskning*, no. 3 (2006), 26.

Similarly, it is possible to research the appropriate dimensions of each of the places needed for the remaining activities. It quickly becomes clear, however, that additional cultural differences that have an impact on the space required come into play. The household objects used in various countries and in various eras play an important part in this.[3] [→ 05-06]

3 A differentiation can be made on a world scale among cultures based on hard and soft furniture. In Western Europe, but also in China, hard furniture has traditionally been used – people sit on chairs – whereas in places like the Middle East, but also in Japan, soft furniture is used, in the form of cushions and floor mats.

The dimensions required for a place or space are determined to a large extent by the objects used to carry out the given activities. These take up space themselves, but also often place demands on the space around them. The space required can therefore be differentiated as follows: [→ 07]

—the dimensions of an object, expressed in length, width and height;
—the emplacement of an object, which is always (a little) larger than the object itself;
—the use space of an object, which is partly determined by the object itself (the drawers or doors of a cupboard) and partly by the user of the object;
—the circulation space needed to reach the object.

Various volumetric analyses of the use of space have been extensively documented in book form and represent a practical resource for many designers (Ernst Neufert's *Architects' Data*, for instance).[4]

4 Ernst Neufert, *Bauentwurfslehre* (Berlin: Bauwelt-Verlag, 1936); third English-language edition: Ernst and Peter Neufert, *Architects' Data* (Ames, Iowa: Blackwell Publishing Professional, 2002).

Quality and Comfort

Generous dimensions alone are not a guarantee for a comfortable home: a large mansion can be horrible to live in while a small flat can be very pleasant. The degree to which an accommodation is liveable is influenced, among other things, by several qualitative factors:

—*Accessibility*. Dwellings and dwelling spaces are easily and logically accessible. This involves not only the size of (doorway) openings, but also whether or not you have to go through a bedroom to reach the toilet, or whether a long corridor is needed to access a particular room, and so on. It is also a matter of safe access to upper floors. For older and less physically able people, proper accessibility requires extra additions from the designer: the elimination of obstacles, the turning circle of a wheelchair, the placement of walkers and scoot mobiles, etcetera.

—*Natural light, views and fresh air*. However logical these may sound, many dwellings are subject to the drawbacks of a lack of

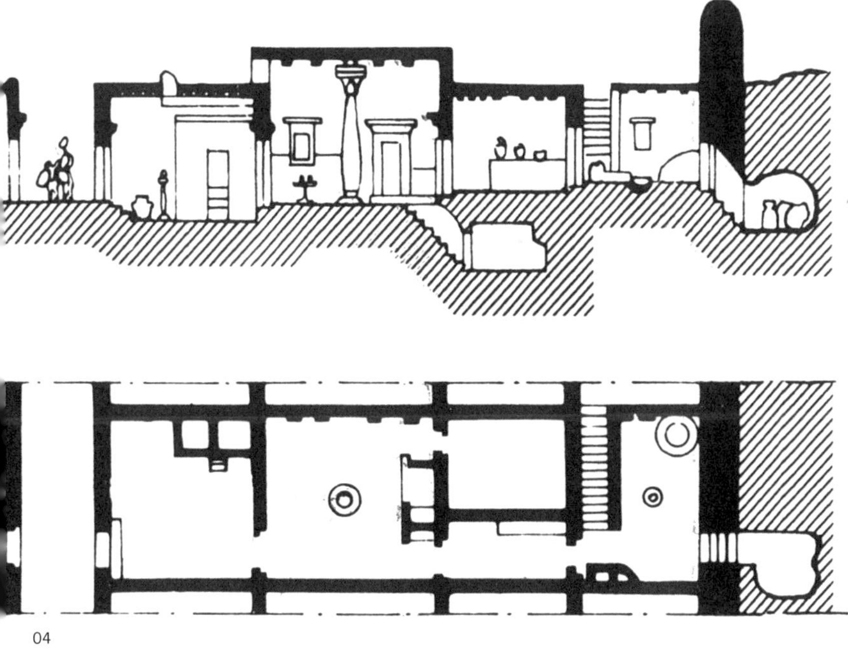

04

05

06

04 Section and floor plan of a typical dwelling in Deir-el-Medina, c. 1400 BCE, with the living room in the middle
05, 06 Dwelling and household goods of a family in Mali and of a family in the US

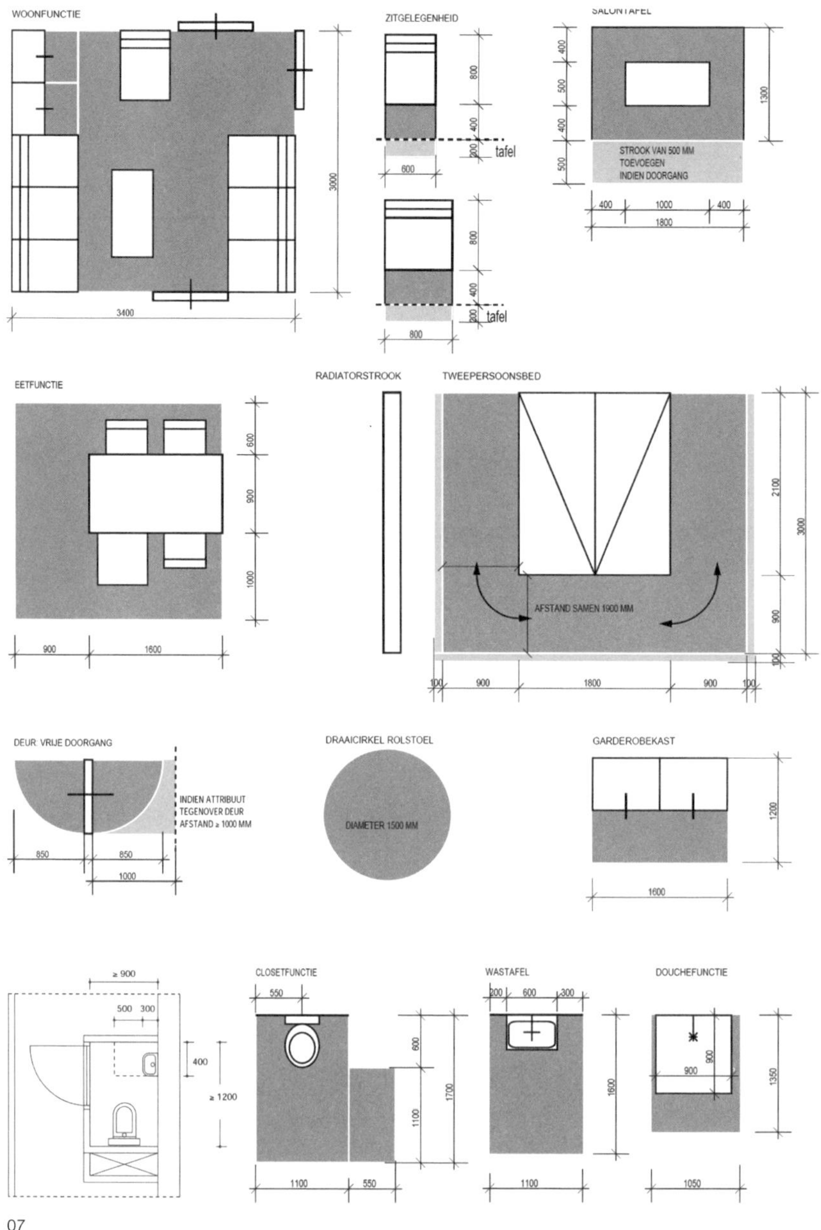

07

07 Indicative schematic overview of different household objects and the space for their optimum use specified by, in this case, the Woonkeur certification panel

these three qualities. This is not simply a question of quantity: think of how attractive a certain incidence of light can make a room, which also affords a spectacular view and ensures comfortable ventilation even in the winter.
—*Temperature*. Warm enough in the winter, cool enough in the summer–a constant interior temperature or one dictated by the season? This also involves the systems and appliances to regulate the temperature, as well as adequate protection from undesirable exterior conditions.
—*Supply of gas, water, electricity and data*. Often invisible to the occupants, but an integral part of the dwelling design: how do you get the necessary conduits to the places you most want them, how do you limit their length and how do you keep them accessible for maintenance and future changes and expansion?
—*Evacuation of fouled air and waste water*. How do you evacuate these outside without obstructions, even when the dwelling has multiple storeys or is situated on top of other dwellings? There is a reason the kitchen, the bathroom and especially the toilet are usually clustered around vertical pipes that use gravity to drain waste water downwards. Unpleasant odours and moisture are also usually extracted here, close to their source.

Rules and Regulations

The minimum dimensions allowable for various dwelling spaces and the minimum level of allowable quality and comfort are stipulated as requirements in national, provincial and municipal legislation and ordinances. In the Netherlands, the Housing Act (*Woningwet*), the Building Code (*Bouwbesluit*) and local building ordinances at the municipal level are the main regulations that govern housing design. Laws and codes are therefore also the expressions of a culture: a place- and time-specific representation of the most commonly shared attitudes towards the minimum level of acceptable housing quality.
Keep in mind that the law prescribes the *minimum* quality and dimensions *allowable*, which is quite a different thing from the ideal quality of comfortable dwelling spaces that can be aspired to. The actual quality of a dwelling, space or place is usually found in spaces that deviate from the minimum requirements. While decisions within a design privilege certain places over others, the law sets out the minimum requirements that the less privileged places must nevertheless fulfil.
In addition, each project also incorporates the wishes of housing corporations, or the certifications of special-interest groups like retirees or the disabled. Sometimes a certification comes with a subsidy–and therefore the financial scope for added quality. This makes certification a political instrument during the design process. The combination of various interests often leads to a maze of

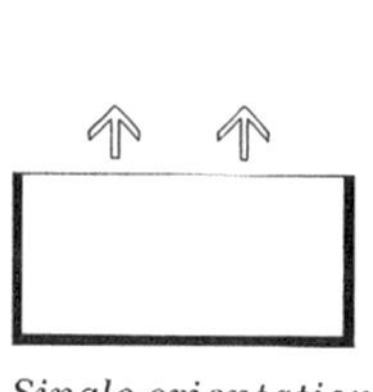

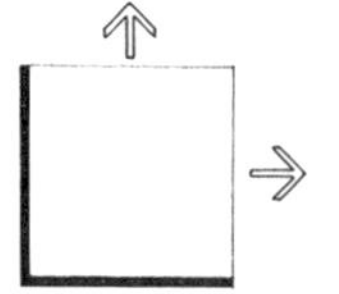

08

08 Schematic representation of Sherwood's categorization of dwellings according to orientation

different set of requirements the dwelling is expected to fulfil. While the value of special certifications is not in question, requirements are often primarily practical in nature. Fulfilling these requirements does not automatically result in a high-quality dwelling, while setting numerous lofty use demands for *every* space – in the case of a limited budget and square footage – can conflict with striving for specific quality in a few spaces that give the dwelling as a whole its quality and character. A designer therefore needs to carefully consider which interests are best served by individual quality requirements.

Orientation

Virtually every aspect of quality and comfort outlined above has something to do with the interaction between the spaces of the dwelling and the world outside. Some of these aspects, such as natural light and sun exposure, views and fresh air, even concern the direct relationship of the occupant(s) with the outside world. The way space in a dwelling is allocated is therefore closely related to the options for creating this relationship.

In a detached dwelling in open terrain, this is not very difficult: the spaces can easily be positioned in a variety of ways along the façades all the way round. Other motivations and factors, like a specific view, the creation of shadow or a certain line of sight, can play a role in the positioning of places and spaces in and around the house. The more a dwelling is surrounded by other dwellings, however, the fewer the options for establishing contact with the outside world. A correct placement of the spaces now becomes crucial to fulfilling the stipulated requirements and conditions. The incidence of natural light, in particular, is a difficult and often determining requirement in this respect. Roughly speaking, we can say that the length of the façade determines the quantity of programme that can be achieved behind it. A dwelling with a façade on only one side is therefore trickier than a dwelling exposed to natural light on two, three or four sides. Its spaces have to be arranged in a different way, in order to be aligned as well as possible towards natural light. We call this 'alignment', or the relationship between the dwelling's floor plan and the façades exposed to natural light, the orientation of the dwelling.

In the book *Modern Housing Prototypes*, Roger Sherwood categorizes housing units according to their orientation. He distinguishes between single-orientation units and double-orientation units. Dwellings with double orientation can be further divided into those with natural light exposure on two contiguous sides (90°) and those with natural light exposure on two opposite sides ('open-ended').[5] [← 08] Although a large proportion of mass-produced housing can be described in this way, there are also dwellings with triple orientation – an end-of-row home, for instance – and in the case of a detached house or a penthouse flat, quadruple orientation.

5
Roger Sherwood, *Modern Housing Prototypes* (Cambridge, MA: Harvard University Press, 1978).

DESIGNING THE DWELLING

There are many possible methodologies for the design of a dwelling. In this book we will confine ourselves to the more complex sort of housing construction, dwellings for unknown users (buyers or tenants). This area also used to be called mass housing construction or housing construction for the anonymous client. Today, however, these labels are no longer sufficient.
What follows is a series of different approaches to the design of housing, including the role played by the programme. We will look in succession at the functionalist approach, design according to criteria, pattern language, the closely related 'designing from place to place', zoning and design using the factor of time.

Designing Based on Function and Scale

Our objects are to be on a human scale, they ought to be but they are not yet, for there is still something nineteenth-century about our furniture, rooms and homes, in our layout of public places and town-planning too. There is not one of us completely free from something that our parents and grand-parents really had in their blood: design for prestige's sake. That is representation and not the human scale, it is excess, it is trying to impress, it is trying to seem more than the truth. And excess is a proof of want of principle and of an antisocial way of life, most of all at a time when the minimum requirements in housing and standard of living of many thousands of the working population remain unsatisfied.[6]
This Mart Stam quotation from 1929 illustrates the passionate commitment of architects in the first half of the twentieth century to the central issue in mass housing construction: how to develop as many good-quality dwellings as possible for the working class, at an acceptable and affordable price. Stam was convinced (along with many of his colleagues at the time) that the solution needed to be found in the precise correlation of the scale of dwelling spaces to 'the human scale'. His statement 'the door is 2 metres high – we know why'[7] is characteristic of his unswerving commitment to design based on the human scale. This statement is not just characteristic; it is now also obsolete in an age when people taller than 2 m are no longer exceptions.
The idea of designing for human dimensions led to numerous studies into the space taken up by our activities. Around 1930 there were various attempts undertaken in Germany to design dwellings that catered to this 'human scale'. There was an effort to arrive at the *Existenzminimum*: the minimum dimensions of dwelling spaces and household objects considered necessary for a standard German working-class family of the period.
In the Netherlands, Willem Van Tijen conducted studies into the activities that took place in the home. [→ 09] He documented

6 Mart Stam, 'Das Mass, das richtige Mass, das Minimum-Mass', *Das Neue Frankfurt*, no. 3 (March 1929), translated by C. van Amerongen as 'Scale – Right Scale – Minimum Scale', in: *Mart Stam: A Documentation of His Work, 1920–1965* (London: Royal Institute of British Architects, 1970).

7 Mart Stam, 'M-Kunst', *i10*, vol. 1 (1927) no. 2, translated by C. van Amerongen as 'M-Art', in: ibid.

domestic life in measurements and motion diagrams.[8] In Germany, Grete Schütte-Lihotzky developed the 'Frankfurt kitchen' based on similar ergonomic analyses. [→ 10-11] After the Second World War, these studies led to codes in the Netherlands such as the 'functional fundamentals of the home'[9] promulgated by the Centre for Building Excellence (*Bouwcentrum*) and the housing ministry's 'Prescriptions and Suggestions' (*Voorschriften en wenken*)[10]. These prescriptions and suggestions, which every subsidized dwelling in the Netherlands had to satisfy, formed the programme of requirements for post-war reconstruction housing. These ergonomic analyses and especially their adaptation into prescriptions and suggestions provide a snapshot of the standard post-war Dutch family. Later regulations set out minimum dimensions in what came to be called *matjes* ('little mats'): specifications outlined for various sub-activities. [→ 12] This approach, exclusively focused on measurements and numbers, eventually attracted substantial criticism, leading to new methodologies.

8
Willem van Tijen, 'Het onderzoek naar de ruimtebehoeften in en om de gezinswoning', in: *De ruimtebehoeften in en om de Nederlandse volkswoning* (thesis proposal) (Zandvoort, 1966), 44 ff and appendix.

9
Bouwcentrum, *Functionele grondslagen van de woning. Algemene inleiding* (Rotterdam, 1958).

10
Netherlands Ministry of Housing and Spatial Planning, *Voorschriften en wenken voor het ontwerpen van woningen* (The Hague, 1965).

Criteria

Another approach to the design of housing is to design according to pre-established internal criteria against which the design can be tested over the course of the design process: if at a given point the design does not satisfy all the criteria, attention can be concentrated on specific points until the design is successful according to every criterion.

One example of this approach is the checklist of the husband-and-wife architecture team of Peter and Alison Smithson. Their 'criteria for mass housing'[11] were intended for dwellings and housing environments in low- and high-rise housing, the occupants of which are not known during the design process and towards whom the architect, in the Smithsons' view, bears a particularly heavy responsibility. They took into account spiritual and emotional well-being and a great number of other psychological aspects. The Smithsons' conclusion was that the criteria represent potential prescriptions that plans must satisfy in order to be accepted as a minimum environment for housing. [→ 13]

11
Alison and Peter Smithson, 'Criteria for Mass Housing', *Architectural Design* (September 1967).

Patterns of Activity

Another, far more systematic and more extensive response to the functionalist approach of housing design came in the 1970s, from American architect Christopher Alexander: 'pattern language'. In his book *A Pattern Language* Alexander outlines a method whereby the design project is examined using a number of activity clusters or patterns.[12] Alexander, one of the first architects to use a computer, endeavoured to apply the principles of computer programming to architectural design. Pattern language is a structured way of describing design problems and sub-problems. Alexander explains the methodology in three steps, as follows:

12
Christopher Alexander, *A Pattern Language* (New York: Oxford University Press, 1977).

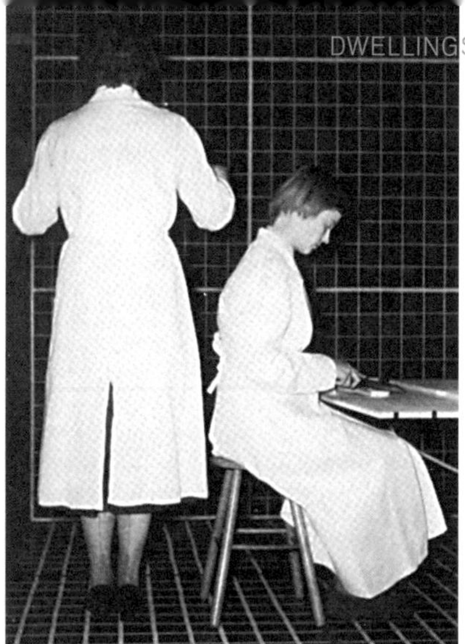

09

III. Küchen und Hauswirtschaft.

1. Die Küche:

In allen Wohnungen ist die sogenannte **Frankfurter Küche** von Frau Architekt Schütte-Lihotzky mit einigen Variationen eingebaut worden (Typ in Bild 25, Ansichten in Bild 26–29).

Bild 25. Frankfurter Küche.

Teil-Abdruck von einem Frankfurter Normenblatt. Die Küche ist 1,87 m × 3,44 m groß und enthält.

1 = Herd mit einer Abstellplatte.
2 = Schubladen für Mehl und Salz.
3 = Kochkiste.
4 = Schubladen für größere Vorräte.
5 = Heizkörper.
6 = Gewürzgestell.
7 = Speiseschrank.
8 = Tisch mit Rinne für Kuchenabfälle
9 = Abtropfbrett
10 = Tellerabtropfgestell.
11 = Zweiteiliges Spülbecken.
12 = Vorratsschrank.
13 = Geschirrschrank.
14 = Topfschrank.
15 = Müll- und Besenschrank.
16 = Schiebelampe
17 = Bügelbrett.

Alle Möbel stehen auf 10 cm hohem Betonsockel, mit Platten bekleidet, der 4 cm zurückspringt.

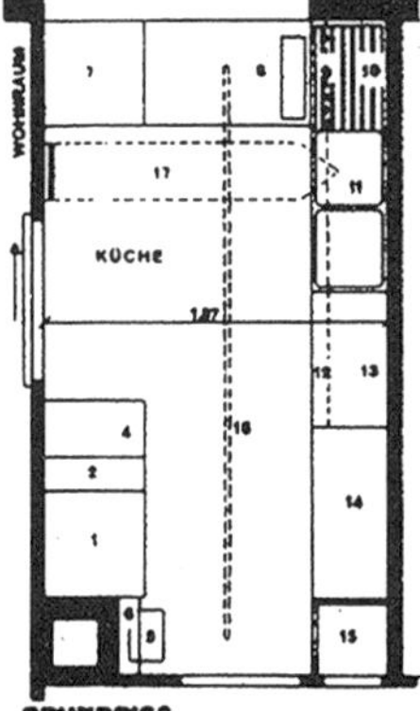

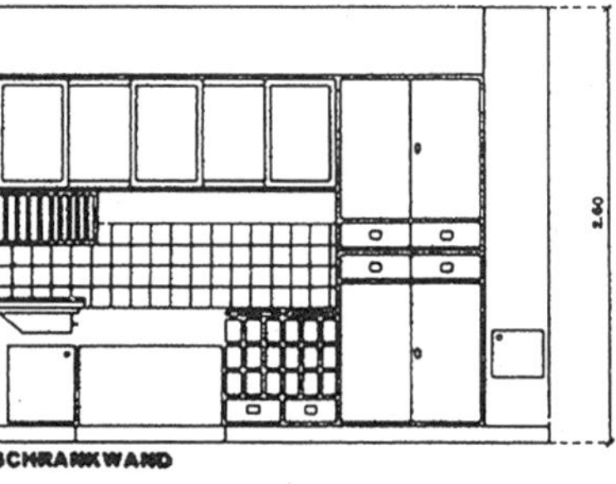

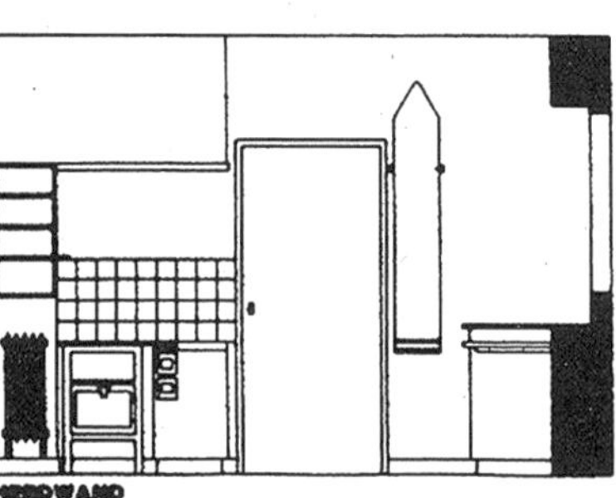

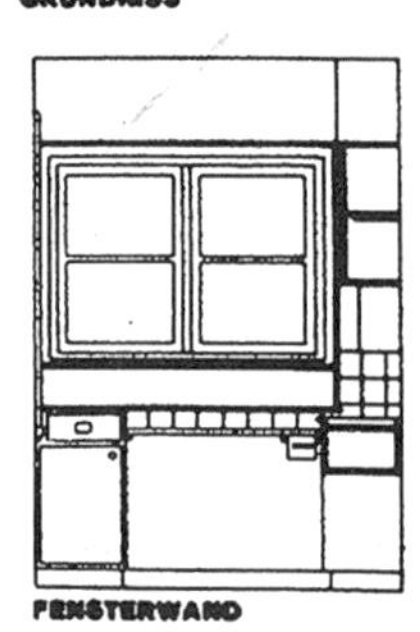

10

11

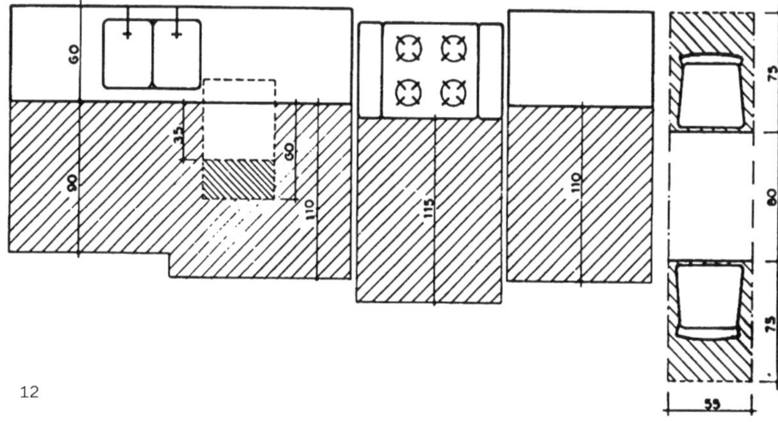

12

:RITERIA FOR MASS HOUSING

evised by A. and P. Smithson for Team X

irst published 1957, revised 1959

he term Mass Housing applies to all dwellings *nct* uilt to the special order of an individual: houses ver which the occupier has no control other than at he has chosen or has been chosen, to live there: ouses for which, therefore, the architect has a eculiar responsibility.

he criteria are intended to apply to all housing respective of number, type of ground occupation, pe of access, etc., etc. The most conventional ouses and layouts, and the most ingenious can qually well come under their scrutiny.

he House

Can it adapt itself to various ways of living? oes it liberate the occupants from old restrictions straightjacket them into new ones?

Can the individual add 'identity' to his house or is e 'architecture' packaging him?

Will the lampshades on the ceilings, the curtains, e china dogs, take away the meaning of the rchitecture'?

Is the means of construction of the same order the standard of living envisaged in the house? the technology *suitable* to house construction: oes it take account of electrical runs and do without traditional 'style-left-overs', such as door ames?

Are the spaces moulded exactly to fit their urpose? Or are they by-products of structural diness or plastic whim?

Is there a decently-large open-air sunlit space pening directly from the living area of the house? there a place in the open-air where a baby can be ft? (0-3 year olds).

Can the extensions of the dwelling (garden, patio, c.), be appreciated from inside?

Can the weather be enjoyed? Is the house insulad against cold weather yet made to easily open up good weather?

Is there a place where you can clean or wash ings without making a mess in the house?

Does it take account of the 3-5 years olds' play?

Is there enough storage? (there is never enough orage)—that is storage not of a purely residual ature (lofts, 'built-in' fittings, etc.). Is there a place r the belongings peculiar to the class of the ccupants—poodles, ferrets, camping gear, geranms, motorbikes, etc.?

Is it easy to maintain (keep fresh looking with st a cleaning down)?

Is the house as comfortable as a car of the same ear?

Can the houses be put together in such a way as contribute something to each other?

The immediate extensions of the dwelling

1 Has the relationship between the dwelling and its means of access been chosen for some good reason?

2 Does this reason include three- to five-year-olds play, if not, where do they play?

3 Does the *idea* for the dwelling produce an absolutely clear external image?

4 Can these images add up to a composite one and is this composite one socially valid (that is, is it done for some present-day *human* reason).

5 Are the extensions of the dwelling—gardens, patios, balconies, streets, access galleries, staircases, etc.—sensible when one considers the existing physical environment of the dwellings and the activities of the occupants (topography and living pattern)? Are the gardens and streets necessary to the life of the occupant or are they irrelevant to it?

6 Is 'delivery' and'collection' antiquated and laborious? (milk, groceries, heat, refuse)?

7 Is there any indication that where people have been put into the air ('flats') that it is really getting them somewhere?
Does the public vertical circulation really work?

8 Is it a labour to go out or return home?

9 If the development was isolated—would it look like a camp?

The appreciated unit

1 Is the scale of the unit related to the size of the parent community? (The pattern of a village can be transformed by the addition of one house; in the great city an equivalent gesture might need a unit of 5,000 houses).

2 Is the work-pattern of the community understood with all its implications for the unit? (A work-pattern of all-family travelling to widely separated places is typical of cities and towns and often also of villages.)

3 Does it fit the site with its climatic and physical peculiarities, its existing built and human structure, and accept their ecological implications *bearing in mind that we are concerned with renewal*?

4 Where do the 5-12 years old's go to? And what do they have to do?

5 Can the unit support shops? And where are the natural 'pressure points' for such facilities? Are the community facilities a social mirage or are they real?

6 Can November 5th be celebrated (or Bastille day or 4th July)?

7 Is there something worth looking at out of every dwelling or does one merely stare out at another dwelling opposite?

8 Does the development offer protection and shelter of the same order as the parent community?

9 Is the unit really generated by an objective study of the situation or are we just saying that it is?

09 Van Tijen, research into minimum required dimensions in the home
10, 11 G. Schütte-Lihotzky, the Frankfurt Kitchen, 1926. Aiming to improve social housing, Grete Schütte-Lihotzky designed this model kitchen as a machine entirely attuned in use of space and ergonomics to the needs of a standard working-class German family.
12 Illustration from Functionele grondslagen van de woning ('Functional Fundamentals of the Home') of specification *matjes* for the various functions centred on preparing food
13 A. and P. Smithson, 'Criteria for Mass Housing', drawn up in 1957, revised in 1959

— identify the usual problems encountered within the area in question;
— describe their most significant features and effective solutions;
— the designer must then work from problem to problem in a logical way, following various paths through the design process.

In *A Pattern Language* Alexander describes many patterns, from city to home. The patterns are arranged in a hierarchical system. One illustrative example is Pattern 130, the pattern for the entrance to a dwelling. [→ 14]
Pattern language is a complex system. It was initially embraced by many people in the 1970s, but its complexity often makes its application problematic. Designing with pattern language makes one yearn for a more self-evident and more architectural way of working.

Designing from Place to Place

For Aldo van Eyck, the concept of place played a vital role.[13] In his 1961 essay 'Interior Art' Van Eyck emphasizes why he prefers the word 'place' to the word 'space':
The word I want to talk about is place. Because, look, the word 'space' has become a sort of academic conjuring word. It means everything and therefore nothing. It is precisely this 'space' in which the mind went astray, and this space has been absorbed into the void along with the mind. One might construct the outline of the emptiness and call this space![14]
Also in 1961, the journal *Forum* put out a special issue with the theme 'Door and Window', in which Van Eyck published 'Place and Occasion' (often referred to by its opening line, taken from a poem by Thomas Campion: 'There is a garden in her face'), a poetic text in which he calls attention to place with sentences such as 'Today, space and what it should coincide with in order to become "space" –humanity at home with ourselves–are lost. Both search the same place, but cannot find it.' And a little way down the page, in big letters, the famous phrase 'make a welcome of each door, a countenance of each window', and then in lowercase: 'make of each a place.' It sounds a lot like Alexander's argument for pattern language: he too made a place of coming in.[15] Van Eyck's text, however, is less systematic and far more poetic.
The concept of place plays an equal role in the way Van Eyck designed and can be described as 'designing from place to place'.[16] This is not so much a method, like pattern language, as it is an attitude towards design. In from-place-to-place design, the place is the locus of operation from which the design is conceived. One or more places form the basis of the space to be created. This also involves the connections among these places, moving from one place to another. This is comparable to some extent to Le Corbusier's

13
Vincent Ligtelijn and Francis Strauven (eds.), *Aldo van Eyck: Collected Articles and Other Writings 1947–1998* (Amsterdam: SUN Publishers, 2008).

14
Ibid., 295. Van Eyck gave a reading of this text on 6 February 1961 at the Royal Academy of Fine Arts in The Hague.

15
Ibid., 295.

16
The concept of 'designing from place to place' has not, as far as we have been able to ascertain, been defined in writing; in the sense associated with Aldo van Eyck it was used frequently in design teaching practice within the Faculty of Architecture at Delft University of Technology throughout the 1970s and 1980s.

5. Interior of the entrance room

(a) Politeness demands that when someone comes to the door, the door is opened wide.

(b) People seek privacy for the inside of their houses.

(c) The family, sitting, talking, or at table, do not want to feel disturbed or intruded upon when someone comes to the door.

Make the inside of the entrance room zigzag, or obstructed, so that a person standing on the doorstep of the open door can see no rooms inside, except the entrance room itself, nor through the doors of any rooms.

6. Coats, shoes, children's bikes . . .

(a) Muddy boots have got to come off.

(b) People need a five foot diameter of clear space to take off their coats.

(c) People take prams, bicycles, and so on indoors to protect them from theft and weather; and children will tend to leave all kinds of clutter—bikes, wagons, roller skates, trikes, shovels, balls—around the door they use most often.

Therefore, give the entrance room a dead corner for storage, put coat pegs in a position which can be seen from the front door, and make an area five feet in diameter next to the pegs.

Therefore:

At the main entrance to a building, make a light-filled room which marks the entrance and straddles the boundary between indoors and outdoors, covering some space outdoors and some space indoors. The outside part may be like an old-fashioned porch; the inside like a hall or sitting room.

BUILDINGS

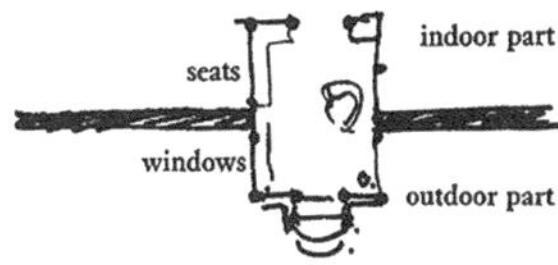

14

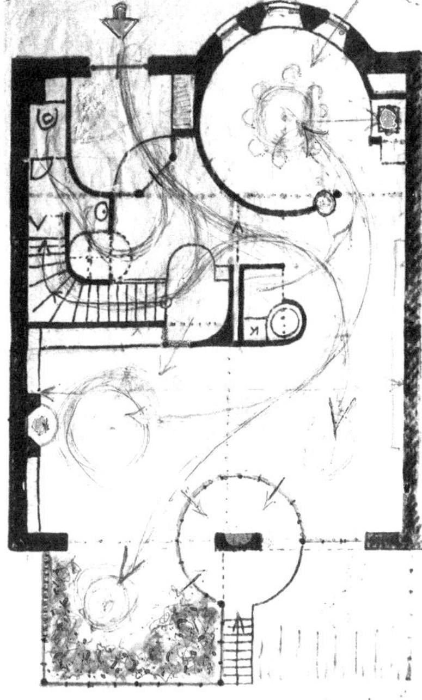

16

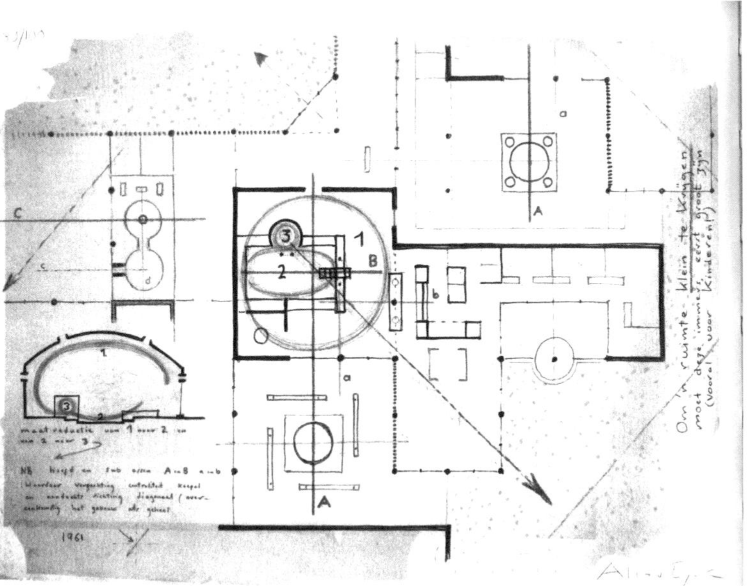

15

14 Pattern 130: the entrance space, from Christopher Alexander's *Pattern Language*
15 A. van Eyck, design sketch for the Amsterdam Orphanage, place within a place
16 A. van Eyck, design sketch for an urban dwelling in London (1969). The sketch clearly shows how Van Eyck investigated circulation lines and places.

route architecturale, with the key difference that the main objective is not the way this progression is experienced: the route is merely a means to connect activities and places.

The design for the Municipal Orphanage in Amsterdam (1955–1959) is predominantly a search for the right configuration and new order of building; at the same time this complex is a fine illustration of 'designing from place to place'. [← 15] In Van Eyck's text on the orphanage in *Forum* in 1961, in which he describes such elements as the design of the interior street, place is an important motif:

> This interior street is yet another intermediary – there are many more. In fact the building was conceived as a configuration of intermediary places clearly defined. This does not imply continual transition or endless postponement with respect to place and occasion. On the contrary, it implies a break away from the contemporary concept (call it sickness) of spatial continuity and the tendency to erase every articulation between spaces, i.e. between outside and inside, between one space and another. Instead I tried to articulate the transition by means of defined in-between places which induce simultaneous awareness of what is significant on either side. An in-between place in this sense provides the common ground where conflicting polarities can again become dual phenomena.[17]

It should be noted that Aldo van Eyck was not simply describing an attitude towards design here; he was also offering a critique of the modernist concept of space, with its continuous, flowing space both through the building and from inside to outside ('call it sickness'). He countered this with his own concept, in which spaces may indeed transition into one another, but only so long as their transitions are clearly articulated. [← 16] Later in the same text he also describes the effect of lighting on place: 'The electric lighting, moreover, is like street lighting in the sense that the child moves from illuminated place to illuminated place via comparative darkness.'[18] His draft designs show how much the search for and the formation of places and their relationships to one another was part of Van Eyck's design process.

One danger in 'designing from place to place' is that the space becomes fragmented and every activity is assigned not just its own place but also its own space, which can hinder future changes in use. This issue is addressed in the following section.

Zoning

In the late 1950s, Dutch architect N.J. Habraken described how the problems of mass housing construction could be resolved.[19] In his book *Supports: An Alternative to Mass Housing* he developed a system whereby the government should provide large structures, called supports, upon or within which occupants could construct their own homes.[20] Together with nine architecture practices and

17
Ligtelijn and Strauven, *Aldo van Eyck*, op. cit. (note 13), 319.

18
Ibid., 319.

19
N. John Habraken, *De dragers en de mensen. Het einde van de massawoningbouw* (Amsterdam: Scheltema & Holkema, 1961). Habraken wrote this book in the 1950s, shortly after completing his architecture studies in Delft. It was not published, however, until 1961. Its first edition in English was *Supports: An Alternative to Mass Housing*, translated by B. Valkenburg (London: Architectural Press, 1972).

20
Ibid., 84.

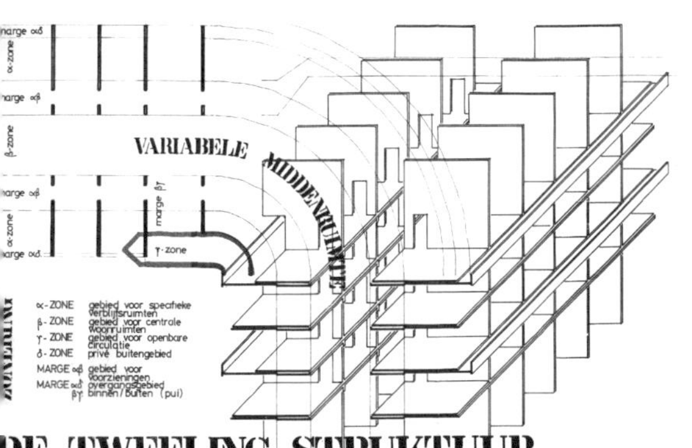

a

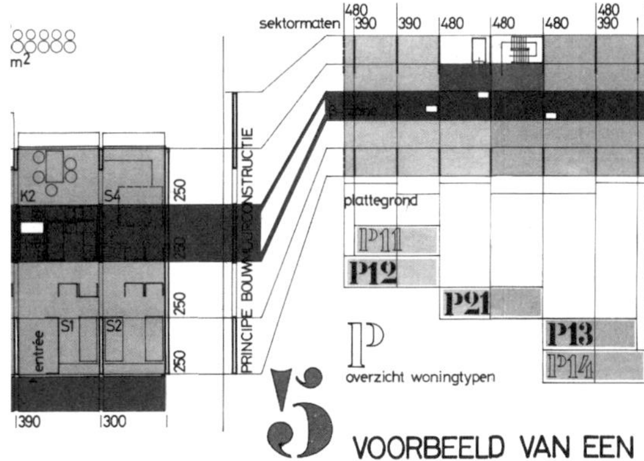

17b

18

19

17 SAR, elaboration of the zoning principle in cooperation with I.B.B.
18 Diagoon house, base principle
19 Ensemble of Diagoon houses

the Royal Institute of Dutch Architects (BNA), Habraken founded the Foundation for Architects' Research (SAR) in 1964. This foundation devoted itself to studying the possibilities for mass production and standardization in housing construction. One of the pillars of this research is a zoning system, the '10–20 grid'. Without going into the specific features and rules of the SAR grid, we can generally agree that working with zones can be useful in housing design. Briefly summarized, this comes down to the following: zones of a specified width are defined, which determine the placement of specific elements of the building or specific kinds of spaces. These can be zones in which material – such as load-bearing walls – as well as space can be located; they can be zones in which access or 'wet areas' are situated (see also CePeZed's Heiwo house, page 325).
We show here an illustration of the zoning system for vertically stacked housing developed by the SAR in the late 1960s in collaboration with the IBB engineering bureau. [← 17] The dark zones in the middle (the β zones) define the location of 'wet rooms' and conduits, the dark zone along the façade (the γ zone) the access or exterior spaces, while the light-grey zone (the α zone) indicates the placement of the habitation spaces.[21]

21
H.W.L. Heyning, *Methodisch ontwerpen in het IBB-gietbouwsysteem* (Leiden/Eindhoven: IBB-SAR, 1969).

Time as a Factor in the Design

Growing criticism of functionalism and the design methods and prescriptions derived from it led to increasing attention among designers towards the treatment of the unexpected and towards the flexibility of the dwelling. A successful dwelling is more than a programme of requirements translated into material form. One of the issues a housing designer has to take into account is the factor of time. Over the course of its lifetime, a dwelling undergoes many changes in use, as well as changes due to cultural, societal and technological developments – changes that the designer cannot predict or identify in any comprehensive way. In order to accommodate the time factor, we must design dwellings that are able to absorb these changes in one way or another. The book *Time-Based Architecture* describes three strategies to accomplish this:[22]
— polyvalent dwellings
— dwellings with a permanent part and an adaptable part, labelled the 'frame concept' in the rest of this discussion
— semi-permanent dwellings.

22
Bernard Leupen et al., *Time-Based Architecture* (Rotterdam: 010 Publishers, 2005).

Polyvalent Dwellings

Polyvalency literally means 'having more than one valency' (valency in this case being the 'relative capacity to unite, react or interact'). In relation to housing, polyvalency means that the dwelling can be used in different ways without requiring adaptations of an architectural nature, thanks to the way activities can be interchangeably carried out throughout the various spaces. Herman Hertzberger introduced this concept into the architecture debate in the early 1960s.[23] We can see some of his ideas on polyvalency in the 'Diagoon' row houses he designed in Delft (1967–1971). [← 18-19] Hertzberger achieves polyvalency here, in the first place, through the spatial organization of the dwelling. The spatial system he has designed can be inhabited in a variety of ways. The dwelling is composed of a number of large habitation spaces, more or less identical in shape, each of which is shifted half a storey in relation to the next. These spaces are also staggered horizontally in relation to one another along the depth of the dwelling.

The spaces are partially separated by two vertical closed elements. The stairs are situated in one of these elements; the other vertical element houses service spaces, including the kitchen. The large spaces for habitation are arranged across from one another diametrically around a central open vertical space (*vide*). This open vertical space allows natural light coming through the roof to reach deep into the heart of the home. It also lets the large spaces communicate visually, which allows the occupants to experience the split-level organization. The play of light engendered by the central open vertical space creates a constantly changing atmosphere in the large spaces. Because the large habitation spaces all have more or less the same dimensions and because their position in relation to the vertical elements housing the service spaces is not unidirectional, their functions are not fixed. The occupant can choose where to live, sleep or work within the home.

23
Herman Hertzberger, 'Flexibility and Polyvalency', *Forum*, no. 3 (1962).

Topological Analysis

The spatial system of a home can be expressed using a topological diagram, a graph. With a graph, the polyvalency of the spatial system of a house can be examined. A spatial system in which various spaces are accessible only through another space, through the living room for example, is less suited to different forms of habitation than a dwelling in which the spatial system offers the option of accessing every space from a central point or by multiple routes. [→ 20]

Two Examples

A classic example of polyvalent housing is the project designed by Duinker Van der Torre in Amsterdam's Dapperbuurt area.[24] The doors, in particular the two sliding doors, play an important role in the manipulation of the spatial system here. Yet the sliding doors are not primarily what make the dwelling polyvalent. Polyvalency is created here by the spatial system itself, which makes it possible to access every space by two different routes (principle graph D). [← 21-23] The placement of the service spaces within a central core is an important facet of this (see also page 108). In order to avoid the route from one room to another leading through too many habitation

24
Han Michel, 'Moderne Beweging in de Dapperbuurt', in: R. Brouwers (ed.), *Architectuur in Nederland Jaarboek 88/89* (Rotterdam: NAi Publishers, 1989), 75.

spaces, the architects have created a shortcut through a small corridor past the 'wet area' (see the section in the upper right of the graph with the little squares representing the spatial system). In practice, the dwelling can be inhabited in different ways. The polyvalency of the spatial system is constrained by the fact that only one space can accommodate the function of gathering (the living room).[25] A more recent example in which polyvalency plays a role is the Straßgang housing project in Graz by Austrian architects Riegler & Riewe (see also page 109). By creating spaces whose proportions do not immediately refer to the usual categories of dwelling space, they invite the occupant to utilize the home in a personal and original way. The architects describe this as follows:

25 Bernard Leupen, *Frame and Generic Space: A Study into the Changeable Dwelling Proceeding from the Permanent* (Rotterdam: 010 Publishers, 2006).

We generated this project with the intention to have a room, which is too large for the entrance, too small for being a living or bedroom, and with the intention to have a service area in the middle of the apartment. As a consequence one has a free choice how to use all the spatial sequences along the facade.[26] [→ 25-26]

26 F. Riegler, 'Is architecture no longer any use?', symposium on Time-Based Buildings, Delft 2004.

The floor plans this produces are more reminiscent of the archaeological digs of Ancient Greek and Roman sites than of the usual modern dwelling floor plan. But perhaps it is precisely in these archetypal features that the secret of the polyvalent dwelling lies. Rather than the floor plan constructed on the basis of modern analyses, it is the arrangements that have proved their value over the millennia that can make a home habitable even over the long term.

The Frame Concept

In the case of the frame concept, a distinction is made in buildings, and in particular in dwellings, between the part of the dwelling that remains constant for an extended time and the part that is subject to change. An obvious example is the common distinction between the shell (the load-bearing structure plus the main access, for instance) as the permanent portion, and the building elements that define the division of space (like partition walls) as the variable portion. Other combinations are conceivable within the frame concept, however, with sometimes surprising results. This concept is developed in detail in the book *Frame and Generic Space*;[27] here we will confine ourselves to one instance.

27 Leupen, *Frame and Generic Space*, op. cit. (note 25).

An illustrative example in which the frame concept can be identified is the Nieuw Australië complex in Amsterdam, which owes its name to the former dockland warehouse Australië. The new structure designed by DKV architecten is situated next to the converted warehouse and part of it is suspended over the old building. Both the old and the new sections consist of shell housing units. In the new section these shells are accessed through a gallery, in the old section through a corridor.

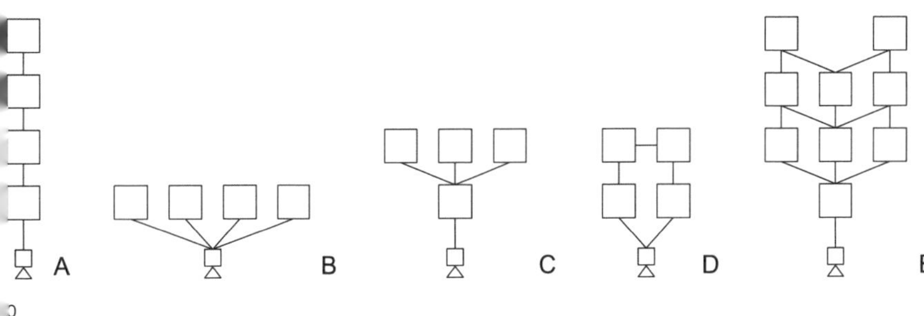

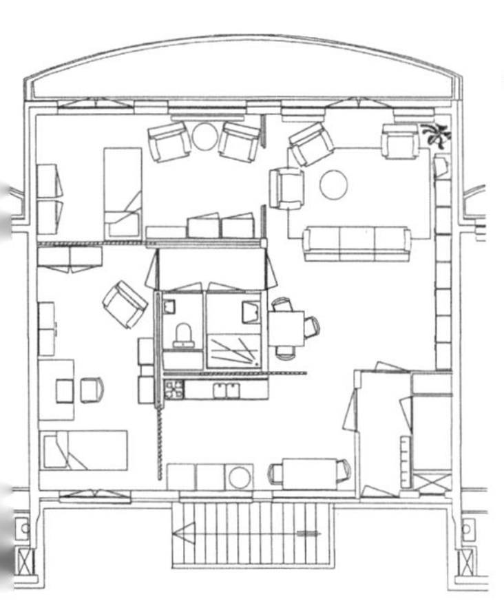

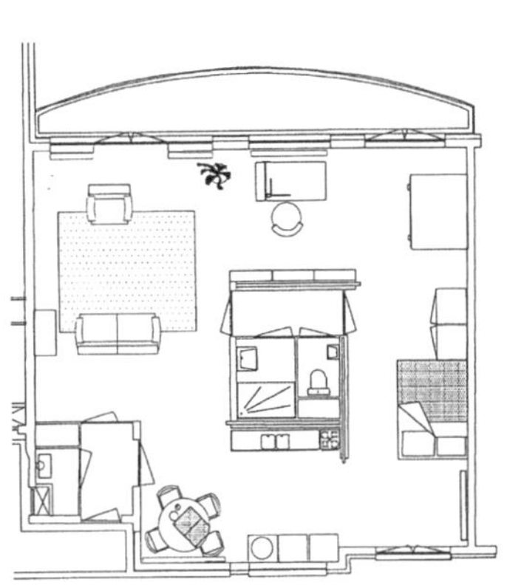

20 Series of graphs representing the organization of space. A represents a spatial system with a low degree of polyvalency: one must go through one room to reach another. Essentially, this implies an increasing sequence in the home from the more communal to the more private. In the other four graphs, the rooms are either organized to coordinate (B and C) or accessible by multiple routes (D and E).
21 Duinker van der Torre, Wagenaarstraat, Dapperbuurt, Amsterdam (1986–1988). Different patterns of use.
22 Graph of the spatial system; the checked boxes are the 'wet cells'.
23 Axonometrics of the spatial system

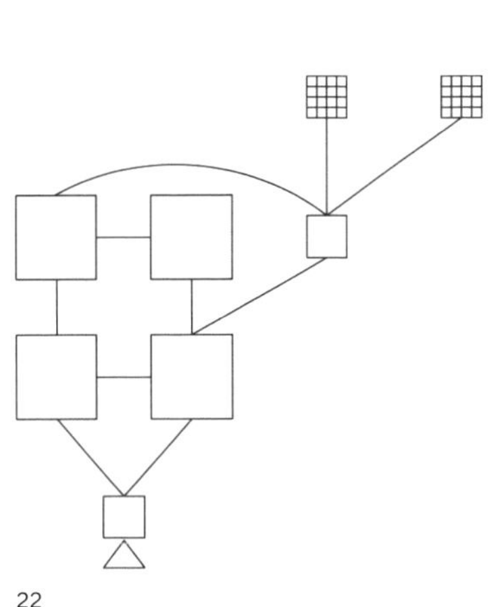

22

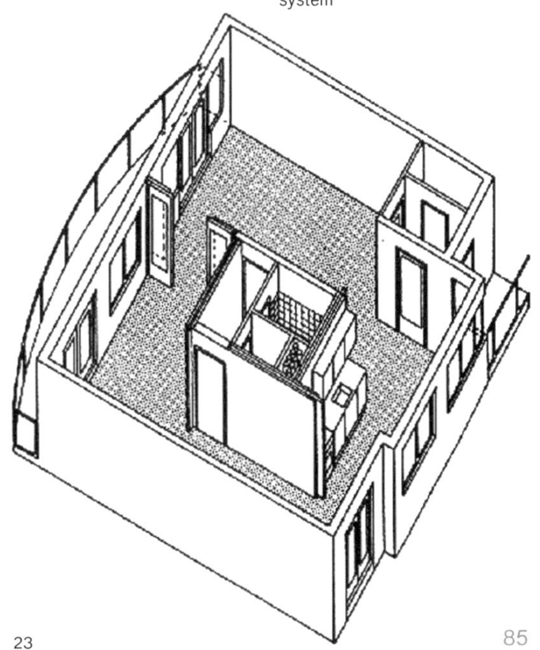

23

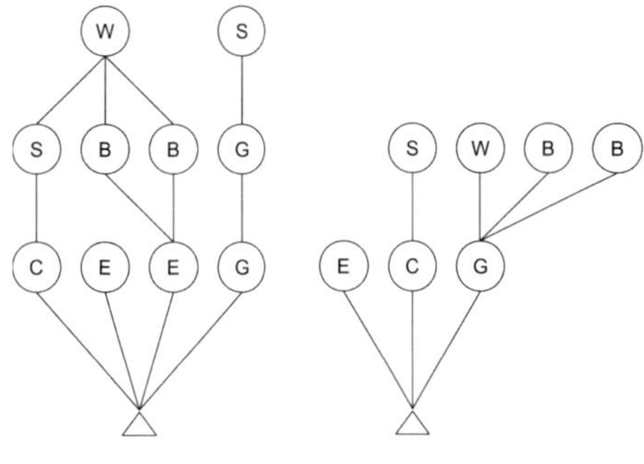

24

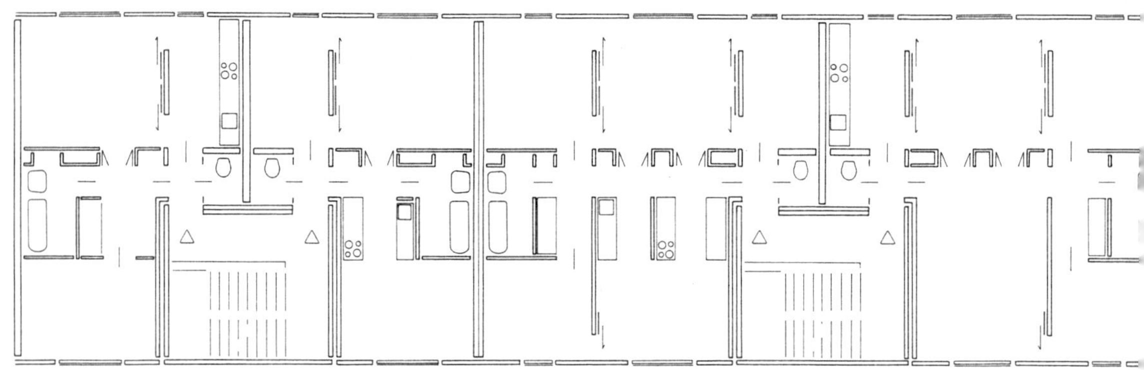

25

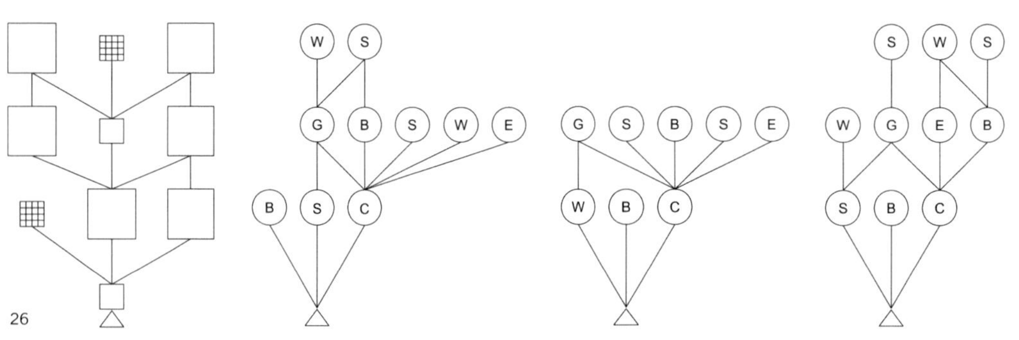

26

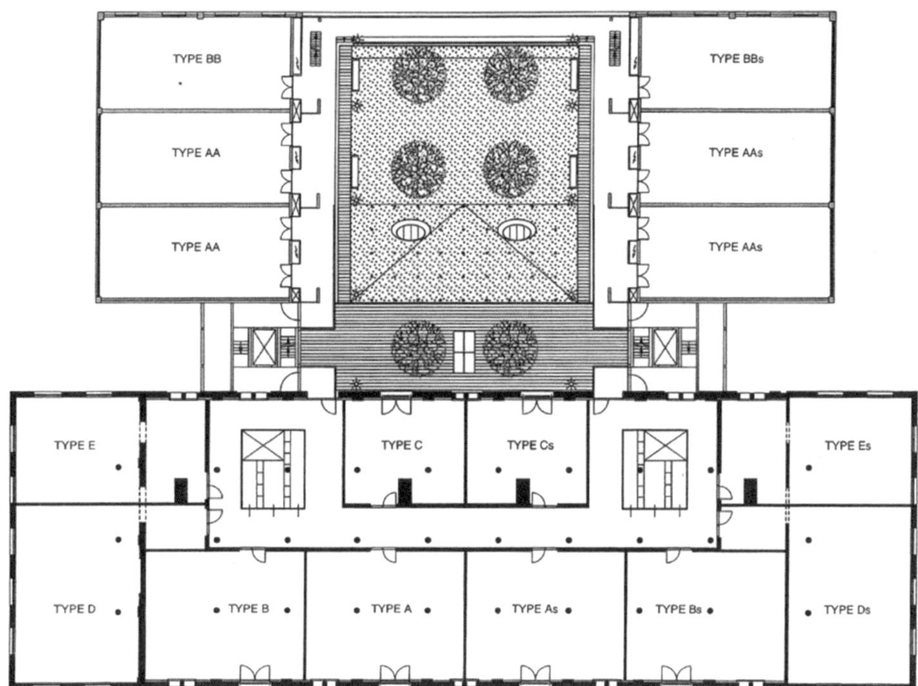

27

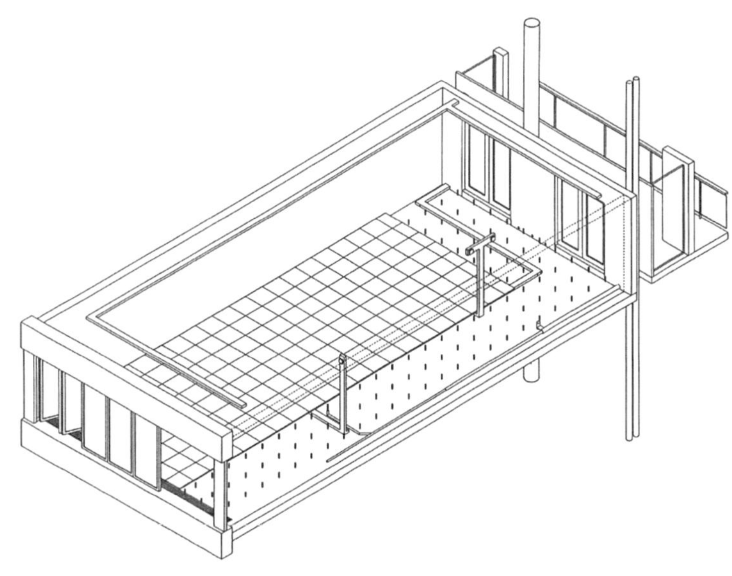

28

24 Two graphs of two different forms of habitation. Legend for the letter symbols in English: Sleeping. Get together. Eating. Cooking. Bathing. Working.
25 Riegler and Riewe, Straßgang project in Graz, floor plan of storey
26 Graph of the organization of space (I), alongside three different graphs of three different approaches to habitation
27 DKV architecten, Nieuwe Australië, floor plan
28 Nieuwe Australië, axonometrics of the frame

The wall between the dwelling (type AA) and the gallery contains the shafts for plumbing and wiring. Here is where the dwelling, so to speak, is plugged into the network of pipes and cables. In order to keep the partitioning of the dwelling as unrestricted as possible, the architects opted for a raised floor. This flooring, of a type often used in computer rooms, is made up of small concrete elements, each 60 × 60 cm, reinforced at the corners by small steel struts.[28] In this project, the permanent part (the frame) consists of the load-bearing structure, the façade (the skin) and the supply and discharge conduits (the 'service elements'). [← 27-28]

The use of this flooring leaves the partitioning of the dwelling entirely independent of the location of the plumbing and wiring. Even the location of the service spaces – toilet, kitchen and bathroom – is discretionary, since in principle the main soil pipe for the toilet can be concealed under the floor. If the toilet is located more than a few metres from the plumbing shaft, however, a system needs to be installed in order to pump waste matter to the main soil stack, so this level of choice does require an additional financial investment. Future occupants can select from a range of prefabricated internal elements, hire someone to build the interior, or build it themselves.[29]

28 It must be pointed out that in the eventual implementation, a foamed concrete flooring was selected, in which channels for plumbing and wiring can easily be excavated.

29 P. de Vroom, 'Australië-Boston Amsterdam', *TBA International*, no. 2 (2008), 17.

Semi-Permanent Dwellings

If future use is undetermined or the function short-lived, the semi-permanent dwelling offers a solution. Semi-permanent dwellings are often designed to meet specific needs on a temporary basis, such as in the aftermath of calamities or to provide a quick solution to a specific problem in the housing market. The example selected here is emergency housing for the victims of the 1995 earthquake in Kobe, Japan. [→ 29] In this case Shigeru Ban designed accommodations that were constructed out of a special cardboard structure. A characteristic of semi-permanent design is the use of provisional, non-durable (in the sense of long-lasting) materials and/or structures that can be taken apart.

29 Shigeru Ban, cardboard emergency dwellings, Kobe, 1995

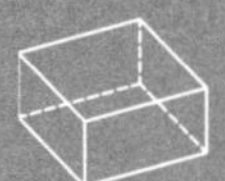

SINGLE-SPACE
WELLING

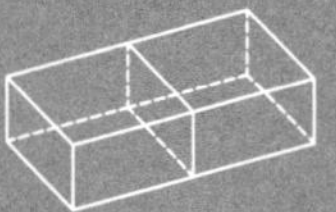

1 ZONE DEEP,
2 ZONES WIDE

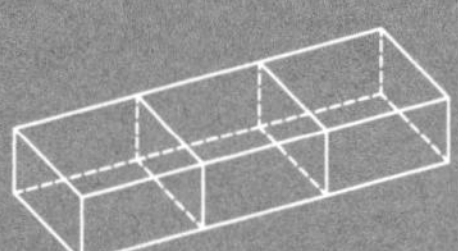

1 ZONE DEEP
> 2 ZONES WIDE

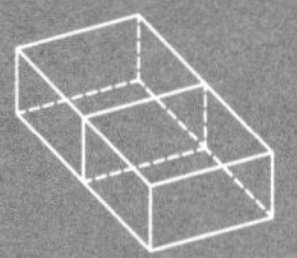

2 ZONES DEEP

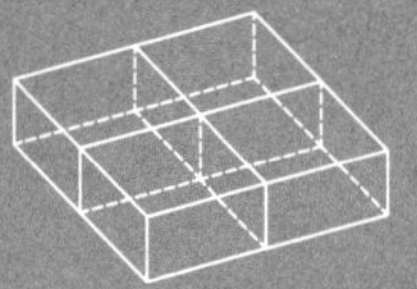

2 ZONES DEEP,
2 ZONES WIDE

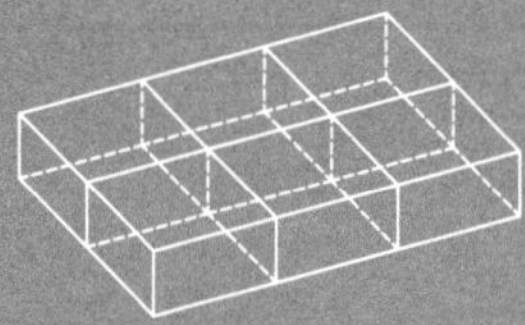

2 ZONES DEEP,
> 2 ZONES WIDE

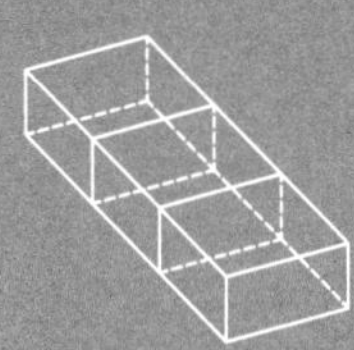

3 ZONES DEEP

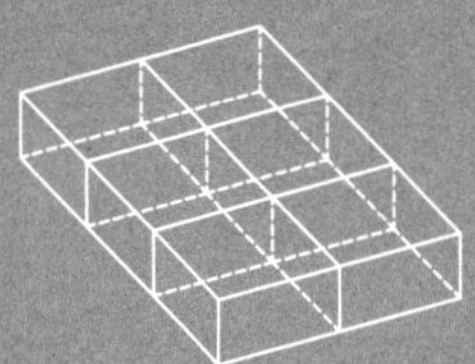

3 ZONES DEEP,
2 ZONES WIDE

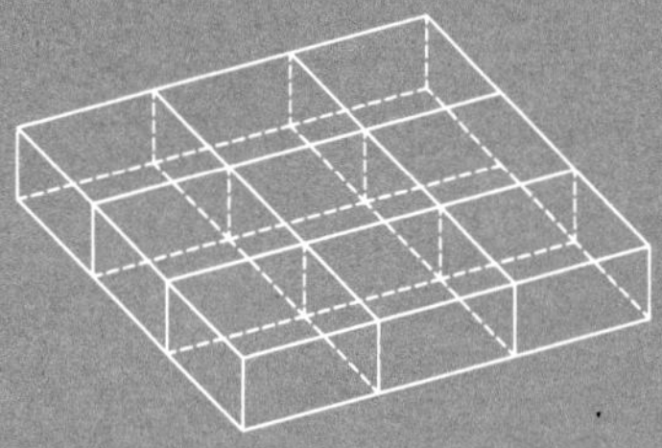

3 ZONES DEEP,
>2 ZONES WIDE

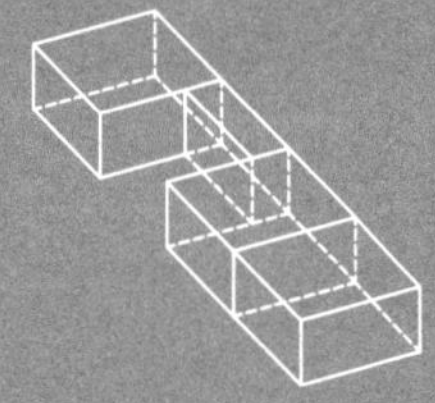

> 3 ZONES DEEP

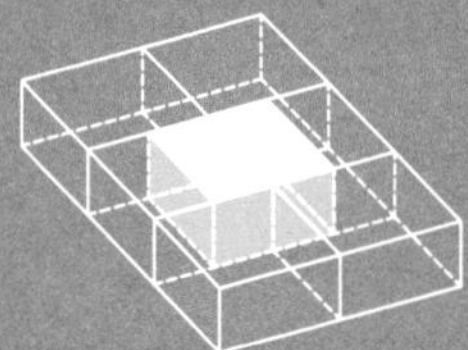

CENTRE: CORE

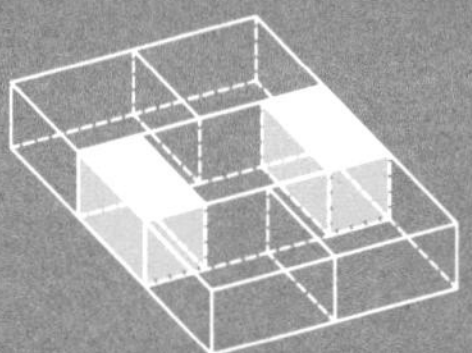

CENTRE: SPACE

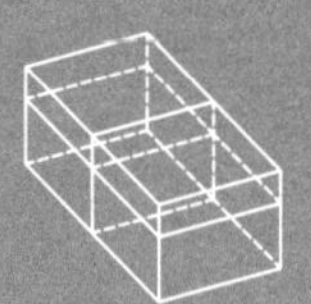

>1 STOREY

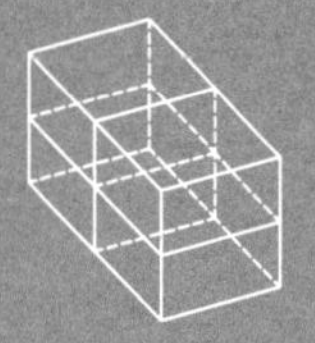

2 STOREYS

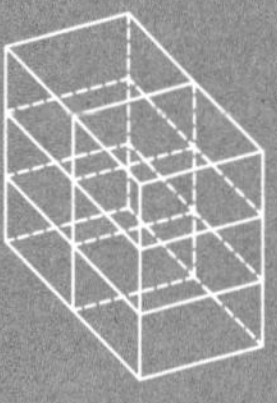

3 STOREYS

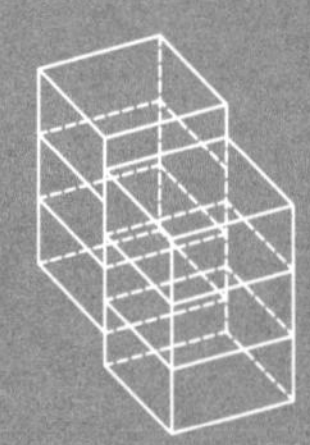

SPLIT LEVEL

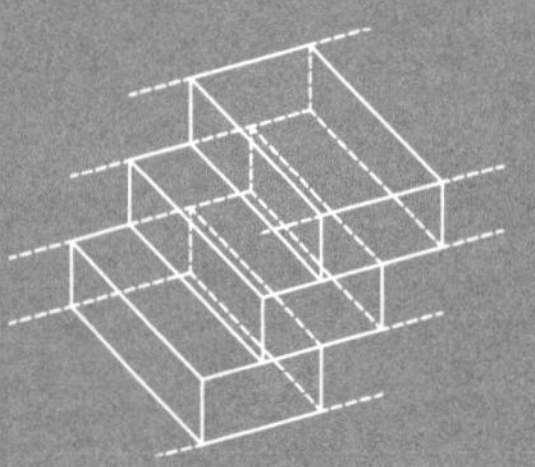

DIAGONAL STACKING

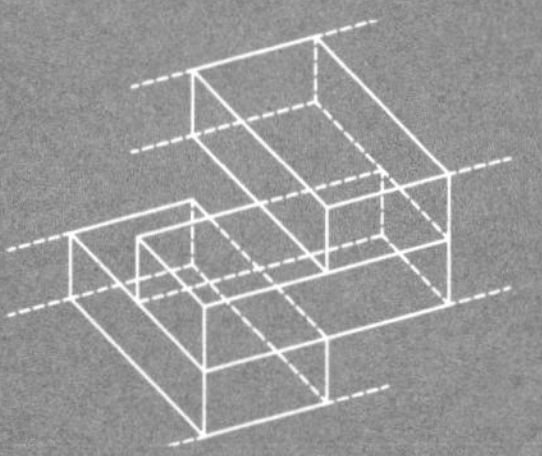

COMPLEX STACKING

SPATIAL ORGANIZATION OF THE DWELLING

In the most general sense, three factors have a defining impact on the partitioning options of the dwelling: its *size*, its *orientation* and its total *façade surface area*:

—The *size* of the dwelling determines the number of separate spaces that can be created inside it. The smallest self-contained dwelling consists of nothing more than a simple space for habitation, supplemented by the minimum amount of facilities necessary. As the dwelling gets deeper, wider or taller, more spaces can be added behind, next to or above this (principal) space.
—The *orientation* of the dwelling determines which side(s) will be exposed to natural light. The spaces that require natural light or views will be grouped here, while the spaces that can do with less natural light are placed in the darker areas of the dwelling.
—The total *façade surface area* determines the maximum quantity of natural light that can be let into the dwelling as a whole. Divided by the ceiling height, this gives the façade length, which determines how many spaces can be positioned next to or on top of one another along the façade.

The façade surface area–and therefore the potential quantity of natural light–is dependent on the size, orientation and shape of the dwelling:

—if the dwelling is made *deeper*, the dwelling floor space increases while the façade surface area remains constant. New spaces can be added along the depth, as long as they can be adequately supplied with natural light;
—if the dwelling is made *wider*, the façade surface area and the façade length increase in direct proportion with the dwelling floor space. New spaces can be added along the width when there is sufficient room along the façade;
—if the dwelling is made *taller*, the façade surface area increases in direct proportion with the dwelling floor space. Higher ceilings allow natural light to penetrate deeper into the dwelling. New spaces can be added along the height when there is sufficient room for an additional storey. The façade *length* therefore increases only in increments.

In the following pages the principles outlined above are illustrated using real-life (design) examples. We begin with the dwelling as a simple space, successively increasing its depth, width and height. The partitioning options produced are directly dependent on the dwelling's size, orientation and available façade surface area.

30a

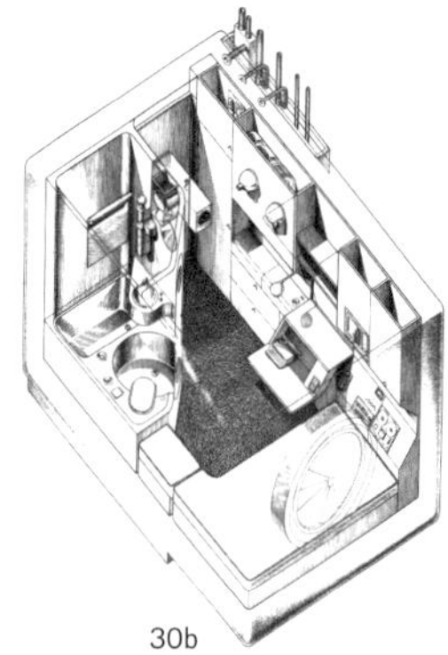

30b

KISHO KUROKAWA, NAGAKIN CAPSULE TOWER (TOKYO, 1970–1972)

In Kisho Kurokawa's Capsule Tower, his single-celled dwellings are clustered as prefabricated capsules around two central stairwells. They are constructed so as to be put in place, taken apart and repositioned as individual units, using only four bolts. The idea was that the dwellings, at the end of their lifespan, could be replaced by newer dwellings, entirely in line with the Metabolist Movement's ideals of interchangeability, reuse and sustainability. The entrance provides direct access from the stairwell to the living space, the wall opposite featuring a single round window. All furniture, including the bed, fold-down desk, television and audio equipment, a cooking facility and closet space, is built into the surrounding walls. A door conceals an alcove for the toilet and bathroom. Infrastructure for the supply and discharge of water and air is also incorporated in the prefabricated wall structure. The dwellings were originally intended for temporary habitation, as an overnight accommodation for business people in crowded downtown Tokyo, for instance. Although these are tiny, single-celled dwellings, all the typical problems of housing design are present here in a nutshell. The dwelling consists of a relatively large habitation space and a smaller service space (the 'wet cell'). The composition of these two spaces can be problematic even on this small scale. The position of the wet cell makes the living space L-shaped. An L-shaped space features multiple directions and is generally perceived as less pleasant, unless there is a subdivision among the different sections of the space, in effect creating different spaces in open communication with one another.

SINGLE-SPACE DWELLING

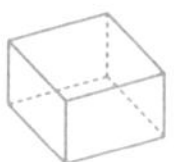

The smallest dwelling possible consists of a single space, in which essentially all activities of dwelling take place. Its dimensions are determined by the most space-consuming activity: gathering. As previously noted, since time immemorial spaces with a diagonal measurement of about 4 m have been reserved for this activity.[30] Facilities and utensils for additional activities are situated around this space. In keeping with hygiene standards, certain facilities (including the toilet and shower) are separated from the living space, so there is really no such thing as an entirely single-celled dwelling.

30 According to Dutch regulations every dwelling must include one space measuring at least 3.3 × 3.3 m. A detached dwelling, as a whole, must provide at least 24 m² of floor space.

31a

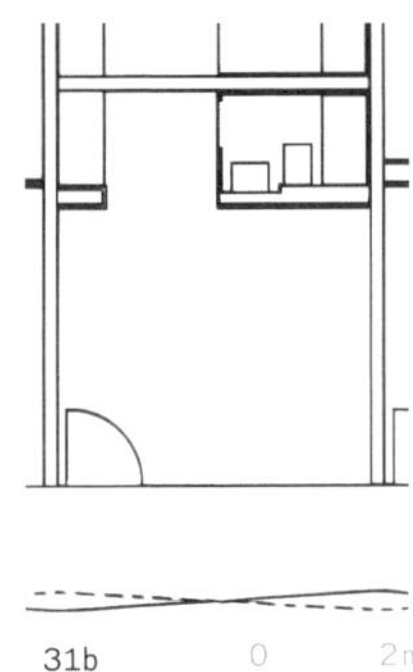

31b

FINK+JOCHER, STUDENT HOUSING (GARCHING BEI MÜNCHEN, 2005)

2 ZONES DEEP

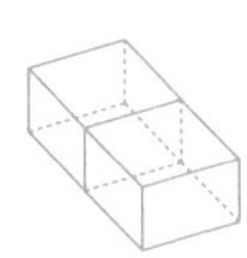

The building consists of a sequence of identical spaces, stacked in four levels. Dwellings of varying size are created by linking these identical spaces, whereby the smallest dwelling consists of only one space with a single orientation. The dwelling is deeper than it is wide, so that facilities can be located in the innermost section of the dwelling. This leaves as much free space as possible along the façade, where a large window provides a view and natural light. This is also where the entrance to the dwelling is located, directly into the living space from a gallery running along the outside of the building. The repetition of the large windows along the façade underscores the uniformity of the spaces behind.

DEPTH

If the dwelling is made deeper, the dwelling floor space increases while the façade surface area remains constant. New spaces can be added along the depth, as long as they can be adequately supplied with natural light. As the depth of the single-orientation dwelling increases, more space is created in the area that gets the least natural light. Locating facilities here frees up the habitation space along the façade.

32a

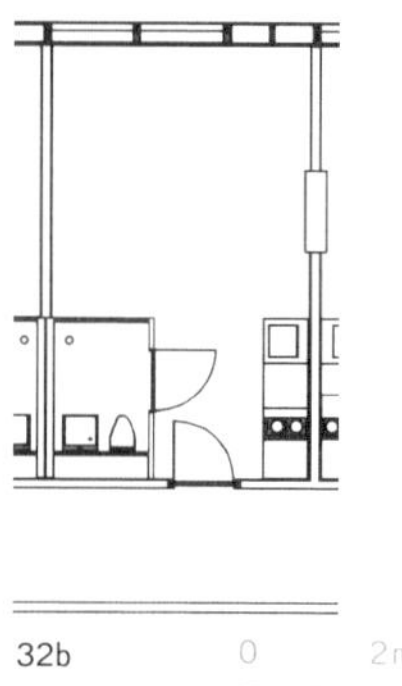

32b 0 2m

2 ZONES DEEP

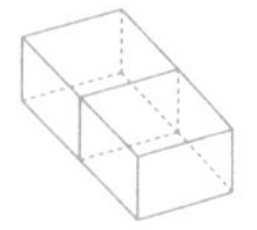

AART A/S, BIKUBEN STUDENT BUILDING (COPENHAGEN, 2006)

This residential building by AART in Copenhagen incorporates dwellings of similar dimensions, orientation and internal organization. Here, however, the dwelling is accessed from a gallery on the inner side of the block, and the entrance is located not in the façade but in the service zone. The living space is therefore the final destination in the dwelling and experiences less disruption from through traffic.[31]

31 This building is also discussed in Chapter 4, 'Residential Building', under the heading 'Block', page 165.

33a

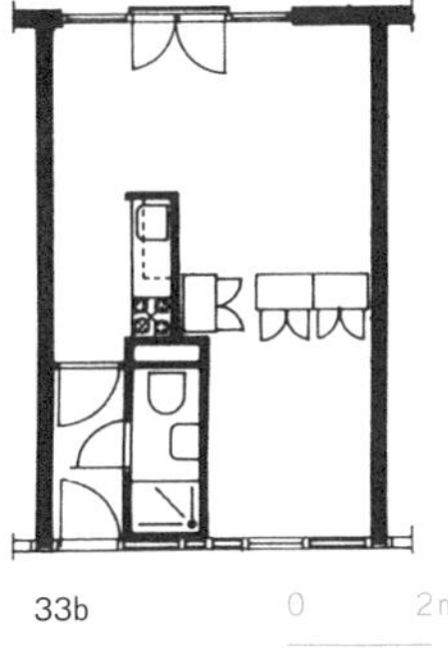

33b 0 2m

CAREL WEEBER, HOUSING, KRUISSTRAAT/MOLSLAAN (DELFT, 1976–1979)

2 ZONES DEEP

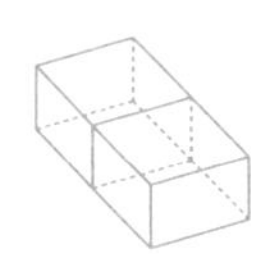

In these dwellings for one- to two-person households, Carel Weeber positioned a living room across the full width of the rear façade and a bedroom in the zone opposite. As sleeping takes up less space than gathering, this zone can also accommodate the toilet and washing space, in addition to the entrance. The principal space is now safeguarded and can focus exclusively on its function as a living room. The cooking facilities are in open communication with the habitation space and at the same time provide a buffer against the entrance. Storage in the form of closets forms the division between living and sleeping spaces, in the darkest part of the dwelling.

In a dwelling with single orientation, a second habitation space cannot be partitioned from the principal space along the depth, since it too needs to be supplied with sufficient natural light. This can be done, however, in a dwelling with double orientation on opposite sides. Given sufficient depth, it becomes possible to allocate one or more activities a space of their own in addition to the space for gathering.

34a

34b Dwelling floor plan, first to third floors
34c Dwelling floor plan, fourth floor

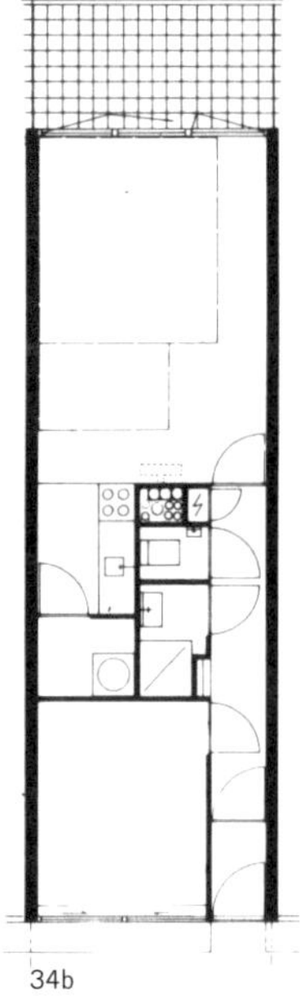

34b

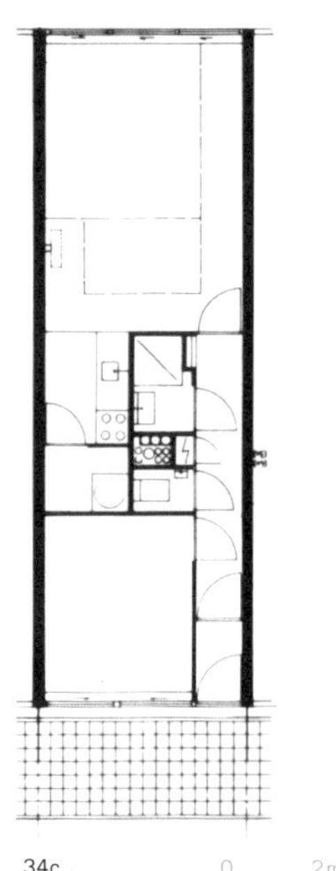

34c 0 2m

3 ZONES DEEP

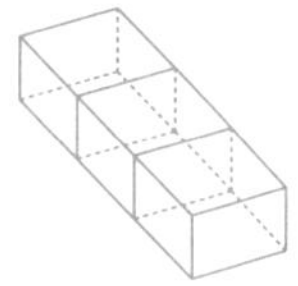

With a standard ceiling height, adequate natural light extends about 5 m from the façade into the dwelling. When a dwelling with double orientation is deeper than 10 m, a zone is created in the middle where natural light penetration is not sufficient. This is the obvious zone to locate spaces that require no natural light: bathroom, toilet, storage, etcetera. The turning point for a dwelling with three zones is therefore a depth of 10 m.

OMA, IJPLEIN OOST III HOUSING (AMSTERDAM-NOORD, 1990)

The dwellings for one- and two-person households that OMA designed in part of this elongated slab on the IJplein in Amsterdam are accessed through a gallery. This means that part of the narrow dwelling façade is already taken up by the entrance. Beyond this are a draught exclusion zone and a corridor that leads to the wide living room on the other side of the dwelling. The middle of the dwelling is occupied by the facilities: a kitchen in open communication with the habitation space, behind it a storage area/laundry room and, accessed from the corridor, the meter cupboard, a toilet and a separate bathroom. The corridor also provides access to the space next to the entrance, which serves as a bedroom. On the lower three storeys the living room is bordered by an exterior space, oriented to the southwest. On the top storey, which rises above the neighbouring residential buildings and affords a more open view, the living room is extended to the edge of the building envelope and the exterior space is situated as a roof terrace on the opposite side, between the gallery and the bedroom. The dwelling is shifted as a whole, as it were, in relation to the dwellings below, while the vertical wiring and plumbing shaft can remain in the same place thanks to a clever redistribution of the facilities. The continuous façade of forward-shifted living rooms on the top storey runs like a connecting cornice across the entire length of the building. On the rear side, the gallery, which is continuous only on this storey, provides the same effect.

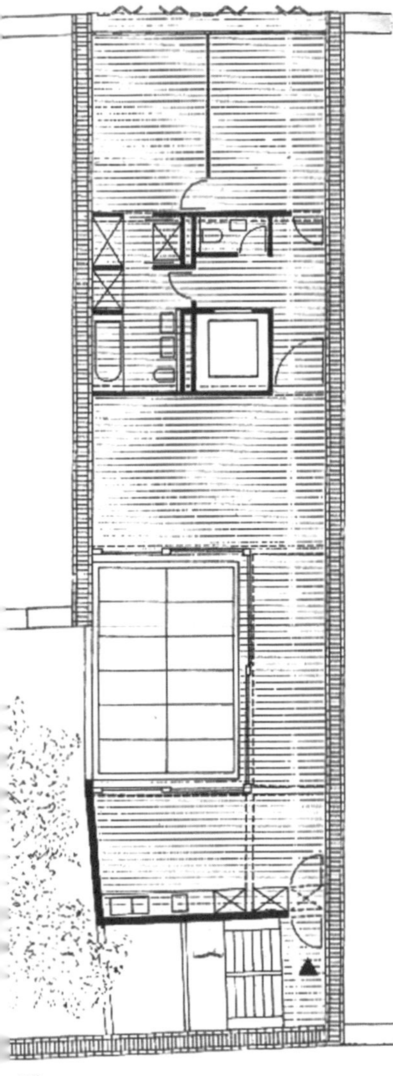

35b

35a

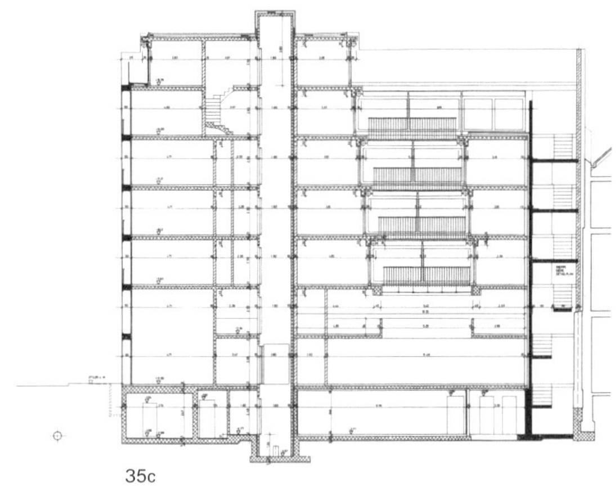

35c

HERZOG & DE MEURON, APARTMENTS AND COMMERCIAL SPACE, SCHÜTZENMATTSTRASSE (BASEL, 1993)

> 3 ZONES DEEP

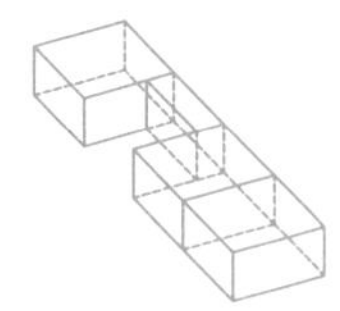

To fill a narrow, deep lot in the midst of an existing line of urban façades, Herzog & de Meuron designed a stack of three apartments and a maisonette, accessed through an internal stairwell and lift alongside a commercial space on the ground floor. The front section of the dwelling is divided into three zones, with the lift opening directly into the flat in the central, darkest zone. This is also where the toilet and bathroom are located, the latter also accessible through a walk-in closet from the bedroom situated along the front façade. The section situated deeper in the dwelling receives light through an internal light shaft along which a narrow corridor links the kitchen and stairs with the rest of the flat.

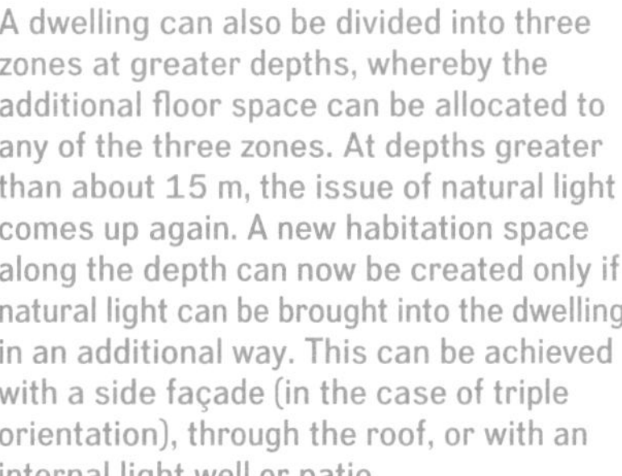

A dwelling can also be divided into three zones at greater depths, whereby the additional floor space can be allocated to any of the three zones. At depths greater than about 15 m, the issue of natural light comes up again. A new habitation space along the depth can now be created only if natural light can be brought into the dwelling in an additional way. This can be achieved with a side façade (in the case of triple orientation), through the roof, or with an internal light well or patio.

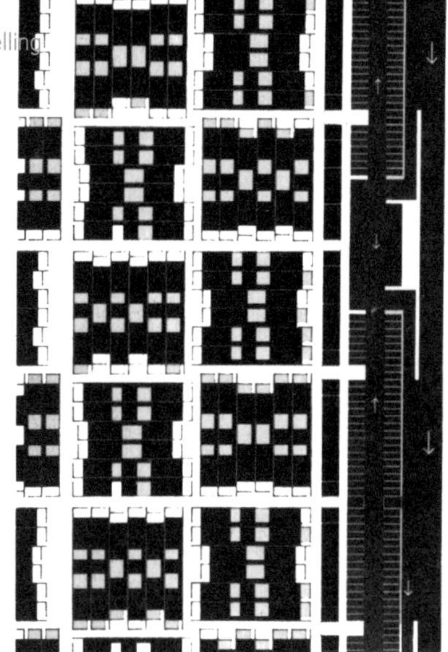

36a Proposed situation: six dwellings together forming one block

36a

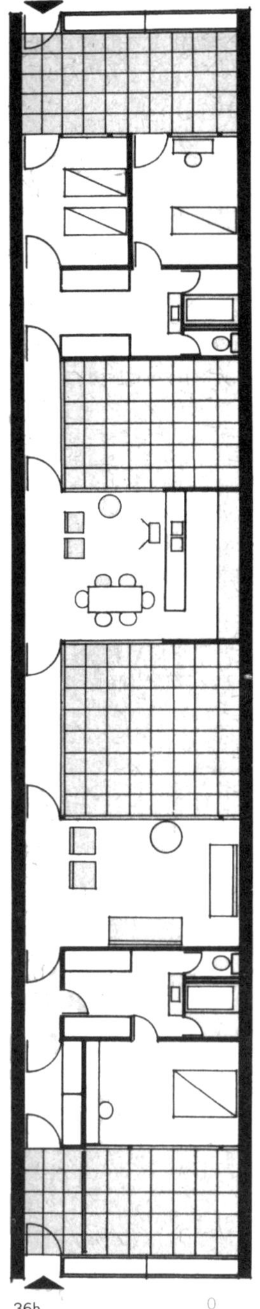

36b

> 3 ZONES DEEP

SERGE CHERMAYEFF, PATIO DWELLING (PROJECT, 1963)

In his patio plan for an urban group home, Chermayeff created a chain of habitation spaces and patios. Every space is accessible through a corridor that spans the full depth of the very elongated dwelling. Habitation and sleeping space for parents and children, respectively, are located at the opposite ends of the house. In the middle is the communal habitation space where the family come together. The patios serve as buffers between the private and the communal spaces and between the dwelling and the street. The nine doors along the corridor also serve as airlocks separating the different spheres of life within the dwellings; they are employed to exclude potential conflicts among the residents and with the outside world.
The design is a response to the rampant tendency, in Chermayeff's view, towards far too open dwellings in the modern city, where nature has vanished, cars befoul the public space and constant noise pollution invades our lives.[32] In an attempt to bring the human need for privacy back into the communal context of the city, Chermayeff designed an urban group home in which six of these dwellings together fill one block within a residential quarter closed to automobiles. The plan was never implemented in this form. Chermayeff did build his own house in New Haven in 1963, elaborating the patio arrangement into a much more nuanced residence, carefully imbedded among existing trees in an otherwise traditional leafy suburb.[33]

32 Serge Chermayeff and Christopher Alexander, Community and Privacy: Toward a New Architecture of Humanism (Garden City, NY: Doubleday, 1963).
33 Dick Van Gameren and Hans Ibelings, Revisions of Space: A Manual for Architecture (Rotterdam: NAi Publishers, 2005).

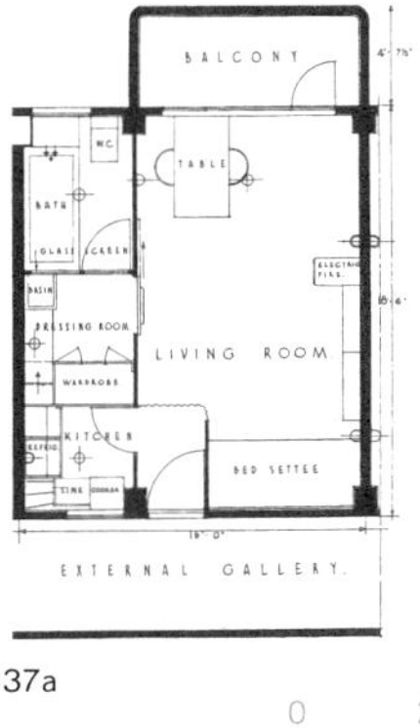

37a

0 2m

37b

WELLS COATES, LAWN ROAD FLATS (LONDON, 1934)

At the 1933 British Industrial Art Exhibition, the firm Isokon (for 'isometric unit construction') exhibited a model of a dwelling for young professionals designed by Canadian architect Wells Coates. According to the client, Isokon's owner, Jack Pritchard, this was intended for 'a new type of man who likes not only to travel light but to live light . . . unencumbered by possessions and with no roots to pull up. For such a person the multiplication of spaces, such as the more expensive architecture usually provides, is not the ultimate luxury but the perfection of service arrangements so as to reduce domestic obligations to the minimum.'[34]
Interest was so great that Coates was immediately commissioned to design the Lawn Road Flats, which include 22 'minimum flats'. It was the first block of flats in Great Britain built in reinforced concrete, with the walls between flats lined on both sides with a thick layer of cork to minimize noise complaints. The flats consist of a wide, open zone as the living space, with a narrow strip alongside housing the bathroom, dressing room and kitchen. Sleeping, eating and gathering all take place in the living space, which is somewhat separated from the entrance by a wall and curtain in lieu of a draught exclusion zone. All necessary furniture is built-in, so that the occupant need only move in his personal possessions. The flats are accessed from a gallery, along which, for the sake of privacy, no façade openings have been made except for the entrance door. On the opposite side, a window across the full length of the dwelling façade provides natural light and a view, and a few flats include a balcony.
As the flats are fairly deep, the gallery side of the dwelling is relatively dark. The architect had to weigh adequate privacy against well-lit space here, and opted for privacy.

34 Richard Carr, 'Lawn Road Flats', Studio International Yearbook (New York: Studio Trust, 2004), 94–99.

1 ZONE DEEP
>1 ZONE WIDE

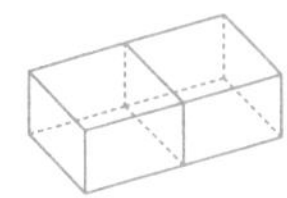

WIDTH

If the dwelling is made wider, the façade surface area and façade length increase in direct proportion to the dwelling floor space. New spaces can be added when there is sufficient room along the façade. In the case of double orientation on opposite sides, the preference is to use both façades as much as possible to accommodate daily use. Facilities can therefore be positioned along a lateral boundary wall, as long as this leaves sufficient width inside the dwelling.

38a

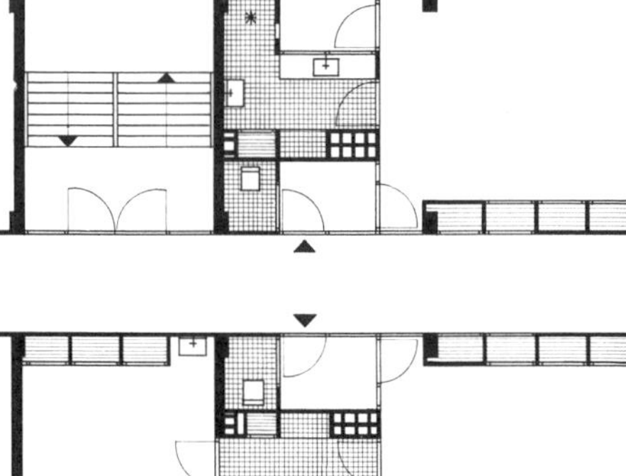

38b

1 ZONE DEEP
2 ZONES WIDE

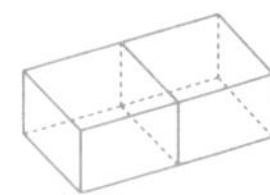

Beyond a certain width, a second habitation space can be created alongside the principal space.[35] As previously along the depth, this makes it possible to allocate various activities a space of their own, allowing a different pattern of use. A zoning of activities can emerge, for instance, whereby a distinction is made between activities that are more private (sleeping, washing) and activities that are more communal (gathering, eating, cooking).

In the Netherlands, the floors in vertically stacked housing traditionally distribute their load laterally, towards the walls separating the dwellings. As the dwelling is made wider, this lateral span increases. At a given point the dwelling becomes so wide that the distribution of downward force is better divided among two or more smaller spans. This creates a structural zoning into two equal or unequal bays or bays: this is known as a two-bay dwelling.

35 Dutch building regulations stipulate that the minimum width of any habitation space must be 1.8 m. Any such dwelling therefore must measure at least 3.3 + 1.8 + wt (wall thickness ≈ 0.07) ≈ 5.17 m in width between the walls separating the dwelling from any adjacent dwellings. For comfort and convenience, greater widths are preferred for both spaces.

JAN RIETVELD, RESIDENTIAL BUILDING (AMSTERDAM-SLOTERMEER, 1955–1957)

The flats for single occupancy that Jan Rietveld designed for the housing cooperative 'Westereind' in 1955 are situated along either side of an internal access corridor and as a result have a single orientation. The structure consists of floors resting on evenly spaced pillars and girders, which divide the dwelling into two (and in the larger flats three) equal bays. Their spatial organization, however, does not follow this sequence: the main habitation space is about one and a half bays wide, while the entrance, toilet, bathroom and balcony together squeeze into half a bay. A space of exactly one bay was added to the larger two-room flats, which serves as a bedroom and is accessed through the bathroom.

39a

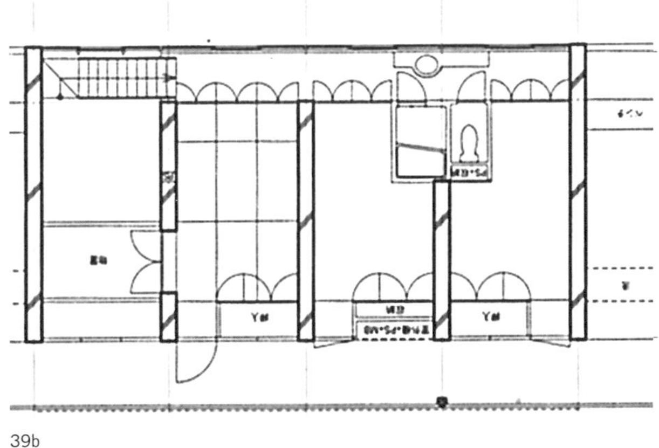

39b

0 2m

KAZUYO SEJIMA (SANAA), KITAGATA (GIFU, 1994–1998)

1 ZONE DEEP > 2 ZONES WIDE

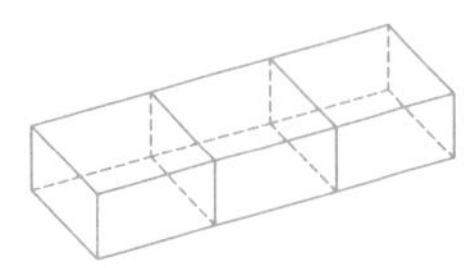

The dwellings in this elongated and shallow slab by Kazuyo Sejima consist of a series of spaces of identical width, separated by load-bearing walls. The apartments vary in their number of rooms and the way in which these are linked: side by side or with a jump to a higher or lower storey, creating a double-height bay. Every dwelling contains at least a kitchen, a 'Japanese room' decorated with simple, traditional furniture, and an open-air terrace; the terraces give the building uninterrupted views and alleviate the massive scale of the slab. The flats are accessed through a gallery, along which continuous stairs adorn the building like long ribbons. Internally, the spaces are connected by a circulation route along the façade, onto which all the spaces open.

As the width increases, the principles outlined above repeat themselves: the façade length increases, so that more spaces can be developed side by side. At the same time, the lateral span increases and this has to be economically divided. Finally, the spaces have to be connected in a meaningful way.

40a

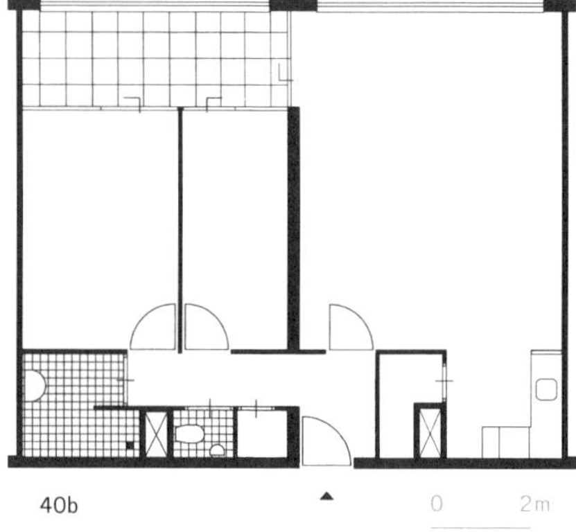

40b

0 2m

2 ZONES DEEP
2 ZONES WIDE
SINGLE ORIENTATION

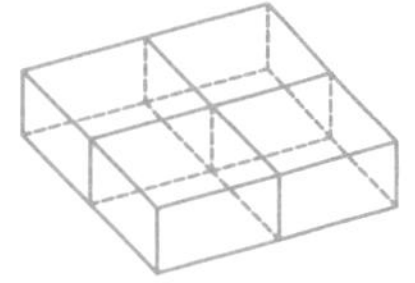

Depth *and* Width
If the dwelling is made deeper as well as wider, the principles outlined above are applicable simultaneously. Various solutions are now often possible, so that the decisions of the designer can be focused more on achieving a particular desired quality.

FRITS VAN DONGEN, BATAVIA (AMSTERDAM, 2000)

In these single-orientation dwellings the facilities zone situated deep within the dwelling is also used to accommodate circulation between the spaces extending along the width of the façade. The short corridor created as a result becomes the functional heart of the home, from which the living space, two smaller (sleeping) spaces, the bathroom, toilet and storage are accessed. The kitchen with adjacent storage is in open communication with the living space. The three principal spaces are additionally connected through a built-in exterior space, making a second route possible.
This also creates a clear zoning within this dwelling into an individual and a more communal use of the dwelling. This partitioning is further reinforced by the structural zoning of two equal bays into which the dwelling is divided: entrance, living room and kitchen in the right-hand bay, with the more private activities situated behind the load-bearing wall in the left-hand part of the dwelling. Whereas in the dwelling discussed in the preceding section partitioning is unrestricted by the lateral load structure spanning its full width, here space is virtually entirely defined by the structural zoning: any other partitioning hardly seems feasible.

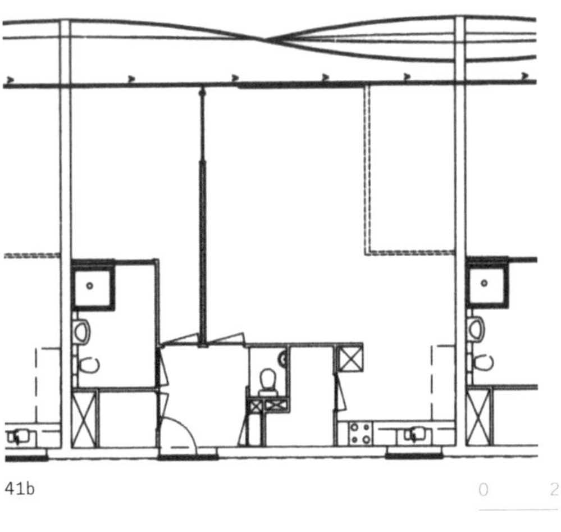

41b

1a

ARONS & GELAUFF, DE PLUSSENBURGH (ROTTERDAM, 2006)

In these gallery-access flats in Rotterdam, Arons & Gelauff attempted to realize several requirements at the same time. For the sake of privacy the façade on the gallery side was kept virtually closed, to all intents and purposes creating a single orientation. This is therefore where the facilities are situated, with the kitchen, in open communication with the spacious living room, nonetheless graced with a window, so that the dwelling does feature natural-light exposure and views on two sides. The entrance is large enough for a small vestibule, which provides access to the living and sleeping spaces, the toilet, storage and bathroom. The latter protrudes rather inconveniently into the bedroom, which as a result does have direct access to the bathroom. The layout therefore features a clear zoning into a private area housing the bedroom and bathroom and a more communal area in which the living room and kitchen are situated. The suggested location for a second bedroom, on the other side of the living room, however, nullifies this zoning. A direct link between the living space and the first bedroom does give the dwelling the option of a double route, with a choice of different uses as a result.

2 ZONES DEEP
2 ZONES WIDE
SINGLE ORIENTATION

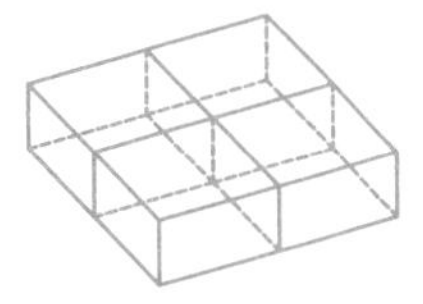

42a

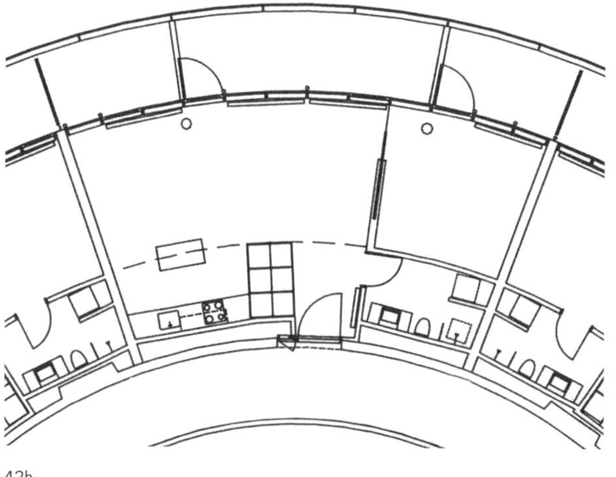

42b

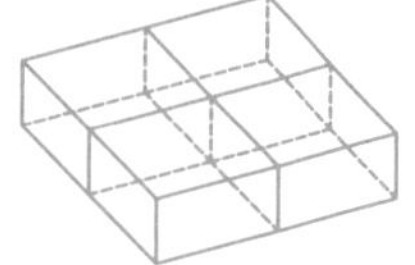

2 ZONES DEEP
2 ZONES WIDE
SINGLE ORIENTATION

MVRDV/JJW ARKITEKTER, GEMINI RESIDENCE (COPENHAGEN, 2005)

This renovation project demonstrates that the previously outlined principles are not just applicable to rectangular dwellings in new-build rectangular buildings. Because the massive concrete walls of the two grain silos limited their ability to cut out openings, MVRDV/JJW arkitekter positioned the dwellings around the outside of this wall, accessed through galleries in the inside, which was left open. This allows the dwellings to benefit to the utmost from the beautiful views, while the spatial character of the industrial cylinders remains spectacularly perceptible on the inside. The access running along this is simultaneously a place for encounter and contact.

In the single-orientation dwellings, the facilities are located along the concrete silo wall, on either side of the entrance. This is in open communication with the principal living space, so that the panoramic view unfolds immediately upon coming in, a view towards which the dwelling is focused with its fully transparent façade. Beyond the façade, around the building, is a zone that provides every dwelling with a full-width terrace. Additional spaces can be divided from the principal living space using sliding partitions. Although the sleeping space created in this way is situated in the same zone as the bathroom, no direct link is created between the two; the route from sleeping to washing runs through the sliding doors and through the living room. The architectural experience of a continuous space along the façade has been favoured over a zoning into individual and communal uses.

43a

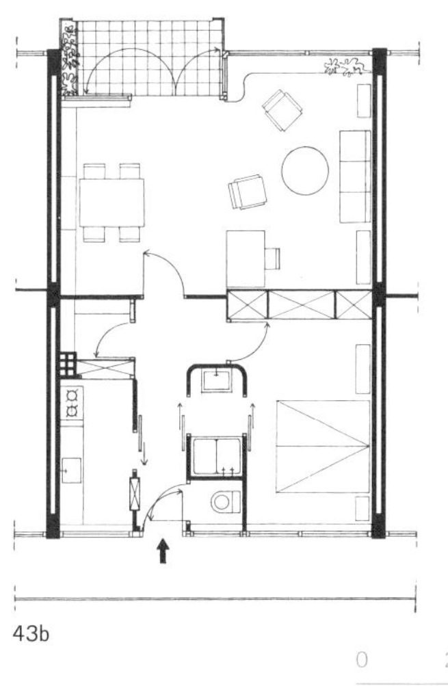

43b

0 2m

W. VAN TIJEN, PLASLAAN BUILDING (ROTTERDAM, 1938)

After his first high-rise on the Parklaan and the first tower block with gallery access, the Bergpolder Building,[36] Willem van Tijen was commissioned to create another high-profile high-rise in Rotterdam-Kralingen, on the Plaslaan. The dwellings are similar in layout but more spacious than in the Bergpolder Building, as the ideal of high-rises for the working class, still cherished at the time, had proved unfeasible. The noise level in the flats in the Bergpolder Building, built using a steel skeleton, led to the use of a concrete structure on the Plaslaan, with the columns concealed in the walls separating the flats.

The dwellings are based on a floor plan of 6.2 × 9 m, accessed through a gallery on the northwest. A separate kitchen, storage and toilet and a bathroom are situated on either side of the entrance and corridor; the bathroom is accessible on the other side from the bedroom situated along the gallery. On the southeast side is the living and eating space, with a half-sunken exterior space and a fine view over the Kralingse Plas lake.

36 See the section on gallery access in the 'Residential Building' chapter, page 187.

2 ZONES DEEP
2 ZONES WIDE
DOUBLE ORIENTATION

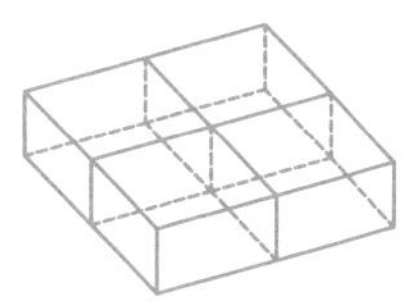

With a double orientation and a depth that allows spaces to be positioned one behind the other, increasing width offers a wide variety in partitioning options. Important spaces and facilities can now trade places along the depth as well as along the width, in accordance to the orientation of the building to views and sun exposure.

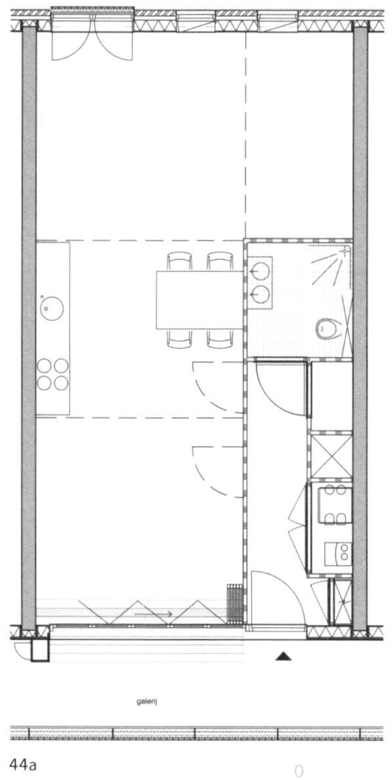

44a

44b

2 ZONES DEEP
2 ZONES WIDE
DOUBLE ORIENTATION

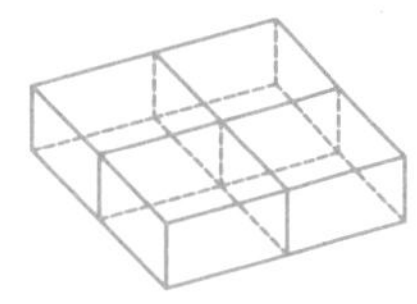

ERIK WIERSEMA, DAPPERBUURT RESIDENTIAL BUILDING (AMSTERDAM 2012)

To replace the existing end of a narrow city block in the nineteenth-century expansion ring of Amsterdam, Erik Wiersema (ADP Architecten) designed a shallow building layer enclosing a consequently larger inner garden. On the ground floor, maisonettes with small private gardens are situated along the north side, the gardens bordering on a communal inner garden for the apartments for elderly residents situated in the south section.

The upper storeys on the north side house relatively narrow and shallow apartments, accessed from the garden façade through broad galleries. In order to restrict internal partitioning as little as possible in spite of the limited dwelling size, the architect opted for double orientation, by making the gallery façade as transparent as possible. The dwelling is divided along its width into a narrow zone and a wide zone, whereby only the entrance and bathroom/toilet are assigned a fixed location in the narrow zone. The rest of the flat can be partitioned in a variety of ways: a front room, back room and side room, a living room stretching from façade to façade with an open kitchen and bedroom, or an entirely open, L-shaped living space.

The gallery façade, thanks to folding glass partitions, can even be fully opened. To provide a modicum of privacy in relation to the gallery, a raised zone has been installed in front of this façade, as wide as the folding partitions. As well as a buffer, this is meant to provide residents on the upper floors with a private place in the open air, overlooking the communal garden.

45a

45b

0 2m

While a double-orientation dwelling is deep enough for three zones, the middle zone, even at greater widths, is the one that receives the least natural light, so that it is where facilities tend to be situated. As this zone gets wider as well, a certain amount of discretion eventually emerges as to the positioning of these facilities within the zone.

OMA, IJPLEIN OOST III HOUSING (AMSTERDAM-NOORD, 1990)

We have already discussed OMA's dwellings for one- to two-person households in the elongated slab of the Oost III sectional plan on the IJplein (see also page 96). The south section of the same slab also incorporates wider dwellings, accessed through a access staircase cutting diagonally across the block (see also the section in the next chapter on dwelling access, 'Staircase, page 183'). On the top floor, this access staircase opens onto the communal gallery, from which the two- and three-room flats situated here are accessed through the balcony.
In addition to the access landing, the entrance vestibule and a sleeping space are situated on the gallery side. The living space and a second sleeping space are located along the other façade. In the middle zone, the facilities are situated between the two bedrooms, accessed from a short corridor that links the two bedrooms with each other and to the facilities. Behind the corridor a set of kitchen units has been positioned along the length, in open communication with the living space. This can now extend deep into the dwelling across the full width and is only separated from the entrance vestibule by a glass partition. This comes visually close, in spite of the internal partitioning mandated by the client, to the desired openness of a New York loft apartment.[37]

37 Bernard Leupen, IJplein. Een speurtocht naar nieuwe compositorische middelen. Rem Koolhaas / Office for Metropolitan Architecture (Rotterdam: 010 Publishers, 1989), 60.

3 ZONES DEEP
2 ZONES WIDE

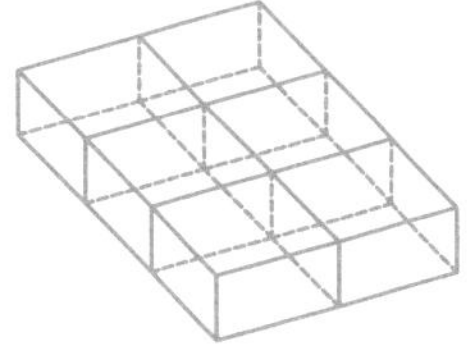

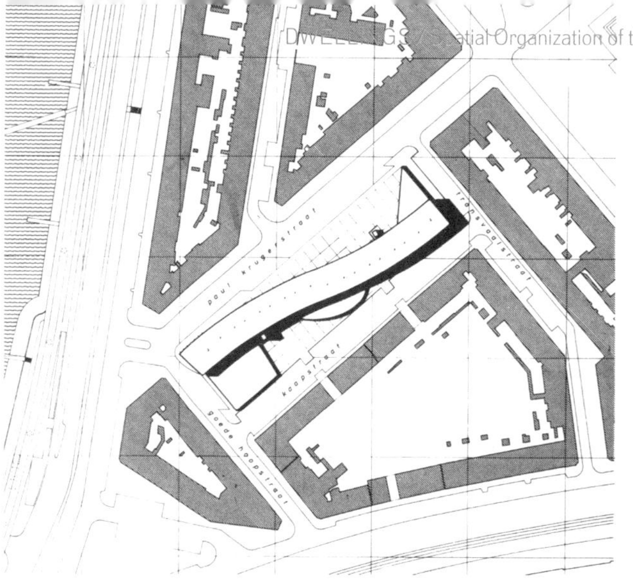

46c

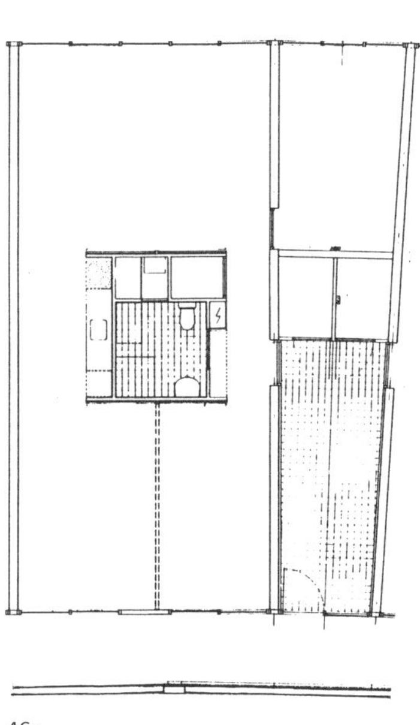

46a

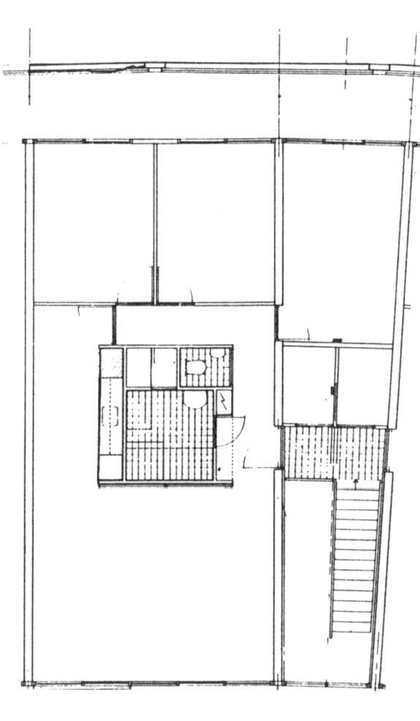

46b

0 2m

FRITS VAN DONGEN, NATAL (ROTTERDAM, 1985–1990)

3 ZONES DEEP
2 ZONES WIDE

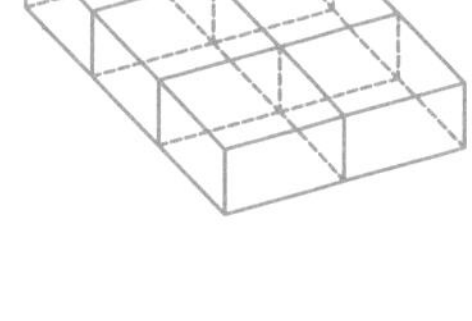

As part of the regeneration of Rotterdam's Afrikaanderwijk area, Frits van Dongen (de Architekten Cie.) designed a slab raised off the ground on a site that formerly housed three small perimeter blocks. The building snakes diagonally across the site, on top of urban facilities on the ground floor, and has no explicit front or back: all sides are oriented towards the urban surroundings. The double-orientation dwellings are also designed in such a way that they can be equally directed in either direction. To achieve this, a core of facilities has been situated in the exact centre of the dwelling; there is sufficient room on either side for a living space or two sleeping spaces, each communicating separately, past the core, with the living room. This narrow side of the core houses the cooking facilities; the other narrow side accommodates the wardrobe, storage and access to the toilet and bathroom. Opposite this, in the middle, is the entrance to the flat, which is accessed from a gallery through a shared landing. The gallery is mirrored by the continuous balconies on the other façade; halfway down the slab, the galleries and balconies switch sides.

46a, 46b Two dwellings with different configurations around the same core
46c Situation

47a

47b

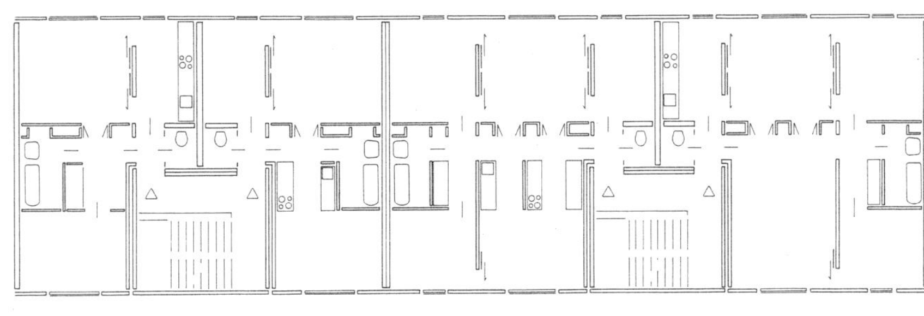

47c

0 2m

RIEGLER RIEWE, STRASSGANG (GRAZ, 2004)

The design of this residential building of three storeys and 27 dwellings is the result of a remarkable combination of conditions: it had to be completed with very minimal finances, as publicly subsidized housing for the Gemeinnützige Eisenbahnersiedlungsgesellschaft, but at the same time there was unprecedented freedom of design in relation to the aesthetics of the suburban context of Graz and the as-yet unknown wishes of future users. The solution was found in a far-reaching standardization of structural and finishing aspects, whereby the structural elements were designed in such a way as to allow flexible use of the different dwellings. The dwellings are divided into three zones along their depth and are two to five zones wide, with three or five habitation spaces, respectively, on either side of the service zone, in which the bathroom, kitchen and toilet are accessible from both sides. Access to the dwelling is through a perpendicularly positioned entrance staircase, which takes up half a bay out of each dwelling.
None of the habitation spaces seems naturally large enough to function as a self-contained living room, but combinations of spaces within the three-bay dwelling can create a living area along the front or rear façade, a living room-kitchen – with or without sun exposure from both sides – in the middle bay or other variations. As desired, one to four bedrooms can be created. As a result, dwellings with the same shell structure are suitable for a variety of combinations of occupants and habitation requirements.
The dwellings have neither balconies nor private exterior spaces; instead, the openings in the façade can be opened down to the floor. Mass-produced, floor-to-ceiling sliding panels are used to keep out the sun and mask the demarcations between individual dwellings.

47c Floor plan of storey

3 ZONES DEEP
>2 ZONES WIDE

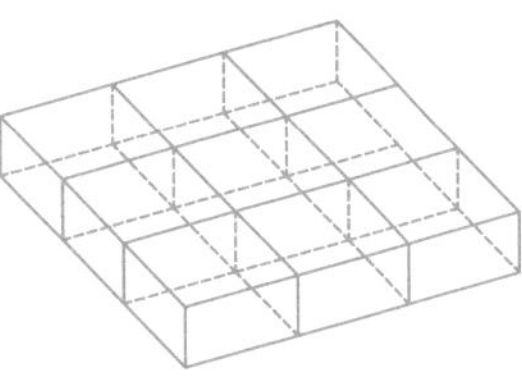

48

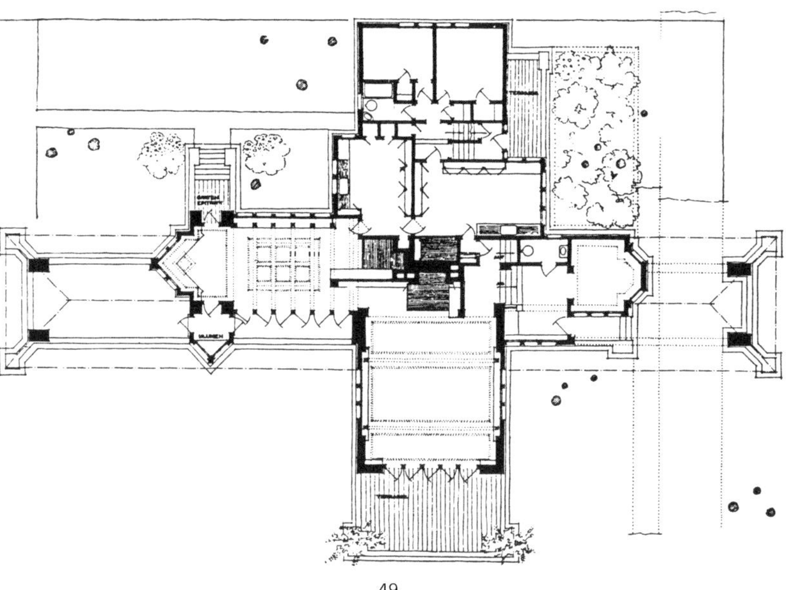

49

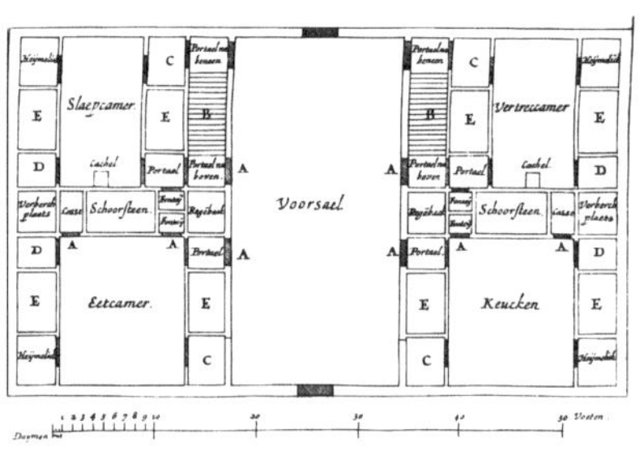

50

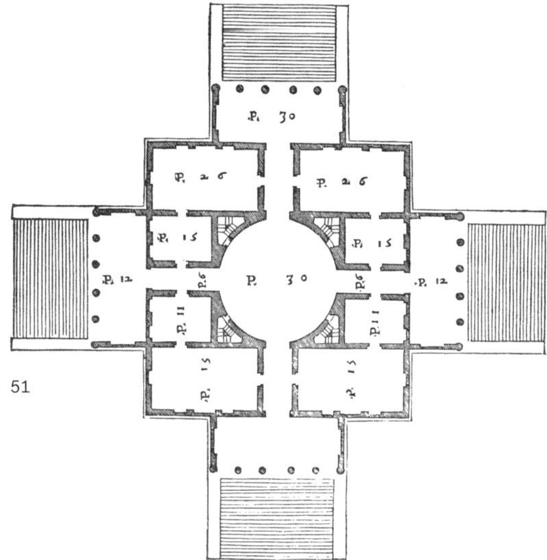

51

48 Sketch of a seventeenth-century farmhouse in Midhust, Sussex. The quarters on different floors are grouped round stove and hearths along the central chimney.
49 F.L. Wright, Ward W. Willits House, 1901, Highland Park, Illinois, floor plan of ground floor. Living spaces spread out in various directions from a central cluster of open hearths.
50 S. Stevin (1584–1620), schematic floor plan of an optimum layout for a residence. The voorsael in the centre is for welcoming visitors and forms a buffer for the private quarters situated on either side.
51 A. Palladio, Villa Rotonda, 1566–1567, Vicenza. A centrally positioned hall divides the house into four quadrants. The hall is oriented toward the house and the surrounding landscape; the other quarters are more introverted.

THE CENTRE OF THE DWELLING: CORE OR SPACE?

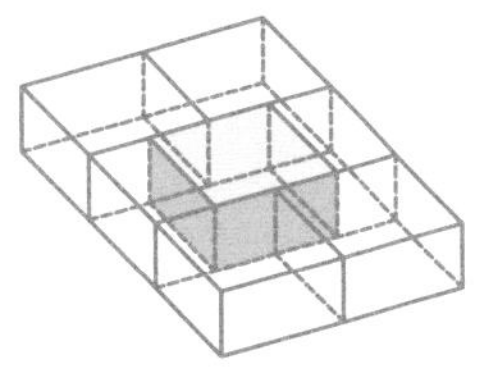

When the dwelling is of sufficient depth and width to allow some discretion in partitioning, the decision of where to position the facilities – with the attendant implications for the course of wiring and plumbing when dwellings are linked horizontally and stacked vertically – plays a vital part in the way the spatial system of the dwelling can be experienced.

Concentrating the facilities in the middle of the dwellings makes it possible to freely organize the habitation spaces around them. The core is accessible from all sides, making a separate route unnecessary. Different sides of the core can be attuned to the desired use of the adjacent space. In a certain sense, such an organization of the dwelling is comparable to the traditional organization of habitation spaces around a central fireplace or hearth, before central heating and electricity came into the picture. The fire supplied heat and light to the surrounding spaces; it was often used for cooking as well, and unpleasant odours and smoke were extracted through a communal chimney. The core divides the dwelling into different areas, each with its own relationship to the facilities.

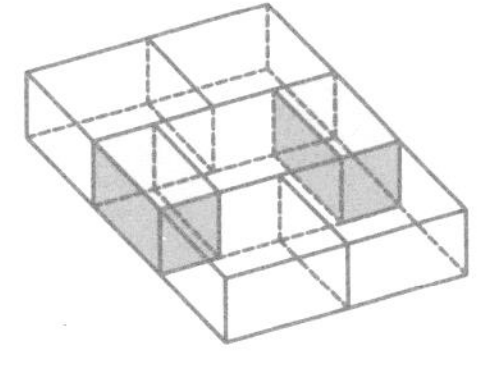

An opposite approach is to create a space in the middle of the dwelling, linking all the other spaces. Rather than moving around a closed core, occupants now move from all the spaces into the central space and out again. This space can be a short corridor or a vestibule, but it can also have greater qualities for habitation. A central habitation space, for instance, can become the cornerstone of daily activities within the dwelling.

In Western homes the hall was originally one of the most important spaces in the house, the occupant's calling card to the guests he received into his home. At the same time, this prominent space played a vital role in the transition between inside and outside; this was still the public portion of the house, where the identification of visitors took place and people could tidy themselves up before entering the domain of the actual home.[38]

From the nineteenth-century onwards, however, the hall was increasingly reduced, in housing projects, to a functional space that provided access to the other spaces in the dwelling, or it shrivelled down to nothing more than a draught exclusion zone, as a remnant of the transition between inside and outside.

38
Irene Cieraad (ed.), At Home: An Anthropology of Domestic Space (Syracuse: Syracuse University Press, 1999), 54.

52a

52b, 52c Different patterns of use

52b

CENTRE: CORE

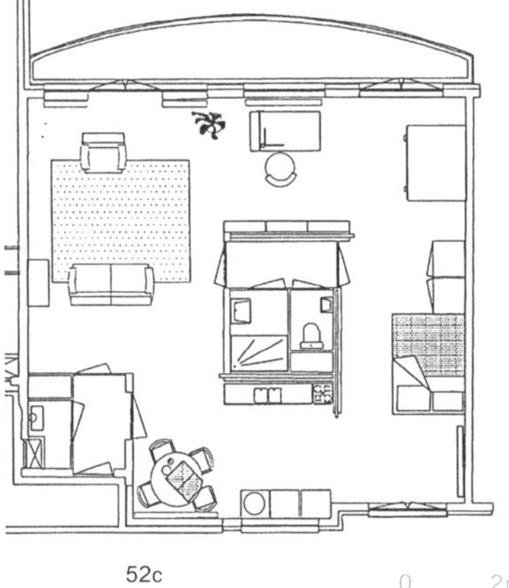

52c

DUINKER VAN DER TORRE, DAPPERBUURT HOUSING (AMSTERDAM, 1986–1988)

The principle of the dwelling arranged around a central core is clearly illustrated by Margreet Duinker and Machiel van der Torre in their project for 49 dwellings on the Wagenaarstraat and Tweede van Swindenstraat in the Dapperbuurt area in Amsterdam. The dwellings are accessed in groups of three through an external entryway with a small landing. The dwelling entrance is located in a small vestibule in the corner of the dwelling. The core housing the facilities is positioned slightly off-centre, so that spaces of varying dimensions are created around it, accommodating various activities. The toilet and bathroom are housed inside the core; the outside of the core accommodates cooking facilities along the edge of the dining room. The spaces flow into one another freely around the core and are only visually divided by it. The core, however, also incorporates sliding partitions, which can be used to divide the dwelling into separate spaces as desired. The spatial system of the dwelling can therefore be continually altered throughout the day by its occupants.

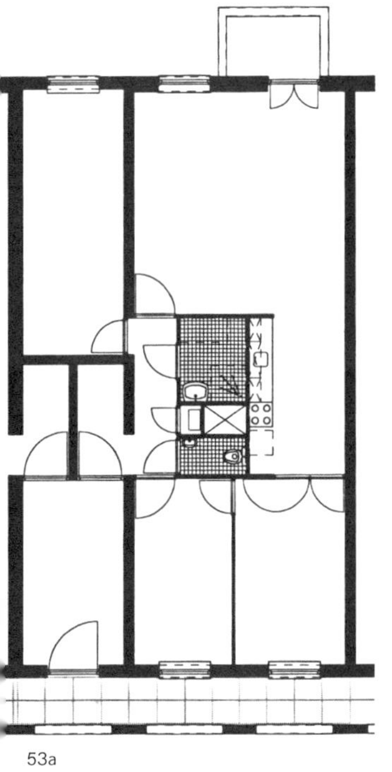

53a

53c

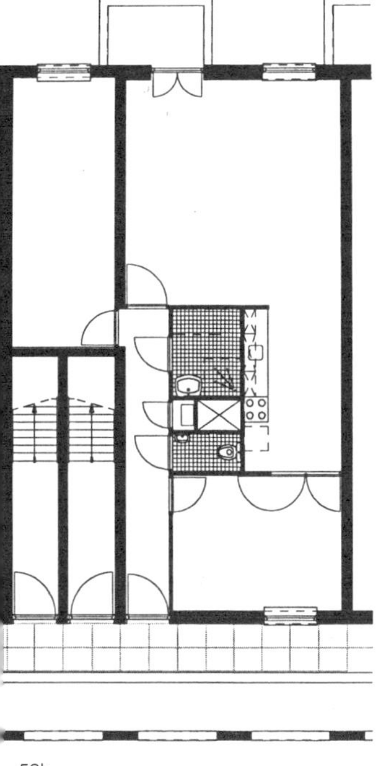

53b

0 2m

HANS KOLLHOFF, PIRAEUS (AMSTERDAM, 1989–1994)

The regular arrangement of the façade of Kollhoff's massive-looking building on the KNSM Island in Amsterdam conceals a total of 304 dwellings, with more than 150 different dwelling configurations. A large proportion of these, however, use the same clever basic configuration, from which the dwellings can be divided in a wide variety of ways within the envelope of the residential building.
This basic configuration consists of a core of facilities including a bathroom, toilet and meter cupboard, all accessed on one side, and the cooking facilities along the opposite long side. This core has been positioned exactly far enough away from the load-bearing wall to leave room for a corridor with doorways on either side; this leaves sufficient room on the kitchen side for a small table, an open-plan kitchen or a set of double doors into an adjacent space. The precise fine-tuning of the dimensions allows the living rooms and bedrooms to be positioned on either side, while communication is always possible around the core, through the corridor or the kitchen.

CENTRE: CORE

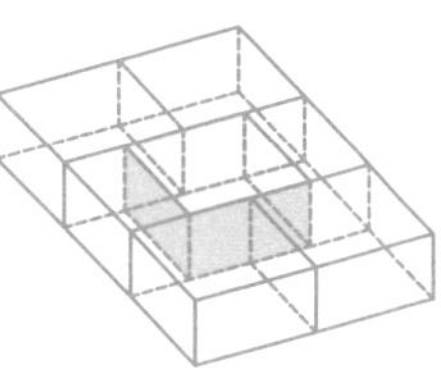

54a

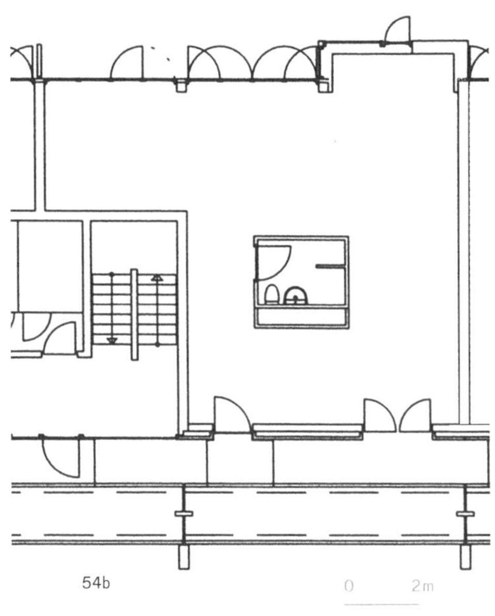

54b

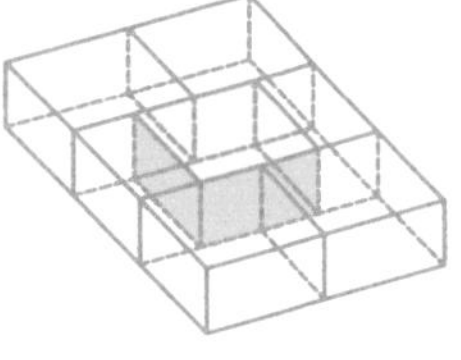

DOMUS ARCHITEKTER, FÆLLEDSHAVEN (COPENHAGEN-BOLIGSLANGEN, 2006)

In the residential building designed by Domus in a suburb of Copenhagen, a core has been positioned in the centre of the dwelling, just as in the dwellings by Duinker Van der Torre. The core is again positioned off-centre, creating different sizes of rooms around it. Here, however, the core contains only a bathroom, which incorporates the toilet. The rest of the organization of the flat, including the cooking facilities and any partition walls required, is left up to the occupants to decide. The core, as the only fixed element, 'frees' the rest of the dwelling from constraints in organization; over the lifespan of the building the flat can be repeatedly partitioned in different ways and adapted to the changing needs of its occupants.

55a

55b

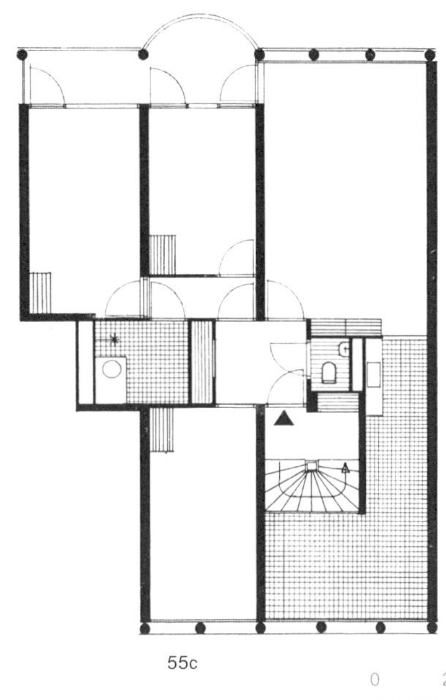

55c

0 2m

FRANS VAN GOOL, HET BREED AND ENVIRONS (AMSTERDAM, 1968)

The high-rise residential district Plan Van Gool, on the edge of the Boven 't IJ shopping centre in Amsterdam, is a remarkable neighbourhood with street names like Het Breed ('the wide'), Het Hoogt ('the high'), Het Laagt ('the low'), Bovenover ('along the top') and Benedenlangs ('along the bottom'). Its 1,161 dwellings were completed in 1972. At the time they were incredibly modern buildings, with glass façades, unique floor plans and collective heating. The experimental housing attracted many artistic and trendy residents, and studio-flats were built especially for artists.

The buildings are situated as modernist slabs in a green setting and express Van Gool's conviction that there must be a clear distinction between the world inside the building and the world outside. Children could play on the broad gallery along the third housing storey, and the baker and milkman could make their deliveries sheltered from the elements by 'jetways' between the buildings. From the internal staircase, the dwelling is entered through a centrally situated vestibule. This is located at the divide between the communal habitation area, where the living room and kitchen occupy the full depth of the flat, and the more individual part of the dwelling, which accommodates three bedrooms and a bathroom. In the vestibule, between the two zones of use, is the toilet. Circulation between the private and the communal and between the dwelling and the outside world always takes place through the central vestibule, giving it a linchpin function within the dwelling. In an earlier phase of the plan, the staircase was rotated a quarter turn and there was direct access from the kitchen to the stairs, which would have essentially given the apartment a back door as well.

CENTRE: SPACE

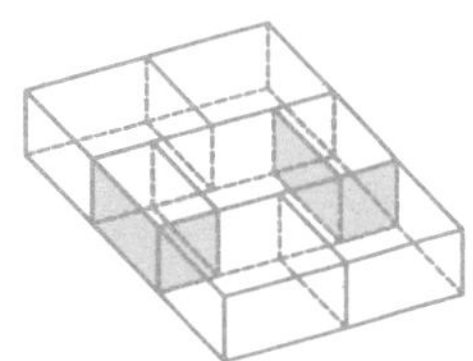

56a

56b

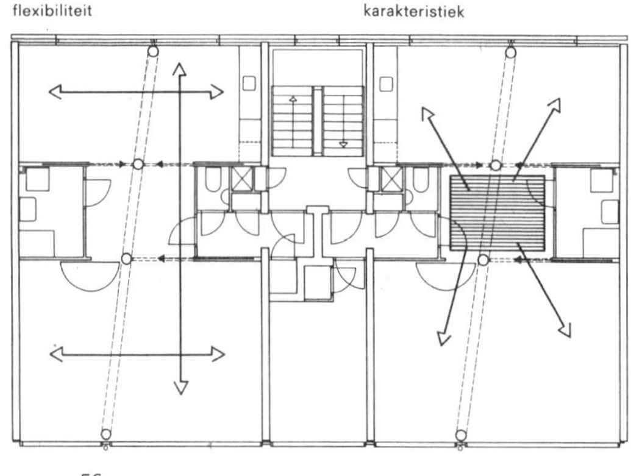

56c

LIESBETH VAN DER POL, PIETER VLAMINGSTRAAT (AMSTERDAM, 1992)

A stone's throw away from the previously discussed project by Duinker and van der Torre discussed on page 112, Liesbeth van der Pol designed a number of dwellings that represent the exact opposite in their spatial organization. Here the centre of the dwelling is not a closed core, but an open space, which links the other spaces in the dwelling.

The dwellings are accessed two by two through a access staircase, so that the entrance opens into the middle of the dwelling. A short corridor leads to the central space, a spacious vestibule in the centre of the flat. The facilities are situated on either side of this, alongside the middle zone. The spaces along both façades can be entered from the vestibule. The dwelling is distributed across two bays, whereby the central support takes the form of a joist resting on columns, so that the spaces on either side can be linked to form a single space. In addition this joist is positioned diagonally, creating a less rigid division of space and allowing the spaces to communicate diagonally as well. These spaces can each be subdivided into two smaller spaces as desired and can be separated from or connected with the vestibule with sliding partitions. The dimensions of the vestibule are enough to add not only circulation space but also spatial quality to the dwelling.

CENTRE: SPACE

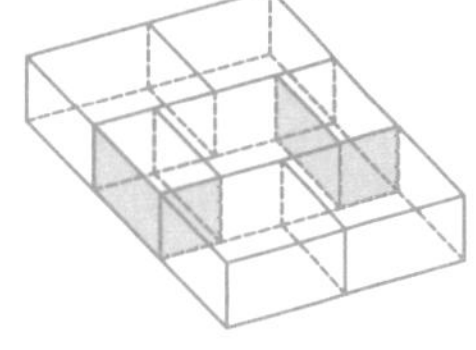

57a

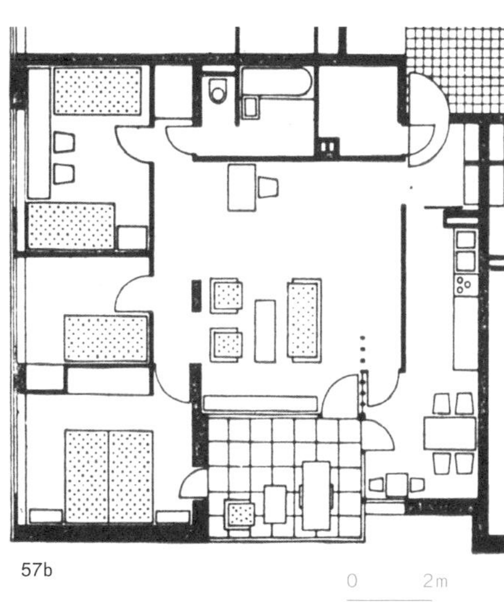

57b

ALVAR AALTO, HANSAVIERTEL RESIDENTIAL BUILDING (BERLIN, 1957)

The apartments in this residential building by Alvar Aalto are also conceived around a central space. Here, however, this is not simply a more generously proportioned vestibule or circulation space linking the most important habitation spaces: the central space has now been upgraded to the principal living space, around which the secondary habitation spaces are grouped. Although the central space also provides access to the other spaces, the route within the dwelling should be interpreted the other way round: the space in the centre has become the final destination, rather than a place of passage. Aalto's concept of a central space in which the phenomenon of dwelling comes together is in fact labelled with the German word *Allraum*. The floor plans shows obvious similarities to Aldo's concept of a courtyard or patio house, as implemented for instance in his own home with studio in Munkkiniemi, near Helsinki (see page 134). There, the various sub-activities of dwelling are situated around a large exterior space, incorporating this into the dwelling as additional habitation space in the open air. In the vertically stacked dwellings of the Hansaviertel, this exterior space has been replaced by the central living space, in which all the surrounding activities come together. There is still contact with the outside thanks to an exterior space pulled deep into the dwelling as a loggia. Short structural wall sections form a subtle separation between the communal living area and the more private sphere of sleeping and washing, while this circulation nonetheless remains connected spatially with the living room.

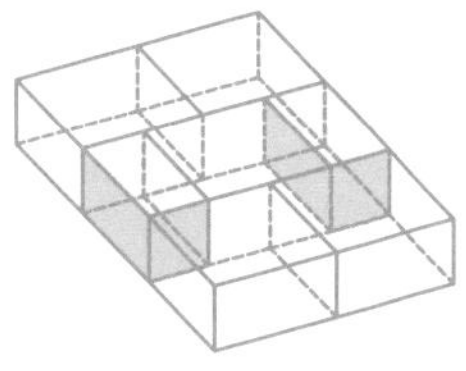

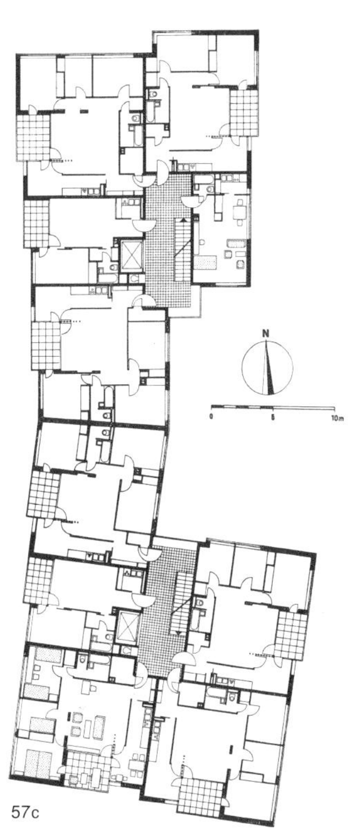

57c

58a

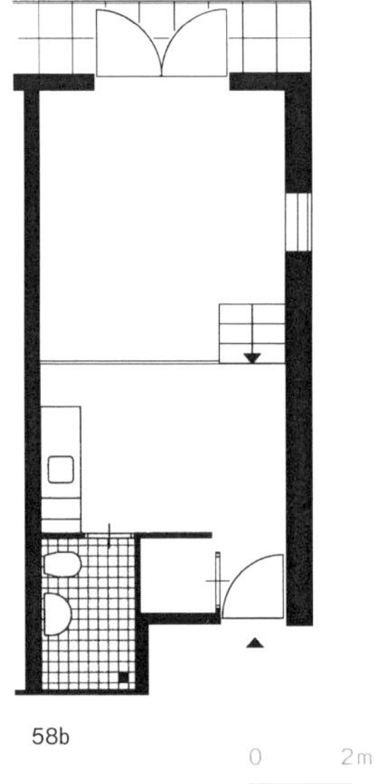

58b

FARO ARCHITECTEN, 4 URBAN ALLEYWAYS (AMSTERDAM, 2003)

The student housing complex on the Grote Bickersstraat in Amsterdam consists of five parallel blocks, in which single-celled dwellings are accessed two by two through small foyers in the side of the building, accessible by a short flight of stairs in the narrow alleyways that separate the blocks. Each block has four dwellings per storey, the top four sharing a kitchen opening onto the roof terrace. The floor of the lowest dwelling is half-sunken, opening onto the street-level terrace through double doors. This creates a division in the dwelling between the section situated deeper inside, with the entrance and facilities including an open kitchen, and the living space situated lower down. While these zones differ in use and experience, spatially and visually the dwelling remains a unified whole.

>1 STOREY

HEIGHT

If the dwelling is made taller, the façade surface area increases in direct proportion with the dwelling floor space. Higher ceilings allow natural light to penetrate deeper into the dwelling. New spaces can be added along the height when there is sufficient room for an additional storey. The façade length therefore increases only in increments.

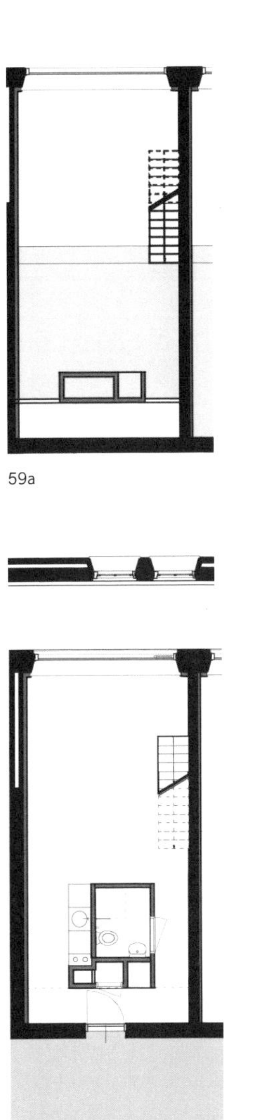

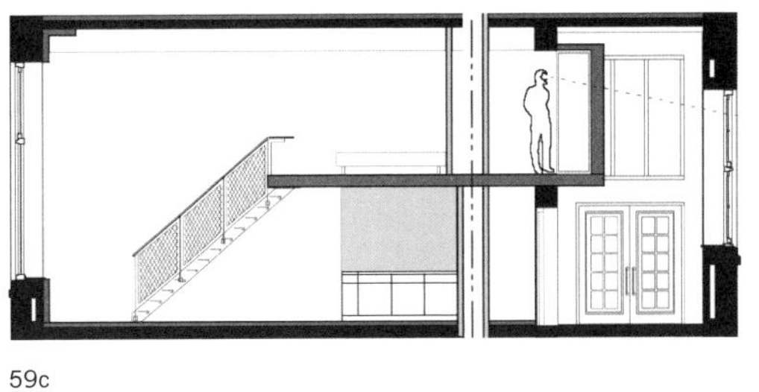

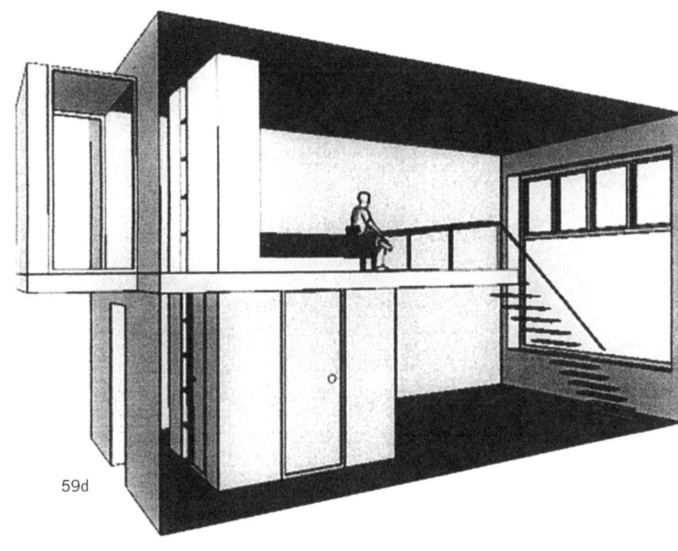

59a, 59b Floor plan of living level and recessed mezzanine
59c Section of a dwelling with mezzanine as balcony in the corridor

KBnG, MIJNBOUWPLEIN STUDENT HOUSING (DELFT, 2010)

The old research and laboratory facilities of Delft University of Technology's former Laboratory for Engineering Physics now accommodate 99 student housing units and three commercial premises. The spaces are 5 m high and have been divided, following the existing distribution of windows, into narrow, tall housing units. This is just under the height needed for two full-fledged storeys, but the clever placement of a mezzanine above the facilities and entrance zone made it possible to increase the usable space of the dwellings anyway. Meanwhile, the habitation zone still has the sense of space afforded by the double height and the large window. A straight set of stairs leads to the mezzanine, where there is sufficient room for sleeping, in open communication with the living space and the view. A few of the dwellings feature an added space up here, which extends over the internal gallery as an overhanging balcony above the entrance and affords a glimpse of the exterior and of the interior common area.

>1 STOREY

60a

LE CORBUSIER, UNITÉ D'HABITATION (MARSEILLE, 1947-1952)

The dwellings in Le Corbusier's various Unités d'Habitation (Marseille, Nantes-Rezé, Briey-en-Forêt, Berlin and Firminy) are accessed through a central corridor. In the most common dwelling type, the single orientation is resolved by organizing the dwelling over two levels: the additional level extends to the opposite façade across the full depth of the building. Two dwellings are therefore wrapped around the corridor: half a storey on either side and a full storey above or below. Because of the shape of their cross section, they are sometimes referred to as 'bayonet' dwellings.

The dimensions of the dwelling are derived from the Modulor, the system of proportions developed by Le Corbusier: they are 24 m deep and 3.65 m wide, with a ceiling height of only 2.26 m. The upper level is recessed away from the two-storey façade, creating a double-height living space. This gives the dwellings of this type a particularly spacious feel, which can be experienced deep inside the dwelling. A significant difference between the bayonet dwellings, intended for families, on opposite sides of the corridor is the location of the entrance within the organization of activities. The dwelling with its entrance on the lower level is entered through the living room and open kitchen. A flight of stairs leads to the upper level, with a bedroom for the parents in the recessed area and two spaces for studies or children's bedrooms on the other side of the home. Private and communal areas are clearly divided and logically sequenced.

The other dwelling is entered on the top level. The kitchen is situated just beyond the door, on the recessed level, overlooking the living room which, logically, is situated one level down in the double-height space. In order to retain the option of two rooms on the other side, however, the living room is linked with the parents' bedroom. The kitchen and the parental bedroom can trade places, reuniting the living room and kitchen, but then the entrance is located on a sleeping level. In either case, the routing and organization of this dwelling are less convenient for the intended user, a problem that vanishes only with smaller occupancy combinations.

2 STOREYS

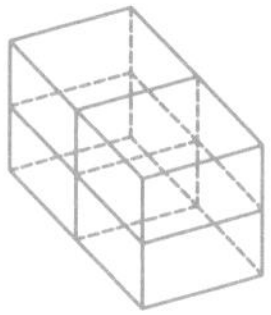

An upper storey does more than increase floor space for habitation; often it separates spaces upstairs and downstairs more than space-partitioning objects and walls do in a horizontal situation. Going up or down a flight of stairs, after all, requires more energy than going through a door. This can be employed to create a marked division between different activities, for instance between the more public or communal and the more private or individual parts of the home. If a hard division is less desirable, then leaving out part of the floor (an open vertical space or *vide*) can restore visual communication between the different levels.

60a Double height in the living room with a wall-to-wall opening into the loggia
60c, 60d Floor plans and cross sections of two bayonet dwellings around the corridor

60b

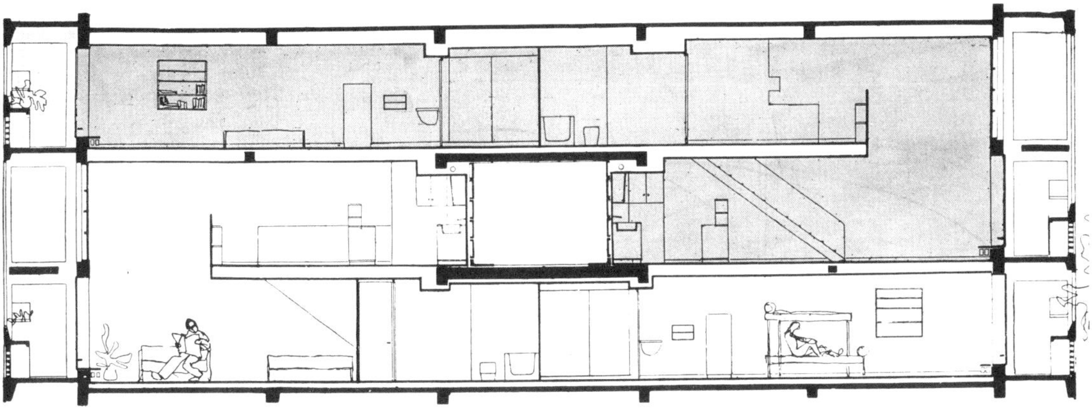

60c

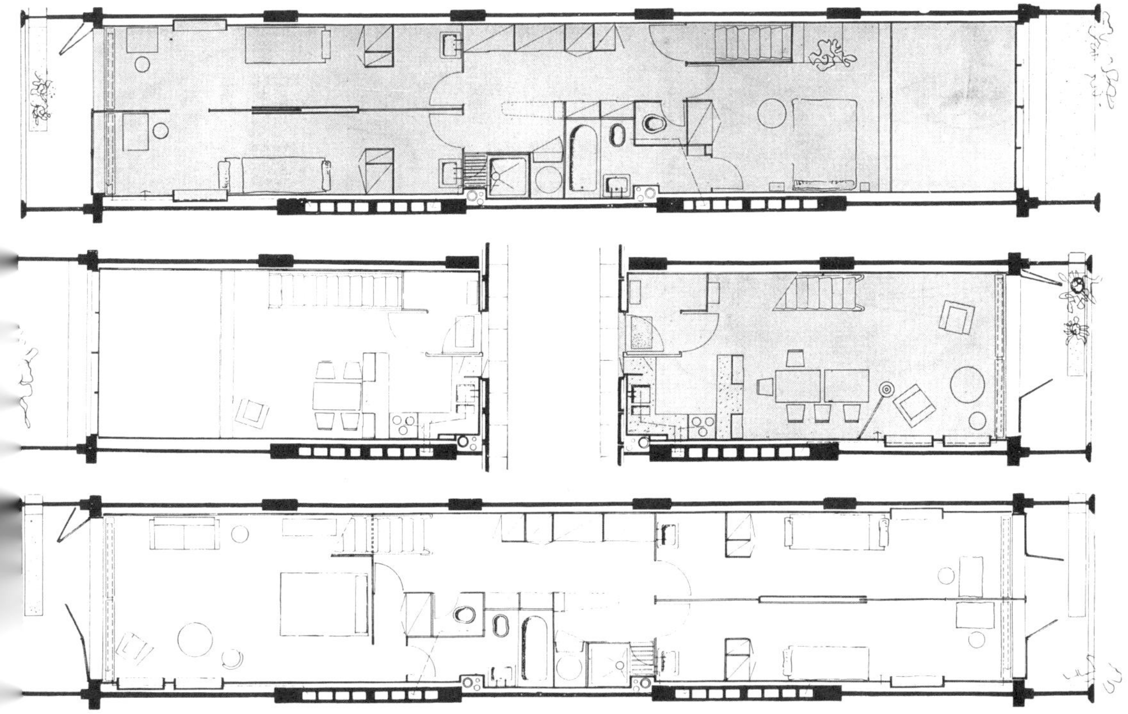

60d

61a

2 STOREYS

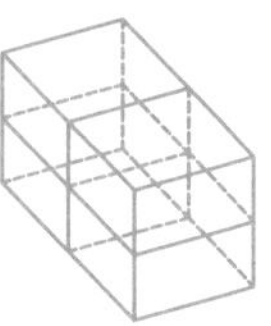

DAVID HELLDÉN & STIG DRANGER, PETERSTORP 3 (MALMÖ-RIBERSHUS, 1938)

Innovative building entrepreneur and inventor Eric Sigfrid Persson commissioned the young architects Stig Dranger and David Helldén to design a residential building in the residential quarter of Ribershus, accommodating nine storeys and a basement. It has a view of the coastline and the sea south-west of Malmö. Inspired by recent housing exhibitions in Stuttgart (1927), Stockholm (1930) and Paris (1937) they designed a building on a functional basis, whose wide variety of dwelling types and sizes is simultaneously a reflection of the Swedish social-democratic ideals of the period.[39]

The most unique of the dwellings is a two-storey maisonette with a living area on three separate levels around a small vertical open space (*vide*). Great spatial effect is achieved with a relatively small 'loss' in floor space for the vertical opening, which gives the dwelling a unique quality. Accessed through foyer stairwells with a lift, the dwelling has two entrances: a main entrance on the lower habitation level and a service entrance on the level above, which provides direct access to the kitchen and the servant's bedroom (the dwelling was conceived for a rather wealthy occupant). Also on the upper level are two (bed)rooms and a bathroom for the occupants, as well as the upper portion (dining room) of the living room.[40]

39 Dick van Gameren, 'Peterstorp 3', in: De woning-plattegrond, standaard en ideaal, Delft Architectural Studies on Housing, no. 4 (Rotterdam: NAi Publishers, 2010), 74.

40 Ulla Hårde, Eric Sigfrid Persson, skånsk funktionalist, byggmästare och uppfinnare (1986); new edition (Malmö: Holmbergs, 2008), 52–79.

61b

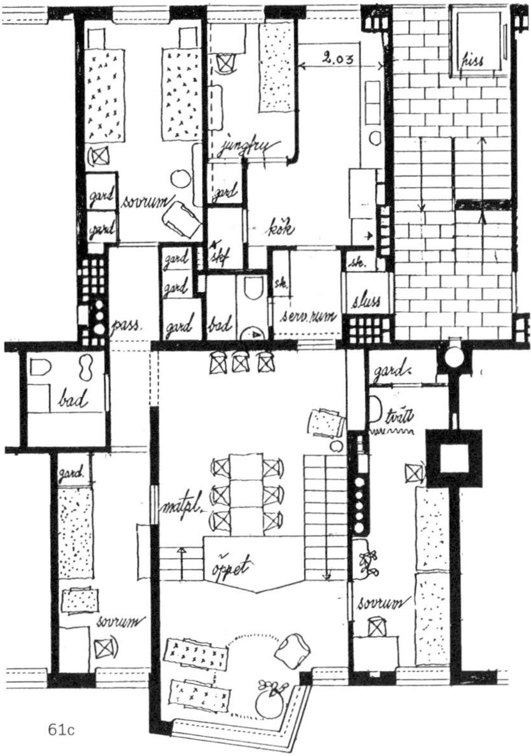
2.03
hiss
jungfru
sovrum
kök
bad
pass.
serv.rum
sluss
tvätt
matpl.
öppet
sovrum
sovrum

61c

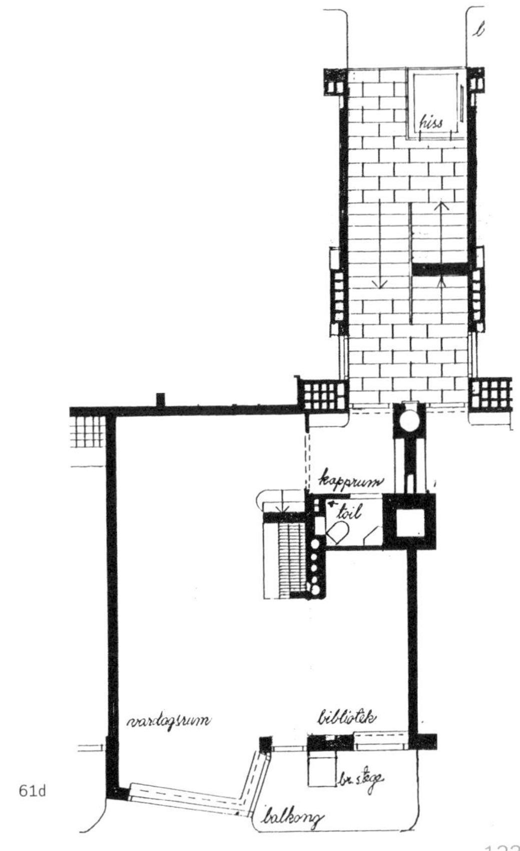
hiss
kapprum
toil
vardagsrum
bibliotek
balkong

61d

62a

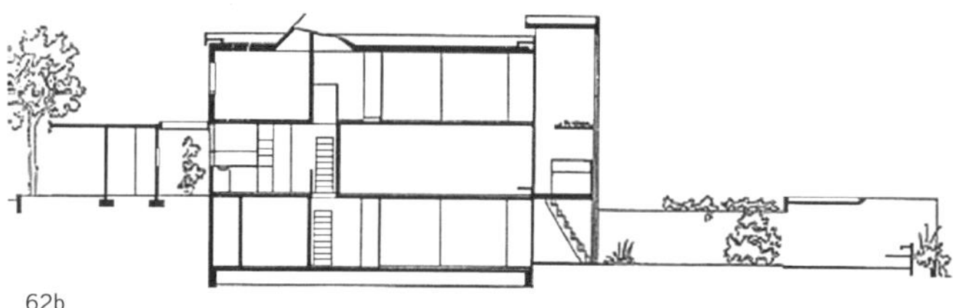
62b

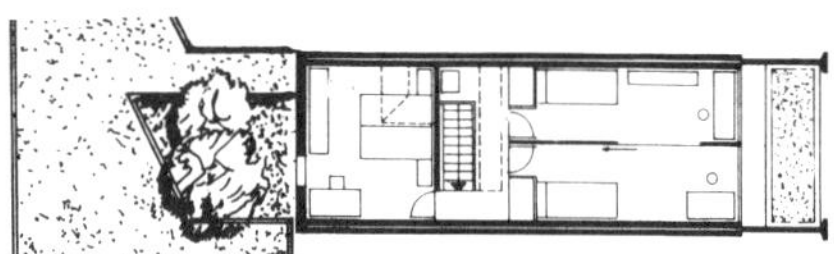
Obergeschoß

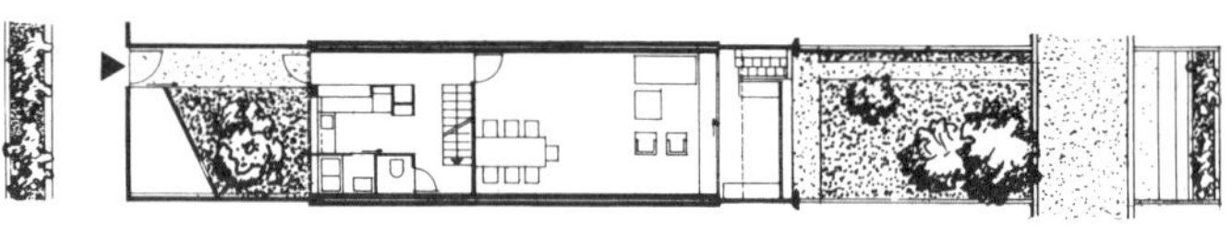
Strassengeschoß

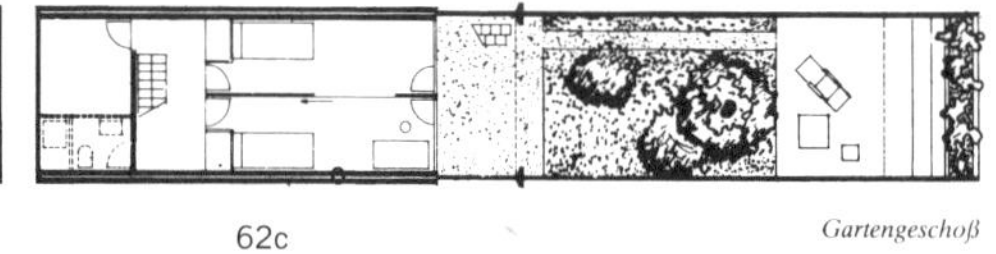
62c

Gartengeschoß

3 STOREYS

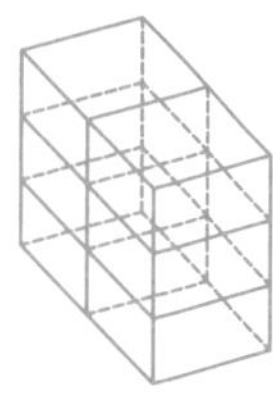

With more than two storeys, the activities within the dwelling are even more separated. Moreover, a more definite hierarchy emerges between the spaces that are close and rapidly accessible and those that are located further away inside the dwelling. This is part of the reason dwellings with multiple storeys are particularly popular for larger occupancy combinations, such as families or group homes, in which the various occupants can claim individual areas within the home. The different floors essentially provide a buffer between the various activities, as the patios and doors did in Chermayeff's elongated ground-floor dwelling (see page 98).

ATELIER 5, SIEDLUNG HALEN (BERN, 1955-1961)

Five architects designed an idyllic residential community in raw concrete on a slope in the midst of woods and green hills. The deep, narrow dwellings are grouped in rows along footpaths and a small communal square. They are parallel to one another, oriented to the south, and thanks to the inclined terrain all have a view over the valley.
The larger dwellings feature three storeys, with the entrance on the first floor, at the level of the footpath. Just beyond the door is the kitchen; the living room is situated further in, with a balcony and a view of the private garden and the valley. Stairs lead up to the children's bedrooms and down to the parents' bedrooms. The latter are situated next to a bathroom and flank the garden, which features a concrete roofed area at the end, offering shade and another view.
This places the middle, communal level between the two private areas. In routing as well as in function, it is the place where the various activities in the dwelling and outside come together, and at the same time it insulates the two bedroom floors from each other.

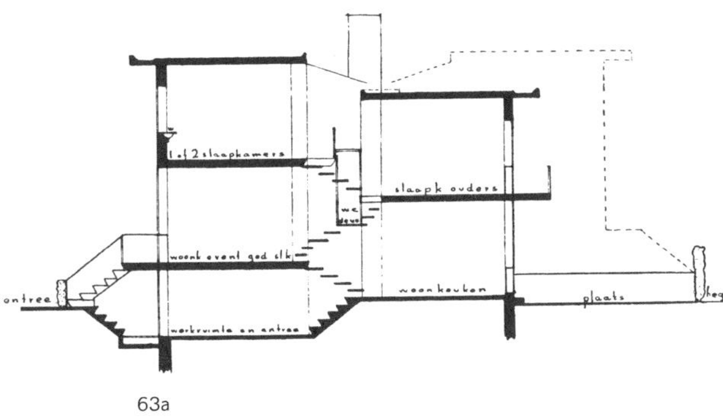

63a

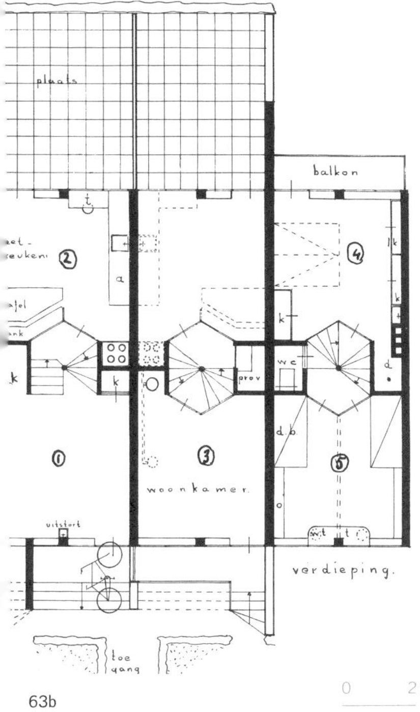

63b

Splitting levels in relation to one another reduces the distances between activities and the division between levels. Visual communication from level to level becomes possible. The degree to which the levels are split can be used to reinforce some connections over others: if the levels are split in increments of a third of a storey rather than half a storey, for instance, the connection between the first level and the second will be stronger than with the next, positioned two thirds of a storey away. A split-level dwelling often creates a linear sequence of activities, reached successively along the internal access.

GERRIT RIETVELD, CORE DWELLINGS (PROJECT, 1941)

A fine example of a split-level dwelling is this design study by Gerrit Rietveld for row houses in an expansion plan for the city of Utrecht. The objective of the study was a design for 'new public housing': a spacious but affordable working-class dwelling, which Rietveld felt could only be achieved by dealing with space in the most efficient way possible.[41] In order to do this, he combined the corridor and stairs into one central spiral staircase that diagonally links the different spaces of the dwelling, which is a mere 4 m wide. The levels to the front and the rear of this staircase are therefore split in relation to each other. The lower space is in the front, half-sunken and intended as a bicycle storage and workshop space, something Rietveld felt was an integral part of working-class life. Cater-cornered behind and above this is a spacious kitchen-diner, at the level of a courtyard. The living room is situated in the front, less than half a storey above the kitchen, creating an easy transition between the two. In addition, this affords the kitchen a view of the main entrance of the dwelling, which opens directly into the living room from a landing. There is a greater distance, however, from the living room to the upper levels, which house the parents' bedroom with shower and above this two children's bedrooms. The dwellings are arranged in rows, staggered two by two with access on alternating sides, creating an extra-wide front garden. They were never implemented in this form. Rietveld had built an early precursor to these 'core dwellings' in 1931, commissioned by Mrs Schröder, on the Erasmuslaan in Utrecht, across the street from the famed Rietveld-Schröder House. These proved much more expensive than anticipated, however, so large-scale construction of this 'new public housing' never materialized.

41 Gerrit Rietveld, 'Een nieuwe volkswoning', de 8 en Opbouw, no. 9 (1941), 122–127.

SPLIT LEVEL

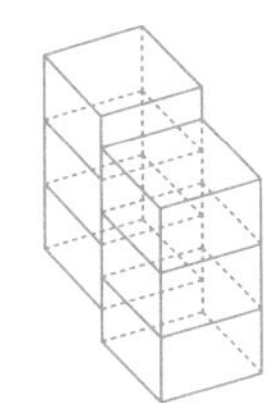

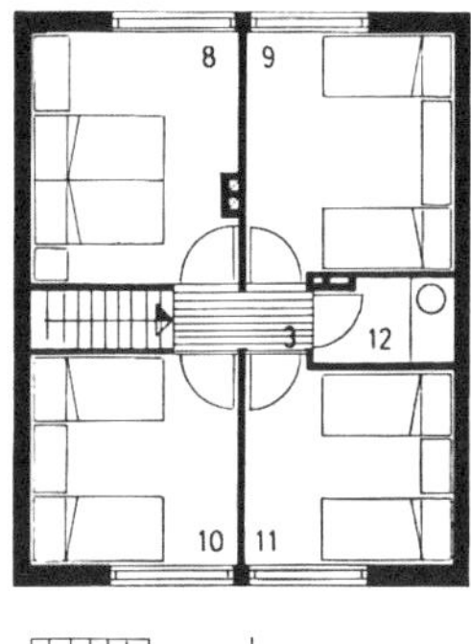

64a

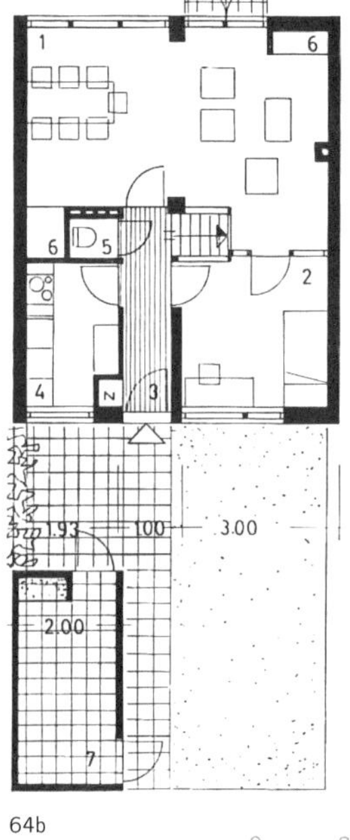

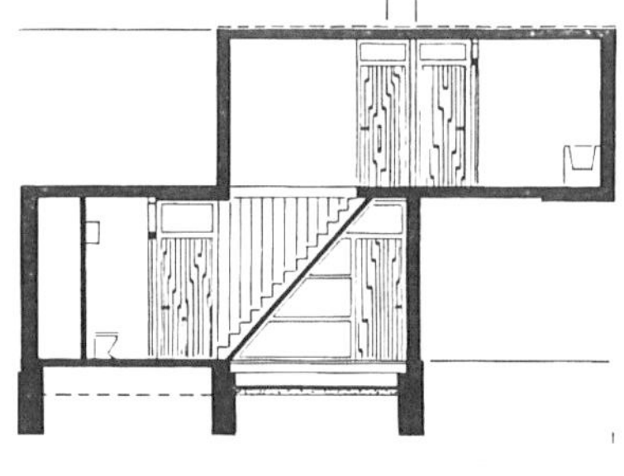

64b

0 2m

VAN DEN BROEK & BAKEMA, KLEI DRIENE (HENGELO, 1951–1956)

In the Klein Driene plan in Hengelo, the architecture practice Van den Broek & Bakema designed a residential area of 6 publicly subsidized dwellings in various configurations. The idea was, on the one hand, to make economical construction possible by repeating the same dwelling types, and on the other to include as mu diversity as possible in the everyday environment of each resident. The resu a clustering of four different dwelling typ in six visually distinctive groups (templat of 91 dwellings, consisting of high-rises a row houses, with sufficient greenery an car-free playing space between the differ housing blocks.[42]

On either side of these six templates, a f type was used in individual rows, intended the largest family units of up to a maxim of nine beds. This 'vertical interlock' typ takes the form of row houses two bays wi the first floor of which is staggered one in relation to the ground floor. The econo in access space this achieves gives the dwellings sufficient room for an extra study/bedroom on the ground floor and f spacious bedrooms on the first floor. In addition, the diagonal communication gi these dwellings an added spatial dimensi

42 J.H. van den Broek and J.B. Bakema, 'Wonin bouw te Hengelo', Bouwkundig Weekblad, no. (1960), 433.

DIAGONAL STACKING

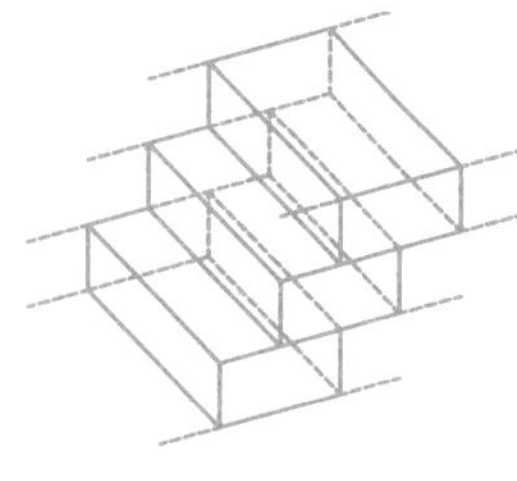

In addition to internal split levels, dwellings in a residential building can be staggered or recessed in relation to one another. This kind of interweaving entails a number of drawbacks, such as a larger contact surface between dwellings, with a greater likelihood of noise penetration, or the fact that ground-connected dwellings now share a common load-bearing structure and are therefore less self-contained. Nevertheless, a desire to provide differentiation among dwellings within a residential building, or to create other unique qualities, can be the inspiration to opt for this arrangement.

65a

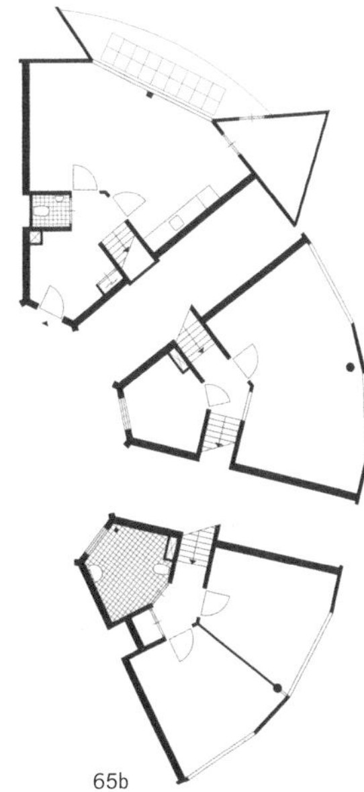

65b

65b Floor plans of ground floor and upper floors of an individual dwelling

LIESBETH VAN DER POL, DRUM DWELLINGS (TWISKE-WEST, 1993)

On a spit of land amid the medieval landscape of perpendicular fields and ditches north of Amsterdam, Liesbeth van der Pol designed 12 round residential buildings, each housing seven ground-connected dwellings. The buildings are situated as individual elements in the public space, so that the landscape of long strips of land and water remains visible throughout. Van der Pol developed the round buildings out of a frustration with the option of either quadrant dwellings, which always entail differences in orientation, or urban villas, in which dwellings are not ground-connected. In order to provide all the dwellings in this water-blessed setting with a garden and yet allow each to enjoy the sun and the view in equal measure, Van der Pol staggered the two levels one circle segment at a time: each dwelling is accessed from the inside of the building, has a garden along the outside façade, and then curves upward diagonally around the 'drum' structure. The straight stairs that provide diagonal communication also separate the small spaces in which facilities are organized from the wide space along the façade on each storey, which can accommodate gathering, eating or sleeping, as the occupants see fit.

DIAGONAL STACKING

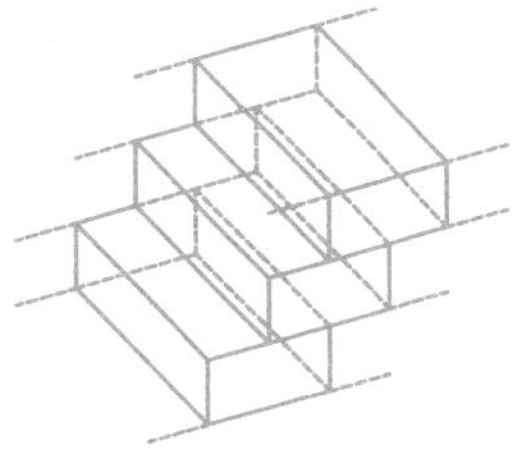

66a

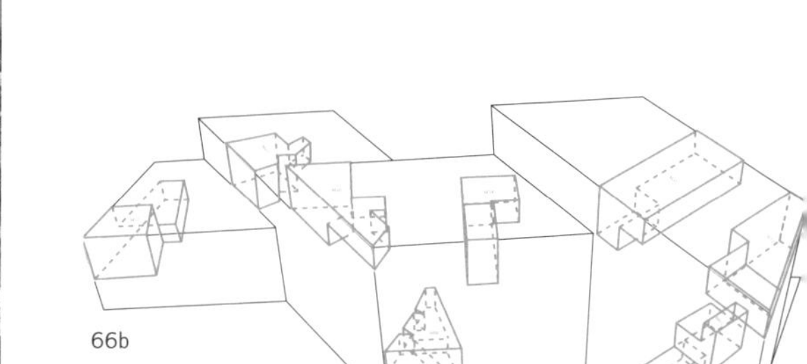

66b

66c

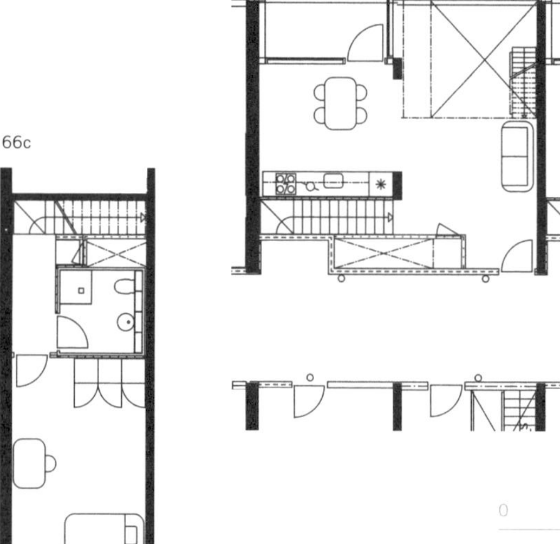

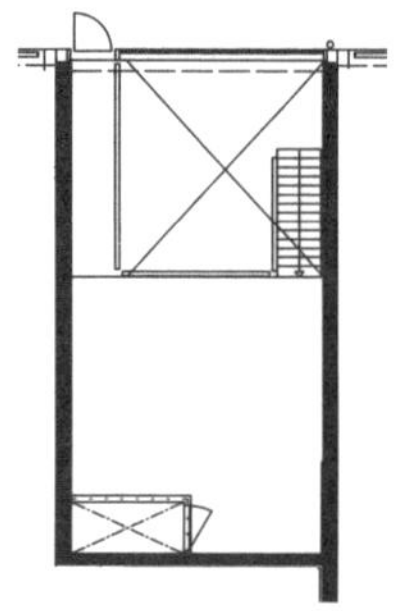

COMPLEX STACKING

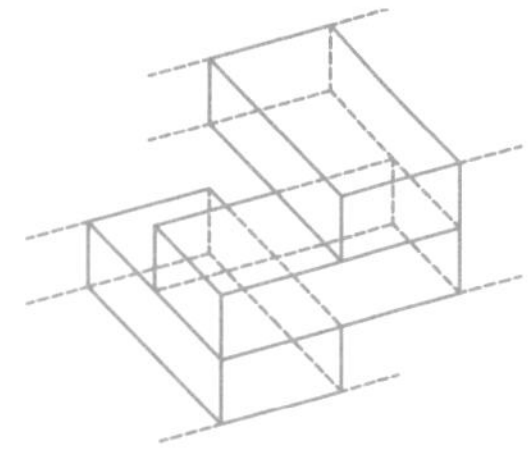

66b Schematic representation of M building, highlighting the position and configuration of individual dwellings
66c Floor plan of three floors of a dwelling around a corridor

PLOT (BIG+JDS), VM BUILDING (COPENHAGEN-ØRESTAD, 2006)

On a narrow strip of land between a metro line and a canal, with an exclusive residential area filled with detached low-rise dwellings on the opposite side of the latter, the architecture practice PLOT designed a pair of buildings that incorporate a wide variety of dwellings and collective facilities. The buildings are lifted off the ground and range from 11 storeys along the railway line to four storeys near the low-rise buildings, in a zigzag progression that gives the pair of buildings its name.
The flats in the M building are accessed through corridors, which cleave one leg of the M on alternate stories. The dwellings have been wrapped around this structure in various ingenious ways, so that a double orientation, an extra-wide façade and/or double-height ceilings can be achieved in each dwelling. The combination of the various design elements leads to a great diversity in dwelling forms and types. (This building is also discussed on page 200 and 307.)

FORM OF THE DWELLING

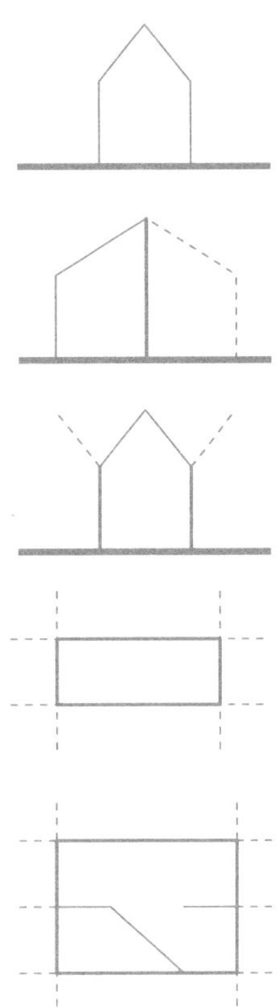

In the preceding sections, the internal organization of the dwelling was discussed based on its depth, width and height. We now move on to the different forms of the dwelling. Naturally these have already been touched upon in our earlier discussions, in relation to the possibilities for internal partitioning of a dwelling. In this section, this relation is examined from the other side. The configuration of the dwelling is discussed according to a systematic categorization of shared characteristics, which have an impact on how the dwelling relates to the space around it and to other dwellings in the immediate vicinity, as well as on the distribution of the dwelling programme over one or more storeys. These relationships ultimately determine, to a significant degree, the parameters of size, orientation and façade surface area that are the basis of the partitioning options of the dwelling (see previous section). The categories within which the dwellings are discussed are:

—*Detached House*

A detached house is ground-connected and has a roof with free clearance. The dwelling does not share any walls with adjacent structures and may consist of one or more storeys.

—*Semi-Detached Dwelling*

A semi-detached dwelling is ground-connected and has a roof with free clearance. The dwelling shares at least one wall with an adjacent structure and may consist of one or more storeys.

—*Row House*

A row house terraced house is ground-connected and has a roof with free clearance. The dwelling shares at least two walls, more or less parallel, with adjacent structures and may consist of one or more storeys.

—*Flat/Apartment*

A flat or apartment is part of a larger (residential) building. The dwelling is spread over a single storey.

—*Maisonette*

A maisonette is part of a larger (residential) building. The dwelling is spread over more than one storey.

DETACHED HOUSE

Of all built structures, the detached house has by far the greatest variety of manifestations. Found in all corners of the world and built since time immemorial, we know it in shapes ranging from a tent to a mansion and from a farmhouse to a palace. These differ to such an extent that a single, unified category is actually impossible. A number of common characteristics, by which they are distinct from other, non-detached dwellings, can nonetheless be identified. One thing detached houses have in common is, in principle, all-round orientation. All the façades are exposed to natural light, which means the dwelling programme can be distributed inside the house as its occupants see fit. Moreover, a detached house, in many instances, is built for (and often by) an occupant who is known in advance. More than in any other kind of housing, the dwelling can be attuned to the individual wishes of its occupant. When this is done well, the home becomes a reflection of the way in which its occupant wants to live. This freedom of individual expression also makes the detached house a favourite assignment for architects who develop and demonstrate their own vision of dwelling by experimenting with form and material. Many innovative ideas about dwelling and dwellings were first brought to fruition in a single detached house, before finding their way into more mass-produced housing construction. Many now-famous villas were created in close collaboration between an enthusiastic client-occupant and an architect with strongly developed ideas.

We should note at this point that despite the exhaustive number of highly publicized examples, such a commission remains a rarity in the conceptual and financial as well as physical domain. By far, most commissions involve dwellings designed in greater quantities and for unknown or serial occupants. The design of the detached residence, in all its facets, therefore falls outside the scope of this book. The few examples included below are meant only to provide illustrations of a number of general characteristics that are identified and pursued in mass-production housing as well, albeit to a less explicit degree.

ADOLF LOOS, HAUS MÜLLER (PRAGUE, 1928–1930)

If any house embodies the idea of shielding a private inner world from the public world outside, it is surely the house Adolf Loos designed for František Müller in 1928, on an open site between the streets Nad Hradním Vodojemem and Střešovická in Prague-Střešovice. Although the house is free-standing, unobstructed all round, and looks out over parts of the city situated lower down, its façades were kept very closed. Moreover, the very few windows included in the composition of the façades seem intended only for natural light and not for a view of the outside: they are fitted with translucent glass or net curtains, while the fixed organization of the dwelling hinders access to the windows.[43]

Everything is indeed focused on the world inside the house. Visual connections between the spaces situated on different levels lead the progress through the house along a course of stairs and turning points, each providing a new glimpse into the spaces just departed or about to be entered. The spaces are organized according to the *Raumplan* principle developed by Loos,[44] whereby spaces are classified in a meaningful order according to their individual heights, each appropriate to its use. In an interview after the house was completed, Loos phrased it himself as follows:

My architecture is not conceived by drawings but by spaces. I do not draw plans, façades or sections . . . for me the ground floor, first floor, do not exist . . . There are only interconnected continual spaces, rooms, halls, terraces . . . Each space needs a different height: a dining room is obviously higher than a larder, that is why the ceilings are placed at different levels. These spaces are connected so that ascent and descent are not only unnoticeable, but at the same time functional.[45]

From the small entrance vestibule a corridor leads to the large reception room at the rear. Cater-cornered above and in open communication with this is the dining room. On the opposite side, a small set of stairs leads to a room to which the lady of the house can retire while still keeping an eye on the reception room. A central staircase leads to the floor above, where the bedrooms are situated. The principal exterior space is located on the roof, next to the breakfast room. Elevated above the immediate surroundings, the occupants can enjoy the view in private.

67a

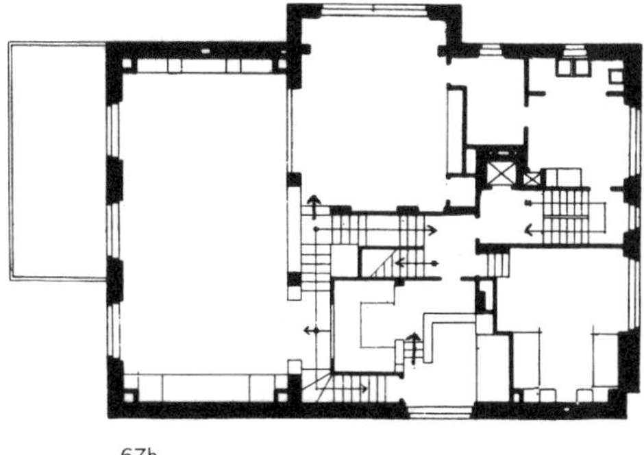

67b

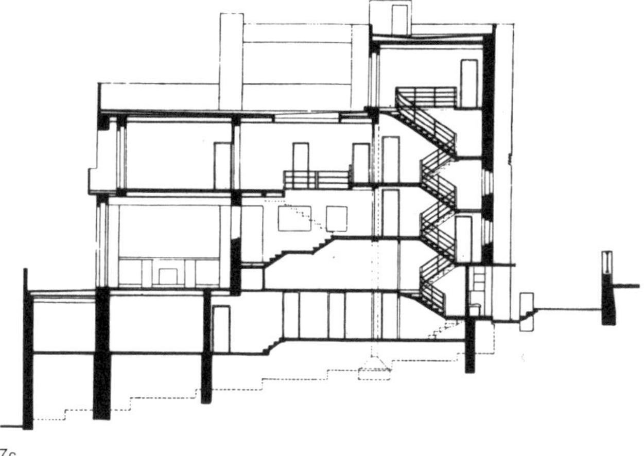

67c

67b Main living level on first floor
67c Long section

43 Le Corbusier said Loos once told him, 'A cultivated man does not look out of the window: his window is a ground glass; it is there only to let the light in, not to let the gaze pass through.' Beatriz Colomina, 'The Split Wall: Domestic Voyeurism', in: Sexuality & Space (New York: Princeton Architectural Press, 1996), 74.
44 Incidentally, the term Raumplan was not applied to this organizational principle by Loos himself, but only later by his associate Kulka.
45 Ivan Margolis, 'Villa Muller', The Architectural Review (November 2000).

68a

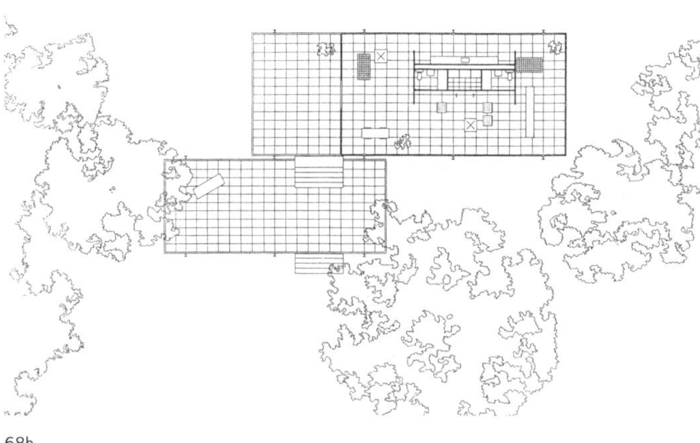

68b

DETACHED HOUSE

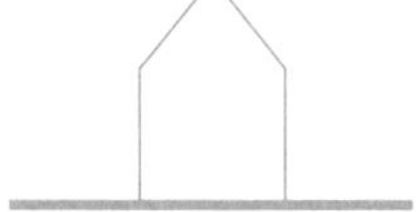

LUDWIG MIES VAN DER ROHE, FARNSWORTH HOUSE (PLANO, ILLINOIS, 1946–1951)

In his house for Edith Farnsworth, architect Ludwig Mies van der Rohe endeavoured to achieve the exact opposite of what Loos was striving for in his Haus Müller. In this private estate along a river, insulated by trees, the modernist ideals of air, light and space are translated into a dwelling in the midst of nature, dematerialized as much as possible. Although protection from the elements is still necessary, every effort has been made to suggest that it is not present. Between an elevated floor platform 8.4 × 23.1 m and a flat roof of equal dimensions, large square glass panels have been placed in minimalist steel frames. On one of the short sides, the façade is recessed to leave room for a covered terrace by the entrance. Parallel to this is a lower open terrace, linked to the house and the surroundings by apparently floating stairs. Slender steel columns on the outside of the glass outline the contours of the house and terrace in a tight rhythm.

Although the entrance is the only physical opening, the impression inside is of being in direct contact with nature all around. This is further reinforced by the location of the fixed core, slightly off-centre in the house, which guides the otherwise open-plan space around it: the entrance with terrace to the west, the kitchen to the north, sleeping quarters to the east and the fireplace with a view of the river to the south. The house is situated among the existing oak trees in such a way that, far removed from the glass façade, they demarcate the spaces of the home. The interior design of the house, which reinforces the composition, was also decided by Mies. The extraordinary openness achieved in the house is due in large part to the precise detailing and choice of materials, which border on perfection. Although the Farnsworth House was of enormous influence among architects, it is perhaps worth noting that in the eyes of the client it was an utter failure. In the summer it was far too hot and difficult to ventilate; in the winter it was impossible to heat. In fact, Farnsworth even sued Mies when the construction estimate was exceeded by 50 per cent.[46] Even light, air and space seem to have a downside and a limit.

46 D. Hauptmann, 'Farnsworth House, 1946–1951, Plano, Illinois, VS', in: W. Wilms Floet (ed.), Het ontwerp van het kleine woonhuis: een plandocumentatie (Amsterdam: SUN Publishers, 2005), 114.

69a

HANS SCHAROUN, HAUS BAENSCH (BERLIN-SPANDAU, 1935)

In most locations there is a clear distinction between the different sides of the dwelling in terms of the relationship between public and private. The use of the dwelling should be a response to this, something a successful design supports. Modernist Hans Scharoun's Haus Baensch demonstrates this in exemplary fashion. Under the Nazi regime of 1930s Germany, modernism was anathema, and a more traditional construction in Heimat style was championed. Scharoun remained in Germany, concentrating on a small number of residential houses for people he knew. His design for a house in Spandau looks, on the street side, almost like a traditional house with a saddleback roof. Behind this formal façade, however, he developed a dwelling that opens out in every way to the surrounding landscape. The service zone with kitchen, immediately behind the front façade, links the entrance to an oval eating area situated on the opposite side, a pivot point that overlooks the dwelling fanning out into three zones. The zones overlap and lead down to the garden, with an elongated sofa providing views of the wider landscape beyond. All around, large glass openings are oriented to different forms of light and views, while sliding partitions and curtains can be used to partition the space. On the upper level, behind the recessed bedrooms, there is a large terrace. The house, so unassuming on the street side, mutates in the back into a multiform volume, directed towards the qualities offered by its immediate surroundings as well as by the wider landscape.

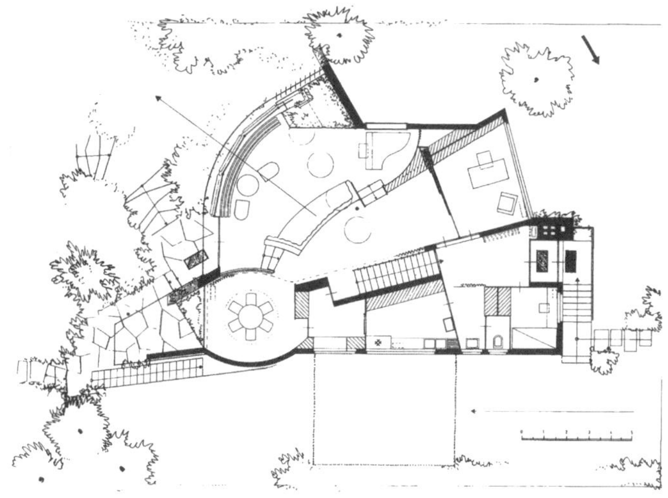

69b

70a

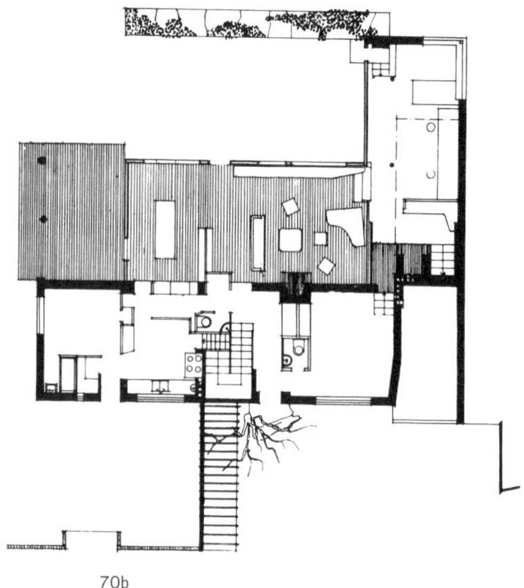

70b

DETACHED HOUSE

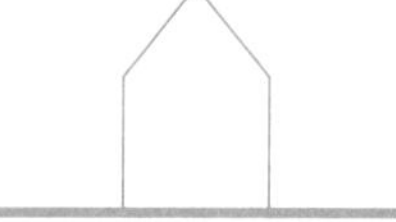

ALVAR AALTO, HOUSE AND STUDIO (MUNKKINIEMI, FINLAND, 1934–1936)

Finnish architect Alvar Aalto considered the relationship between the dweller and the natural environment to be of preeminent importance. In his view, the primary concern in housing construction for both architects and occupants should be an intimate connection between man and the natural environment, inside as well as outside the dwelling. His experimental quest to give shape to this link between inside and outside at a profound level begins with his own modest house with studio on the Riihitie in Munkkiniemi, a suburb of Helsinki.[47] The house is made up of a number of volumes that differ in form and material and together enclose an exterior space in a U-shaped formation. This layout is partly inspired by the configuration of a small farmhouse around a farmyard, as the archetypal form of dwelling in proximity with nature.[48] The entrance provides access to the central section of the house, where, on the ground floor, a service zone including a kitchen is situated. A staircase leads from here up to a small private living room with a terrace, as well as to the sleeping quarters. The other wing houses the studio, which takes up two storeys, looking out onto the sheltered exterior area through abundant amounts of glass. The studio is accessible separately from the entrance, but a sliding door also connects it to the central space of the house, the general reception and living room or *tupa*, which is situated in the lee of the inner angle, flanking the enclosed exterior space and also directly accessible from the entrance zone. A half-wall and a curtain form the communication with an adjacent dining room, also accessible from the kitchen and also flanking the exterior space. The latter is bordered at the opposite end, near the end of the studio, by an elevation planted with shrubbery, separating it from the rest of the outside space and making it, as it were, part of the dwelling itself. This creates a habitation space in the open air, which can be used as an extension of the living and dining rooms in fine weather. Together, they fulfil the function of Aalto's centrally situated dwelling space or *Allraum*, which incorporates a relationship with nature into the house.

47 Sarah Menin and Flora Samuel, Nature and Space: Aalto and Le Corbusier (London: Routledge, 2002), 133.

48 Ibid., 135.

71a

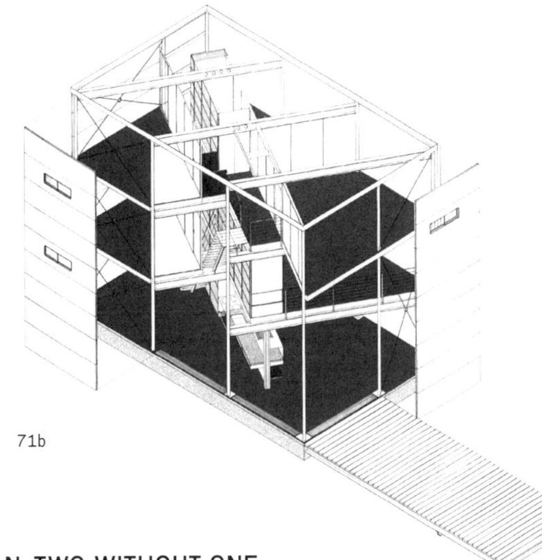

71b

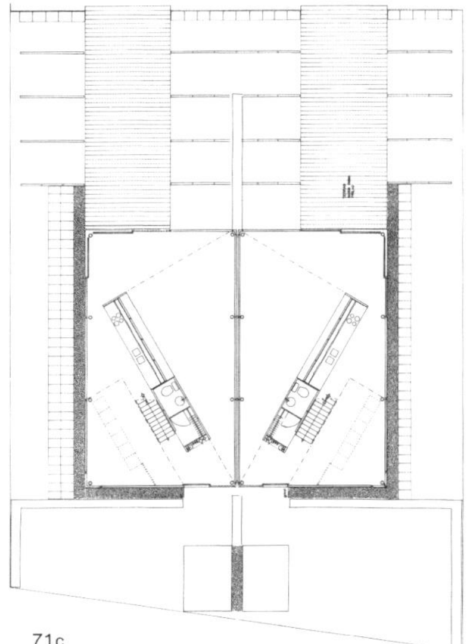

71c

JAN PESMAN, TWO-WITHOUT-ONE-ROOF (DELFT, 1988)

In 1989 the Delft-based designers association Delft Design launched a competition for its members to design a double residence. The competition, entitled *twee-zonder-één-dak* – 'two-without-one-roof', as a variant on the traditional semi-detached double house known in Dutch as a *twee-onder-een-kapwoning* or 'two-under-one-roof dwelling' – was intended to generate new designs featuring the qualities of a shared villa, for a row of 24 lots along the southern edge of the Tanthof area, with unrestricted views towards Rotterdam. The winning designs were implemented, including the dwelling Jan Pesman (CePeZed) designed for himself (and a neighbour). The volume looks like a severe, rectangular box of glass and stainless steel, each half of which is a mirror image of the other. In the front, the doors to both dwellings are located fraternally side by side in a single entryway, which gives the ambiguous suggestion of a single villa and also affords each of the dwellings a fairly continuous side and back garden. A brick cavity wall splits the volume spatially and acoustically, while each of the two dwellings is constructed out of one steel frame.
Each steel skeleton encompasses a single, large space three storeys high. Inside, a fixed core has been positioned diagonally along the middle, dividing the dwelling into different zones. From the entrance, the wardrobe and kitchen as well as the stairs, suspended from the core, are directly visible, while the spacious living room, with its view over the fields, is still hidden. The core also creates different rooms on the upper floors. The staggered floors create open vertical spaces (*vides*) and sightlines that connect the levels within the dwelling in exciting ways.

There are various conceivable reasons to trade the significant benefits of a detached house for a configuration in which multiple dwellings are grouped within a single volume. First of all there is an economic benefit, based on the fact that fewer construction materials and costly façades are needed than for the same number of detached dwellings. The dwellings are therefore more likely to be affordable for more people. At least as important, however, is a qualitative consideration. At too high a density, a paltry amount of space is left over around detached dwellings, adding little enjoyment value to the home. Clustering the dwellings can ensure that every home features a high-quality exterior space.

SEMI-DETACHED DWELLING

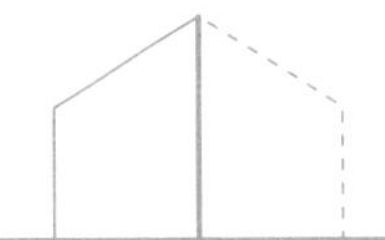

72a

72b

ROW HOUSE

The row terrace house, built in vast numbers in the Netherlands, is based on the principle of a repetition of the same housing unit in a continuous building volume, the row of linked houses. It was first applied on a large scale during the industrialization of the nineteenth century, in order to provide a large number of affordable working-class dwellings in short order. The major motivation here was the low construction costs rather than the quality of housing for the occupants. It remains a popular dwelling type today, thanks to the fact that it combines the economic advantages of mass-produced housing with a ground-connected structure; for relatively little money, occupants can live in a house, often with a garden, at street level.

Due to sequential horizontal linking, the row house shares its two outer side walls with adjacent dwellings and features a double orientation through opposite sides. It often has an exterior space at the front and back, whereby the space at the front also serves as a buffer between the street and the home. The narrower the dwelling, the more dwellings can fit in a row. This comes at the expense of the façade length and therefore constrains the partitioning possibilities of the dwelling. The entrance is usually positioned to one side, to leave as much free space as possible along the front façade. Dwellings can be linked in a uniform sequence or mirrored two by two along the row; in the latter case two entrances are positioned side by side.

The drawbacks of the row house include a loss of individual visual differentiation when the repetition is too uniform; there can also be a lack of privacy, in that the dwellings or exterior spaces are too exposed to the street or their immediate neighbours. Both drawbacks can be resolved through well-designed interventions.

J.J.P. OUD, WEISSENHOFSIEDLUNG ROW HOUSING (STUTTGART, 1927)

In 1927, an international exhibition by the Deutsche Werkbund opened in Stuttgart, entitled 'Die Wohnung'. An international selection of architects was invited to implement solutions to 'the problem of the dwelling' within an urban design plan by German architect Ludwig Mies van der Rohe. The exhibition demonstrated, for the first time, the similarities in thinking about new architecture at the time. There turned out to be an international consensus of ideas, which would become known as the Modern Movement and *Neues Bauen* ('the new way to build').

In the design by Rotterdam architect J.J.P. Oud for a small row of five ground-connected dwellings, the organizing principle is the orientation of the dwellings to the sun. The dwellings are positioned on a north-south axis, whereby the habitation space is situated in the south-facing portion and the service spaces in the north-facing portion. Even the dwelling access is part of this: the entrance for residents is through the garden on the private south side, while access for deliveries is planned through a walled courtyard on the north side; goods can be delivered directly to the kitchen. The orientation regulates the circulation

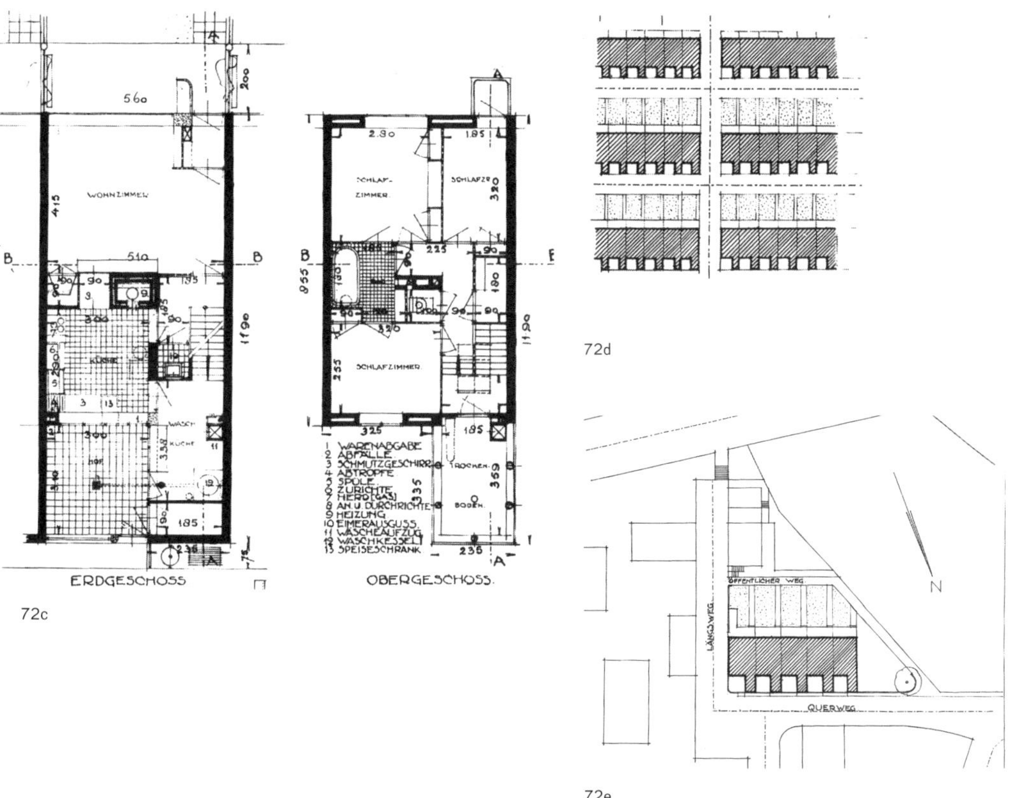

flows of the dwelling, so that hardly any room for circulation is needed inside. The kitchen developed by Oud plays a vital role in this. Unlike the 'Frankfurt kitchen' developed a few years earlier, Oud's kitchen is spacious enough to eat in, and it is positioned between the living room and the courtyard. Deliveries are taken in through the kitchen window, and rubbish can be sent back to the courtyard through a hatch. On the opposite side of the kitchen, the living room can be served through an opening large enough to keep an eye on children playing in the living room and garden.[49] Cater-cornered behind the kitchen and flanking the courtyard is a projecting volume housing a laundry room and scullery as well as bicycle storage, with a drying space above. Thanks to this volume and a slightly stepped arrangement due to the slight incline of the terrain, the dwellings are legible as individual units.

An accompanying situation drawing shows that Oud intended the dwellings to be part of a larger plan, in which the streets are lined with front and rear dwelling sides in equal measure. The south-facing gardens line the north side of every street, across from the closed façades of the walled courtyards. According to Oud this would 'produce a lively streetscape, presenting, instead of the tedium of façades of formalist design, the wealth of variety of a grouping based on organic principles'.[50] In this respect the plan is akin to Ernst May's developments for housing in parallel lines in Frankfurt (see also 'Parallel Line Development' in Chapter 5, 'Urban Ensemble', page 227). In the Weissenhofsiedlung only one row of houses was built, and the street providing access to the gardens was narrowed to a path, in order to leave more room for the gardens here.

49 Richard Pommer and Christian F. Otto, Weissenhoff 1927 and the Modern Movement in Architecture (Chicago: University of Chicago Press, 1991), 119.

50 J.J.P. Oud, explanatory text accompanying his design, in: Deutscher Werkbund, Bau und Wohnung. Die Bauten der Weißenhofsiedlung in Stuttgart, errichtet 1927 nach Vorschlägen des Deutschen Werkbundes im Auftrag der Stadt Stuttgart und im Rahmen d. Werkbundausstellung 'Die Wohnung' (Stuttgart: Wedekind, 1927), 87.

72b View from the kitchen in the courtyard on the north side
72c Ground floor and upper floor
72d Diagram of an ideal situation
72e Situation in the Weissenhofsiedlung, Frankfurt

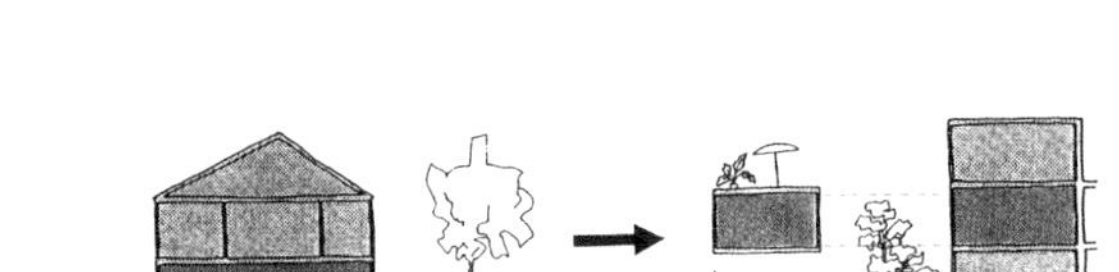

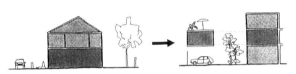

73a

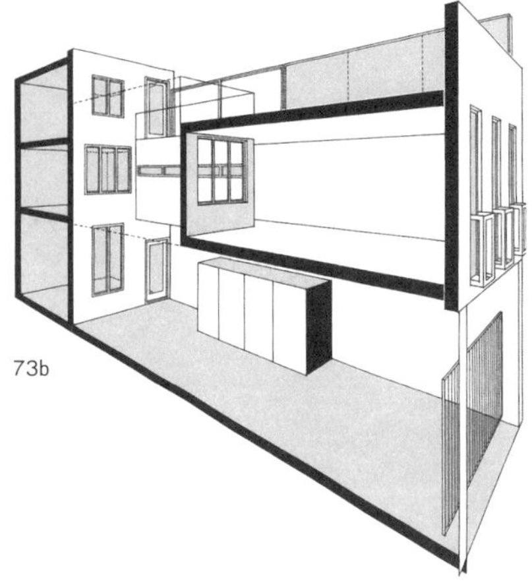

73b

73c

KÖTHER & SALMAN ARCHITECTEN, SINGLE-FAMILY HOMES, ERTSKADE (AMSTERDAM, 1994–1999)

After a successful building programme that covered the KNSM Island with cosmopolitan blocks and the Java Island with a subdivision inspired by Amsterdam's historic city centre, the city decided to fill the subsequent islands in its new Eastern Harbour District with high-density low-rises. To this end, the subdivision of the – by now traditional – row house was mutated into a configuration that would permit this higher density. West 8's master plan called for the parking and exterior space to be situated within the volume, and the dwellings placed back to back, creating relatively narrow, automobile-free streets between dwellings strung together in deep blocks. Diverse subdivision principles and a variety of architects provided a different interpretation for each block. The dwellings by Köther & Salman architecten on Borneo Island represent a clear illustration of the aforementioned mutation of the row house. On the ground floor, the car is parked behind a gate at the front, and access then progresses through to an open patio, vital in bringing light into the deep, single-orientation dwellings. This is the entrance to the three-storey rear section of the house. On the first floor, a narrow corridor along the patio links the kitchen with the living room situated at the front. Above, the same route provides access, through the bedroom, to the large roof terrace that, in addition to the patio, affords the dwelling a large, sunny exterior space with a view over the water. In spite of the high density, these dwellings feature a high degree of privacy.

ROW HOUSE

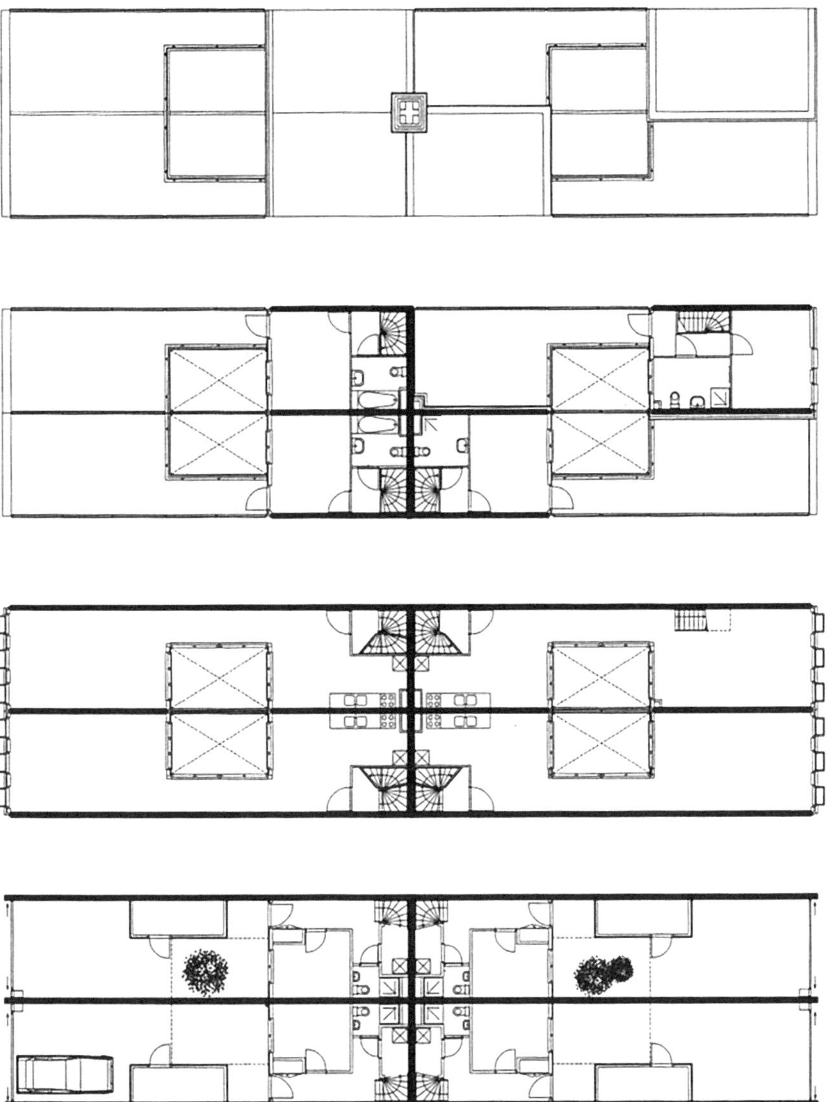

73d

73a Diagram by West 8. Transformation of a standard row house into a patio dwelling
73d Four row houses in a back-to-bacl configuration. Floor plans of ground floor, upper floors and roof.

74a

APARTMENT

As more and more people want to live in the same place, it becomes necessary not only to link dwellings horizontally but also to stack them vertically. The non-ground-connected dwellings created in this way allow for construction up to very high densities. The same plot of land is built upon multiple times, which produces significant economic advantages. A relatively large dwelling space can be realized for relatively little money, for instance. In addition, the concentration of collective facilities can produce greater dwelling comfort than would be feasible in low-rise housing.

Stacking also makes it possible to develop dwellings spread over a single storey: a flat or apartment. This is usually wider than a dwelling in which the same programme is distributed over several storeys. If desired, a sense of great space can be created here, making apartments highly suitable for open-plan living. Their absence of internal elevations also makes them convenient for elderly or disabled occupants with limited mobility. One drawback to apartments is often the result of an unfavourable combination with the dwelling's access: in combination with a gallery, privacy soon becomes an issue, while a corridor turns single-storey apartments into single-orientation dwellings.

JOHANNES DUIKER, NIRWANA (THE HAGUE, 1929)

In the 1920s, when rising wages made it more difficult for wealthy families to employ sufficient domestic staff for the upkeep of a detached house, living in luxury apartment buildings became a trend throughout Europe. Imported from the Roaring Twenties culture of America, these combined the luxury of collective facilities like staff and upkeep with living in a metropolitan atmosphere. Persuaded by the accounts brought back from the USA by his colleague Jan Wiebenga, Duiker decided to join him in developing an independent plan for luxury full-service flats for the wealthy residents of The Hague. The original plan consisted of five buildings, arranged in a checkerboard pattern along the Benoordenhoutseweg and linked by continuous balconies on all sides. The apartments were spacious and luxurious, with a large hall, drawing room and 'gentleman's study' and amply furnished with glass on all sides. After many changes, arguments and a parting of the ways between the architects, only one building was eventually built, with smaller apartments and without continuous balconies. Due to the input of buyers early in the design process, the floor plans vary substantially behind the regularly ordered façades.

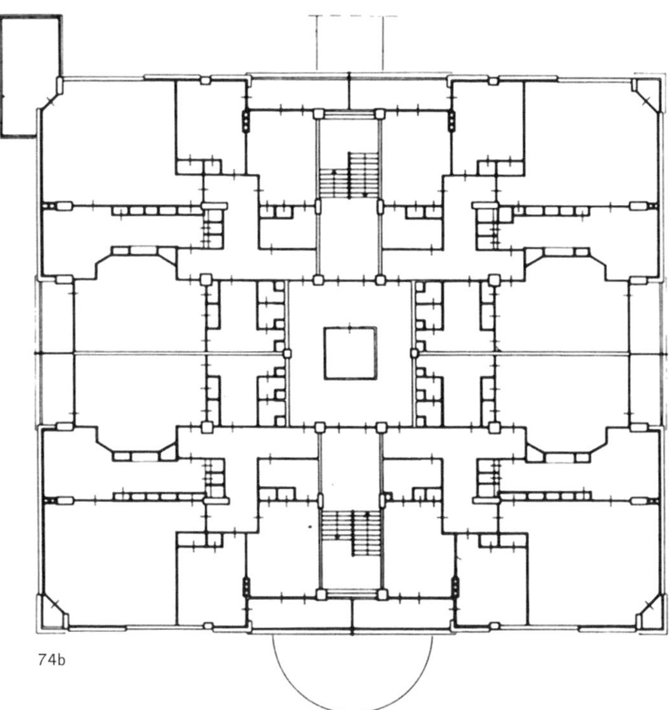
74b

In the 'ideal plan' the dwelling is entered from the central stairwell and lift through a spacious hall that provides access to the rest of the premises. The open angle accommodates the living room, with an adjacent kitchen and a lounge with balcony along the side façade. Two bedrooms share a balcony on the other façade, while the facilities are concentrated in the dark internal angle. Communal facilities included chutes for rubbish and dirty laundry, a house telephone, a goods lift and central heating. Originally there was a kitchen downstairs, from which orders could be placed with the house telephone and delivered to the correct apartment using the goods lift.
The construction of a residential building in reinforced concrete was also a first for the Netherlands. The choice of this kind of construction came out of Duiker's search for lightweight construction and materials, his 'conceptual economy'. Over the 'insipid construction in brick walls so heavy they kill off any joy of life inside', he opted for 'a system of floors and columns', still in development in high-rise construction at the time, 'that bears its own load and that of the connected walls. As a result, the highest standards of hygiene are automatically fulfilled even on the lowest storeys, since on every storey the openings for light can be made as large as is required for every space.'[51] The structural beams, which are visible as parapets in the front façade, are suspended on the columns with an overhang, which helps the distribution of downward force and contributes to an economy of materials. The angle that is left free as a result accommodates the building's iconic corner balconies.

51 Johannes Duiker, 'Ingezonden brief aan Collega Van der Steur', Bouwkundig Weekblad Architectura, no. 2 (1928), 63-64.

74b Typical floor plan of a storey with four identical apartments. Due to the input of initial buyers during the design and implementation, the arrangement of the storeys actually deviated from this.
75b Living and sleeping level in a maisonette

75a

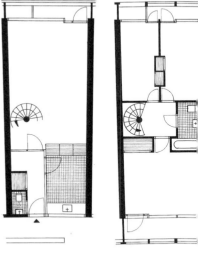

75b

75b Woon- en slaapverdieping in een maisonnette

Like the apartment, a maisonette is part of a larger residential building and therefore shares its advantages in economy and density. The word maisonette means 'little house' in French, making its essential feature immediately evident: a miniature house, a dwelling with multiple storeys, incorporated in a residential building. A maisonette with two storeys is sometimes called a 'duplex', one with three storeys a 'triplex'. As the dwelling programme is spread over several levels, these dwellings occupy less space per storey than an apartment with the same programme. For reasons of economy (to limit the façade surface area and achieve as many dwellings side by side as possible) this usually results in narrower dwellings. Internally, a good division between the private and the communal parts of the home can be effected, making maisonettes suitable for families. The additional storey can also serve to redress the disadvantage of apartments in combination with a gallery or corridor: the entrance level remains constrained in privacy and/or orientation, but the façades of the other storey(s) can be kept free of traffic flows. On the contrary, a combination with access through a staircase is less advantageous, unless the maisonettes are confined to the top storeys: in the lower levels the collective stairwell would run parallel to the internal dwelling access, which requires twice the amount of space and produces long vertical distances between dwellings.

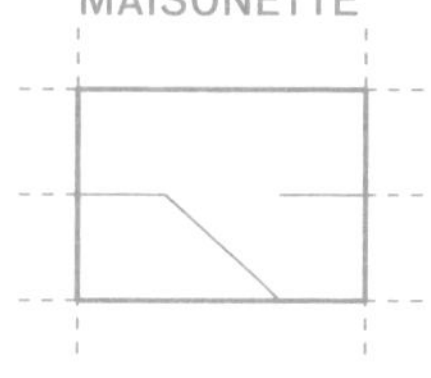

INGWERSEN & DE GEUS, AUTOPON (AMSTERDAM, 1961)

At the end of the Overtoom in Amsterdam, where this avenue curves towards the Amstelveenseweg, Ingwersen & De Geus designed a building for dwellings and commercial premises that follows the curve of the street. In composition and use of materials, the building is clearly inspired by Le Corbusier's Unité d'Habitation and originally had an automobile showroom on the first floor, for which an expressively projecting display window was created to put the latest car model on show for the city. The residential programme consists of apartments and maisonettes that, unlike in the Unité, are accessed through galleries at the rear of the building. In the maisonettes, the kitchen and toilet are positioned along the gallery side, with a spacious living room with balcony along the unobstructed front façade. An open spiral staircase leads to the sleeping level. Here, three bedrooms are distributed along both unobstructed façades, whereby the master bedroom is situated on the quiet rear side and the other two share a balcony on the street side. On this level, the middle zone is the obvious place for a bathroom and vertical circulation, which determines the placement of the spiral staircase.

RESIDENTIAL BUILDING

DETACHED HOUSE

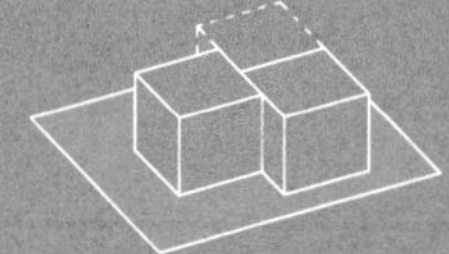

CLUSTERED LOW-RISE

ROW

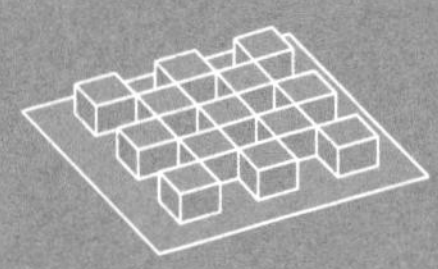

MAT

URBAN VILLA

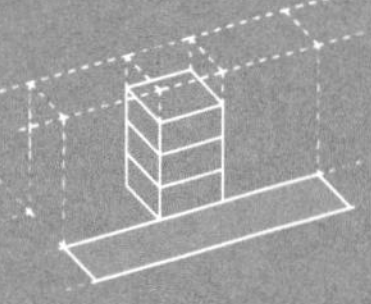

INFILL

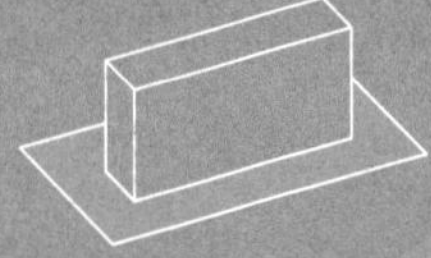

SLAB

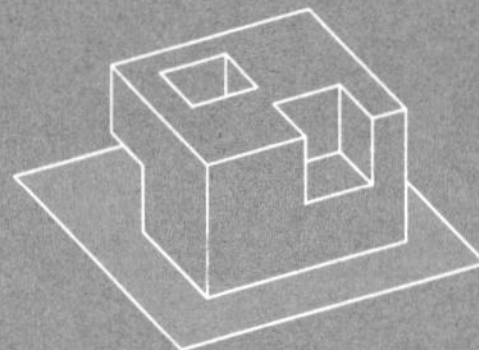

BLOCK

TOWER

As more and more people want to live in the same place, it becomes necessary to link dwellings horizontally and at higher densities to stack them vertically as well. The ensemble of linked and stacked dwellings is now manifested as a shared volume: the residential building. We call the way in which the individual dwellings are arranged and accessed within this the residential building configuration. In principle, this configuration can be described geometrically, whereby the simplest residential building consists of a single home. Linking dwellings width-wise and depth-wise produces, respectively, line and plane formations of ground-connected dwellings. If a vertical component is then added, volumes in line, plane and block formations of stacked dwellings result. Each of the volumes obtained in this way has its own logic in regard to the organization and access of the individual dwellings.
This chapter begins by discussing the characteristics and qualities of various combinations of linking and stacking. We then turn to the different ways of providing access to the dwellings.

LINKING AND STACKING

In practice, a residential building is not usually designed based on the linking and stacking of a desired number of dwellings; instead, contextual (see Chapter 7, 'Context') and aesthetic aspects commonly determine the form and shape of the building volume. Only then are dwellings fitted into this: stacked, linked and accessed as is most desirable in the given situation. Nevertheless, the same principles can be identified in the building in its final form as in the theoretical series of geometric building volumes used here. Even a complex building form can often be read as a combination of simpler forms and organizational principles.
Based on the aforementioned geometric categorization, we can distinguish the following categories at the level of the residential building:

—*Detached House*	—*Mat*	—*Slab*
—*Clustered Low-Rise*	—*Urban Villa*	—*Block*
—*Row*	—*Infill*	—*Tower*

The characteristics of the various categories are discussed below using examples. Because the residential building as a detached house coincides with the category of the detached house at the dwelling level, we refer readers to its discussion in the section on the detached house in the preceding chapter.

01a

WINGENDER HOVENIER ARCHITECTEN, STELLINGHOF (VIJFHUIZEN, 1998–2004)

Wingender Hovenier Architecten's winning design in the multiple commission for the expansion of Vijfhuizen is based on a strong relationship between the dwelling and the exterior space. Rotating the standard layout of the narrow, deep row house a quarter-turn produces a dwelling that communicates with the street and garden over an extended width. This dwelling is then linked, in various dimensions and combinations, with dwellings in the publicly subsidized rental sector as well as medium- to high-end buying market. The publicly subsidized rental homes are grouped as groups of four corner dwellings in single volumes, staggered a little in relation to one another and shifted away from the centre, in order to create lot sections of different sizes. The dwellings with the smallest exterior space have their bedrooms on the ground floor and a spacious open-plan kitchen and living room on the first floor. The other dwellings have their living space on the garden level and the sleeping quarters upstairs. Double dividing walls and separate entrances afford each dwelling within the shared volume a substantial degree of privacy.

CLUSTERED LOW-RISE

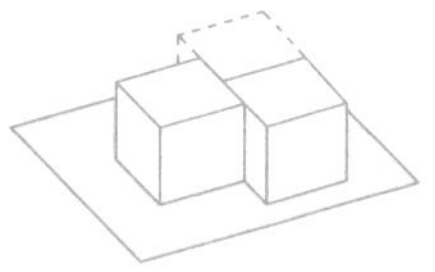

This category includes various building volumes in which two or more ground-connected dwellings are linked, but not in any explicit direction. These commonly semi-detached dwellings share a number of structural walls, but each is usually focused on the exterior space around it. A communal entryway is possible, but access is usually privately organized as well, in one of the open façades of the dwelling. The most important advantages of this configuration are the shared construction costs, in combination with the relatively sizable open space around the building.

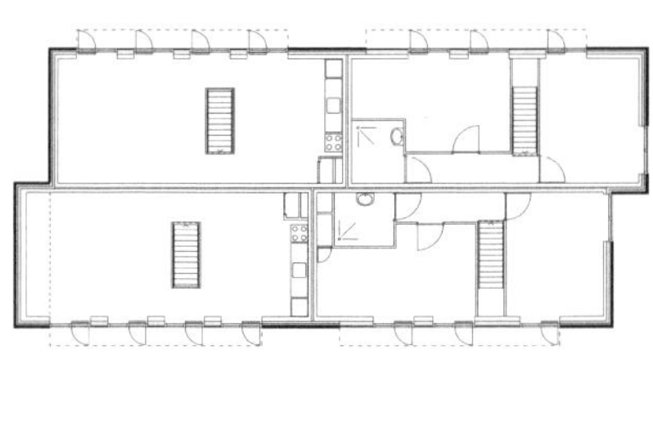

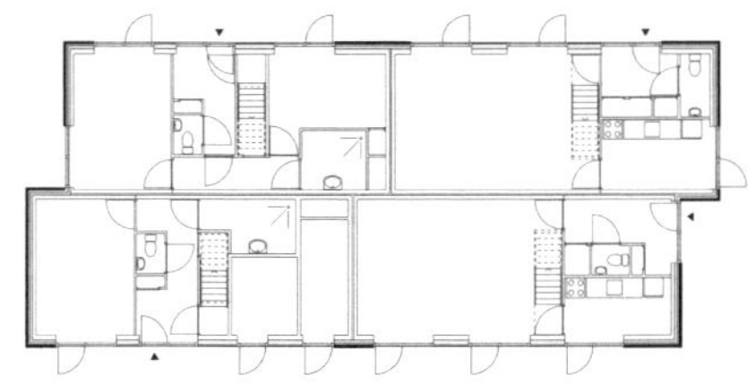

01b

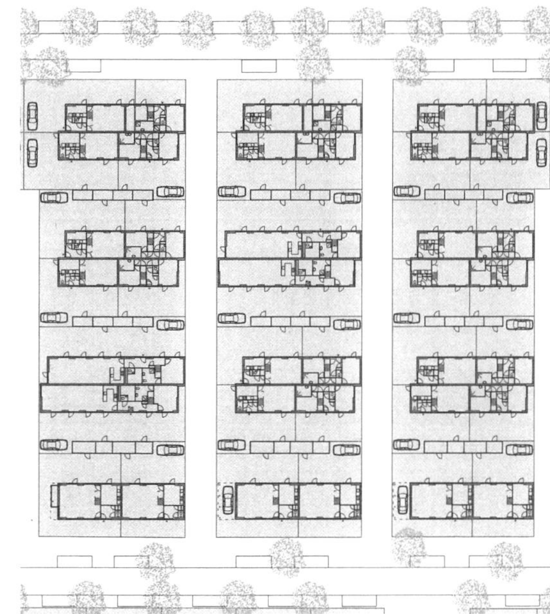

01c

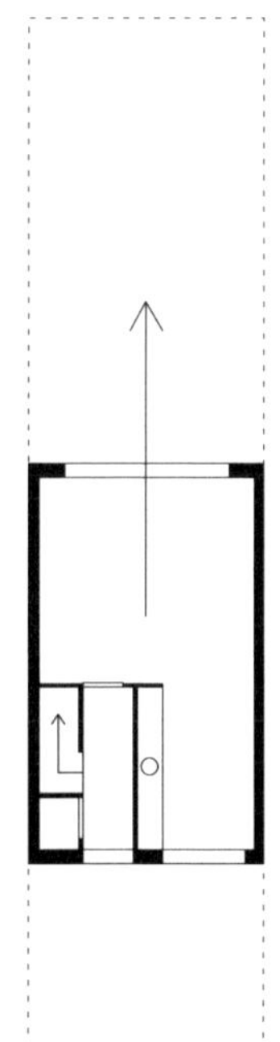

01d

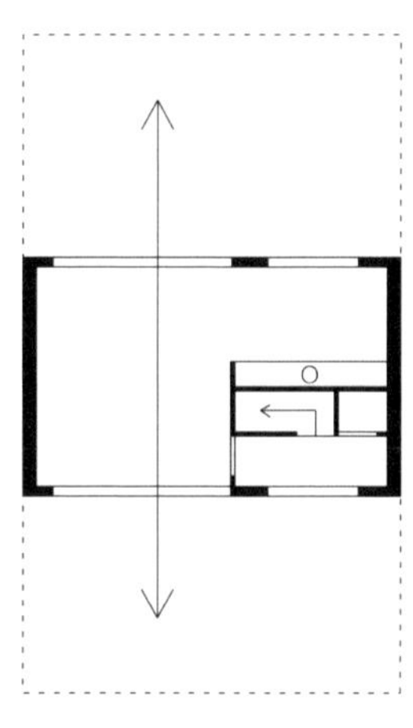

01b Cluster of publicly subsidized rental units, floor plans of ground floor and first floor
01c Part of the completed situation
01d Rotation of the row house

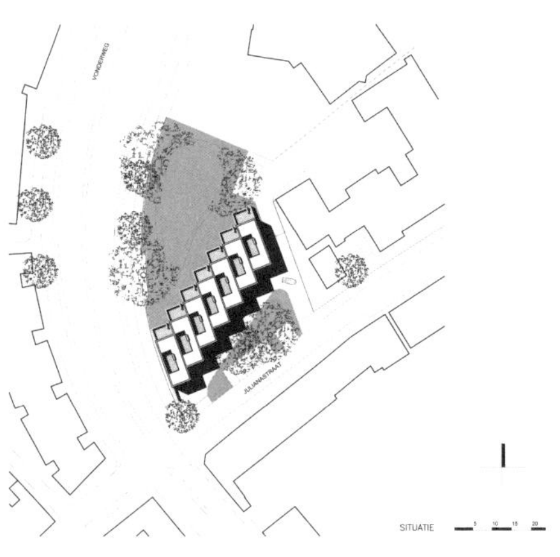

02a

02b

ROW

A row terrace involves more than two ground-connected dwellings linked together in a line. The dwellings in the middle of the line are double-orientation row houses, those at either extremity end-of-row houses with triple orientation. The dwellings are accessed parallel to the street through entrances in the front façade. On the street side a small exterior space often serves as a buffer, while a more private garden is located at the rear. As we noted in the section on the individual row house, the row runs the risk of a loss of visual differentiation and identity when its repetition is too uniform. Privacy is constrained when entrances and exterior spaces directly border the street or neighbouring properties. Solutions for these issues can be provided in the row design. Arranging the dwellings in mirrored alternating formations allows the entrances to be grouped two by two, lending the row a varied rhythm. The row can be broken up by staggering its elements, which also creates different spaces at the front and the rear of the building. Differentiations in volume, façade composition, material and finish, at the level of the individual dwelling or for larger sections of the building, offer plenty of options to arrive at a successful contemporary solution for the row.

GROSFELD ARCHITECTEN, URBAN HOMES (EINDHOVEN, 2000–2003)

In the fragmented setting of a pre-Second World War neighbourhood of buildings dating from different eras, cut in two by a busy roadway, the architects designed seven new-build ground-connected homes in an autonomous volume. The volume is positioned at an angle in relation to the surrounding streets, leaving a triangular plaza with trees at the front, around which a one-way street provides access to the buildings.
The individual dwellings are strikingly distinguishable in the block in that each projects 3 m from the next, giving the block a highly serrated outline. The entrance to the dwelling is sheltered under the living room on the first floor, which also projects 3 m, providing a roof above the carport. At the rear, the projection of the volume provides privacy for the house terrace flanking the kitchen, positioned half a storey above ground-level in a split-level configuration and looking out onto the open field between the residential building and the busy road.
The rest of the composition and the choice of materials reinforce the sculptural quality of the block as a whole. The front and rear façades of the homes in rough-sawed cedar wood alternate with the dark brick of the side façades. A full-height window opens the living room across its entire width and wraps around the corner in the side façade. In view of the traffic noise, the façades of the sleeping storey have been kept solidly closed: a patio lined with glass partitions provides the necessary natural light here.

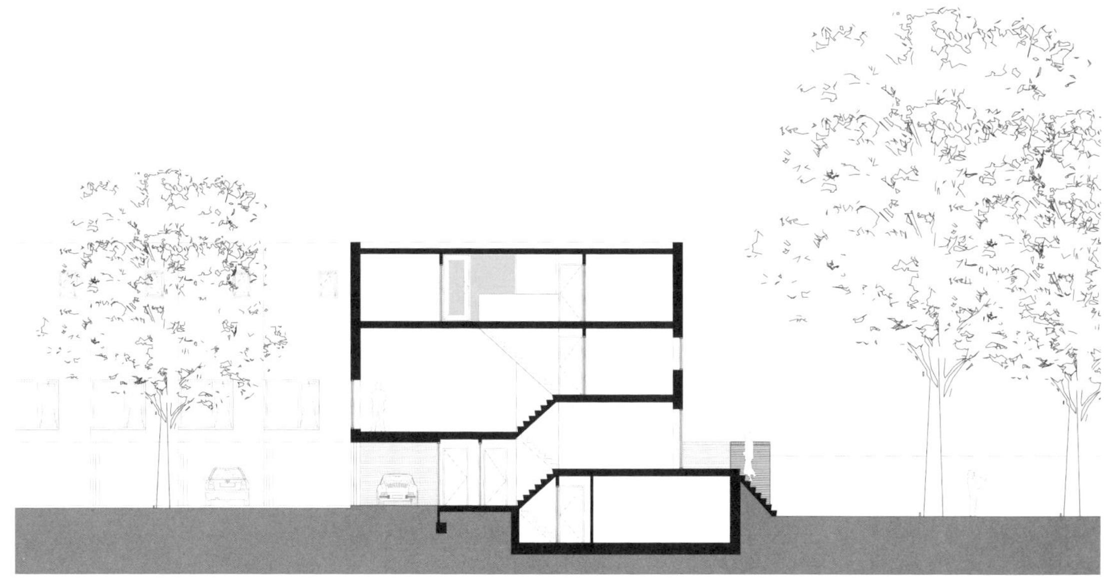

02c

02a Situation
02b Projecting front façades with covered entrance
02c Cross section of a dwelling with a view of the dwellings behind
02d Floor plans of ground floor and upper floors

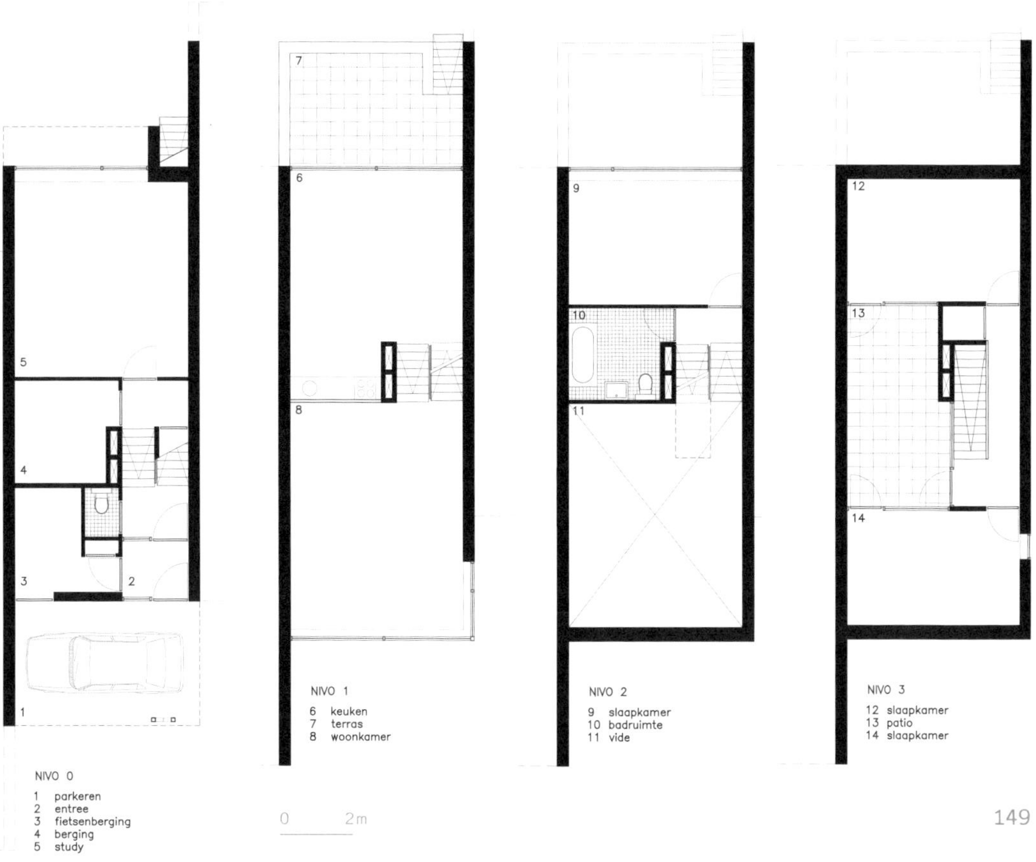

02d

NIVO 0

1 parkeren
2 entree
3 fietsenberging
4 berging
5 study

NIVO 1

6 keuken
7 terras
8 woonkamer

NIVO 2

9 slaapkamer
10 badruimte
11 vide

NIVO 3

12 slaapkamer
13 patio
14 slaapkamer

0 2m

03a

03b

03c

DICK VAN GAMEREN ARCHITECTEN, SINGELS II (YPENBURG, THE HAGUE, 1997-2002)

This design for 650 dwellings at the point of the De Singels subarea in the Ypenburg suburban residential district in The Hague is predicated on the connection of the district to its surroundings. The housing blocks are linked on one side to the rectilinear structure of the adjacent buildings, but open out on the other side towards the green waterside area on the point. The folds in the building volumes allow a maximum number of dwellings to face the fringe of greenery and, conversely, allow the green zone to reach far into the neighbourhood.
These folds are echoed in the elaboration of the buildings, which reinforce the dynamics of the subdivision with their continuous lines of eaves and roof peaks, giving each of the volumes an individual identity. Each row of homes is shaped as a morphological unit with a pattern of continuous lines and consistent use of materials in the roof and façades, nonetheless concealing a wide variety of dwelling types. This underscores the continuity of the exterior space, while the streets remain distinguishable from one another by their outlines, differing choice of materials and alternating plantings and trees. At a higher level of scale, the form and subdivision of the rows link each part of the neighbourhood with its wider environs.

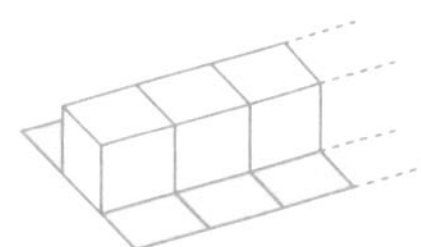

03a Situation, with the section of the plan fanning out towards the surroundings on the left
03c Façade views of a number of rows
03d Floor plans and cross sections of six dwelling types included in the plan

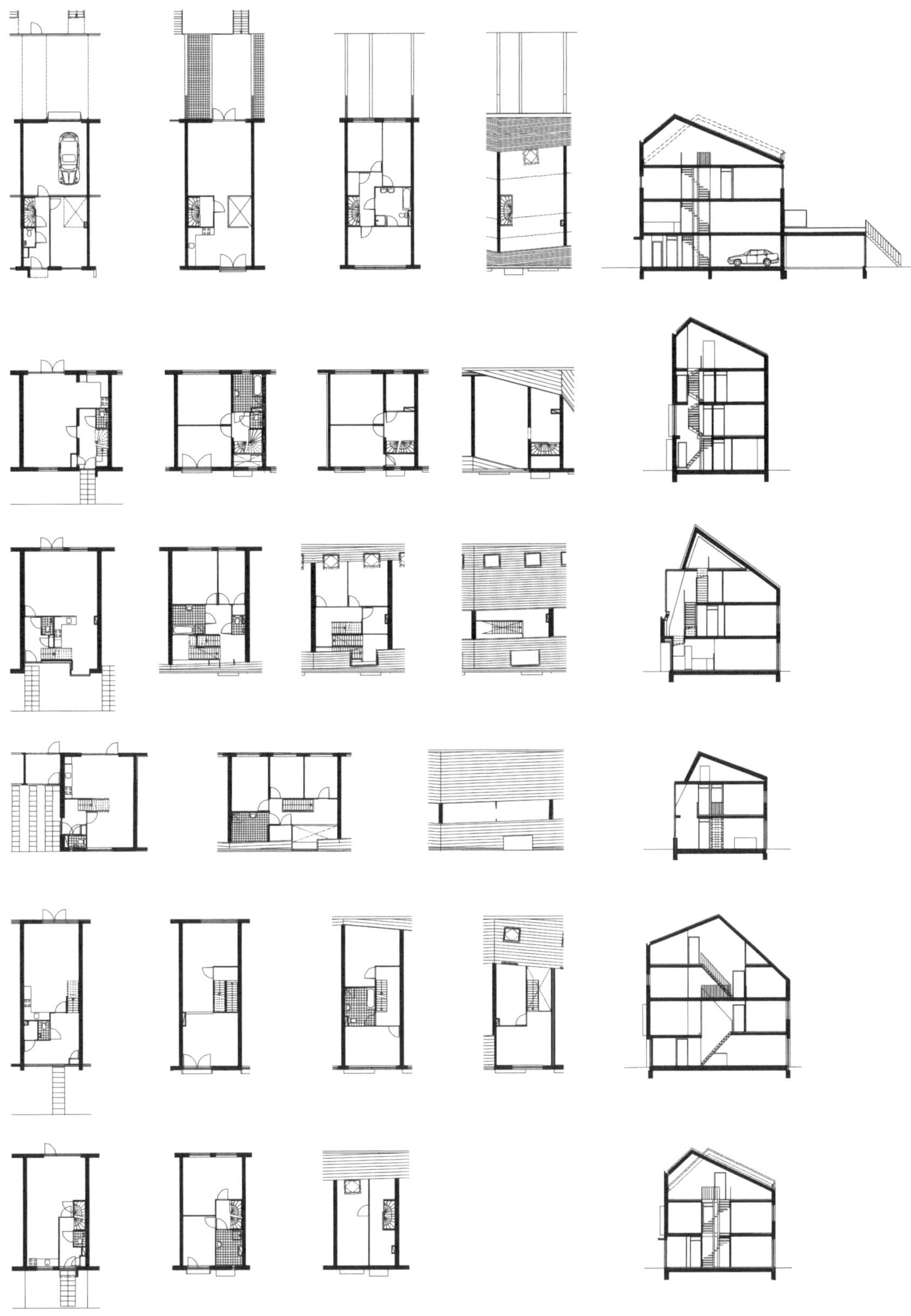

03d

04a

MAT

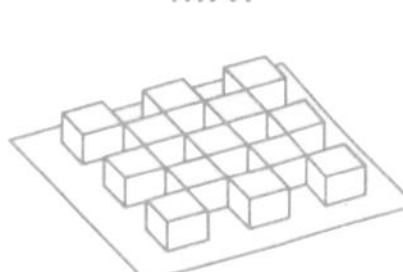

When ground-connected dwellings are linked not only width-wise but also depth-wise, the double-orientation row house turns, in the most basic instance, into a back-to-back configuration with single orientations. The deeper the dwellings are made, the less adequate the natural light exposure through the façade becomes, so that additional light must be introduced with patios or skylights. The dwellings can still be accessed privately from the street on either side of the building. Further linking along the depth creates dwellings that no longer border the contours of the building volume. Not only do the 'hemmed-in' dwellings lack views and natural light, additional infrastructure is needed to access them. Structural solutions for this produce a 'mat' configuration, which in principle can be expanded width-wise as well as depth-wise. The dwellings are accessible through an access route that connects them under, through or over the building to the public space. Natural light penetration can be addressed, and a usually limited view is balanced out by a significant degree of privacy in each dwelling.

PIET BLOM, KASBAH (HENGELO, 1973)

In this Piet Blom design inspired by North African housing communities, 184 connected dwellings are lifted off the ground on concrete columns. This is an expression of Blom's vision of 'dwelling as a city rooftop', in which such themes as densification and the blending of functions play a significant role. The raised dwellings leave the ground level free for a lively urban environment where parking and communal facilities like shops could find a place, supported by a high density of about 100 homes per hectare. The dwellings are linked horizontally around light yards of varying size and accessed from ground level by means of stairs. Three basic types designed by Blom are combined into a total of five different dwelling types.
The public ground-level area connects the light yards with one another and with the adjacent buildings. The architect hoped that the residents would come up with their own uses for this urban space once construction was complete. That a bustling urban environment failed to materialize and that the initially opened shops quickly closed down has been attributed to the fact that the design, originally intended for a city centre, was ultimately built in a suburban area.

04b

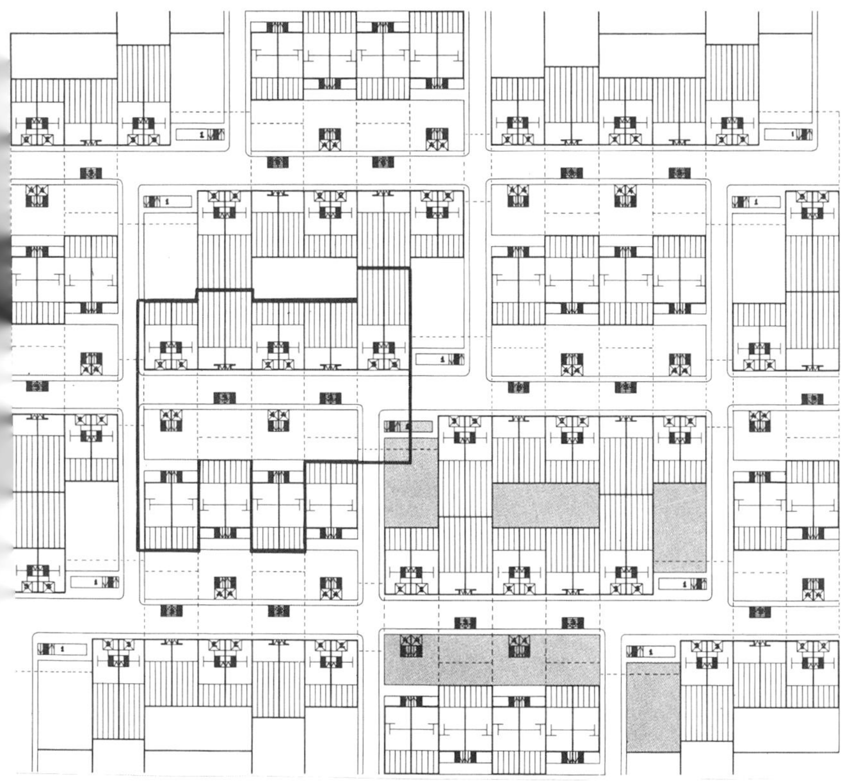

04c

04a The open space flows freely under the dwellings
04b Floor plan of the dwellings, accessed from the open ground level

05a

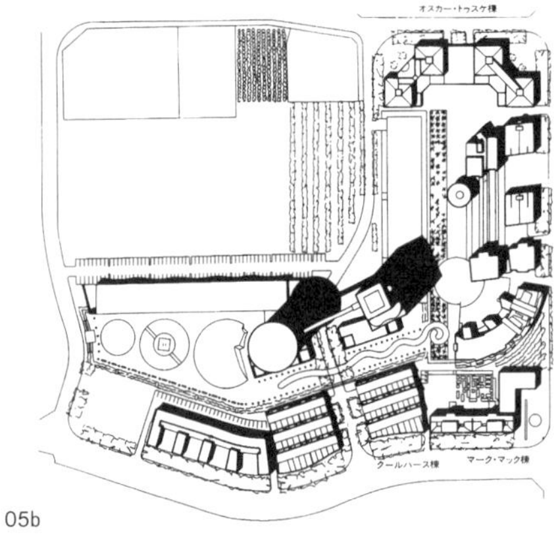

05b

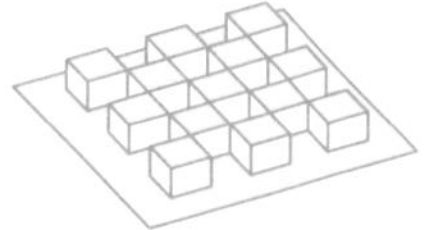

OMA, NEXUS WORLD HOUSING (FUKUOKA, 1991)

OMA's design for a client that wanted to introduce a 'new urban lifestyle' in Japan consists of 24 dwellings of three storeys each, grouped in a linkage of three by four in two autonomous volumes. Closed off all round by a rough, solid wall, the dwellings are very introverted and not individually distinguishable; only small openings afford the outermost dwellings a glimpse of the exterior.
Diagonal inclined footpaths traverse each block at ground level and provide access to the dwelling entrances. Narrow slits from top to bottom allow natural light to penetrate down to this access route. Inside each home, a vertical light shaft brings natural light into the habitation spaces on every floor. The bottom of this light shaft, directly behind the front door, is covered in white stones like a Zen garden. A continuous stairway leads to individual rooms on the first floor and communal habitation spaces on the top floor, where the open space spanning the full width of the dwelling and flanked by the exterior house terrace can be partitioned into various configurations with Japanese curtains and screens. The vegetation-covered roofs arch in a unidirectional upward sequence, so that all the dwellings are ensured added natural light, views and a substantial sense of space without sacrificing privacy.

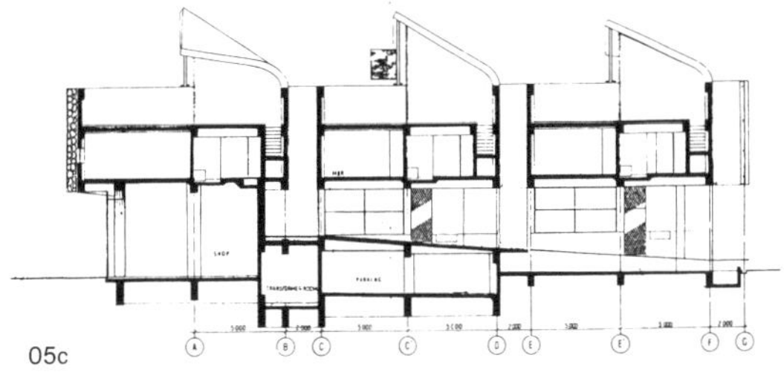
05c

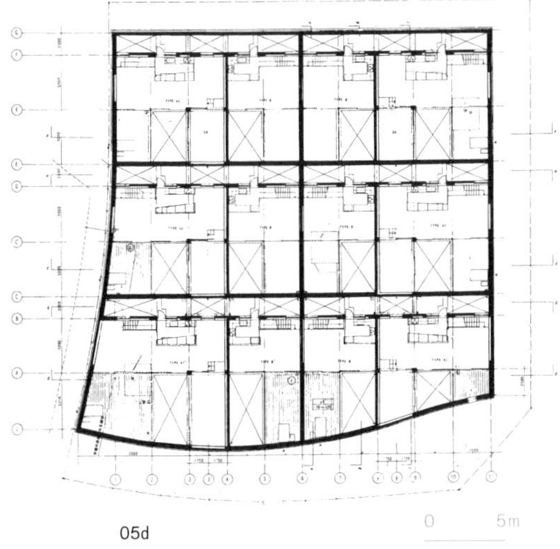
05d

0 5m

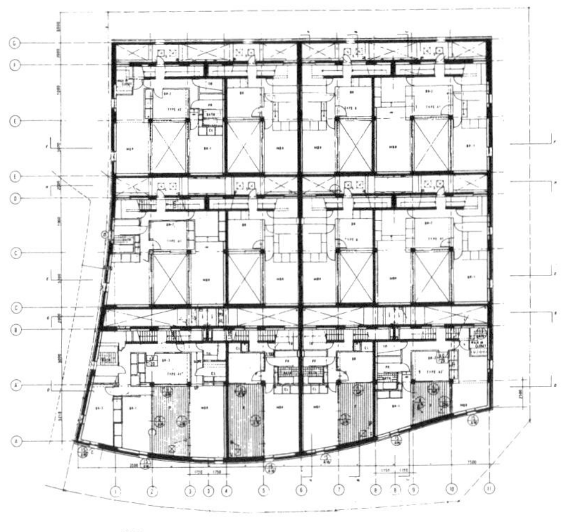
05e

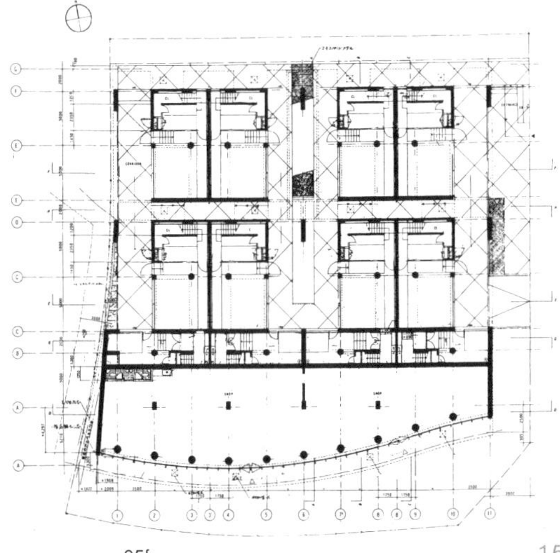
05f

05b Situation of Nexus World Housing, with the two OMA residential blocks at bottom centre
05c Cross section
05d Second floor
05e First floor
05f Ground level

06a

Like the urban housing blocks built around courtyards found in more southern parts of Europe, the urban villa is a distant descendant of the Roman *insula*, a more affordable variant of the patrician villa, housing several families in a single building volume. Spatially, the original access courtyard is gone, but the principle of communal access from the inside out is retained, so that the façades of the dwellings grouped around this central vertical access channel are kept entirely free for habitation spaces. The typology of the urban villa began to attract interest as a solution for inner cities approaching saturation in part thanks to studies presented in the 1970s by Oswald Matthias Ungers and Hans Kollhoff.[1] The stacking of dwellings makes it possible to incorporate urban facilities in the bottom level, revitalizing the dynamism of the inner city. An essential characteristic of the urban villa is its morphological autonomy. Unlike the more or less continuous row façade of the city block, the urban villa is a detached object, an eddy around which the urban space swirls. There is no definite distinction between the front and the back, no screening between the publicly and more privately situated exterior space: the urban villa stands exposed to the public environment in all directions. Given the absence of an inner courtyard, any private exterior space is likely to be situated along the external façade of the dwelling, in direct confrontation with the public street. Although urban in origin, the urban villa is often built in more suburban and even rural settings, where space that is less dynamic, but green, forms the context for these autonomous residential buildings.

1 O.M. Ungers, H.F. Kollhoff and A.A. Ovaska, 'The Urban Villa – A Multi-Family Dwelling Type', *Cornell Summer Academy 77* (Berlin series) (Cologne: Studio Press for Architecture, 1977).

URBAN VILLA

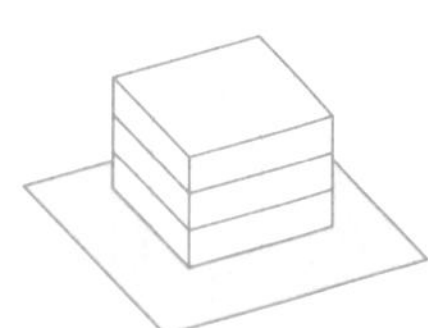

BAUMSCHLAGER & EBERLE, ACHSLENGUT HOUSING (ST GALLEN, 2002)

On a green slope in a suburb of St Gallen in Switzerland, eight free-standing building volumes in bright white concrete rise five storeys high. Four apartments per storey are accessed from the inside through a lift and stairwell. Projecting floors around all the façades provide a shallow exterior space around the whole of each dwelling, which widens towards the corners. Along the exterior, floor-to-ceiling sliding panels of frosted and transparent glass have been fitted, making it easy to choose views or privacy. The blocks have been positioned to afford as many dwellings as possible a view of the lake below.

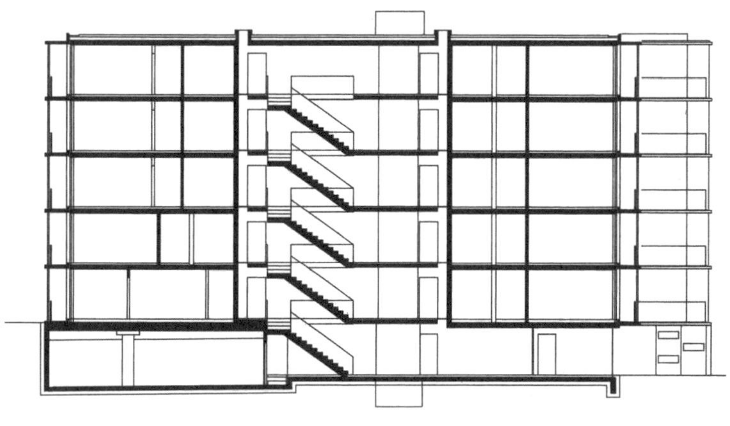

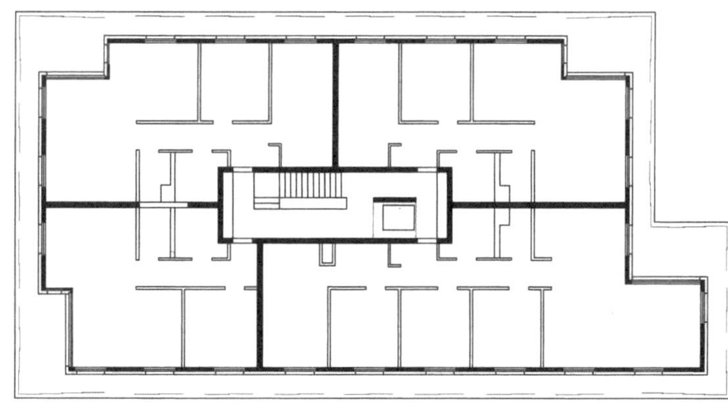

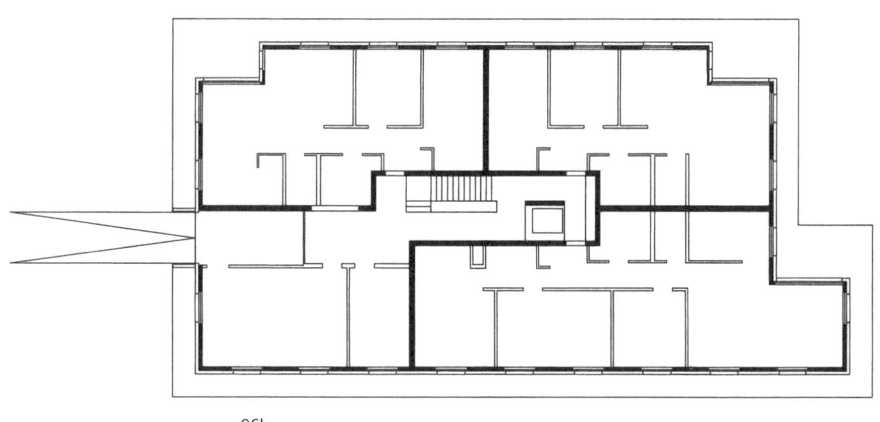

06b

06b Floor plan of ground floor and upper floor, and long section

07a

07b

INFILL

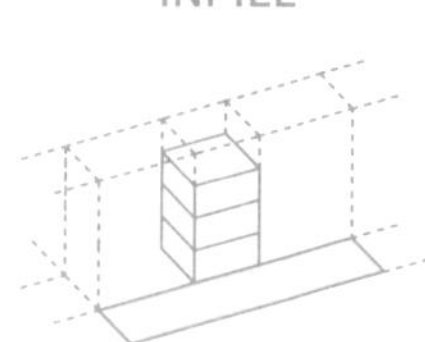

This category includes housing construction projects that do not form a whole residential building in themselves, but rather are an element of a greater volume which is not covered by the same commission. This may be the replacement of an existing section of a building, for instance in urban regeneration projects, but it may also mean filling in a vacant lot sandwiched between adjacent buildings. The project and the design of the new construction are self-contained, but they are linked to the pre-existing built environment to a far greater degree than the design of free-standing residential buildings. In most cases, the building alignment and the building height are predetermined factors, and the façade rhythm of neighbouring buildings also guides the heights of the floors or the eaves. Moreover, the limited volume of the new construction usually offers little financial manoeuvring room for variety. Yet these constraints often produce interesting solutions that lend a unique character to a previously less remarkable place.

PHILIPPE GAZEAU, APARTMENTS FOR POSTAL EMPLOYEES (PARIS, 1993)

Inspired by the densely packed and multifaceted buildings on the Rue de l'Ourcq in Paris, Philippe Gazeau designed an apartment block that stands out in many ways from the street wall in which it is inserted. The building is set back from the street between the buildings on either side, leaving room for a small café with a terrace on the pavement, as well as for the entrance to a parking garage underneath the building. In between, the building is split in two over its full height and depth by a spacious and transparent entrance zone, creating in effect two building volumes, 3.5 and 7.5 m wide. Broad wooden platforms span the open zone on every storey, recessed along the depth of the block every other storey, so that the apartments can be accessed on both sides of every floor. They communicate with the ground level by means of open stairs and a lift and afford a spectacular view on both open sides of the infill.

07c

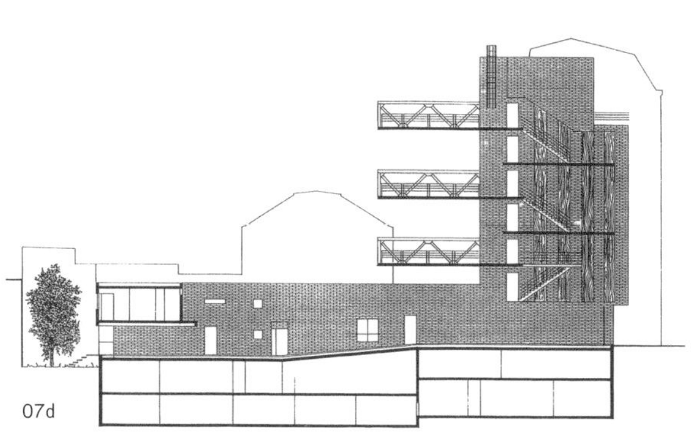

07d

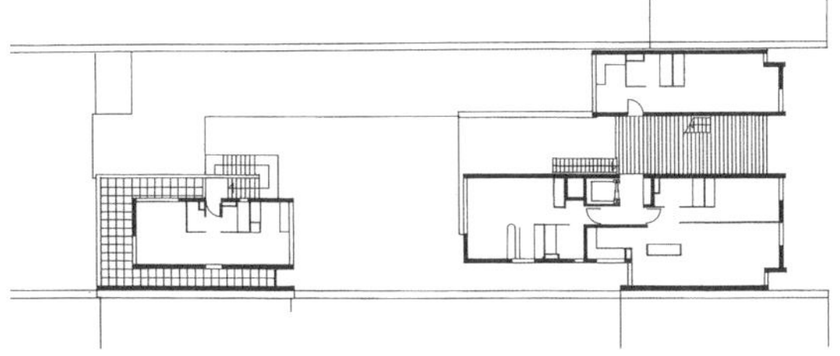

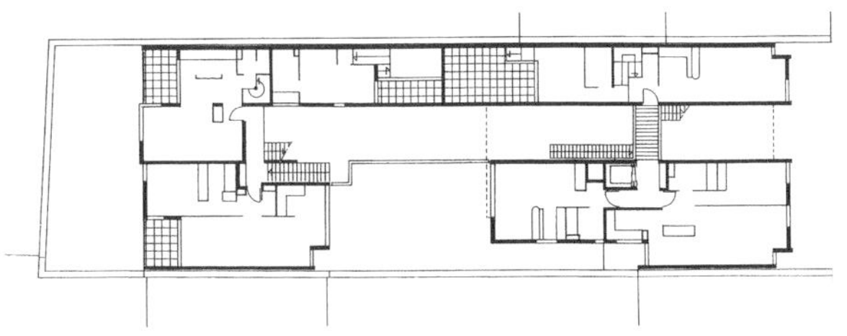

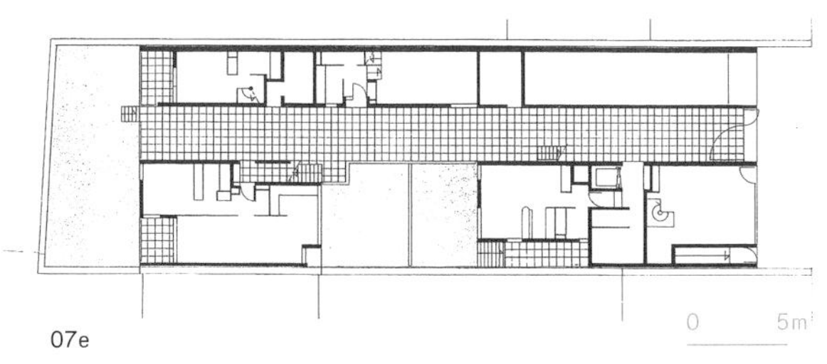

07e

07a Situation
07c Rear view from the wide terrace
07d Long section
07e Floor plans of ground floor, first floor and higher floors

A slab is created when dwellings linked in a horizontal line are also stacked vertically. The type, in its inner-city form, goes back to the multistorey housing that emerged in the wake of industrialization. A continuous wall of nineteenth-century buildings housing ground-level as well as walk-up flats can be seen, in principle, as a simple slab. The construction of multistorey working-class housing marks the beginning of a widespread application of the slab as a volume in urban planning. Originally inserted into the urban pattern of the old inner cities, the slab grew to become a crucial building block of modernist urban design. Stacking dwellings in volumes in slab form allows a larger proportion of the ground level to remain unbuilt, which implies the promise of light, air and space in the dwelling environment for everyone. Ground-breaking examples include (again) Le Corbusier's Unités d'Habitation, which as autonomous volumes lifted off the ground promise every occupant light and a view, far above the noise and pollution of the traffic or inner city. The Unité in Firminy, in particular, a colossal free-standing volume on a hilltop surrounded by woodland, makes its promise of liberated living in a green setting visible in a persuasive way.

Because of its size and its capacity to incorporate urban facilities, the slab fit the ideal of an urban design of separate volumes in a green park, an idea adopted all over the world. In the Pendrecht area in Rotterdam, slabs of varying sizes were used to form residential ensembles that, repeated as templates, were a modernist answer to the saturated quarters of the inner city. A notorious exponent is found in the – now largely demolished – slabs of the Bijlmer housing estate south-east of Amsterdam, where the ideal of serpentine slabs in a green park setting fell victim to issues of anonymity and of the manageability of the uncontrolled area at ground level. This gave the slab as a free-standing volume a poisonous reputation for several decades. Neither did its widespread application as part of a more traditional urban pattern, as cheap walk-up and gallery-access apartment buildings in the (semi-)open and closed blocks of the post-war reconstruction period, result in the desired quality of urban life, bringing the slab into further disrepute. In the 1990s, the slab began making a comeback, including as a free-standing volume; no longer so much as a building block for an ideological urban design, but rather as an often unique and successful solution within a given situation.

Depending on size, virtually every type of access is applicable within the slab. Street access is possible up to two or three storeys, followed by access using a foyer and stairs, sometimes supplemented by a lift. In wide slabs of more than four storeys, a gallery or corridor provides access to a large number of dwellings from a single vertical access channel.

SLAB

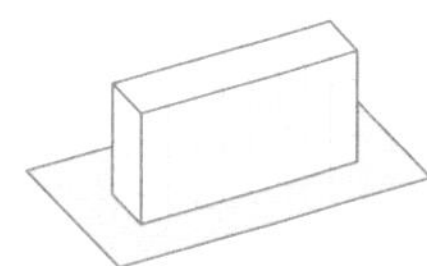

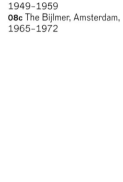

08a Rough sketch of the idea behind the Unité d'Habitation
08b Pendrecht, Rotterdam, 1949–1959
08c The Bijlmer, Amsterdam, 1965–1972

08a

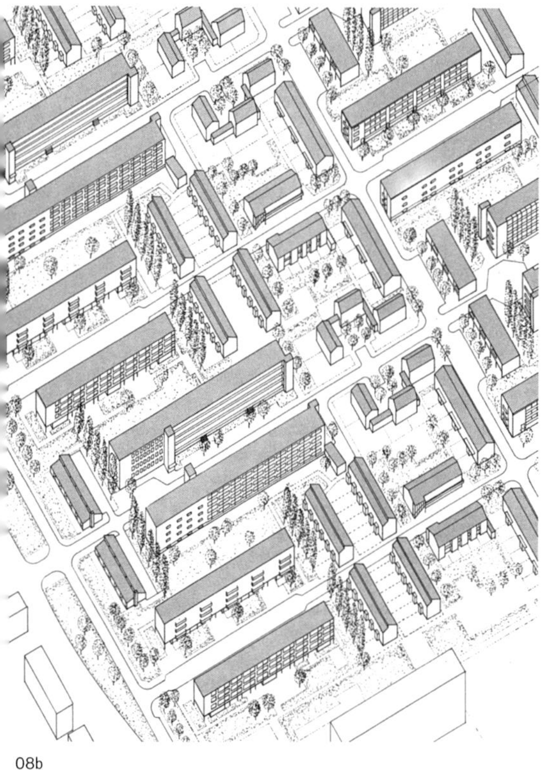

08b

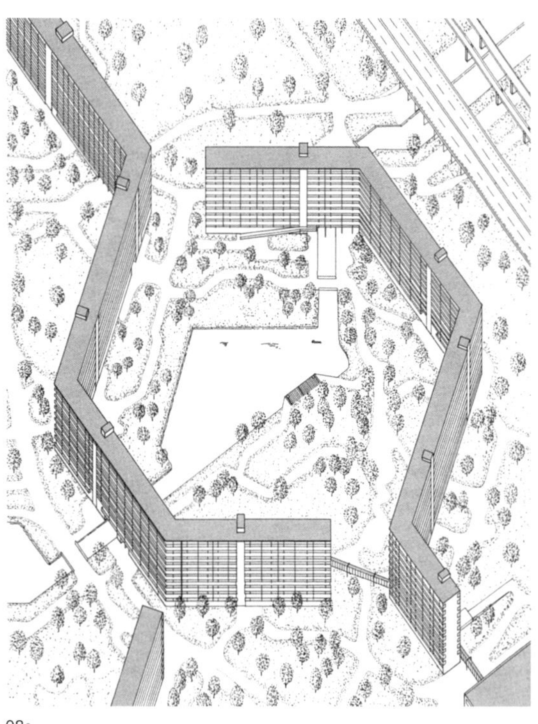

08c

09a

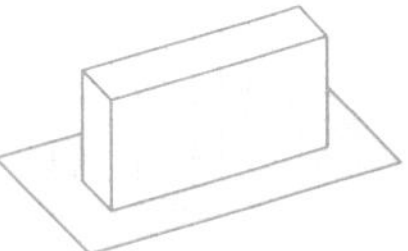

KEES CHRISTIAANSE & ART ZAAIJER, LOT 25 (THE HAGUE, 1988–1992)

In 1989, to mark the 200,000th home built in The Hague, a 'housing festival' was held on a strip of land 30 m wide along the Dedemsvaartweg, under the supervision of Kees Christiaanse, who at the time was working at OMA. The design Christiaanse and Zaaijer implemented here is an edifice inspired by the Unité d'Habitation, lifted off the ground on slab-like columns. This residential building is pierced by two huge cavities so as not to entirely deprive the neighbourhood across the street of a view of the greenery behind the building. In total, 45 dwellings in 11 different types are distributed over six storeys and accessed by a combination of access principles, giving each area of the building a unique character and making alternate routes to the various dwellings possible. An open stairway with landings in one opening of the building and a lift in the other connect a gallery on the lowest residential level and two corridors higher up in the building with the ground level, where a parking facility is incorporated underneath the edifice.

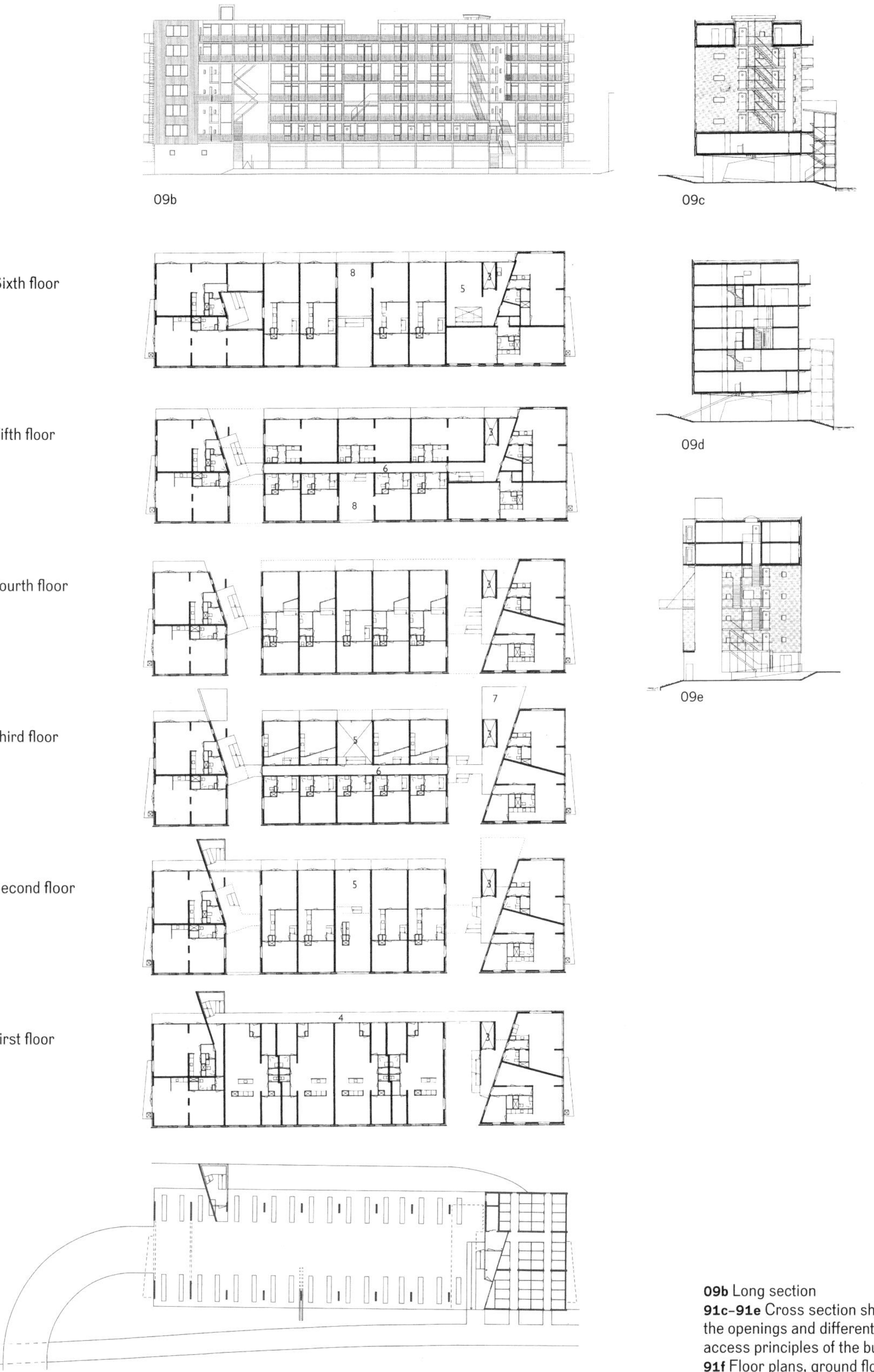

09b Long section
91c–91e Cross section showing the openings and different access principles of the building
91f Floor plans, ground floor to sixth floor

LOFTS	HUTS	PATIO	MAISONETTE
GYMNASIUM	HOBBY	X-HOUSE	OFFBEAT 3 ROOM
PANORAMA	UNITE	BALCONY	PANORAMA
PANORAMA	SENIOR	SENIOR	GARDEN HOUSE
HOBBY	STUDIOS	LIVE & WORK	DOORZONE
VALERIUS PLEIN	STUDIOS	WORKLOFT	3 BEDROOM FLAT
VENETIAN WINDOW	HALL + TRAY	MARINA	FAMILYHOUSE
	STORAGE		LIVE & WORKLOFT

10a

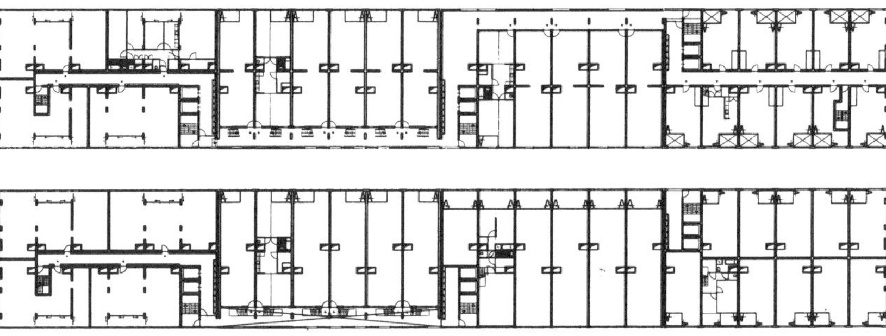

10b

10c

SLAB

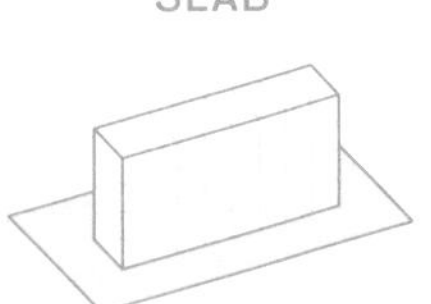

10a Façade arrangement, organized into 'neighbourhoods'
10b Floor plans of fourth and fifth floors

MVRDV, SILODAM (AMSTERDAM, 1995–2002)

Situated in an open position at the end of a levee with panoramic views of the IJ waterway, this cosmopolitan residential and commercial building by MVRDV is set just above the water on concrete columns. In terms of appearance as well as organization, it represents a combination of a wide variety of dwelling types, access types and commercial spaces, reducing the massive scale of the complex to diverse domains with individual characters. In each case, similar dwelling types are organized around one access, creating a stack of little 'neighbourhoods', each with its own atmosphere and character.

The dwellings vary not only in size and number of rooms, but also in height and number of floors, while the access facilities of alternating galleries and corridors connect them along meandering paths with three vertical access channels. Within each residential domain, the access has been given a unique finish and colour. In the façade, the stacking of the different 'neighbourhoods' is made visible by giving each its own façade cladding. The total of 17 different façade sections are a reference to stacked containers on a cargo ship.

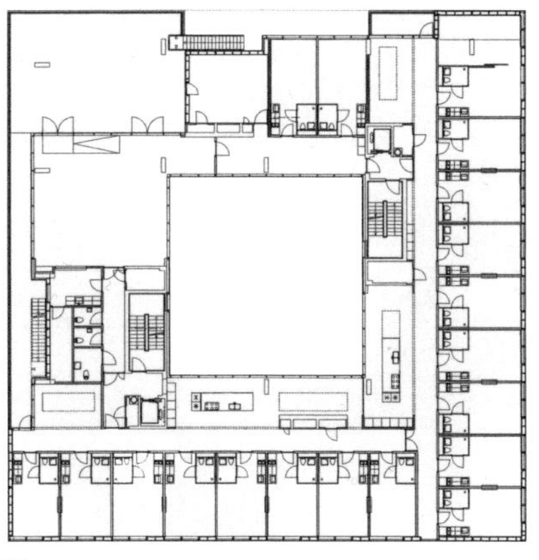

11a

11c

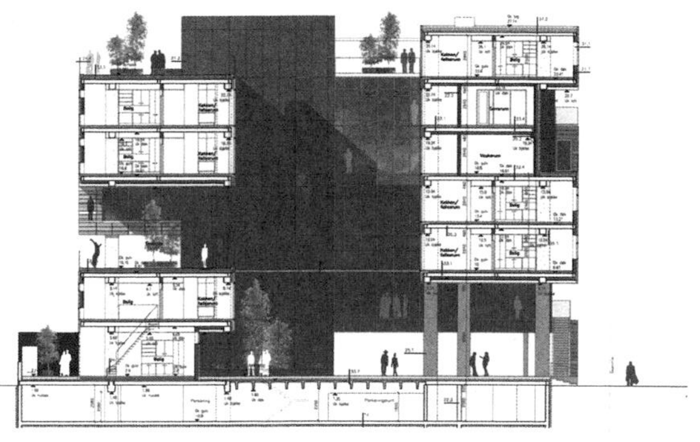

11b

11a Fifth floor
11b Cross section

Not to be confused with the city block (discussed in the following chapter), the building volume in block form can be seen as a stacking of the mat configuration or as an expansion of the slab along the depth. These are stacked residential buildings that can contain more than two dwellings across their width as well as along their depth. While resolving issues of access and natural light penetration adequately in a mat configuration is already difficult, in a multistorey version this becomes practically impossible. The block-form volume needs to be mutated through the use of openings or incisions so that a proper scale and sufficient façade space can be achieved for the dwellings it must accommodate.

AART A/S, BIKUBEN STUDENT HOSTEL (COPENHAGEN, 2006)

In an effort to counter the loneliness and social isolation students can experience during their time at university, aart designed a collective residential building in which student dwellings are mixed with communal spaces and facilities. The building is free-standing on a plaza and is lifted off the ground on concrete slabs, which provide open access to a central atrium.
The dwellings and communal facilities are stacked around the atrium, the access route connecting the individual dwelling entrances with adjacent communal facilities in a double spiral. The dwellings flank a gallery situated along the outer façade but looking out onto the atrium. This runs along the exterior of the building past the communal spaces, where a recessed façade allows additional natural light to penetrate the atrium and where interaction with the plaza predominates. As a result, maximum privacy for the dwelling is combined with maximum interaction in the rest of the building, whose varied incisions give it a lively and characteristic appearance.

BLOCK

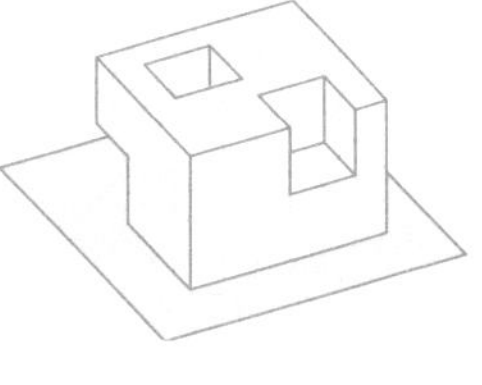

12a

12b

BLOCK

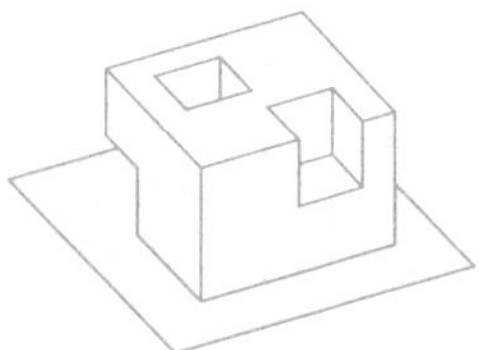

DICK VAN GAMEREN, HAARLEMMERPLEIN HOUSING (AMSTERDAM, 2004–2012)

The project consists of the replacement of a housing block demolished in the early 1970s, on the north side of the seventeenth-century Haarlemmerplein square on the western edge of Amsterdam's city centre. The building shields the square from the railway line and a busy roadway and contains 70 apartments, commercial spaces on the ground floor and a four-storey underground car park. A load-bearing structure of parallel walls produces narrow apartments whose stacking is a reference to the seventeenth-century subdivision of narrow, tall residences. Three internal courtyards cut into the volume and provide the deep apartments with adequate natural light and a façade sheltered from the traffic noise. The courtyard on the side facing the square forms the communal main entrance to the individual dwellings, which are accessed on each floor by internal galleries.

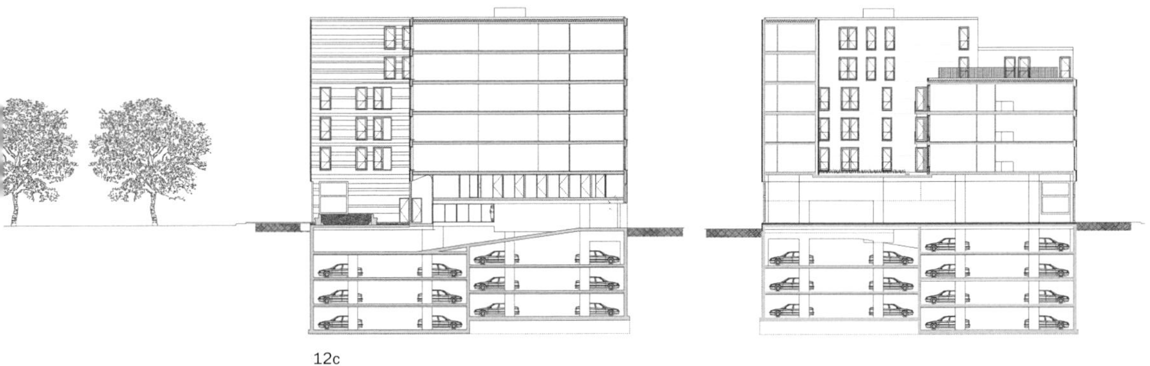

12c

12d

12e

12a Entrance court
12b The building on the Haarlemmerplein
12c Cross sections
12d Floor plan of upper storey, with dwellings around three recesses
12e Situation

13a

Vertical access with a lift makes it possible to stack dwellings up to very great heights. As dwellings are kept clustered around this vertical access channel, a vertical building volume is created, with a communal entrance at ground level, as in the urban villa, and a landing around the lift on each level where the individual dwelling entrances are located. For reasons of safety, a double evacuation route by means of enclosed staircases is mandatory in the Netherlands, in addition to the (stretcher-sized) lift. These can be combined into a double-helix staircase structure, in which the two staircases lead down in two separate, enclosed stairwells wrapped around each other. As the tower gets taller, additional lifts become necessary, and the dimensions of the structure and support elements at the base increase. As higher elevations are reached, the number of lifts and conduits can be reduced and the structure can taper off, leaving gradually increasing amounts of space for dwellings. The use of residential towers allows for very high housing densities. On the other hand, the great advantage of living in a tower – a free and unobstructed view – is best served by a great deal of open space around the tower. Towers are therefore often situated in strategic places with great views, on the water or as an iconic landmark in an urban design. The vast number of dwellings on a relatively small area of land makes a good parking solution an absolute necessity. Dwellings in a tower have little connection left with the street or the immediate environs of the building. Instead they are focused to a maximum extent on the views of the wider surroundings and the quality of life within the dwelling. Large exterior spaces can compensate for a potential sense of claustrophobia, although this is constrained by climactic conditions at high elevations. Communal spaces and facilities located elsewhere in the building can expand the residential domain inside the tower. Given their distance from the street, the dwellings often enjoy supplementary services, varying from rubbish disposal to electronic ordering facilities for grocery deliveries.

TOWER

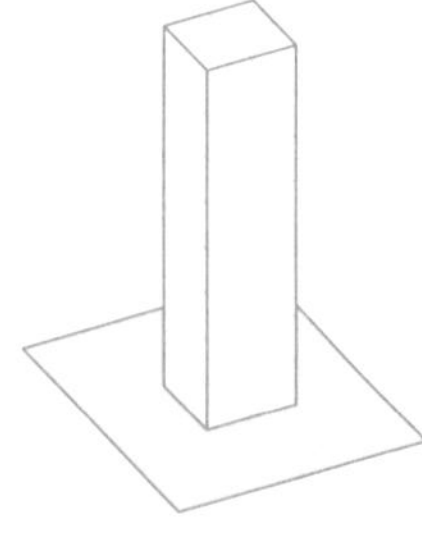

CINO ZUCCHI, NUOVO PORTELLO (MILAN, 2002–2007)

On the site of the former Alfa Romeo car factory in what was until recently an industrial zone around Nuovo Portello, in the north-western section of Milan, Cino Zucchi designed a housing ensemble in five towers and three slabs, supplemented by a commercial building. Two towers of publicly subsidized rental housing stand on either side of a diagonal axis linking the area with a large new park to the south and a nearby shopping centre to the north. The other three towers contain apartments for the private sector and are grouped on one side of the axis in their own green setting. The different towers have a comparable layout, organized around an internal core housing two lifts and a staircase. In the publicly subsidized buildings these provide access to three flats per storey, each with a loggia behind the façade as exterior space. These loggias are staggered across the storeys and give the brick towers a sculptural façade. In the private-sector towers, the core provides access to two larger apartments per storey, with triple orientation and surrounded by different exterior spaces projecting from the volume. The higher the storey and the more tenuous the connection with the surrounding park, the larger and further projecting the exterior spaces become; if desired they can be enclosed in glass. The varying placement and dimensions of these projecting volumes reinforce the plasticity of the three towers, which are positioned at slight angles to one another.

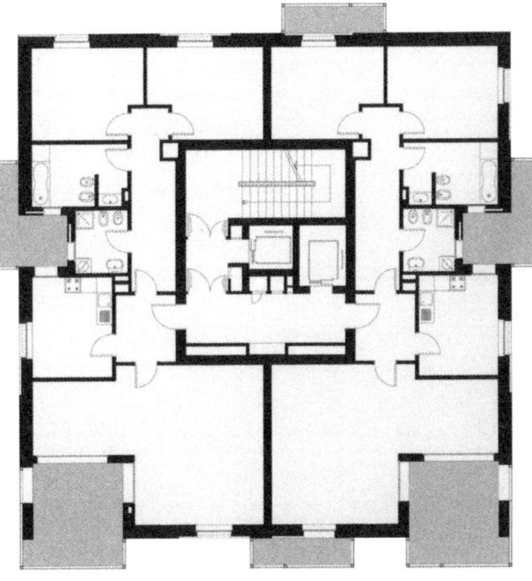

13b

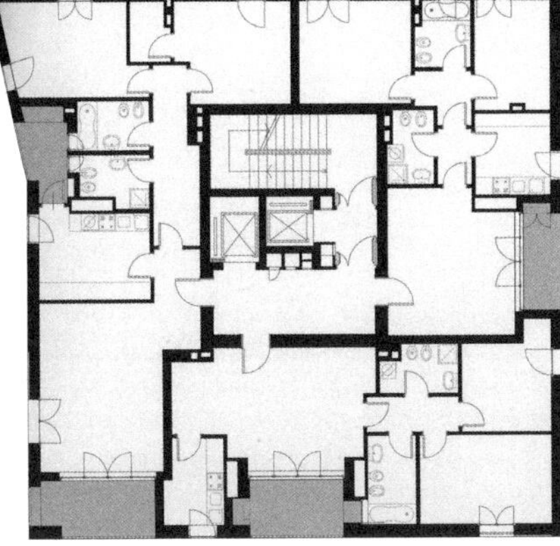

13c

13d

13a Situation
13b Typical storey in a tower for the private sector
13c Typical storey in a tower for publicly subsidized housing
13d The towers for the private sector
13e The towers for publicly subsidized housing

13e

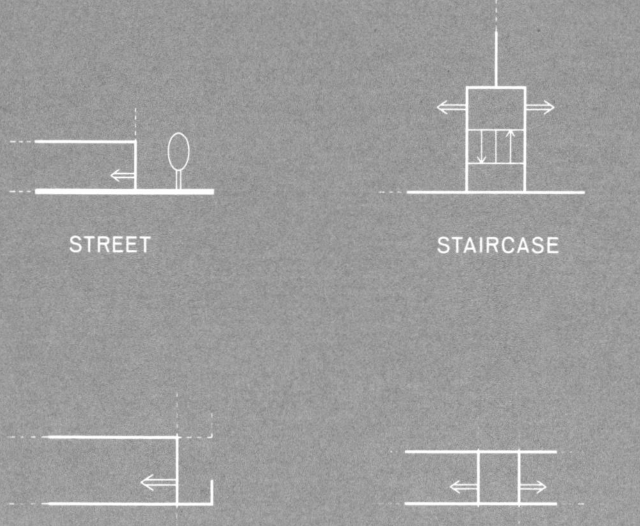
STREET
STAIRCASE
LIFT
GALLERY
CORRIDOR

DWELLING ACCESS

Entering and leaving the dwelling takes place through the entrance. As the examples in the preceding chapter ('Dwellings') have shown, the location of the entrance has a significant impact on the organization of the spaces within the dwelling. Outside the dwelling, the organization of the spaces that provide access to it is no less important. These spaces form a daily part of the lives of the building's occupants and are of great significance to the quality and the perception of the experience of dwelling.

To begin with, the dwelling entrance must be reachable from the outside. For ground-connected dwellings this seems a simple matter: a doorway in a façade on the ground floor will suffice. As soon as dwellings are stacked, additional facilities are needed to reach the higher dwellings. Stairs and lifts transport people vertically to the upper storeys, while horizontal circulation routes inside or outside the building can link a greater number of dwellings to a communal vertical access channel.

We call the combined system of facilities that provide entry to the dwelling–in other words the connection from the front door of the building to the front door of the dwelling–the access. When dwellings are reached exclusively by means of stairs or a lift, this is called vertical access. When the dwellings are lined along a gallery or corridor, this is horizontal access, even if this connects at some point to a vertical access channel. We distinguish the following access types, identified by the way in which the individual dwelling is accessed:

—*Street*

The dwelling is directly accessible at ground level.

—*Access Staircase*

The dwelling is accessed through a communal staircase.

—*Central Lift Access*

The dwelling is accessed through a communal lift (and [emergency] stairs).

—*Gallery*

The dwelling is accessed through a communal horizontal circulation route along the dwelling façades.

—*Corridor*

The dwelling is accessed through a communal horizontal circulation route inside the building, not situated along the façade.

The access forms a zone between the dwelling and the public realm outside. It is no longer a private area, but in most cases it is not accessible to just anyone. This creates a collective domain shared by all the individual users, where they run into one another and, if they wish, may spend time together. The design of the access creates conditions that invite people, to a greater or lesser degree, to use it as a space for collective habitation.

At the same time, how the collective area relates to the privacy of the individual dwelling is a vital consideration. Where circulation zones run alongside a dwelling, privacy is constrained, and a certain level of shielding is desirable. In addition, the access often determines the placement of the entrance in the dwelling, and therefore some of its internal organization options. Even in a row house with direct ground-level access from the street, the placement of the entrance is limited to a spot in the narrow façade. Each type of access comes with its own implications for privacy and for the place where the dwelling is entered, so that access type and dwelling floor plan often come in pairs: the access staircase with a single-storey flat, or a corridor with a 'bayonet' apartment.

Although Ancient Rome featured dwellings stacked in residential buildings, the *insulae*, this mode of construction fell into disuse in western parts of Europe after the fall of the Western Roman Empire. Under the legal system of the Middle Ages, rights of citizenship in a city were limited to those who had their own home on a piece of the city's land.[2] This meant every dwelling was directly accessible from the street, and there were no collective access facilities of any kind. The residential building reappeared in European cities like Paris, Berlin, Helsinki and Milan in the eighteenth century. Like the *insulae*, these were arranged around communal inner courtyards, along which access was also situated. The Netherlands, however, retained a strong tradition of ground-connected dwellings, often with a semi-public workplace on the ground floor. The necessity to accommodate housing in stacked dwellings would only emerge in the wake of industrialization towards the end of the nineteenth century, leading to the development and application of other types of access.

The great advantage of the individual front door on the street over other access principles is its association with the independence of the individual dwelling. Not having to share facilities with others means no unwanted encounters or shared organization of maintenance and management; instead there is individual control and privacy in entering and leaving the dwelling.

The tensions between the private and public are mediated in the area of transition between the dwelling and the street. Direct street access entails an abrupt transition between the home and the public environment, and privacy suffers from the traffic of random passers-by. A private exterior zone can be used as a buffer, as can a recessed entrance or a raised ground-floor storey. Dwellings can also be accessed at the rear through a sheltered square or courtyard, which thus forms a collective area of transition between the street and the home. Although there is a great variety of accesses at ground level and they are certainly not all situated on the street, they are nevertheless grouped, in relation to the other types of access, into one category.

Private street access is valued so highly that even dwellings on upper storeys sometimes have a street-level front door. Almost immediately behind this is a flight of stairs leading up to the dwelling level. The dwelling next door features identical stairs and, if the dwellings on the storey above also have direct street access, their private stairs vault two storeys. Double staircase structures like this take up a lot of space, but they do afford every home a private entrance. The façade then displays a 'battery of doors'.

2 Bernard Leupen, *Frame and Generic Space: A Study into the Changeable Dwelling Proceeding from the Permanent* (Rotterdam: 010 Publishers, 2006), 126.

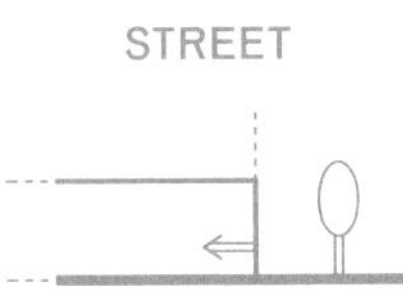

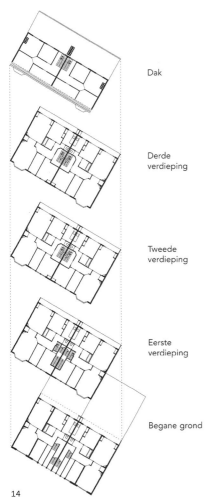

Dak

Derde verdieping

Tweede verdieping

Eerste verdieping

Begane grond

14

14 Stacked dwellings with street access

15a

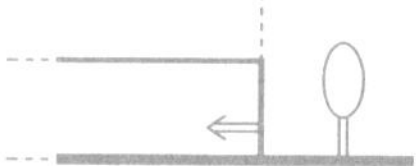

15a The split-level solution produces 16 entrance doors side by side, providing access to the different dwellings.

NEUTELINGS RIEDIJK, GWL SITE (AMSTERDAM, 1994–1998)

Starting in 1994, the former site of the municipal water company (GWL) in Amsterdam, on the western edge of the city centre, was transformed into a car-free and environmentally friendly residential area under the supervision of Kees Christiaanse. In addition to sustainable materials and substantial green exterior space, Christiaanse commissioned the various architects to fit in as many ground-connected dwellings in the five-storey residential buildings as possible. This ground connection and the private exterior spaces associated with it were meant to encourage a shared commitment among all residents to the maintenance of the ground-level area. Blocks 8 and 15, designed by Neutelings Riedijk, represent an exploration of the flexibility of the traditional one up-one down arrangement. In a split-level configuration, a total of 16 dwellings per block have their front doors side by side, behind which parallel stairs subsequently give each dwelling a different configuration. Four dwellings accessed side by side each have a large living space, one on top of the other, spreading across their full width and facing the four entrances. Spaces of different shapes in each dwelling are linked to this, half a storey up or down. The two bottom dwellings have a private garden at ground level, the other two continue up to the top of the building, where their individual roof terraces are situated. In Block 8 the entrances of all the dwellings are located at ground level and the gardens are accessible by means of stairs from the first floor. In Block 15, shown here, the entrances are organized side by side on the first floor, accessible by means of stairs from the adjacent pedestrian and bicycle path. Here the bottom dwellings duck under the entrance to their garden situated immediately alongside the façade.

15b

15c

Ground floor
First floor
Second floor
Third floor
Fourth floor
Roof

3 Ibid., 128.
4 Dutch building regulations stipulate that dwellings more than 12.5 m above ground level must be wheelchair-accessible – in other words, have access to a lift.

In the late nineteenth century, when housing the mass influx of workers migrating to the city in the wake of industrialization turned into an urgent problem, residential buildings of stacked dwellings began to be built in the Netherlands as well.[3] One-room, usually single-orientation flats were built at the lowest possible cost, with (poorly ventilated) box beds or a sleeping alcove and sometimes a tiny kitchen. These small dwellings were stacked back to back within the familiar typology of the nineteenth-century double-bay town house. On each floor, two flats were accessed through an internal staircase that connected on the ground level with a hallway to the communal front door. [→ 16a] A more upscale variant on this emerged in the form of the stacked town house, still a feature of many nineteenth-century middle-class districts in larger cities. Through the addition of an extra staircase in the narrow bay, the house is split into an upstairs and a downstairs dwelling, each spread over two storeys. Both dwellings have their own front door on the street, side by side in a shared 'niche' behind the façade wall. This niche serves as the architectural articulation of a shared entrance: the suggestion of a single entryway for the town house as a whole is maintained, while the recessed front doors divide the house in two. [→ 16b] Giving the dwellings alternating mirror layouts makes it possible to expand the number of front doors in a shared niche, while the same principle is also applicable to stacked apartments or combinations of apartments and maisonettes. In all of these instances there is still direct access from the street. If more than two dwellings positioned one on top of the other are accessed, however, the separate flights of stairs take up an inconvenient amount of space. The next step in development was therefore the addition of a communal staircase in the façade opening, leading to an enclosed landing one storey up. Whereas the dwellings on the ground floor are accessed individually, this landing is for the front doors to the second and third residential level, the latter accessed by means of an additional private staircase behind the front door. The façade opening could now be constructed to span two storeys, giving this kind of access its characteristic appearance. Because of its widespread use in three-storey housing in The Hague, this access type is also known in the Netherlands as a *Haagse portiek*. [→ 17a,b] This access has different implications on each storey for the location of the entrance and the form of the remaining floor space of the dwelling. This means the dwellings positioned one on top of the other also vary in their organization. The disruptive impact, however, is confined to the service zones and bedrooms situated around the access, while the bay with the *en suite* living room is identical on every storey. The complex structure of the *Haagse portiek* began to conflict with the development of rational dwelling floor plans during the first half of the twentieth century. The search among functionalism-oriented architects for clarity and repetition led to a new type for vertical access, the *moderne portiek* or 'modern access staircase'. A communal front door provides access to a collective staircase that leads in two half flights to two apartments per storey. The placement of the entrance in the flat is the same on every floor and set deep in the flat, keeping both façades free for habitation spaces.

The resulting single-storey flat accessed via a entrance and stairs lacks the division between private and communal habitation space that another internal level can provide. In the example by J.H. van den Broek shown here, this is compensated with sliding partitions and fold-away furniture, creating a dwelling that is open during the day and divided into separate rooms at night. The *moderne portiek* is often characteristically discernible in the façade as a vertical band running from the ground floor to the top, with the horizontal façades of the apartments on either side. Although a 'niche' in the façade is not necessarily a feature, in the Netherlands the name *portiek* ('portico') has remained associated with this access principle. [→ 18a–b]

In principle, the rational separation of access from dwelling floor plan makes stacked dwellings accessible up to very significant heights. Regulations, however, protect occupants from having to climb endless flights of stairs by mandating a lift above a prescribed height.[4] Accessing two dwellings per storey with a lift is very costly, however, and as a result a different access principle is usually chosen. Access via a staircase is economically advantageous in combination with relatively large apartments, sometimes topped by a maisonette. Maisonettes positioned at lower levels lead to double flights of stairs and great vertical distances between dwellings. In combination with small dwellings, the proportion of habitation space to access space becomes skewed, and opting for a horizontal access is recommended.

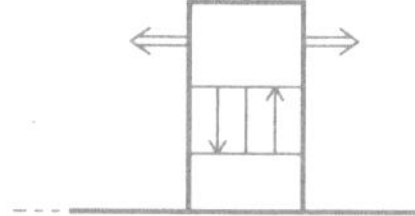

16a Standard floor plan for working-class flat in the Pijp area of Amsterdam, late nineteenth century
16b Nineteenth-century double townhouse, Concertgebouw area, Amsterdam
17a Façade view of a building with a *Haagse portiek*
17b Gulden & Geldmaker, residential building accessed by *Haagse portiek*, 1915, The Hague
18a, 18b J.H. van den Broek, De Eendracht housing, 1931–1934, Vroeselaan, Rotterdam

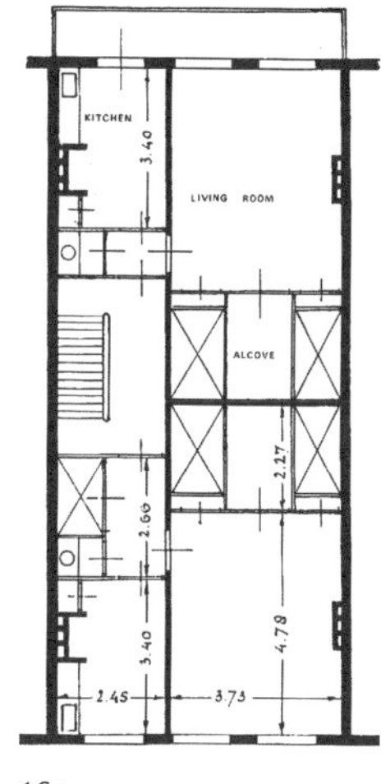

16a

Ground floor

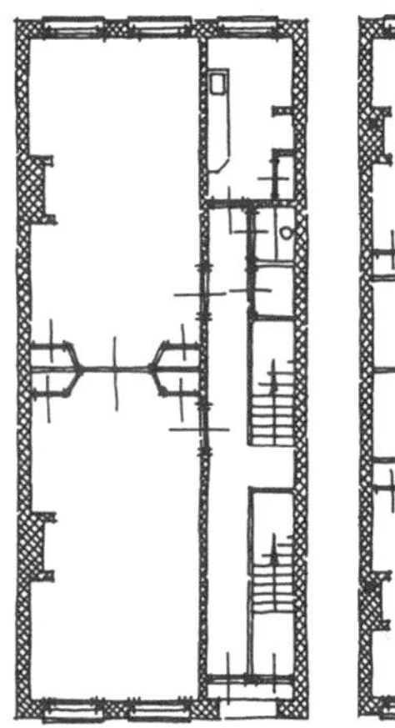

First floor

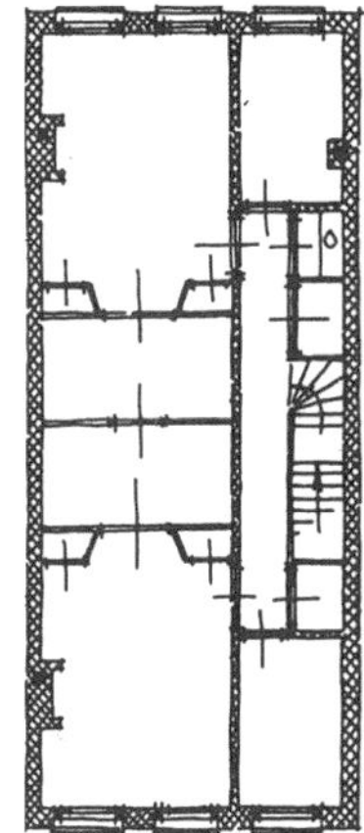

16b

17a

Ground floor

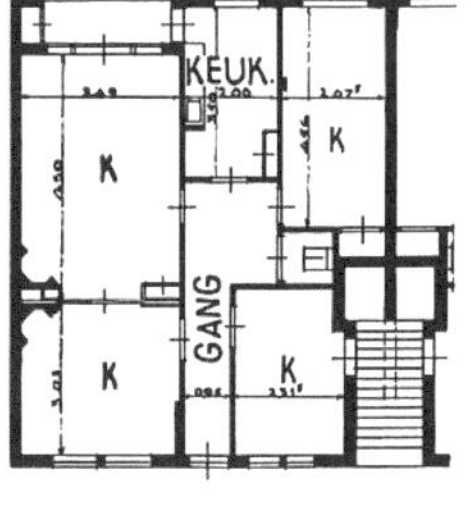

First floor

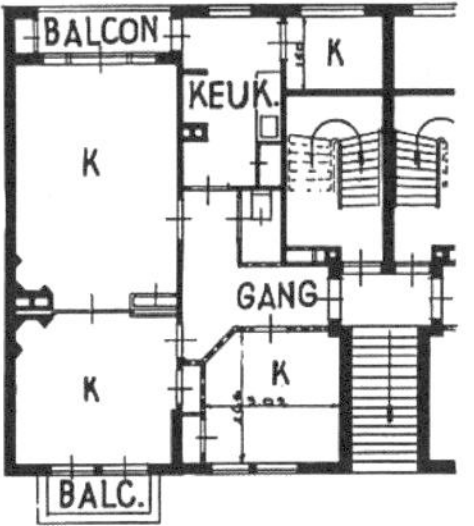

Second floor

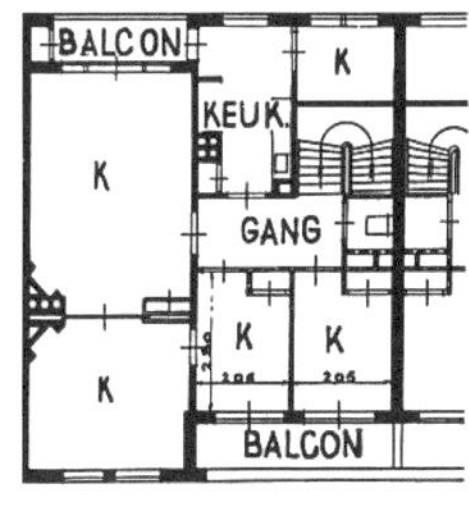

17b

18a

18b

19a

ALVARO SIZA VIEIRA, PERIOD AND COMMA (THE HAGUE, 1985–1989)

As part of the urban regeneration of the multicultural Schilderswijk, Portuguese architect Alvaro Siza Vieira designed two buildings with a total of 106 dwellings that had to be suitable for occupants of diverse cultural backgrounds. Unlike the usual urban regeneration floor plans in the Netherlands at the time, in which a hallway with a toilet and bathroom provides access to the remaining spaces, Siza developed flexible floor plans with separate circuits between the private and the communal areas of the home. The living room and kitchen are located at the front, while the bedrooms with individual access to the bathroom are situated on the quiet garden side. Sliding doors connect the two circuits as the occupants see fit. In a cross-pollination of cultural integration, the access is inspired by the *Haagse portiek*, with six front doors on the landing on the first storey. On every floor, the entrances open into the communal area in the middle of the dwelling. Even in the ground-floor flat with its own access from the street, a narrow hallway leads first to the middle, to reinforce the division into front and rear zones. The space under the ingeniously interlaced staircases is used for large storage spaces in each dwelling.

STAIRCASE

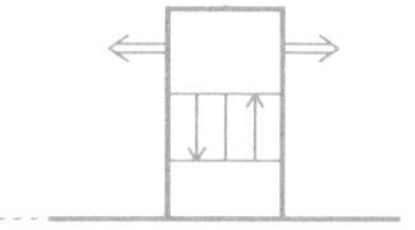

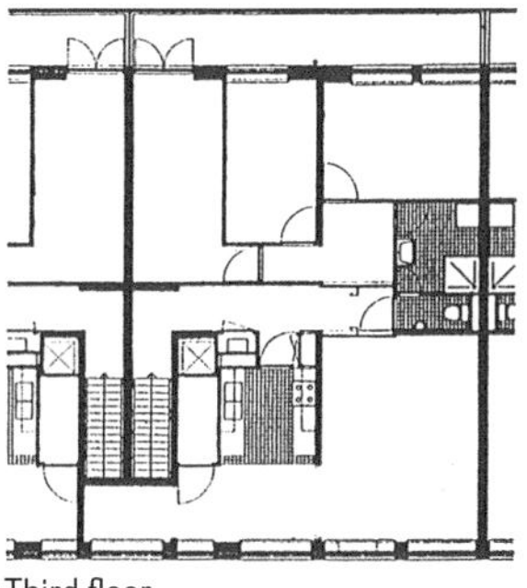

Third floor

Second floor

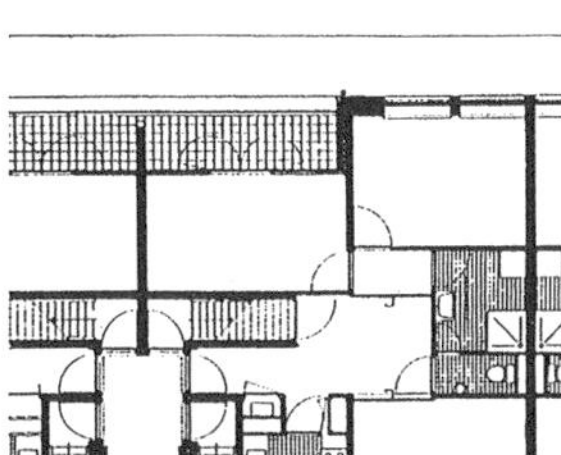

First floor

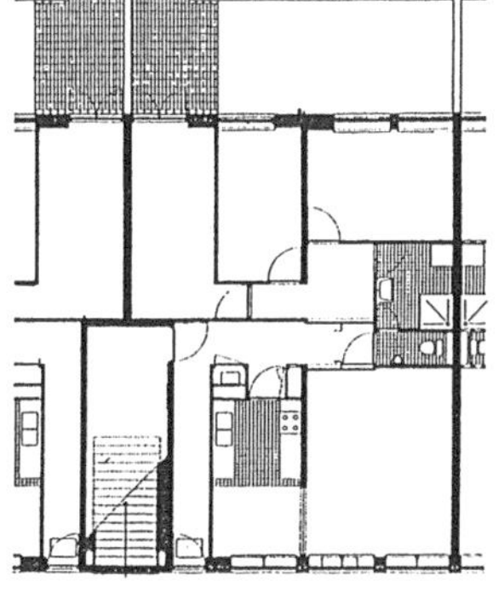

19b

19c

19c Siza's version of the
Haagse portiek

20a

20b

WOLFGANG POPP, ESTRADENHAUS (BERLIN, 1998)

The Estradenhaus designed by Wolfgang Popp in Berlin can be seen as a contemporary reinterpretation of the block of walk-up flats with an access staircase. The seven-storey building contains retail and office space as well as a total of 10 apartments in the private rental and buying market. The dwellings are accessed by staircase with a lift, situated off-centre in the structure, which divide the floors into larger (108 m^2) and smaller (79 m^2) apartments. The combination of the stairwell and lift requires a deeper accommodation for the stairs, so that people can walk past the staircase on the ground floor to reach the lift.
The service spaces are housed in a narrow zone on either side of the access, leaving the rest of the apartment open across its entire depth. Revolving floor-to-ceiling wooden panels allow the connection to the different spaces in the service zone to be modified as needed. Various configurations like an open kitchen, a vestibule or an open entrance area, or even an open bathroom, can be created simply by sliding or turning these panels. The open floor plan and the choice of access to the various service spaces means the way the dwelling can be used is not predetermined. Additional moveable wall elements are optional, in order to partition the open space into separate areas. Along both façades, a special area has been demarcated by a podium 1.8 m deep with a raised ceiling along the entire width of the flat. It is this raised zone or *estrade* that gives the building its name.

STAIRCASE

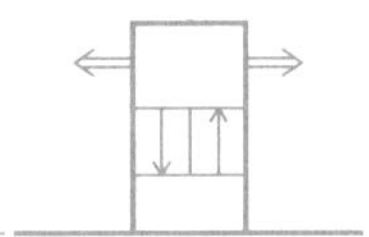

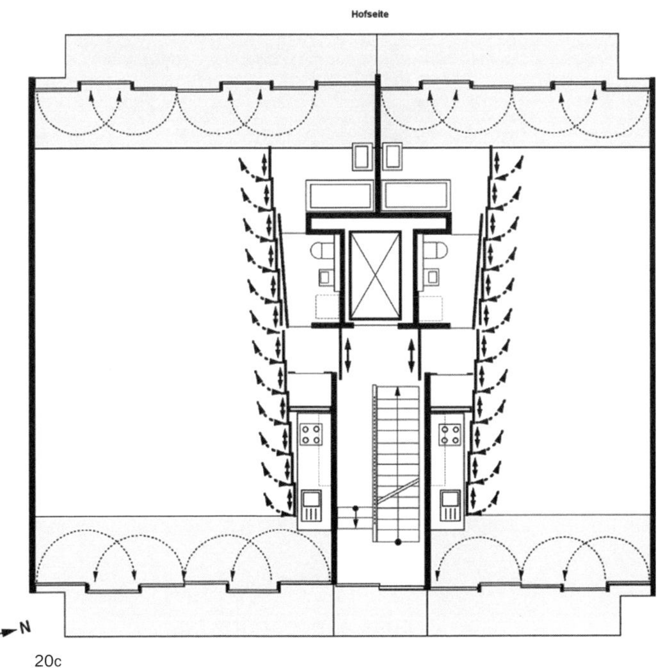

20c

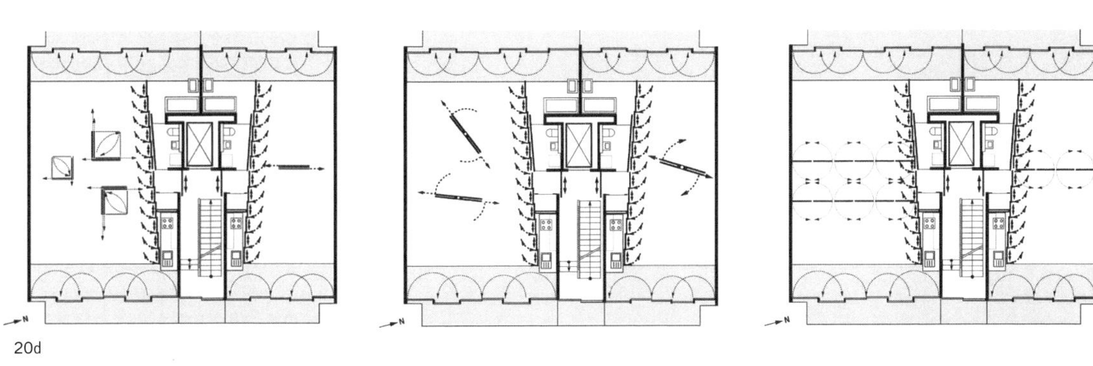

20d

20a The revolving and sliding panels allow different uses of the dwelling.
20c Floor plan with apartments of different sizes on either side of the access staircase
20d The space can be further divided with optional revolving wall elements.

21a

21b

OMA, IJPLEIN OOST III (AMSTERDAM-NOORD, 1986)

When the Office for Metropolitan Architecture was selected as coordinating architect for the IJplein site in Amsterdam-Noord, there was already a plan from the city's spatial planning department that called for a repetition of semi-open blocks of walk-up single-storey flats. To avoid a tedious succession of entrance lobbies and draw the IJ further into the residential area in a perceptual sense, the architects designed a new structure of open blocks and urban villas, in which a variety of access types were used to create differentiation among the dwelling typologies and in the streetscape.[5]

The building OMA itself elaborated, which is lifted off the ground, includes three different access types: the single- and double-occupancy units in the front section are accessed through a gallery, the middle section features an internal access staircase, and in the rear section the dwellings are accessed through a staircase running diagonally across the building. As the flights of stairs are set in a line, the whole of the staircase along every storey can be seen at a glance, and light reaches to the bottom of the stairs zone. At the same time, the entrances, grouped in facing pairs, open into the dwelling in a different place on each floor. A staircase in half-flights extending at an angle under the building leads to the ground level, where the communal entrance is located.

5 Bernard Leupen, *IJ-plein. Een speurtocht naar nieuwe compositorische middelen. Rem Koolhaas / Office for Metropolitan Architecture* (Rotterdam: 010 Publishers, 1989), 10.

STAIRCASE

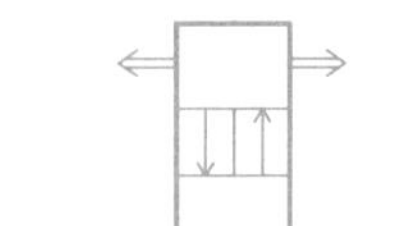

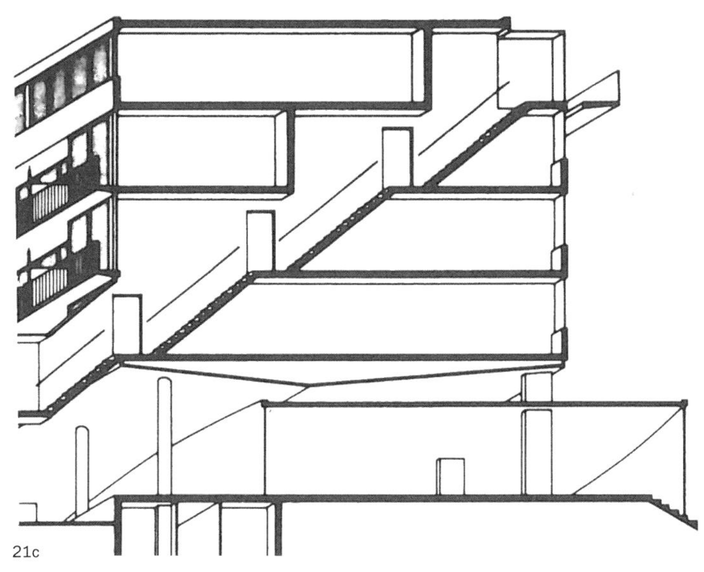

21c

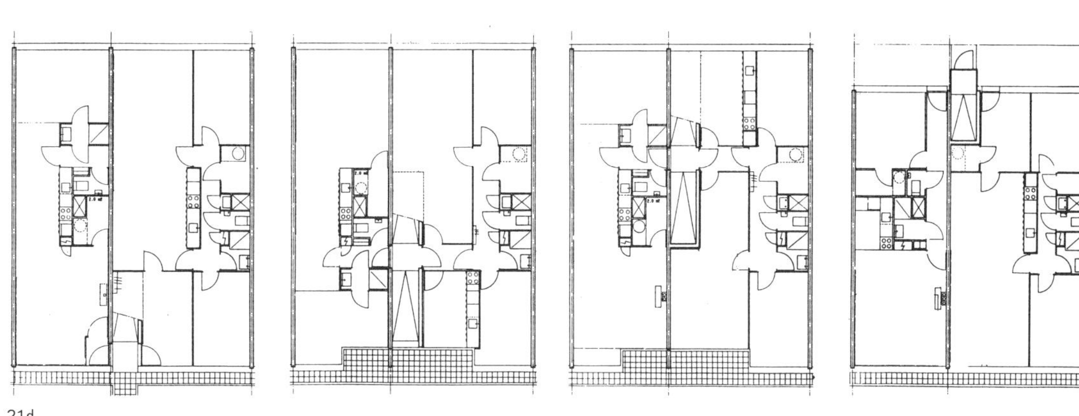

21d

21a Upward view of the stairway
21b From the entrance, the stairway extends at an angle under the building and then turns back and leads up diagonally through the volume.
21c Cross section of the diagonal access stairway
21d First to fourth floors. The entrances to the dwellings on either side of the stairway are located in a different place on each floor.

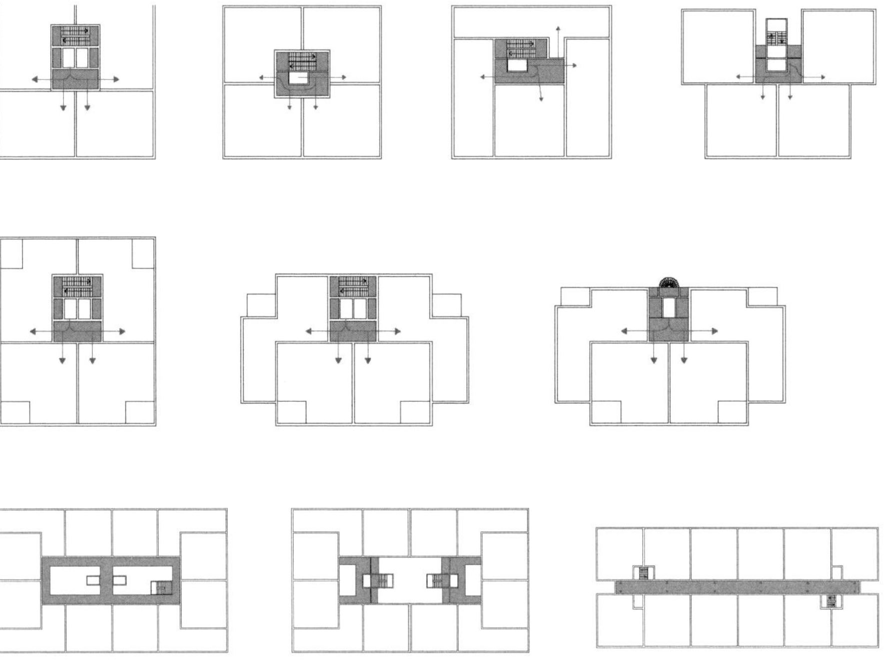

22

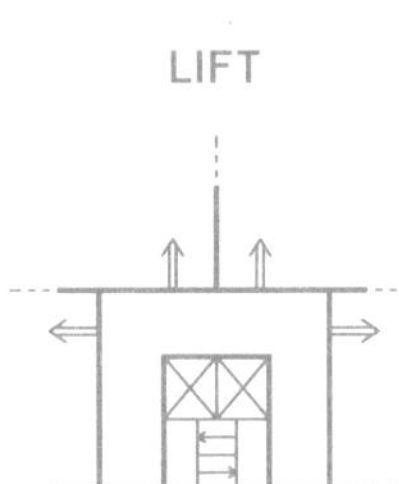

Elisha Graves Otis's presentation of the first lift with a brake mechanism at the Crystal Palace in New York in 1854 marks the advent of the construction of tall office and later residential buildings. The lift made it possible, for the first time in history, to make buildings of great heights easily and safely accessible for people and goods. Although the lift as a mechanical instrument has had many applications since, and can be used to supplement other types of access, we only speak of lift access in housing construction when the dwellings are more or less directly accessed from the lift, clustered around the central vertical access channel in which the lift is housed. For safety reasons, (emergency) stairs are also installed, the function of which becomes more secondary as the building increases in height. At ground level, there is a collective entrance for all the dwellings served by the lift. Because a lift is relatively expensive, an attempt will be made to have one lift serve as many dwellings as possible. This will be to the detriment of the potential orientation of the dwellings, unless solutions are found through clever configurations. In order to reach all the dwellings, a collective area is also created on each storey, which, as a communal reception or habitation area or in combination with collective facilities, can improve the quality of the residential environment. As the number of dwellings increases, this collective area also increases in size and is used by more people. At a certain point, the distance between the dwelling and the lift is such that the situation becomes one of horizontal access in the form of a gallery or corridor.

23a

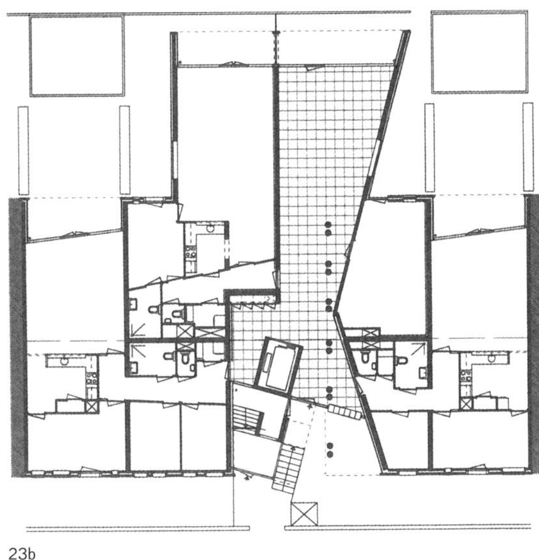

23b

KCAP, JAVA ISLAND HOUSING BLOCK (AMSTERDAM, 1992–1998)

The dwellings in the eight-storey block by KCAP are accessed from its centre through a lift and stairwell. Rather than hide this away in the darkest heart of a configuration based on maximum floor space, the architects opted to make the entrance zone into something special. Natural light falls diagonally into the block from both façades into the communal lobby, where a panoramic view over the water and the public gardens at the rear of the building can be enjoyed. The lift, positioned diagonally, shields the separate dwelling entrances to a certain extent, while the fully glassed-in staircase provides an appealing alternate route. Situated at an angle between brightly coloured internal walls, the vertical entrance zone is strikingly accentuated in the dark composition of the façade.

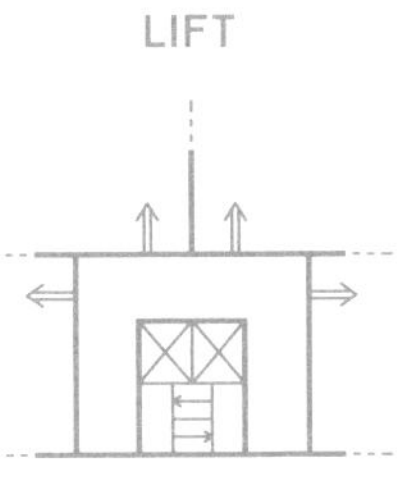

Around 1807, the French utopian socialist Charles Fourier developed ideas for housing the proletariat. His *Phalanstère* consisted of a number of large residential blocks set in a pastoral landscape, together forming a great 'palace of the worker'. Over 1,600 people were meant to live here communally, working the land for their own development and happiness. Inspired by these ideas, the industrialist Jean-Baptiste André Godin designed and built his own accommodations for the workers of his factory in Guise, in northern France, between 1859 and 1885. The dwellings in Godin's Familistère are grouped around covered inner courtyards in three connected blocks of four residential levels and a peaked roof. Inside the courtyard, all the dwellings are accessed through a gallery on each level, itself reached by stairs in the corners of the block. The gallery in the inner courtyard also serves as a collective balcony and a place for collective events and festivities. [→ 24a–b]

Gallery access was not an entirely new phenomenon: the Roman *insula* featured a kind of gallery, and the cloister as an open ambulatory running along cells encircling an inner courtyard can also be seen as a precursor. What was new in the edifice in Guise was the gallery applied in a structural way on a large scale as a self-contained type of access.[6]

We can find an early Dutch example of a gallery in Michiel Brinkman's unique residential block in the Spangen area of Rotterdam (1919–1921). Elongated four-storey building volumes housing stacked maisonettes are arranged around a large semi-public inner area, from which the lower dwellings are accessed. The upper-storey dwellings are accessible via a pedestrian walkway running all the way around the second storey, which is very wide and was genuinely intended as an elevated street: the baker and the milkman still made their deliveries door to door here as late as the 1950s. [→ 25a–b]

GALLERY

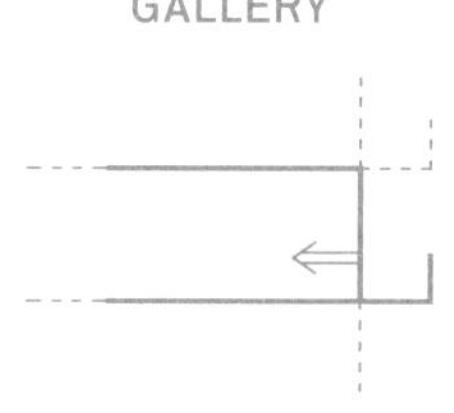

The first structural application came over a decade later, with the first gallery high-rise in the Netherlands, Willen van Tijen's Bergpolder Building in Rotterdam (1933–1934). Here, identical apartments are rationally linked and stacked into a slab 10 storeys high, onto which galleries are suspended on every storey to provide access to the flats. An equivalent zone on the other side houses balconies. This configuration is characteristic of the countless gallery high-rises that subsequently formed the expansion districts of many Dutch cities and towns. [→ 26a–b]

A significant drawback to the gallery in combination with flats is already discernible in the floor plan of the dwellings in the Bergpolder Building. The gallery runs directly along the façades of the flats and disrupts the privacy of the habitation spaces situated there. In addition, part of the front façade is taken up by the entrance, along with the circulation space required to penetrate deeper into the dwelling. Habitation spaces can be situated along the opposite façade as much as possible and the window openings on the gallery can be kept small, as though the dwelling had a single orientation. In dwellings of more than one room this is not always possible, and one or more (sleeping) spaces suffer from noise and exposure to passers-by on the gallery. A gallery running along the façade also interferes with natural light penetration into the storey below. The situation is somewhat improved when the gallery is further removed from the façade, which unfortunately entails a view into the downstairs neighbours' homes. [→ 27]

Privacy improves noticeably in combination with maisonettes. Now there are three façade sections in addition to the gallery façade along which to accommodate the dwelling programme. And the number of galleries required is cut in half. The façade of the upper level can be extended over the gallery, so that the latter is incorporated into the block and does not take natural light away from the lower storeys. If the dwellings alternate up and down, only one gallery is needed for every three storeys, and the maisonettes, from a narrow entrance level, can expand above or below across a double width. [→ 28]

Finally, a noteworthy cross section is the gallery in combination with two split-level apartments, in which the gallery and the two service zones together occupy the same height as the two more spacious habitation zones along the opposite façades. This two-on-three solution was identified as the most economical for relatively small working-class dwellings in a 1928 study on dwelling typology carried out by the Stroikom committee of the Gosplan planning institute in the former Soviet Union. Soon thereafter, the 'Stroikom type F' was actually implemented in the Narkomfin Building (Moscow, 1928–1932) by architects Moisei Ginzburg and Ignaty Milinis. [→ 29a–c]

6 Leupen, *Frame and Generic Space*, op. cit. (note 2), 133.

24a

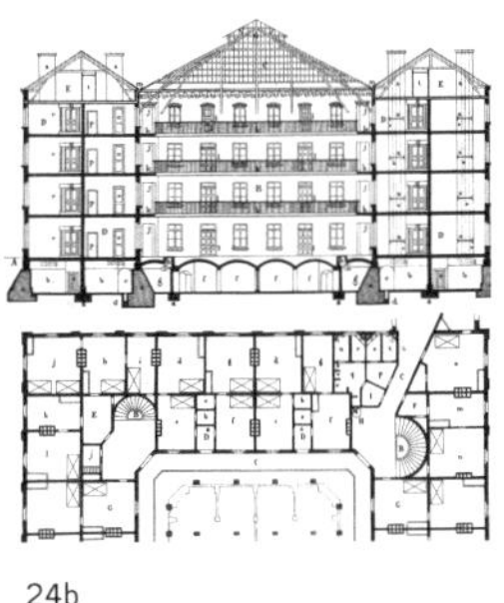
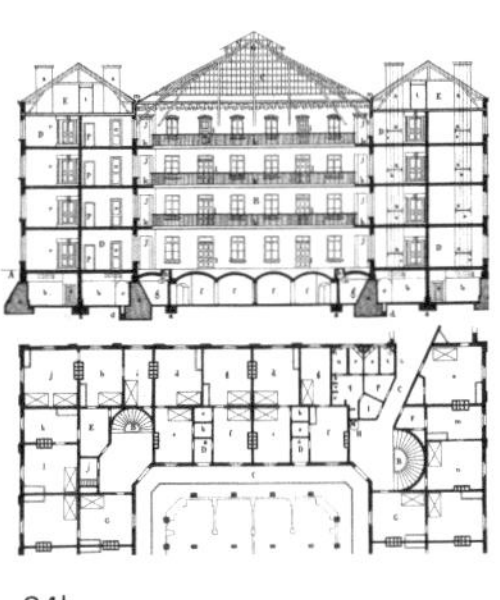

24b

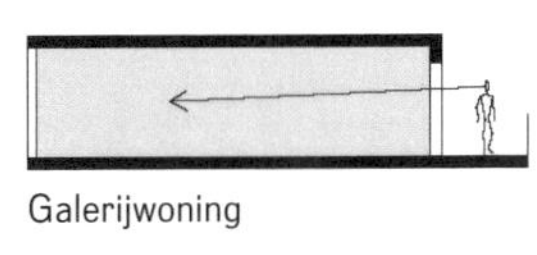

Galerijwoning

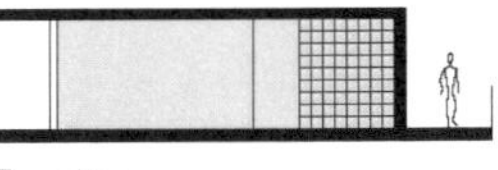

Zonering

Kleine ramen

Afstand van gevel

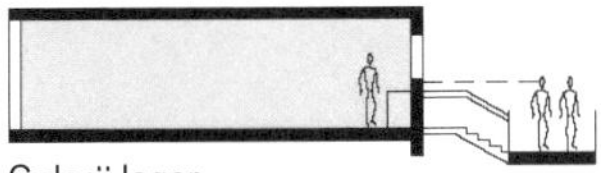

Galerij lager

27

25a

25b

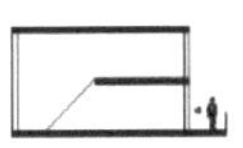
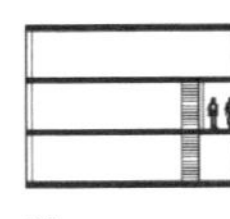

28

26a

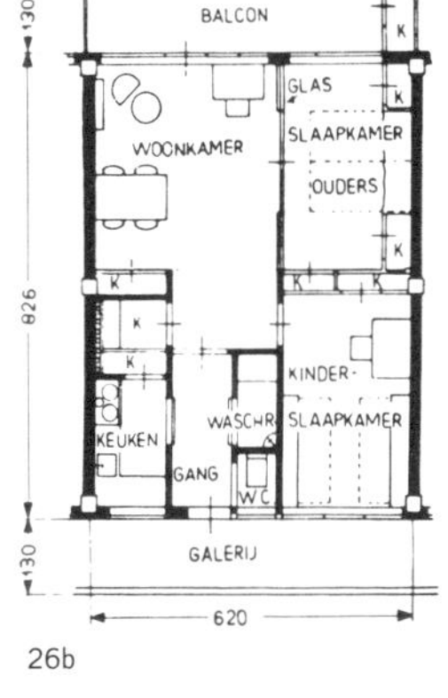
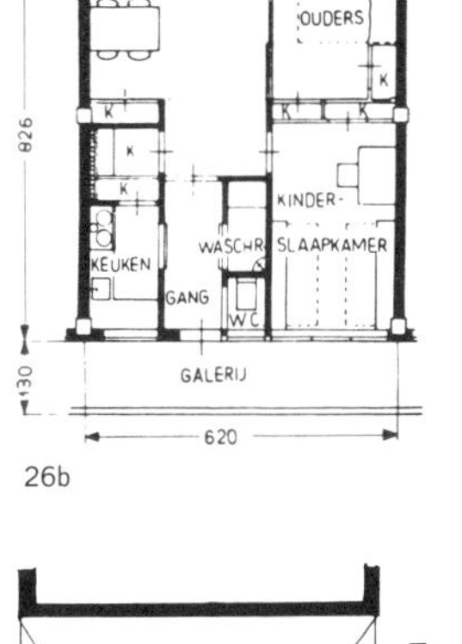

26b

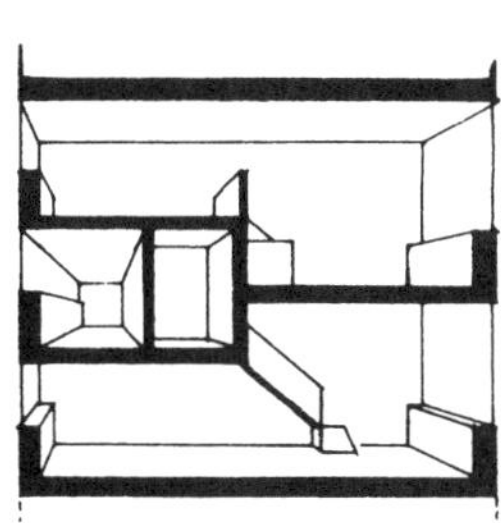

29a

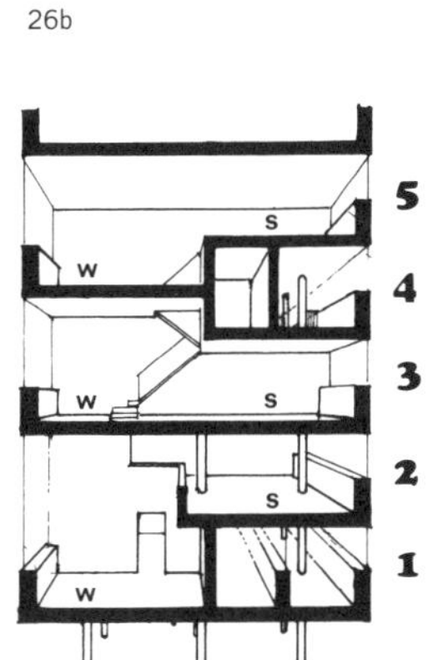
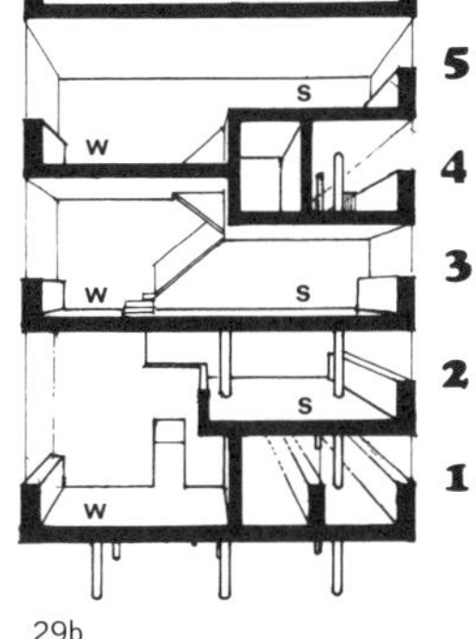

29b

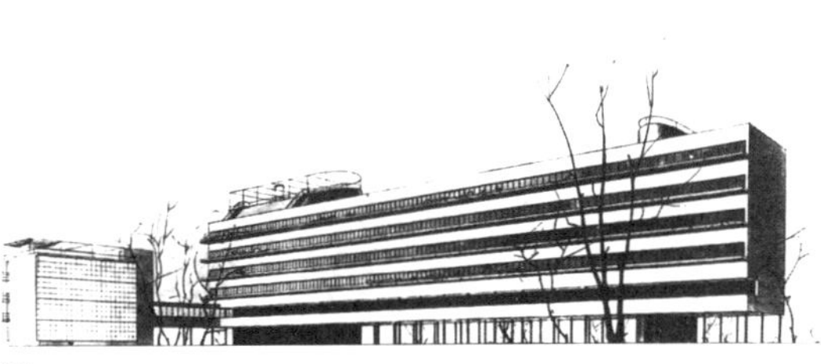

29c

24a, 24b J-B.A. Godin, Familistère, 1859–1877, Guise, France
25a, 25b M. Brinkman, Justus van Effen Block, 1919–1921, Spangen, Rotterdam
26a, 26b W. van Tijen, Bergpolder Building, 1933–1934, Rotterdam
27 Design tricks for gallery flats
28 Gallery serving one or more floors
29a Stroikom type F, 2:3 cross section
29b M. Ginzburg & I. Milinis, Narkomfin Building, 1928–1932, Moscow. Cross section including the Stroikom type F configuration.
29c Narkomfin Building

30a

30b

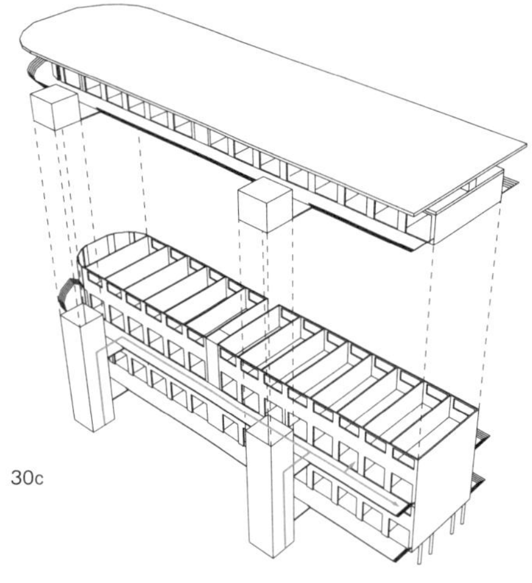

30c

GALLERY

JEAN NOUVEL, NEMAUSUS I & II (NÎMES, 1985–1988)

Jean Nouvel's two futuristic-looking residential blocks in Nîmes represent a radical break from the tradition of publicly subsidized housing built in small dwellings of stuccoed low-rise housing blocks. The premise was the definition of a good apartment, which the architects felt had to be as large as possible, adaptable and not expensive. Industrial construction in thin prefabricated concrete and aluminium cladding was used to build a total of 114 dwellings of 17 different types, each one to three storeys and on average 40 per cent larger than a standard publicly subsidized rental home. The dwellings are accessed on every other floor by a gallery 3 m wide that, like a street in the air lined with benches along the railing, affords sufficient room to serve as a comfortable extension of the home. On the other side, an equivalent zone provides large terraces for the dwellings, appropriate to the way of life in this Mediterranean climate. The façades of the dwelling are made up of panels two storeys high, which can open up the whole home to the terrace like garage doors. The broad galleries also provide protection from the heat of direct sun exposure.

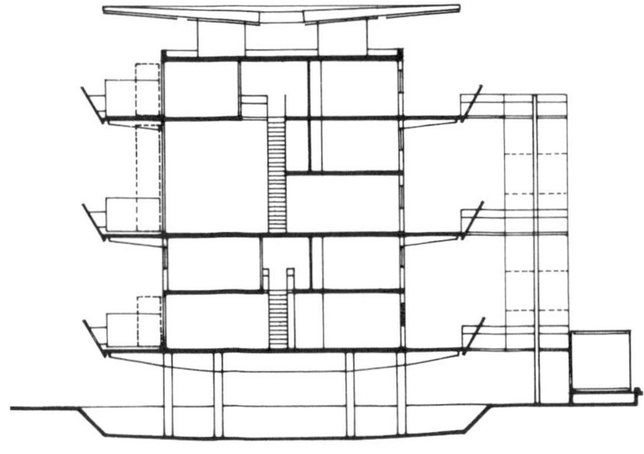

30d

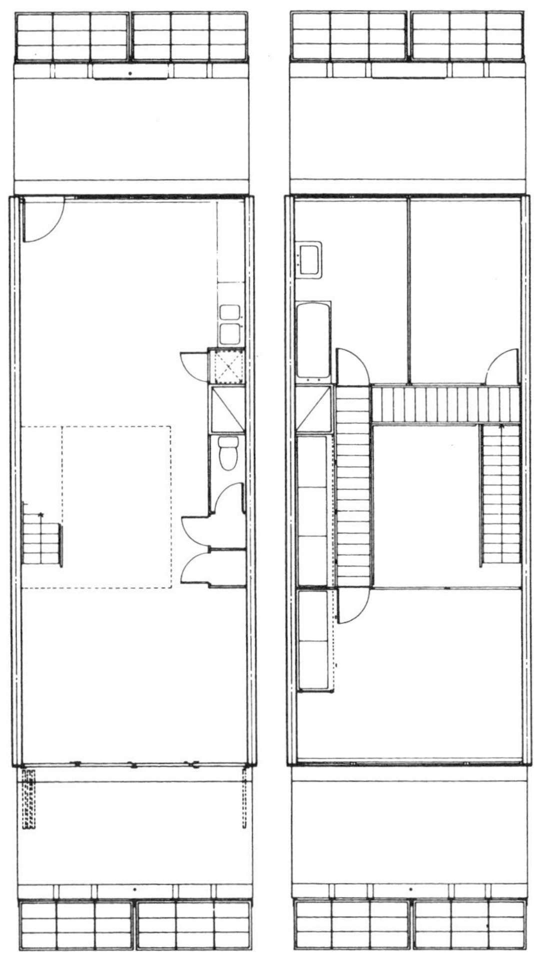

30e

30b The broad gallery of Nemausus
30c Plan of the access
30d Cross section with balconies on the left and the gallery on the right
30e Floor plan of a maisonette

31a

31b

PI DE BRUIJN, HONINGERDIJK (ROTTERDAM, 1981–1983)

This seven-storey residential building by Pi de Bruijn (de Architekten Cie.) forms a buffer for the residential area situated behind it against the traffic of a busy access road into the city. Within the block, two double-height galleries on the second and fifth storeys serve the same function for the dwellings behind them. The galleries are situated within the contours of the block and are lined with glass to keep out traffic noise, creating an internal street that emphatically feels like part of the collective dwelling area. The galleries provide access to three storeys: a three-room apartment on the gallery level, a three-room apartment on the floor above, reached by means of a flight of stairs leading from the gallery, and a four-room apartment one floor below, with a private staircase behind the entrance door situated on the gallery. Combining the access to multiple floors on one gallery means the latter is used and monitored more intensively, to the benefit of its security and quality as a supplemental dwelling area.

GALLERY

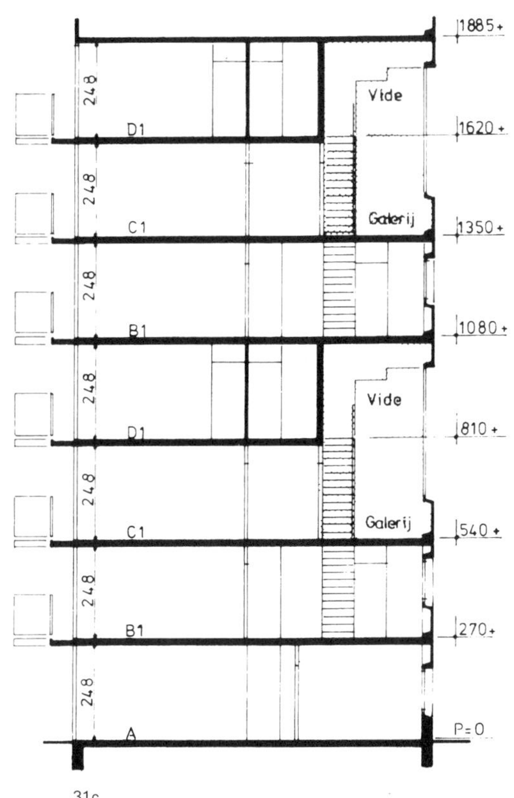

31c

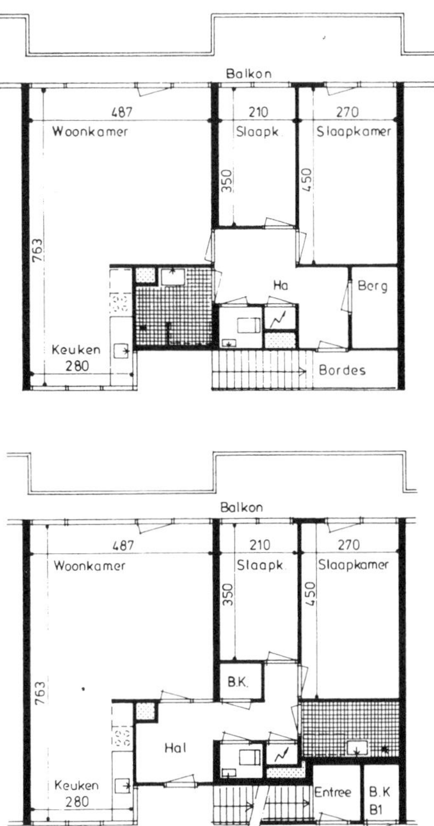

31d

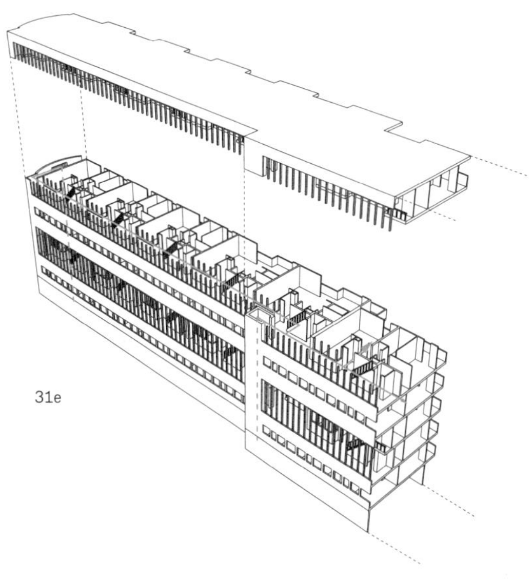
31e

31a The internal double-height gallery
31c The cross section shows both double-height internal galleries
31d Floor plan of the dwellings alongside and above the gallery
31e Diagram of the access

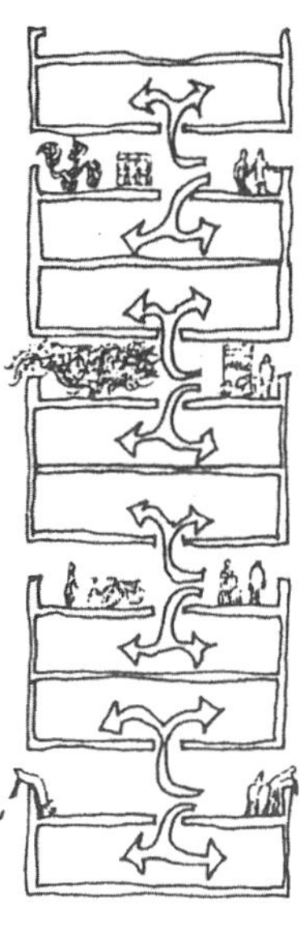
32a

32b

ALISON & PETER SMITHSON, ROBIN HOOD GARDENS (LONDON, 1966–1972)

For a competition in 1952, as a commentary on the traditional gallery-access building, in which a bleak gallery provides access to a series of apartments, Alison and Peter Smithson designed an alternative solution for the reconstruction of the war-ravaged areas of London. In the Golden Lane project, access is provided by open decks across the entire width of the building, affording entry to the dwellings above and below. In addition to the dwelling entrances and a broad walkway, these 'streets in the air' also contain storage sheds and private gardens, which give the block a breezy diversity. Many of the ideas in this never-implemented project form the basis for the building on Robin Hood Lane. This too incorporates broad open residential streets providing access to dwellings on several levels. The dwellings, however, are now maisonettes organized alternately upward or downward. To reinforce the sense of a street beyond the front door, all dwellings feature a kitchen-diner along the gallery, and the shallow entrance alcoves form a differentiated 'street façade'. Yet nowhere does the complex achieve the scale of transparency and diversity suggested by the Golden Lane project.

GALLERY

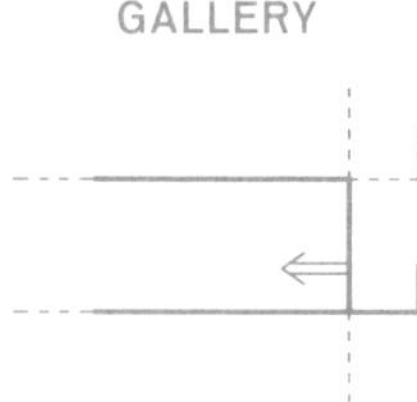

2c

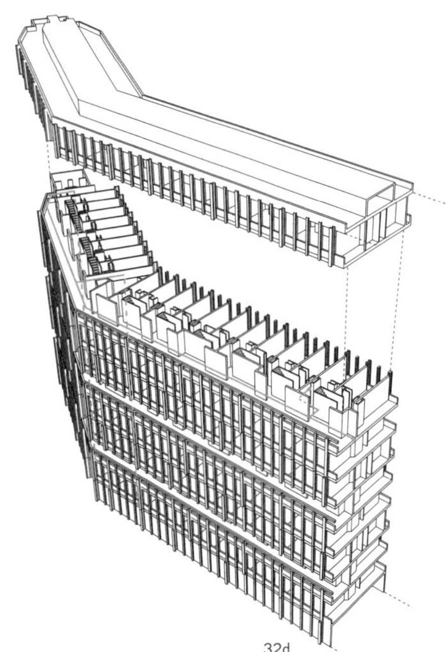

32d

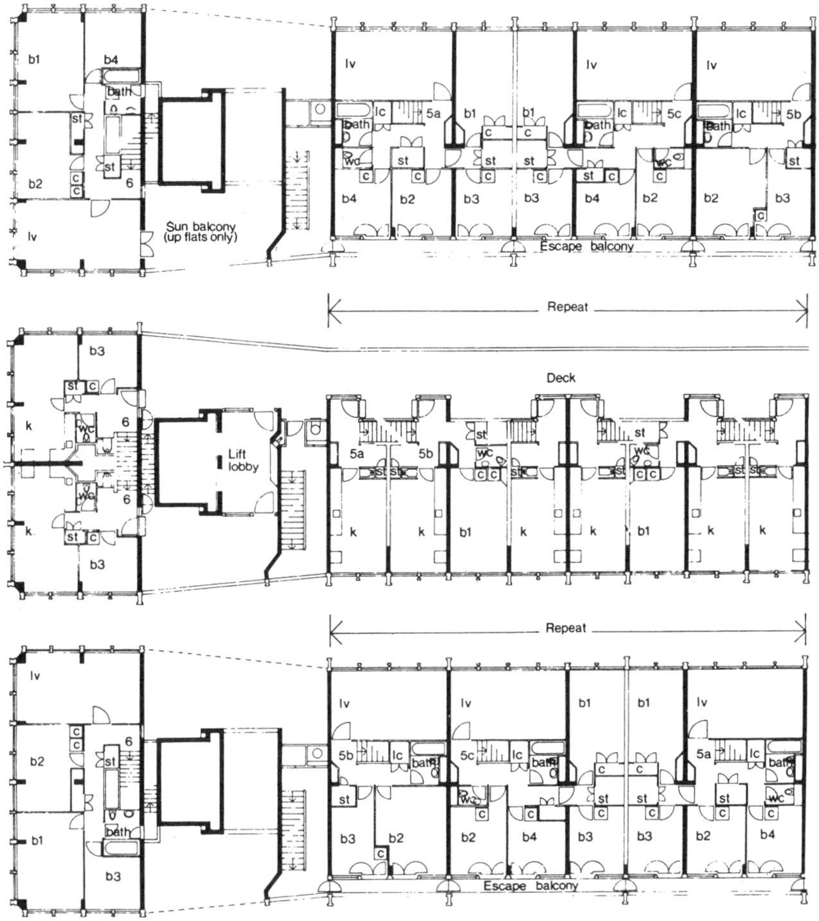

32e

32a Diagram of the plan for Golden Lane
32c The broad deck of Robin Hood Gardens
32d Diagram of the access
32e Floor plans of a section of the building with dwellings under, alongside and above the deck

CORRIDOR

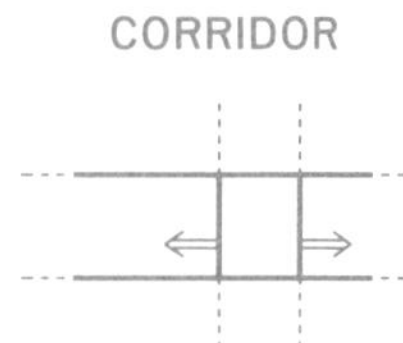

Access through a gallery constrains privacy, because the gallery runs immediately alongside one of the façades. This problem can be addressed by shifting the access to the middle of the building, where access is provided to dwellings on both sides of an internal central hallway or 'corridor'. This combination has long been familiar from prisons and hotels, where the single orientation it produces does not raise insurmountable objections. In housing construction, the effort to provide double orientation leads to more complex solutions. In 1927, the OSA, the Russian Organization of Contemporary Architects, held a competition for a new type of residential building, the communal house. Andrej Andrejewitsch Ol's entry [→ 33] shows a residential building in three levels, in which a corridor on the first storey provides access to dwellings on the ground floor as well as the upper floor. The double orientation is resolved through the 'bayonet' cross section: a dwelling with a truncated section flanking the corridor and a level that extends over or under the corridor to the opposite façade. While entry directly from outside would certainly be feasible for the ground-level dwellings, the corridor leads all residents to a central entrance building housing day nurseries and collective kitchens. The access in this never implemented project therefore serves a mainly social function. The corridor and the 'bayonet' dwelling would become widely known later because of Le Corbusier, who demonstrated their possibilities in his Unités d'Habitation. Not only does the corridor improve privacy, it also positions the entrance on the inner side of the dwelling, so that no habitation space is lost along the façade. The dwelling entrances are not visible from the outside, and even the corridor is only perceptible in the end façades. This allows a building with corridor access to appear quite solid and autonomous. Conversely, there is the danger that no natural light can penetrate the access zone, turning the corridor into an unpleasantly dark hallway. Like the gallery, a corridor can in principle provide access to more than one residential level. One corridor per level is not very economical and produces exclusively single-orientation dwellings. A corridor for every two levels already offers room for alternating combinations, in which dwellings can be interlaced not only transversely but also lengthwise. Three levels produce the most economically advantageous solution with a double 'bayonet' cross section, although other combinations are possible as well. Finally, a split-level solution is also possible, whereby the dwellings, from the corridor, go up or down half a storey, and then extend over or under the corridor a further half-storey above or below. [→ 34]

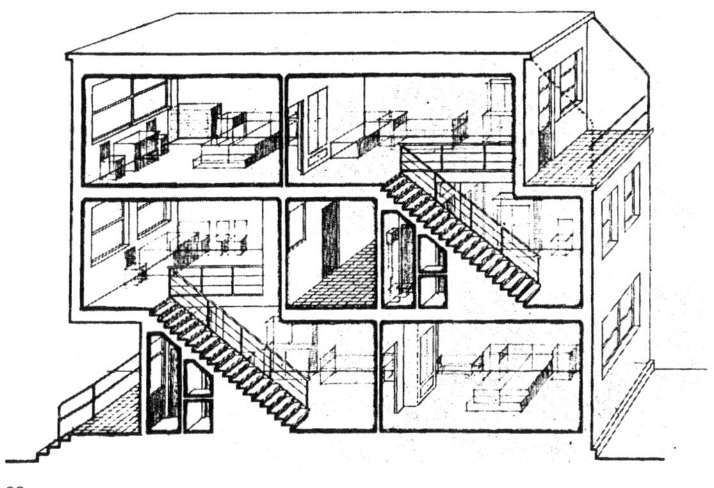

33

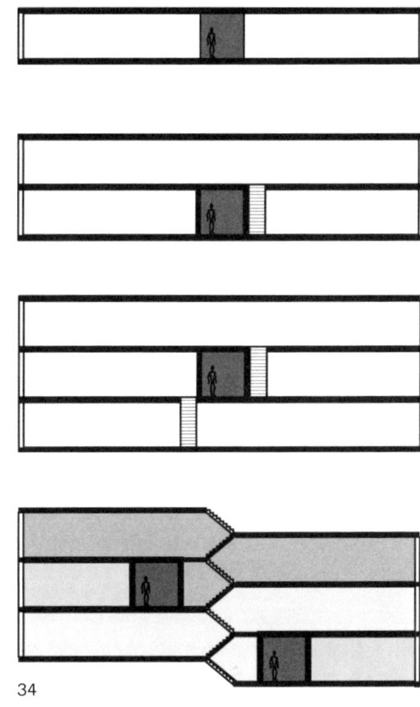

34

33 A.A. Ol, competition entry for communal dwellings, 1927, exploded cross section of one part of the building
34 Corridor serving one or more storeys

35a

LE CORBUSIER, UNITÉ D'HABITATION (MARSEILLE, 1947-1952)

A total of 337 dwellings are distributed over 16 storeys in 23 different configurations, varying from one to ten occupants, accessed by seven central corridors. These are situated at irregular intervals over the height of the complex, creating diverse dwelling cross sections from top to bottom. In the lower six storeys we find the 'bayonet' cross section twice, with a corridor in the middle of three habitation levels. Above this are two storeys with one corridor each, with single-orientation spaces on either side. Then one corridor for three storeys twice more, and finally two storeys containing apartments and maisonettes accessed from a corridor on the top storey.

CORRIDOR

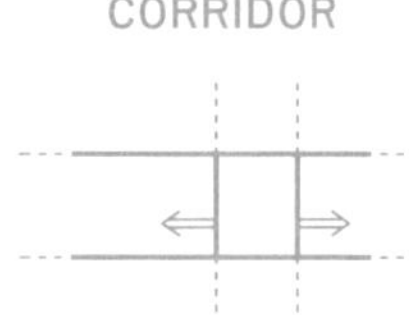

Le Corbusier saw the access corridor as a *rue intérieure*, a residential street within the building along which the residents have their own individual front doors. A relatively generous width (3.25 m, with ceilings 2.26 m high), varied colours and striking letterboxes are meant to visually reinforce this idea of a street. Similarly, the lift serves only seven stops in the stacked 'neighbourhoods'. A certain amount of natural light falls past the lift into the residential street, but because the latter leads to wrap-around end dwellings at one end and to a blank wall at the other, the way from the lift to the dwelling is quite dark. On the 'third floor' (seventh habitation level) the residential street turns into a commercial street, with amenities like a café-restaurant, bakery and various shops.

35a Corridor in the Marseille Unité d'Habitation
35b Diagram of the access
35c The cross section shows the positions of the different corridors.
35d Cross section of the 'bayonet' dwellings in the building

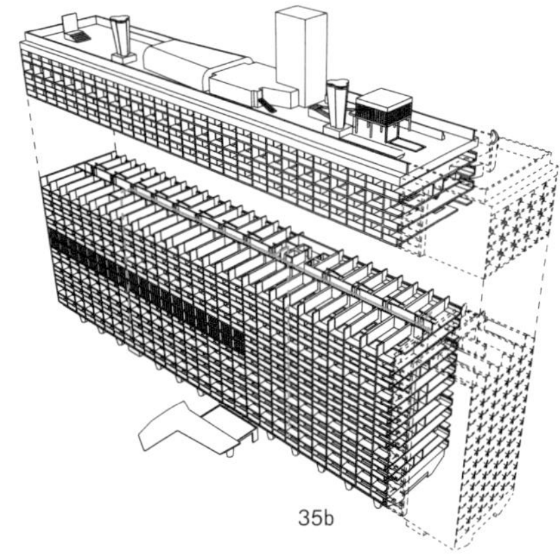

35b

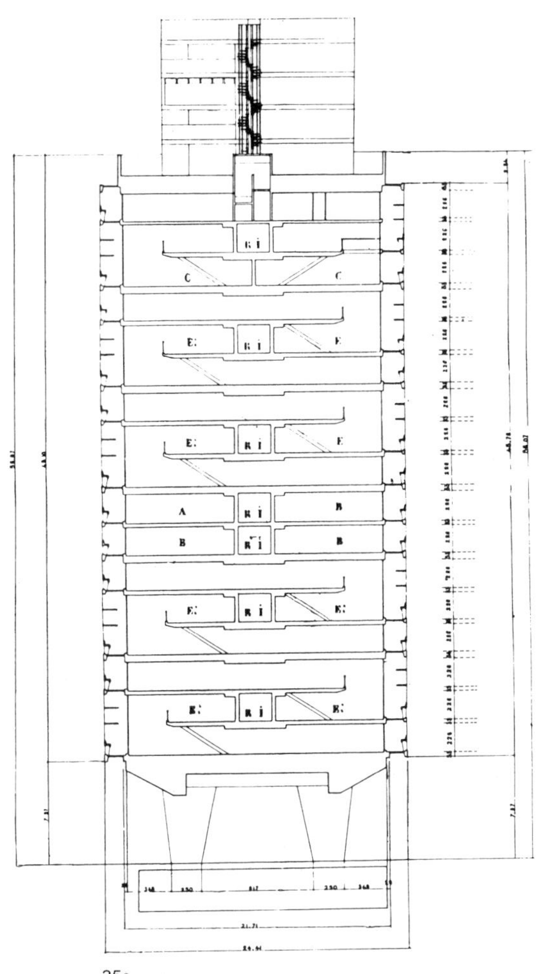

35c

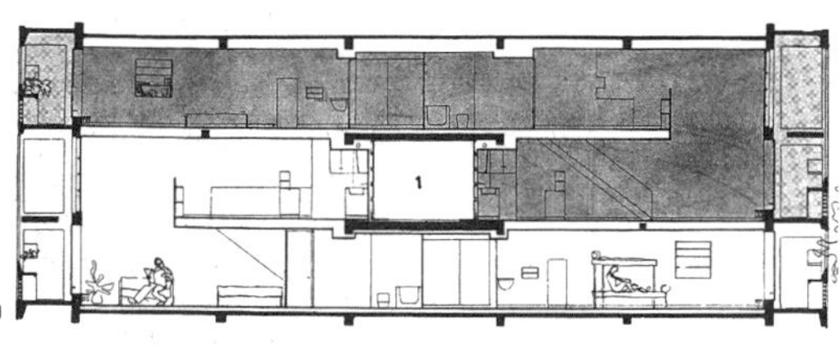

35d

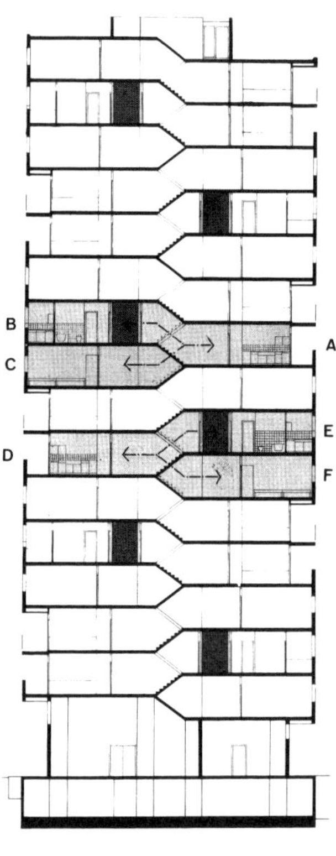

36b

36b Cross section with the alternately spaced corridors lined by split-level dwellings
36c, 36d The stairs that direct the split-level dwellings around the corridor
36f Diagram of the access

36a

CORRIDOR

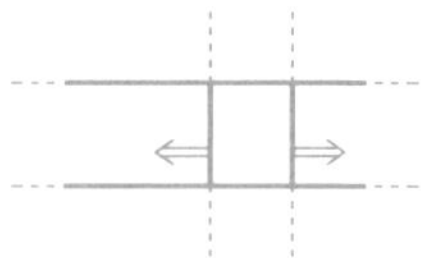

VAN DEN BROEK & BAKEMA, HANSAVIERTEL HOUSING (BERLIN, 1957)

For the international building exhibition Interbau in Berlin, Van den Broek & Bakema designed a residential tower of split-level dwellings accessed by corridors. The advantage of the split-level configuration – bringing different levels closer together – is used here to make it easier to circumnavigate the corridor. Six corridors are distributed at regular intervals over a total of 15 storeys, or two and a half storeys per corridor. The staircase in half flights is located in the middle of the dwellings, while the corridors alternate to its left and right. From each corridor, two sets of four split-level dwellings are accessed by narrow staircases set side by side, which open into wider dwellings along the façade. An equally narrow stairway extends to the other side, so that the split-level here does not have the spatial effect it otherwise would. The corridors are relatively short and open out on a wide communal balcony in the end façade, allowing adequate natural light to penetrate, so that the relatively narrow corridor is a pleasant place to be.

36c

36d

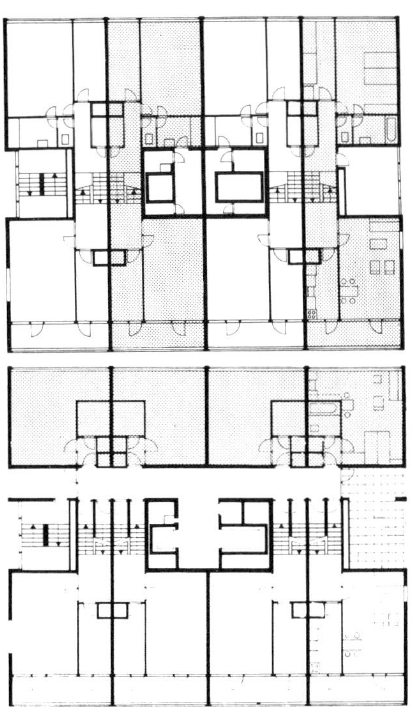
36e

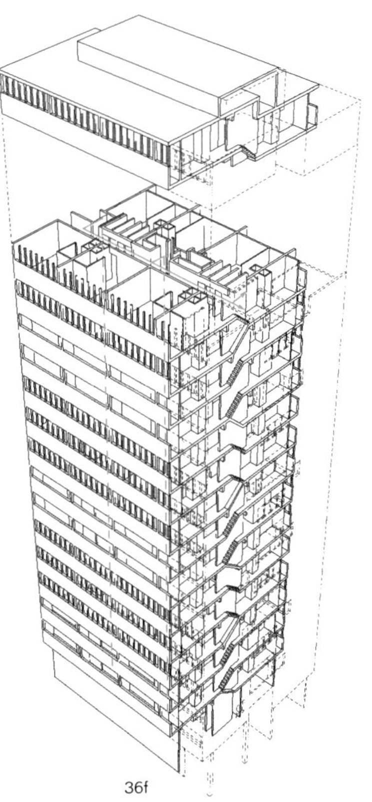
36f

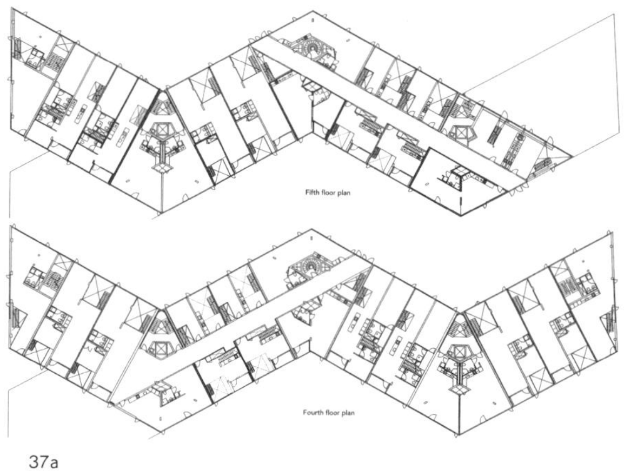

37a

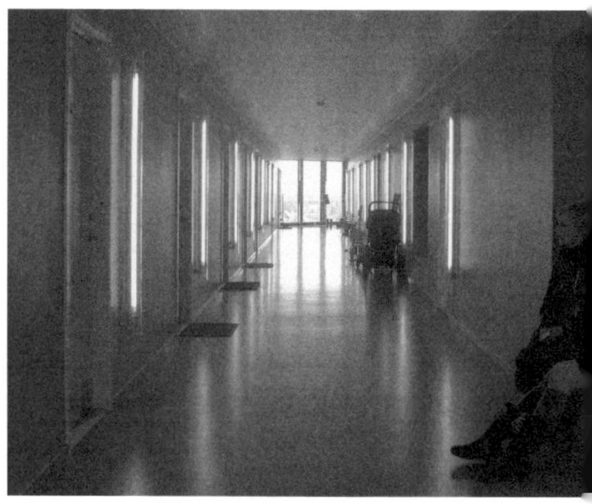

37b

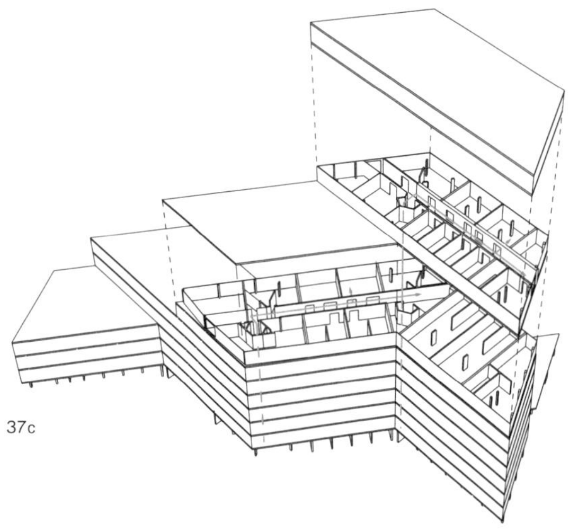

37c

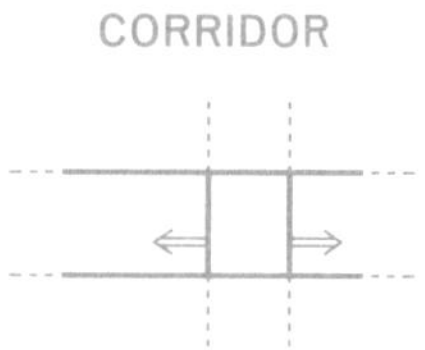

PLOT (BIG+JDS), VM BUILDING (COPENHAGEN-ØRESTAD, 2006)

Of these two buildings whose footprints form the letters V and M, it is the M building in particular – with its wide variety of dwellings and collective facilities, the stilts that lift it off the ground and its corridor access – that can be seen as a contemporary homage to the Le Corbusier's Unités d'Habitation. Based on one access level for every three storeys, the dwellings are wrapped in ever more ingenious combinations around the corridor, which here too has been elaborated as a residential street within the building. One important difference is that each of the corridors in the M building is only as long as one stroke of the M and opens at both ends onto a glass façade, allowing natural light to penetrate deep into the edifice. This turns the broad residential street into a pleasing place to be, an aspect seized upon to make alcoves in the walls that invite people to sit. The corridor is situated on a different floor in each adjacent building section, so that the scale of the hallways and the number of residents remains small enough to avoid anonymity. At the points where the corridors, running one above the other, intersect, vertical access channels connect the 'little neighbourhoods' to one another and with the ground level.

37a Floor plans of the fourth and fifth storeys, each with a corridor in a different part of the building
37b A corridor in the M building, with alcoves and natural light
37c Diagram of the access

Comparing the different galleries

38a

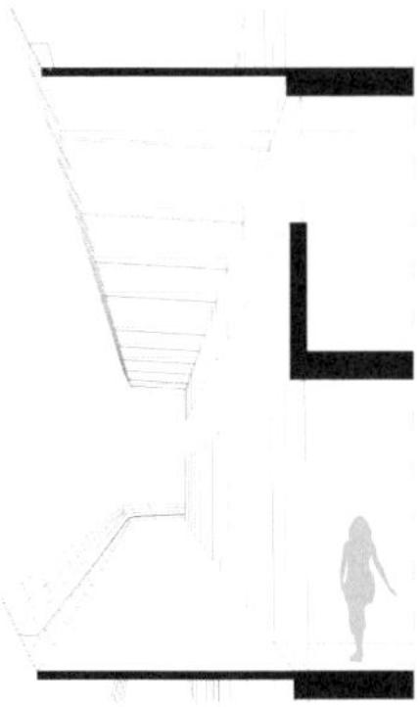

38b

38c

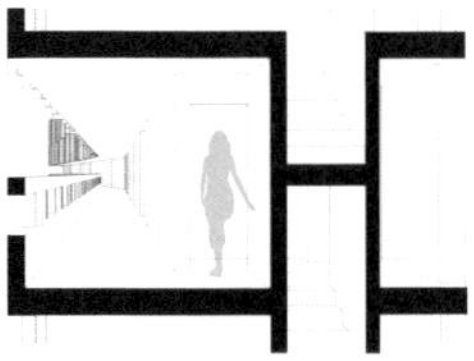

38d

Comparing the different corridors

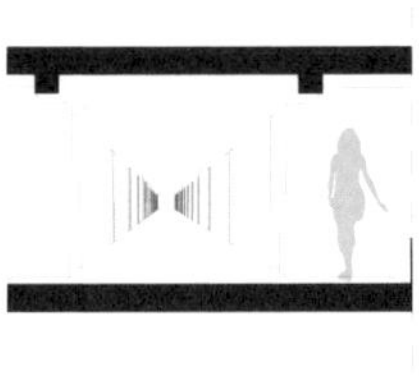

39a

39b

39c

38a Bergpolder Building gallery
38b Nemausus gallery
38c Honingerdijk gallery
38d Robin Hood Gardens gallery

39a Unité d'Habitation corridor, Marseille
39b Hansaviertel residential building corridor, Berlin
39c M building corridor, Copenhagen

URBAN ENSEMBLE

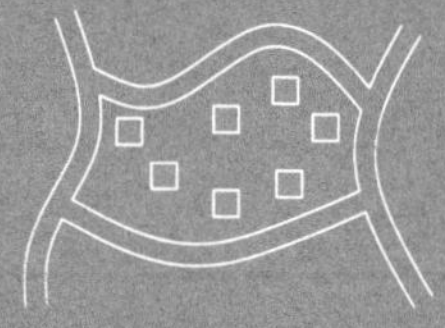

VILLA PARK

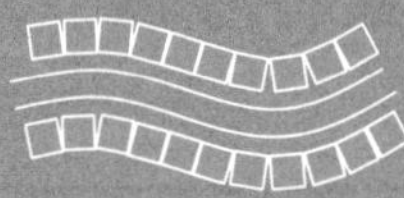

RIBBON DEVELOPMENT

PERIMETER BLOCK

SEMI-OPEN BLOCK

OPEN BLOCK

SUN ORIENTED
PARALLEL ROWS

FREE-STANDING OBJECTS

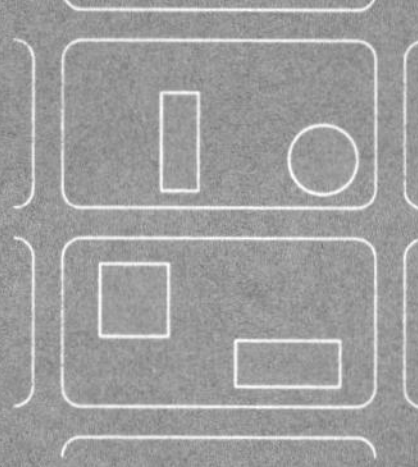

FREE COMPOSITION

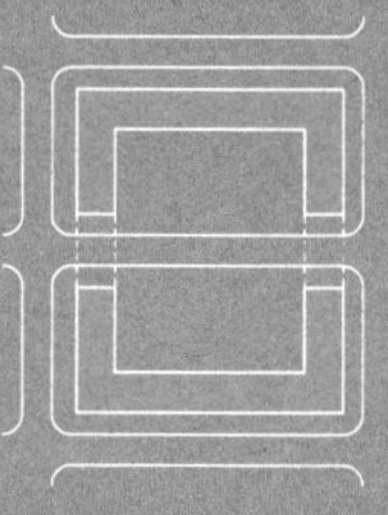

SUPERBLOCK

The environment in which we dwell is formed by an array of different residential buildings. The configuration of this urban ensemble determines the qualities that shape the dwelling condition. The dimensions of the individual volumes, and the way in which they relate, define the relationships between inside and outside, such as views, the penetration of natural light and noise tolerances, but also the relationship between public, collective and private domains and the degree of shielding between them. The access principles in the various residential buildings determine the everyday use of the public space, while their connections to parking infrastructure, urban amenities and green space can make or break the quality of a residential area. Every configuration has its own specific qualities, always at the expense of others. Every situation is different from the previous one, in dimensions, orientation and objectives. Every project, therefore, requires a new examination of the various possibilities a potential building site offers.
In order to select a suitable configuration for an intended residential programme and to make the best use of its qualities, it is vital to recognize the specific qualities of a number of basic configurations. To this end, we distinguish the following categories at the level of the urban ensemble:

—*Villa Park*
—*Ribbon Development*
—*Perimeter Block*
—*Semi-Open Block*
—*Open Block*
—*Sun Oriented Parallel Rows*
—*Free-Standing Object*
—*Free Composition*
—*Superblock*

In the pages that follow, these are explained in greater detail in terms of the history of their development and principles, illustrated with a few examples. We should emphasize that this concerns the model of the urban ensemble, not the elaboration of the architectural design. In principle, the urban ensemble can be filled in by several different architects, just as in the past individual dwellings or groups of dwellings inside the perimeter blocks were designed by different architects. Even when an urban ensemble is designed and elaborated by a single designer, as is more often the case today, the distinction between the urban ensemble and the residential building remains a crucial one.
Obviously the categories listed above do not represent all the possible configurations of an urban ensemble, by any means. Every built environment has its own characters traits. Moreover, many configurations, implemented or conceivable, do not fit into any of the categories above and perhaps cannot be identified according to one particular morphological typology. This chapter aims to highlight some of the characteristic features of the types that can.

1
Refers to the German *Zeilenbau*, usually applied to housing slabs several stories high, arranged in parallel rows in an East-West orientation with two-sided open-ended dwellings, a type commonly associated with functionalist/ *Neue Sachlichkeit* housing projects of the 1920's beginning in Germany but used in many countries; see also R. Sherwood, *Housing Prototypes*. Online. Available HTTP: http://housingprototypes.org/ glossary (accessed 28 September 2011).

The villa park is characterized by a seemingly independent distribution of free-standing volumes in a commonly scenic setting. The open spaces separating the volumes may be private property or publicly accessible. The sizable space of each dwelling is coupled with very low density, making the villa park configuration primarily suited to suburban areas. Its major quality is living in a green and leafy setting, which usually also means that many urban amenities are unavailable or accessible only by car.

The villa park has its origins in the industrialization of the nineteenth century and is therefore linked to the rise of a new middle class of wealthy citizens. Their professions tied them to the city, and they initially resided in relatively mixed proximity with working-class people in the same neighbourhood: the bourgeoisie in the more exclusive houses along a street or canal, the workers in the smaller back streets and alleys. Only a tiny upper crust of industrialists could afford to spend a few months outside the city during the summer, on their own country estates. New forms of transport, the construction of railroads in particular, brought nature areas situated near the cities within reach. Areas of land that had hitherto been unsuitable for reclamation and agriculture were bought up by investment companies for little money and developed into residential areas of spacious lots in park-like settings. The rise in the standard of living allowed the upper middle class to imitate the wealthy upper class and settle outside the city. This gave rise to the romantic ideal of the well-to-do gentleman who comes to town to do business, but whose private life unfolds in 'the open countryside'. The villa park offered the illusion of a pastoral existence, in the necessary vicinity of the city and within the financial limitations of the urban middle class. As they were usually unable to afford two homes, these well-to-do people deserted the city, which increasingly became the abode of the working class. A system of socially homogeneous residential areas emerged, a deliberate choice in the suburban neighbourhoods of exclusive villas.[1]

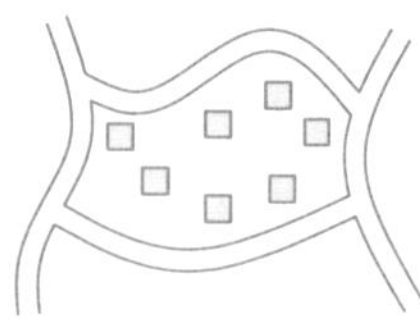

These developments first took place in Great Britain, for many years the only major industrial power in the world. To keep wealthy residents in the city, parks within or on the outskirts of the city were soon developed as a response to the suburban villa parks: exclusive residential areas with large lots and a great deal of greenery, where the proximity of urban amenities compensated the less bucolic setting.

Well-known villa parks around London include such districts as luxurious Hampstead Heath and Bedford Park, the latter initially intended more for the middle class. The rise of the middle class also found expression in the architecture of the new residences. In contrast to the often neoclassical or Gothic Revival monumental country houses of the wealthy upper class, the 'country houses' by architects such as Richard Norman Shaw, William Eden Nesfield, George Devey and Philip Webb were developed in a new style based on rural housing and building traditions. The floor plans they developed were revolutionary as well, and laid the foundations for middle-class suburban housing in the centuries that followed.[2]

Industrialization only began to spread in the Netherlands towards the end of the nineteenth century, whereupon the development of villa parks – often modelled on British examples – accelerated between 1895 and 1914. In the Netherlands, the influx of workers did not result in teeming cities of millions of people; the growth in population was mainly absorbed by smaller cities and towns.[3] Villa parks were created in numerous natural areas in the vicinity of railroads and stations, not too far from city centres.

The great success of the villa parks rapidly drove up land prices. The growing demand could only be met by reducing the size of the lots. As a result, many now-unaffordable villas were demolished after the First World War, so that the subdivision of the parks could be redrawn and the land made available for sale once more.[4] In new residential areas too, the desire to live in the country was constrained by the financial resources of an increasingly numerous but also less wealthy target market. This gentrification of countryside dwelling bears a kinship to the residents of today's leafy suburbs commuting to work in the cities.

Parallel to the development of villa parks, the socialist ideal of dwelling in nature for the lower classes emerged. Stimulated by Ebenezer Howard's *Garden Cities of Tomorrow* (1902) and the garden city movement that followed, several progressive factory owners and major industrialists developed working-class neighbourhoods in green settings, often featuring single-family homes with individual gardens. Some of these 'garden villages' were based on the same structure as the villa parks, except that a 'villa' now usually included more than one dwelling.

1 Jannes De Haan, *Villaparken in Nederland. Een onderzoek aan de hand van het villapark Duin en Daal te Bloemendaal 1897–1940* (Haarlem: Schuyt & Co., 1986), 15–19.

2 Ibid., 73–90.

3 C.S. Kruyt, De verstedelijking van Nederland (Assen: Van Gorcum & Comp. NV, 1961), 10.

4 De Haan, *Villaparken in Nederland*, op. cit. (note 1), 28.

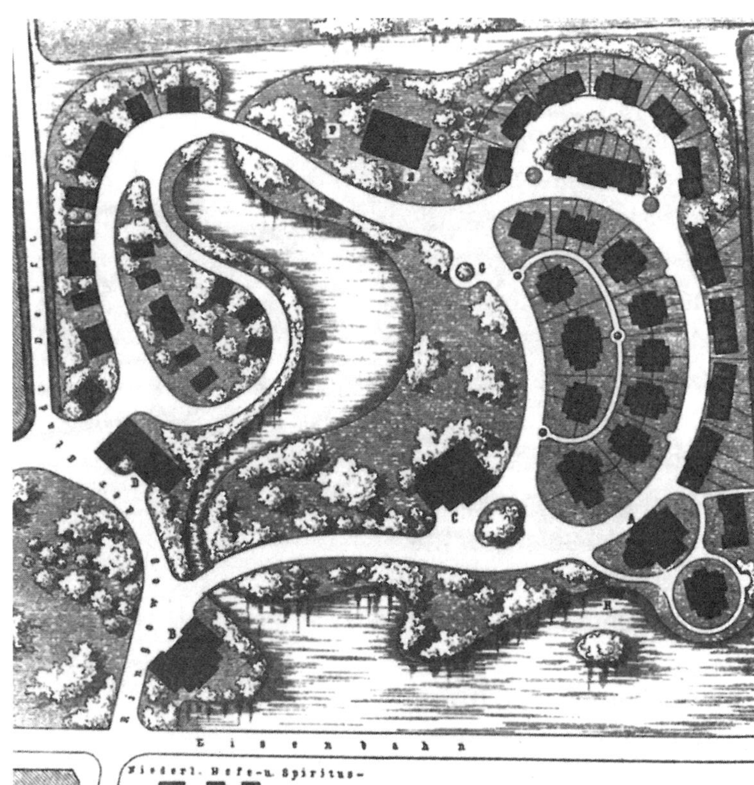

02

01 J.L. Ritter, sales lithograph for the villa park Het Bloemendaalsche Park, 1882
02 L.P. Zocher, Agneta Park, Delft, 1884. Workers' villas with up to four dwellings per volume, in a villa park layout.

03a

VILLA PARK

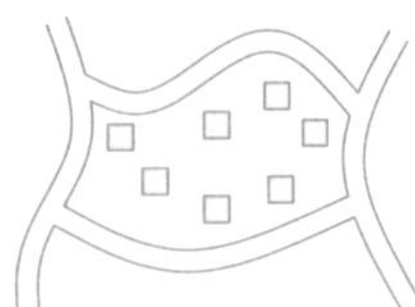

L.A. SPRINGER, DUIN EN DAAL VILLA PARK (BLOEMENDAAL, 1897–1914)

The development and operation of villa parks in and around the town of Bloemendaal is representative of the situation in the Netherlands during the transition from the nineteenth to the twentieth century. The first of these, Het Bloemendaalsche Park, was founded in 1882, just before a major economic recession. As a result it had little initial success and remained for a long time the only villa park in Bloemendaal. Immediately next to it, between the woods of the Bloemendaalsche Bos and the tall dunes, lay the country estate Duin en Daal, 'one of the most picturesque country estates in the whole of the Netherlands, with running water in abundance, consisting of beautiful meadows, alternating with wheat fields, encircled by a semi-circular ring of dunes rising like an amphitheatre, with at the very top a summer house, from which one can see as far as Amsterdam on one side and out to the ships at sea on the other'.[5]
In 1824, the renowned landscape architect J.D. Zocher Jr had transformed the site into an Arcadian scenic park, including a country house, modelled on the English 'Picturesque Movement'. By 1895, its heirs had let the estate fall into disuse, whereupon the specially created property development venture N.V. Binnenlandsche Exploitatie Maatschappij van Onroerende Goederen ('De Binnenlandsche' for short) was able to acquire it in successive purchases in order to develop a villa park. The design was entrusted to the young but already renowned garden architect Leonard Springer.[6]
Springer's most important and most difficult challenge was the access to the area, in order to ensure commercial success, as it was surrounded on all sides by private estates, woodland and sea, as well as by the still less than flourishing villa park Het Bloemendaalsche Park to the southeast. After various negotiations and supplemental acquisitions, Duin en Daal was connected to the roadways of Het Bloemendaalsche Park and, via the Hoge Duin en Daalseweg, to the Overveen train station to the south. To the north, land purchases made it possible to run a link to the Zomerzorgerlaan, so that the area could be accessed from that direction as well. Springer laid new roads in the park, endeavouring to retain as many of Zocher's scenic qualities as possible. Except as a necessary evil for the sale of land lots for villas, he felt that 'roads . . . in a garden or in a park are only necessary to point the visitor toward the finest observation points'. The roads could be slightly curved, so that 'one can see trees, copses from multiple sides and in multiple combinations, and the play of light and shadow can have greater impact', but he was a fierce opponent of having roads and paths meander without reason, purely for the sake of a pastoral style. He had great admiration for the unforced, elegant lines in Zocher's design.[7]
The result was a villa park that did justice to both parts of the term: a charming park landscape containing generously spaced lots for villas. The beauty of this villa park was appreciated by many of its contemporaries, and the sale of lots and the construction of villas proceeded at a rapid pace until the First World War. In the 1960s and 1970s, building density increased dramatically as a result of re-allotment, which eroded the park's original character;[8] however, the central vale has remained unbuilt, and many of the area's buildings are concealed by the abundant vegetation.

5 J.L. Terwen, *Het koningrijk der Nederlanden – voorgesteld in eene reeks van naar de natuur geteekende schilderachtige gezigten, en beschreven door J.L. Terwen* (Gouda, 1858) (reprint: Groningen: Foresta BV, 1979), 76.

6 De Haan, *Villaparken in Nederland*, op. cit. (note 1), 31–35.

7 Ibid., 46–47.

8 Ibid., 48.

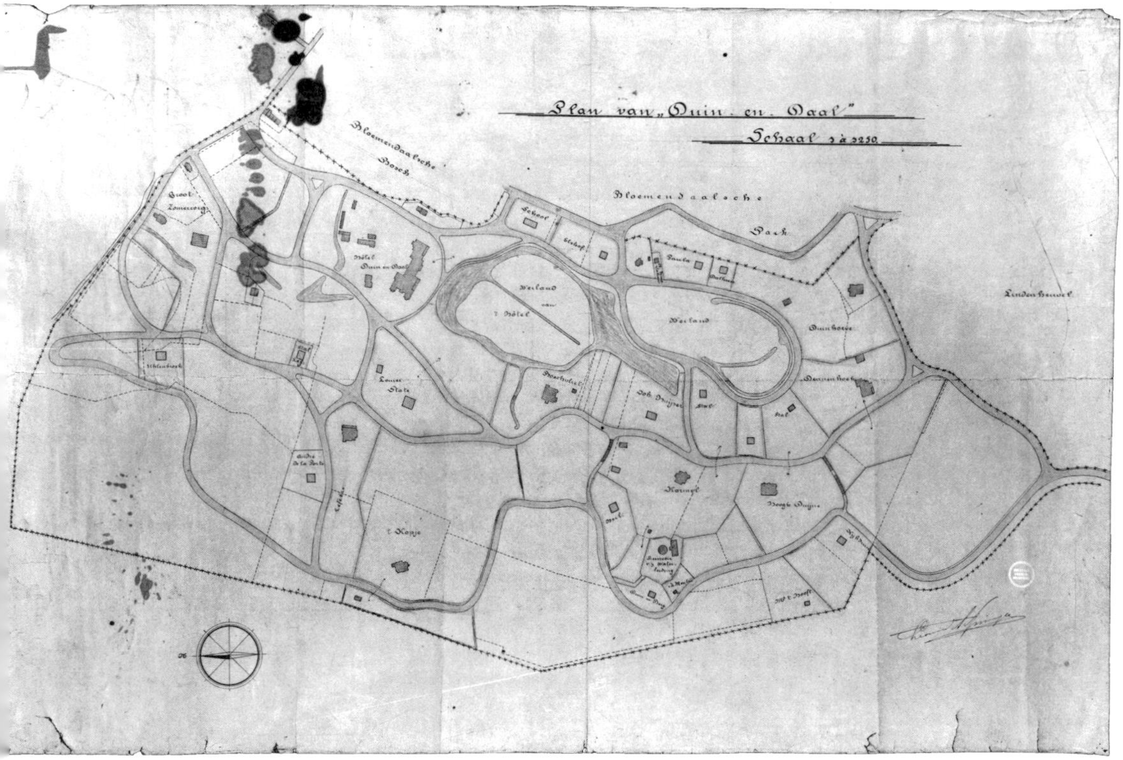

03a The villa park Duin en Daal at the beginning of the twentieth century
03b L.A. Springer, plan for Duin en Daal showing sold lots, circa 1905
03c L.A. Springer, sales lithograph for Zuid-Duin en Daal, 1897. The illustration shows a possible subdivision for villas in the wooded setting. The road with hairpin turns over the tall dunes was never built.

VLUG & PARTNERS, FLORIANDE ISLAND 5 (HOOFDDORP, 2001–2009)

Floriande is a large new-build residential district (a Vinex district, in current Dutch parlance) on the west side of Hoofddorp, consisting among other things of 12 parallel 'islands'. Each of these rectangles of land, bounded by ditches of virtually identical dimensions, has been built up according to an individual type of urban subdivision. The urban design by VLUG & Partners for the ground-level area of Floriande's Island 5 is an interesting illustration of how the ambitions and temptations of an old-fashioned villa park relate to the possibilities and mechanisms of today's economy.

The design brief contained a number of essential and potentially contradictory quality requirements. The site had to be a villa park in which houses would be built free of building standards commission regulation, laid out in imitation of the organic forms and the park-like character of the villa parks in Bloemendaal and Aerdenhout. At the same time, financial considerations dictated as large an area of privately marketable land as possible, meaning as little public space as possible. This had to fit within a rigidly demarcated piece of land of about 7.7 hectares.

The design rests on an avenue planted with native oaks on both sides, providing access to the 66 independent lots of 600 to 1,200 m^2 in a slightly meandering loop. In the narrow area inside the loop is a small park with footpaths and bicycle paths, which together with the trees represents the public green space. To reinforce the visual ambiance of a villa park and to conceal the expected wide diversity in the unregulated architecture of the villas, green amenities have been provided on the privately marketable land as well, in the form of hedges of mixed vegetation along the property lines. Planted embankments shield the lots on the outer sides of the plan area from the adjacent islands. The green amenities on private land were planted in the pre-building phase and are to be maintained by the city for the first five years following the completion of construction.

Originally a residential tower of 10 'stacked villas' was planned in the southwest corner, in which each storey would be considered an independent lot to be developed as buyers saw fit. In the course of the process, however, this was implemented as a regular block of 20 apartments, enabling the plan area as a whole to achieve a density of 11 dwellings per hectare.

VILLA PARK

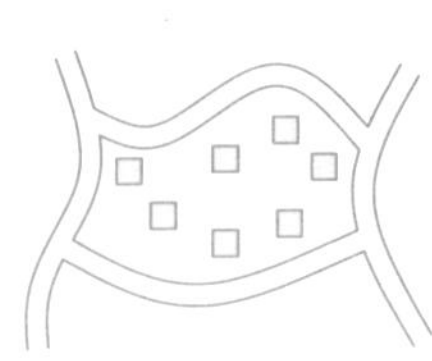

4a

b

04a Development along the Eikenlaan
04b Urban design for Floriande Island 5

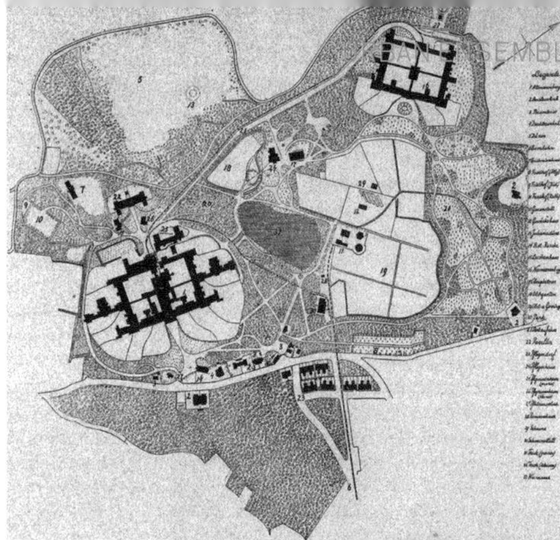

05a

DS LANDSCHAPSARCHITECTEN, BREDERODE PARK (BLOEMENDAAL 2003–)

On the vast site of the former provincial psychiatric hospital on the north side of Bloemendaal, a new villa park is currently under development, designed by DS landschapsarchitecten (dsla). Ever since the construction of the hospital in its corresponding park – both designed by J.D. Zocher Jr – in 1849, the site had been entirely cut off from its surroundings. Over time many outbuildings and extensions were added, as well as a park designed by L.A. Springer, until the care of psychiatric patients was gradually – and in 2002 definitively – relocated elsewhere.
A redevelopment master plan was drawn up, predicated on how the site looked in Zocher's day. The main building was stripped of its later extensions and renovated by Rapp + Rapp into a free-standing edifice (a *buiten*, or Dutch country house) amid greenery, housing 60 luxury apartments. The twentieth-century hospital outbuildings on the rest of the site were removed. Remarkably, the land use plan for redevelopment into a villa park allowed one quarter less built square footage than in the site's pre-redevelopment situation. The land use plan also stipulated requirements in terms of landscape quality, maximum gross building surface area and building heights, but the exact implementation of these were left to be decided during the design phase. In order to reconnect the isolated area with its wider surroundings, dsla has based its design on the landscape characteristics of the different subareas of the site. For instance, the residential area Duinzicht, situated in the east, is grafted onto the park Springer designed here, significant sight lines and trees of which have been rediscovered and reused. The street patterns, with its curved lines, follow Springer's style, while the villas (both detached and semi-detached) are set not along the roadway, but in an autonomous grid, so that each can be approached from a different angle. Despite relatively small lots (300 to 350 m^2) and partly thanks to the tall hedges and replanting of 'Springer trees' from elsewhere on the site, an atmosphere of living in a meandering park has been created.
The design of the residential area Duin en Beek, on the west side of a green, open central core in the publicly accessible park, is based on the special qualities of the dune landscape. From the roadway, wooded banks and the contours of the dunes allow only fragmentary glimpses of the architecture. The vegetation-rimmed lots on either side of a sand flat are positioned so that no view from any property is obstructed by any other buildings. Because the plan here, in contrast to Duinzicht, is for individual development, additional regulations have been put in place in order to vouchsafe a subdued overall look. Swimming pools and summer-houses are not permitted, for instance, and the individual dwellings are being designed in close collaboration with a quality control team. The objective is not the atmosphere of a park of villas, but of living in the dunes.
South of Duin en Beek, on the edge of the dunes behind the old hospital, several apartment complexes are being developed, including one destined for publicly subsidized housing. The plan area as a whole rests on the design of the landscape, much of which was completed prior to the development and sale of the subareas (and prior to the current economic crisis). A great deal of modern-day engineering know-how was needed to preserve existing ecological structures. A vast replanting programme was implemented, new water features excavated, tunnels drilled under ancient root systems for residential wiring and sewers, as well as tunnels to allow toads to safely cross under the new roads. This shows that the development of a villa park, perhaps even more today than in the past, remains an exclusive affair.

VILLA PARK

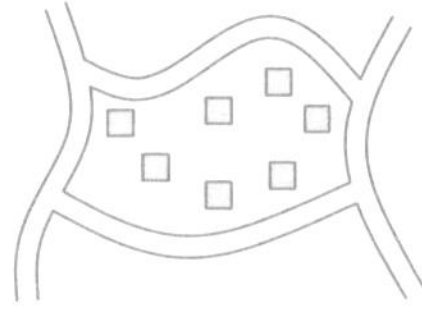

5b

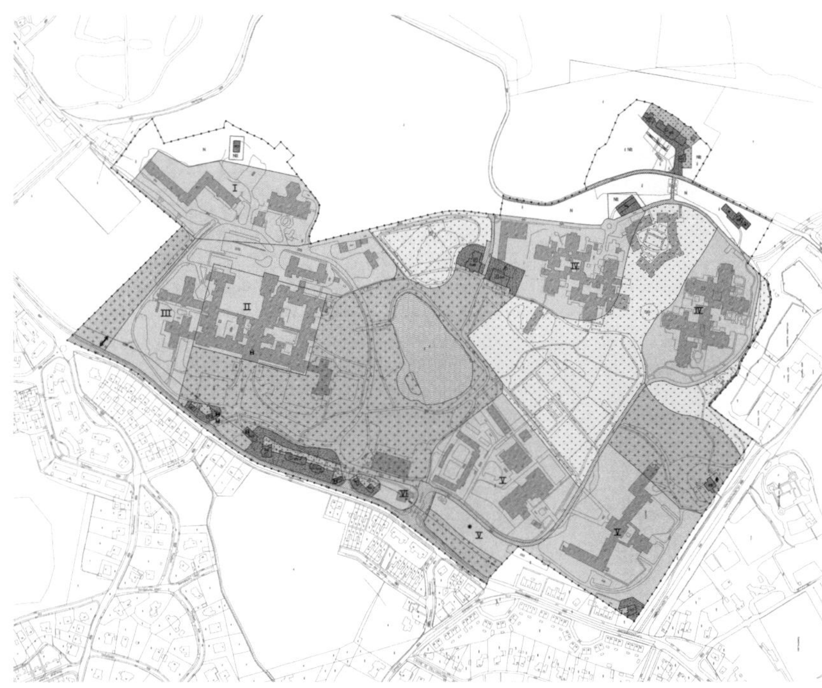

05c

a Plan of Meerenberg,
spital and outbuildings, about
10
b Design for Brederode Park,
luding landscaping, sight
es and various residential
eas
c Meer en Berg land-use
n in 2004

06

RIBBON DEVELOPMENT

One of the earliest forms of built environment consists of detached dwellings set side by side along a roadway or canal. This mode of construction is found along the arterial exit roads of many towns and villages and has often developed as a result of a gradual growth in the local population. New structures are added to the end of the existing series of building, following the line of the road or canal. The newer dwellings are situated further and further away from the (historic) village or town centre with its communal facilities, but on the other hand in an easily accessible, scenic and open setting. Independent control over one's own dwelling is coupled with the company of neighbours and a collective interest in the maintenance and use of the access road.
The natural, unplanned way this type of built environment develops means it can be found in diverse regions virtually across the entire world. At the same time, it is seldom employed as a planning strategy for the development of new residential areas.

During the reconstruction period in Europe in the wake of the Second World War, when many new residential districts were built and old residential districts modernized, both with limited economic resources, the existing ribbon developments attracted a great deal of criticism. The rather inefficient organization of far-flung, single-orientation buildings made the construction of roads, sewers and cabling for electricity and television much more costly than in compactly designed residential areas.
Since then, many existing ribbon developments have become part of the characteristic heritage of village and town conservation areas. As a result, while they are not part of an active strategy for design, they are an element of the urban design preconditions within which any new design must be created.

06 Characteristic ribbon development in the Krimpenerwaard area of South Holland

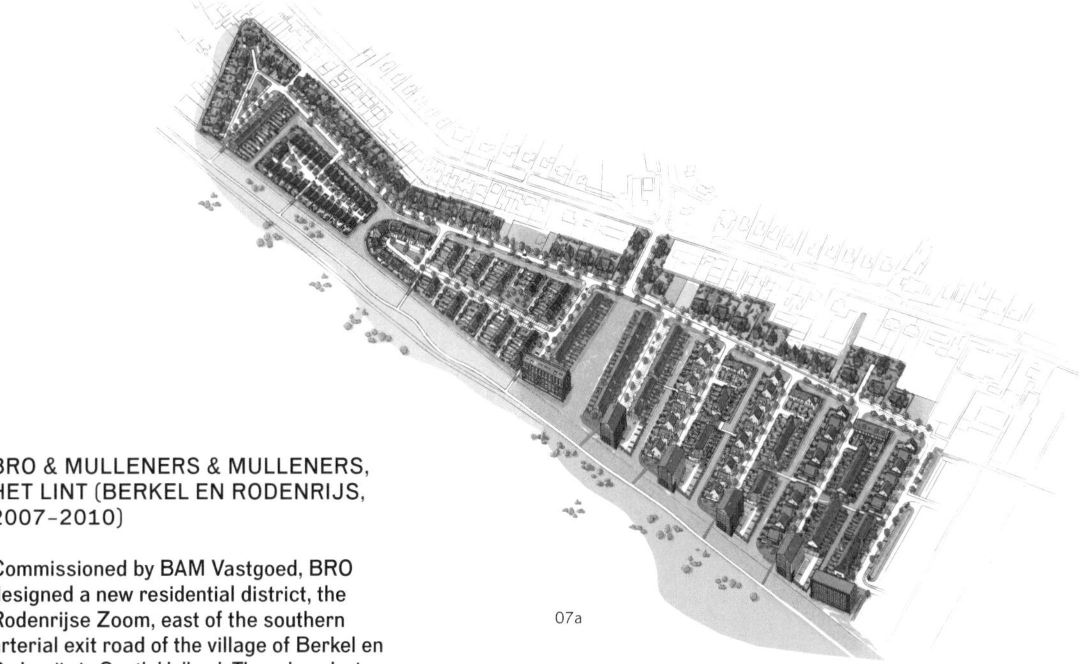

07a

BRO & MULLENERS & MULLENERS, HET LINT (BERKEL EN RODENRIJS, 2007–2010)

Commissioned by BAM Vastgoed, BRO designed a new residential district, the Rodenrijse Zoom, east of the southern arterial exit road of the village of Berkel en Rodenrijs in South Holland. The urban design was partly based on two aspects of the area's history: the system of waterways that typifies the old polders of Berkel en Rodenrijs, and the village's ribbon development.
Berkel en Rodenrijs was settled in the eleventh century when the marshy soil was made suitable for farming by digging small drainage ditches. By the fifteenth century, when continuing subsidence had once again made the soil too wet, the inhabitants switched to cutting peat, which caused the settlement, over time, to grow into a ribbon village lining several roads amid excavated expanses of water. In the eighteenth century the peat ran out and the land was drained to form polders. Since its designation as a site for new development (Vinex district) at the end of the twentieth century the village has undergone explosive growth, of which the Rodenrijse Zoom is a part.
The urban design consists of several residential islands of varying shapes and sizes, separated by ditches that are a reference to the old polder landscape. Each of the islands has been filled in by a different architect, to create a suggestion of gradual, historic growth. The connection of the islands to the village was resolved by laying out a narrow strip of ribbon-development structures parallel to the existing ribbon development along the Rodenrijseweg. The sub-plan Het Lint ('the ribbon') is filled in with 30 semi-detached dwellings and nine detached villas designed by Mulleners & Mulleners. The homes, following the wishes of the client, are traditional in appearance, with an alternation of basic-gable and cross-gable roofs and brickwork that fits in with that of existing buildings.

07b

07a Bird's-eye view of new development in the Rodenrijse Zoom, showing the sub-plan Het Lint along the top, parallel to the existing ribbon development along the Rodenrijseweg
07b New houses in Het Lint

PERIMETER BLOCK

The perimeter block is characteristic of the classic European city as it developed during and after the Middle Ages. Its essential feature is a continuous line of buildings along every side of the city block. The outer side of these buildings therefore defines the streets and public spaces, while the open space inside the block is shielded from the activity of the city. Originally made up of linked row houses, the same structure was later filled by stacked housing as well.
Although perimeter blocks are part of virtually every European city, clear differences exist among them. For instance, in many cities outside the Netherlands, starting in the eighteenth century, apartment complexes were built around small inner courtyards, linked to form a block containing many small light yards. The access to each block takes place through these courtyards, as collective transitional zones between the city and the dwelling. In the Netherlands, the block continued to develop out of ground-connected row houses, each individually accessed from the street and featuring a private garden in the sheltered inner area. On the street side, the dwellings are concealed behind a formal façade, while on the garden side a simpler and less formal façade mediates access to the garden or balconies. From the outset, therefore, the dimensions of the blocks and the transition from private to public in the Netherlands have been substantially different from those in neighbouring countries.
Significant issues with the perimeter block centre on the orientation of the dwellings and the solutions for corners. The dwellings do not all receive equal sun exposure, a problem that is exacerbated in the corners. Moreover, the corner dwellings have little if any communication with the inner domain, let alone an exterior space in the sun. The issue of the corner and poor sun exposure led, at the start of the twentieth century, to the opening up of the block in favour of an urban design more focused on the quality of the dwelling: the open or semi-open block and parallel line development (see below).
In the 1980s, at the second Berlin International Building Exhibition, architect Rob Krier led a reintroduction of the perimeter block. Spaciously proportioned 'urban villas' around semi-public inner courtyards were used to redefine the city street as a response to the open subdivision of the modern period. The corners accommodated vertical access channels and well-conceived apartments. This led to a revival of the perimeter block throughout Europe.
Another development in the perimeter block was the opening of the inner area to collective and even public use. The entrances to dwellings can be relocated here and the original rear façades can become formal front façades around a courtyard, a domain shielded by buildings, quiet and free of cars. Because the street side is also a public side, the dwellings have two front façades, as it were, with all that this implies in terms of use and privacy. This forces a re-examination, in every project, of the relationship between the quality of the dwelling and the quality of the city, and by extension the relationship between private, collective and public areas.

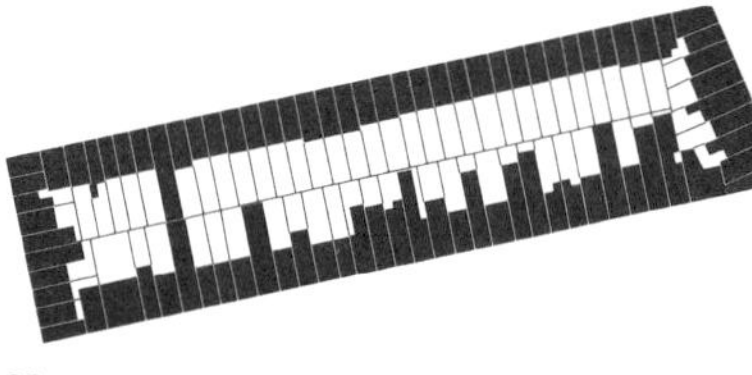

08a

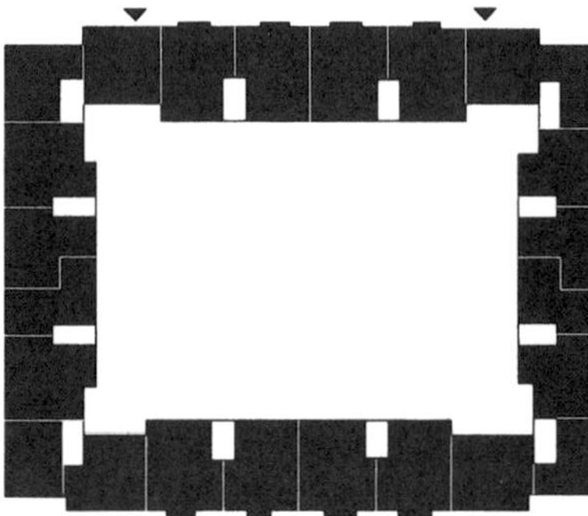

08b

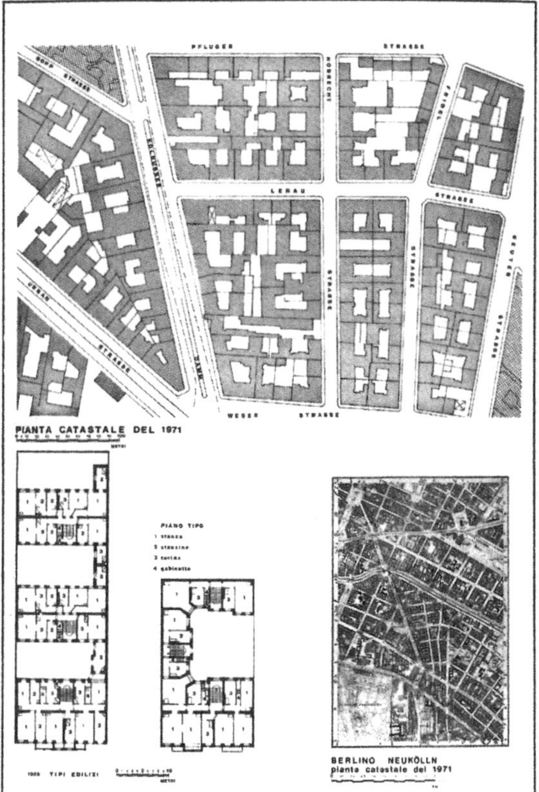

08c

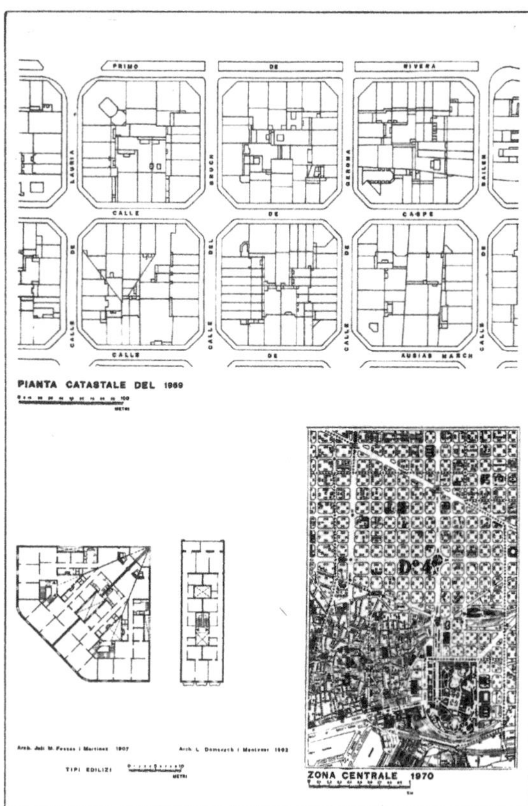

08d

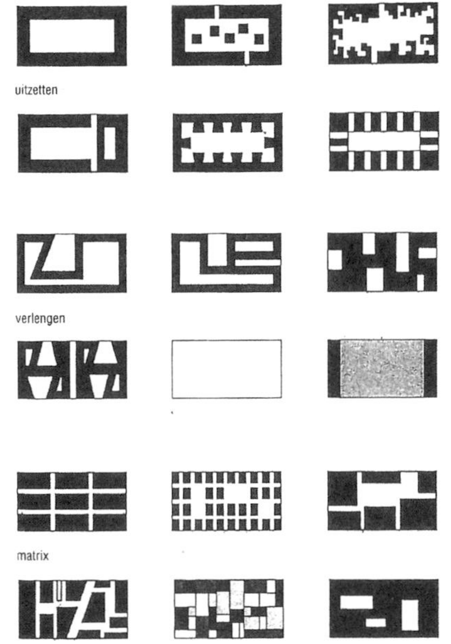

08e

08a Schematic plan of a traditional Dutch city block, made up of individual row houses
08b Schematic plan of a traditional German city block, made up of apartment buildings with clustered entrances
08c City blocks in Berlin
08d City blocks in Barcelona
08e Diagram of the various ways the city blocks on Haveneiland (Harbour Island) have been filled, Amsterdam-IJburg, 1999–

09a

09b

09a View of the 'Golden Bend' (*Gouden Bocht*) of the Herengracht by Gerrit Adriaansz. Berkheyde, 1672. The individual uses of space in the separate lots of the perimeter block can easily be seen.
09b Detail of the city map of Amsterdam by Balthasar Florisz. van Berckenrode, 1625.
The division between the representative façades on the street sides and the quiet world of private gardens inside the perimeter blocks is clearly visible.

HERENGRACHT-KEIZERSGRACHT BLOCK (AMSTERDAM 1614-1625)

The traditional Dutch perimeter block is characterized by a continuous line of connected individual houses that together define the four sides of an area of land in a city or town. Each dwelling has its front door directly on the street, so that the public portion of daily life takes place on the outer side of the block. Together, the dwellings form the separation between the public side and the inner domain, to which, in principle, only their occupants have access. Various perimeter blocks together define the street pattern of the city.
This model can be found in many places in the world in organically evolved medieval inner cities, where the internal areas, due to a shortage of space, were gradually built up to the point of saturation. In the 1614 expansion of Amsterdam, the model, as a deliberately applied urban building element, was part of the biggest new-build operation of its time: the *Grachtengordel*, the city's now-famed ring of inner canals. This plan, conceived on a highly rational basis, is also seen as an adaptation of Simon Stevin's ideal urban model, published around the same time – a rational, orthogonal grid of streets and perimeter blocks – to the semicircular layout of Amsterdam.
Several parallel canals were dug around the old city centre to form a direct connection to the IJ waterway: the city's expansion plan was directed at merchants and tradesmen whose stores or workshops were part of their homes, and the main form of transport was over water. The canals were interlinked at strategic points. For the efficient transfer of goods, quays and streets were built along all the canals, interconnected by cross-streets as well. The rectangular plots of land left over were divided into lots and sold to accommodate housing. The lots directly on the canals were intended for wealthier merchants and were larger than the lots lining the side streets, where more modest tradesmen opened their shops. In some places, the distance between two canals was enough to lay an additional back street between two blocks, again accommodating smaller lots. This is where the mews were originally located. In order to sell as many lots as possible, those on the canals were made narrow and deep. In virtually all cases, the idea was to build up the street side, concealing long, narrow gardens behind the line of buildings. By buying several contiguous lots, a prosperous merchant could have a wider and more imposing residence built, with a wider area at the back. To this day, these green inner domains of the blocks remain hidden from passers-by.

PERIMETER BLOCK

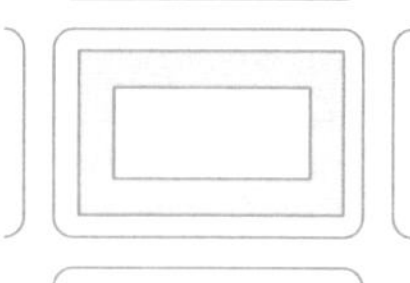

10a

10b

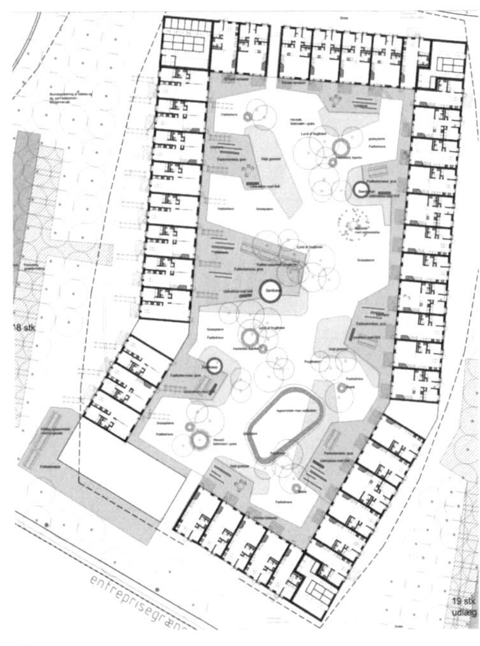

10c

10a Communal inner area, viewed from the low side
10b Outer façade on the high side
10c Plan of Lange Eng with a designed, communal use of the inner area

DORTE MANDRUP, LANGE ENG (ALBERTSLUND, DENMARK, 2009)

A modern-day example of a perimeter block in an entirely different setting is the Lange Eng project by Danish architect Dorte Mandrup in Albertslund, a suburb of Copenhagen. The project is part of Herstedlund, a new scenic residential area under development, consisting of eight egg-shaped sites for different types of residential construction in a newly planted forest. One of these sites was purchased by a collective of private clients, who asked Mandrup to design a collective residential building of 54 self-contained dwellings with a number of communal functions and a collectively shared exterior space.
The basic configuration of the building is a perimeter block that takes up virtually the entire building site. The building slopes from two storeys on the east side to three on the west side and follows the direction of the site with a bend, so that the volume, standing free among the trees, presents a different appearance from each side. The continuous building shell shields a large inner domain from the public domain of the woodland park. Except for a narrow band of private patios along the inner façade, the entire inner area has been laid out as a communal garden, with sandboxes, playground equipment, benches, outdoor cooking facilities and communal picnic tables, imbedded in a landscape of fruit trees, vegetable and herb gardens and lawns.
The perimeter block is not actually closed: the inner area is directly accessible from the outside through various portals. The dwellings, of eight types in all, can all be accessed from the outside as well as the inside of the block. The lower sections of the block contain maisonettes; the taller sections contain apartments on the ground floor with maisonettes above. These upper dwellings are accessible through outside staircases on the inner and outer façades that stick out diagonally from the façades and seem to anchor the building to the ground. The corners of the building accommodate collective functions, like a communal area, storage facilities and guest quarters.

PERIMETER BLOCK

11a

SEMI-OPEN BLOCK

The semi-open block is an adaptation of the perimeter block, in which the sheltered nature of the inner domain is sacrificed by eliminating one of the four sides or by positioning the different sides separate from one another. The missing side is usually oriented towards the sun or an adjacent urban space. The loss of privacy in the inner area is balanced by better views and better sun exposure for the three remaining sides. The inner domain is more easily accessible than in a perimeter block, which can provide the impetus to create a collective or semi-public garden here, possibly flanked by smaller private gardens behind the ground-floor dwellings. At the extremities of the U-shaped volume, instead of the problematic corner dwellings of the perimeter block, triple-orientation end dwellings are created.

The semi-open block came out of the search by architects in the 1920s and 1930s for new alternatives to the often small, dark and stuffy working-class dwellings of the inner cities. The standard urban structure of shallow perimeter blocks in working-class residential areas left at least one side with poor sun exposure, while the quality of dwelling in or near the corners left even more to be desired. The semi-open block does not present these issues: either not all of its sides are built up, or it is transected in order to avoid poor orientation in problematic corners. At the same time, its configuration lends itself to the same overall urban layout as the perimeter block.

11b

11c

VAN DEN BROEK & BAKEMA, DE EENDRACHT (ROTTERDAM, 1934)

W.G. Witteveen's 1931 urban expansion plan for the north and northwest parts of Rotterdam called for a symmetrical pattern of perimeter blocks on either side of the Statenweg. One of these blocks was designed by the firm of Van den Broek & Bakema, who were active in international debates on the improvement of housing conditions of the period. They developed a variant on the perimeter block in which only three sides of the block are built up and are separated from one another, so that the plan features no corner dwellings. The unbuilt side is situated to the southwest and – given that an ideal orientation in relation to sun exposure was not feasible within the urban design parameters – focused on the Vroesenpark located in that direction.
The structure consists of a half-sunken basement with storage spaces and covered laundry and play areas, supporting three storeys of apartments. As a result, none of the apartments has a direct connection to the inner area, which is designed as a collective garden. Each dwelling does have a balcony that looks out onto the inner garden and the Vroesenpark beyond it. Along the Statenweg the fully built side of the block fits into the symmetry of the urban ensemble. The apartments are accessed two by two through entrances and stairs, discernable in the outer façade as fully glazed vertical elements that divide the block into segments. These stairs also provide access to the basement and from there to the inner domain, which is not publicly accessible; a fence along the open side on the Vroesenlaan makes it clear that the inner area is spatially, but not functionally, connected with the park.

11a Situation, with underneath the suggestion for a whole series of open blocks along the park; only one was implemented in this way.
11b De Eendracht housing block, see from the Vroesenpark
11c The cross section shows the relationship between the dwellings and the communal inner garden, accessible through the basement.

12a

SEMI-OPEN BLOCK

BATAVIA BUILDING, FRITS VAN DONGEN (AMSTERDAM, 2000)

On a former railroad yard in Amsterdam's Eastern Harbour District, a U-shaped residential complex was designed whose open side looks out onto the Entrepothaven harbour. The U consists of a continuous sequence of buildings in which a great diversity in dwelling types has been achieved. Access to these dwellings varies from entrances and stairs to galleries and corridors. Large access staircasees are situated at the corners of the building, providing a welcoming entrance to the corridors and galleries; from inside, these work as windows onto the city, while at night they serve, conversely, as an urban lighting element.
A half-sunken car park is located under the building. Its wooden roof also forms the surface of the raised inner courtyard. This is where the private terraces of the lower dwellings are located, as well as a garden with trees, which serves as an ornamental garden for the apartments on the upper floors. These feature a conservatory as exterior space, which also serves as a sound buffer; the wooden folding panels of the conservatory can be opened fully. A fence separates the open side of the block from the publicly accessible pedestrian area along the water of the harbour.

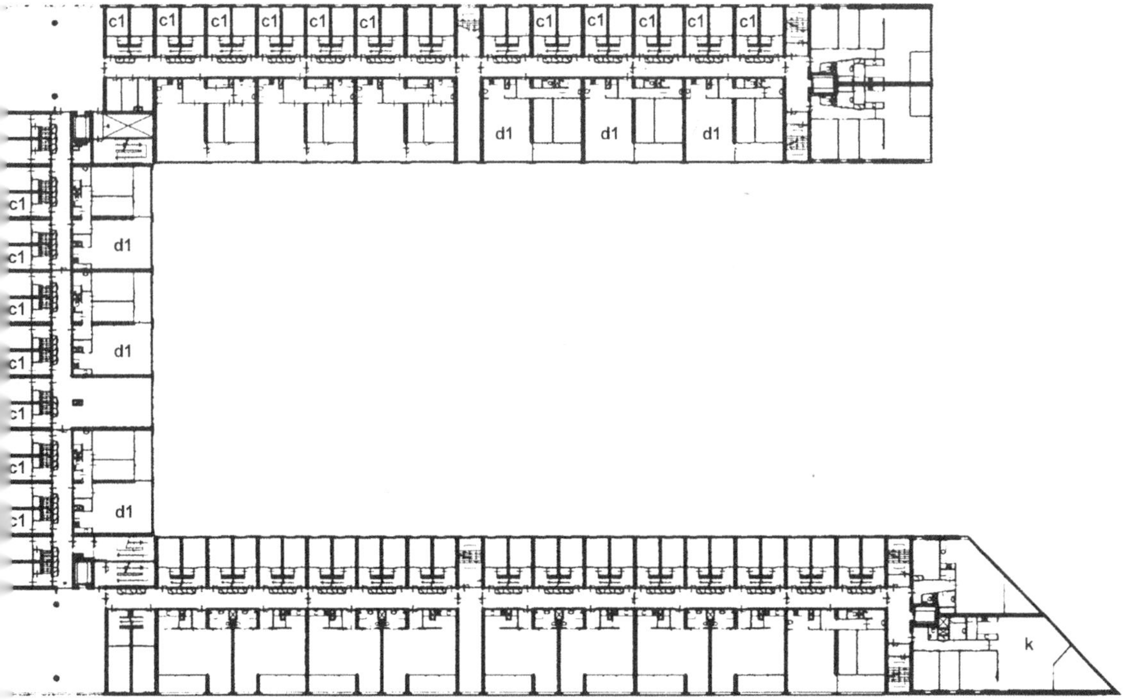

12b

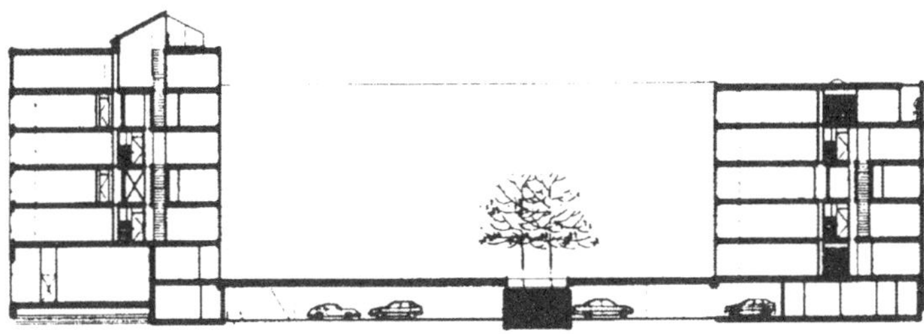

12c

12a The open side of the block, seen from the opposite bank of the water
12b Floor plan of the ground level, with the open corners
12c Transverse cross section showing parking garage and the garden deck

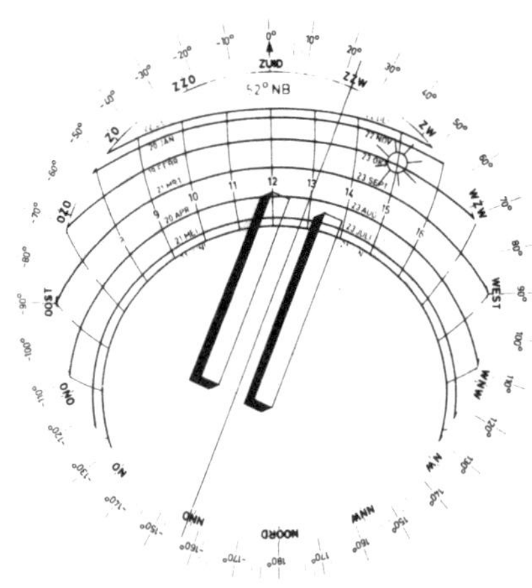

13b

13a Schematic plan of the Praunheim residential area, Frankfurt (1927). Open-block subdivision by E. May in two separate directions.
13b E. May and W. Schwagenscheidt, schematic plan for an ideal orientation of the open block

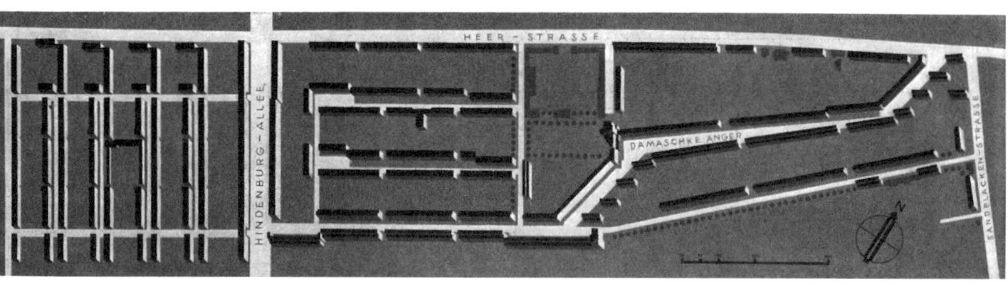

13a

OPEN BLOCK

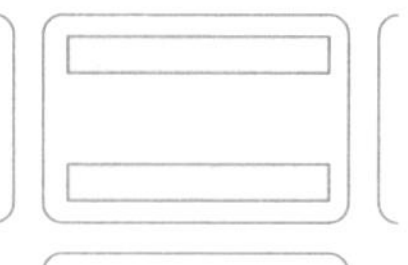

In the 1920s and 1930s, architects associated with the Congrès Internationaux d'Architecture Moderne (CIAM) developed alternatives to traditional urban design in perimeter blocks. The challenge of creating mass-scale public housing and the control of urban problems formed the driving force behind a grand quest for new ways of building high-quality, affordable dwellings based on rational principles.
The architects and urban planners involved in the expansion plans for Frankfurt under the Weimar Republic (1918–1933) came up with very definite ideas to meet this challenge. The group centred round Ernst May considered the orientation to the sun to be of the most crucial significance for housing quality. This was not so much a case of sunbathing in the garden as of the general health benefits that would come from sunlight penetrating directly into the habitation spaces. The perimeter block defined by the urban space, with its dark corners and inherent orientation issues, was dismissed to make way for a subdivision focused on the quality of the dwelling.[9]
A vital step in this direction was the development of the open block. In this, dwellings are positioned in two parallel terraces or slabs facing each other. Both are set on the edges of the city block and define the public space on the street side. At the back, an informal rear façade flanks a more privately situated zone with individual exterior spaces. The two remaining sides of the block are open, which gives the configuration its name. For optimal sun exposure, it was calculated that the best orientation for the open block could be achieved with a rotation of 22.5° (clockwise) from the north-south axis to a northeast-southwest axis. When the average number of active hours per day is balanced against the number of hours of daylight, this allows both of the dwelling spaces facing each other to receive equal, maximum sun exposure.

9 For a detailed study of the opening up of the traditional urban block into an open subdivision, see also Jean Castex, Jean-Charles Depaule and Philippe Panerai, *Urban Forms: The Death and Life of the Urban Block* (Oxford: Architectural Press, 2004), original French edition: *Formes Urbaines, de l'îlot à la barre* (Marseille: Parenthèses, 1977).

14a

14b

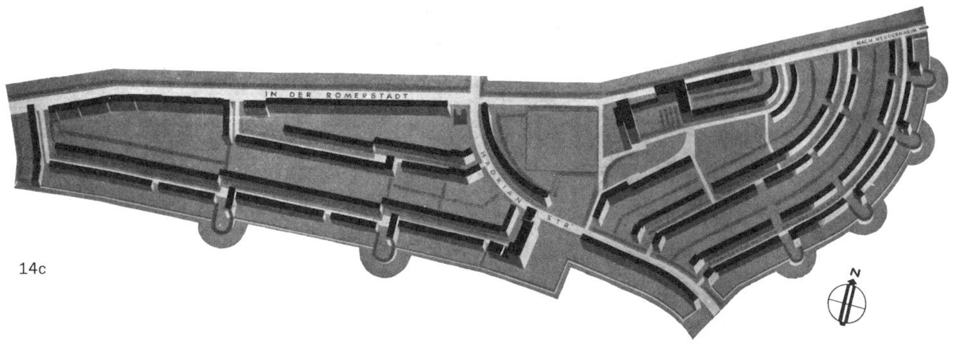

14c

ERNST MAY, RÖMERSTADT (FRANKFURT, 1927)

One of the first and most convincing examples of the new, open configuration of city blocks in the early twentieth century is the Römerstadt area in the new expansion districts of Frankfurt am Main dubbed *Das Neue Frankfurt*. Architects and urban planners came from all over the world to see the developments Ernst May and his associates had achieved here. What makes Römerstadt different from other new areas like Praunheim and Westhausen, which display a purer or perhaps more radical implementation of modernist principles, is the way the residential area fits into the relief of the existing landscape. Römerstadt, named after a nearby Roman archaeological site, lies curved on gently sloping hills along the Nidda River. The street pattern follows these slopes, creating a curved subdivision that was subsequently filled in with a structure of open blocks. The hillside location affords the top floor of every dwelling a view of the Nidda Valley over the dwellings situated lower down. Crossing these curved streets, radiating footpaths lead to observation points at the edges of the residential area, each marked by a block of flats. The area is divided in two by a larger main road, flanked by gracefully curving apartment buildings.

Ideal orientation towards the sun, prescribed by the designers themselves, was thus subordinated here to the positioning in the landscape. As a result, the dwellings on opposite sides of the streets were designed differently: the dwellings on the south side are oriented towards their back gardens and feature only a small entrance zone, demarcated by a little wall, on the street side. The dwellings on the north side have larger front gardens, which are elevated above the street thanks to subtle differences in height. A richly varied dwelling environment was created with relatively modest means, employing systematic application and repetition to arrive at a composition full of subtlety and diversity.

14a Bird's-eye view of Römerstadt around 1930; the Praunheim residential area is in the background.
14b Street view in 2010: the various connections to the north and south sides of the street
14c Plan of the Römerstadt residential area

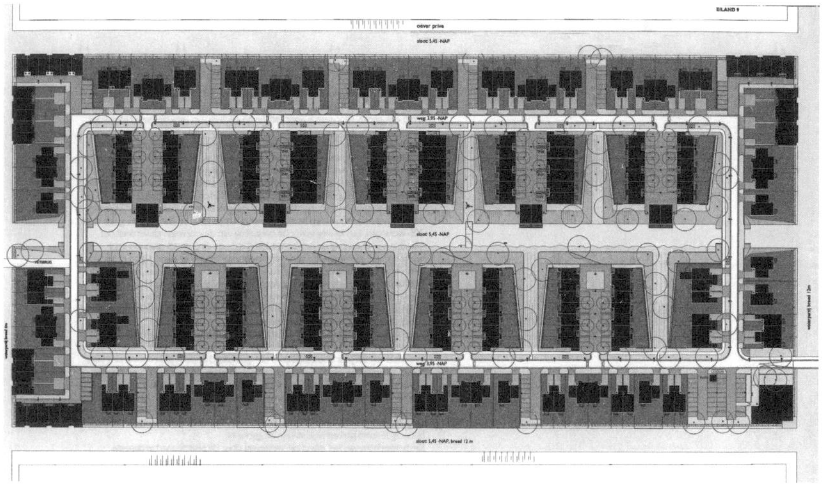

15a

15b

15a Plan
15b The collective inner area

HEREN 5 ARCHITECTEN, DE COLLECTIEVE TUIN (HOOFDDORP, 2002)

The Vinex district of Floriande, west of Hoofddorp, consists among other things of 12 parallel rectangular 'islands' separated by ditches, each with its own urban design. Heren 5 Architecten's plan for Island 8 was named De Collectieve Tuin ('the collective garden'), immediately signalling that the designers had concentrated on the communal use of the exterior space. Its clear layout consists of a rectangular ring road leaving a strip of land on the outside where boundary structures are organized in small volumes. The focus, however, is on the inner side of the ring road, where the communal green space is located. Here, a repetition of virtually identical open blocks has been arrayed, each grouped around its own car park and with its outer sides situated in an area of open greenery. Seen from the road, the car parks and bands of green space alternate. They both afford a view of a connecting greenbelt along the open side of the blocks, where a wide ditch splits the island in two. The blocks are set at staggered intervals on either side of the ditch, so that from a car park you have a view of the band of green space on the opposite side. In the bands of green space, tapering zones of private terraces afford all the residents a view of the central garden. Between the terraces, a sunken green playing field runs down to the open central zone along the ditch. The end of each northerly blocks is bordered by a free-standing little block of flats with broad balconies facing the green space to its south; in principle, therefore, this is really more a semi-open block configuration.

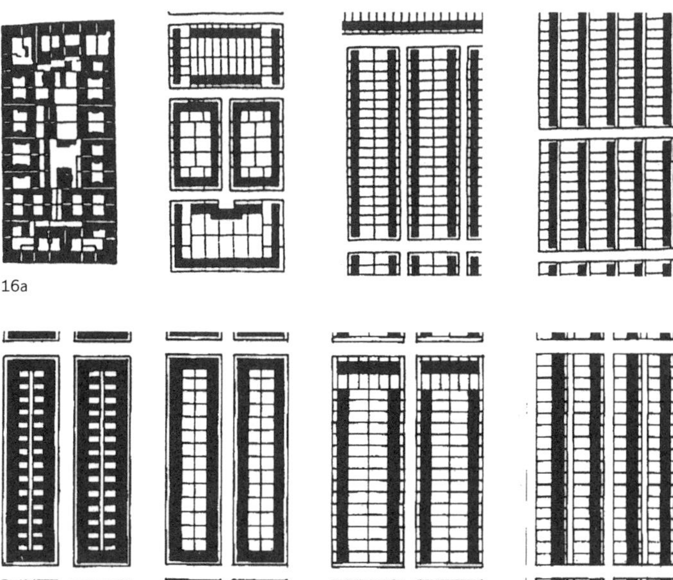

16a

16b

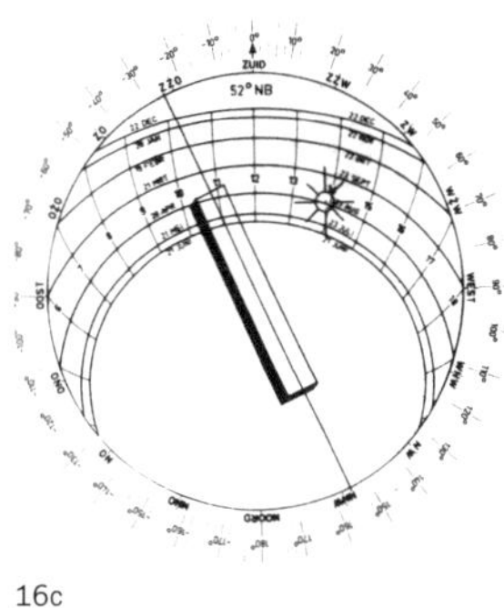

16c

The next stage in the optimization of dwelling orientation was the development of a configuration in parallel lines. This represented a definitive abandonment of the block as an organizational entity to mediate between the private and the public, and the premise became the ideal situation of each dwelling. The rows or slabs of parallel-linked dwellings no longer face one another in mirror formations, as in the configuration of the open block, but are equally spaced one behind the other, all with the same orientation.
Ernst May and Walter Schwagenscheidt calculated an ideal orientation for this configuration as well, this time 22.5° in the other direction, on a northwest-southeast axis. The habitation spaces of all the dwellings face the afternoon sun in the southwest, while the service spaces, and often the entrances as well, are housed in the northeast-facing zones. In principle, every row is approached from the same side. This has major implications for the organization of the block: there is no longer an inner area shielded from the street, where the exterior spaces of the dwellings occupy a private domain. The private side of one row flanks the public access way of the next, in a configuration than can be repeated endlessly according to rational principles. As a result, this optimization of the dwelling turned the traditional organization of the city on its head and introduced new issues of privacy. Many variants have been developed and implemented since, bringing some nuance into the open-row subdivision of parallel lines, from secondary access paths to mixed forms incorporating open and perimeter blocks, in order to reconcile the ideal of the optimally oriented dwelling with the quality of the public space and the need for privacy.

16a Schematic representation of the evolution from the perimeter block to a subdivision in open rows, according to E. May
16b Application of E. May's schematics to the Dutch city block, according to M. Risselada
16c E. May and W. Schwagenscheidt, schematic plan for an ideal orientation of parallel-line development

17a

17c

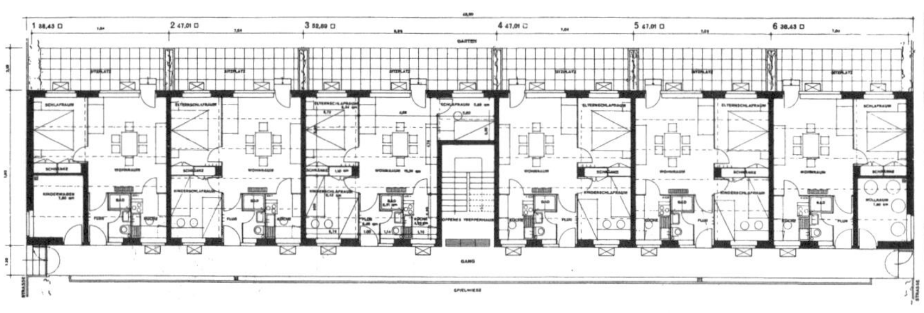

17b

17a Plan of the residential area
17b Plan of a block with six dwellings and a circulation corridor
17c Bird's-eye view of Westhausen in 1932; some of the high-rises have not yet been built.

SUN ORIENTED PARALLEL ROWS

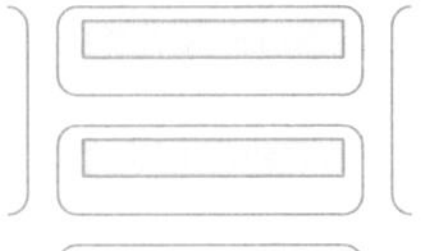

ERNST MAY, SIEDLUNG WESTHAUSEN (FRANKFURT, 1929)

Following the successful application of the new urban design principles of open blocks in places like Praunheim and Römerstadt, the designers around Ernst May dared to implement an even more radical break with classical urban design. An opportunity presented itself in the development of the Westhausen residential area, also northwest of Frankfurt. Here, a configuration could be designed based on a theory and calculation of ideal orientation, to give all dwellings maximum sun exposure.
A revolutionary innovation for the time was to separate the dwellings from the street pattern; in the traditional city these had been closely linked – and still were, even in open-block configurations. In Westhausen the rows of dwellings are perpendicular to the streets, and they are accessed by a new, independent layer of footpaths and open spaces. For reasons of economy and efficiency, every row of dwellings was built in an identical way. The urban design unity now consisted of a row of seven dwellings with an access path and public green space on the northeast side and private gardens on the southwest side, as well as identical floor plans, in mirrored pairs and always with southwest-facing living rooms. This configuration could now be repeated ad infinitum within a framework of perpendicular access roads, without any loss of quality for the individual dwellings.
In Westhausen, the district consists of seven groups of nine of these rows, accessed by four perpendicular streets. The pattern of rows is situated on a slight incline, which led to two dwellings to be set higher in each row. In the middle, green zones run perpendicular to the rows between two access roads. The district is bordered by a composition of taller buildings, set at right angles to the parallel line development pattern. The composition, differences in height and refined detailing at the smaller scale ensure that the district, in spite of its high degree of repetition, seems less rigid and has remained popular with residents.

18a

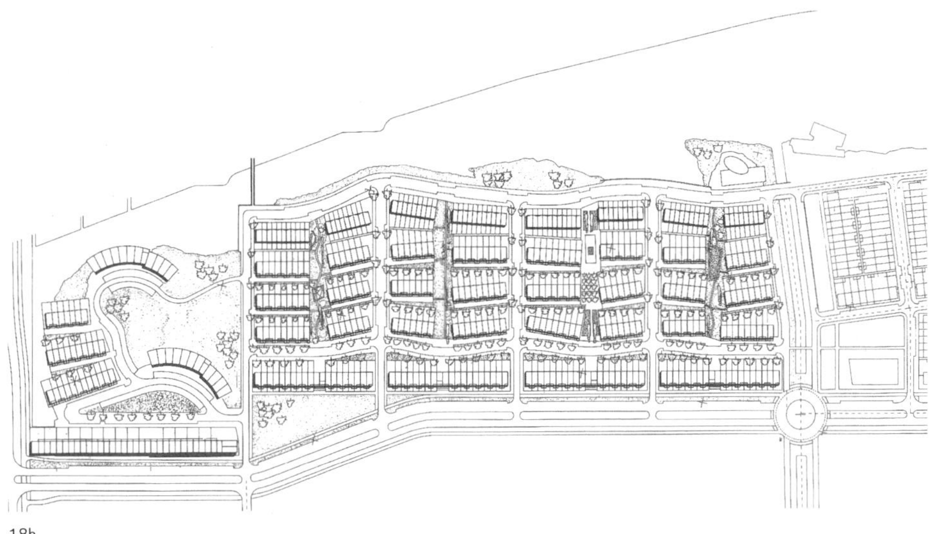

18b

SUN ORIENTED PARALLEL ROWS

MECANOO, RINGVAARTPLASBUURT-OOST (ROTTERDAM-PRINSENLAND, 1993)

For a new residential neighbourhood in the Prinsenland area of Rotterdam, Mecanoo faced the challenge of designing 550 more or less identical dwellings with enough variations and differences to stimulate a sense of community. The solution chosen shows a clear affinity with the garden cities of the early modernist era, Siedlung Westhausen in particular, transplanted to the soil of a Dutch polder. Four slabs of six storeys shield the neighbourhood from the major arterial road running alongside. Between the slabs, six streets divide the neighbourhood into more or less equal areas of land, in which short rows of dwellings have been set perpendicular to the streets. The rows seem to vary in length at random and are slightly rotated in relation to one another, creating a playful variety of directions and intermediate areas. Each of the four sections features a communal green zone as a collective garden in its centre, between two streets; each collective garden has its own planting theme: French, Dutch, Japanese and English. These gardens connect the neighbourhood visually with the Ringvaartplas lake situated to its south.

19 The ideal of a free-standing building rendered in Le Corbusier's sketch for the Unité d'habitation

FREE-STANDING OBJECTS

A different answer to the pollution and poor living conditions of the traditional inner city was significantly influenced, at the beginning of the twentieth century, by Le Corbusier's ideas for the *Cité Radieuse*. With his Unités d'Habitation, but also in urban plans for cities like Paris and Saint-Dié, he championed an urban design involving tall residential buildings set as free-standing volumes in a green environment. In this, dwellings are elevated above the traffic noise and abundantly provided with light and views, while the ground level is left free for parking and other open-air facilities. Although his ideological plans called for a repetition of such volumes in an immense open area, the projects that were implemented were built as single free-standing volumes, often in an urban setting.

The free-standing volume in the form of a slab or tower, in an urban context, often also leaves more room at the public ground level than an open or perimeter block configuration. This urban space can be put to use as a park or square with public facilities. If no other solution is provided, however, this space quickly clogs up as a sorely needed car park. Other benefits of the free-standing object include dwellings well-supplied with natural light and situated away from city noise, as well as the high density that can be achieved.

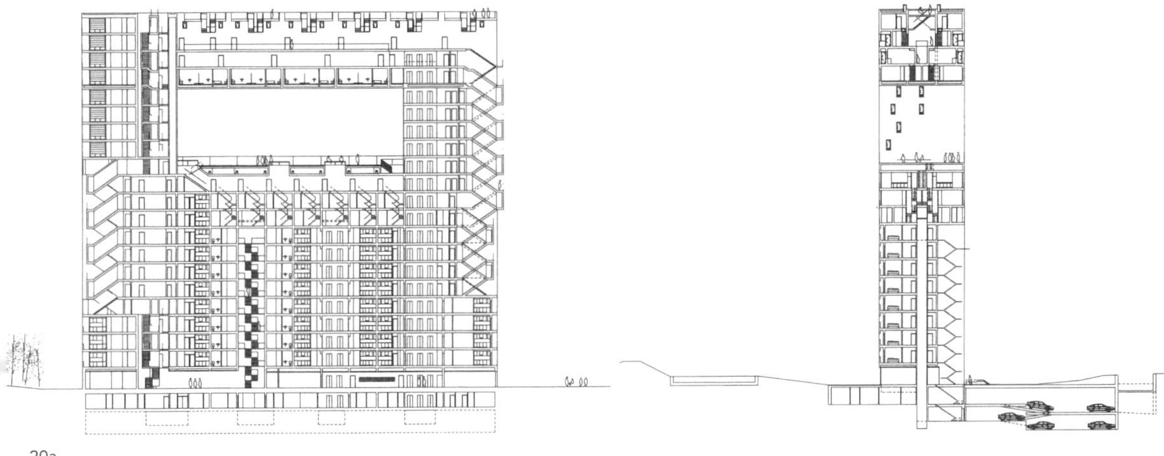

20a

20b

MVRDV & BLANCA LLEÓ, MIRADOR, SANCHINARRO (MADRID, 2005)

In a suburb northeast of Madrid, MVRDV and Blanca Lleó designed a tall and striking residential building as a response to the monotonous housing blocks of this area. For its architects, the building was also meant as a beacon for the new expansion districts, visible from the arterial roads leading out of Madrid. Instead of a perimeter-block structure, a vertical slab of 22 storeys was chosen, with a huge opening cut into it at a height of 40 m. With a little imagination, it can be seen as a perimeter block set on its side. A plaza in the opening, accessible to all occupants, affords panoramic views of the surrounding area and the mountains further on. The building houses 165 apartments, grouped in various sizes and types in separately identifiable, smaller building sections. As a result, the edifice seems to be literally made up of a stack of smaller buildings, linked around the elevated communal plaza.

21a

21b

21c

FREE COMPOSITION

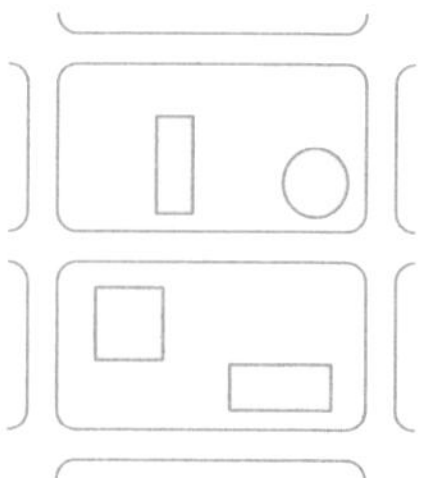

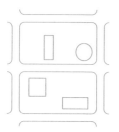

When free-standing volumes such as slabs, blocks or towers together form a larger compositional entity, the greater whole of the urban ensemble can be seen as a free composition of residential buildings. The ground-level area between the volumes is often a collective or even public space, where the absence of private gardens is compensated by the quality of a larger-scale facility for all the residents. The positions of the separate residential buildings form open spaces within the city, often shielded from the commotion and noise of traffic.

ÉMILE AILLAUD, LA CITE DE L'ABREUVOIR (PARIS-BOBIGNY, 1960)

In the latter half of the twentieth century, French architect Émile Aillaud designed and built a number of residential areas that share strong similarities and are illustrative of his vision of a successful dwelling environment. The residential areas are composed of various types of residential buildings, with star-shaped and cylindrical towers and long, interconnected, serpentine slabs as recurring elements. With these compositions, which he called *grands ensembles*, Aillaud aimed above all to create a pleasing and attractive urban exterior space, a green residential park its residents could enjoy together. The residential buildings themselves, and definitely the individual dwellings, were subordinate to this.
An evocative example of his work can be found in Bobigny, a suburb northeast of Paris. Here a serpentine block forms the northwest boundary of a publicly accessible green park, in which several star-shaped and cylindrical towers seem to have been set at random. The composition of their façades, in which the individual dwellings are not discernible, underscores the position of the buildings as autonomous volumes.
In spite of the vast quantity of open green space, the scale is definitely urban, with a unique atmosphere.

22a

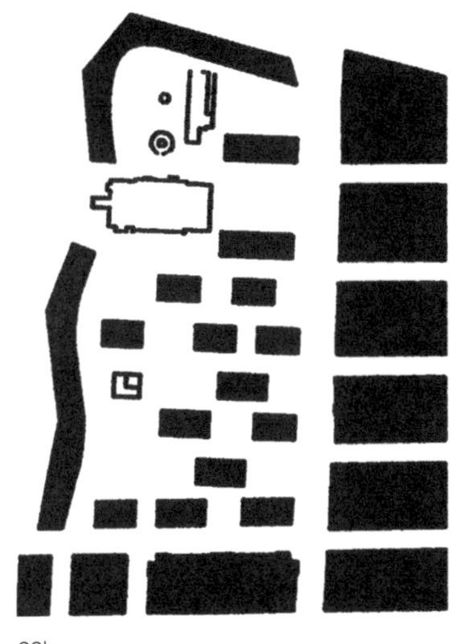

22b

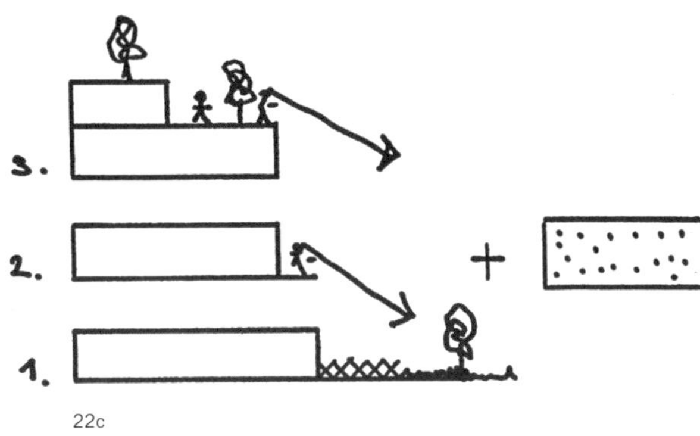

22c

KCAP & WEST 8, GWL SITE (AMSTERDAM, 1998)

On the former site of the municipal water company (GWL) KCAP designed a car-free and environmentally friendly residential area in collaboration with West 8, in a zone forming a transition between the perimeter blocks of the city centre and the industrial estates to its west. A tall, meandering slab shields the area from the busy traffic on the Haarlemmerweg and the adjacent industrial activity. The slab climbs from four storeys in the south to nine storeys in the north and houses about 57 per cent of the dwellings. Within its outline, 14 little residential blocks four to five storeys tall have been set in a free configuration in a green park. These have been designed by different architects, with the stipulation that as many dwellings as possible should be accessed at ground level, which produced ingenious layouts. The dwellings either have a private garden at ground level or can make use of garden allotments situated elsewhere in the plan area. Thick hedges around the gardens provide privacy and reinforce the green character of the area. A few old buildings and a water tower serve as historic reference points in the district, which despite a density of 100 dwellings per hectare retains a relaxed and open character.

22a Aerial photograph of the GWL site
22b, 22c Subdivision principle and diagram of connections between buildings and communal exterior space

FREE COMPOSITION

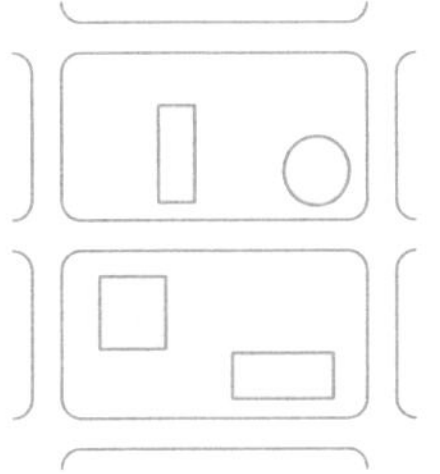

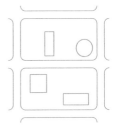

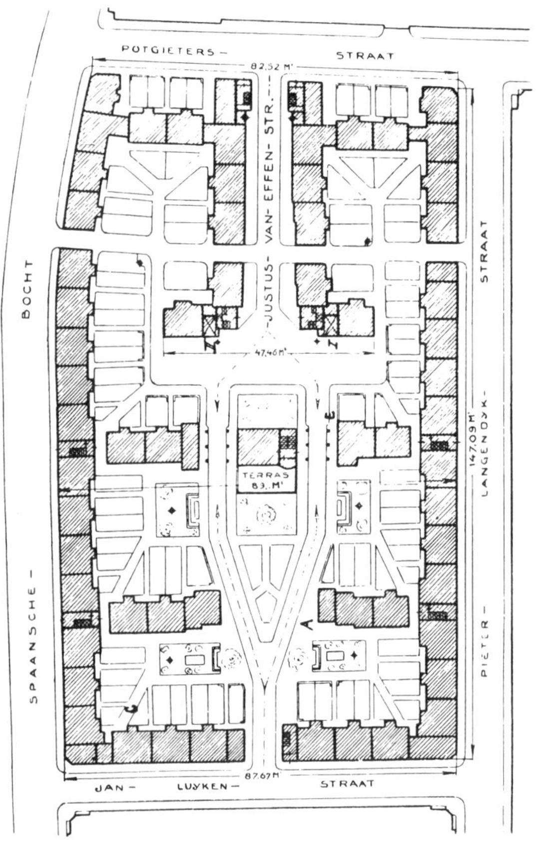

23a

23b

SUPERBLOCK

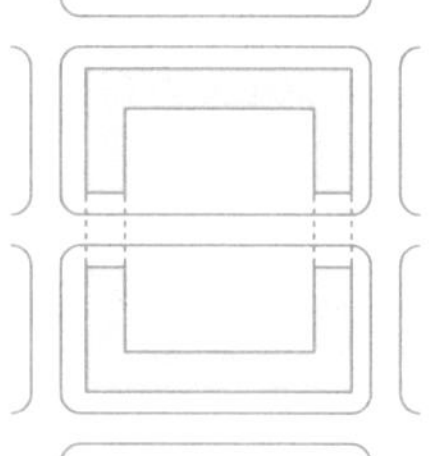

In some instances the scale of a housing project is such that the design of a residential building encompasses several urban lots, and the urban pattern of circulation links and public space is continued within it. While the structures on the edges form a clear separation from the greater urban space, within the complex a fascinating interaction between private, collective and public areas often emerges.

In spite of the public network of streets, the access to public space through private dwellings creates an inner area that makes people feel like someone else's guests. For the residents this urban space is an everyday extension of their dwelling. The privacy of the area can be increased by putting up barriers between the street and the inner space, or by extending the structures into the block along the street, in effect creating different building sections connected across the street.

MICHIEL BRINKMAN, JUSTUS VAN EFFEN BLOCK (ROTTERDAM-SPANGEN, 1922)

In the Spangen area of Rotterdam, Michiel Brinkman designed a residential complex in four storeys on either side of the Justus van Effenstraat. Instead of a traditional layout of several perimeter blocks with public outer sides and private inner courtyards, he connected the outer building structures across the street to form a superblock, the inner part of which was now publicly accessible. In order to reinforce this public character, he also located the dwelling entrances on the inner side of the block. Supplementary structures inside the block divide the whole into a complex sequence of inner courtyards, linked by the public street that continues beyond the other side of the block.

The dwellings on the ground level and first floor are apartments spanning two naves, each with its own front door directly on the street. These dwellings also have a private garden in the inner area. To provide access to the single-bay maisonettes above, Brinkman designed a wide gallery that runs along all the sides of the block and connects its various parts, contributing to the liveliness of the inner domain. Two goods lift initially allowed the milkman to make his deliveries door to door with his cart.

24a

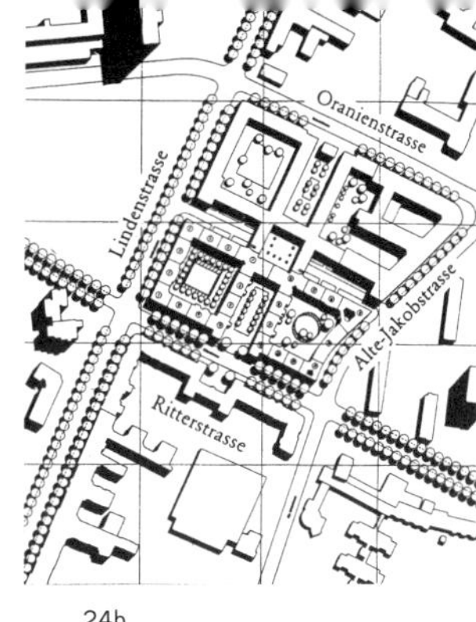

24b

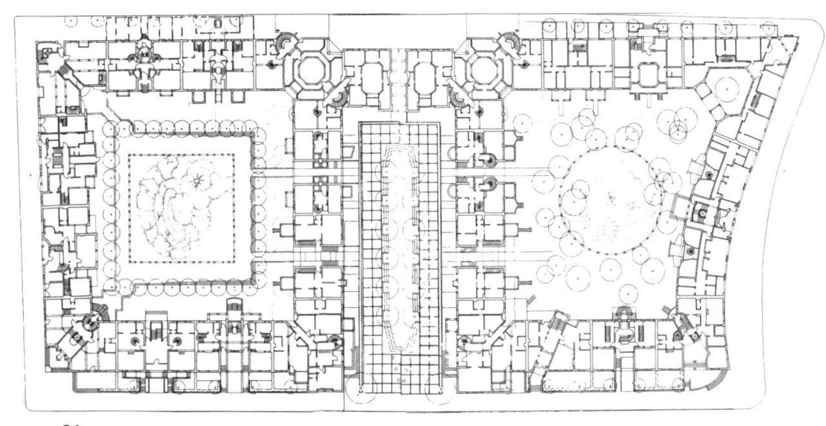

24c

24b Situation
24c Partial plan for the Ritterstrasse project, with dwelling floor plans drawn in
24d Long section

24d

ROB KRIER, RITTERSTRASSE (BERLIN, 1983)

In 1977, Luxemburg architect Rob Krier won the competition for the development of an area north of the Ritterstrasse in Berlin with a plan centred on repairing the traditional city. His plan consists of perimeter blocks in a square formation, connected at the corners where they meet, creating an enclosed domain in their midst, at the intersection of two public routes. One of these routes is a public roadway, crossed at this point by a route for pedestrians and bicycles. The four perimeter blocks have four to five storeys and their contours follow the street pattern, so that they vary in shape and size. The blocks are built of brick on the outside, but the walls facing their various inner gardens are clad in light-coloured stucco, with bright yellow accents here and there. The government provided support for underground parking, the use of passive solar energy, a mixture of dwelling types and the intensification of the use of exterior spaces through the application of gardens, loggias and conservatories.

The blocks were filled in by several young architects, and Krier himself designed the structures spanning the streets in the central section. For this he developed dwelling floor plans with a large vestibule as a central space for gathering, around which the various sleeping and living spaces are arranged. As a result, which is the front and which is the rear façade is not pre-determined, and neither is the use the occupant should make of the spaces.

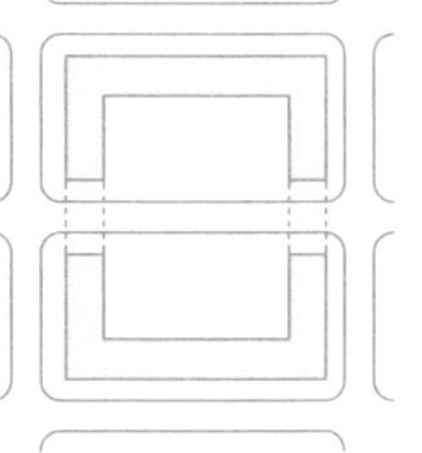

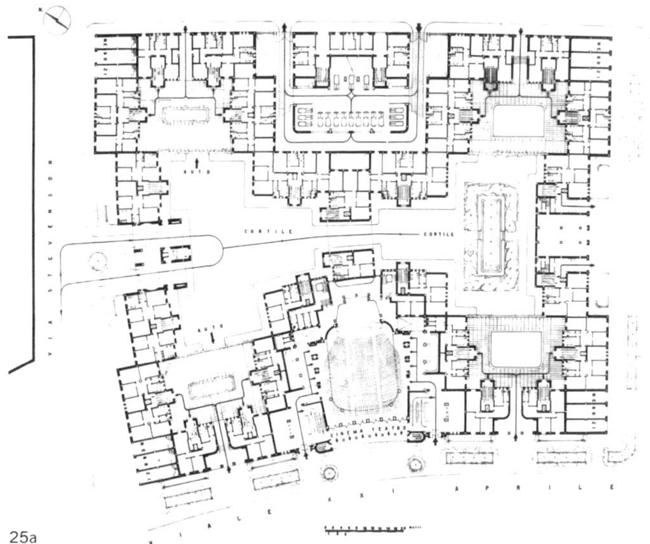
25a

25b

25c

MARIO DE RENZI, CASE CONVENZIONATE FEDERICI (ROME, 1937)

SUPERBLOCK

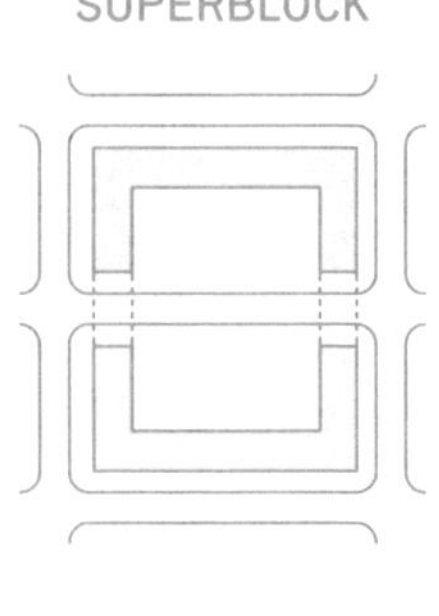

Around the 1930s, to ease an acute housing shortage for the growing working class, the Fascist regime in Rome developed an incentive programme for high-density multistorey housing in the inner cities. Commissioned by the Federici company, Mario De Renzi designed a residential complex on the Viale XXI Aprile featuring a wide variety of dwelling types, suitable to different target customers and incomes. The building encompasses several city blocks and contains a total of 442 dwellings, 70 shops, a parking garage and a 1600-seat cinema. Two building sections, each forming a double S, are positioned in a mirror formation, so that the structure enfolds a varied system of inner courtyards and at the same time avoids forming a solid street wall on its outer sides. At the transition between the two sections, a street cuts through the inner courtyards of the complex, which remains a unified whole thanks to structures that span the street. On each storey, two or three dwellings are clustered around communal stairwells with a lift, the semi-circular and fully glassed-in landings of which give the courtyards a monumental vertical articulation. They also reinforce the communal character of the edifice, in which collective routes and spaces are tightly connected visually both inside and outside.[10]

A suggestion of what it was like to live in the building at the time is given in Ettore Scola's famous film *Una giornata particolare* (1977) with Sophia Loren and Marcello Mastroianni, which was filmed in the complex.

10 Jana Kuhnle, 'Tre edifici residenziali degli anni '20 e '30 a Roma di Mario De Renzi', in: Milena Farina (ed.), *Studi sulla casa Urbana – sperimentazioni e temi di progetto* (Rome: Gangemi, 2009), p 157–173.

25a Floor plan of ground level
25b, 25c Inner courtyard with the glassed-in stairwells

TECTONICS

There are various reasons to devote a chapter to the tectonics of the residential building in a book on housing design. The Norwegian architect Christian Norberg-Schulz defines dwelling as identifying with a place.[1] This includes identifying with one's surroundings, the context, as well as with the object in which dwelling actually takes place: the home. The relationships between inside and outside, or between the dwelling condition and the garden, the street and the landscape all play a key role in identifying with the place. It is governed in no small measure by that part of the home that mediates between the inside and outside, that is the façade, as well as the entrance, itself a part of the façade. Identifying with the dwelling is largely governed by what encases the dwelling condition: the interior, the cladding of the rooms in which our private activities take place.

The finishing of the rooms and the materials used for this acquire their meaning in the act of dwelling: the wooden floor with the thick carpet, the ceramic tiles beneath the natural stone counter where the cooking is done, the French windows in the load-bearing façade, the weathered timber on the balcony where we have a drink in the sun, the glass brick in the tiled bathroom. The perception of a space and its finishing changes in the act of dwelling, making it very different from the perception of the theatre, the town hall or the office. It must therefore meet different requirements.

Another issue comes into play in housing, and in particular mass housing: repetition. Duplication of the same programme as well as the production method of the dwellings and the configuration of the components and elements that make up these dwellings can easily result in repetition on a mass scale. This repetition of elements or of entire dwellings is primarily expressed in the façade. How to handle this comes under the tectonics of housing as well. On the one hand, it is about common construction methods, structures, façade systems, galleries, staircases and even summer-houses; on the other hand, it is about the control of all of these elements and the way in which they are put together to arrive at the composition of the residential building. Rhythm and proportion are important ingredients here: they turn a residential building into an experience, into architecture. At the end of the day, architecture is all about combining materials and components, about arranging them.

The term tectonics often, and erroneously, evokes the engineering of the building. Engineering certainly comes into it, but tectonics is first and foremost about the architectural and aesthetic quality of this engineering. Yet architectural quality is a broader concept. Besides tectonics, it also encompasses the quality of the spatial arrangement in relation to the building's purpose, the quality of the building in its context, its beauty, meaning and emotion. In short, architectural quality still revolves around Vitruvius's three points: durability, functionality and beauty.

1
Christian Norberg-Schulz, *Genius Loci: Towards a Phenomenology of Architecture* (New York: Rizzoli, 1979).

The word tectonics comes from the Greek word *tecton*, meaning carpenter or builder. The nineteenth-century architect and theorist Gottfried Semper saw tectonics as the art of assembling. Semper defines the concept in his book *Der Stil in den technischen und tektonischen Künsten* (Style in the Technical and the Tectonic Arts, 1860–1863) as 'the art of assembling stiff, planklike elements into a rigid system'.[2] Other authors have described the concept as a kind of mediator between creation and outward form or that which brings about form. In *Die Tektoniek der Hellenen* (The Tectonics of the Hellenes, 1843–1852) the German art historian Karl Bötticher deploys the twin concepts of *Kernform* (the core form) and *Kunstform* (the art form), in which the core form, in the analysis of the Greek temple for example, stands for the wooden structures of the original temples, whereas the art form refers to their artistic representation.[3] The German architecture historian Fritz Neumeyer takes this one step further by linking creation with the perception of the art form.

2
Hans Kollhoff (ed.), *Über Tektonik in der Baukunst* (Braunschweig: Vieweg, 1993), 7.

3
Kenneth Frampton, *Studies in Tectonic Culture* (Cambridge, MA: MIT Press, 1995), 4.

The core (essence) of the concept 'tectonics' refers to the mysterious relationship between the creation and the visible expression or perception of things (objects) and concerns the relationship between the order of the built form and the structure of our perception. This relationship between the appearance of something that is built and our emotional experience of it is governed by its own dialectic. We do not experience everything that is technically or structurally feasible and that might be useful as pleasant or even beautiful – and vice versa.[4]

4
Fritz Neumeyer, 'Tektonik: Das Schauspiel der Objectivität und die Wahrheit der Architekturschauspiels', in: Kollhoff, *Über Tektonik*, op. cit. (note 2), 55.

Neumeyer's statement captures the relationship between creation and perception, between the order of the building and the structure of our perception. Our experience of a building, and in particular an individual dwelling, is mediated by perception. Visual perception is paramount, but the non-visual – smelling, feeling, hearing and so forth – also shapes our perception. Finnish architect Juhani Pallasmaa draws our attention to this in his book with the illuminating title *The Eyes of the Skin*.[5] Perception and experience are bridged, to a significant extent, by the meanings that we read into a building. We 'read' the façade and the cladding of the rooms. Depending on what we know or have experienced before, we recognize, interpret and – in our own, personal way – experience.

5
Juhani Pallasmaa, *The Eyes of the Skin* (London: Academy Editions, 1996).

FOUR LAYERS

To further explore the tectonics of the residential building, we have classified its constitutive elements into four groups or layers. The composition of each of these layers and their relationship to one another determines the tectonics of the building and hence its architecture. Our classification is based on the writings of Gottfried

Semper, Adolf Loos, Francis Duffy [→ 01] and Stewart Brand, among others:[6]

1 The *structure* (columns, beams, load-bearing walls, trusses, structural floors). The structure transfers the building load down to the foundation.
2 The *skin* (cladding of the façade, roof and belly). The skin separates the inside from the outside and presents the building to the outside world.
3 The *scenery* of the indoor space (cladding, inner doors and walls, the finishing of floors, walls and ceilings). The scenery arranges and defines the space.
4 The *services* (pipes and ducts, appliances and other facilities). The services control the supply and drainage of water, energy, information and fresh air and include the appliances and rooms associated with these tasks.

Needless to say, the building is in a particular location, the site. The site, however, is not part of the building itself and should not be seen as one of the material layers. The aforementioned four layers are the subject of this chapter.

6
Bernard Leupen, *Frame and Generic Space: A Study into the Changeable Dwelling Proceeding from the Permanent* (Rotterdam: 010 Publishers, 2006), 26–32.

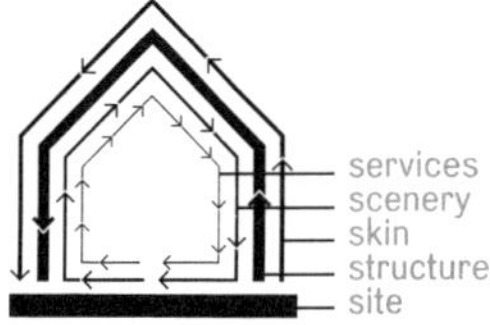

01 Four layers that together define the dwelling

MONOLITH / MONOLITH

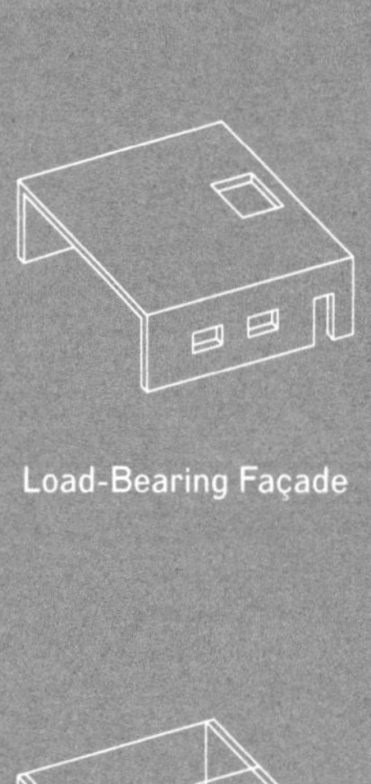

Load-Bearing Façade

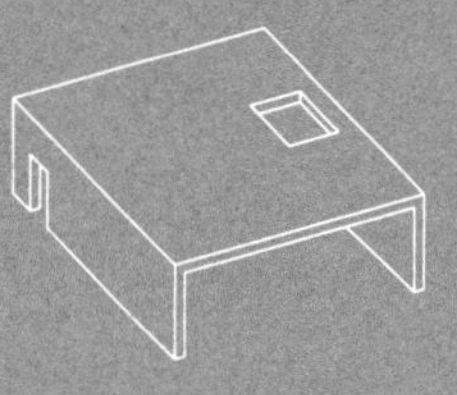

Load-Bearing Dividing Wall,

Box Structure

MONOLITH / SKELETON

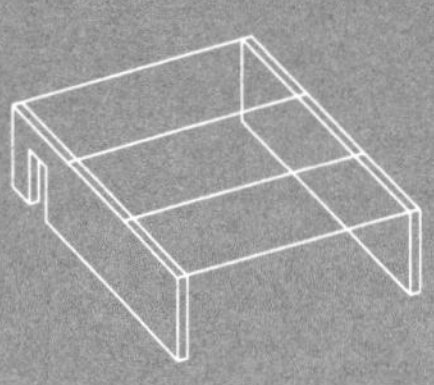

Load-Bearing Dividing Wall

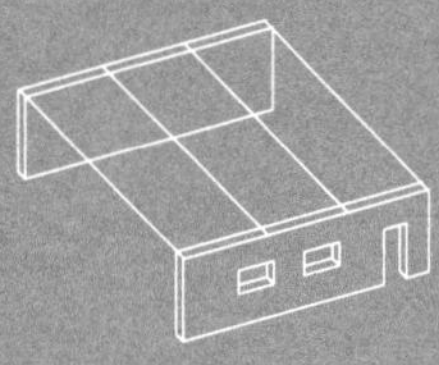

Load-Bearing Façade

SKELETON / MONOLITH

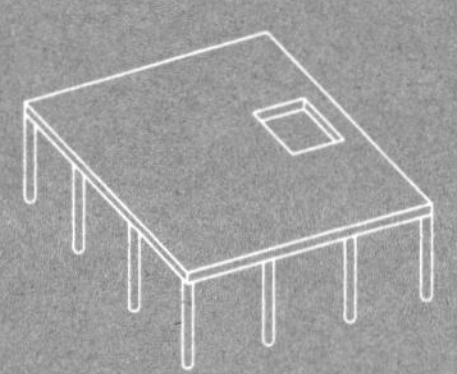

Dom-ino skeleton

Reticulated Structure

SKELETON / SKELETON

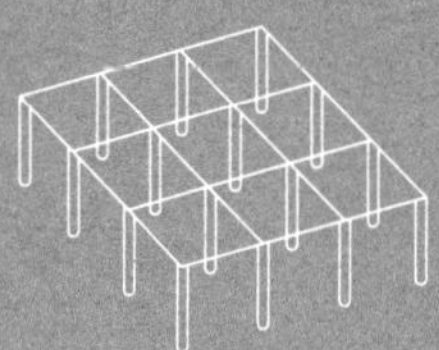

3d-skeleton

02 Basic types of structur

STRUCTURE

When we talk about the tectonics of the structure in housing we are referring to the configuration of walls, floors, columns and beams that transfer loads down to the foundation or that ensure the stability of the building. The particular configuration of the structure has a significant impact on the spatial organization within a building. Although variations and combinations can prompt new and unique solutions in each project, in theory these solutions can always be traced back to a few types of structural system.
The eighteenth-century French architecture theorist Antoine Chrysostome Quatremère de Quincy identifies two main principles underlying the structure of buildings: the monolithic method of construction and the skeleton-like structure.[7] Both methods have their own history. The skeleton construction, as found in medieval timber houses, dates back to the primitive hut, the subject of Semper's analysis in *Der Stil in den technische und tektonische Künsten*.[8] The monolithic construction can be traced back to primitive stone dwellings such as the grotto and the *trulli* in southern Italy. Monolithic construction returns in monumental stone buildings. In fact, until the nineteenth century this was the most common method of construction for monumental edifices throughout most of Europe. Swiss architect Andrea Deplazes makes a similar distinction between 'solid versus filigree' in his hefty handbook *Constructing Architecture*.[9] Based on these two principles, we can identify the following types in contemporary house building: monolith and skeleton. [← 02]
A residential building can be built according to one of these construction principles, or combinations of the two. This classification is therefore a theoretical one. In brick and block building especially (construction using large or small blocks such as bricks, sand-lime bricks or natural stone), intermediate forms are possible, as the example of Adolf Loos's design for Haus Moller suggests. Assuming that the walls and floors can each have their own construction principle, we can identify the following combinations:

Monolith / Monolith
—Load-bearing façade
—Load-bearing dividing wall and solid floor
—Box structure

Monolith / Skeleton
—Load-bearing façade
—Load-bearing dividing wall

Skeleton / Monolith
—Dom-ino skeleton
—Reticulated structure

Skeleton / Skeleton
—3-D skeleton

7
Antoine Chrysostome Quatremère de Quincy, *De l'Architecture Égyptienne, considérée dans son origine, ses principes et son goût, et comparée sous les mêmes rapports à l'Architecture Grecque* (Paris, 1785).

8
In *Der Stil in den technische und tektonische Künsten* (Kollhoff, *Über Tektonik*, op. cit. (note 2), 29), Gottfried Semper describes the Caribbean hut at the Great Exhibition of 1851.

9
Andrea E. Deplazes, *Constructing Architecture: Materials, Processes, Structures: A Handbook*, transl. G.H. Söffker (Basel: Birkhäuser, 2005), 13.

03

04

MONOLITH / MONOLITH

The monolithic structure is characterized by a unity between the load-bearing and dividing elements. Walls are both load-bearing and dividing. In the most consistent examples all the load-bearing elements are made of the same material. A traditional example would be the *trulli* in southern Italy, but the Herzog & De Meuron house in Leymen (France, 1996–1997) is also quite homogenous in its use of materials. Indeed, the example shows that with the use of thick insulating concrete, monolithic structures are still possible in this day and age.

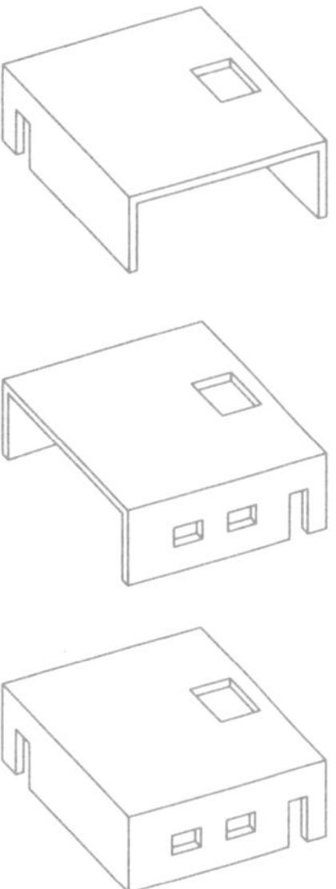

03 Herzog & de Meuron, private house, Leymen, France
04 Monolith: *trulli* in southern Italy

05a

DKV ARCHITECTEN, KOP VAN HAVENDIEP (LELYSTAD, 2004)

The housing block designed by DKV is situated at the tip of the Havendiep waterway, wedged between the water and the railway tracks. Because the noise levels at this location beside the tracks are extremely high, especially for housing, only an unorthodox solution would do. The designers started from the premise that none of the living spaces could face the tracks. The façade on this side would have to be a 'blind façade': a façade without windows that open. Such a façade is the ideal load-bearing façade. The sun and the view are on the quiet, western side of the building, which can therefore be extremely open. But if the blind façade is load-bearing, then the sun-oriented façade must be load-bearing as well. This has been achieved by constructing this façade with a series of slabs with large openings that accommodate generously proportioned French windows. Attached to these slabs are beams that support the floor. The structure can also be described as follows: the front façade, like the rear, consists of a large concrete wall with a series of large vertical openings. These openings were fitted with glass doors that provide access to the balcony as well as plenty of sunlight and a view.

MONOLITH/MONOLITH

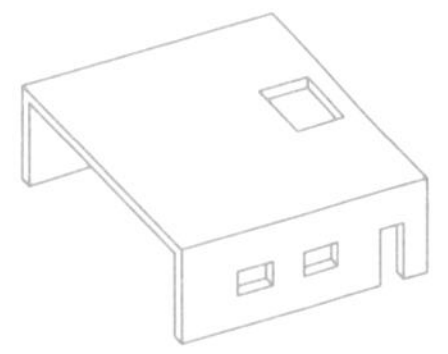

Load-Bearing Façade

The storeys of the building are arranged in a straight line. The combination of the longitudinal structure and the load-bearing façades – the latter is unusual in Dutch housing – has created a great deal of flexibility. The standard storey accommodates two apartments which have been divided into two linear areas. Halfway along the track side we find the building's vertical access system, a lift and stairwell. Situated on either side of this core are the bathrooms and toilets, the service ducts, storage spaces and, in the corner, the open-plan kitchens. The area on the sunlit western side of the building can be freely adapted, enabling different layouts, because both the installation of the services and the construction as a whole are based on a standard grid. In one instance, one apartment occupies an entire floor.

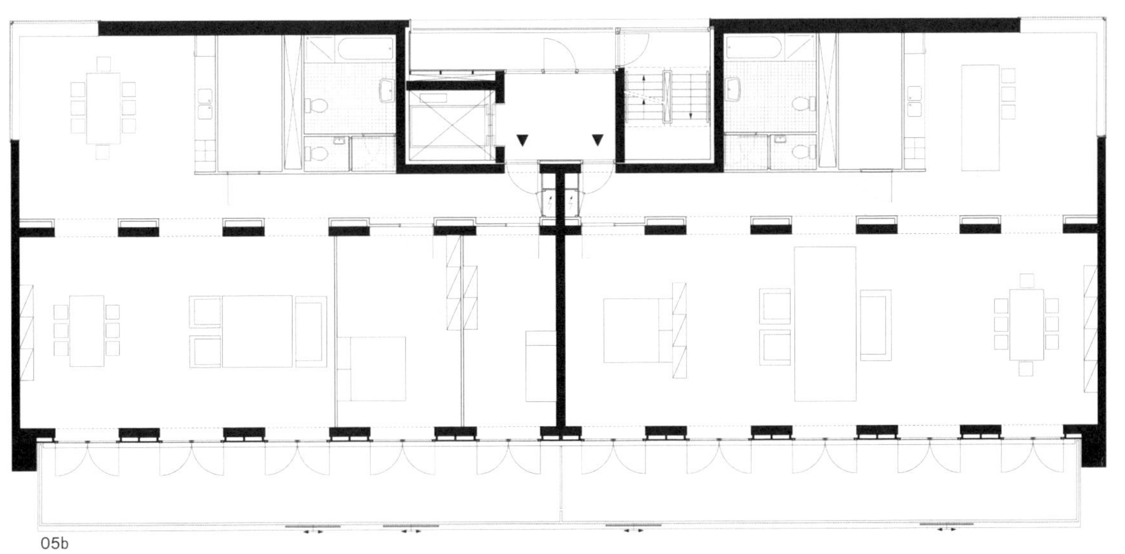

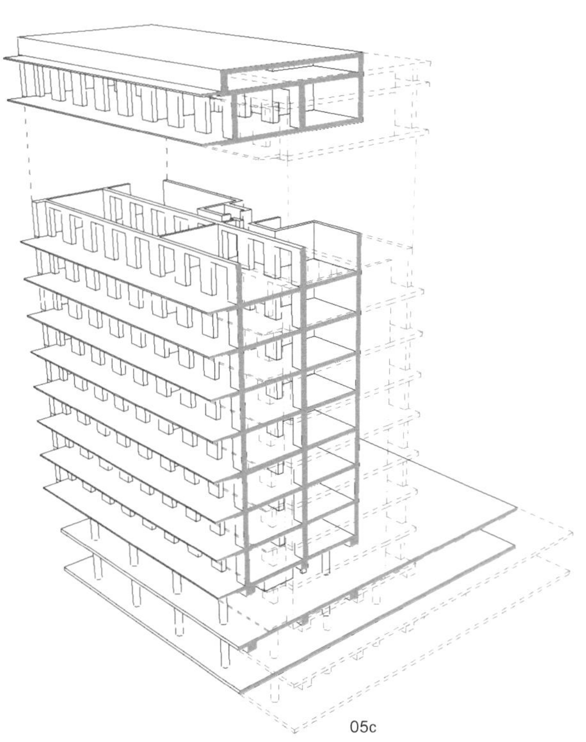

05b Regular floor plan
05c Analytical drawing

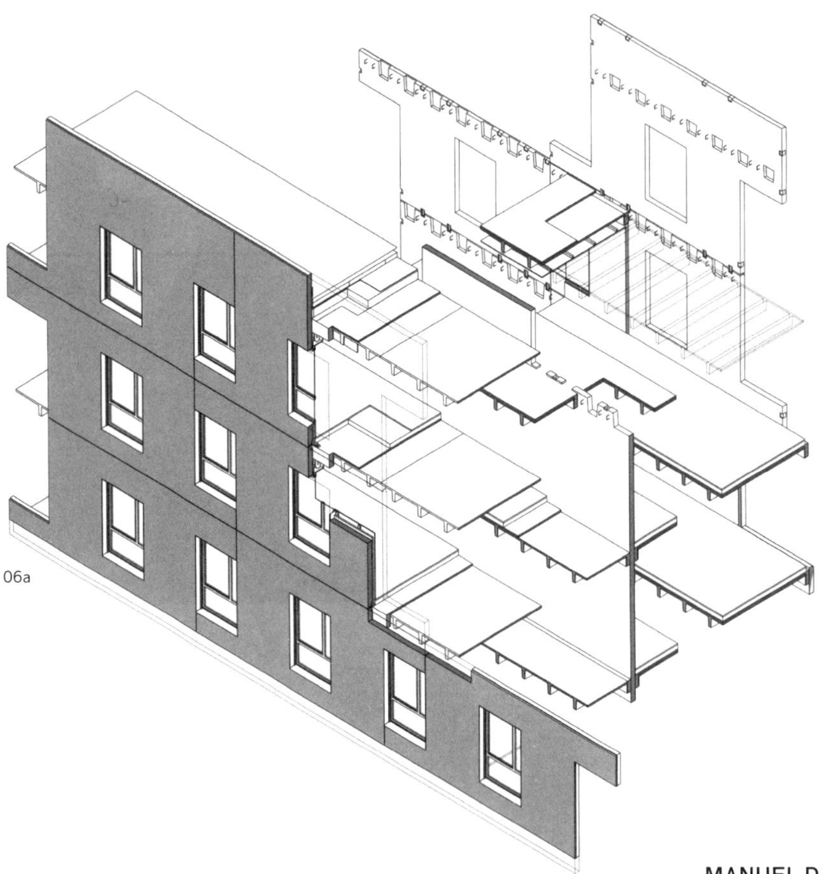

06a

MANUEL DE LAS CASAS, 198 DWELLINGS, MARQUÉS DE LA VALDAVIA (MADRID, 1996)

System building is a method of building in which the structure is made of large, storey-height prefabricated concrete elements. This system, developed among others by the French company Coignet, was widely used in the countries of the former Eastern Bloc, where it is known as *Plattenbau*.
An interesting, recent housing project based on this principle was designed by Manuel de las Casas in Madrid. In this project, the large prefabricated concrete elements remain visible, because the insulation has been applied on the inside of the walls. Because insulation on the inside requires great care, this reverse façade system is most common in countries with a meticulous construction track record, such as Switzerland.
By reversing the package, the prefabricated elements can be displayed on the outside, giving the building its typical semi-prefabricated look. The seams between the elements form a pattern, which Manuel de las Casas has highlighted in his composition. This and the perfectly balanced proportions have turned a simple idea into an impressive project.

MONOLITH/MONOLITH

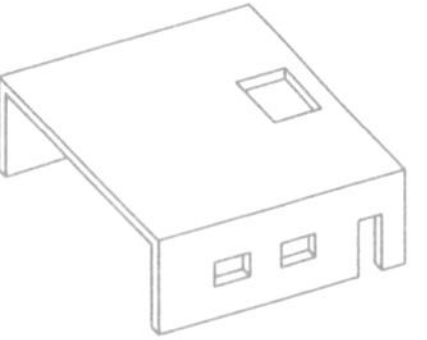

Load-Bearing Façade

06b

06a Analysis of prefabricated concrete structure

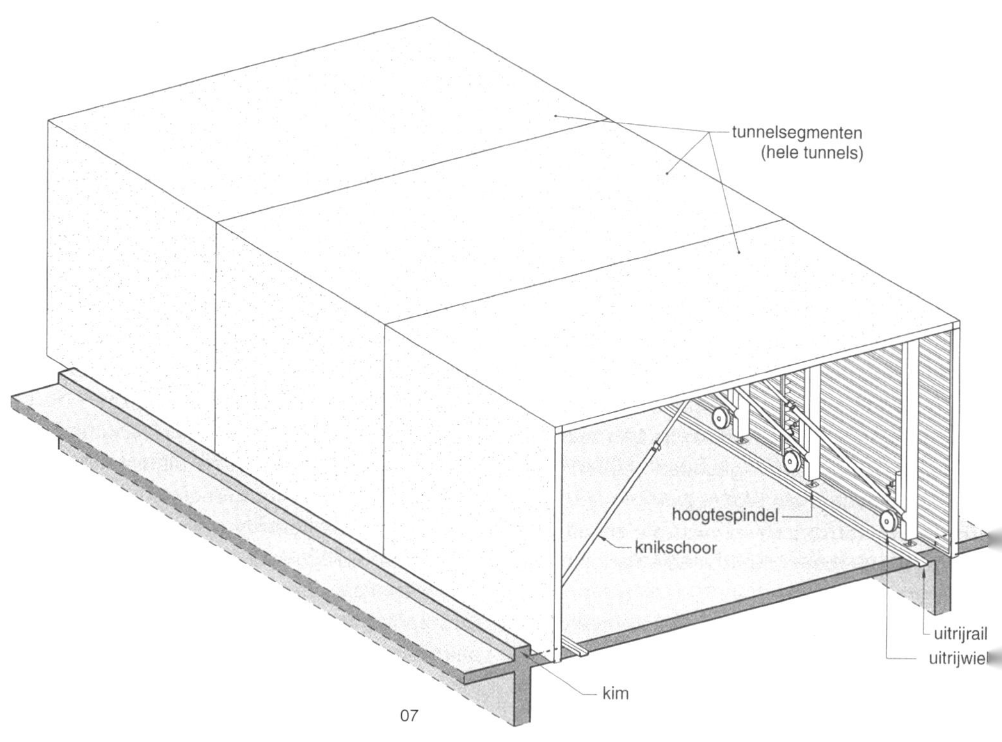

07

08

07 Tunnel-form principle
08 Bijlmermeer, Amsterdam. One of the examples of where tunnel-form construction was applied during the post-war reconstruction period.

MONOLITH/MONOLITH LOAD-BEARING DIVIDING WALL AND SOLID FLOOR

The Tunnel-Form Structure

A common building method based on the monolith/monolith principle with load-bearing party wall is tunnel-form construction. Tunnel-form construction originated in the desire for rationalization and industrialization in post-Second World War housing. Tunnel-form construction remains the dominant method of production for structures in housing in the Netherlands, hence our special attention to the tectonics of this building method. [← 07]

In the tunnel-form system, load-bearing walls tend to be rigidly tied to horizontal floor slabs. The whole is cast *in situ*. Entire floors can be cast in one go using standard steel formworks. Because the formwork is heated it can be removed after a few days. The floor and wall constitute one monolithic whole, but this monolithic structure can be punctured both horizontally and vertically for windows, doors, lifts and stairs. These punctures are subject to restrictions, however: there must be enough wall and floor left to ensure an even load transfer.

As the ultimate monolithic structure, the tunnel can be seen as an extension of the monolithic structures with domes, such as the aforementioned *trulli* and the loam houses of the Mexican pueblos. The main difference between these archetypal monolithic structures and the modern tunnel-form method is that the latter produces a fixed-moment structure.

Tunnel-form construction allowed the ideas of Ludwig Hilberseimer and CIAM – the large-scale duplication of the ideal dwelling – to be implemented, thus bringing a home in a high-rise with a view of the horizon and surrounded by green space within everybody's reach. In the end, the implementation of this idea would meet with less appreciation than the many ideologues, planners, architects and builders had anticipated at the time. [← 08]

Tunnel formwork involves a fixed-moment connection between walls and floors, which then form a monolithic whole. This fixed-moment connection gives tunnel structures, unlike their stacked counterparts, a clear span direction, at least up to a point.

The advantages of tunnel-form construction are:

– Cost-savings on large production runs.
– Rapid output (the formwork can be removed after a few days). The entire process can be done in two production runs of five tunnel bays, for example.
– Smooth walls and ceilings.
– The concrete load-bearing wall and floor comply with noise regulations.
– The concrete load-bearing wall and floor comply with safety regulations regarding fire compartmentation.

The disadvantages of tunnel-form construction include:

– Only suitable for highly repetitive construction.
– Rigid structure.
– Demands great uniformity.
– Creates a single type of space (tunnel).

Some of these disadvantages can be overcome with the necessary know-how and clever uses of the tunnel-form system. A span of over 7 m, for example, is quite easy to achieve nowadays, giving designers the freedom to choose their preferred layout. It has also become easier to make the openings in the wall between two tunnels wider than a single door.

The following examples demonstrate that within the strict discipline of tunnel-form construction there is still some flexibility in building design. It can be seen as a kind of minimalism: playing with the basic unit of the tunnel's standard dimensions.

MONOLITH/MONOLITH

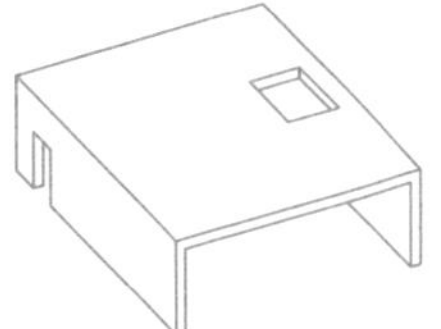

Load-Bearing Dividing Wall and Solid Floor

09a

RUDY UYTENHAAK, HOUSING BORNEO-EILAND (AMSTERDAM, 2000)

MONOLITH/MONOLITH

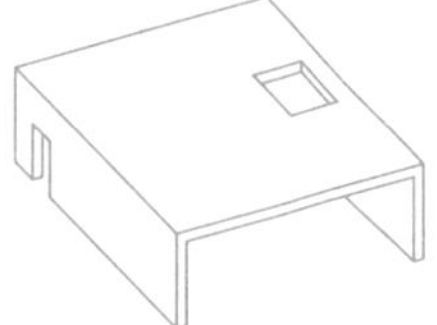

Load-Bearing Dividing Wall, Tunnel with Intermediate Space

The use of cut-aways in the floor slabs – which is also done for stairwells – makes it possible to realize entire *vides* in tunnel-form systems. It also enables the creation of double-height rooms. If so desired, secondary, lighter and more flexible floors can be inserted into these double-height rooms to create interesting and transformable structures. In his project on Borneo Island in Amsterdam's Eastern Harbour District, Rudy Uytenhaak alternates the tunnel with partially unfilled zones, thus creating an extremely complex fabric of dwellings. For every two bays, five dwellings are interlinked, four of which are served by a small courtyard that can be entered from the east side. The fifth dwelling is on the west side and has a patio for the car. The dwellings all have a large terrace on the second floor, a secondary construction inserted between the tunnel-form structural walls.

09b Analysis of the structure including tunnels and open zones
09c Floor plan

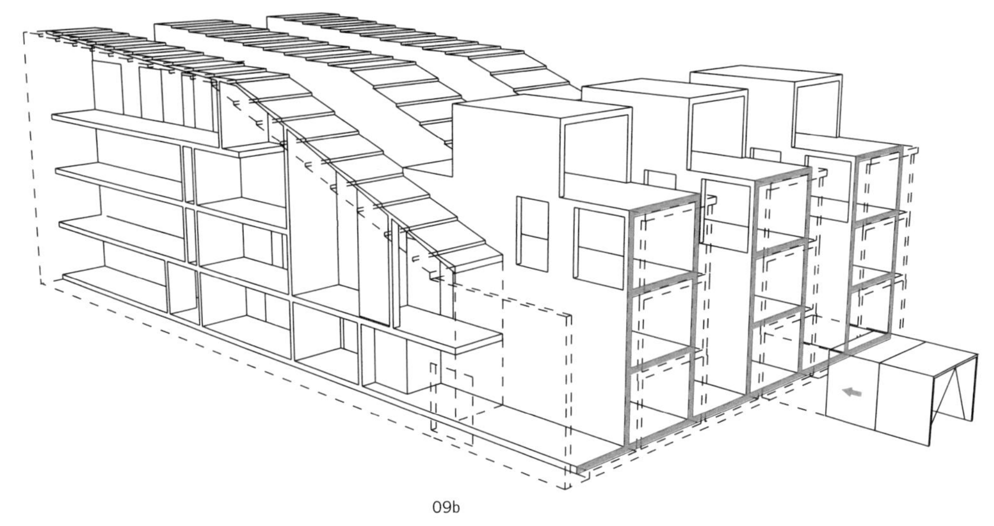

09b

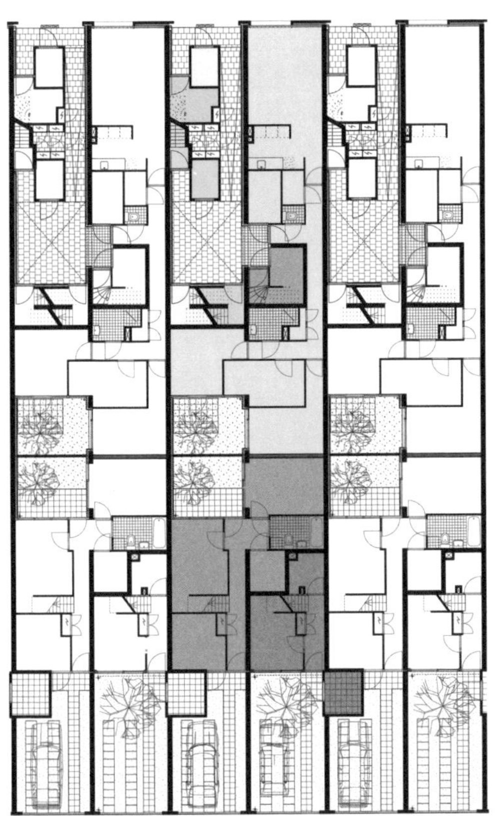

09c

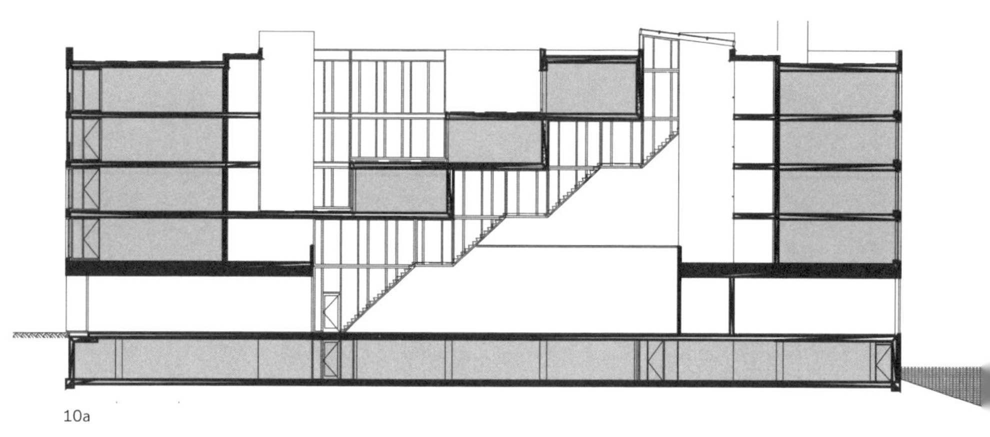

10a

DE ARCHITEKTEN CIE, FRITS VAN DONGEN, BOTANIA RESIDENTIAL BUILDING (AMSTERDAM, 2002)

Botania, in Amsterdam's historic city centre, accommodates a wide range of luxury apartment types. The brick façades with white and dark-green window frames allude to the city's old canal houses. The 40 apartments are grouped ingeniously around the spacious access staircase. Particularly striking are the three façade-to-façade apartments, each 33 m long. Placed diagonally above one another, they divide the block's central open space into two stepped spaces: a patio that widens towards the top and an indoor space that tapers towards the top and forms the access staircase. This project showcases the possibilities of tunnel-form construction. Most of the building is composed of tunnel elements, even its ends, where the tunnel has been rotated 90 degrees. At first sight, the 33-m dwellings that stretch from façade to façade appear to be made of tunnel elements as well. But while this is true for the extremities of these apartments, which are part of the tunnel-form system of the block's long sides, the middle part was built using a steel skeleton. The main reason for the different method of construction is that these apartments are entirely open on one side. The open parts are fitted with glass fronts that provide access to large roof terraces. These window walls are topped by a large steel section to absorb the load (see detail 10b).

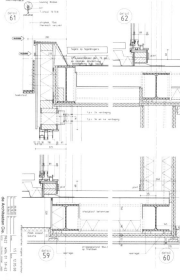

10b

MONOLITH/MONOLITH

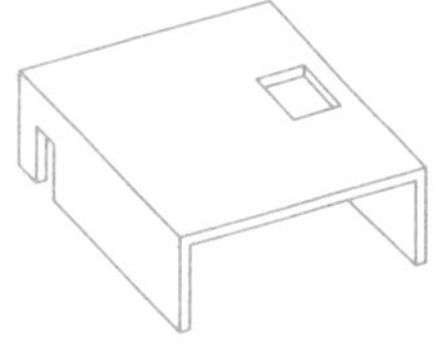

Load-Bearing Dividing Wall, Tunnel with Intermediate Space

10c

10a Cross section of the façade-to-façade apartments
10b Detail of the structure of the façade-to-façade apartments
10c Interior of the cross-block apartment
10d Floor plan of second storey
10e Floor plan of fourth storey

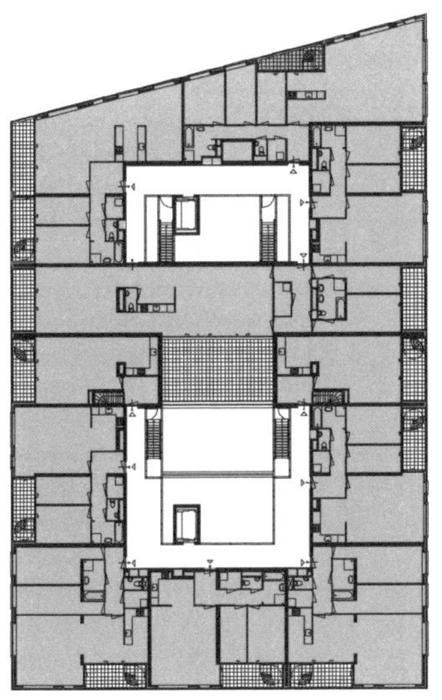

10d

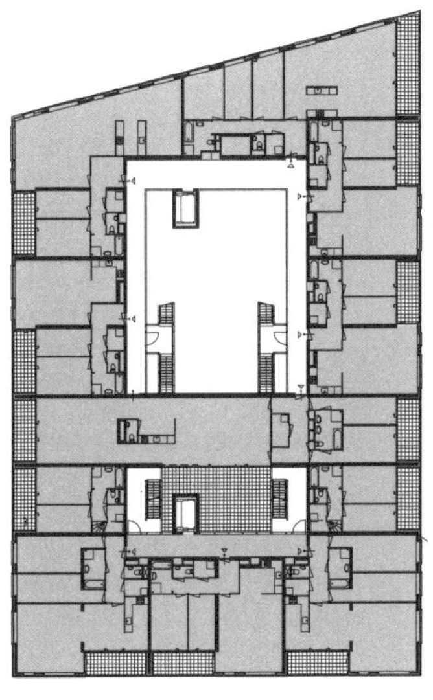

10e

11a

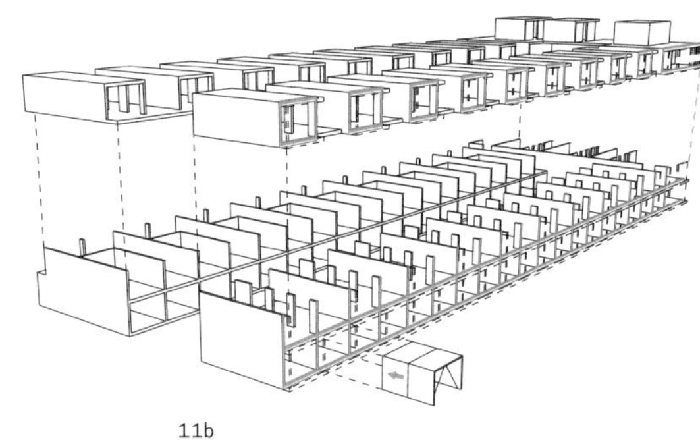

11b

NEUTELINGS RIEDIJK ARCHITECTEN, SPORENBURG HOUSING (AMSTERDAM, 1995)

It is also possible to use inserts in the formwork to create cut-aways for doors and windows. In fact, these cut-aways can be made big enough to allow rooms to be built across two bays.
This is what Neutelings Riedijk architecten did on the Sporenburg peninsula. The first-floor living room straddles two bays with a relatively narrow width of 4.2 m each. This width was created using a large cut-away in the structural wall. The result of this intervention is a puzzle of dwellings. One dwelling has a large living room on the first floor, parallel to the street and partially above the neighbours' carport. A west-facing balcony stretches across the entire length of the living room. The other dwelling has a large living room on the second floor, perpendicular to the street. Parallel to this room, and on the neighbours' roof, is a large roof terrace. The interweaving of the homes invites comparison with Neutelings Riedijk's Panorama dwellings in Huizen (see Chapter 2, 'Typology', page 53).

MONOLITH/MONOLITH

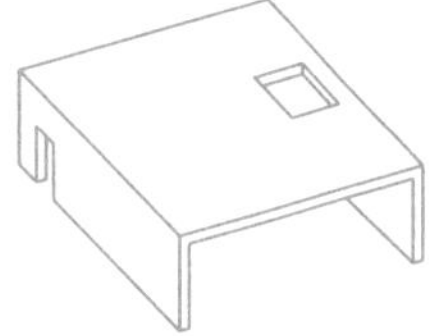

Load-Bearing Dividing Wall, Tunnel with Transverse Space

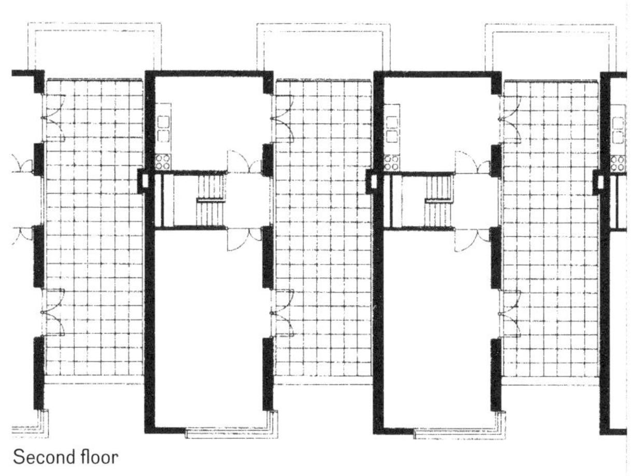
Second floor

First floor

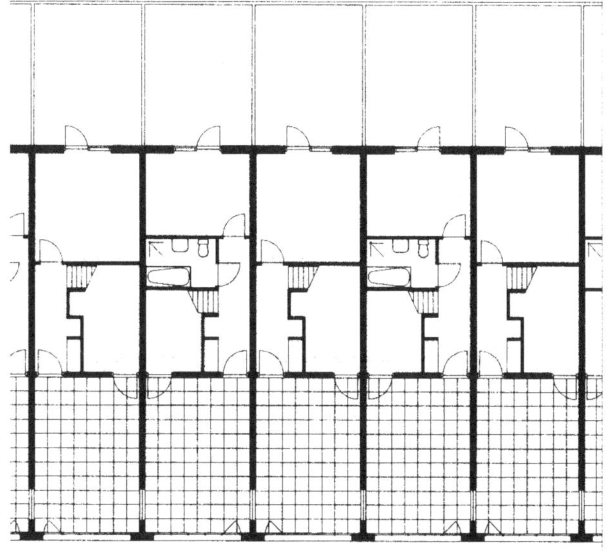
Ground floor

11c

11a Front elevation
11b Analysis of the structure

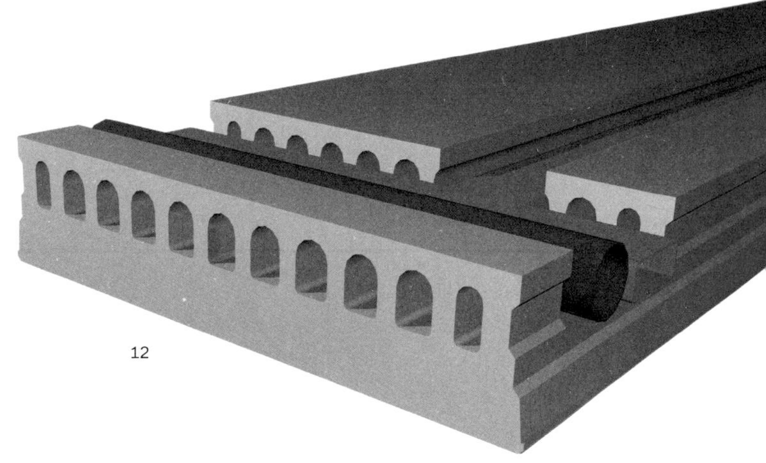

12

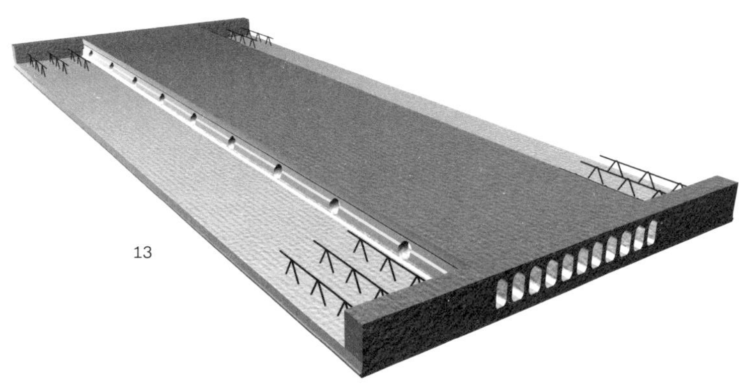

13

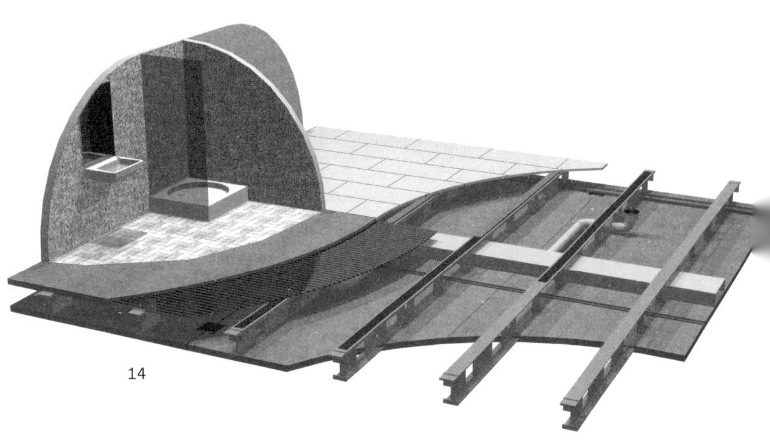

14

12 Services flooring or apartment flooring
13 Wing-flooring slab system
14 INFRA+ flooring system

FLOOR TYPE INTERLUDE: BETWEEN TUNNEL-FORM AND PREFAB

Alongside the widely used tunnel-form system and prefabrication with large elements (see below), there are all kinds of hybrid construction systems in use in house building. The range of floor systems is particularly extensive. Although the focus of this book is not on construction techniques, a brief look is useful. The following criteria play a role in the choice of floor system:

- Mode of construction (dry or wet assembly)
- Span
- Flexible installation of ducts for plumbing and wiring
- Sound insulation
- Efficiency
- Flexibility

Many new flooring systems seek to strike a balance between light, rigid designs that enable larger spans, space for ducting in the floor and sufficient sound insulation, that is to say, sufficient weight per square metre. The building sector has come up with two different solutions. The first is a floor made of a thin prefabricated subfloor and reinforcement joists. This is often covered *in situ* by a structural layer. The familiar wide-slab flooring is a good example of this type, while the Infra+ flooring is a contemporary variation of it. When these wide-slab floorings are made, the ducting is poured into the compression layer at the same time. The Infra+ flooring, on the other hand, leaves space between the steel joists to install and, if necessary, move ducting (see also Uytenhaak's La Fenêtre, p. 278). Whereas the wide-slab flooring only provides the flexibility to arrange the ducting before or during construction, the Infra+ flooring also provides flexibility in use.
The second solution comprises floors made of a structural layer topped by a non-structural layer of lighter foamed concrete. The light top flooring can be hacked away quite easily to install ducting. This type of flooring also allows adjustment to the service ducts. The services flooring is a good example.

MONOLITH/MONOLITH

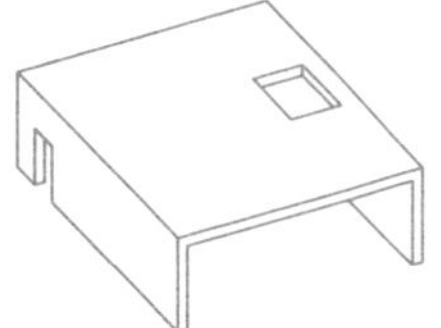

Load-Bearing Dividing Wall, Prefab Tunnel Elements

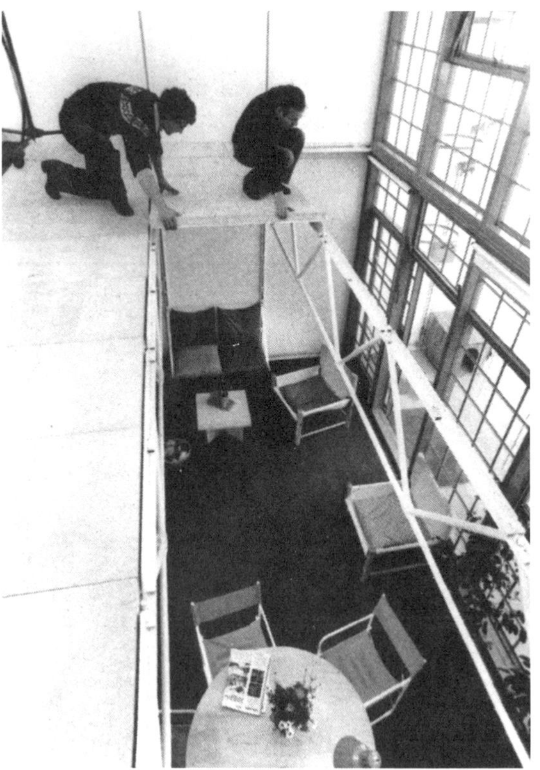

15a

15b

MONOLITH/MONOLITH

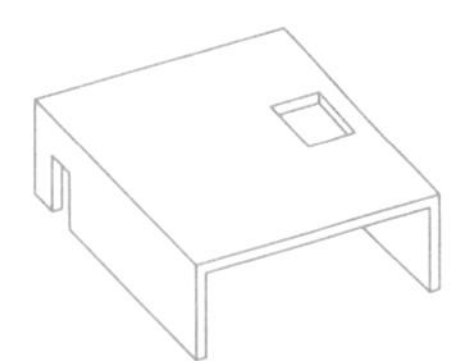

Load-Bearing Dividing Wall, Prefab Tunnel Elements

RENZO PIANO, IL RIGO HOUSING (CORCIANO, ITALY, 1978)

The housing project by Italian architect Renzo Piano in Corciano-Il Rigo near Perugia is a remarkable project with a tunnel-form structure. The project was informed by the idea that it is relatively easy to produce a cheap shell with a prefabricated structure.[10] The shell of the building designed by Piano is made of floor-to-ceiling prefabricated U-shaped concrete elements that are stacked on top of one another. Turning the top elements upside-down results in a tall and freely subdivisible space.[11] The resulting tunnel is 6 m wide and 6 m high on the inside. A floor can be installed in this 6-m high room using light open-web steel joists and small prefabricated floor slabs. The open-web steel joists are connected to a section attached to the U-shaped elements 3 m above the floor. The idea is that a developer constructs the shell, after which the occupants can install the floors and window walls at their own discretion. The two U-shaped elements that make up the shell are visible on both the inside and the outside and clearly articulated. Even the finishing of the links between the concrete elements is a prominent feature of the interior. The stacking receives even more emphasis on the outside because the end window walls are recessed 1.2 m from the end of the tunnel.

10 Toshio Nakamura, 'Renzo Piano Building Workshop 1964–1988', *A+U* (March 1989), 104–113.

11 Consider for instance the design that Le Corbusier submitted in 1964 for the competition for the Palais des Congrès in Strasbourg.

15a, 15b Assembly of the prefabricated tunnel-form elements and the prefab flooring elements
15c Axonometrics

15c

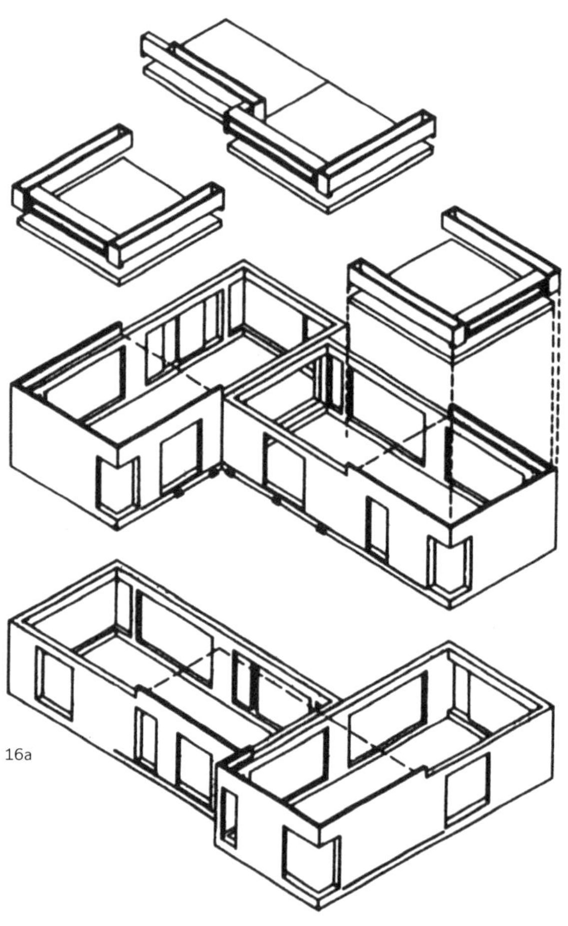

16a

MONOLITH/MONOLITH

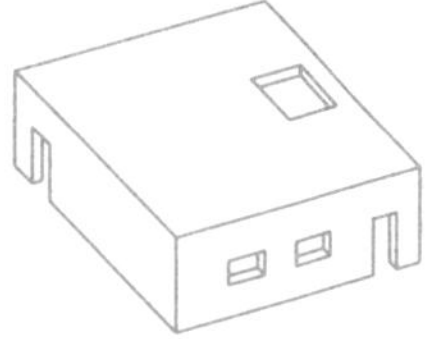

Box Structure

MOSHE SAFDIE, HABITAT '67 (MONTREAL, 1967)

In the box system all the walls are load-bearing. In more or less square spaces, the floor spans in two directions, a 'two-way slab'. One of the few buildings to have been designed according to this principle is Moshe Safdie's Habitat '67 in Montreal. It was built as a model for the housing of the future at the World Exhibition site in Montreal in 1967. This arresting stacked development attracted a great deal of attention and was seen as a fine alternative to the many familiar forms of stacked housing, such as slabs and towers.

The dwellings in the Habitat project were prefabricated as boxes and lifted into place. This may sound simple enough, a bit like stacking matchboxes, but complications set in as a result of the various forces that the box has to absorb. The boxes at the bottom have to carry the entire building, those at the top only themselves. Another problem is the fact that in this kind of stack the structure is doubled. To prevent this, all the boxes were designed with their position in the stack in mind. In actual fact, these are not proper boxes; each has one missing part, which is then formed by the adjacent box or the box on top. The roofs and the balconies were either added as separate elements or formed by the dwelling above.

16b

16a Analysis of the structure
16b Stacking of the dwellings

17

17 Wooden skeleton of a medieval house

MONOLITH / SKELETON

The third type of structure consists of load-bearing walls with beams supporting the floors. Many people see the archetypal building as a kind of 'stack', more specifically a stack of bricks that are more durable when fired than as clay. In this method of construction, the walls are relatively closed and space-defining. The position of the wall, the dimensions and the span (bay size) are largely determined by the structural possibilities of the materials used. Openings in the walls are possible, but bound by the limitations of the materials used. Unlike the walls, the installation of the floor slabs is subject to fewer restrictions. As long as the floor has a clear span, its vertical position is free. The only restriction here is the slenderness ratio of the load-bearing wall. The stability of the load-bearing wall depends on the material used: a reinforced concrete wall can be tied rigidly, unlike a stacked wall, which will therefore be restricted in height.

Monolith / Skeleton, Load-Bearing Dividing Wall

Since the seventeenth century, the load-bearing dividing wall between two houses has been the structural principle of urban development in the Netherlands [← 17]. Since the great city fires in the sixteenth century, the walls dividing dwellings have been made of masonry. The narrow lot made it possible to have beams parallel to the front façade spanning the dividing walls. The dividing wall became a so-called structural wall, which transferred the load down to the foundation. Because the front and rear façades were not load-bearing, they could be fitted with large openings, resulting in the characteristic Dutch townhouses with large and numerous windows.

MONOLITH / SKELETON

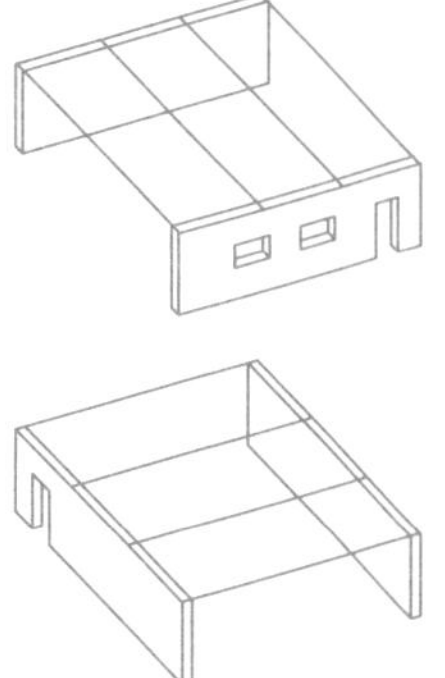

Load-Bearing Dividing Wall

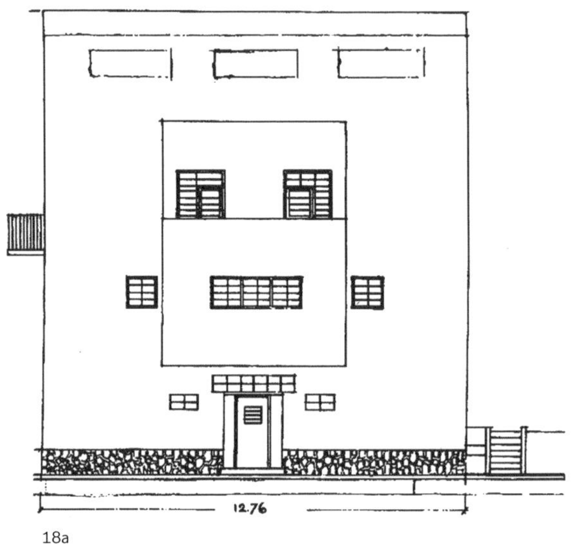

18a

ADOLF LOOS, HAUS MOLLER (VIENNA, 1927–1928)

With relative freedom in the placement of the floors it becomes possible to create all kinds of interesting spatial relationships. Split levels, *vides* and even sloping floor decks are among the possibilities. Haus Moller, designed by Adolf Loos, is a fine example of this. The basic structure of Haus Moller consists of load-bearing stone walls combined with timber floor joists. This method of construction makes it possible to create rooms with different heights. Loos used this type of construction to realize his beautiful spatial designs, known as the *Raumplan*.[12] In Haus Moller this produces a wealth of spatial relationships in which the many facets of urban dwelling can be played out against the backdrop of the bustling metropolis Vienna.

The load-bearing walls are made of brick. In this kind of stacked construction it is often difficult to pinpoint where the load-bearing function of the brickwork ends and where it merely serves as a partition between inside and outside. The load partially spans the corner here, while part of the side wall adds strength. This is why we decided to include both pictograms here, that of the structure with load-bearing façades and that of the structure with load-bearing party walls. All the walls of a detached house such as the one shown here are façades, making the façade load-bearing by definition.

12 See also Max Risselada (ed.), *Raumplan versus Plan Libre* (New York: Rizzoli, 1987).

MONOLITH / SKELETON

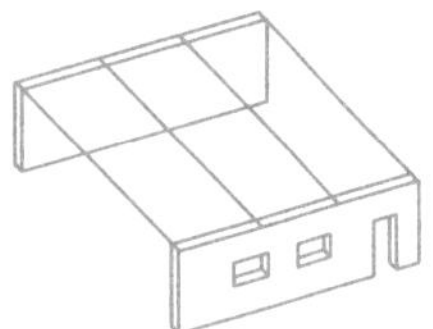

Load-Bearing Façade

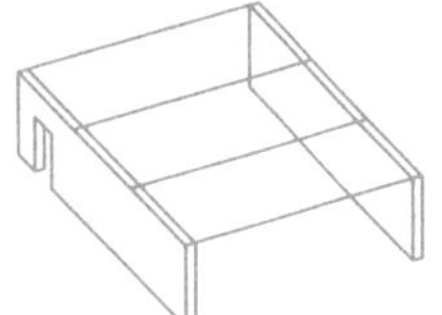

Load-Bearing Dividing Wall

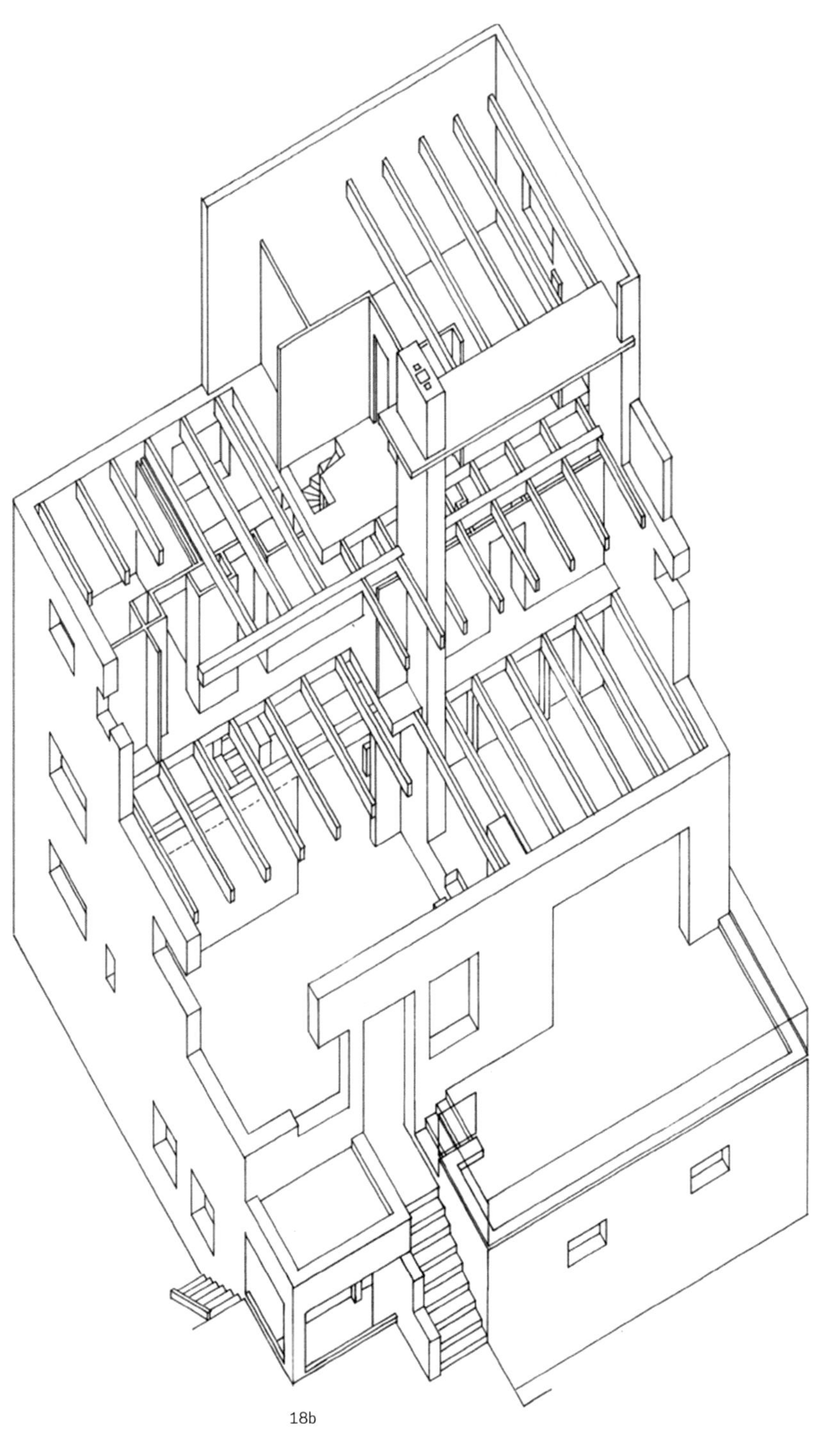

18b

18a Front elevation
18b Analysis of the structure

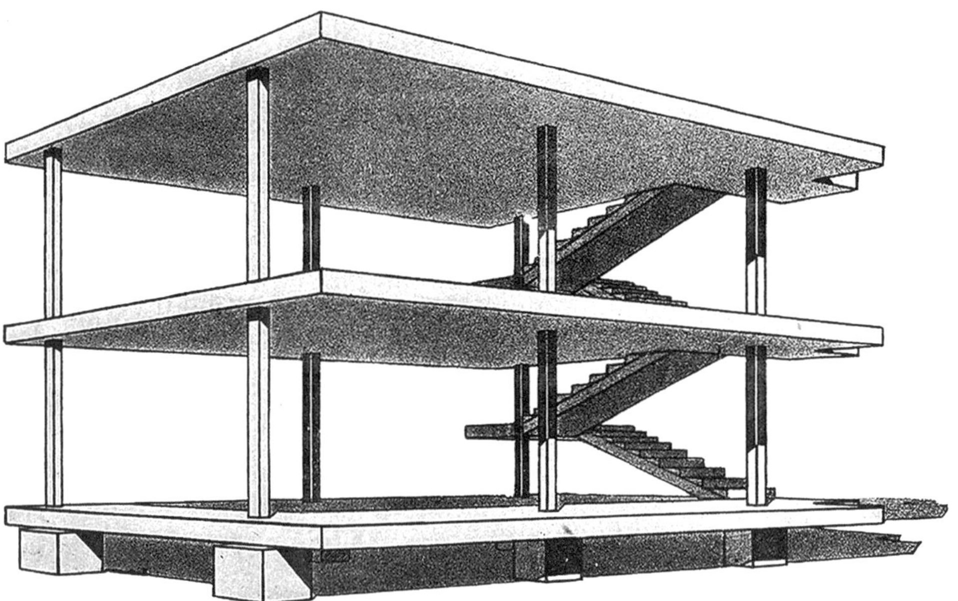

19

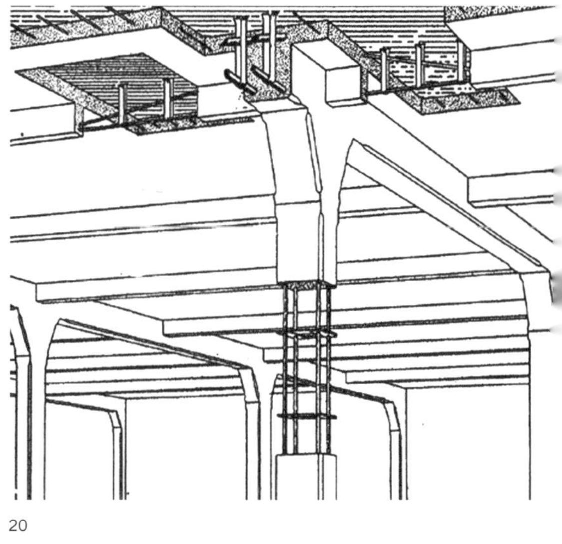

20

19 Le Corbusier, Dom-ino principle
20 F. Hennebique, reinforced concrete principle

SKELETON / MONOLITH

Dom-ino Skeleton

This type of structure owes its name to Le Corbusier's Maison Dom-ino (1914). [← 19] The Dom-ino principle features rigid floor slabs supported by columns. The floor slabs determine the overall structure here and cannot be adapted very easily. The partition walls, however, can be placed anywhere within the open-floor plan, so that the preferred horizontal relationships can be achieved.

The Dom-ino house is based on a standard reinforced concrete skeleton according to the Hennebique system. [← 20] When Le Corbusier opted for reinforced concrete, he assumed that this technique would enable rapid and efficient house building.[13] The Dom-ino principle can be summarized in the following four points:

– The structure is independent from the final layout.
– The skeleton is poured *in situ* without complex formwork.
– A company can manufacture the structure *in situ* and on demand.
– The production of the fittings and fixtures, such as standard wardrobes, doors and windows, can be done by another contractor.[14]

13 Le Corbusier developed the Dom-ino principle to facilitate the rapid reconstruction of Flemish towns and villages devastated in the First World War.

14 W. Boesiger, *Oeuvre complète de 1946–1952: Le Corbusier et Pierre Jeanneret, vol 2* (Zurich: Artemis, 1964), 23.

SKELETON / MONOLITH

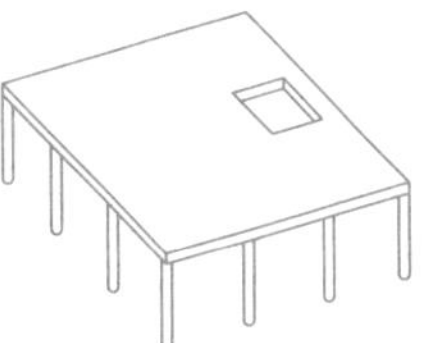

Dom-ino skeleton

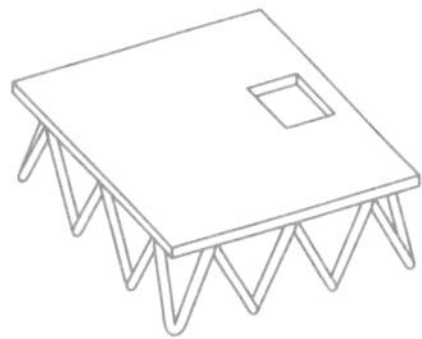

Reticulated Structure

21a

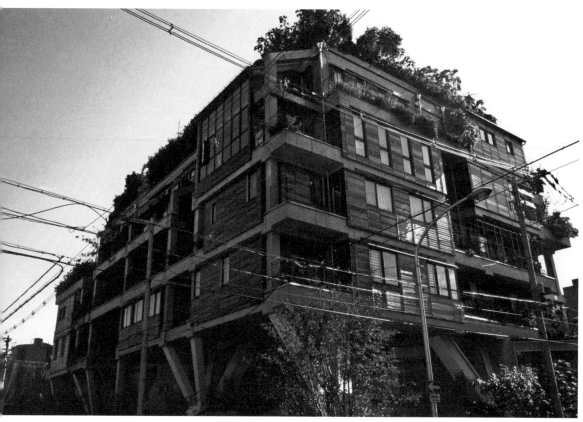

YOSITIKA UTIDA AND SHU-KO-SHA ARCH. & URBAN DESIGN STUDIO, NEXT 21 (OSAKA, JAPAN, 1994)

Next 21 was built as the housing of the future for the Japanese Osaka Gas Company. The building is an experiment in the field of energy and water management. It incorporates environmentally friendly features and integrates vegetation on the roof and in the façades. The longevity of the building has been extended by separating the support from the internal layout.
To achieve maximum flexibility on each floor, the designers opted for a main structure based on the Dom-ino principle, with floors and columns made of concrete. But unlike the Dom-ino skeleton, the floors have been partially lowered or raised to accommodate the service ducts. The dividing walls between the dwellings are part of the infill kit. Support and infill have been constructed in such a way that the joint structure and adjacent dwellings will not be affected by any alterations to the individual units. The service ducts, for example, have been separated from the main structure. The electric wiring, water and sewage pipes have been worked into the lowered floor of the galleries and the corridors. The ventilation system has been concealed behind the lowered ceiling of the dwellings and the smaller pipes and ducts have been integrated in the raised floor inside the dwellings. To demonstrate the feasibility of the concept, Osaka Gas has actually made adjustments to some flats. However, so far no residents have come forward with plans for major modifications. The use of a Dom-ino skeleton with dividing walls between dwellings that are not made of reinforced concrete is quite exceptional given contemporary fire safety and noise insulation standards. In that respect, Next 21 is a unique project.

SKELETON / MONOLITH

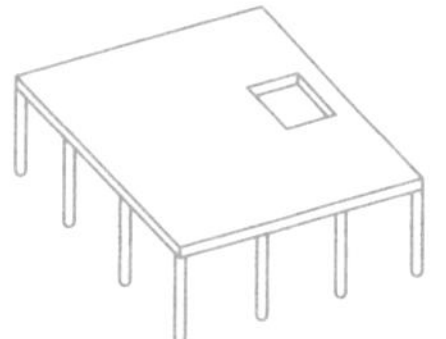

Dom-ino skeleton

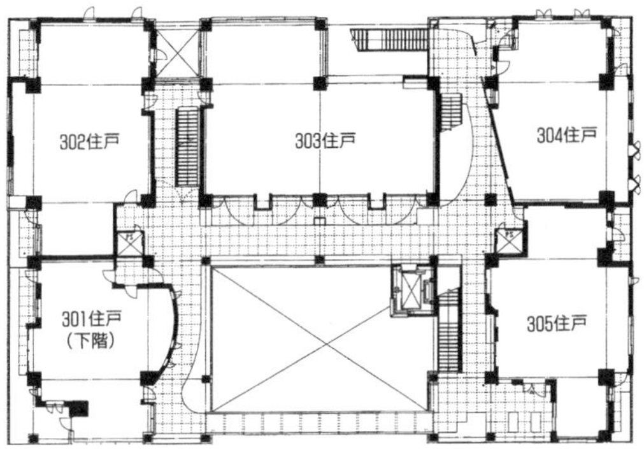

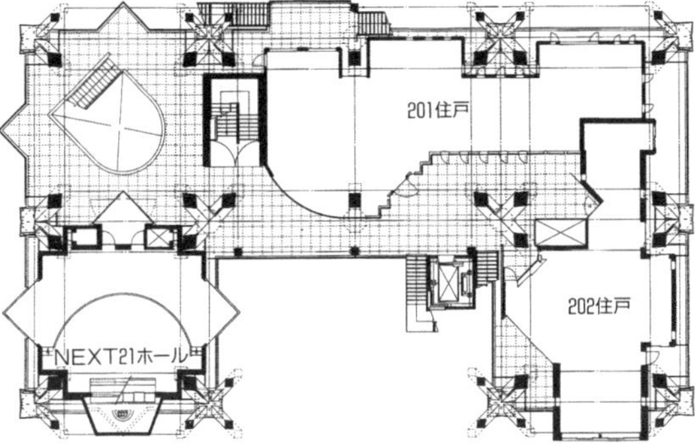

21b

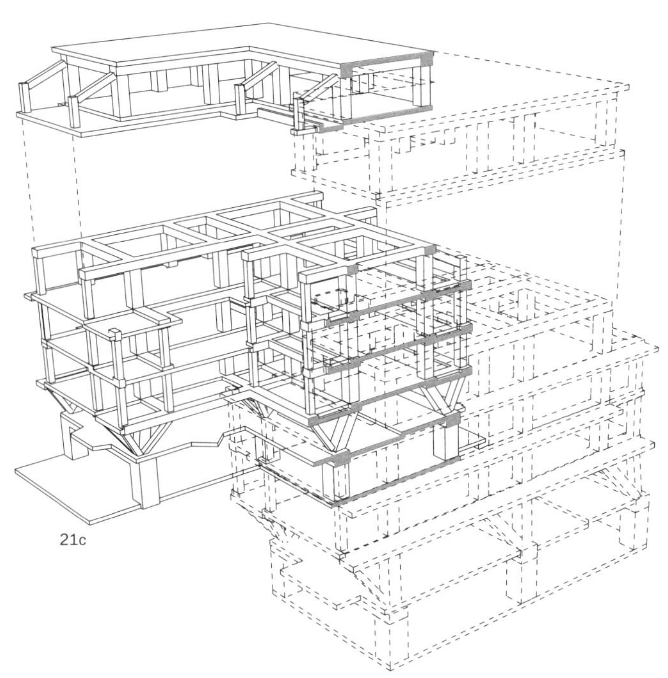

21c

21b Ground-level and first-storey floor plans
21c Analysis of the concrete skeleton

22a

XAVEER DE GEYTER, CHASSÉ PARK APARTMENTS (BREDA, 2001)

SKELETON / MONOLITH

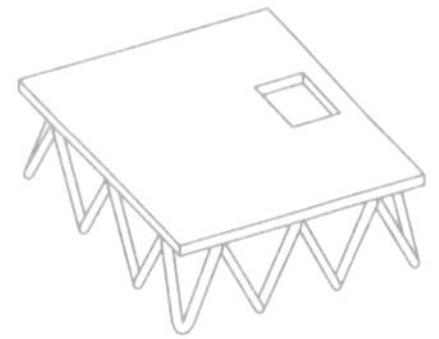

Reticulated Structure

In recent years we are seeing more and more buildings with a reticulated structure.[15] The principle is used in housing as well. In this kind of construction the load is not absorbed by vertical columns but by a criss-cross pattern of columns or beams. Angling the load-bearing elements and interlinking them in several directions produces a rigid surface. Because this network can be made relatively lightweight, it is transparent enough to be placed in the façade. The result is a building with load-bearing as well as transparent façades that can support large floor slabs without columns.

One of the residential buildings in the project shown here, by Xaveer de Geyter on the Chassé site in Breda, was built using a load-bearing grid, in this case a concrete grid. This grid is positioned immediately behind the façade. The reticulated structure appears to be confined to the south side. However, the other, more closed façades are built in the same way, albeit that the reticulated load paths have been concealed in the rectangular cladding panels. These panels have been stacked diagonally. With the load-bearing line in the façade, the open floor plan offers great flexibility.

15 Cecil Balmond, in his *Frontiers of Architecture 1* (Humlebæk: Louisiana Museum of Modern Art, 2007), speaks of a reticulated structure.

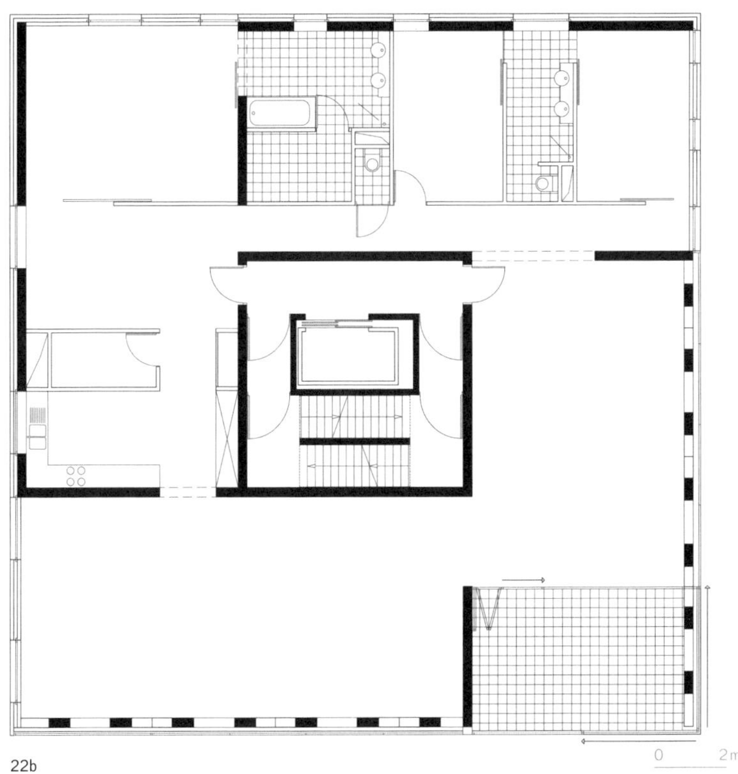

22b

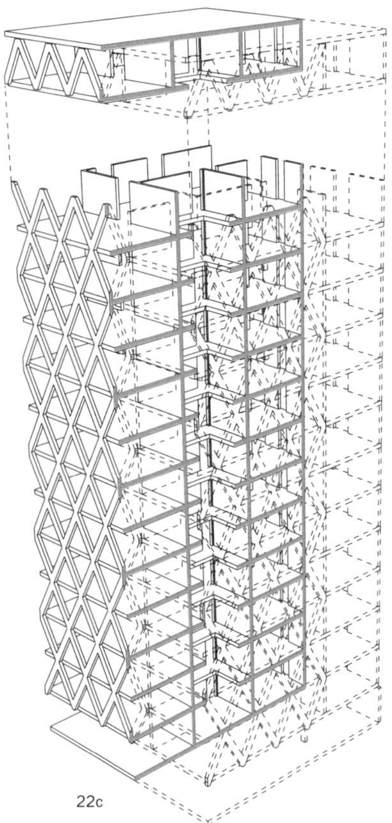

22c

22b High-rise floor plan
22c Analytical drawing

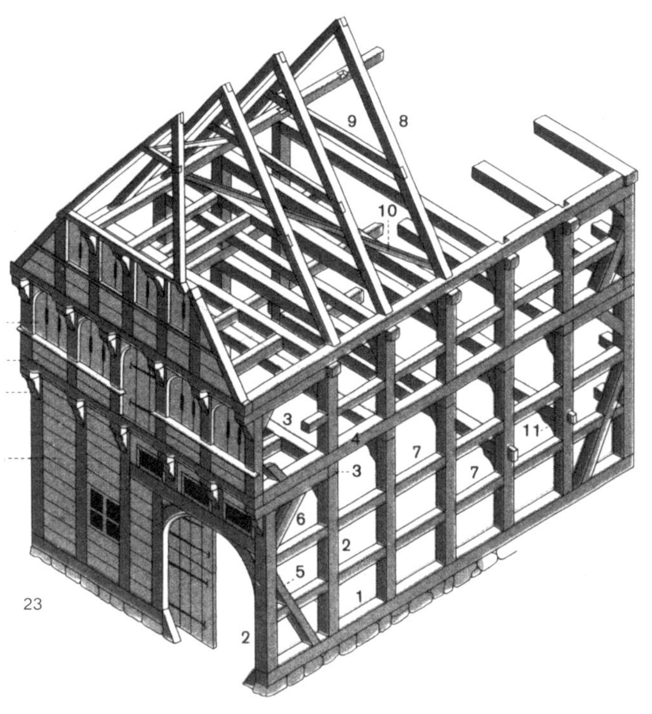

23

24

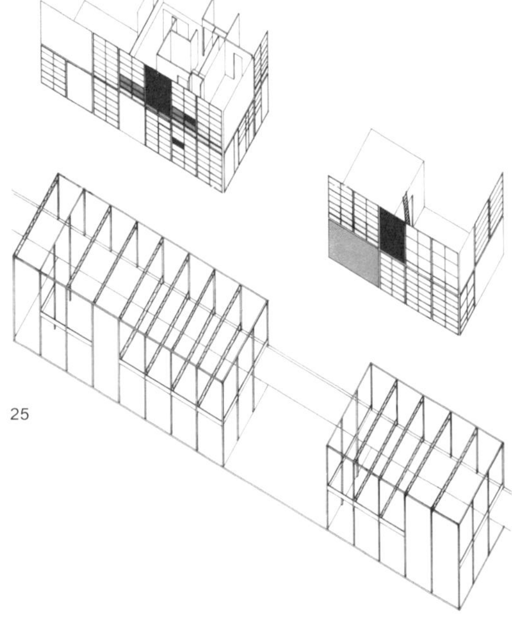

25

SKELETON / SKELETON

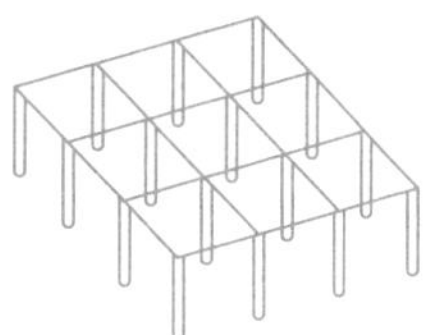

3d-skeleton

3-D Skeleton

The skeleton construction consists of a three-dimensional skeleton made of beams and columns. If it is built as an open, three-dimensional skeleton, both the space-defining walls and, to a certain degree, the floors can be positioned freely.

The half-timbered house emerged in the late Middle Ages in North-West Europe, especially around the major river deltas. Like their common ancestor, the primitive hut, these houses are made up of two separate layers: the structure consisting of the timber skeleton on the one hand, and the skin made of the clay, stone or timber infill and the tiled roof on the other. The skeleton as structuring principle is palpable throughout these houses: timber columns in the wall, heavy main and secondary beams against the ceiling, buttresses, corbel stones, roof trusses, you name it, all of which shape our perception. The structure of these houses therefore leaves an indelible impression. [← 23]

A more recent example, albeit in steel, is the house that Ray and Charles Eames designed for themselves (Santa Monica, 1945–1950). This house was built using a steel skeleton: steel I-beams as columns with lattice girders on top. [← 24–25] The skeleton is covered with standard cladding. The floors and roof panels are made of profiled sheets for extra rigidity.

23 Farmhouse in Lower Saxony
24, 25 R. and Ch. Eames, private house, 1945–1950, Santa Monica. On the right the axonometrics of the structure.

26a

LE CORBUSIER, UNITÉ D'HABITATION (MARSEILLE, 1947)

After the Second World War, Le Corbusier's study of mass housing edifices resulted in the Unité d'Habitation, a residential building accommodating 321 apartments, shops, a nursery school, a hotel and a fitness centre.[16] Le Corbusier managed to implement several of his ideas in this Unité. The separation between skeleton and internal layout, for example, which Le Corbusier had first explored in the Maison Dom-ino, returns in the separation between the carcass of the skeleton and the production of the individual housing unit in the Unité. The double-height living quarters and the *pilotis* were first used in the Maison Citrohan. The main structure of the Unité consists of a gigantic concrete skeleton cast *in situ*. The individual apartments have been placed within this concrete skeleton. The structure of the apartments themselves consists of steel I-beams and light box girders. In theory, the concrete skeleton of the Unité in Marseille provides three-dimensional freedom, which Le Corbusier exploits to design various, differently linked dwelling types. [17]

The Unité is one of the few examples of a 3-D concrete skeleton used in housing. For sound insulation and fire safety reasons, the floors tend to be poured at the same time as the skeleton. Every three storeys, the Unité features a thin fire-resistant flooring layer. As this is too thin to support habitation, it was then covered with the same type of flooring as in the other storeys.

16 H. Engel, 'Veertig jaar Unité d'habitation een nieuwe formule voor stedelijkheid', *OASE* 37/38 (1994), 32–67.

17 Leupen, *Frame and Generic Space*, op. cit. (note 6), 154 ff.

SKELETON / SKELETON

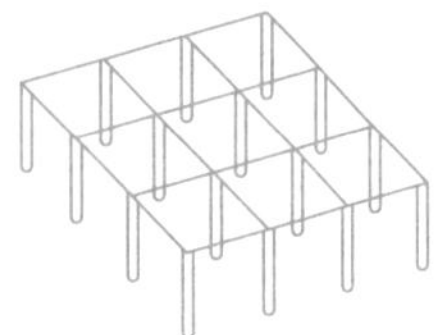

3d-skeleton

26b Concrete skeleton during construction

27a

27a Steel skeleton during construction
27b Infra+ flooring during construction
27c Initial design of seventh floor, tunnel system shown in secondary colour
27d Definitive design of 23rd floor, more flexible layout

SKELETON / SKELETON

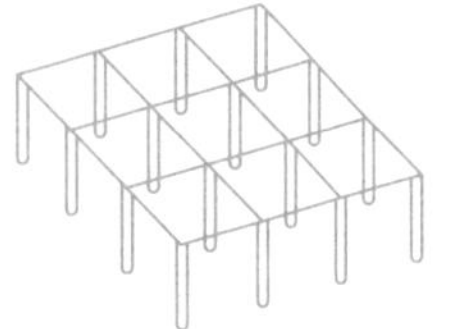

3d-skeleton

RUDY UYTENHAAK, LA FENÊTRE (THE HAGUE, 1998–2005)

On a narrow plot, wedged between a busy street and the Dutch National Archives, the site of La Fenêtre was extremely tight. To complicate matters even further, a route for slow-moving (pedestrian and bicycle) traffic had been planned to run underneath the building. The architect soon decided to use a steel skeleton, not just because of the small site, but also because steel is easier to dismantle and reuse if necessary.[18]

In a steel skeleton, the distinction between load-bearing and dividing elements is absolute. As in the Unité, the structural skeleton forms the framework within which the walls and floors separate the dwellings from one another. The steel skeleton creates an open floor plan with plenty of flexibility for installing partitions and service ducts. In practice, however, this flexibility has not been exploited. Because the initial design was based on a tunnel-form concrete skeleton, the definitive design still features the typical tunnel-form floor plan with parallel walls. However, this layout has been abandoned in a few places, most notably on the 23rd floor, where the zoning is less rigid. The floors were made using the Infra+ system, a prefabricated flooring system that consists of a concrete subfloor with steel I-beams for reinforcement. These I-beams are then covered with a top flooring layer. Depending on the quality and weight of this top flooring, the resulting package should provide sufficient sound insulation for use in housing. The cavity between the Infra+ flooring and the top flooring offers space to tuck away a flexible set of pipes and ducts. The service ducts can also be inserted through the oval opening in the I-beam and installed across the length of the I-beam. In theory, it should be possible to remove the top flooring at a later date to adjust the service ducts, for instance for a new apartment layout. However, in the case of La Fenêtre it was decided to use a top flooring layer made of steel dovetail sheeting (Lewis sheeting) covered with a sand cement top flooring layer. This type of top flooring is difficult to remove. The designer opted for this system because the client objected to changes to the flooring after completion, as the re-laying of the top floor by non-professionals could result in noise seepage.

18 Huub Smeets et al., *La Fenêtre Den Haag* (Maastricht: Vesteda architectuur, 2007), 12.

7b

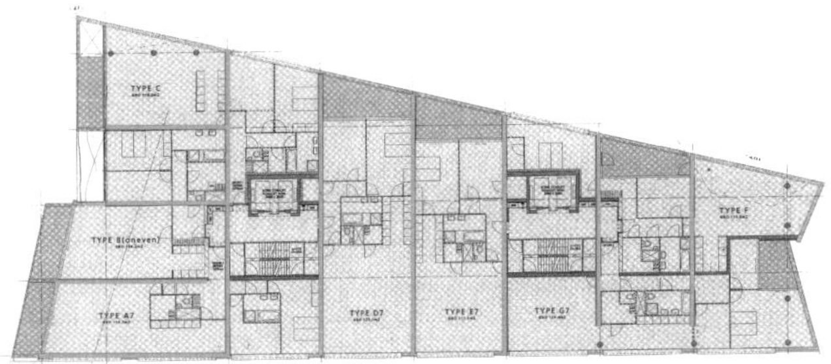

27c

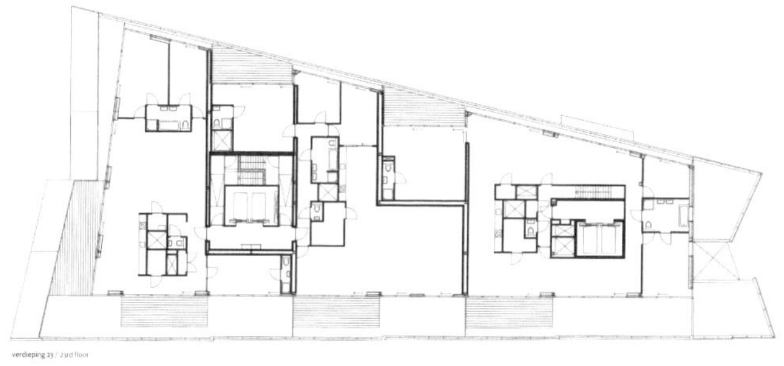

27d

0 7,5m

28a

HERZOG & DE MEURON, HEBELSTRASSE 11 HOUSING (BASEL, 1988)

Herzog & De Meuron opted for a timber structure in their design for six dwellings around a courtyard on Hebelstrasse in Basel. Their decision was inspired by the old timber sheds in the courtyard of this housing block.
The first two floors of the building are made of timber. A series of support columns, some of which are partly visible as the beautiful, slender cigar-shaped wooden columns facing the courtyard while the others are concealed within the wall, transfer the load down to the foundation. At the rear of the building a large wall built with chunks of natural stone – alluding to the old garden walls in the area – ensures stability.
Large main beams constitute the main span between the wall and the columns. Secondary beams support the floor slabs, as they do in a traditional house with stone walls and timber floor joists, making this timber skeleton a three-dimensional skeleton. However, the structure is not made entirely of wood: only the floors and part of the main structure are. On the building's third floor, the timber skeleton makes way for a steel skeleton. Because this skeleton supports only the roof, it does not have to be fire-proofed and can therefore be left showing.

SKELETON / SKELETON

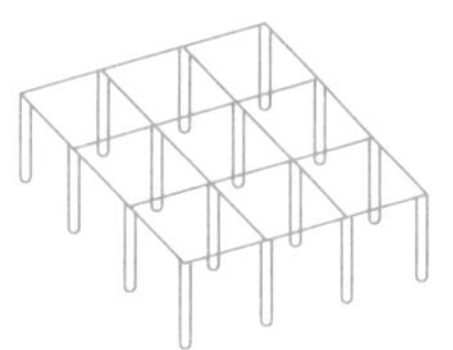

3d-skeleton

28a Entrance on courtyard
28b Ground floor and first flo
28c Cross section
28d Analytical drawing

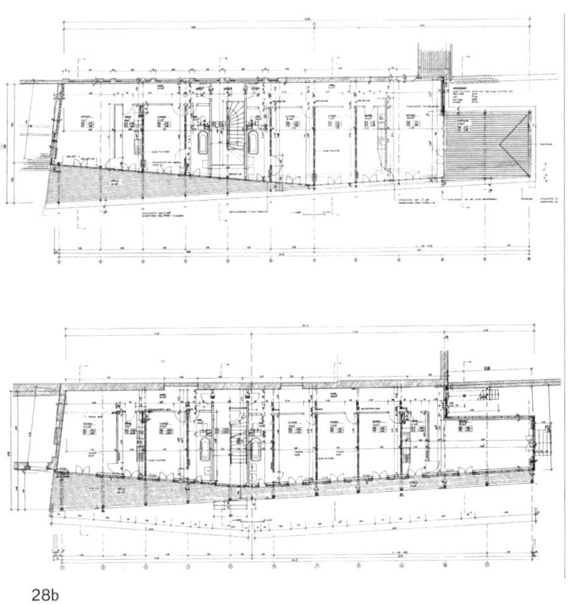

28b

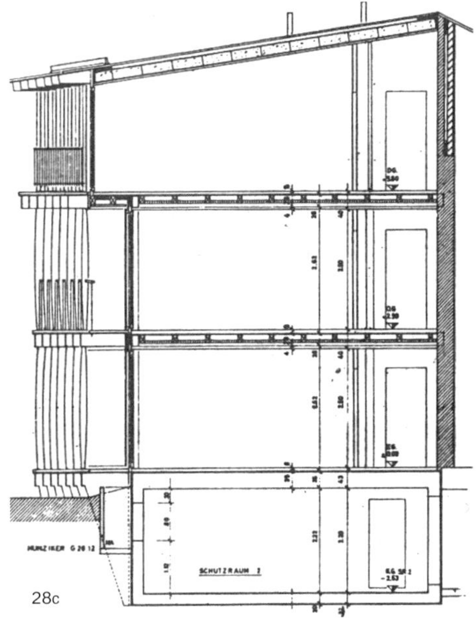

28c

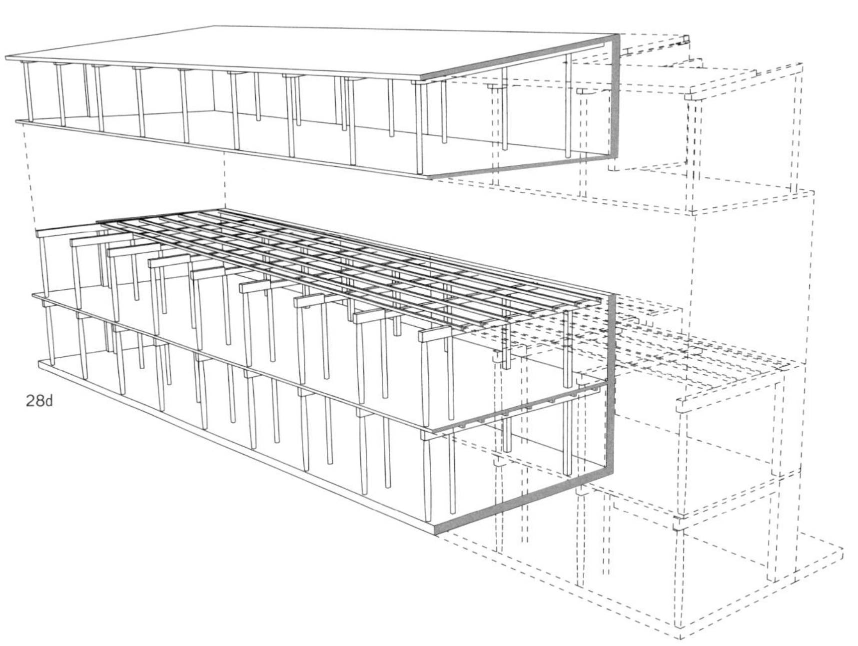

28d

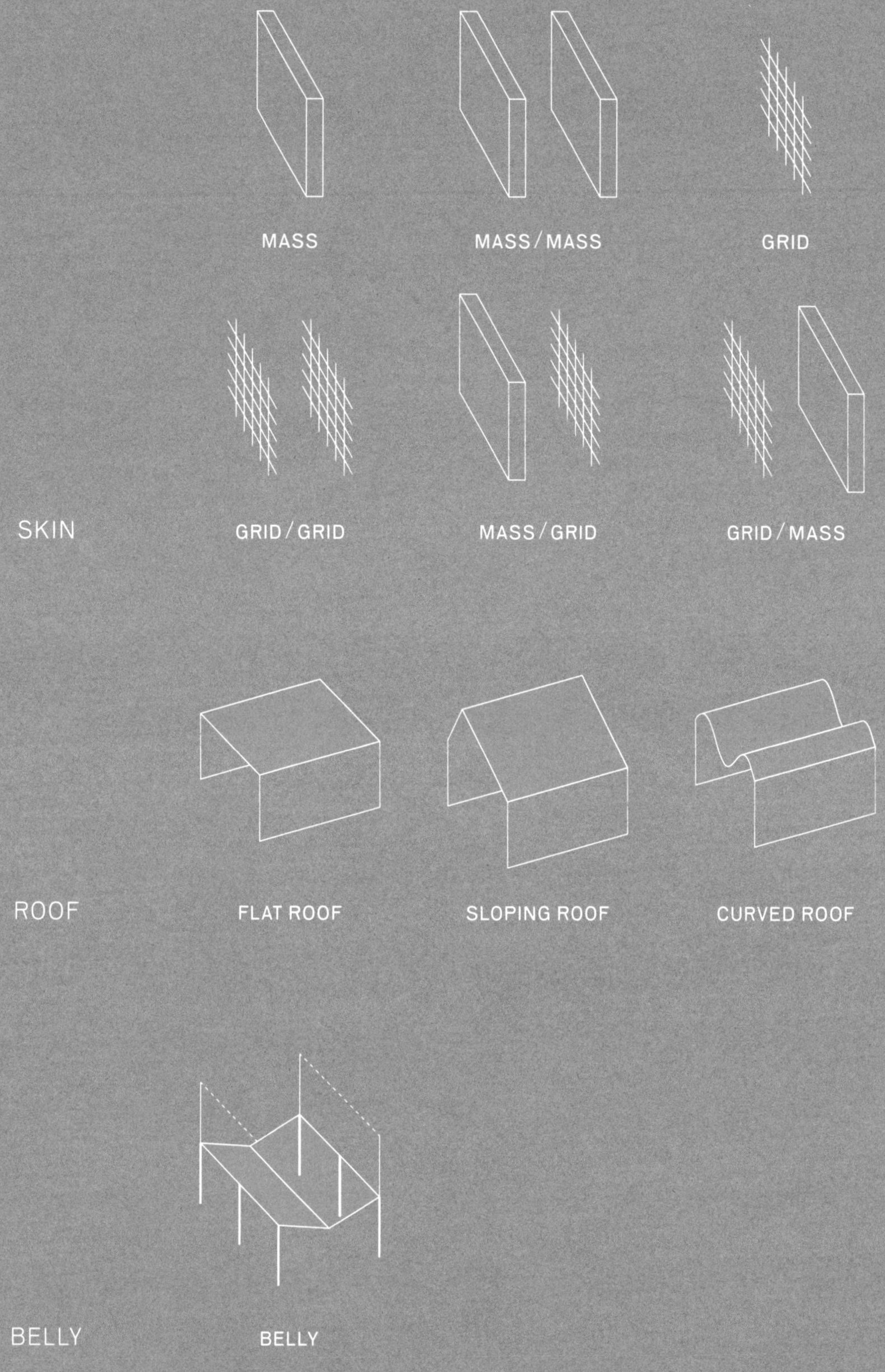

MASS MASS / MASS GRID

SKIN

GRID / GRID MASS / GRID GRID / MASS

ROOF

FLAT ROOF SLOPING ROOF CURVED ROOF

BELLY

BELLY

SKIN

The skin separates the inside from the outside, while also presenting the building to the outside world. The skin comprises the arrangement of all those materials and elements that define the separation between inside and outside. Sometimes this is a single layer, such as a glass pane, and sometimes it is a complex package with inner and outer cladding, insulation, vapour barrier, substructures, etcetera, as it is in a roof. Sometimes the skin, contrary to what the word suggests, is actually a complex spatial system in which physical and spatial dividing lines do not coincide. All of these constellations will be discussed in this part of the chapter. We can also break the skin down into the skin underneath, on top or at the side of the building. If the skin is a more or less vertical plane, we refer to it as the *façade*. If it covers the top of the building we speak of the *roof* and if it encloses or bounds the underside of a building we call it, somewhat expressively, the *belly* of the building.

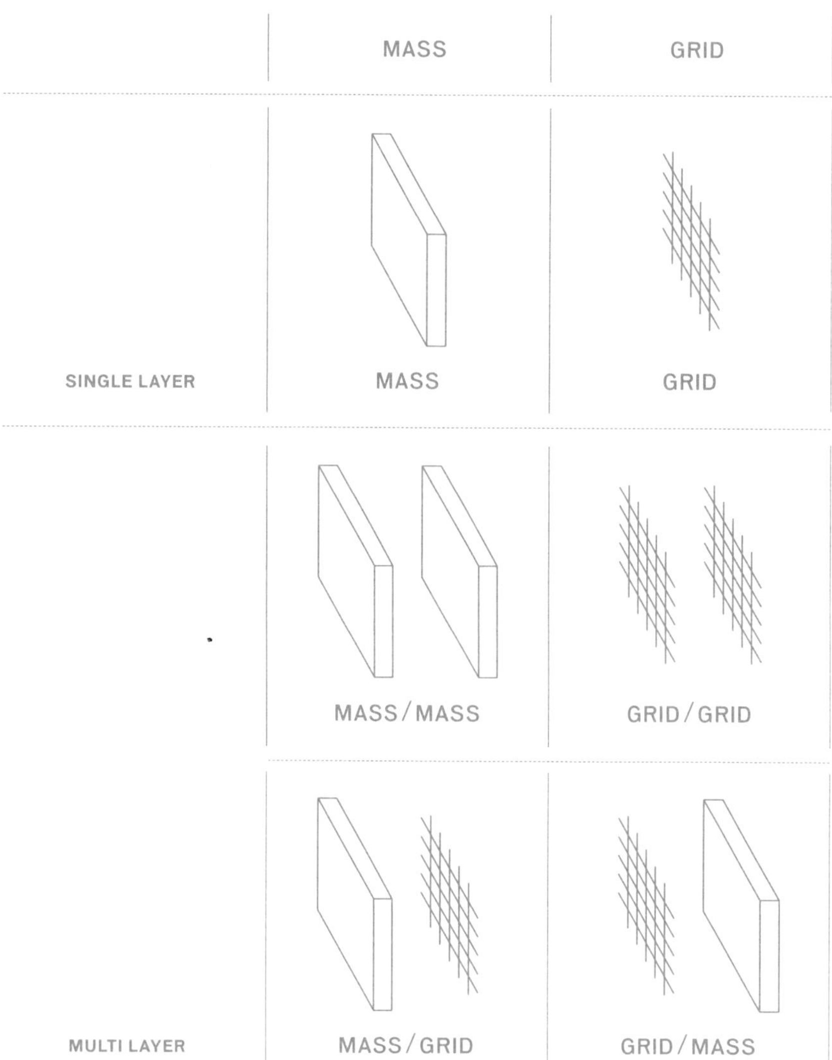

29 Matrix of six façade types

The Façade

—*Mass*
—*Grid*
—*Mass/Mass*
—*Grid/Grid*
—*Mass/Grid*
—*Grid/Mass*

Like the structure, there are two basic façade types: the monolithic wall (the 'mass') made of a single material, and the membrane-like façade (the 'grid'), which is made of a skeleton and sealed with a transparent or opaque sheet-like material.[19] The contemporary façade serves a multitude of functions. It has to transfer load, insulate against noise and heat and be wind- and water-proof. Because few materials can meet all of these requirements, façades are increasingly made of different materials with different properties, with each layer fulfilling a different task.
The various layers can be both monolithic and membrane-like. The matrix diagram on page 284 represents all of these combinations. The following examples illustrate the different positions within the matrix.

19
Deplazes, *Constructing Architecture*, op. cit. (note 9), 13.

30

MASS

BEARTH & DEPLAZES, HOUSE, MEULI (ST GALLEN, SWITZERLAND, 2001)

Meuli in Switzerland is home to a private house with façades made of a single material. Its architects, Bearth & Deplazes, who specialize in unusual methods of construction, built the house with thick concrete walls. These walls are made of a specially prepared concrete and, at 50 cm, thick enough to be insulating. An admixture makes the concrete lighter while adding extra insulation properties. The walls are a part of the structure. The special concrete meets most of the requirements of a façade, that is to be load-bearing, insulating, watertight and windproof. Small windows have been inserted for light and a view, with their free composition expressing their subordination to the main material: the insulating concrete.

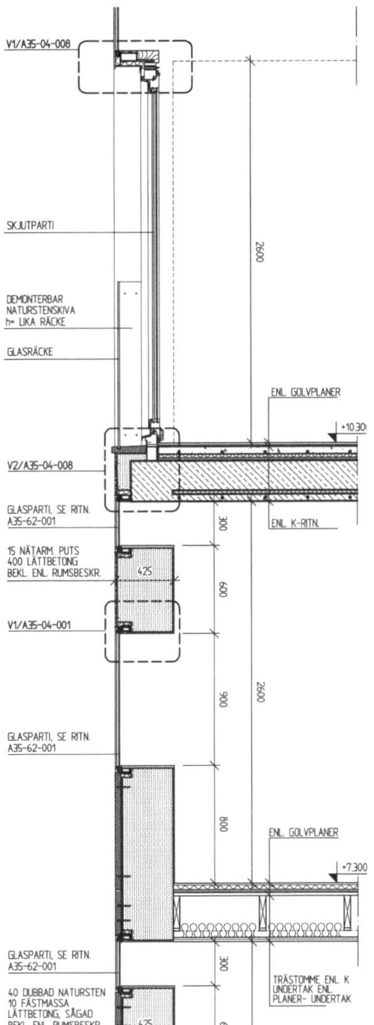

31a

31b

GERT WINGÅRDH, BO01 (MALMÖ, 2001)

For Gert Wingårdh, durability means first and foremost solidity.[20] He drew on natural materials and sturdy building techniques to design a residential building for the building exhibition 'BO01' in Malmö, Sweden. The residential building, which is to last hundreds of years, is a prominent part of a residential neighbourhood designed by Klas Tham. It looks out across the Sundet, the strait between the North Sea and the Baltic Sea. Building Bo01 consists of two parts, with the tallest part like a fortress screening the adjacent neighbourhood with its narrow pedestrian streets from the raw sea wind. The courtyard immediately behind the fortress accommodates the second, lower apartment building. The façades of this building are made of a lightweight concrete brick. Thanks to the use of insulating concrete in the thick façade, no extra insulation is needed. Like the ground-level floor, the base of the apartment building is clad in limestone. In contrast to the house in Meuli, discussed above, the façade here is not load-bearing. This is reflected in the generous window openings that Gert Wingårdh has introduced.

20 Bernard Leupen et al., *Time-Based Architecture* (Rotterdam: 010 Publishers, 2005).

MASS

31a Vertical façade detail

32a

32b

VANDKUNSTEN, ÆBLELUNDEN (COPENHAGEN, 2008)

The façades of this building are made of prefabricated concrete sandwich (layered) panels. The external leaf includes brick. These two stone-like materials envelop a layer of insulation material. This sandwich with a stone-like material on either side is typical of prefab elements.
The façade is not part of the main structure and only supports itself. The prefabricated standard floor elements are parallel to the façade and have been fixed to the structural walls, which are also dividing walls. The architect has opted for a prefabricated sandwich panel to create a stony exterior with brick panels.
The façade has a puzzle-like pattern. The openings for windows and balcony doors and the balconies themselves are staggered, creating a vivid picture. It also means that the façade no longer reflects the individual housing units, the way it does in traditional mass housing.
Given the staggered pattern of the openings in the façade, the façade could be constructed using relatively small prefab elements. The large openings are created by open spaces between the elements instead of cut-aways in the elements themselves. This means that less lost space (cut-away material) has to be transported by road. Although the façade is not part of the main structure, it does support itself. With the sandwich panels placed in a checkerboard pattern, the load lines run straight down.

MASS / MASS

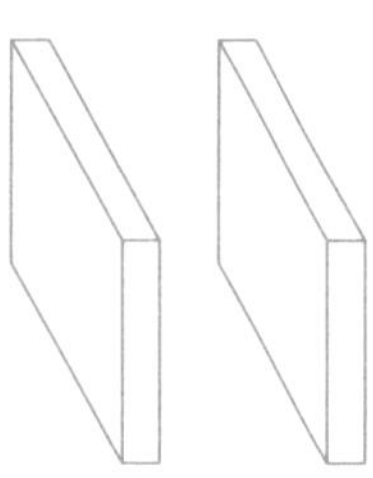

32a Façade structure principle: prefabricated panels stacked in a checkerboard pattern with vertical load lines
32b Rendering of western façade

33a

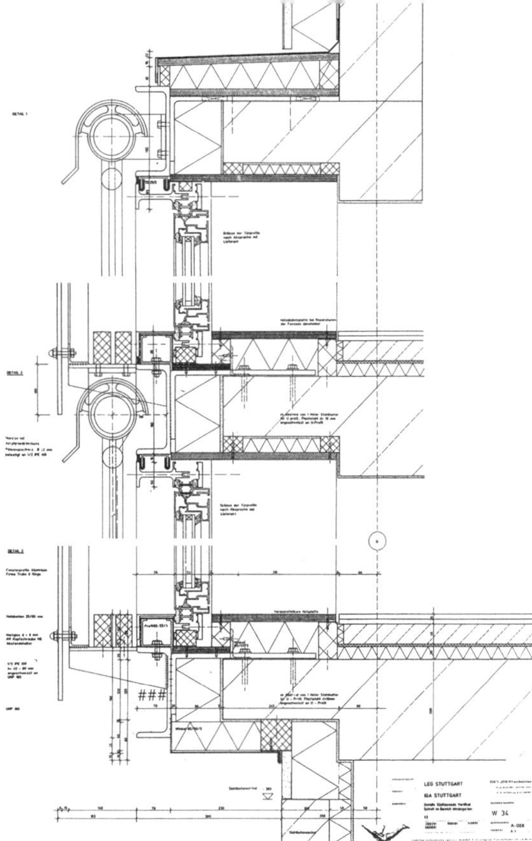

33b

MECANOO, HOUSE 13 (STUTTGART, 1989–1993)

House 13 formed a part of the Internationale Garten Ausstellung, a housing exhibition with an environmental focus in Stuttgart. It is a good example of an apartment block with a single-layer façade. The tunnel-form structure, cast *in situ*, has three closed sides and one open side. The closed sides with load-bearing walls are punctured in a few places by a door, a small window or just a tiny hole closed off with a glass brick. The two short sides have been treated differently: the rear, which faces northeast across a communal garden, is closed. This wall was cast *in situ* as a stabilizing wall. The side walls are clad in façade insulation and plaster, while the park-oriented rear elevation is clad in zinc with underlying insulation. The sun-facing open side is enclosed with a continuous glass front. The timber window frames on each floor are fitted with insulating glass, imbuing the façade with a degree of layeredness. The glass front contains rotating elements so that the winter garden behind it can be opened across its entire width. The winter garden and the living quarters are separated by a single-glazed folding partition.

33b Vertical detail of south façade

34a

34b, 34c Metal shutters
34d, 34e Vertical cross sections of front façade and side façade behind building with wooden roll-down shutters

HERZOG & DE MEURON, RUE DES SUISSES (PARIS, 1996)

In some multilayered façades the external layer is not the waterproof and windproof layer. In some cases, such an 'outer skin' is purely aesthetic, in others it serves as a sun blind or privacy measure. Herzog & De Meuron fitted an outer skin that alludes to the traditional shutters found in various forms of European housing. The windows of traditional houses in Europe are fitted with shutters to keep out either the sun or the cold. In France we find shutters with horizontal tilted slats that admit some light and air during the day, while houses in colder regions have closed shutters with the sole aim of keeping out the cold.

In many Dutch canalside houses, the shutters are on the inside of the windows. These shutters can be folded away in an alcove in the wall beside the 'window seat'. In French boulevard blocks from the early twentieth century, such shutters were sometimes made of metal. This was the inspiration for Herzog & De Meuron when they chose the façade cladding for their housing project on the Rue des Suisses in Paris. When closed, the perforated steel shutters admit filtered light. Instead of mounting the shutters in the usual way in the window recesses, Herzog & De Meuron fit them as a kind of net curtain 50 centimetres in front of the climate-proof façade. When closed, this smooth façade covers the entire building, making it look quite abstract. When the shutters are opened, the windows appear and the façade displays an alternating open-and-closed pattern. A balustrade turns the narrow strip between the window and the shutter into a Juliet balcony.

GRID / GRID

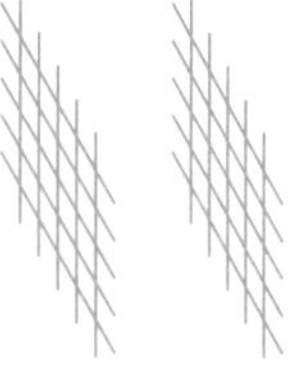

34b

34c

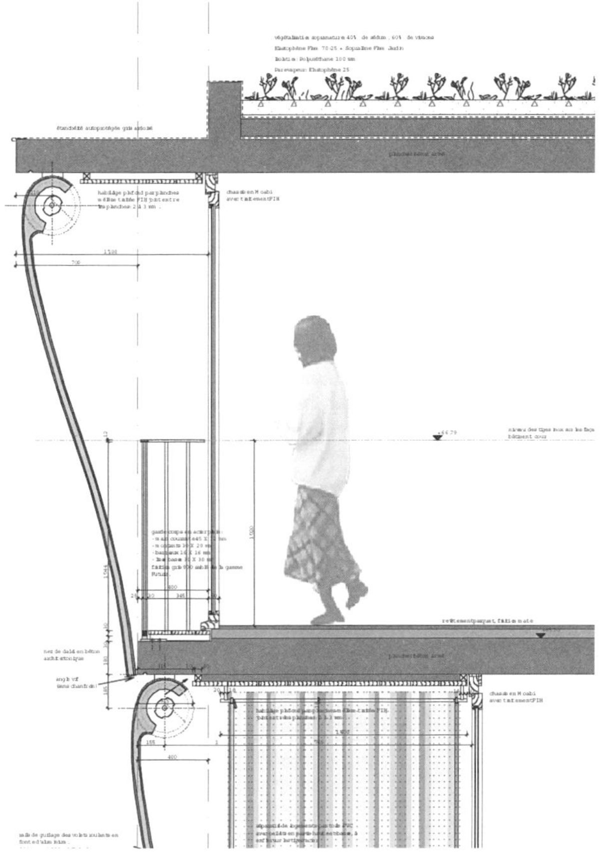

34d

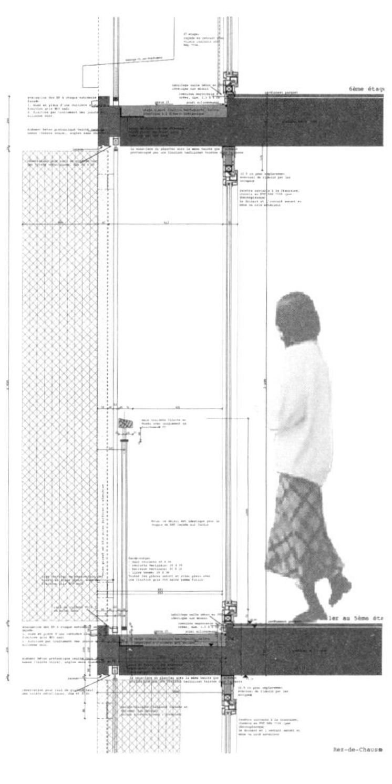

34e

35a

MASS / GRID

GRID / MASS

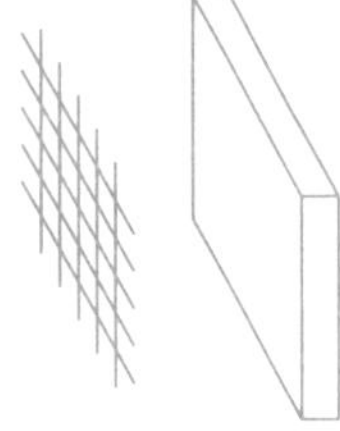

35a Façade fragment with the continuous load-bearing façade surface clearly visible around the windows
35b Vertical cross section of south façade

DKV ARCHITECTEN, KOP VAN HAVENDIEP (LELYSTAD, 2004)

The Kop van Havendiep was discussed under the section on structures as an example of a load-bearing façade. The façade of this building is indeed load-bearing, but its layered composition conceals the structure. The first thing one notices are the sliding panels that provide shelter on the balconies. Sets of double French doors give access to these balconies. The doors are alternated with closed walls clad on the outside with multiplex with insulation underneath. These wide piers constitute the load-bearing façade. Because the piers are alternated with the openings with the French doors, the façade, at first sight, does not appear to be a part of the main structure. The façade therefore consists of a mass on the inside and a grid on the outside – a grid made of two layers, one of which is the kind of 'external skin' we saw in the previous project.

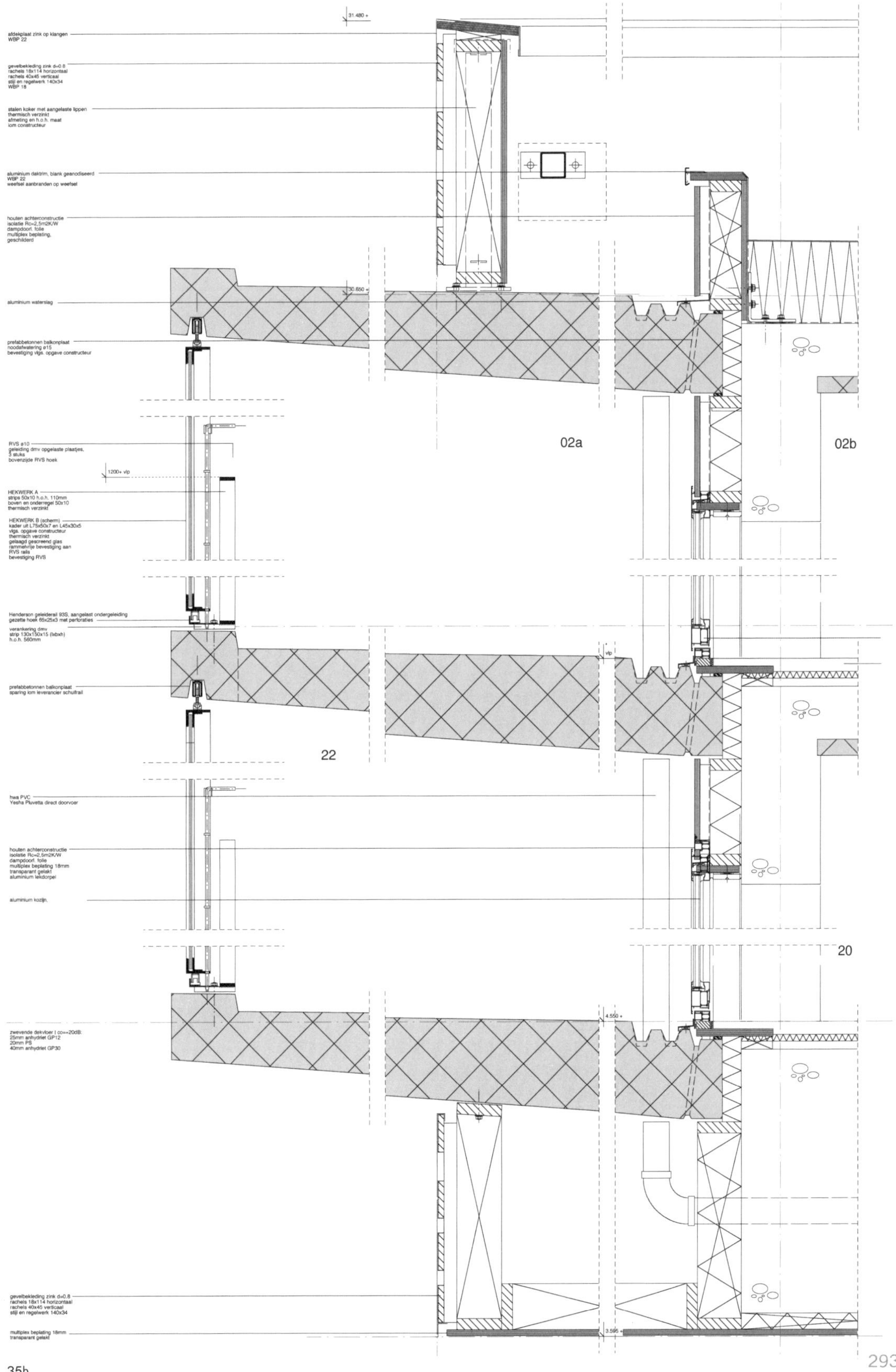
31.480 +
afdekplaat zink op klangen
WBP 22
gevelbekleding zink d=0.8
rachels 18x114 horizontaal
rachels 40x45 verticaal
stijl en regelwerk 140x34
WBP 18
stalen koker met aangelaste lippen
thermisch verzinkt
afmeting en h.o.h. maat
iom constructeur
aluminium daktrim, blank geanodiseerd
WBP 22
weefsel aanbranden op weefsel
houten achterconstructie
isolatie Rc=2,5m2K/W
dampdoorl. folie
multiplex beplating,
geschilderd
30.650 +
aluminium waterslag
prefabbetonnen balkonplaat
noodafwatering ø15
bevestiging vlgs. opgave constructeur
02a
02b
RVS ø10
geleiding dmv opgelaste plaatjes,
3 stuks
bovenzijde RVS hoek
1200+ vlp
HEKWERK A
strips 50x10 h.o.h. 110mm
boven en onderregel 50x10
thermisch verzinkt
HEKWERK B (scherm)
kader uit L75x50x7 en L45x30x5
vlgs. opgave constructeur
thermisch verzinkt
gelaagd gescreend glas
rammelvrije bevestiging aan
RVS rails
bevestiging RVS
Henderson geleiderail 93S, aangelast ondergeleiding
gezette hoek 65x25x3 met perforaties
verankering dmv
strip 130x150x15 (lxbxh)
h.o.h. 560mm
vlp
prefabbetonnen balkonplaat
sparing iom leverancier schuifrail
22
hwa PVC
Yesha Pluvetta direct doorvoer
houten achterconstructie
isolatie Rc=2,5m2K/W
dampdoorl. folie
multiplex beplating 18mm
transparant gelakt
aluminium lekdorpel
aluminium kozijn,
20
4.550 +
zwevende dekvloer I co=+20dB:
25mm anhydriet GP12
20mm PS
40mm anhydriet GP30
gevelbekleding zink d=0.8
rachels 18x114 horizontaal
rachels 40x45 verticaal
stijl en regelwerk 140x34
multiplex beplating 18mm
transparant gelakt
3.595 +

35b

36 Mansard roofs in Paris
37 Detail of a mansard roof
38 Le Corbusier, Unité d'habitation, Marseille, roof with children's paddling pool

36

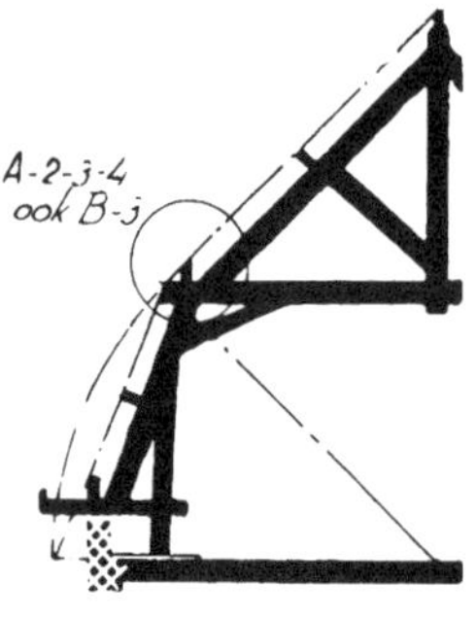

37

38

The Roof

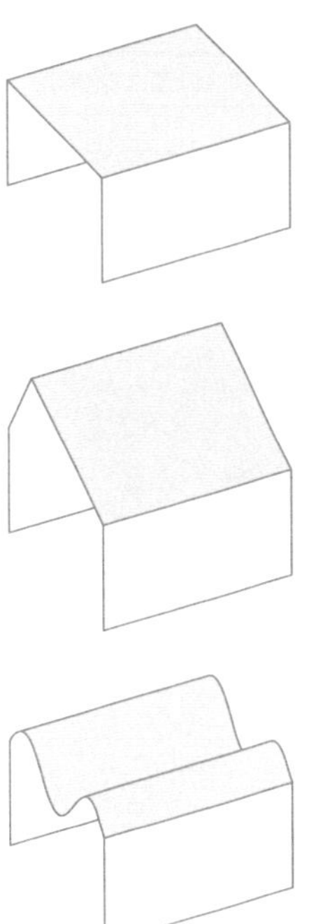

Forms of Roofs

The sloping roof plane–the pitched roof especially–is an archetypal roof form in the northern climate zone. This form of roof–usually covered with tiles–is good at keeping out rain and snow. Originally such roofs were not insulated. Underneath the often attractive roof structures would be the attic, a buffer zone, suitable for storing household or commercial goods. The attic did not always stay dry, because the roofs were usually not weatherboarded. Once roofs were fitted with boarding and later with insulation as well, the attic became a habitable space. In this case, dormer windows provide the necessary light and increase the standing room. The desire to increase the effective floor area in the attic inspired French architect François Mansart to develop roofs with cantilever trusses. These mansard roofs top many nineteenth-century buildings in Paris. Because part of the roof surface is too steep for tiles, zinc cladding is used.
With the emergence of modern architecture at the start of the twentieth century, the roof on top of stacked housing fell into disuse. Modern architects saw the attic–with or without a mansard roof–as second-rate living space. Their solution was the flat roof, which soon became the standard of modern housing. Le Corbusier saw the flat roof as an opportunity for reclaiming space for roof terraces and children's playgrounds, as the roof of the Unité in Marseille illustrates.
There are minor regional differences in the adherence to the dogma of the flat roof. In the Netherlands a flat roof is well and truly flat. A pitch of one degree takes care of the necessary drainage. In Germany, the flat roof tends to have a substantial slope of some 10 degrees. To achieve the desired rectilinear building shape, the walls are extended. Designers in Scandinavia are less radical. Modern or not, a lot of post-Second World War stacked housing is topped with a pitched roof with a gentle slope of 15 degrees, with a wink and a nod to tradition.

The Fifth Façade

Because tiles cannot be used on a gently sloping roof, let alone on a flat roof, and because many modern architects have preferred the abstraction of the smooth plane to the ceramic tile, mastic or rubber-like roofing is the most obvious solution.
By the end of the twentieth century, the roof was no longer just the top of a building, but also something that was looked out upon (from an even taller building). This gave rise to the idea of the fifth façade. The roof deserves as much attention as the façade composition. Taken one step further, the roof is viewed as a landscape. It can be covered with grass or moss, which is ecologically friendly and insulating at the same time.

39

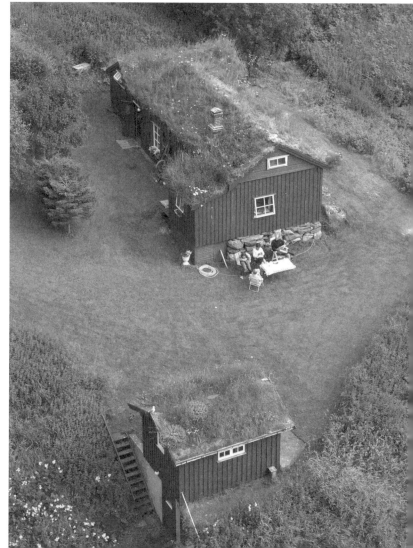

40

39 Grass roof that can be walked on
40 Grass roof of a Norwegian house

The roof can now also be curved or undulating, thanks to modern techniques such as the computer-controlled production of roof trusses or the construction of curved panels using sprayed concrete. The 1990s introduced special roof forms in housing. The following examples cover the most important roof forms and their specific tectonics. We identify the following three roof forms:
—*Sloping roof*
—*Flat roof*
—*Curved roof*

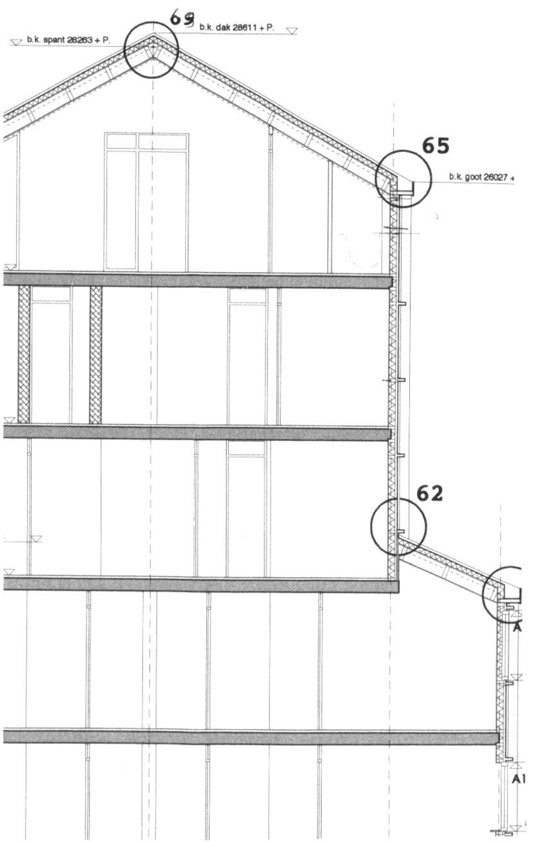

41a Vertical cross section

41b

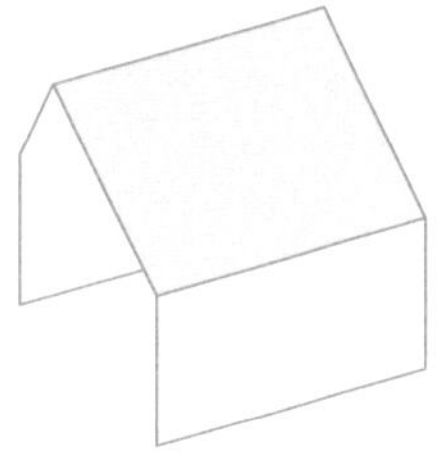

LIESBETH VAN DER POL, ROOIE DONDERS (ALMERE, 1998)

To achieve a distinctive and expressive building shape, Liesbeth van der Pol decided to fit the residential buildings on the Aakweg in Almere with sloping roofs. The building has been topped with a huge pitched roof, under which unusual living spaces are situated, right up to the rafters. It means that this expressive shape is interesting both outside and inside. It is interesting to think that the distinctive shape of the space underneath the roof is particularly appreciated these days.
To further emphasize the striking quality of the three residential buildings in Almere, they have been clad in red corrugated sheeting. To create the pitched roof, steel rafters have been placed on the tunnel-formed structural walls. These rafters are supported by timber purlins. The purlins are topped by 16 mm of underlayment and insulation. The roof is covered with plastic roofing in the same colour red as the façade's corrugated steel sheeting. For the lower roof surfaces the purlins have been placed directly on the concrete structural walls that are cut slantwise.
The Rooie Donders ('red rascals') derive their powerful impact from the systematic use of the colour red and the sloping roofs.

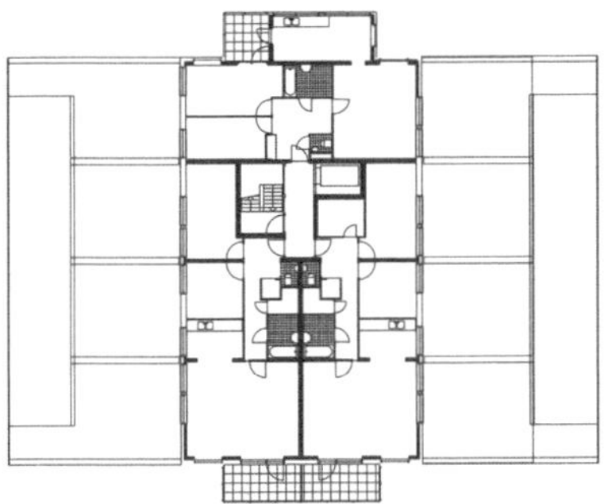

Third to sixth floor

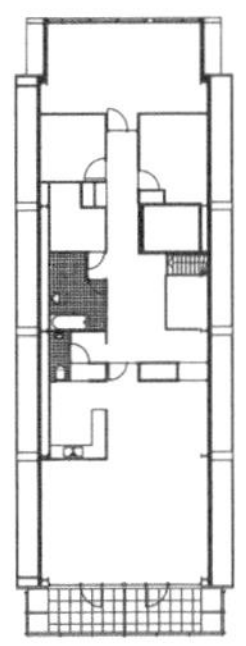

Ninth floor

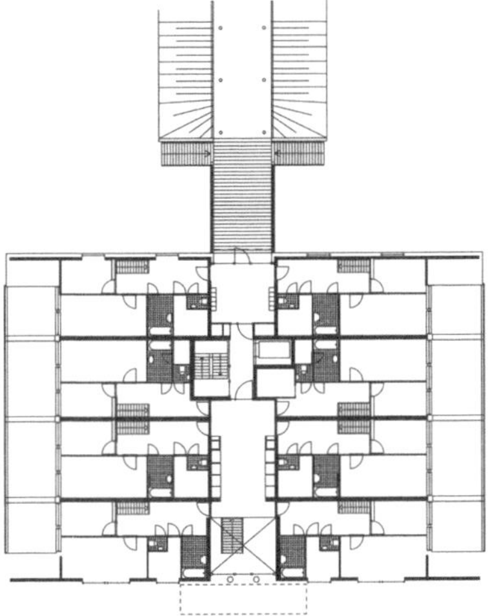

Second floor

Eighth floor

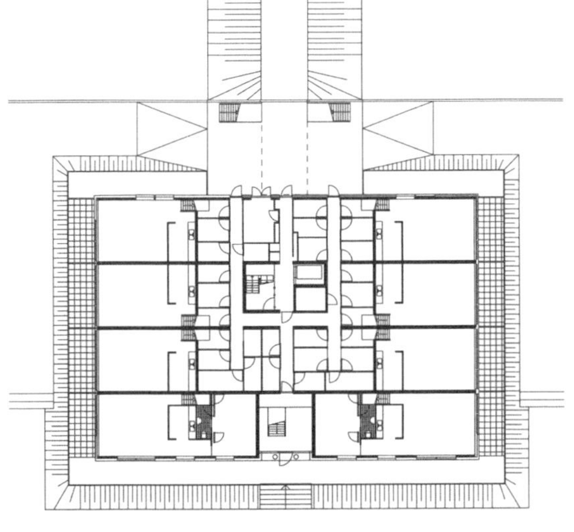

41c First floor

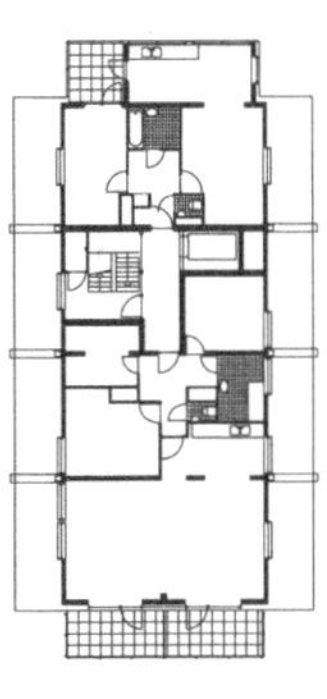

Seventh floor

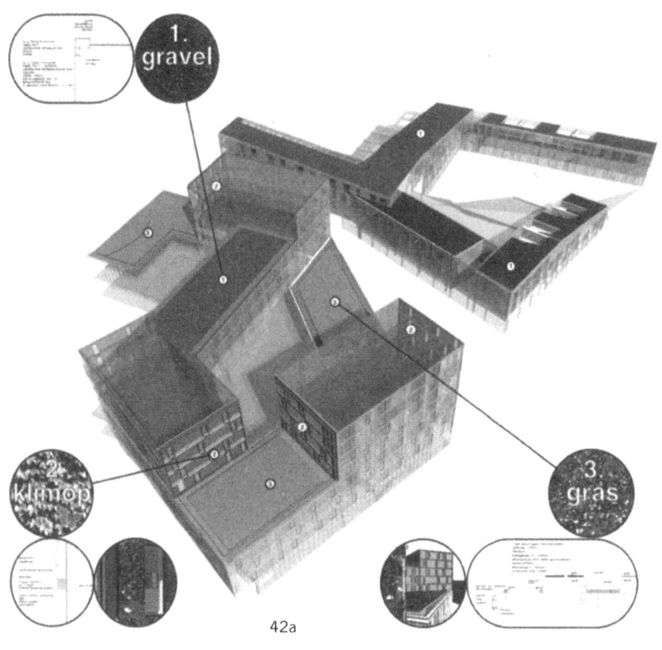

42a

FLAT ROOF

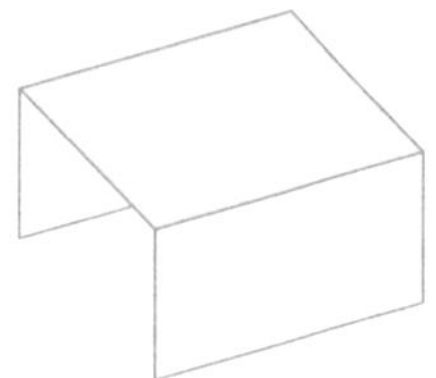

S333, SCHOTS 1 AND SCHOTS 2, CIBOGA SITE (GRONINGEN, 2003)

The form of the development of Schots 1 and Schots 2 on the Ciboga site in Groningen originated in the desire for an open development on the one hand and a complex programme on the other (see also Chapter 7, 'Context', p. 366). To realize a substantial number of homes, together with shops, supermarkets, car parking and plenty of outdoor space, architecture firm S333 created a large urban landscape. Part of the programme has been accommodated beneath sloping terraces and other surfaces. The form of the housing blocks follows these landscape features. Flat and sloping roofs with special vegetation define the place where the residential development ends and the landscape continues. Most of the roofs here are flat. The initial plan was to use different types of roofing to create a varied roof landscape. Some of the roofs were conceived as grass roofs and some were to be covered in gravel, resulting in a red-and-green composition of planes. Unfortunately, the actual implementation of this roof landscape was sacrificed in order to cut costs.

42a Proposed roof landscape
42b Details of roof

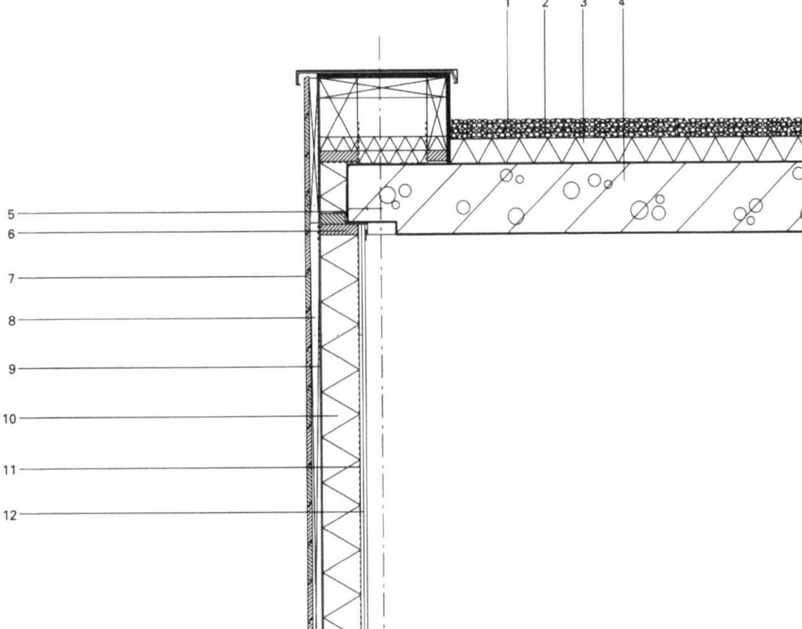

1 GRAVA
2 MEMBRANA IMPERMEABILIZANTE
3 AISLAMIENTO 90 mm
4 FORJADO DE HORMIGÓN
5 PERFIL METÁLICO EN L
6 ARMAZÓN DE MADERA 38 x 140 mm
7 TABLAS DE CEDRO ROJO COLOCADAS EN HORIZONTAL19 mm
8 RASTRELES VERTICALES Y CÁMARA DE AIRE 34 x 71 mm
9 BARRERA DE VAPOR
10 AISLAMIENTO 140 mm
11 MEMBRANA TRANSPIRABLE
12 DOBLE PLACA DE CARTÓN-YESO 25 mm

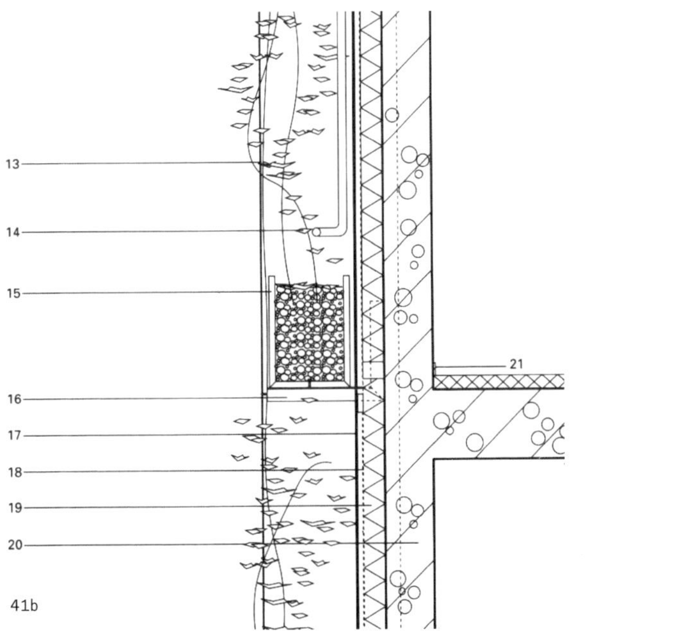

43

CURVED ROOF

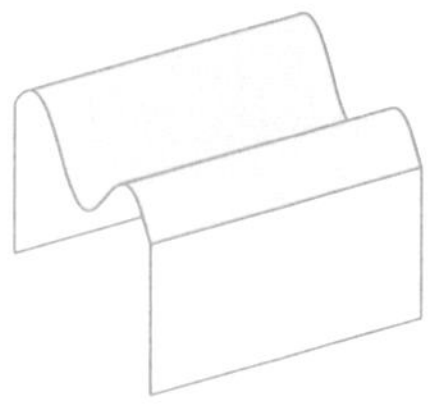

43 Curved roof made of sprayed concrete

REM KOOLHAAS/OMA, NEXUS WORLD HOUSING (FUKUOKA, JAPAN, 1991)

At the close of the twentieth century many architects seemed to have shaken off the modernist dogma of the flat roof. When flat is no longer obligatory, a world of possibilities opens up – aided by the computer as well as new construction techniques such as sprayed concrete. Rem Koolhaas chose to give the roof of the patio housing at Nexus World in Fukuoka an undulating line. To provide the introverted homes with a glimpse of the sky – the horizon is well and truly out of the picture – the flat roof is slit and curled upwards, as it were. The colliding waves increase the view of the sky from the living area. In between the concrete waves the odd glimpse of a small grass roof is visible. Underneath these domes are the 'contemplation rooms' of the homes.

44a

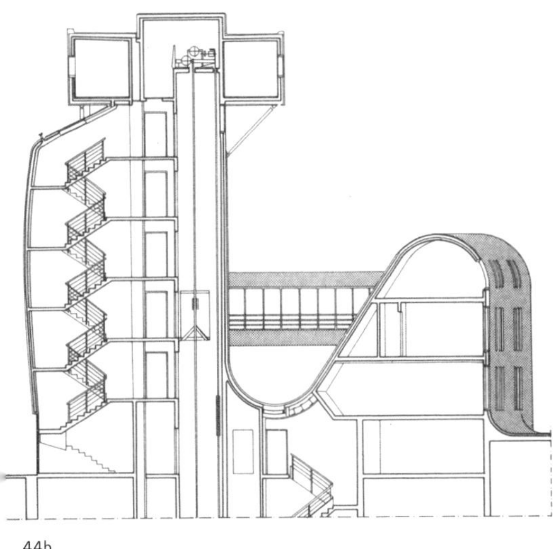

44b

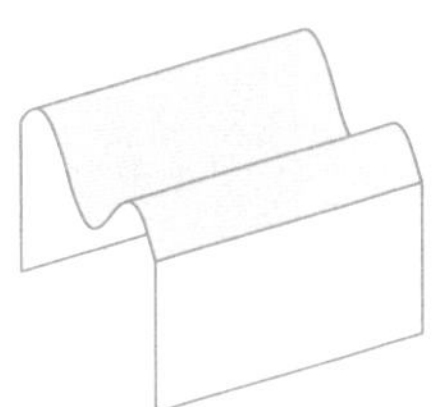

MASSIMILIANO FUKSAS, ÎLOT CANDIE, PASSAGE RUE SAINT BERNARD (PARIS, 1992)

Italian Massimiliano Fuksas is another architect who has turned to waves. When, in the late 1980s, he was commissioned to design an entire perimeter block in the 11th arrondissement in Paris as part of urban regeneration efforts – a block containing housing, work space and sports facilities – he used the form of the wave to bind all the different elements together. Following the traditional Parisian mansard roof, the entire wave has been made of zinc. However, Fuksas has not only clad the roof in zinc, he also uses it on some of the façades.

44b Cross section

45

The Belly

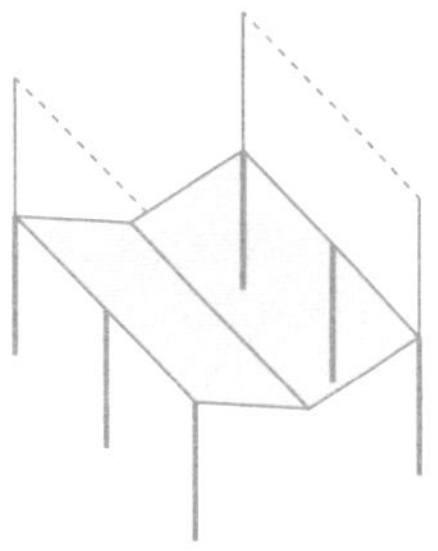

There where the building ends at the bottom, something special begins: a cellar or an unusual kind of floor. We are generally not aware of this, because these parts of the building are hidden from view. But as soon as housing blocks are pierced by a pedestrian way, placed on *pilotis* as in Le Corbusier's Unité, or given overhangs, the underside or the 'belly' of the building becomes visible. This raises the question: What material is used for this underside? Is the cladding extended or will a new material be introduced? Cladding of the underside of residential buildings introduces two problems. First of all, there is usually a dwelling on the floor above the underside to be clad, which means that this floor needs proper insulation – preferably on the underside of the floor. Insulation material is not very nice to look at, so one option would be to use sheet material for a proper finish. The second problem stems in part from the first and has to do with attaching the materials. Attaching a cladding material such as brick or natural stone to the underside of a horizontal surface is not easy. Whereas the bricklayers of the Amsterdam School did not hesitate to extend brickwork on the underside of projecting bay windows, sticking brick to the underside is no longer an option when insulation materials have been used. The use of such heavy materials on the underside of a building calls for special methods of securing them. It is often better to opt for lighter sheet-like material.

45 Underside of the Unité d'habitation on *pilotis*. The belly of the building is made of *béton brut* (raw concrete) and forms a part of the heavy structure that must bear the load of the 17-storey building.

46a

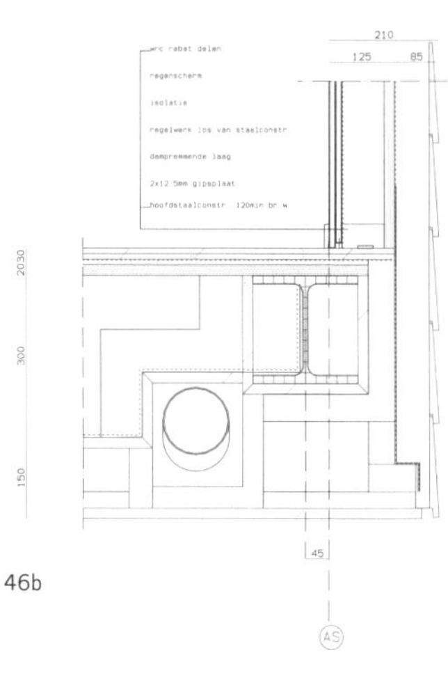

46b

MVRDV, WOZOCO (AMSTERDAM, 1997)

In the late 1990s, Rotterdam-based architectural firm MVRDV designed a remarkable residential care home (in Dutch a *woon-zorgcomplex* or *wozoco*). To comply with the planning conditions of Cornelis van Eesteren's famed 1935 urban expansion plan for the Westelijke Tuinsteden (a 'garden city' expansion district in the west of Amsterdam, ultimately built in the 1950s and 1960s), MVRDV decided to suspend some of the dwellings from the building. The firm was thus able to achieve the required number of dwellings within the plan envelope. The projecting homes were attached to the load-bearing walls of the high-rise using a steel skeleton and were timber-clad on all sides. This timber panelling has been continued on the underside of the projecting dwellings, so that they look like large wooden chests.

BELLY

46a The projecting dwellings are timber-clad on all sides.
46b Façade detail of the projecting wozoco dwellings showing one of the structure's heavy I-beams. The timber siding is rabbeted and continues on the underside with long boards. The timber boards are fixed to a grid.

47a

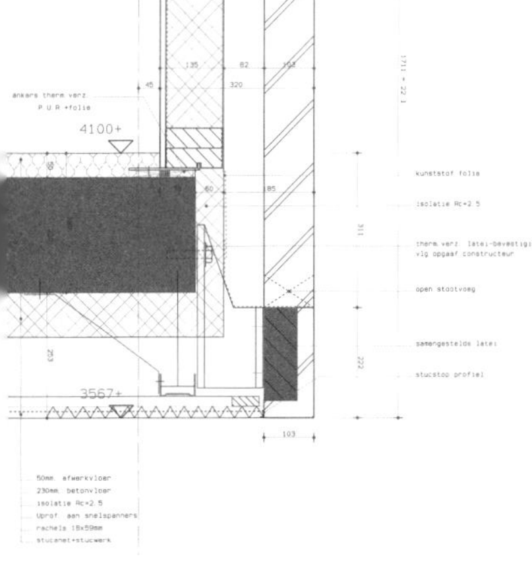

47b

DIENER & DIENER, HOOGKADE EN HOOGWERF (AMSTERDAM, 2001)

If the cladding consists of brick, as it does in this housing block in Amsterdam's Eastern Harbour District, there is another problem to contend with: capping the external wall leaf. In principle, a steel corner profile attached to the underlying floor will suffice. The disadvantage: the steel corner profile will be visible on the underside. Designers may want to keep the detailing 'simple' here by extending the brick to the underside. This is what Diener & Diener did at their residential buildings on the KNSM Island. However, this seemingly simple solution calls for a special detail. A slender reinforced concrete lintel has been attached to the adjacent floor using steel anchor plates. This concrete lintel is clad in brick strips, making it look as if the brick continues down to the bottom.

BELLY

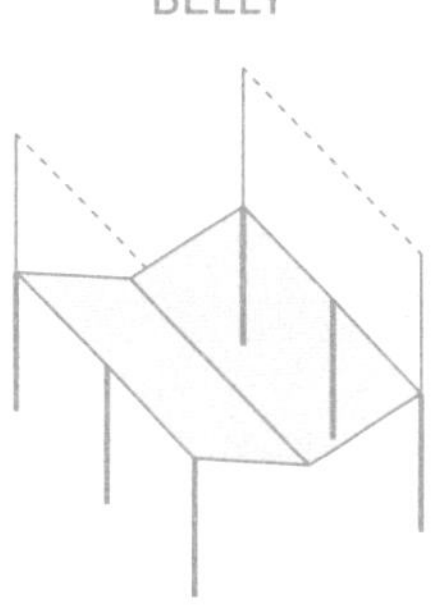

47a Vertical detail woth prefabricated concrete lintel clad in brick strips
47b Concrete lintel clad in brick strips

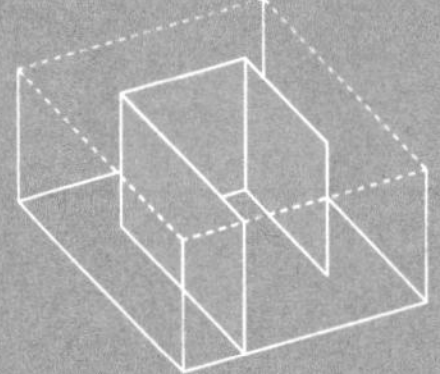

SCENERY

SCENERY

The scenery divides and defines the space. The scenery consists of the cladding of the walls, of interior doors, floors, walls and ceilings. In private houses before 1600, the structure (stone walls or timber skeleton) was directly visible. The space was defined by unrefined materials such as the oak boards and beams of the ceiling, timber boards or flagstones on the floor and rammed earth or brick walls. Between 1600 and 1800 the interior underwent a major transformation. In the Netherlands in the seventeenth century, builders started covering masonry walls with whitewash. The ceiling beams disappeared under fine suspended plaster ceilings. In the eighteenth century, a new generation of artists began to specialize in the decorating, painting and sculpting of interiors. Jacob de Wit was one of the period's best-known painters, renowned for the so-called *witjes*: small paintings in medallions above doors. With the introduction of paintings and sculptures the scenery acquired its own visual imagery. Fabric was stretched across the walls and painted. The lower part of the wall was covered in exquisite panelling, so-called wainscoting, to prevent damage to the fragile fabric covers.

48

49

50

SCENERY

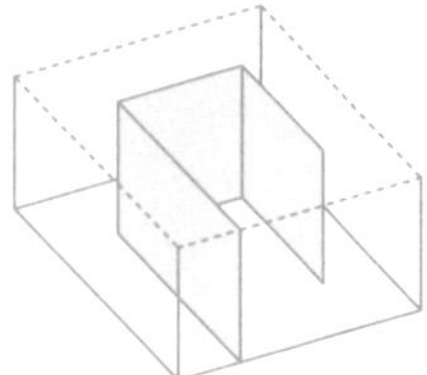

HAUSSMANN INTERIOR

In the nineteenth century, the scenery developed into the standard cladding of the bourgeois house. All the dwellings on the boulevards designed by Georges-Eugène Haussmann in Paris were fitted with parquet flooring, wooden wainscoting and stucco ceilings. The scenery was more or less elaborate in accordance with the residents' social status.

48 Haussmann interior
49 Pieter de Hooch, interior of an seventeenth-century home
50 Front room, Herengracht 168, Amsterdam. Wall hangings painted by Jacob de Wit (figures) and Isaac Moucheron (landscape) (1738–1734).

51

DAS PRINZIP DER BEKLEIDUNG

In his text 'Das Prinzip der Bekleidung' ('The Principle of Cladding'), Adolf Loos described the relationship between the scenery as the definition of the space and the structure.[21]
Loos's argument was informed by the needs of the occupant. It is the occupant who wants a soft and warm environment: carpets.[22] In Loos's view, the structure is of secondary importance, necessary to keep the scenery in place.

21 Adolf Loos, 'Das Prinzip der Bekleidung' (1898), *Sämtliche Schriften* (Vienna/Munich: Verlag Herold, 1962), 105. See also Adolf Loos, 'The Priciple of Cladding' in: *Spoken into the Void: Collected Essays 1897–1900* (Cambridge, MA: Opposition Books, MIT Press, 1982), 66–69.

22 It is not surprising that Loos reached this conclusion in 1898, because by that time he was working almost exclusively on designs for new interiors in existing private houses, such as the design for the apartment for Leopold Lange (1901) and his wife's bedroom (1903).

SCENERY

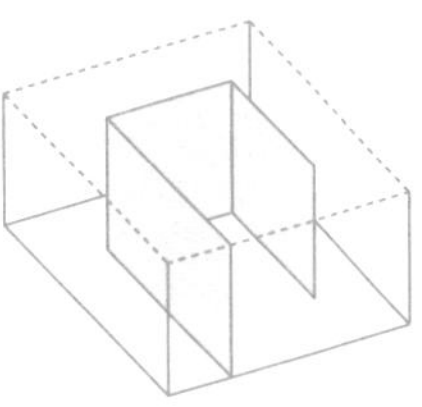

51 A. Loos, Haus Moller, 1927–1928, Vienna, interior

52

53

52 H.P. Berlage, Villa Henny, 1898, The Hague, interior
53 A. Warners, private house, Noordwijk aan Zee, interior

SCENERY

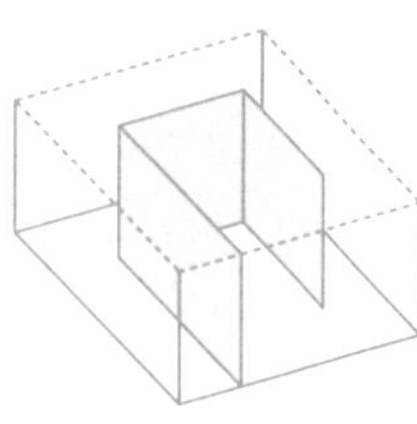

BERLAGE

At the time when Loos was pronouncing autonomous scenery to be the foundation of architecture, H.P. Berlage and Victor Horta were designing buildings in which, on the contrary, the definition of space coincided with the structure. Both in Berlage's Villa Henny (1898) and Horta's own house (1898–1901), the space was defined by load-bearing brick walls. Newer, more delicately finished building materials such as glazed brick and finely wrought iron beams made it possible to integrate the scenery and the structure. This development had an immense impact on the Moderns. This new perspective in architecture appeared to spell the end, at least for the time being, of the scenery as an autonomous layer. For the time being, because with the application of new concrete or steel skeletons, the non-load-bearing inner wall (the new scenery) becomes indispensable for the definition of space.
In mass housing with masonry walls and timber floor joists the scenery usually consists of timber flooring and plastered walls. The timber flooring is made of either floorboards – a structural top layer – or an extra finishing layer of a good quality wood: parquet. In countries where the floor slabs have traditionally been made of stone-like structures, as in many parts of southern Europe where vaulted floor structures are common, a stone-like finishing of the floor makes sense. Indeed ceramic tiles or marble are widely used in these regions. In a warm climate, finishing with stone-like materials on a stone structure has the necessary cooling effect; the structure retains heat, but warms up more slowly during the day. In post-Second World War stacked mass housing, the interior becomes increasingly makeshift. [53] The architect appears to have withdrawn entirely. The bare concrete is covered with a thin layer of plaster to form a ground for wallpaper, while the concrete floor is given a thin finishing layer as a ground for modern and hygienic materials such as linoleum. In mass housing the interior ceases to be the domain of the architect and passes to the housing corporation instead. In the Netherlands this is taken to such an extreme that even the type of window skeleton and interior door is prescribed by the housing corporation. The flush-mounted door is exchanged for an often ugly rebated door with rounded plastic finishing. It is too time-consuming to have a carpenter hang the flush-mounted door, whereas anybody can install a rebated door in no time. However, in many parts of Europe the architect is now regaining control over the interior of mass housing. Below are a few examples that illustrate this trend.

54

JUUL & FROST, BILLIGERE BOLIGER (KØGE, DENMARK, 2004)

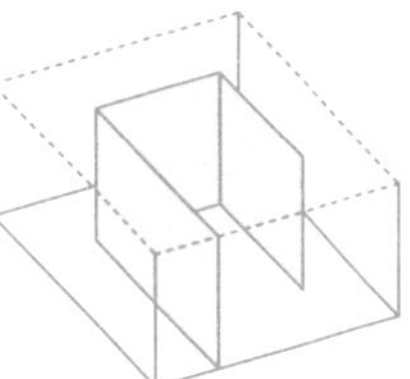

The Billigere Boliger ('cheaper houses') by Juul & Frost were designed as cheap and flexible starter homes for young people and families.

The choice of flooring in this project, a parquet floor, is quite unusual. The flooring was relatively cheap thanks to a seemingly roundabout method of procurement. The timber was cut in Poland and then shipped to China for processing. The homes, which were handed over as empty shells, have wall-to-wall parquet flooring. Partition walls and kitchen units will be placed on this solid wooden floor, so that future rearrangements of the apartment layout will not result in strange grooves or cracks in the floor.

54 Interior with parquet strip flooring

55

HANNE KJÆRHOLM, INTERIOR, LØVENBORG (COPENHAGEN, 2003)

In the centre of Copenhagen we find a fine example of a high-quality interior finish. The Danish School of Architecture has a guest accommodation in a 1906 Jugendstil building on the Vesterbrogade, decorated by Danish interior designer Hanne Kjærholm. The designer has left her mark throughout the apartment, determining not just the scenery but the furnishings as well. She chose her materials and furniture very carefully. The floor is made partially of wood and partially of stone: large Norwegian slate tiles for the kitchen and a wooden parquet floor for the living quarters. The sink area of the kitchen has been fitted with a large granite worktop, while the cooking area with built-in appliances has been finished in stainless steel. Finally, all the furniture is perfectly matched. All its pieces are crafted by – who else – Poul Kjærholm, Hanne's husband.

SCENERY

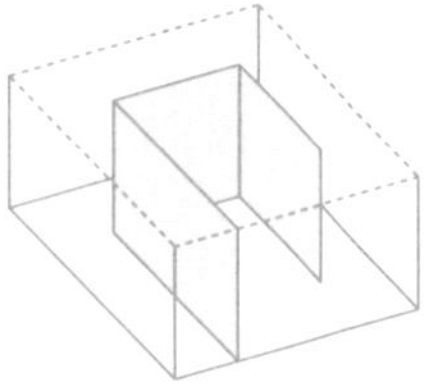

56

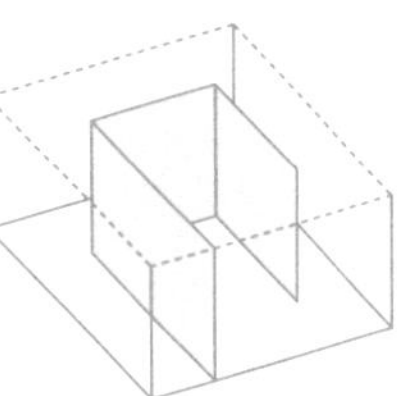

GERT WINGÅRDH, BO01 (MALMÖ, 2001)

As part of Malmö's urban expansion along the Sundet, Swedish architect Gert Wingårdh designed a quayside housing project. In this project, previously discussed for its façade, Wingårdh used a hard-wearing interior with a wooden staircase. Durability was the guiding principle here, and the solid wooden staircase and banister exude solidity. The same is true of the kitchen, in which large wooden cabinets and a solid stainless steel worktop stand out.

56 Interior with solid wooden staircase

57

ALVAR AALTO, BANISTER

Finally, a brief look at the function and meaning of materials in terms of tactility, hygiene and presence. Aspects such as texture, aging and patina, colour, natural or treated finishing lend material an articulated expression. Surfaces can be either polished or lacquered, painted or bush hammered. Different senses can be targeted through reflection, transparency, heat conductivity, noise absorption and smell (parquet, beeswax, wood, moisture, stone, etcetera). Such non-visual aspects of architecture are the topic of Juhani Pallasmaa's aforementioned book from 1996, *The Eyes of the Skin*.
Alvar Aalto's copper banister is a good example of both expression and the relationship between hygiene and tactility. The copper kills off any bacteria on the hands, but thanks to its exclusivity copper's hygienic properties have acquired additional connotations of luxury. Copper door handles, for example, become all shiny due to the oil on the skin of people's hands and acquire a lovely patina. Door handles tend to be made of stainless steel or chromed metal, but door handles made of ivory, Bakelite or wood feel warmer. Alvar Aalto designed leather door handles and handrails to make them more pleasant to the touch. The architects associated with the Amsterdam School liked to use wood for handrails, because it is oilier and therefore slides better. The wooden floor, marble wainscoting, solid stone steps – all combine functional and representational qualities with their place in the scenery.

SCENERY

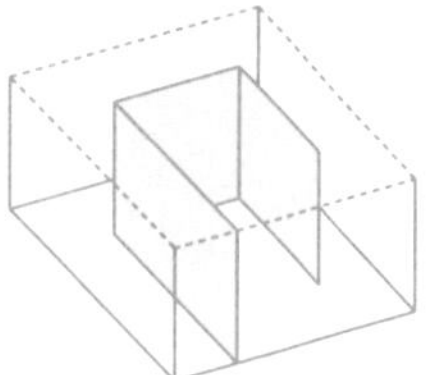

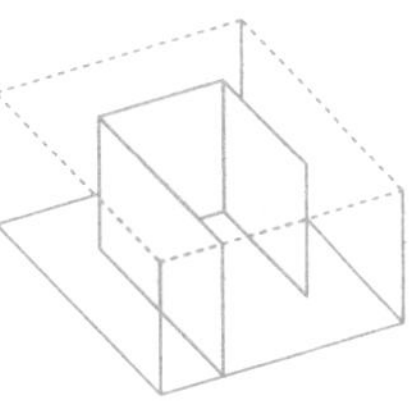

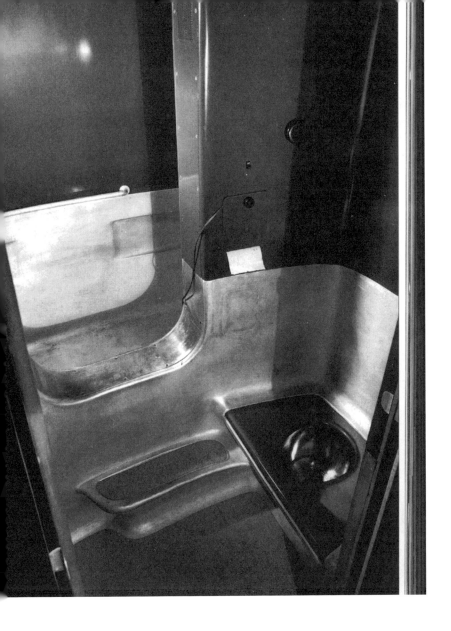

RICHARD BUCKMINSTER FULLER, DYMAXION BATHROOM (1939)

When, in 1939, Buckminster Fuller decided to make the Dymaxion bathroom of aluminium, he assumed that bathrooms would become ready-made industrial products, straight from the factory. The pressing of aluminium sheeting into a three-dimensional product creates smooth transitions. But the question is how the consumer experiences such an aluminium space. In terms of tactility (touch) and acoustics especially, this concept is extremely different from the customary bathroom design using stone flooring (terrazzo or tiles) and tiled walls.

59

SCENERY

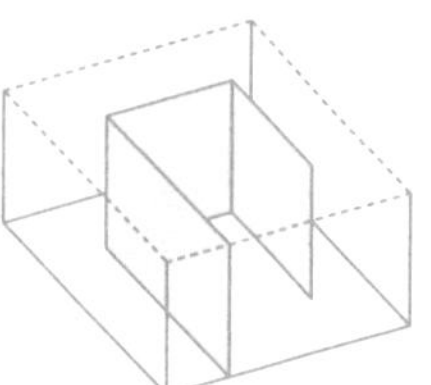

59 Interior with wall decoration by François Seigneur

JEAN NOUVEL, NEMAUSUS (NÎMES, 1987)

On the one hand, Jean Nouvel's project in Nîmes can be seen as an extreme example of the bare interior associated with mass housing, while on the other it marks the reintroduction of decoration in mass housing. The idea underlying the project was: 'A good dwelling is a large dwelling.' Applied to publicly subsidized housing this meant: efficient and cost-effective building. As a result, the scenery as added layer was left out completely. Instead, the structural materials determine the interior. A return to Berlage, with this difference that we are not talking about refined glazed brick here, but unfinished concrete, straight from the formwork and including rock pockets. Nouvel used this basic level of finishing as the foundation for a new form of decoration. He invited artist François Seigneur to paint the walls. Seigneur introduced lines and shading that emphasize the imperfections of the poured concrete.
Responding to criticism of this new form of decoration, Nouvel referred to the scenery of Haussmann's boulevard housing in Paris: 'If you live in a Haussmann, all the ceilings will have mouldings and plaster. You have the right not to like them, but seldom the right to remove them.'[23]

23 Lionel Duroy, 'Liberté, de qui ?', *L'Architecture d'Aujourd'hui*, no. 252 (September 1987), 10.

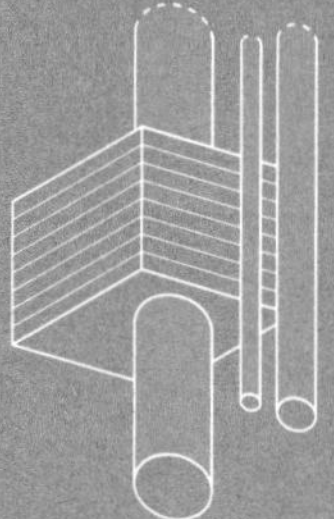

SERVICES

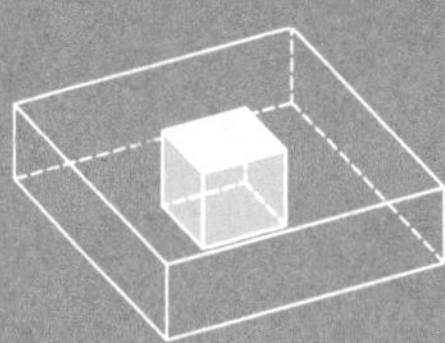

SERVICE CORE

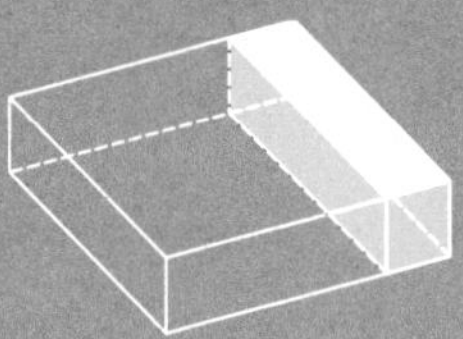

SERVICE ZONE

THE FLOOR AS
SERVICE ZONE

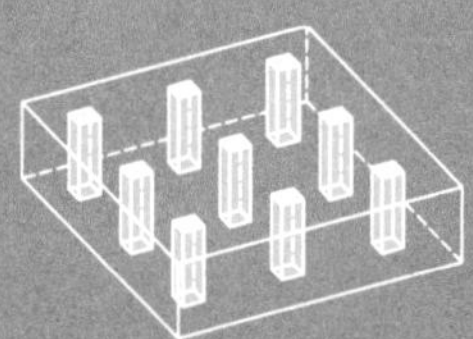

DUCTING IN A COLUMN

SERVICES

In the eyes of the English architecture critic Reyner Banham, one of the most important requirements that a building must satisfy is a 'well-tempered environment'. In the introduction to his book, Banham laments the fact that the services that provide comfort in buildings are not a subject of architectural history.[24] And when they do become a topic of discussion, they are included in the chapter on technology. Although we are not really concerned with the well-tempered environment here, we are citing Banham to bring a frequently neglected layer to our readers' attention: the services. The services do more than just climatize the indoor spaces. Whereas Banham focuses mainly on heating and air conditioning, in our definition the services layer incorporates all those issues associated with the supply and drainage of energy, water, air and information.

The services layer can be subdivided into three different sets. To start with, the pipes and ducts for the supply and drainage of energy, information, air and water. Secondly, the appliances associated with these pipes and ducts that control the supply or drainage or that require energy. Thirdly, the dedicated rooms for these facilities and appliances, such as the kitchen, bathroom and toilet. However, this only becomes interesting from an architectural perspective when these pipes and ducts, and the appliances associated with them, require special adjustments to the spaces where we find these appliances, such as bathrooms and kitchens. This is why these spaces require special finishing and detailing.

24
Reyner Banham, *The Architecture of the Well-Tempered Environment* (Oxford: Architectural Press, 1969), 9.

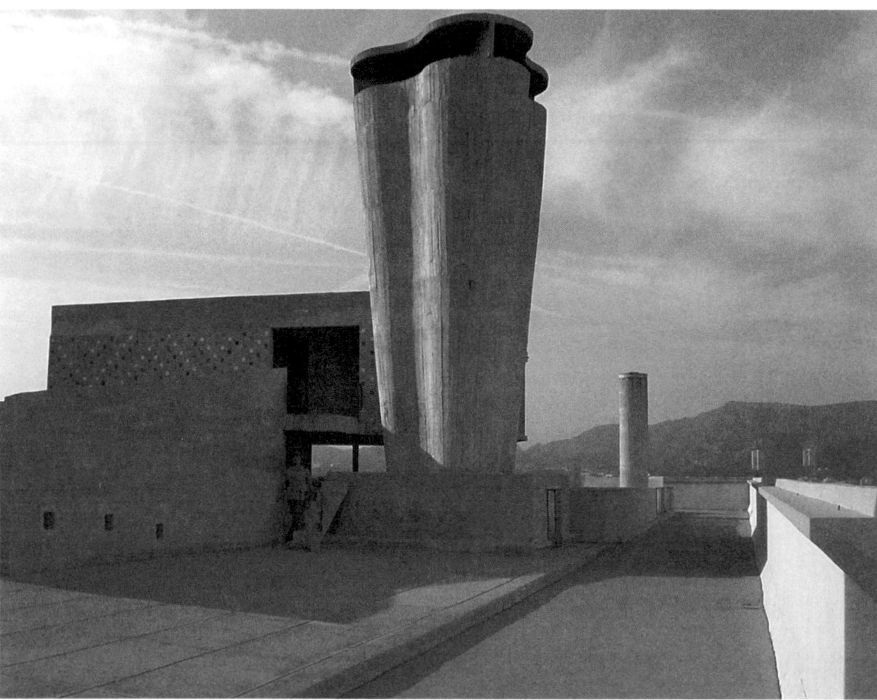

60

SERVICES

LE CORBUSIER, UNITÉ D'HABITATION (MARSEILLE, 1952)

Ever since pipes and ducts entered our homes, we have tended to conceal them as much as possible. In the nineteenth century, service ducts were concealed behind wainscoting and wallpaper. Following the disappearance of these forms of scenery in the standard dwelling, pipes and wiring for water and light were worked into the plaster or brickwork. The advent of modern concrete structures called for yet another solution. In many cases, electric wiring is now incorporated in the reinforced concrete. Empty pipes and sockets are inserted into the formwork during construction and poured into the concrete. Shafts are created for the other service ducts (gas, water and ventilation). However, the services are rarely given proper architectural expression.
In the Unité in Marseille, Le Corbusier turned the chimney into a major architectural statement. Inspired by the big ocean liners of his day, he placed a giant chimney in the centre of the roof. Curiously, in this day and age, with energy use and the climatization of the home the focus of increasing attention, there is no equivalent to such an architectural articulation of heating, ventilation or insulation of housing. To what extent will the climatization of space play a role in the architecture of housing in the future?

60 Roof structure with ventilation pipes

61

PIERRE CHAREAU AND BERNARD BIJVOET, MAISON DE VERRE (PARIS, 1931)

Although service ducts and the appliances associated with them are not the most exciting architectural elements, there are some twentieth-century precedents in which they form a part of the architectural composition. A nice example is the way in which the electric wiring has been isolated and articulated in the Maison de Verre in Paris, designed by Pierre Chareau and Bernard Bijvoet.
To showcase the modernity of the lighting system, the architects placed a tube with electric wiring at some distance from the wall. Attached to this tube is an oblong metal box, containing the switches and a socket. The switches are of the type that was then commonly used in electronic equipment, such as tuners. The whole looks unusually high-tech for the period.
This articulation of the wiring and switches is first and foremost an architectural gesture. To achieve a strong effect, the wiring has been completely detached from the wall. And just like the column frees the wall from its load-bearing task, so does this tube with wiring free the wall from fulfilling this role, so that it can be moved or removed without any consequences for the services.

At the same time it can be argued that this foregrounded electric wiring gets in the way and interferes with a flexible use of the space. To mitigate this effect, the architects decided to put it next to the steel column that is also detached from the wall. Perhaps we ought to go back to Chareau and Bijvoet and make the services visible again. However, contemporary wall-mounted systems are often so poorly designed that architects are unlikely to do so. Besides, many residents prefer to have everything concealed behind the wallpaper. Here lies a new challenge for product designers.

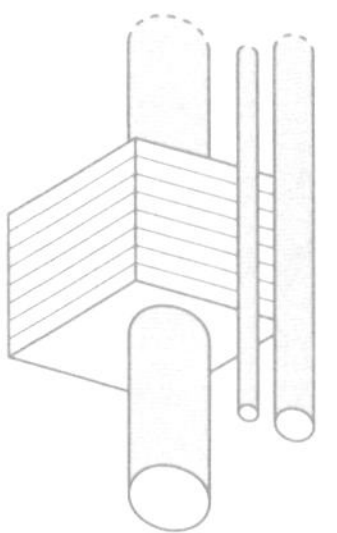

61 Duct with clearly articulated light switch

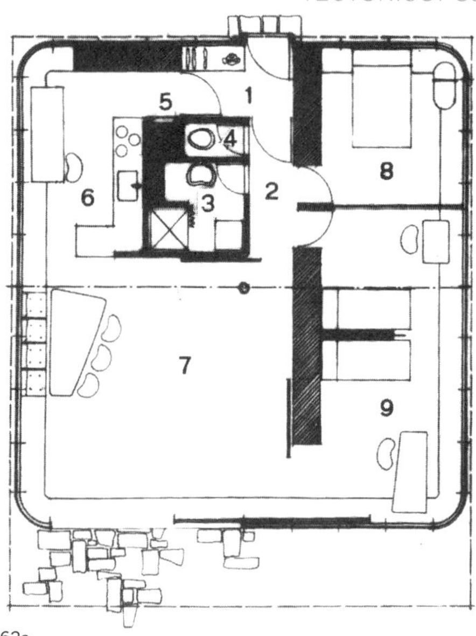

62a

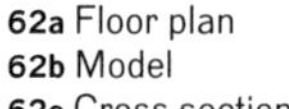

62a Floor plan
62b Model
62c Cross section

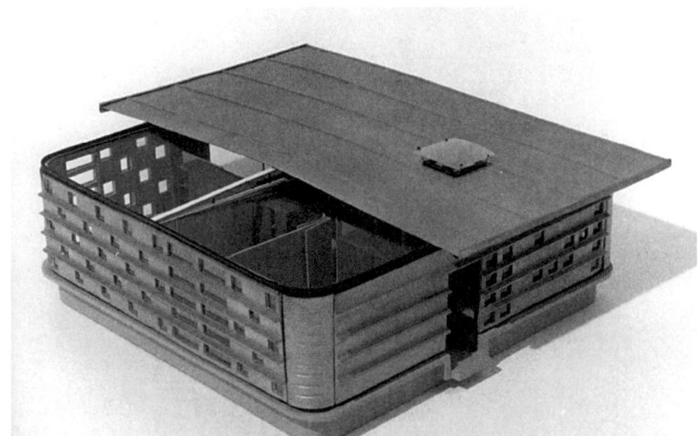

62b

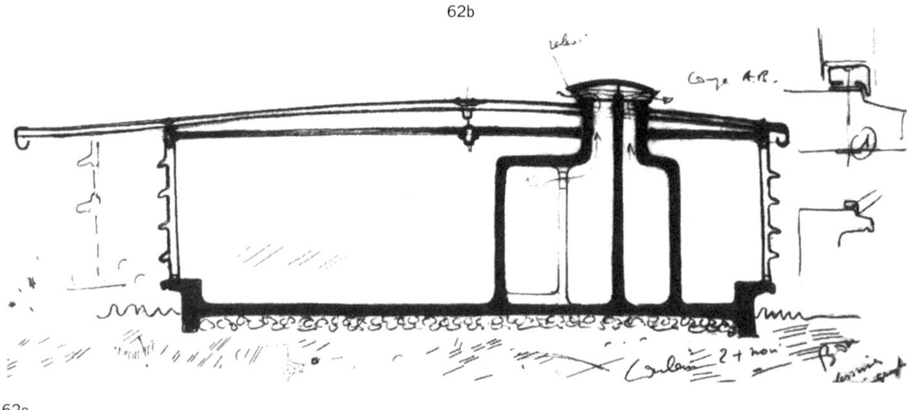

62c

SERVICE CORE

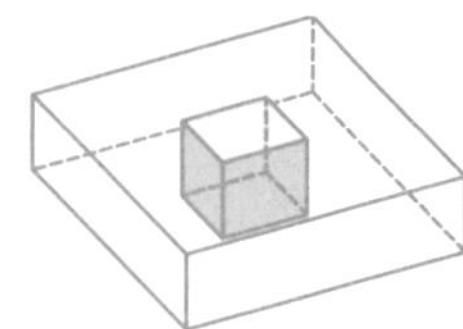

JEAN PROUVÉ, MAISON ALBA (1950)

In 1950 Maurice Silvy and Jean Prouvé designed a house that sought to address the housing shortage among the poorest segments of the population in post-war France. This Maison Alba is a typical example of a house with a service core. With the services in a core, the surrounding space is freed from wires, pipes and ducts, all of which can obstruct layout flexibility. The articulation of the core as an autonomous element brings its liberating effect even more to the fore.

SERVICE CORE OR ZONE

The arrangement of the service ducts, and especially the clusters of service ducts in shafts, requires attention. A service shaft in the middle of the home will have other implications for the layout and transformability than a shaft along one of the walls or in the façade area. Depending on dwelling size, bay width and structural principles, each of these options has its own advantages and disadvantages. The installation of shafts and cores raises the issue of zoning. The arrangement of the services and their associated spaces such as bathrooms and kitchens in particular zones or in a core creates duct-free areas and hence flexible dwelling layouts.

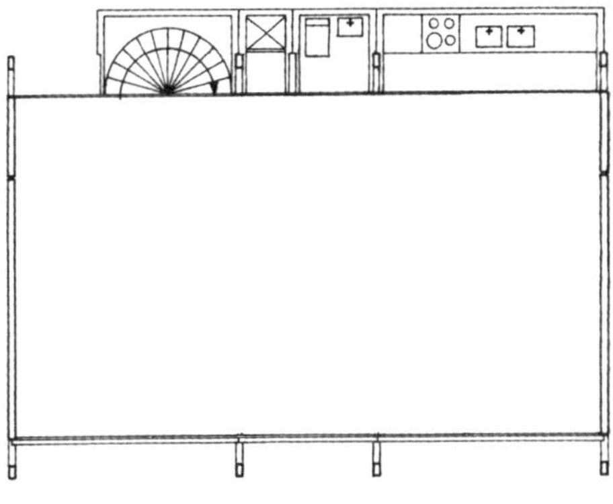

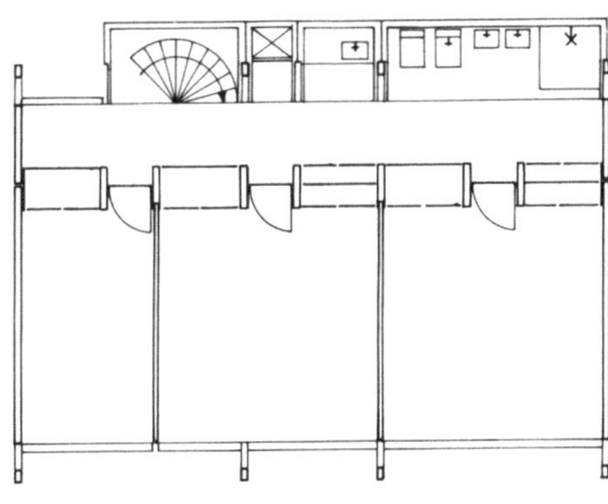

63a

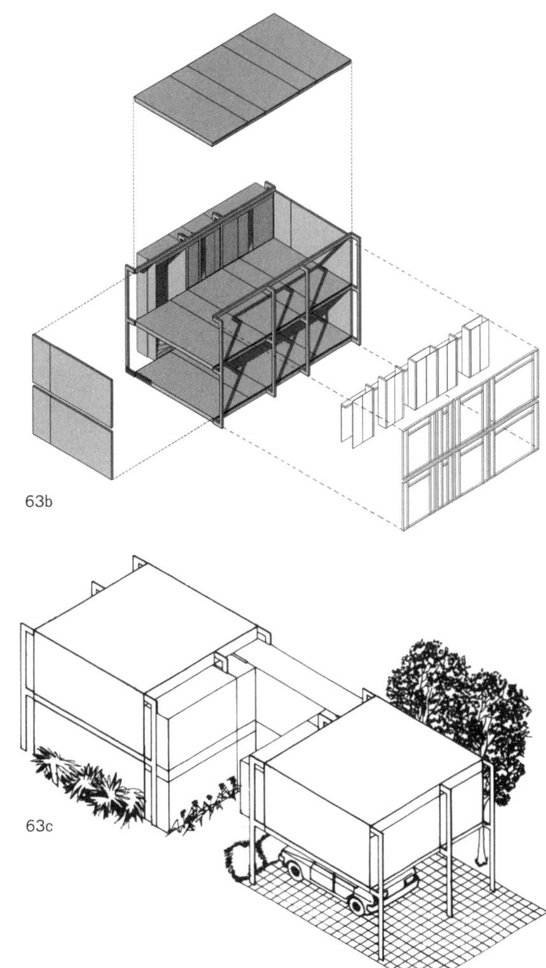

63b

63c

CEPEZED, HEIWO HOUSE (1980)

The construction system that CePeZed developed for the Heiwo company has a dedicated service zone. The homes consist of a light steel skeleton that creates two parallel free floor slabs. Because the skeleton is outside the building volume, the indoor spaces are entirely free of columns and even the façade layout is independent from the skeleton. On one side of the skeleton, prefabricated plastic cells have been suspended from a zone. These cells contain the services and access to them. The architects have designed the dwelling in such a way that there are no pipes, ducts or sockets in any of the living areas. In that sense the service zone is a kind of plug-in wall that supplies electricity and air. The heating (air conditioning) of the rooms is also controlled from this zone. If users want to arrange the large open-plan space, they can do so using light partition walls and a wall cabinet. As this wall cabinet does contain wires and ducts for the electricity and air conditioning, it is then plugged into the service zone.

SERVICE ZONE

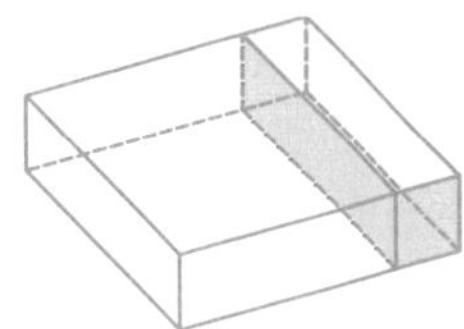

63a Ground floor and first floor
63b Exploded axonometrics
63c Axonometrics of Heiwo dwelling with annex

64a

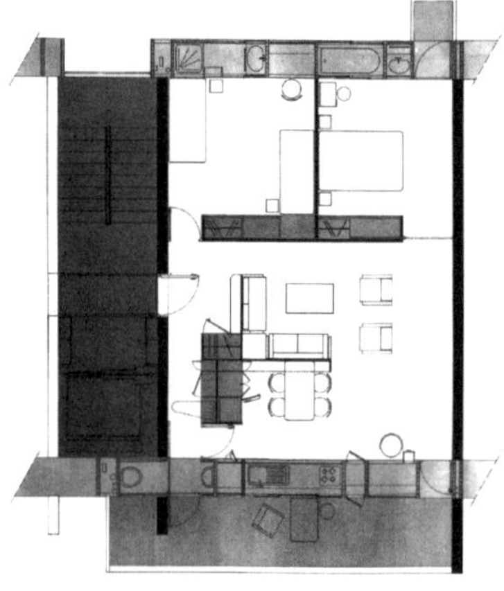

64b

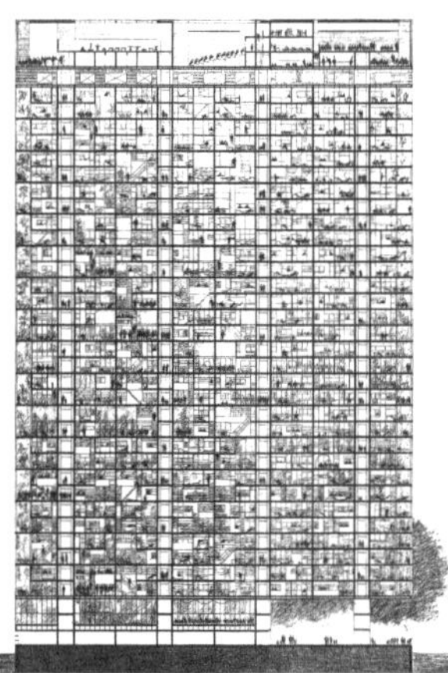

64c

YVES LION AND FRANÇOIS LECLERCQ, DOMUS DEMAIN (PROJECT, 1992)

French architects Yves Lion and François Leclercq took a different approach to the ducting challenge. In their design for the Domus Demain project, the services have been integrated in the façade area. The bathroom, the kitchen units, the lavatory and the service ducts have all been worked into this area. The architects describe it as an 'active layer'. Does the façade take over the role of the services or vice versa? Neither: the façade and the services are fully integrated. The façade has become the intermediary between inside and outside in the broadest sense of the word. It controls not only the insulation, ventilation and penetration of light, but also the supply and drainage of clean water and waste water, information and energy. The façade area is completely separate from those elements of the scenery that determine the room layout, making the space between the two service façade areas completely transformable.

SERVICE ZONE

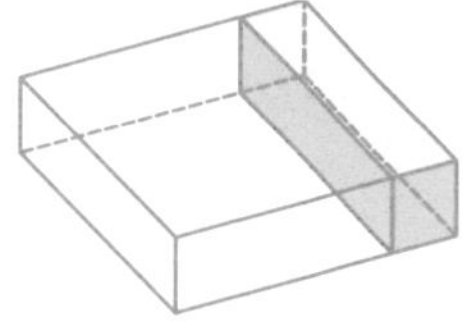

64a View of the façade from the inside out
64b Apartment floor plan with sanitary facilities along the façade
64c Cross section

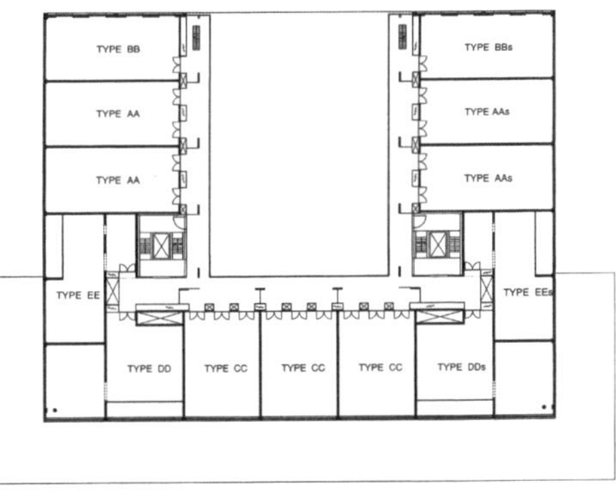

5a

65c

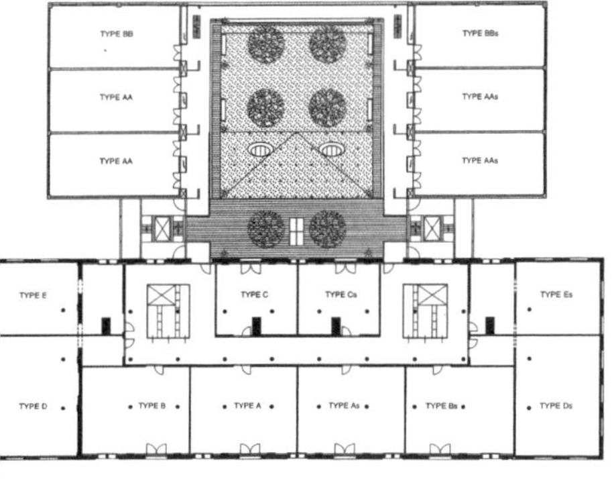

5b

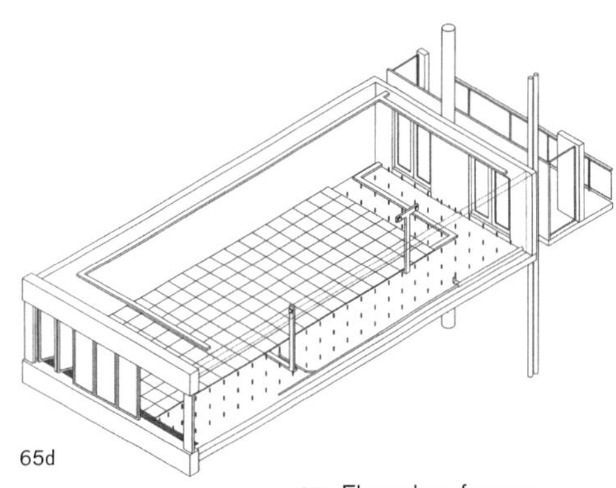

65d

65a Floor plans for new construction, floors 7–10
65b Standard storey, floors 1–4
65c Nieuw Australië
65d Axonometrics of the dwelling with flooring system and ducting

DKV, NIEUW AUSTRALIË, OOSTELIJKE HANDELSKADE (AMSTERDAM, 2000)

The increasing diversification of the housing market has resulted in a demand for an ever wider range of dwelling types. Complex stacks are a direct consequence of this. Developers trying to meet the demands of this complex and changeable housing market are increasingly interested in flexible floor plans and projects using the shell principle. The development group Nieuw Amerika (OCNA),[25] for example, developed shell-system housing on the Oostelijke Handelskade in Amsterdam. The Nieuw Australië project derives its name from a former dock warehouse named Australië. This warehouse has been integrated in a new residential building. The new part of the building stands next to and partially overhangs the former warehouse, like a lion grasping its prey.
In order to keep the partitioning of the dwelling as unrestricted as possible, the architects opted for a raised floor. This flooring, of a type often used in computer rooms, is made up of small concrete elements, each 60 × 60 cm, reinforced at the corners by small steel struts. For cost-related reasons, a foamed concrete flooring was eventually selected, with integrated service ducts. Because channels for new service ducts can be easily excavated in this flooring, the layout of the dwelling is essentially flexible, including the location of the service spaces (toilet, kitchen and bathroom). If needed, the service run can be moved relatively easily. Future occupants can select from a range of prefabricated internal elements, hire someone to build the interior, or build it themselves (see also Chapter 3, 'Dwellings', p. 87).

25 The participants in this development alliance include the housing corporation Het Oosten, the former municipal housing development agency Woningbedrijf Amsterdam (now privatized and merged with other entities) and the project developer Johan Matsen Projectontwikkeling.

THE FLOOR AS SERVICE ZONE

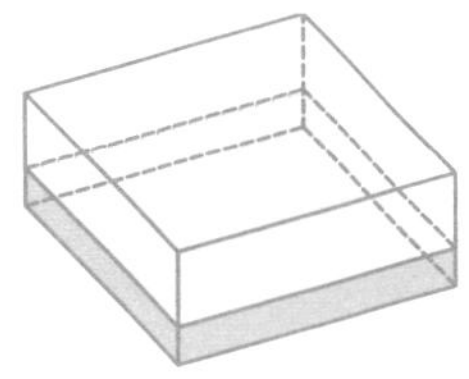

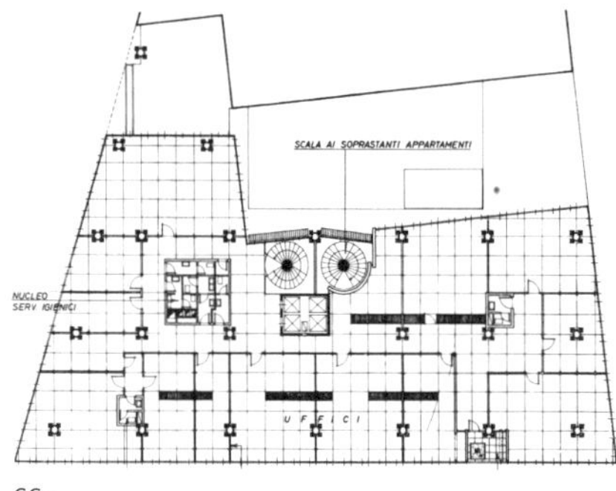

66a

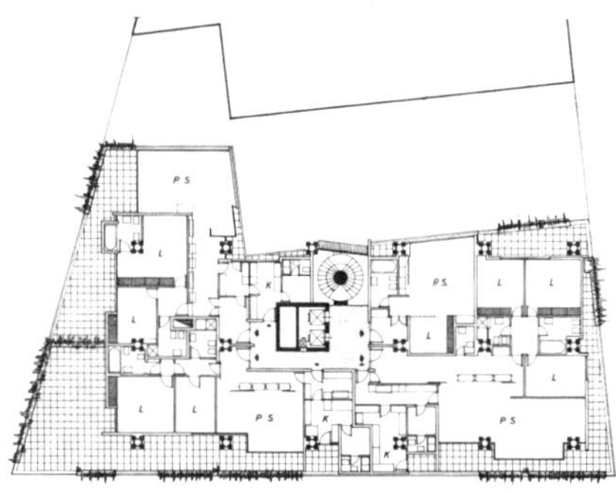

66b

VINCENZO, FAUSTO AND LUCIO PASSARELLI, VIA CAMPANIA (ROME, 1965)

Finally, ducting can be arranged as a *plan libre*. The building designed by Vincenzo Fausto and Lucio Passarelli on the Via Campania in Rome is a good example of this. Here the ducting has been worked into the column. The building has quite an unusual design. It accommodates four different functions: a car park on the bottom two underground storeys, shops on the lower ground level and the ground level, while the next three storeys are given over to office space. The top five storeys accommodate luxury apartments.

The building has a different architecture for each part of the programme. The ground level has a recessed shop front while the offices are enclosed by a curtain wall. This curtain wall follows the building lines of the adjacent buildings. The dwellings above do not conform to the shape of the block and the urban space it creates. With their generous roof terraces, the dwellings create the impression of a collection of hanging gardens far above Rome's streets.

The entire building is based on a structure with columns. From the street level upwards, prefabricated concrete columns have been used; each column itself consists of a system of four slender columns, with space in the middle for pipes and ventilation ducts. The grid has been dimensioned in such a way that the position of the column and the position of the partition walls are not linked. Sometimes the columns are detached; sometimes the column abuts the wall. The four-part structure of the column makes it possible to connect the partition walls in four directions. Due to the stepped structure of the dwellings, some of the columns are outside the building volume, lending the residential part of the building an unusual character.

DUCTING IN A COLUMN

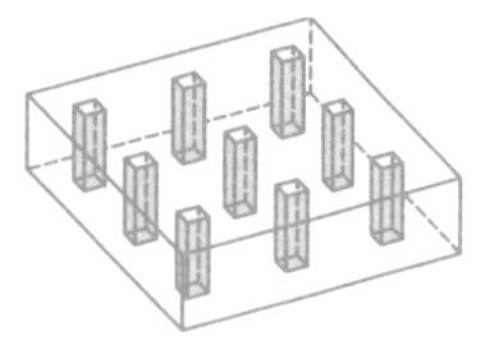

66a Office storey, floors 1–3
66b Fourth storey, residential
66c View from street level
66d Roof structure with dwellings, note the columns with ventilation shafts

66c

66d

CONTEXT

In the south of France houses have a different appearance and layout compared to those in Ireland. Likewise, houses in Groningen used to be different from those in, say, Limburg and Zeeland, or even Drenthe, which is barely a stone's throw away. Traditionally, people have built their houses with materials that were locally available, widely used and familiar, building on local knowledge, customs and traditions.
Differences in climate, culture, political situation and landscape, among other things, can prompt an architect to take a different approach and lead to regional differences in the built environment. At the same time there is a tendency to harmonize national and international legislation. Architects are increasingly operating on an international platform and inclined to impose their ideas on the various contexts they are working in. And although legislation plays an important role, it is ultimately up to the architect to decide how to respond to the context. This chapter seeks to provide the necessary tools for looking at, 'reading' and responding to the context.

ASPECTS OF CONTEXT

In 1997, in an attempt to structure the spatial planning field in the Netherlands, Dirk Sijmons introduced a model for government policy.[1] He identified three layers, all of which, on their own level and within their own specific time span, have an effect on our built and natural environments:

1
Dirk Sijmons, *Landkaartmos en andere beschouwingen over landschap* (Rotterdam: 010 Publishers, 2002).

Physical Context (according to Sijmons)
—Substratum, or the geological patterns of soil and water conditions;
—Networks, the pattern of links;
—Occupation, the different forms of built development and settlement.

This tripartite division is a useful starting point for an analysis of the physical context of a new design location. It allows us to read the existing situation as a map, put together from layers of physical patterns. But designing for a particular context also depends on other local factors: the climate as well as the political and cultural context. These six aspects will be explored in more detail below.

Substratum and Geology

We need a proper understanding of the substratum on which we build and live, so that we know both the bearing capacity of the soil and substratum as well as the morphology of that substratum. Whereas the substratum in the Netherlands is seemingly always flat and level and the bearing capacity of higher ground in, say, France and Scandinavia always allows building without extra foundations, the reality is often different. An old riverbed in rocky

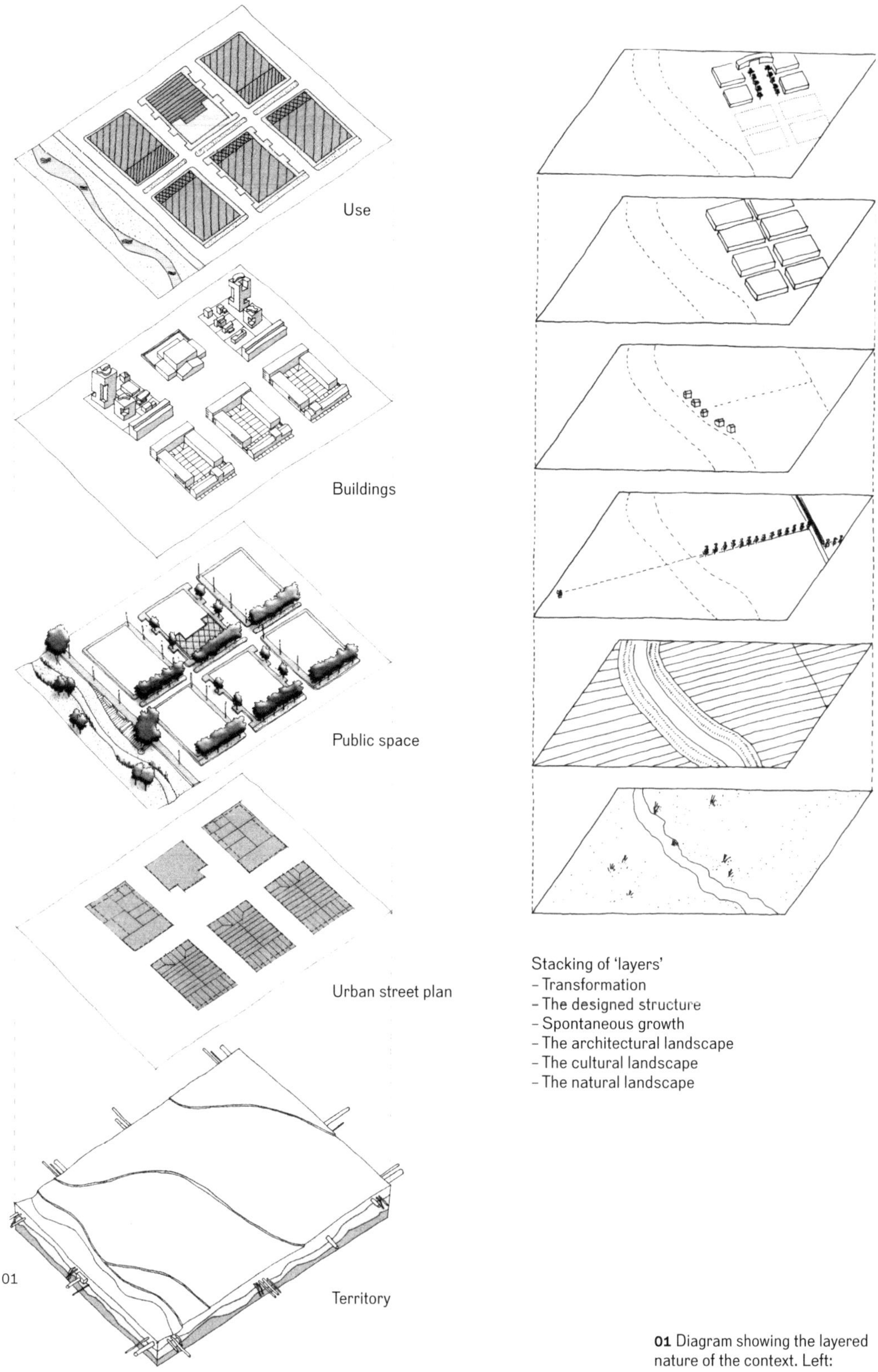

Use

Buildings

Public space

Urban street plan

01

Territory

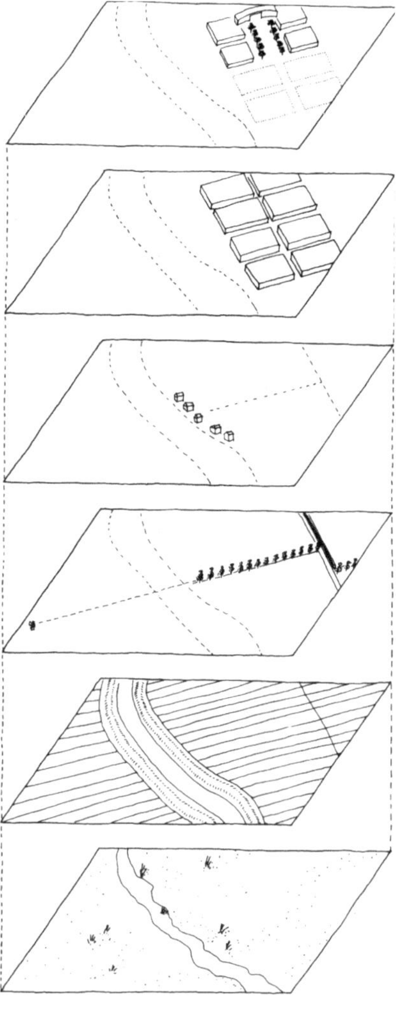

Stacking of 'layers'
- Transformation
- The designed structure
- Spontaneous growth
- The architectural landscape
- The cultural landscape
- The natural landscape

01 Diagram showing the layered nature of the context. Left: layers of the urban street plan according to Heeling et al., 2002. Right: from natural landscape to buildings and their transformation.

terrain can have disastrous consequences if it goes undetected. A 50-cm disparity in what appears to be a flat polder can lead to entirely different design ideas.
Moreover, the form and nature of the substratum and the surrounding landscape are often a source of inspiration. A view of a lake, dale or brook adds value to the design, while differences in level can inspire special solutions. In urban areas these aspects can be difficult to pinpoint, because so many original landscape elements are covered by a carpet of buildings.
But with a few relatively simple tools and, above all, a good eye, many important aspects of the geological and landscape context can be mapped. To start with, all relevant information must be collected with the help of soil maps, geological maps and, where available, geomorphological maps. Soil maps give an impression of the substratum's top few feet. Such maps, which provide information about the types of soil in the top layer, are not only useful for the farming industry. However, this information is unfortunately not available for urban areas.
Geological maps provide information about deeper layers and, in combination with cross sections, show the substratum's composition. The geological map shows us whether the substratum contains sand, peat, clay or rock, while also indicating the origins of these layers. For example, it tells us whether we are dealing with sea or river clay. For building purposes it is particularly interesting to know at what depth we will find the right substratum for the foundation. While in the Netherlands this tends to be the Pleistocene sand deposit, in other countries it can be primary, secondary or tertiary rock. Needless to say, this type of information must be supplemented with exploratory drilling.
As the name suggests, a geomorphological map combines geological information with the form (morphology) of the land. In the Netherlands these kinds of maps tend to cover the hillier areas, such as those in the east and south of the country. Finally, areas rich in water benefit from a groundwater level map. Such maps show the differences in water level in various waterways, for example in a polder. These differences determine whether the surrounding area must be drained or, on the contrary, irrigated.

Networks and Links

To some extent urban agglomerations can be read as networks composed of lines and nodes, of links and access points to those links, or connections between the various kinds of links. The lines include the roads, navigable rivers and waterways, rail networks and flight paths. The nodes include the slip roads, ports, stations, bus and tram stops, park & ride facilities and airports.
The design of a new housing project must consider the project's location in relation to the urban network. How accessible is the

02

03

Vitruvius on the directions of the streets, with remarks of the winds
The town being fortified, the next step is the apportionment of house lots within the wall and the laying out of streets and alleys with regard to climatic conditions. They will be properly laid out if foresight is employed to exclude the winds from the alleys. Cold winds are disagreeable, hot winds enervating, moist winds unhealthy. We must, therefore, avoid mistakes in this matter and beware of the common experience of many communities.[2]

2 Vitruvius, *The Ten Books on Architecture*, Book I, Chapter 6

02, 03 Wind catchers on top of dwellings in Yazd, in southern Iran. The wind is blown into the house through a damp cellar, creating a natural air conditioning.

future project, what is the site's potential within the urban network? Is the location next to a busy metro station or only served by a bus twice a day? What could the site's relation to the network mean for the creation of functions other than living? But also: To what extent could the project be hindered by these networks, for instance by noise or particulates?
By mapping these networks and nodes, the city can be made readable. In some cases, additional, invisible information will be necessary, such as the number of decibels produced and pollution caused by the link. Any possible risks (transport of hazardous goods, for insance) must also be recorded.

Settlement and Built Development

To understand the form and organization of the surrounding built development, we need to learn more about its morphology and typology. This requires analysis of the neighbouring parts of town. To start with, we have to look at the structure of those parts of town: its orientations, transport axes, different spaces, and so forth. The neighbouring urban fragments often appear to be entirely random. But an urban fragment can be seen as an organism, a set of objects and spaces, which, on closer inspection, can be reduced to familiar principles. A thorough analysis can produce a better understanding of the underlying structure of the urban development. Its form is often the outcome of the application of previously used design principles or types, in which case we speak of urban plan types. In the section 'Analysis and Design' we will look at this in more detail.

Climate

Of old, the elements have had a determining effect on house construction. Protection from the sun, wind, precipitation, humidity and temperature–or, by contrast, the capture and retention of these–has prompted a variety of constructions, ranging from screening from the sun and wind to orientation towards the sun or prevailing wind direction to generate more warmth, ventilation, etcetera. Roofs in Mediterranean countries need little more than a gentle slope with Roman tiles. In northern countries, on the other hand, we find steeper slopes with interlocking tiles that provide proper water drainage. Sometimes the extreme cold requires special provisions, in other circumstances the heat. In dry southern regions the wind is used to cool the house. In southern Iran, for example, houses are fitted with windcatchers, towers that channel the wind via an ingenious system down to the cellar, where water basins cool the air before it is brought up into the living areas. [← 02-03]
A south-facing kitchen is probably not a good idea in the northern hemisphere. However, a bedroom facing east is probably a good choice wherever you are. People perceive and experience being in

a north-facing room very differently from being in a south-facing one. A different aspect can influence a room's depth, height or colour scheme. A south-facing conservatory can have a pleasant buffer effect. During the cold season the conservatory adds passive solar energy, while in summer, provided the necessary shading is in place, it actually keeps out the heat.
The orientation also plays a role in the way the residential blocks are positioned. The CIAM functionalists propagated good sun exposure, which in those days was less about enjoying the sun than about its effects on hygiene. The architects and planners who were involved in the expansion of Frankfurt in the 1920s and 1930s had very pronounced ideas about this. Ernst May and Walter Schwagenscheidt propagated an orientation which would give the bedroom side of the house enough sun to ensure a beneficial effect, while the side with the living room – and any adjacent outdoor areas (garden or balcony) – was to have sun for most of the day (see also Chapter 5, 'Urban Ensemble', page 224–225). Building in large open areas or near the sea requires special attention to weather extremes. When it is windy in the city, a gale is blowing up on the coast. Whereas in sheltered areas precipitation will be more or less vertical or oblique if it is windy, in open spaces the rain will be horizontal in heavy winds. This calls for extra attention to detail when positioning residential blocks and streets. How is the street laid out in relation to the prevailing wind direction? What effect do high-rises have on the microclimate around a building?

Political Context

The architect's sphere of activity is subject to political forces. Because politics are an important factor, especially in major commissions, we need to understand the balance of power. Who are we dealing with, what is the position of the client and of local government, who is in charge? In the Netherlands the municipal alderman for spatial planning or public works usually plays a key role in major commissions. In France, mayors, directly elected, will often refer to their electoral mandate to try to influence proceedings. But more often than not the client, project developer or housing corporation will call the shots. Larger urban developments increasingly draw on the services of a so-called supervisor, an architect-planner who has not only drawn up the masterplan, but who, in dialogue with the architects of the sub-plans, also tries to keep track of the overall picture during the implementation. As a rule, the supervisor answers to the local political leaders, i.e. the city council's executive committee. A city tends to draw on the services on a supervisor when it has particularly ambitious plans for a new development.
It is crucial for an architect to find out what political forces might impact on any given project. Is the project part of large-scale urban ambitions – is it, for instance, meant to put the city on the map?

–or is it part of a comprehensive urban redevelopment informed by sociodemographic rather than architectural concerns (the redevelopment of a post-Second World War neighbourhood, for example)? Is the project prompted by infrastructure modernization and implemented at the expense of an old neighbourhood (for example the construction of the Amsterdam metro system in the 1970s) or is it prompted by the transformation of a part of town into a business district (such as the office district near Brussels-North station)?
A key question here is: Should the architect choose sides in such political and conflict-ridden processes and if so, how?

Cultural Context

In addition to political circumstances, cultural values and the overall cultural climate play an important role in the realization of a project. Is the cultural climate of the location progressive or conservative? Is there a sense of great cultural optimism, of hope for a better future? Can society be described as forward-looking, as in Frankfurt towards the end of the 1920s, when the likes of Ernst May developed new social housing concepts, or is there a sense of nostalgia, of wanting to go back to the row housing of the 1930s? Of course the architect plays a role in this, but more often than not he or she is not free to choose between avant-garde and bourgeois traditions.
Some cultural aspects are of a more local nature or associated with the site of the new project. These include:
—Language, dialect
—Local rituals
—History of the region, town or site
—Significance of the region, town or site, often historically determined
—Dwelling culture

The cultural stratification of the site plays a role too. Over time, different cultures have settled in the area earmarked for design. After these earlier cultures went into decline or left the site, they became what we can describe as the compost, the foundation for new developments. The result is an archaeology of lost cultures that have left traces in the built environment. The challenge is to read the meanings that these earlier cultures have carved into the open spaces and buildings.

ANALYSIS AND DESIGN

Incisive analysis of the adjacent built environment, in both the immediate surroundings and further afield, is crucial for good housing design. It should be noted, however, that such an analysis of the

context does not imply an unambiguous position on contextualism. It is up to the designer to decide what to do with the conclusions of these analyses and what choices to make on the basis of these conclusions.
Before delving deeper into the various techniques for analysing the existing development, we would like to raise two issues: What does the existing built environment consist of, or, more generally, what does the city consist of? And what means do we, as designers, have at our disposal within a given context and commission with which to add to or change the built environment?
The built context can be seen as a complex, multilayered system. It encompasses the three aforementioned aspects outlined by Sijmons. For our purposes we have further subdivided the aspects 'networks' and 'occupation'. By analogy with the layers we have used in Chapter 6, 'Tectonics', we can identify the following layers here:

— Substratum, soil
— Networks
  - access: roads, cycle paths, etc.
  - technical infrastructure
— Occupation
  - buildings
  - design of the public space
  - programme: what functions are available?

These layers can be present in varying combinations, densities and manifestations. Differences in architectural style, degree of obsolescence, intensity of use and age lends colour to the differences between neighbourhoods and urban fragments. Sometimes buildings form a street frontage together and are joined up into residential blocks, as in the old city centres. The spaces between the blocks form streets and squares that provide access. Above or below the streets and squares we find the technical infrastructure. The many suburban developments of the twentieth century have an entirely different configuration of buildings. Here they are separate elements or else clusters or ensembles on a continuous foundation: the urban field. Access and infrastructure choose the line of least resistance here and form an autonomous fabric that bears no relation to the fabric underlying the buildings.

An architect will have to develop an eye for all of these differences in order to arrive at a beautiful and solid design. As we noted earlier, architects can decide how to deal with these differences after contextual analysis. But they can do this within the freedom offered by the land use plan and those supervising the master plan, among them supervisors, building inspectors and other quality assurance agents. Likewise, an architect of considerable standing will often have

04

04 Comparison of the structure of Amsterdam's city centre with that of Amsterdam-Zuidoost, Bijlmermeer. From the top: urban green space, roads, buildings. In the city centre these three layers all have a similar structure, whereas in the Bijlmermeer district they are more or less autonomous.

(or take) more room for manoeuvre than a less experienced counterpart. So provided he has the freedom, what choices can a designer make? In principle, the following strategies are possible: he can adjust to the surroundings, opt for contrast or steer a middle course between these two extremes. This is obviously a truism that requires some elaboration. Complete adjustment to or assimilation with one's surroundings is an illusion. New times demand new techniques which in turn lead to new materials and details. The longer the time lapse between the existing and the new development, the greater the difference between all these.
An adjusted design raises the question: adjusted to what? If the architect adjusts the building to its surroundings, does he adjust the programme, the composition, the building height, the building mass, the use of materials or the detailing? Does he adjust to the neighbours on the left or right or to the surroundings in general? The latter case raises the question: What is typical for the broader physical context? The construction of a new property along a canal in Amsterdam could raise the question of whether there is such a thing as a typical Amsterdam canalside house and, if so, what it looks like. What appears to be the simplest strategy of adjustment involves many different choices. This also applies – probably even more so – to the designer who seeks a contrast with the surroundings. The first question here is: Why opt for contrast? Again, this is a matter of interpretation. What is the context of the design, what choices are being made and why? The answers to these questions will have to reflect all of these facets of the building: its position, form, volume, articulation, façade structure, position of the entrance, composition, use of materials, access, detailing, etcetera.

DESIGN TOOLS

The tools with which the architect can shape the brief are many. The overview below is far from exhaustive. Depending on the potential of each individual location and brief, designers of new housing projects have a combination of programmatic, morphological and architectural tools at their disposal.

Programmatic Tools

The choice of dwelling size and dwelling types and the degree of variation in them says something about the intended target group, whether the new residents fit in with the neighbours or differ from them to add variety or bring about a change. The intended density, measured per square metre and in homes per hectare, plays a key role in shaping the urban fabric, as does the public-private distribution of property: are there any public squares or parks, communally managed spaces, or are most of the properties privately owned?

Although the programme is often predetermined, it remains important to cast a critical eye over it and, should this lead to better, more beautiful solutions, put forward other proposals. In the following pages, three projects are examined as examples of the application of the various design tools.

Morphological Tools

This category covers all the different components of the urban design: the urban plan type within the urban fragment, the fabric of streets, squares and residential blocks, the direction, rhythm and profile of the streets, the grain, form, geometry and articulation of the building volumes and the positioning of the buildings within the block.

Architectural Tools

When it comes to the architectural elaboration of the block or building the opportunities for articulating a relationship with the surroundings are almost infinite, at different levels of scale and ranging from powerful statements to subtle nuances. At the level of the design as a whole, there is the differentiation of the various side walls and façades, articulation of the building mass and the dimensions and arrangement of façade surfaces and openings. The experience of the building up close is determined in part by the materiality and expressiveness of the façades and, where relevant, decorative layers and elements. Even the detail of a connection can say something about the relationship with the built environment, history or culture of a place, neighbourhood or city.

05

EDITH GIRARD, BASSIN DE LA VILLETTE (PARIS, 1985)

By stacking different dwelling types Girard has put her own stamp on the composition of this residential block. The façade parallel to the Bassin de la Villette accommodates apartments. Its two upper floors contain gallery-access maisonettes that top the block like a colourful cornice. The block at right angles to the canal is made up of maisonettes of the Unité type, served by an internal corridor.

06

HERMAN HERTZBERGER,
WEESPERSTRAAT STUDENT HOUSING
(AMSTERDAM, 1959–1966)

At first sight, this early design by Herman Hertzberger for a student hall of residence raises the question what a block inspired by Le Corbusier's Unité d'Habitation is doing in Amsterdam's city centre. On closer inspection, however, it becomes apparent that Hertzberger has linked the morphologies of two different contexts. Whereas the tall building on the Weesperstraat is in step with the rhythm of the large office blocks on the east side of the street, its corner complements the buildings on the Nieuwe Keizersgracht. The roof terrace at the corner of the hall of residence is the same height as the adjacent canalside houses, and this is extended to the wide fourth-floor gallery. Another special detail of the way the hall complements the buildings on the Nieuwe Keizersgracht is the strongly articulated eaves line of the small pavilion on the roof terrace.

07

MASSIMILIANO FUKSAS, ÎLOT CANDIE, PASSAGE RUE SAINT BERNARD (PARIS 1992–1996)

In his infill block, designed for the 11th arrondissement in Paris, Fuksas combines adjustment to the existing architecture with an entirely unique form. The architecture of the block bears a great resemblance to the existing late nineteenth-century architecture, a structure of whitewashed façades, orthogonal windows, zinc roofing and open fronts at street level (see left on the photograph). This architecture – including the fenestration – returns in Fuksas's design, albeit with a twist. For example, on the corner, at the entrance to the building, the windows are different, while the zinc roofing has been transformed into a large zinc box that contains an entire floor (see also Chapter 6, 'Tectonics', page 00).

TYPOLOGICAL AND MORPHOLOGICAL ANALYSIS

Because a proper typological and morphological analysis is crucial to a good design, we are devoting a separate section to it.
Not every city or village expansion will readily submit to typological analysis. The pattern of built development can be so chaotic as to defy any kind of meaningful conclusion about the relationship between the urban plan type and the city's actual form. But again, appearances are often deceptive. With a bit of help and interpretation, we can find a well thought-out design concept in the most chaotic parts of the city. Sometimes the design has been partially realized or else fundamentally changed at a later date. Careful consideration of the details and the style of the buildings will ultimately yield some cohesion.
The problem with typological analysis of urban fragments is that it requires a thorough knowledge of the history of the urban design to assess whether a certain part of town contains any fascinating elements. At the same time, once our eyes are opened, this type of analysis could be a fun introduction to such a history.

Typological Analysis

As with dwelling types, the typological study of urban fragments boils down to the reduction of the object under analysis. Given the fact that the plan type that governed the urban fragment is not always immediately apparent, a drastic reduction of the fragment may be needed to reveal it. There may be a number of different causes for this ambiguity. Unskilled use of plan types may have resulted in a barely recognizable version or else the concept may have been left unfinished; that is to say, an essential part of the plan type has been left out so as to make the end product unintelligible. Finally, a plan type that was realized at a later date may have more or less eliminated the earlier plan type (see page 204).
To distil the applied plan types, it may be necessary to remodel the indistinct urban patterns into a more regular pattern. This reconstructed regular version will often be hypothetical, but that need not be a problem. What matters is that we have a reference against which to set the erosions, transformations and ruptures. In the example of the Concertgebouw neighbourhood in Amsterdam-Zuid, this remodelling did not have to be very comprehensive, because the plan type had been implemented fairly rigidly. Ultimately these analyses are all about recognizing the underlying structures and urban configurations (see also Chapter 4, 'Residential Building', page 143).
As outlined above, a plan type can be described as a system consisting of two or more layers. We could be dealing with a strict and balanced relationship between dwelling and lot type, linkage, block layout type and urban plan type (roads, green spaces, the relationship between

city and landscape). Alternatively, perhaps the only thing we can say about a particular part of town is that the plan type consists of a spaghetti of roads, sprinkled with random property. That is why the analysis must start with the typology of dwelling and lot (linkage). In some situations a typological analysis on this scale will suffice. In the example of the ribbon villages developed along roads in rural areas of parallel fields, the typology of house/business and lot can be determined quite easily. The village's basic structure is nothing other than a linear succession of this type and directly reflects its specific form. However, in many cases the typological analysis will have to be carried through to the next level, block level (block pattern), after which the third level, the urban plan, can be described in relation to the first two. It is often helpful to illustrate the typological features in several complementary drawings. [→ 08-09]

Morphological Analysis

The city's actual form can be described as the outcome of a series of erosions of the typological diagram. This method of morphological analysis has been inspired by the likes of Jean Castex, whose work includes a number of influential studies of the form of the city, including the book *Lecture d'une ville: Versailles*.[3] In these studies, Castex and his associates link typological analyses at building level with the analysis of urban fabrics and urban plan types. At the end of this section, we will discuss a few other methodologies.
Morphological analysis may seem like an attempt to reconstruct the design process of the part of town in question, but that is emphatically not its intention. On the contrary, the analysis is aimed at identifying any regularity in and erosions of the urban pattern. We can identify the following types of erosion:

Connections
—Ruptures (where the influence of two adjoining parts of town is felt).
—Barriers (canal, railway and motorway, industrial estate).
—Change in direction: how has this been dealt with in relation to the two colliding fragments?

Omissions
In many cases essential parts of a plan have never been implemented (the boulevard between Station Zuid and the Rijksacademie in Berlage's Plan Zuid of 1915, for example), while some plan types are ill-considered or badly understood. [← 10]

Transformations
Deliberate erosion of a plan concept by superimposing a new concept is a common occurrence in city centres. In such a case, comparison between different stages of the plan (available from the municipal archives or planning agency) should clarify matters.

3
Jean Castex et al., *Lecture d'un ville: Versailles* (Paris: Moniteur, 1980).

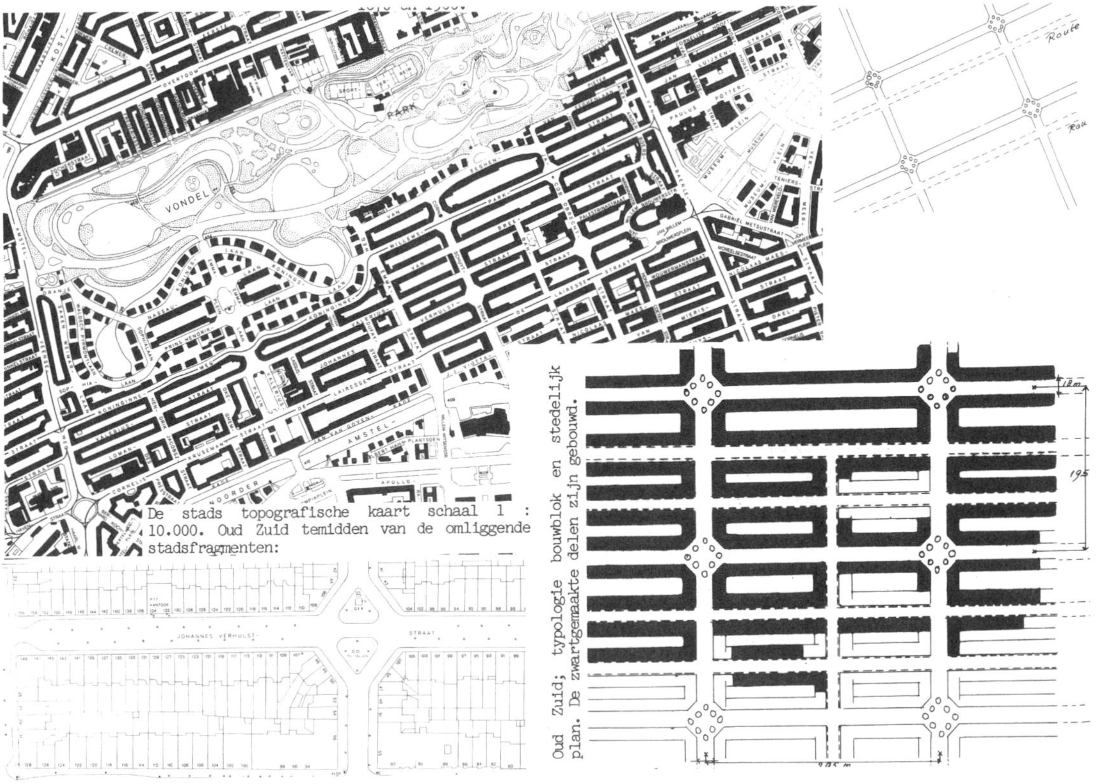

08

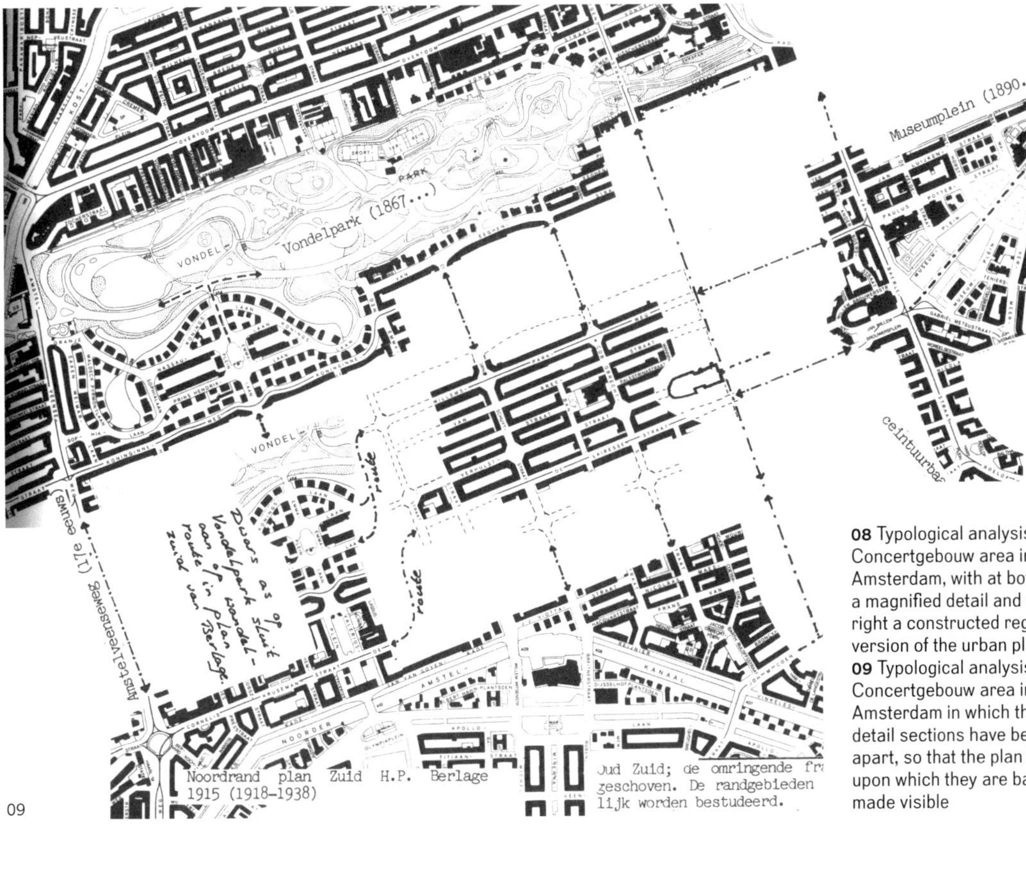

09

08 Typological analysis of the Concertgebouw area in Amsterdam, with at bottom left a magnified detail and at bottom right a constructed regular version of the urban plan type
09 Typological analysis of the Concertgebouw area in Amsterdam in which the various detail sections have been pulled apart, so that the plan types upon which they are based are made visible

10

10 H.P. Berlage, Plan Zuid showing the Station Zuid-Rijksacademie axis.

Analysis of the morphology of the city on a larger scale, and in particular those elements that define its structure, requires a thematic reduction of its topography. This step allows us to determine our position vis-à-vis the spatial structure of the city and/or the landscape. In their day-to-day, casual use of an area, residents do not gawp at the highlights, like tourists do, but tend to be more or less oblivious to them (it can be a fascinating experience to suddenly be a tourist in one's own city again, for example when we show foreign visitors around). Nonetheless, in everyday use the architectural features of a space do play a role in how its structure is memorized. These architectural features include: the form of the space, the landscaping, the water, the form of buildings and objects. Ultimately, orientation and recognition will always be linked to a limited number of spatial elements within the urban fabric. Which elements these are will vary, depending on the way the city is used. Trying to identify the structuring elements of the city or landscape is one way of ascertaining the spatial cohesion of a particular area.
It is possible to make a reduction drawing of an urban development plan by only highlighting the structuring elements at the various stages of development. This method casts the city as a text that has been amended, edited and added to over a long period of time. Combined with the analysis of the historical development, this can produce a clear picture of the way in which, over time, a series of essential elements has taken shape as a result of deliberate design interventions, coincidence or lucky accidents. As the examples of Copenhagen and Breda demonstrate, a reduction drawing can be quite clear, even on the detailed scale of 1:20,000. [→ 11-13]

'Figure-ground'
To arrive at a better understanding of the morphology of the city, and especially the new city, American theoretician Colin Rowe[4] drew the buildings as black volumes (*figure*) against an empty background (*ground*). By reducing the urban fabric to this black-and-white 'figure and ground' pattern, he was able to highlight the difference between the traditional city with its perimeter blocks and the modern city with its autonomous objects. In the example here, Rowe placed the city of Parma, which has a traditional, continuous structure, next to Le Corbusier's design for Saint-Dié-des-Vosges. In the latter image, the solitary buildings emerge as separate elements against the large urban field with roads and green spaces. [→ 14-15]

4
Colin Rowe and Fred Koetter, *Collage City* (Cambridge, MA: MIT Press, 1984).

Morphological Analysis of the Modern, Dynamic city
The morphological analysis discussed above focuses first and foremost on static buildings, without taking the movement of and through the city into account. The 1960s and 1970s saw the development of a number of analytical methods that looked at the city from other perspectives.

11

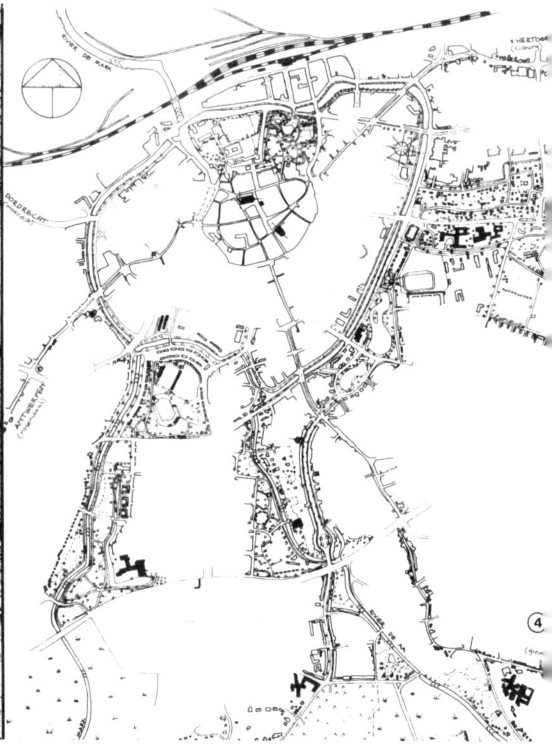

12

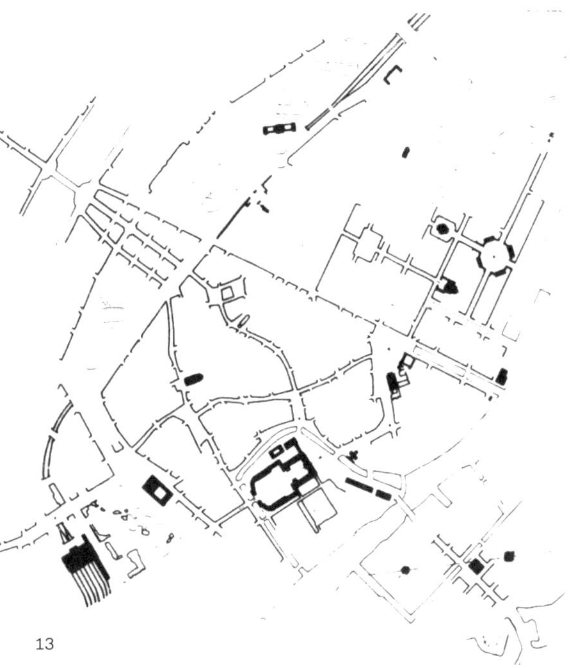

13

11, 12 Morphological analysis of Breda; left, a reduction of the topography in which all buildings are indicated. This reduction method can be seen as derived from the figure-and-ground analyses.
13 Morphological analysis of Copenhagen, in which the topography has been reducted to the contours of the most significant urban spaces. The buildings that serve as landmarks are indicated.
14 C. Rowe, figure-and-ground plan of Parma, 1984
15 C. Rowe, figure-and-ground plan of Le Corbusier's Saint-Dié-des-Vosges, 1984

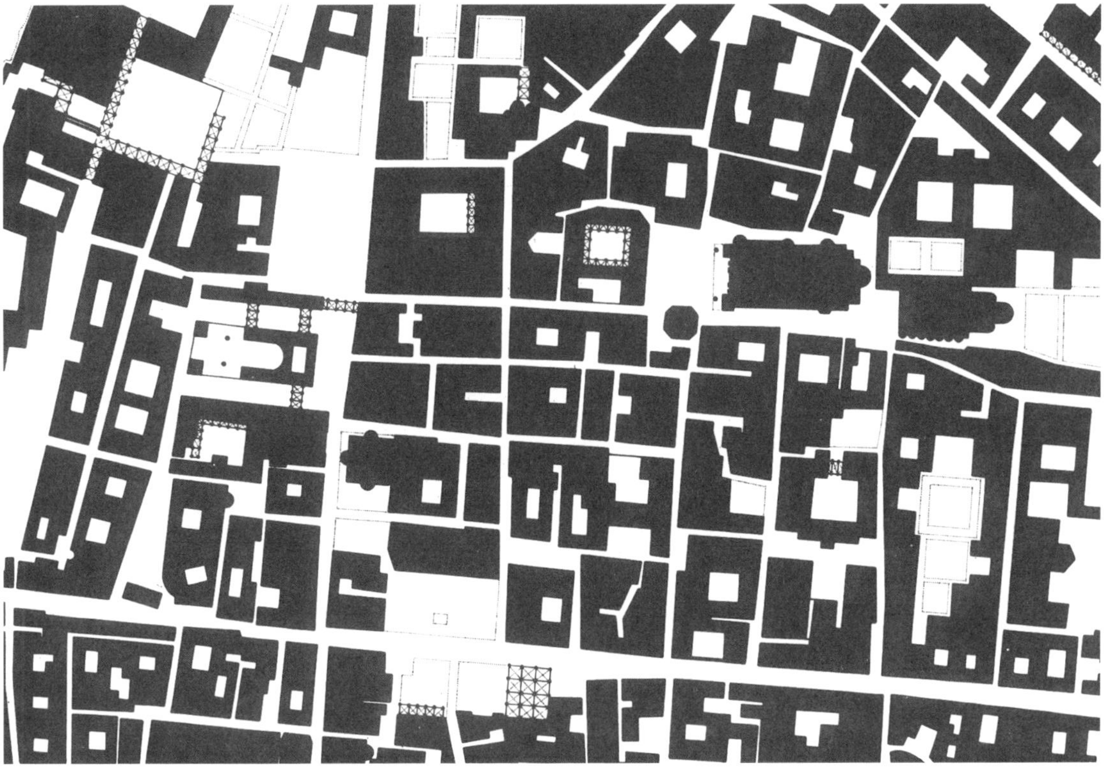

14

15

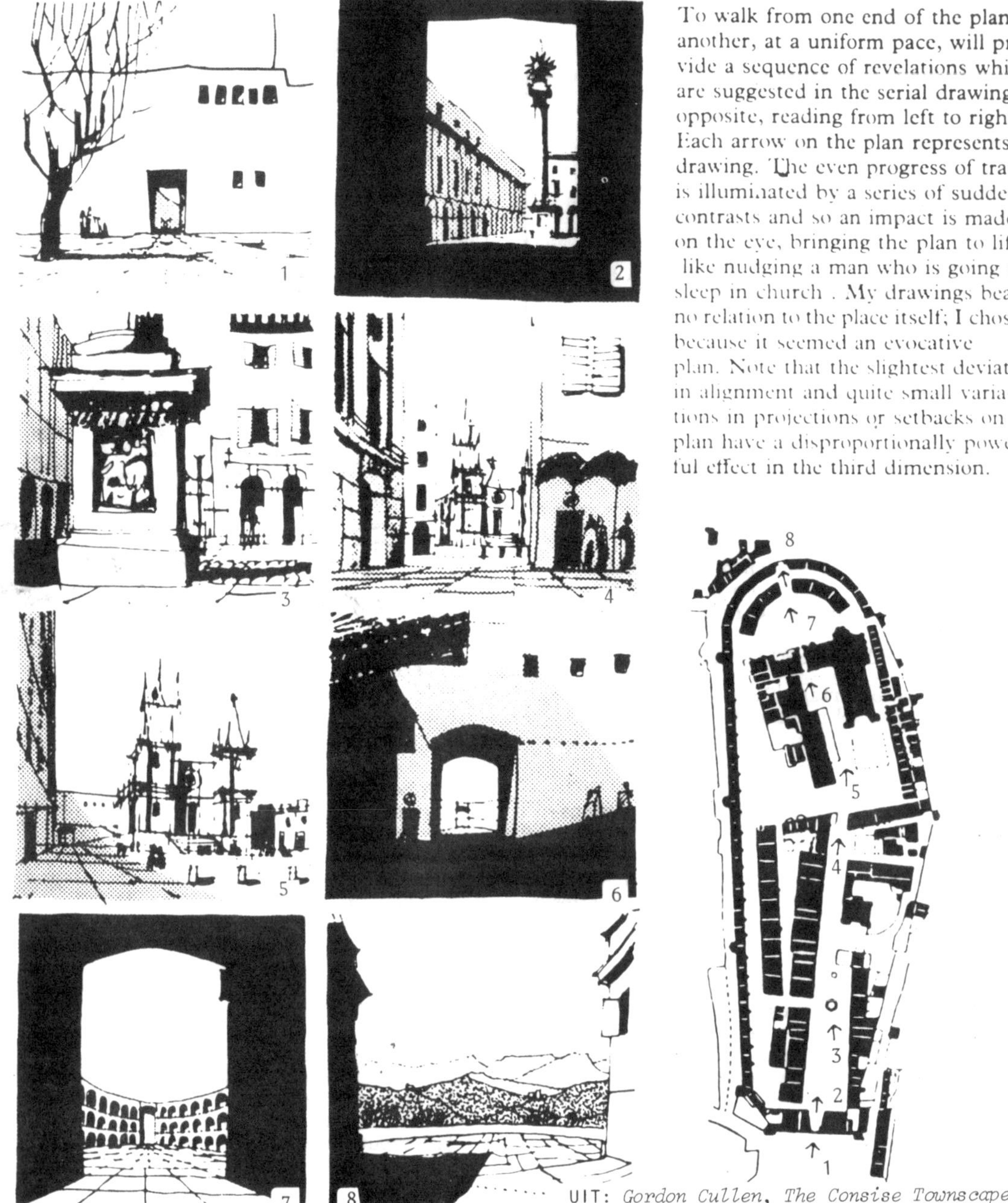

CASEBOOK: SERIAL VISION

To walk from one end of the plan to another, at a uniform pace, will provide a sequence of revelations which are suggested in the serial drawings opposite, reading from left to right. Each arrow on the plan represents a drawing. The even progress of travel is illuminated by a series of sudden contrasts and so an impact is made on the eye, bringing the plan to life like nudging a man who is going to sleep in church . My drawings bear no relation to the place itself; I chose it because it seemed an evocative plan. Note that the slightest deviation in alignment and quite small variations in projections or setbacks on plan have a disproportionally powerful effect in the third dimension.

UIT: *Gordon Cullen, The Consise Townscape*

16

16 G. Cullen's 'serial vision' from *The Concise Townscape*, 1961

In his book *The Concise Townscape* Gordon Cullen adopts a series of changing perspectives ('serial vision') to define the visual perception along certain routes. He is particularly interested in the perception of the old city from the slow progression of, say, a pedestrian. [← 16] Kevin Lynch focuses on the modern city with opaque patterns. Lynch's most famous work, *The Image of the City*, is the result of many years of research. His object of study encompassed three very different cities: Boston, Jersey City and Los Angeles. [→ 17] According to Lynch, residents understand their complex surroundings through what he labels 'mental maps', a mental construct of their surroundings.[5]
These mental maps contain five elements:
— 'paths': streets, pavements, tracks and other routes along which people travel
— 'edges': borders such as walls, buildings and coastlines
— 'districts': urban fragments, neighbourhoods, etceter with a distinct character
— 'nodes': focal points, junctions, sites
— 'landmarks': important objects that function as reference points in the city

Lynch's collection *City Sense and City Design* includes a 'mental map' in which he recreates its dynamic perception as experienced from inside a car.[6] It shows the sequence of impressions of the 'motion space' along a planned highway through the city. The image shows the experience of space and motion. [→ 18]

In *Learning from Las Vegas*, Robert Venturi and Denise Scott Brown describe and analyse the 'non-city' Las Vegas, a city whose appearance is first and foremost determined by ephemeral objects such as giant billboards and vast car parks. Their conclusion is that in a city such as Las Vegas (ephemeral) images have a much greater impact on perception than the architectural form.[7]
They use the 'Las Vegas Strip' as a metaphor for the everyday and the ugly. Venturi and Scott Brown posit a distinction between the 'decorated shed' and the 'duck'. Whereas the 'duck' represents modern architecture that tries hard to express the function of the building, the 'decorated shed' represents architecture in which the exterior bears no relation to the interior.
To understand the strip, Venturi and Scott Brown draw a series of diagrammatic maps, starting with a Rowe-style figure-and-ground map. They then draw a negative of this map, shifting the emphasis to the unbuilt spaces. The subsequent series depicts only the asphalt, uncultivated land, ceremonial places such as wedding chapels, cars, illumination and written texts visible from the car. [→ 19-20]

5
Kevin Lynch, *The Image of the City* (Cambridge, MA: MIT Press, 1960).

6
Kevin Lynch, *City Sense and City Design*, in: *The Writings and Projects of Kevin Lynch* (Cambridge, MA: MIT Press, 1990).

7
Robert Venturi and Denise Scott Brown, *Learning from Las Vegas* (Cambridge, MA: MIT Press, 1977).

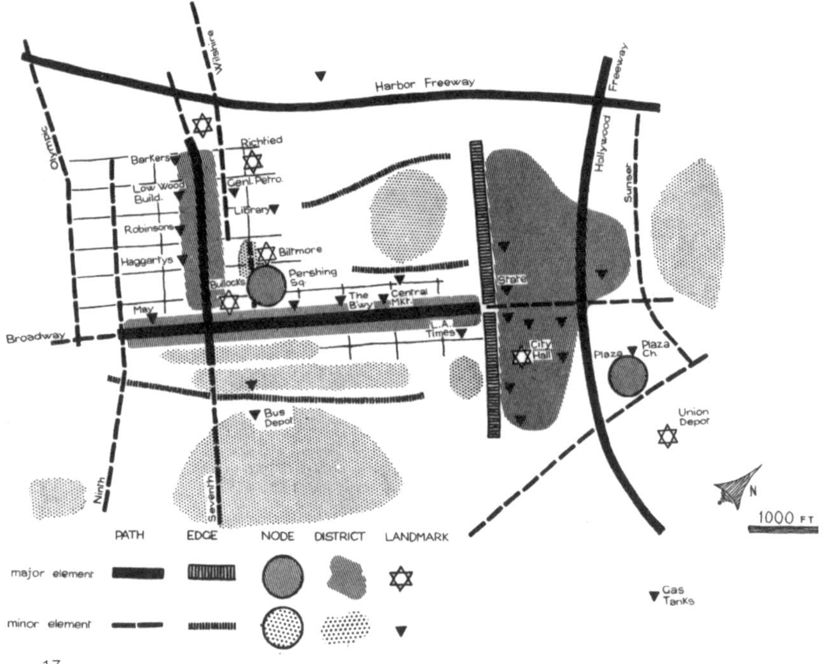

17

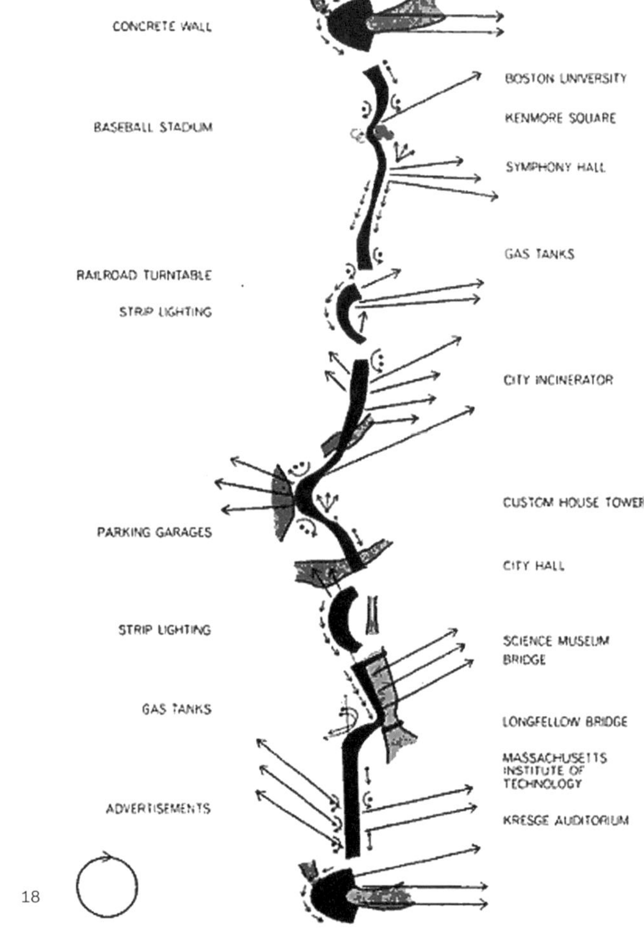

18

17 K. Lynch, 'The visual form of Los Angeles', 1960
18 K. Lynch, representation of the sequence of impressions of the 'motion space' along a planned motorway through the city

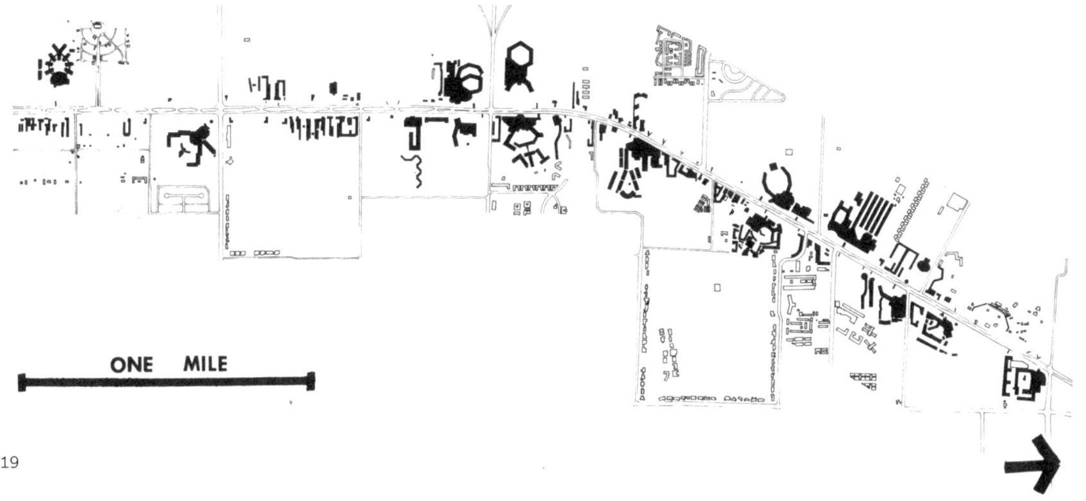

19

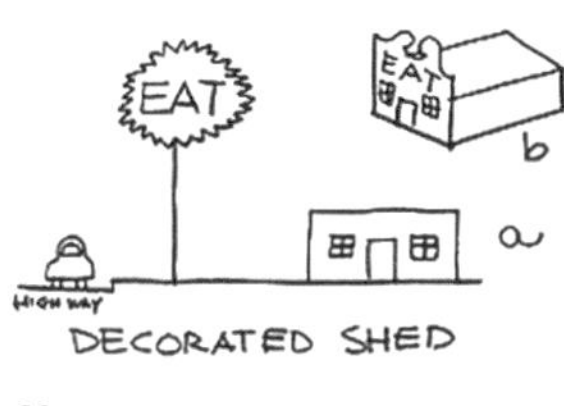

20

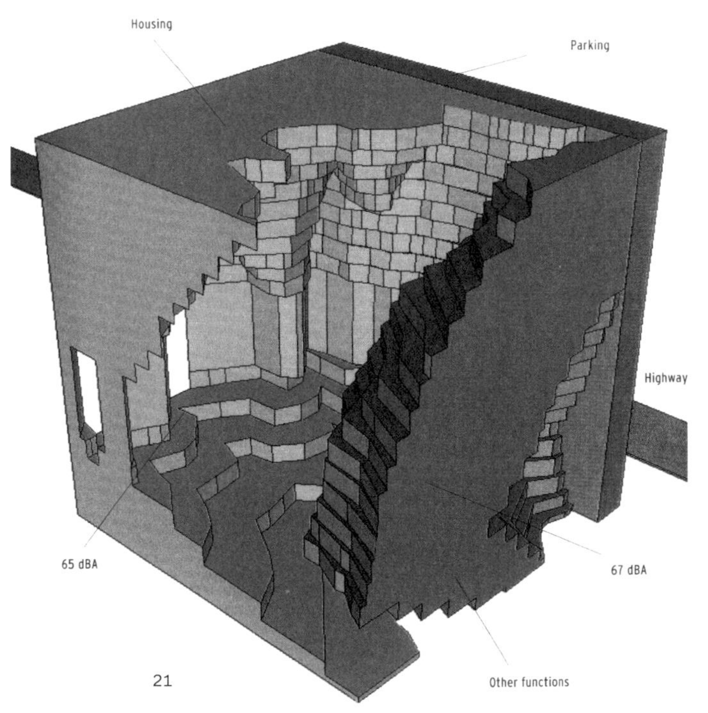

21

19 R. Venturi and D. Scott Brown, map of the Las Vegas Strip, 1977
20 The 'decorated shed' and the 'duck'
21 MVRDV, datascaping baed on the sound pressure level in housing, 1998

GIS and Datascaping

Finally, a brief look at more recent techniques for documenting the context, known collectively as geographical information systems (GIS).[8] A geographical information system makes it possible to store, manage, process, analyse and present spatial data or information about geographical objects, so-called geo-information.

8
This part of the text draws on the Wikipedia entry for GIS.

GIS has three practical functions:
—the digitization of large amounts of topographical data;
—the development of a relational database;
—contextual output such as plans, maps and 3D representations.

Because the systems contain spatial information, they can give information a place on a map before linking it spatially.
Sources of geographical information include: digital maps, aerial photographs, height maps, densities, composition of the population, land use, plant and animal life per square kilometre, air quality and noise levels. GIS lends itself extremely well to organizing the multilayered analytical models described at the start of this chapter. Architecture firms such as OMA and MVRDV use GIS to process and manipulate contextual data. One example is the map of Europe that OMA used in the development of Euralille. On this map the distances within Europe were expressed in temporal units. The arrival of the high-speed rail link will transform the face of Europe; while some distances will be reduced, other areas will seem further away.
GIS is used not only to present and analyse data but, as with OMA and MVRDV, also as a tool with which to manipulate data and make design choices. With the help of this method, better known as *datascaping*, data is processed in such a way as to produce a possible new building design. For example, data on levels of sound pressure, particulates and the penetration of natural light can be converted into building volumes. Datascaping literally means designing on the basis of data, or in other words: *form follows data*. [← 21]

THE BRIEF

The urban design is an important contextual aspect and element of the architect's brief. To begin with, the planning regulations for a particular location include the legally binding rules set out in the land use plan. However, these regulations can also offer a certain degree of freedom and provide an arena where the urban planning agency or supervisor and architect enter into a discussion to arrive at a good solution. In this process, the planning agency or supervisor enjoys the backing of politicians.

In this part of the chapter we will look at the different kinds of briefs, categorized according to the type of location and the planning tools specified in the town plan. The locations are subdivided into two main groups: tabula rasa locations and redevelopment areas.
Tabula rasa locations are literally 'empty' areas, where every last trace of the past has been erased and is often covered by a layer of sand. True to the spirit of the word, there are no references to substratum, growth or water courses. This kind of location offers the architect few starting points in terms of size, direction or scale. The tabula rasa location is quite common in the Netherlands, for two reasons: soil conditions and impoldering. Because of poor soil conditions a foundation on piles is a necessity in large parts of the western and northern Netherlands. It is impossible to build on the poor substratum, which consists for the most part of thick peat formation and other weak substances. Only the underlying substratum of sand provides sufficient support. Often the soil is not just unsuitable for building, but also too soft for paving or planting green spaces and gardens. Many of the areas earmarked for urban expansion are former peat fields. Soil consolidation is needed to prepare this ground for building. The appropriate method for this is the application of a thick layer of sand. In large areas this is done by rainbowing sand: sand is dredged up from another location and transported in liquid form through thick pipes. The application of sand, especially through rainbowing, erases the landscape's original structure and morphology, leaving the designer with few starting points for his new housing design. All traces of the past have been rubbed out.
We find a similar scenario in most Dutch polders, especially those in the former Zuiderzee. After reclamation the virginal seabed emerges, a clean slate without any clues, giving the designers carte blanche. The only thing that really matters here is the drainage system: ditches, canals and the reservoir canals that drain away the rising water and precipitation to the pumping stations so as to keep the polder dry. Like a strict Mondrian, this mathematical polder structure dictates the position of roads, fields, farms and cities. Everything here is designed, even the departures from the norm and the quasi-randomness; everything has been dreamt up at the drawing table; nothing is organic or accidental.
It is an entirely different story in redevelopment areas, which tend to harbour lots of traces of the past: old buildings or fragments of buildings, ancient trees, water courses, quay walls, and so forth. Likewise, adjacent buildings and the landscape loom larger. In the 1970s, entire neighbourhoods and districts were improved or else demolished and replaced. Urban regeneration took place in many large European cities, with nineteenth- and early twentieth-century housing, in particular, given overhauls. The following decade saw the rise of a new form of urban restructuring. The restructuring of old industrial sites, ports and railway yards freed up large areas close

to urban territory. These areas were transformed into residential neighbourhoods, business districts, parks and other urban facilities. The presence of older buildings, industrial monuments and hard boundaries provides interesting contexts for new neighbourhoods or districts. That said, some restructuring projects are so immense that they acquire the nature of a tabula rasa.
In addition to the distinction between a tabula rasa and a restructuring project we can make a distinction based on the level of planning, from neighbourhood level via the block or sub-plan to the infill of one or more properties in a larger context. Each task at a particular level will have its own character. Finally, this chapter also contains a classification based on planning tools, especially those employed in the land use plan. In some cases the local planning controls have been described in more detail with the help of the town plan. These descriptions are referred to as the 'planning framework' (see matrix on page 363).

Planning Tools

Sector Plan
A land use planning method in which only the function and perhaps the density is specified, it avoids making any kind of statement about form. In the Netherlands in the 1970s and 1980s it was a common response to the *plan masse* (see below), which was considered too rigid.

Building Line
One of the oldest planning tools in Dutch town planning is the building line or alignment, the line or more accurately the plane that specifies the position of the building, the plane that must be materialized. As a rule this tool is applied only to continuous façades in urban areas. The *Grachtengordel*, the historic ring of canals in the centre of Amsterdam, was planned on this basis, as were many nineteenth-century neighbourhoods. If this principle is applied in combination with a maximum building height and maximum building depth, as is often the case, it is referred to as a 'zoning envelope'.

Zoning
The concept of zoning comes from American urban planning and specifies a zone for the development. In principle this tool is always combined with a land use plan. Unlike the building line, zoning indicates the area where you are *allowed* to build instead of where you *have* to build. Zoning is the foundation of the American urban plan, but it can also be found in many European land use plans.

Zoning Envelope
We speak of a 'zoning envelope' when the zoning is supplemented with three-dimensional rules that exceed the prescription of a maximum number of floors. The zoning envelope is the tool with which cities with many high-rise buildings, such as New York, are regulated. In this system a so-called envelope, an imaginary volume, is defined within which the building must be realized. The concept of Floor Area Ratio (FAR) plays an important role in the specification of the envelope. The FAR expresses the floor area divided by the building's surface area. It also defines the angle at which the building must recede to allow sufficient light in the street. The zoning will often prescribe a recessed plane that guarantees enough daylight at street level.

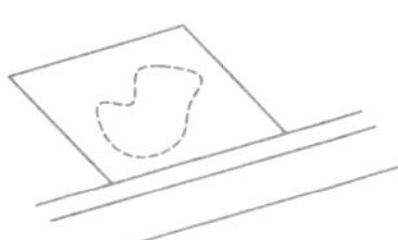

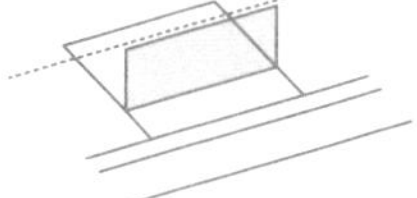

Plan Masse
In contrast to the zoning envelope, the *plan masse* defines a volume for the new building. While not the maximum volume, it defines the form of the building. In the Netherlands this tool was used on a large scale, for instance, by Hendrik Petrus Berlage to determine the form of the buildings of Plan Zuid in the south of Amsterdam.
The diagram in Figure 17 groups the types of briefs according to location and planning tool. Where possible we have tried to select a project for each type of brief, but this does not make sense for all combinations. For example, infill projects based on sector plans are very thin on the ground. The infill of, say, a single gap in an existing block is nearly always subject to detailed regulations, such as a building line, zoning envelope or *plan masse*, as well as regulations concerning the gutter height, the position of the window frames (the reveal) and the cladding.

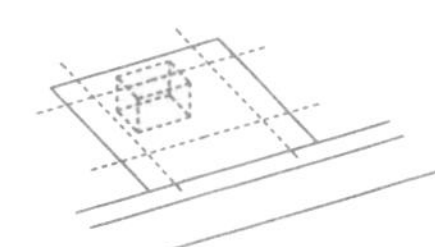

Planning Tools Involving a Supervisor
Besides the planning tools discussed above, there are two other tools in which inspection by a building standards commission and/or a supervisor plays a role. We are referring here to the 'city image plan' and the negotiation model.

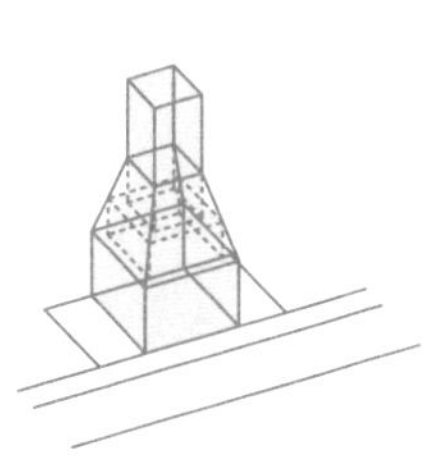

City Image Plan
The city image plan is not an independent planning tool, but more of a supplement to one of the aforementioned tools. The city image plan dictates the appearance of the urban space and buildings, including the colour, material and rhythm. The city image plan has no legal validity, but it can be influential as part of the aesthetic control bill. It gives the building standards commission an instrument with which to control the aesthetic quality of urban space. One problem, however, is that whereas the committee has a say in building

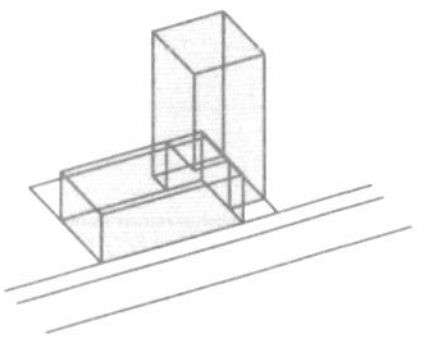

applications and hence the buildings bordering the public space, it has no control over the design and layout of that public space. The design and layout and furnishing of the public space are a matter for the municipal authorities.

Negotiation Model
Finally, there is a planning tool that we have called the negotiation model. This model, in which the plan takes shape through the constant interaction between the planner and supervisor, also tends to supplement one of the other tools. The negotiation model is common in new developments. The development and detailing of the urban design comes about, in part, through the negotiations between the plan supervisor and the architects of the various sub-plans.

The next section is devoted to the analysis of a wide variety of projects, in a range of contexts with different local planning controls. We will describe the context and planning controls for each project and indicate how each design responds to them.

URBAN PLANNING METHODOLOGY	area	housing block or sub-plan area	interpretation
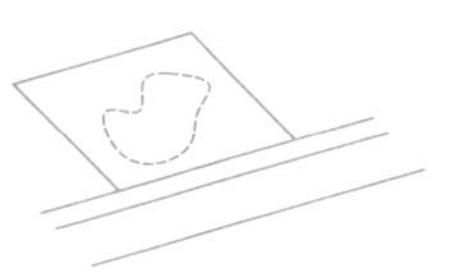 SECTOR PLAN	 p. 364		
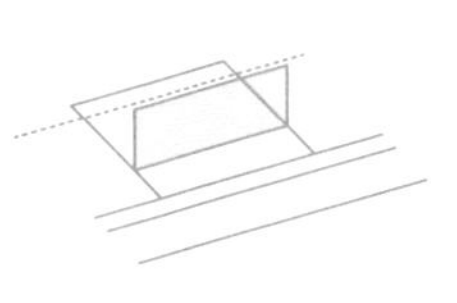 BUILDING LINE			 p. 367
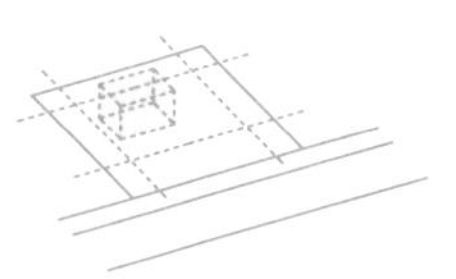 ZONING	 p. 366		
ZONING ENVELOPE		 p. 372	 p. 370  p. 368
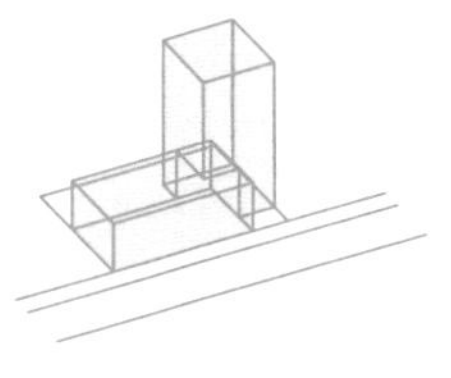 PLAN MASSE	 p. 378	 p. 376	 p. 374

trix of housing briefs, including sample plans. In the project discussions t follow, we indicate, as much as possible, what sort of brief was olved and what set of tools was employed to determine the urban nning conditions. In addition, we describe how the designers erpreted the brief.

23a

23b

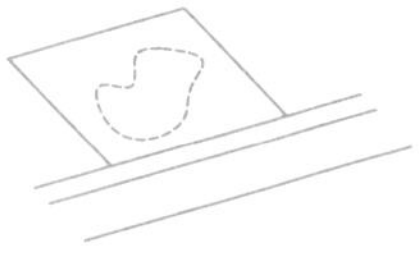

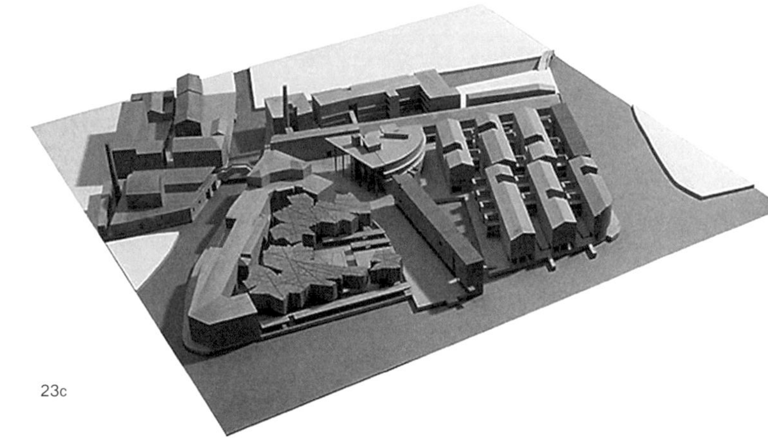

23c

23a Central square
23b Articulated façade openings
23c Competition plan by Cino Zucchi
23d Original situation
23e Current situation

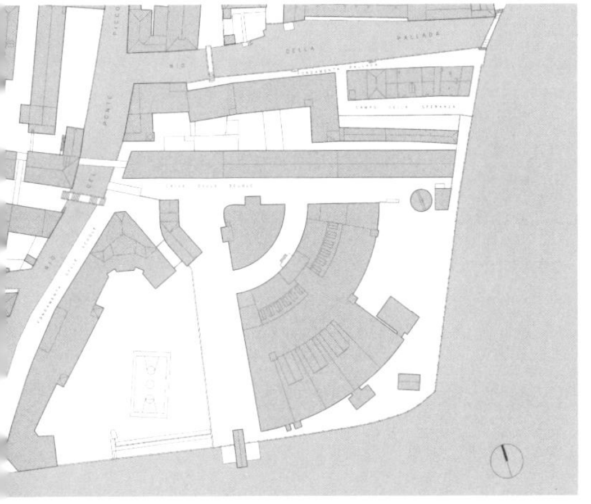

23d

23e

CINO ZUCCHI, CAMPO JUNGHANS (VENICE, 1998–2003)

In 1995 a closed competition was held for the redevelopment of the former industrial estate of watch manufacturer Junghans on the Venetian island of Giudecca. The Italian architect Cino Zucchi beat five colleagues to win the competition. There was no land use plan for this archetypal restructuring area, only a programme and of course the existing buildings. Because there were no formal guidelines for the new design other than the programme, the planning framework can be described as a sector plan.

The brief for the 3-hectare area stipulated the following: 150 homes, 40 urban facilities and small commercial spaces, 160 student flats and a theatre with rehearsal rooms.

Giudecca is an elongated island south of Venice. Its north side is accessed by a long quay with a series of narrow alleyways perpendicular to it with wide but shallow buildings. Here and there the island is bisected by north-south canals. This structure has been disrupted on the site of the Junghans factories. Here, the canals bend while the former factory buildings fan out to the tip of the island.

The absence of a formal planning framework for this new neighbourhood provided an ideal competition project, allowing all the designers to give free reign to their visions. In his competition plan Zucchi leaves some of the existing buildings intact, including the monumental school along the canal and an oblong industrial building at right angles to the island's structure. The fan-shaped factory makes way for a series of long, narrow housing blocks. The centre of the fan had been home to the old factory headquarters. In Zucchi's plan its shape returns in the form of a theatre.

For the most part, Zucchi uses two types of housing that are typical of Venice: the long, narrow blocks that tend to be accessed by small stairwells, and the block-shaped buildings or urban villas. He situated a striking block of the latter type at a corner where two canals meet, close to the bridge that provides access to the main part of the neighbourhood. Its façade openings are clearly articulated through wide frames.

The bridge takes us to the central square between the school, the theatre and one of the long residential blocks. The urban space here opens up towards the south and the lagoon and part of it has been turned into a small park. The entire plan is characterized by an archetypal Venetian mix of narrow streets, water, bridges and open spaces with views of the vast lagoon.

Most of the housing has been developed by Zucchi in collaboration with others.

The restoration and conversion of the long former industrial building was done in cooperation with Pietro Nicoline, one of the five architects who entered the competition.

Contrary to Zucchi's wishes, the site of the original fan-shaped factory was given a different interpretation.

24a

24b

S333, CIBOGA SITE, SCHOTS 1 AND SCHOTS 2 (GRONINGEN, 2002) PLANNING FRAMEWORK: CIBOGA SITE (GRONINGEN, 1998–2002)

In northeast Groningen, a mixed-use project has been realized on the site of a former gasworks called the Ciboga site (from Ci*rcus-,* bo*den- en* ga*sfabriekterrein*, meaning 'circus, freight and gasworks site'). The Ciboga site is set within the nineteenth-century city ramparts; situated on the edge of the city centre, it has a strategic location for housing. But while a high urban density is required here, the area is also part of the city's ecological infrastructure.

One of the benefits of twentieth-century mass housing was that it provided for both collective amenities and infrastructure. This advantage was at risk of being lost as a result of the privatization of house building in the 1990s. Groningen is now experimenting with buildings that cater to urban lifestyles while also including communal spaces. Inspired by British examples, spaces have been developed that can be managed well in the long term and also accommodate a varied urban life.

ZONING

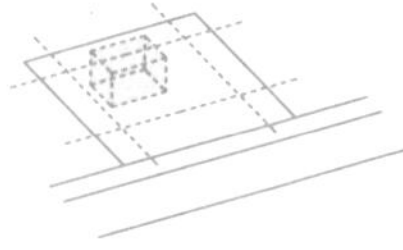

Maarten Schmitt, Groningen's urban planner at the time, designed a layout for the Ciboga site consisting of 11 *schotsen* or floes. The *schots* design can be characterized as a zoning plan. The plan defines the contours (zoning) of the splotches (floes) to be built on, but includes few formal specifications. However, the plan does include functional requirements regarding density and mixed use. For the northern-most floes, Schots 1 and Schots 2, the number of dwellings to be realized has been set at 150, while a total of 4,500 m² of shops and services is required.

In 1992, the Ciboga site was the location for the Europan competition, which was won by architecture firm S333 architecten. S333, led by Jonathan Woodroffe, developed Schots 1 and Schots 2 with the aforementioned local planning conditions in mind. The two S333-designed blocks consist of meandering rows on a continuous green, urban landscape. The blocks accommodate a great variety of dwelling types (ranging from live-work units to a large five-storey mansion), winter, roof and patio gardens, two supermarkets, a police station, a playground and a glass arbour. The blocks are part of Groningen's ecological corridor, giving the public and semi-public areas as well as the many private gardens and patios an important, 'green' role. The *schots* concept that S333 developed for the Europan location has a strong urban design component: large urban blocks with smooth, relatively neutral façades that fit well in the urban context. But the concept stands out for its landscaping too. The traditional sequence of public, semi-public and private (outdoor) space and the related set of street, square, internal courtyard and front and back garden have been replaced by a continuous landscape with indistinct transitions.

The two floes by S333 share urban and landscape features as well as an underground car park. Architecturally, however, they have been treated as two separate entities. Schots 1 is robust and has higher sections and a glass façade, with dwellings sporting floor-to-ceiling windows. The use of different kinds of glass has introduced a great degree of variation in transparency and reflection, muted and colourful hues. Schots 2 is clad in cedar wood panels and has a distinctive, gently sloping landscape in the internal courtyard, which rises incrementally from street level to the first-floor entrances.

25

CEES DAM IN COLLABORATION WITH KAREL BODON, AMSTEL 270 RESIDENCE (AMSTERDAM, 1988)

On the banks of the Amstel River in Amsterdam stands a striking house – striking because it is a remarkable reinterpretation of the canalside house. Since the development, in the seventeenth century, of the ring of concentric canals, the building line has been the organizing principle for street frontage in Amsterdam. As well as the building line, there are maximum building heights and building depths for each lot, while a detailed land use plan specifies the permitted functions. Last, but certainly not least, Amsterdam's city centre has strict building standards. A building line not only stipulates that no part of the building may project beyond this line, but it also imposes limits on recessed elements. In fact, a building line is not so much a line as a plane, an imaginary plane that specifies the position of the façade; it is the plane that must be built.

The only part beyond the building line that may be built on is the pavement. Since the Middle Ages, people in Amsterdam have had rights to the strip of ground in front of their house. This area is part of the house and may be used for access steps, doorsteps and cellar entrances, but it is also publicly accessible, unless clearly closed off by a fence, for instance. Another typical feature of the canal house is the large open front on the ground floor and perhaps a mezzanine. Again, these elements go back to the late-medieval house in Amsterdam, where business was conducted on the ground floor. The upper storeys often have more closed façades consisting of brickwork with windows. Since the eighteenth-century, the front elevation of a canal house in Amsterdam has been topped by a cornice. In this new house along the Amstel, the architects have integrated all of these traditional features in quite a remarkable way. On the ground floor a double-height window wall has been constructed using large I-beams. Behind this front we find a double-height entrance hall with a mezzanine. Because the lower floor is the main floor, it has been raised slightly above street level. A monumental doorstep provides access to both the office and the private house above. The upper storeys have large, closed façades with one large window in between. In contrast to the traditional canalside elevation, this elevation is asymmetrical. The top floor is slightly recessed and, with its narrow vertical window arrangement evokes associations with the eighteenth-century cornice.

BUILDING LINE

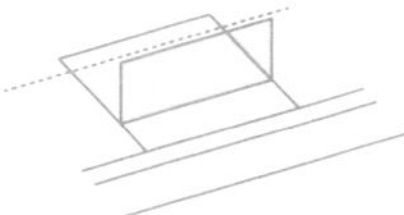

26a

SHOP ARCHITECTS, THE PORTER HOUSE (NEW YORK, 2002)

At the corner of Ninth Avenue and 14th Street in New York, SHoP Architects has realized an extension on top of an existing building. The project is part of the transformation of Manhattan's former Meatpacking District. This area west of The Village, where the meat-processing industry was traditionally based, has been transformed into a modern residential neighbourhood with lots of galleries, trendy furniture shops, bars and restaurants. The existing building, which used to house a meat-packing business, has been converted into a residential building with offices on the lower floors. To create additional homes, the designers made the most of the maximum building volume permissible, as laid down in the 'zoning law'.

The zoning law is a legal instrument that specifies the so-called 'zoning envelope' (the description of the maximum building volume). Here, at the corner of Ninth Avenue and 14th Street, category C6-2A from the New York City zoning handbook is in force [→ 22c].[9] 'C' stands for Commercial and '2a' permits mixed use. The permitted FAR is 6.0, which means that the gross floor area here can be six times the surface area. The New York City zoning handbook also stipulates a number of rules on building height and recessed building lines, to ensure sufficient light in the street.

Architecture practice SHoP made clever use of the rules by pushing the new building volume back, something that is permitted under zoning. In this way, they managed to create the maximum possible volume. To facilitate rapid construction at this busy location and to limit the weight of the new block, the façade was made of prefabricated elements with steel cladding. Thanks to its façade pattern and dark colour the new block fits in well with the sturdy brownstone buildings that are such a distinctive feature of the neighbourhood.

ZONING ENVELOPE

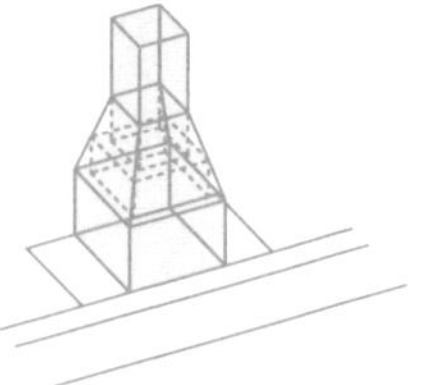

9 Department of City Planning, New York City, 2006.

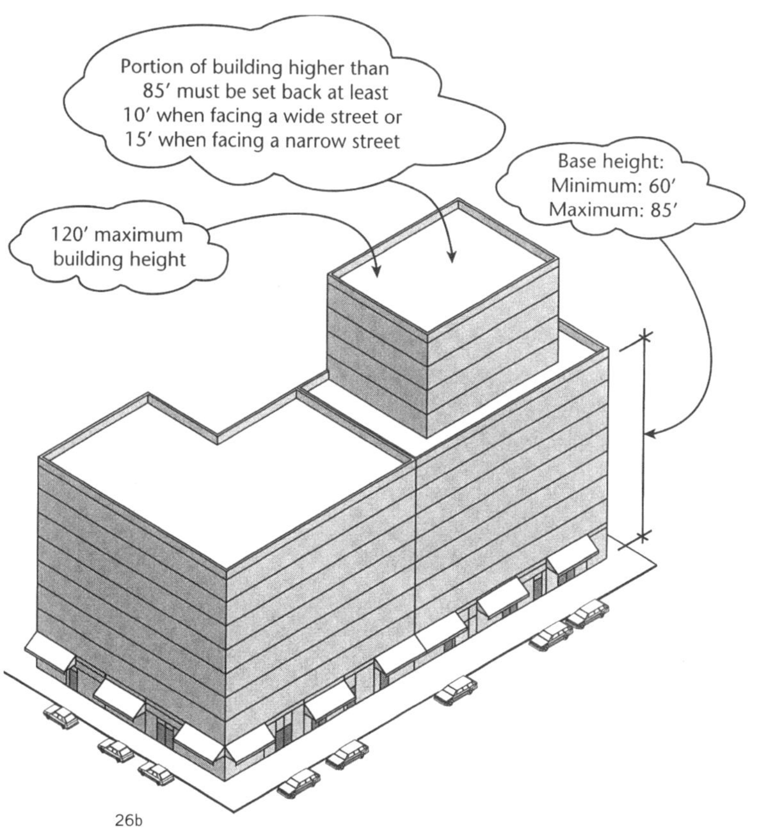

26b

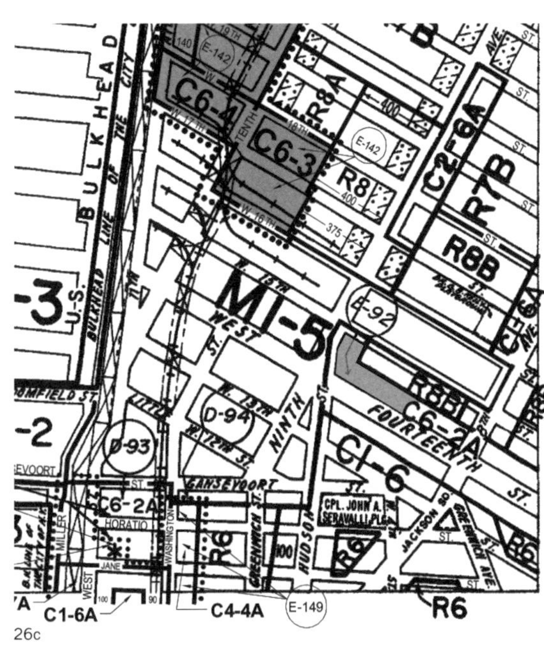

26c

26b Zoning envelope of zones C6-2A, New York City Department of City Planning, 2006, p. 63
26c Detail of the zoning map around the The Porter House site

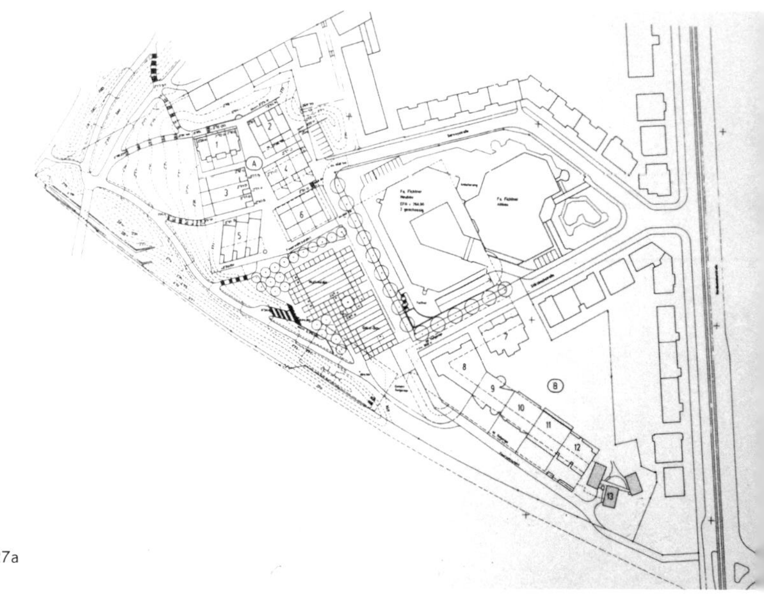

27a

MECANOO, HOUSE 13 (STUTTGART, 1989–1993)

A more idiosyncratic interpretation of the zoning envelope can be found in Mecanoo's design for the House 13 project in Stuttgart (see also Chapter 6, 'Tectonics', page 289). House 13 was part of the Internationale Gartenschau in Stuttgart in 1993 (IGA). The theme of the international garden show was sustainability. Under the heading 'responsible approaches to nature' several architects were invited to design experimental ecological homes, ranging from energy-saving single-family homes to flexible dwellings for new forms of cohabitation. Mecanoo saw this challenge as an opportunity to explore the possibilities of linkage. When homes or parts of them can be attached or detached, both vertically and horizontally, the resulting rearrangement will lead to ever new uses.
The starting point was an envelope that defined a wall that closed off an existing block. Mecanoo had been allocated a lot somewhere halfway down this wall. The idea was that every participating architect would develop a small section of this wall. The standard dwelling type was based on the 'troika' or three-point access system: a central stairwell with lift providing access to three dwellings per floor.
In an attempt to achieve greater freedom, Mecanoo pulled apart this typically German 'troika' structure. The separate components were then regrouped in a composition made up of three free-standing towers, varying in height, and linked to a similarly free-standing transparent lift shaft via slender bridges. The *exploded* 'troika' block contains 13 small apartments and three maisonettes. Separate units can be combined with the help of the spiral staircases inside the towers. With the building's components pulled apart, the neighbourhood's green spaces can snake through the composition.
Because this exploded 'troika' block did not fit within the specified envelope, after some negotiation Mecanoo's lot was moved to the top of the block, where the intervention would not disrupt the principles of the master plan but would enrich it instead. Stripped of the traditional, central staircase, what remained were slender stacks of residential units. The abstract façades reinforce the object-like character of the towers. Each of the towers has one glass façade. The other three are all closed, save for a few carefully chosen windows and balconies that enhance the composition.
In this project Mecanoo sought sustainability in flexibility and the linkage of dwellings. With hindsight it is doubtful whether the project is genuinely sustainable. Pulling apart the building volume and distributing it across three small towers has resulted in an adverse relationship between floor and façade surface and will certainly have a negative effect on energy use.

ZONING ENVELOPE

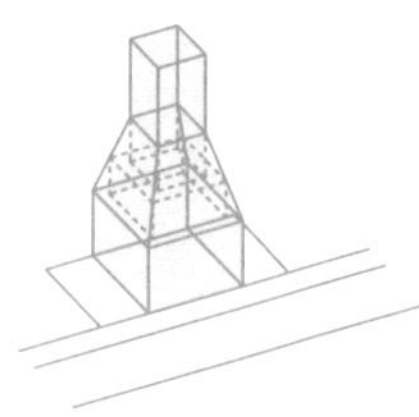

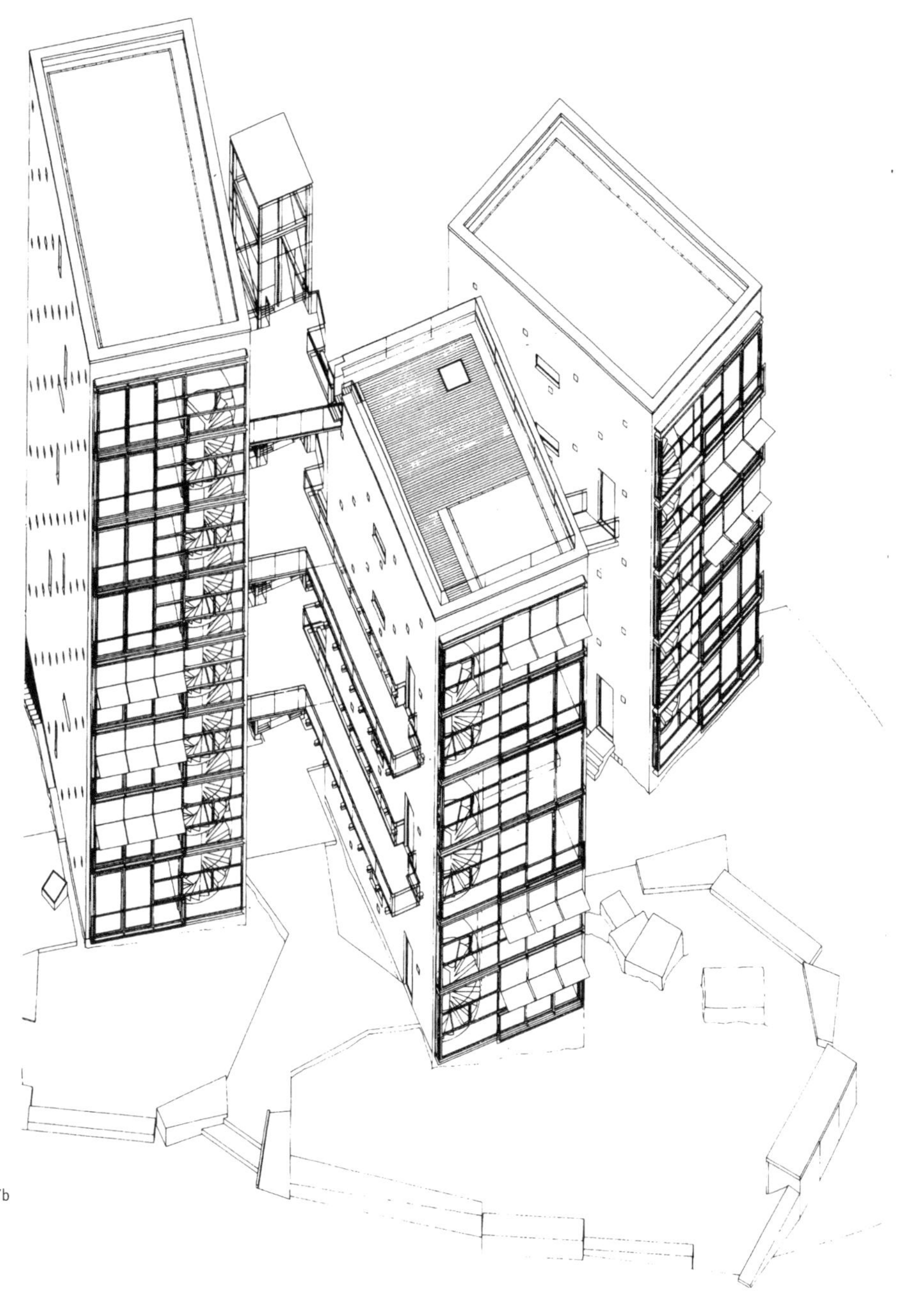

27b

27a Final composition of the urban design, with the three little towers at bottom right
27b The slender towers with detached lift shaft

28a

28a V building balconies
28b The slope of the building is visible
28c Imaginary envelope within which PLOT developed the building (I) and transformation of the proposed row subdivision
28d Urban plan for Ørestad, building height chart. See secondary colour.

ZONING ENVELOPE

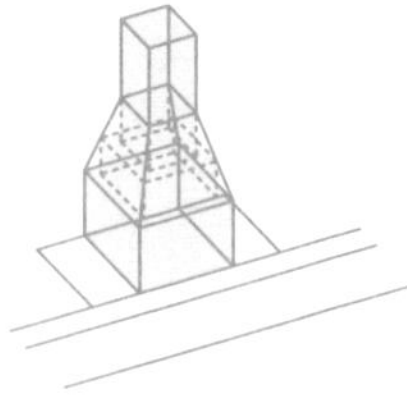

PLOT (BIG + JDS), VM BUILDING (COPENHAGEN-ØRESTAD, 2006)

South of Copenhagen, on the island of Amager, a new neighbourhood called Ørestad is being built. An ultramodern metro links the urban area with the heart of the capital. The relatively new architecture practice PLOT was commissioned to design the first housing block. PLOT's founders, Julien De Smedt, a Belgian, and Bjarke Ingels, a Dane, met at OMA in Rotterdam. Inexperienced but brimming with ideas, they embarked on the commission. The site is wedged between the metro line and low-rise development with a lot of bungalows. The master plan proposed a layout with two parallel lines, sloping down in height from 12 storeys along the metro line to six adjacent to the low-rise buildings. Although these planning regulations can be translated into an envelope, the planning tool used here is best described as zoning with a maximum number of storeys. PLOT questioned the proposed parallel-line layout, criticizing in particular its face-to-face positioning, giving the residents no view but that of one another. Manipulation of the blocks, carried out in a number of steps, led to a plan with two different blocks, a V-shaped and an M-shaped one, giving the development its name. This intervention created diagonal sight lines. The modification of the blocks and its step-by-step illustration are reminiscent of the adjustments with which Hans Kollhoff put his own stamp on Jo Coenen's proposed building mass for the Piraeus building on KNSM Island in Amsterdam.[10]

The tabula rasa context of Ørestad did not immediately suggest any particular architectural expression. But the combination of new urban development and a youthful architecture practice led to an explosion of ideas. The building would become a showcase of new ways of living. The anticipated residents (the pioneers of Ørestad, among them many urban professionals) were the ideal target group for this experiment. The total number of 209 houses, including some for private ownership, is divided across the two blocks. Each has its own access system and a unique character. The V block is accessed by galleries on the north side, whereas the M block features Unité-inspired access corridors. Because of the block's zigzag structure the central corridors are short and illuminated from both ends of the building. The beautiful, broad central corridors contain recesses, emphasizing the fact that the central corridor is more than just a means of access. In the architects' view these corridors are communal spaces where residents can meet. The bright colours are meant to stress the festive character of such encounters.

But most experimental of all are the dwellings themselves. Set foot in the various homes and you will find a true smorgasbord of types. The V building features 40 different dwelling types, as does the M building. Again, a comparison with Piraeus presents itself, as Kollhoff accommodated 135 different dwellings there. The homes designed in Copenhagen are directly inspired by Le Corbusier's bayonet-shaped flat in the Unité, although the Danish versions have undergone a further transformation. Not only are they spread across several floors, but they also make audacious horizontal movements (see also pages 120 and 196). Finally, De Smedt and Ingels opted for extremely transparent façades with large expanses of glass, as if to display these new dwelling concepts to the world. To underline this statement, the sharp, triangular balconies of the V building are thrust into the air like knives.

10 Maurits Klaren (ed.), *Piraeus. Een woongebouw van Kollhoff* (Rotterdam: NAi Publishers, 1994).

28b

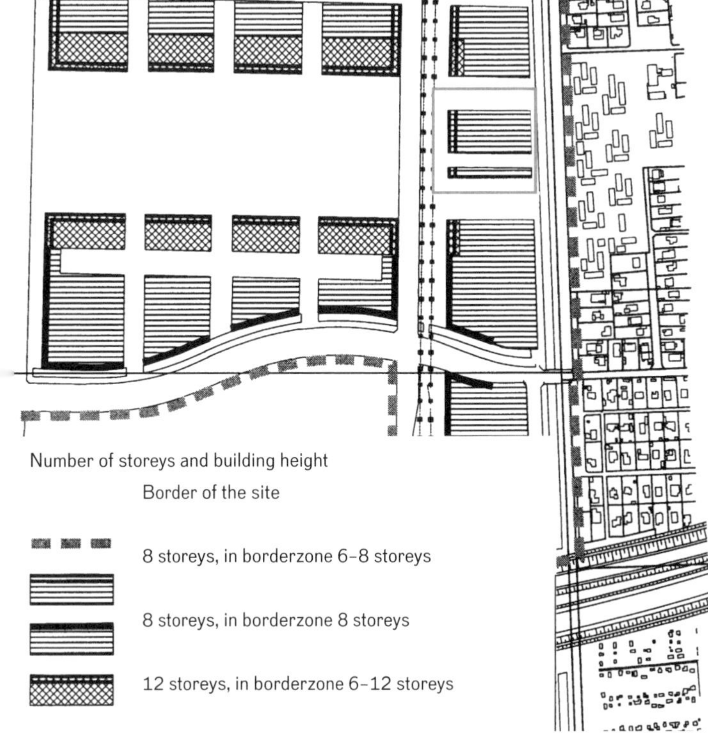
Number of storeys and building height
Border of the site
8 storeys, in borderzone 6–8 storeys
8 storeys, in borderzone 8 storeys
12 storeys, in borderzone 6–12 storeys

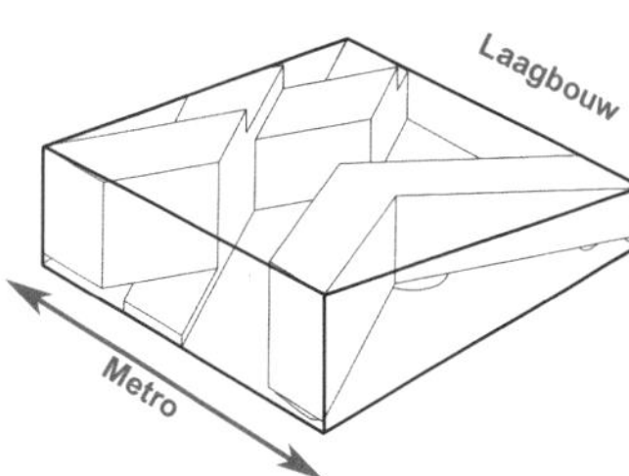
Laagbouw
Metro

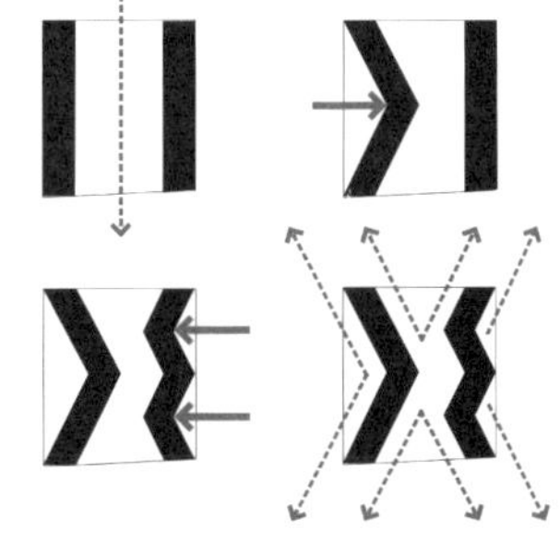

28c

28d

DKV, VICTORIEPLEIN (AMSTERDAM, 1993) PLANNING FRAMEWORK: H.P. BERLAGE, PLAN ZUID (AMSTERDAM, 1920–1940)

In the early 1990s, part of the north side of the Victorieplein in Amsterdam-Zuid was demolished because of poor foundations. The square is part of the celebrated Plan Zuid, which was developed under the supervision of H.P. Berlage. Plan Zuid is remarkable for its architectural unity, which was established in the master plan and reinforced as a product of the close collaboration between the supervisor and the architects. Most of the buildings are in the style of the Amsterdam School. To achieve architectural unity, the master plan for Plan Zuid drew on new tools. It did not restrict itself to defining the building line and the maximum building height, as was usual at the time. Instead it relied on the *plan masse*: a precise specification of the form of the blocks that the architects were to develop. The architectural form of the project was described through specification of the profiles, gutter heights and roof slopes and supported by fine aerial perspectives of the building shapes. And as if that was not enough, diagrams of the new façade composition were drawn up in collaboration with the city architect.

The circumstances were very different when, 75 years after Plan Zuid was designed, a closed competition was held for a design to replace a few buildings within this master plan. Realizing that a city continues to develop, the client, Woningbedrijf Amsterdam, deliberately opted for 'unassimilated infill'.[11] The local planning conditions had changed too. The building line was maintained, but there was no longer a specified building mass or façade composition. The designers were free to do as they saw fit within the following programme:

– The construction of eight three-room flats, 11 four-room flats and one six-room flat;
– Maximum building height: 16.25 m and, in places, 17.25 m;
– A maximum of five storeys;
– A maximum distance of 15 m between the front and rear façades.

Rotterdam-based architecture firm DKV won the closed competition and designed a five-storey building. The lower floor can be accessed from the street; the next four have an access gallery on the north side. The flats have large balconies facing the square, which are partially integrated in horizontal strips, lending the façade a strong and horizontal articulation. In the right-hand corner the balconies gave way to recessed balconies to ensure the best possible connection with the adjacent building. The flats themselves have been rotated in relation to the front façade, with DKV following the orientation of the adjacent building to the west. This angle of rotation has been partially absorbed by the large balconies. The result can be described as a contemporary interpretation of Berlage's dominant plan. It is not a clean break with the past, because the plan's continuous lines have been preserved, but a refreshing take on the original Plan Zuid.

11 L. Pouw, 'Voorwoord', in: *Victorieplein, niet aangepast inpassen* (Amsterdam: Woningbedrijf Amsterdam, 1990), 2.

PLAN MASSE / BUILDING LINE

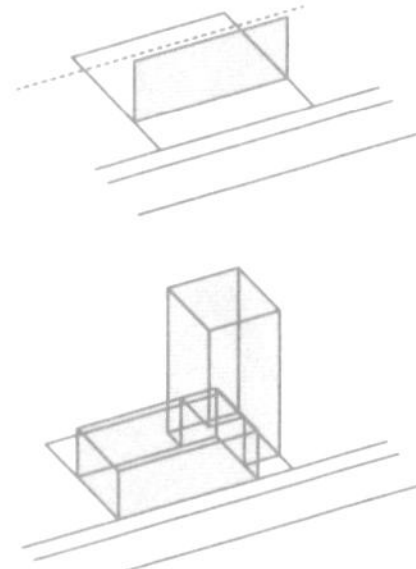

29a

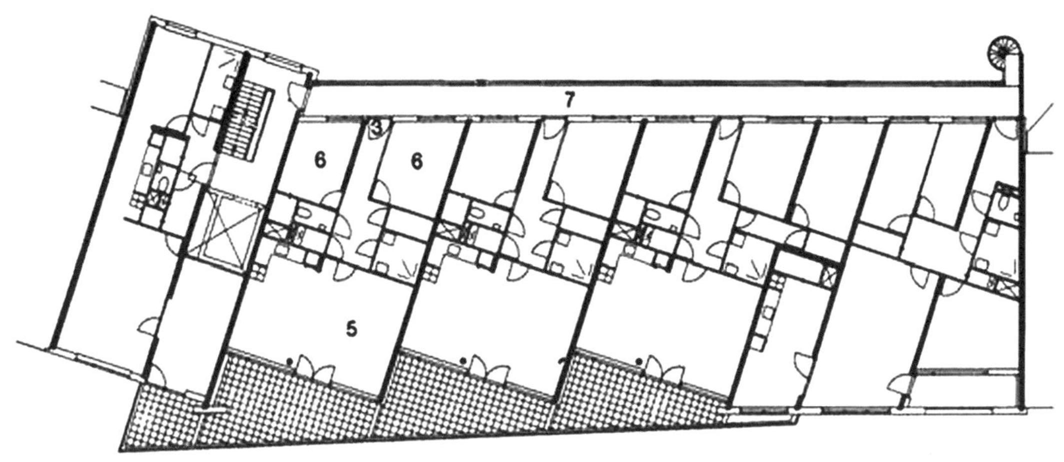

29b

a Design sketch for
e Victorieplein
b Plan of buildings on
e Victorieplein

30a

PLAN MASSE

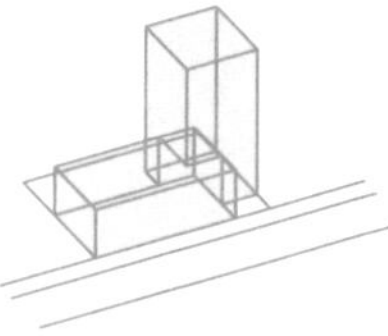

DICK VAN GAMEREN ARCHITECTEN, IJBURG SUB-PLAN 23B1 (AMSTERDAM, 2006)
PLANNING FRAMEWORK: DE ARCHITEKTEN CIE., IJBURG BLOCK 23 (AMSTERDAM 1996–)

A new residential district has been created on a number of artificial islands in the IJmeer, east of Amsterdam. The resulting tabula rasa provides the foundation for a master plan with a grid-pattern layout. Haveneiland, the largest of the islands, is filled with elongated blocks of an average 90 m deep, comparable in size to the blocks in the seventeenth-century ring of concentric canals in Amsterdam's city centre.
IJburg has two levels of planning: island level and block level. Each block has a coordinating architect, who develops the block with two other architects. At the island level of planning the building line has been fixed, as well as the maximum building height, which ranges from 10 to 15 m. In some places 'accents' of up to 24 m are permitted. To ensure that the blocks look varied enough, the master plan includes a programmatic trick: the programme for each block is so extensive that it cannot possibly be realized by building only on the perimeter of the block. To achieve the desired result, the land use plan provides three strategies:
– extending the perimeter through the creation of, for instance, interior streets;
– increasing the depth of the blocks;
– maximizing the entire block surface by introducing a fabric of buildings in the interior courtyard.

Mindful of the prescribed regulations and proposed strategies, De Architekten Cie. drew up a design for the block. They opted to broaden the perimeter with three accents. The block is bisected by a waterway and consists of three separate buildings, each to be built by a different architect. Each building has a hybrid form, consisting of a low-rise section and a raised end section, to be realized in three and eight storeys respectively. The low-rise and high-rise should merge seamlessly. Each hybrid derives its distinctive form from its 'raised head'. An open interior street in the low-rise provides access to two rows of houses, with a dual orientation on the inside and outside of the block. This proposal resulted in an envelope within which De Architekten Cie., VMX Architects and Dick van Gameren architecten each developed their own sub-plan.
Sub-plan 23B1 was designed by Dick van Gameren. It includes 26 low-rise homes, 52 apartments, a commercial space and a half-sunken car park. Although the building envelope and the façade material (brick) had been specified, the architect still faced a tabula rasa context. That is to say, when he started designing there was hardly any built environment or other physical context; no roads, only designs: a paper context. This gave the architect a great deal of freedom, albeit within the confines of the plan at block level and the coordinating architect. A comparison between Van Gameren's building and that of VMX Architects shows just how much freedom the architects had when interpreting the brief. While these buildings share the same envelope, they are clearly different in terms of typology as well as colour and material. Van Gameren, for example, introduced an interior street, while VMX Architects provide access to some of the dwellings from the interior courtyard. These different solutions were inspired by the different locations of the two buildings. Block 23B1 is located on the central boulevard, with commercial activities on the ground floor. Access to the dwellings above is via a semi-raised interior street at the rear. As a result, the dwellings opposite back onto the interior courtyard, where they have their own outdoor space.
Another difference between the two blocks is their materiality and colour scheme. The use of brick was prescribed, but in order to achieve greater transparency VMX pushes the envelope by using large expanses of glass in the courtyard. Van Gameren, on the other hand, adheres to the brick theme by designing a solid, brick-clad block. The might of these blocks is reinforced by the many incisions made by the interior streets and patios.

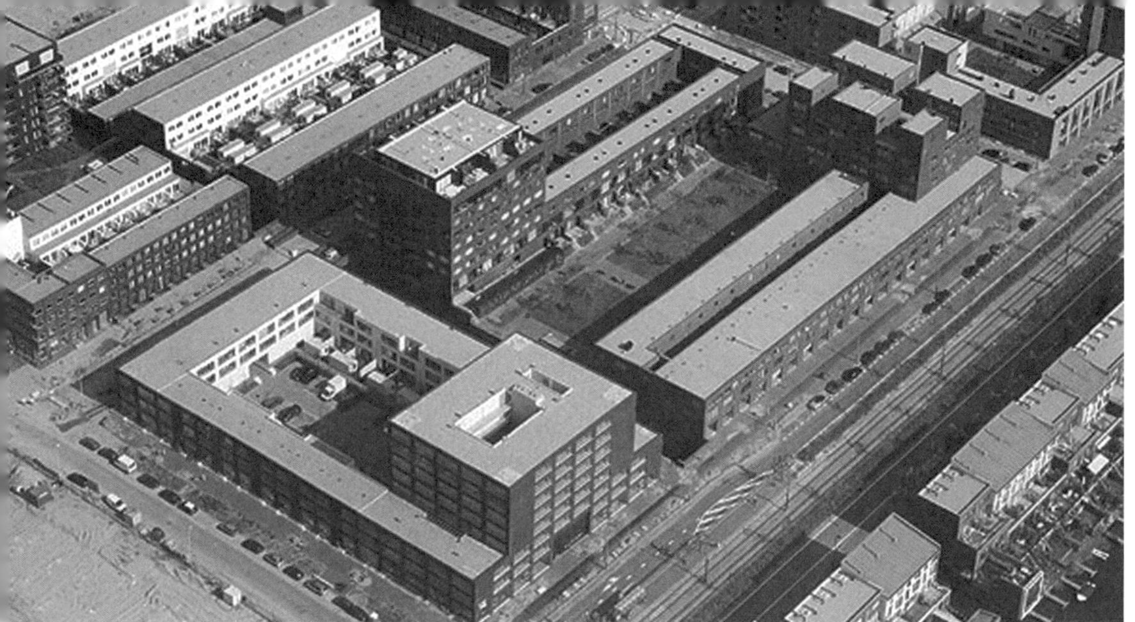

30b

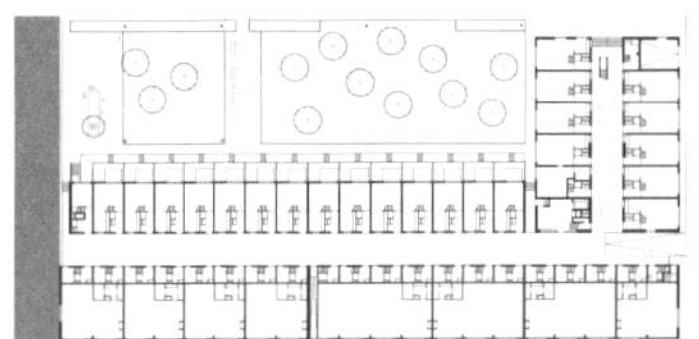

Ground floor

Ground floor

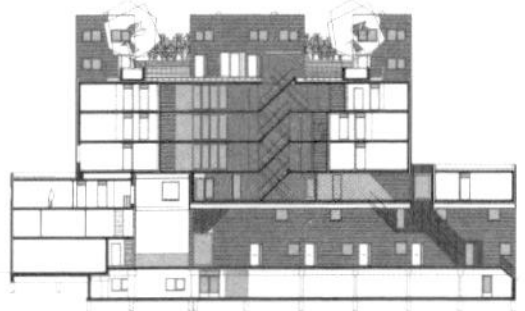

Cross section

Second floor

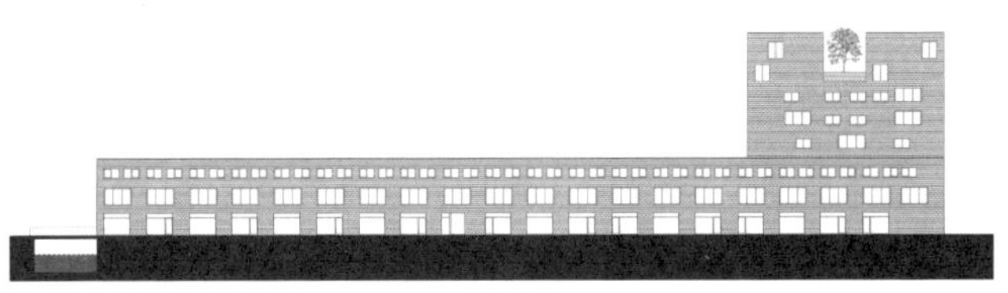

South elevation

30c

30c Floor plans, cross section and elevations

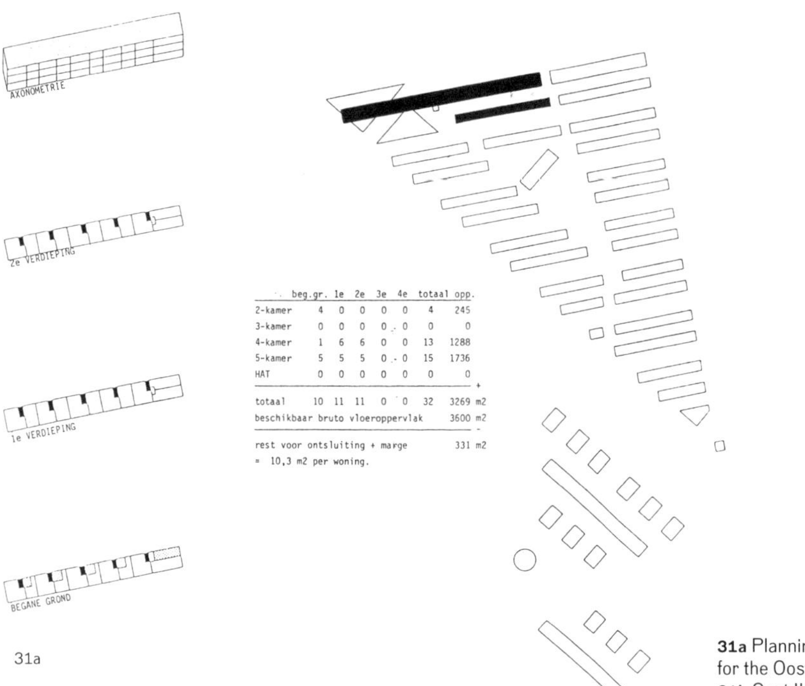

	beg.gr.	1e	2e	3e	4e	totaal	opp.
2-kamer	4	0	0	0	0	4	245
3-kamer	0	0	0	0	0	0	0
4-kamer	1	6	6	0	0	13	1288
5-kamer	5	5	5	0	0	15	1736
HAT	0	0	0	0	0	0	0
totaal	10	11	11	0	0	32	3269 m2
beschikbaar bruto vloeroppervlak							3600 m2
rest voor ontsluiting + marge							331 m2

= 10,3 m2 per woning.

31a Planning stipulations for the Oost IIIa sub-plan
31b Oost III sub-plan

PLAN MASSE

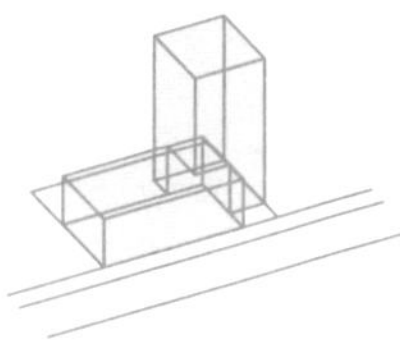

OMA, IJPLEIN, OOST III (AMSTERDAM-NOORD, 1990)
PLANNING FRAMEWORK: OMA, IJPLEIN (AMSTERDAM-NOORD 1983–1990)

In the early 1980s, the city of Amsterdam decided to redevelop the site of shipbuilding company Amsterdamse Droogdok Maatschappij (ADM). This location in Amsterdam-Noord offered a terrific view of the IJ inlet and the historic city centre. It was decided to treat the site as a tabula rasa. All existing buildings were demolished and the dock basin was filled in to create space for as many homes as possible. After an initial attempt by its own urban development agency, the city eventually asked Rem Koolhaas/OMA to draw up a master plan. The local planning conditions amounted to little more than the brief – 1,750 dwellings in the publicly subsidized housing sector – and might be described as a sub-plan.[12]

As well as a detailed land use plan, the commission included the architectural design of the outdoor areas. Because OMA also served as supervisor, the design for the square included the detailing of the building mass, access, the colour of the plaster and the brick. IJplein marks a watershed in the Dutch tradition of designing new residential developments. On the one hand, it is among the last new residential areas made up almost entirely of publicly subsidized housing, while it is also one of the first post-Second World War neighbourhoods with compositional ambition. The design breaks with the common functionalist practice of templating an ideal layout. OMA's proposals resulted in a planning map and axonometrics that specified the form of the blocks and an access system for each sub-plan.

So there was a simple document specifying the access system, the number of dwellings and the building mass before work on each sub-plan commenced, including Oost III, which was developed by OMA itself. Koolhaas described the planning method used as a zoning envelope, but the programme for each sub-plan has the same volume as the envelope, so strictly speaking it is a *plan masse*.

It is fairly unusual for the access system to be specified, but this was done with a view to creating a varied streetscape. Unlike the city's erstwhile Department of Spatial Planning, OMA did not want an endless succession of access staircases. A mix of galleries, staircase and more unusual means of access, such as the diagonal staircase, was to produce a richer streetscape.

b

Sub-plan Oost III, which OMA designed with project architect Kees Christiaanse, consists of a longer and a shorter block. The longer block, which alone has three types of access, is partially raised with its northern end resting on two triangular elements: the community centre and the supermarket. Two oval-shaped elements have been slipped underneath the southern tip. Because the sub-plan's entire composition was laid down in the aforementioned document, OMA had set itself a nice little puzzle. The idea of creating variation through different means of access has been taken to extremes in Oost III. The southern part of this block is served by five internal access staircases and seven diagonal access staircases. The top floor is served by a gallery that can be reached via a lift and a stairwell at the northern tip. The intervening section with small flats is also accessed by galleries.

12 The City of Amsterdam's Spatial Planning Department had initially drawn up its own master plan. After a lengthy tussle between the alderman for spatial planning and the alderman for public housing, the commission was given to OMA. See also Bernard Leupen, *IJ-plein. Een speurtocht naar nieuwe compositorische middelen. Rem Koolhaas / Office for Metropolitan Architecture* (Rotterdam: 010 Publishers, 1989).

REGULATIONS AND NEGOTIATIONS

The examples discussed here show that regulations are not always very stringent. Depending on the legal status and, equally importantly, the position of the architect, there is usually some scope for negotiation. Often the degree to which regulations are negotiable also depends on the phase of development. If the plans concern an established part of the city, say the city centre of Amsterdam or Manhattan, the regulations will have been in force for a long time and are not open to interpretation. But if the plans concern a new urban development or a large-scale urban redevelopment, such as Ciboga in Groningen (see pages 300 and 366) or the Quartier Massena in Paris (see page 402 ff.), the urban planning regime and the architects of the sub-plans are more likely to interact. Changes in the housing market can have a similar effect, as they did on IJburg in Amsterdam. In-depth analysis of three projects in the next chapter will reveal where regulations are set in stone and where they can be adapted, with or without some negotiation.

THE DESIGN PROCESS

Now that we have discussed the various aspects of housing design, this final chapter presents the design process in its entirety, using three different projects. Aspects from earlier chapters relevant to each of these projects will come into play, and they will be discussed as a whole, in contrast to the preceding chapters. In addition, we will provide insight into the different steps involved and into the choices made by the designers.
In describing these processes we concentrate on broad outlines. The standard professional literature in this field usually features merely a description of the outcome of the process: the definitive design. Yet what makes the study of the design process interesting is the way it reveals the winding roads designers travel in order to reach their goal. A final design may look crystal-clear and self-evident, but it turns out many steps were needed to achieve its apparent simplicity and its 'self-evident' solution. To get to the ultimate solution, quite a few obstacles need to be overcome and a number of – shall we say – little inventions cooked up. The more experienced the designer, the more sure-footed the approach to the process. At the same time, experienced designers will set their sights higher and venture down new, unexplored avenues. We have seen the process take whimsical detours even with well-established architects.

STARTING POINT OF THE PROCESS

This chapter does not aim to prescribe a standard procedure for the design process. Although in principle the design process begins with a commissioning client, a programme of requirements and a location, the process can start in many different ways. The housing project Le Medi in Rotterdam, for instance, only had an initiator at the outset; the client, the location and the architect were still to be found. After several changes of line-up, the location was finally chosen. Once a client, a programme of requirements and a location are in place, you can concentrate on producing the preliminary and definitive designs, but even then there is no set formula for arriving at a successful plan.
Anyone who has visited different architecture offices knows that every practice has its own approach and way of working. There are practices that base their work on the choice of a particular dwelling type, and practices that start by defining the form, the volume and the plasticity or materiality of the residential building. One will focus on type; another may work based on the concept or on the urban space. Differences in working methods are also partly the result of differences in culture and geography.
For many years in the Netherlands – in particular during the reconstruction period in the aftermath of the Second World War – the dwelling type was of primary importance. Once a type

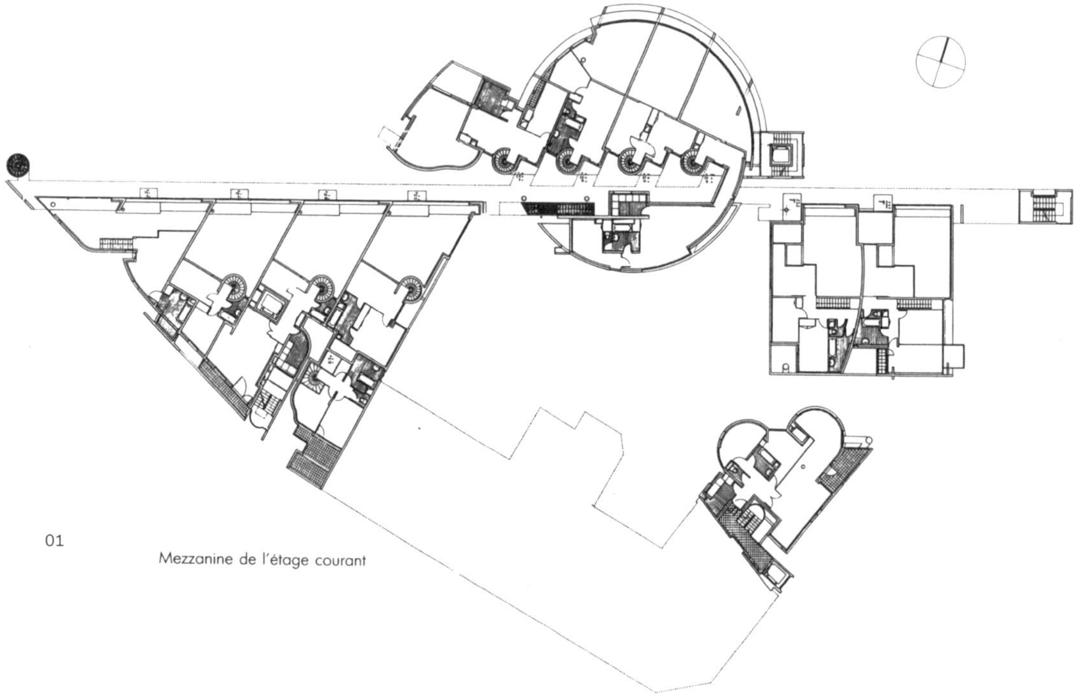

01

Mezzanine de l'étage courant

02

01 Michel Kagan, Cité d'artistes (Paris, 1990), first-storey floor plan
02 Jean Nouvel, Nemausus (Nîmes, 1985–1987), gallery

was properly developed and conceived, it could be repeated into horizontal links and vertical stacks in order to produce a housing block, a division of lots and a street pattern. This emphasis on dwelling typology in the Netherlands resulted, from the 1980s onward, in a display of genuine virtuosity in the linking and stacking of various dwelling types. Architecture firms such as Mecanoo, DKV, Neutelings Riedijk and MVRDV are prime exponents of this. But we also find it in the Piraeus housing project in Amsterdam, designed by German architect Hans Kollhoff in collaboration with Delft-trained architect Christian Rapp (see page 313 ff.). Nor was virtuosity in the linking and stacking of dwellings limited to the Netherlands. The Danish practice PLOT (later BIG and JDS) demonstrates a complex combination of types in the VM project in Copenhagen we discussed earlier (see pages 128 and 373). In this its founders reveal their Dutch connections: both once worked at OMA in Rotterdam.
In post-war France, with its tradition of *grands ensembles*, the starting point of the design process has often been the morphology of the ensemble. If we look at the work of French architect Emile Aillaud we see first a composition of different, often free-form blocks and towers (see page 318). The dwelling design then follows, more or less as a matter of routine, the contours of the block. An extreme example of this approach is Michel Kagan's Cité d'Artistes in Paris. Three building blocks – a cube, a cylinder and a prism – linked by a communal gallery, form an ensemble of studio-flats. [← 01-02] Kagan manages to design interesting studio-flats inside each of these primary shapes. Curiously enough, the flats inside the difficult shapes, the cylinder and the prism, look more self-evident than those inside the cube.

In his design for the Îlot Candie (also in Paris), Italian architect Massimiliano Fuksas starts with a concept for the materiality of the skin: zinc and whitewash (see page 303). The choice of these materials, so characteristic of Paris, leads him to wrap the entire complex inside one huge wave of zinc. We see a comparable approach in Jean Nouvel's design for the Nemausus in Nîmes (see page 318). Here the concept first guides the materiality of the project and then the entire structure, the dwelling type, the stacking, the linking and the access. Nouvel's concept is as simple as it is effective. 'A good dwelling is a large dwelling,' he said. This raised the inevitable question: How do you create as large a dwelling as possible in publicly subsidized housing? The answer: By building as cheaply and as efficiently as possible.
How does Nouvel do this? First with a rational load-bearing structure, namely a tunnel-form concrete skeleton. Secondly by using mass-produced façades, stairways and galleries. In the Nemausus this led him to choose aluminium façade cladding,

using standard garage doors in order to allow the flats to be opened up as much as possible in the summer. Steel mass-produced stairs and galleries, also clad in aluminium, provide access. The use of maisonettes saves on dwelling access. The maisonettes make it possible to run a gallery on every other storey only: as many front doors as possible per metre of gallery. Finally, the balconies are constructed in exactly the same way as the galleries.

Whatever the starting point, all aspects will eventually come up and have to be balanced with one another. If you start with materiality, the design of the individual dwelling still has to be addressed at some point. If the dwelling is the starting point, then sooner or later the skin, the façade and the roof come up for discussion, and if you begin with the urban space, you will also have to reach a conclusion about the dwelling, the building volume, the dwelling access and the skin. The starting point is merely the beginning of a complex process in which all these aspects have to be brought into balance. Nevertheless, the starting point of the design process will often determine the character of the design.

Forms of Commission

Then there are the various commission situations within which the design is created. Normally, a commission is assigned directly to a single architecture firm. Sometimes a study is first commissioned from one or more practices, in order to investigate the possibilities for a new type or a complex location. Witness, for example, the many studies that preceded the designs for the Borneo Sporenburg area in Amsterdam's Eastern Harbour District.

It can happen that the process begins with a 'multiple commission', whereby a number of firms are asked to submit a design proposal. Open competitions are also used quite regularly in housing construction. The most famous and most popular are the Europan competitions: design competitions for young architects (under 40 years of age) organized every two years in various locations distributed across many European countries. For many renowned architects, this has been the stepping stone to the founding of their own practice.

And finally this caveat: the design process can unfold in unexpected ways. Anything can change over the course of the process. In the first place, the commission may change: the programme of requirements may be altered, from rental to buying-market units or from large to small dwellings, for instance. The location may change; the budget, the completion deadline, the land use plan, but also the architect or the client may be replaced. And in the worst-case scenario the project is simply cancelled: no money, no market, contaminated soil, a lawsuit . . .

Using three projects that differ from one another in a number of ways, we will now demonstrate how the process can unfold in real-life practice. The first residential complex, Hans Kollhoff's Piraeus, is the oldest of the three. Its design process is interesting in two aspects. First there is the adaptation Kollhoff applies to the envelope spelled out in Jo Coenen's urban design; secondly, the way in which the dwellings are stacked and linked in cohesion with the access is a textbook example of what we have dubbed the *rules of combination*. You might say Piraeus is a typical example of a virtuoso exercise in dwelling typology.
The second project is an ensemble of three small tower blocks in the Logements PLUS sub-plan by Badia Berger architectes in the Quartier Massena in Paris, following an urban design by Christian de Portzamparc. In this design process the emphasis is on the interaction between the interpretation of the architects and the evolution of the urban design.
The third project, Geurst & Schulze's Le Medi in Rotterdam, is also a superblock, but of an entirely different kind–condensed low-rise construction in an urban regeneration area–and with a different design process. Here, ethnic and cultural motivations play an important role in the design process; moreover, the start of this process is marked by numerous uncertainties and changes.

PIRAEUS, HANS KOLLHOFF (AMSTERDAM, 1989–1994)

304 dwellings, including 22 dual-use (work/residence) dwellings

The Challenge

In March 1994 a striking residential building reached completion in Amsterdam's Eastern Harbour District. This residential building is part of the redevelopment of the KNSM Island, a manmade peninsula where the Royal Netherlands Steamship Company (KNSM) used to be based. The Piraeus block, designed by Berlin architect Hans Kollhoff, forms a crucial link in Jo Coenen's urban design for the KNSM Island.
This urban design–a *plan masse*–called for two identical, massive blocks on the south side of the KNSM Island. The building mass for both elongated blocks was specified. In this *plan masse* the two enormous blocks were planned with a cylindrical element and a round public space in the middle, a configuration comparable to Karl Friedrich Schinkel's Altes Museum in Berlin. Belgian architect Bruno Albert implemented the easternmost block in keeping with Coenen's urban design. On the site of the western block, however, there remained an old harbour building, whose occupants–squatters–had successfully campaigned for its preservation. Coenen's urban design consequently incorporated the building as a disruption to the central cylinder.

Initially, the programme for Piraeus was a standard housing programme for its time. The urban design stipulated the usual 80 per cent for three- and four-room flats, with the leftover space to be filled with larger and smaller dwellings. In itself not exactly an earth-shattering programme. Over the course of the process, however, there was a shift towards a more complex differentiation in dwellings. One of the reasons for this was the idea of exploiting the varying qualities that could emerge as a result of the urban structure. This afforded the opportunity to make room for new insights into housing construction and public housing practice, which ultimately produced unique results in the elaboration of the dwelling types.

Interpretation of the Specified Building Mass

From the moment Hans Kollhoff was designated the architect of Piraeus, he questioned the urban design. While Kollhoff felt Coenen's plan was a positive starting point for the creation of a massive block, the proposed mass presented too many issues to develop successful dwellings; the mass was also far from ideal for the angle of light and sun exposure of the rear dwellings and the courtyard. In addition, there was the contradiction between the formal perimeter block with a central courtyard and the block's position on the waterfront. These considerations and the need to preserve an old harbour building on the site of the cylinder were sufficient reason for Kollhoff to put the specified building mass up for discussion. Through an interesting process, various options were explored, in an effort both to preserve the old edifice and to provide proper sun exposure for the northern section of the block.
Once the basic form for the block was set, an elaboration phase followed: kneading and sculpting this basic form to achieve the final result. [→ 05a–c] This phase ran parallel to the development of the dwelling types and the 'filling' of the block with dwellings.
In this process of sculpting and kneading, two crucial openings were made in the block: a wedge-shaped incursion in the middle created the necessary space for the preserved harbour building and afforded the flats in the rear a view of the water. Where the wedge-shaped opening protrudes into the block, it creates an opening that connects the area in the rear, along the KNSM-laan, with the waterfront. There was a small park at the western end of the block, designed by landscape architect Mien Ruys. A massive portal on the west side of the block allows the renovated park to flow into the western courtyard. Finally, the top of the block was sliced off at an angle, and the slopes of the roof were directed inward, in order to produce the best possible natural light incidence and sun exposure.

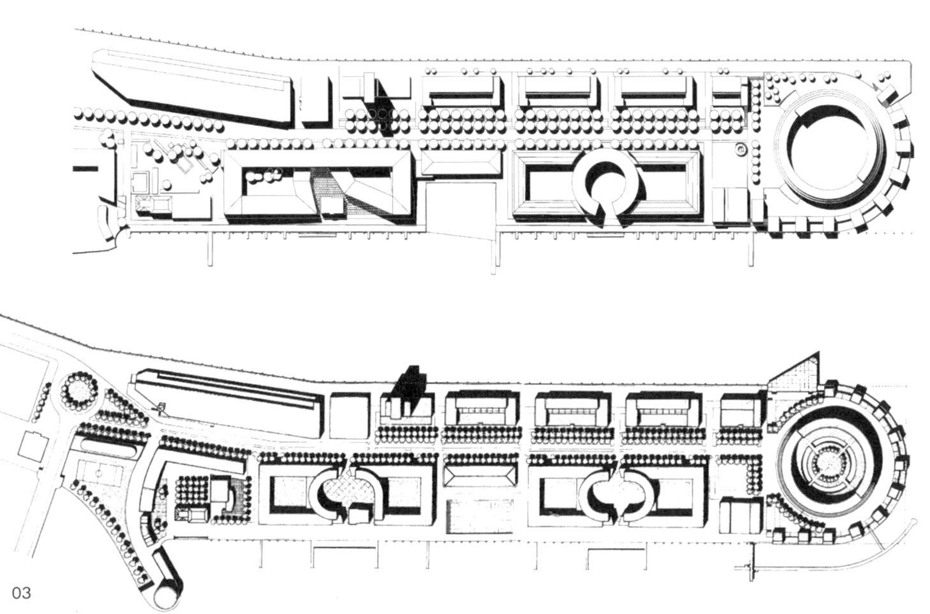

03

04

03 Jo Coenen, urban design (1989) and modified urban design (1994) for the KNSM Island
04 Hans Kollhoff, Piraeus (Amsterdam, 1989–1994)

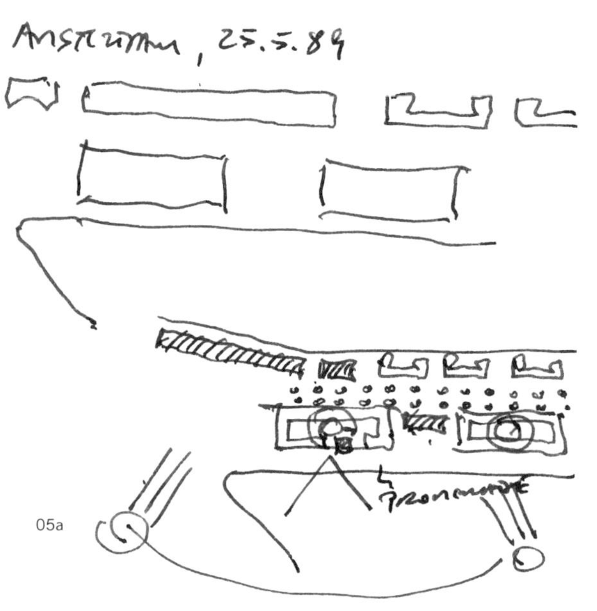

05a

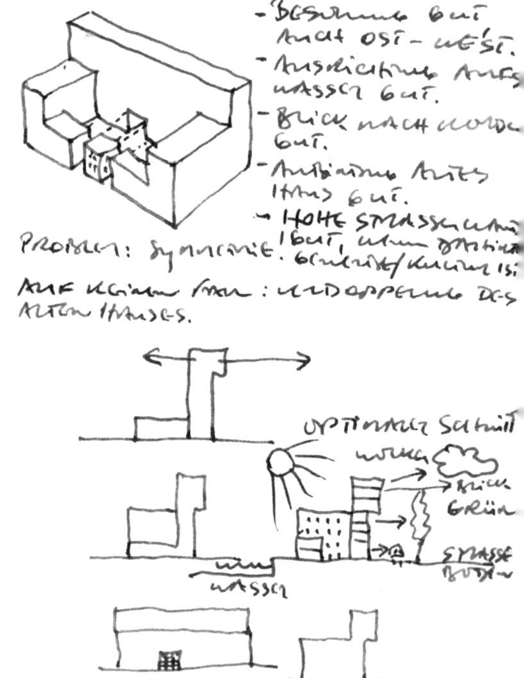

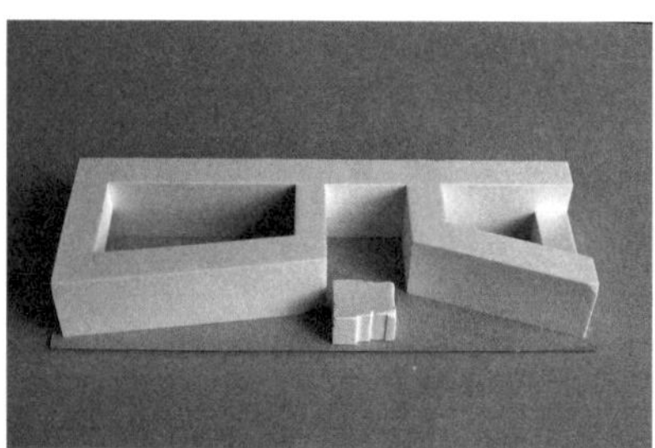

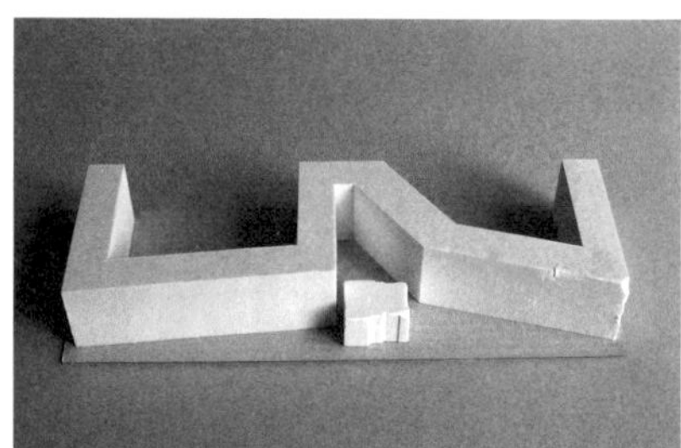

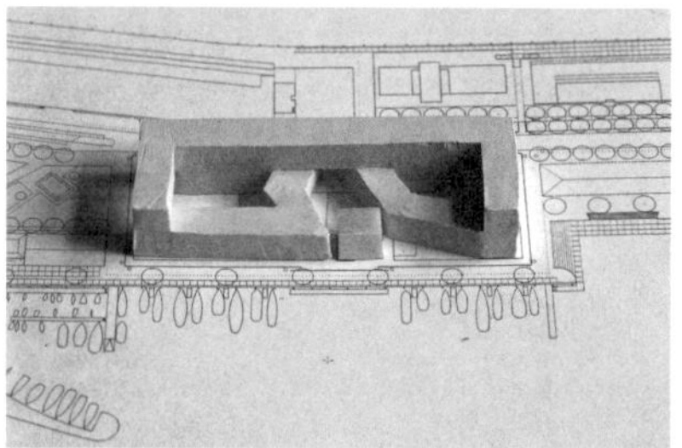

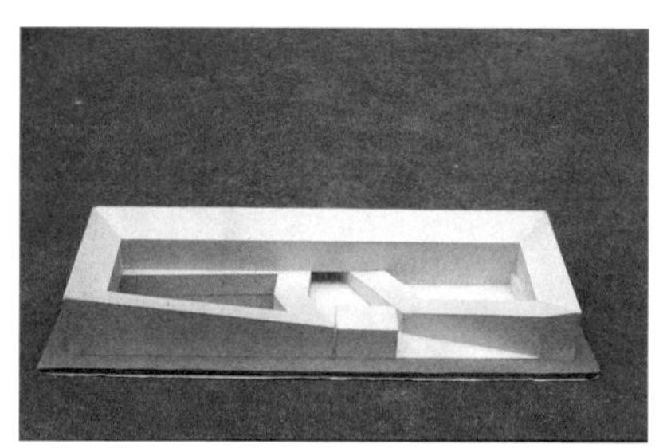

05b

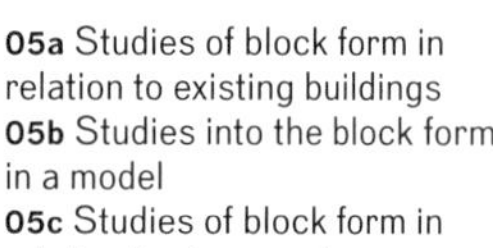

Piraeus

05a Studies of block form in relation to existing buildings
05b Studies into the block form in a model
05c Studies of block form in relation to views and sun exposure

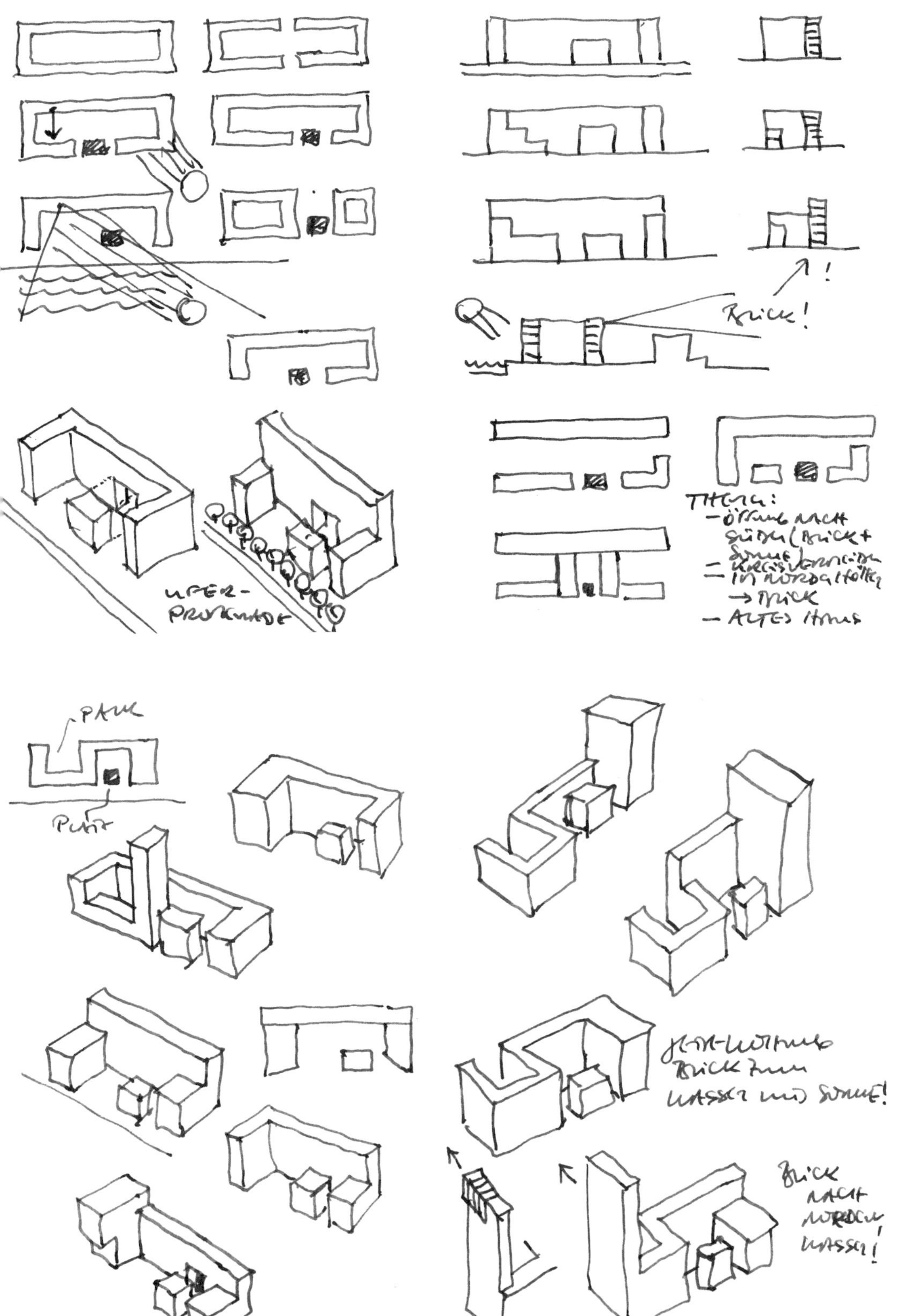
BLICK!
THEMA:
– ÖFFNUNG NACH SÜDEN (BLICK + SONNE)
→ BLICK
– ALTES HAUS
UFER-PROMENADE
PARK
PLATZ
BLICK ZUM WASSER UND SONNE!
BLICK NACH NORDEN WASSER!

The Dwelling Type

For Piraeus, the form of the building predominated. The dwellings were developed after the basic form of the building had been set. Christian Rapp played an important role in the elaboration of the dwellings. This German architect, who had trained in Delft, was working with Kollhoff at the time. Because Rapp speaks Dutch, he was able to research complex Dutch housing construction regulations and he was the one who communicated with local authorities.

Kollhoff and Rapp initially wanted to develop split-level flats. They felt this would be a good solution for the top storeys, directly below the angled roof. Unfortunately the drawings of these studies have since been lost. Neither the client nor Amsterdam's municipal department of public housing liked the idea: they did not want flats with multiple floors. Kollhoff had great difficulty accepting this rejection. Rapp, who was better acquainted with the specific character of Dutch housing construction, now had to find alternatives. He found the solution in the work of DKV architecten, specifically in their floor plans for the building on the St. Janshaven harbour head in Rotterdam. Their bays, 5.1 m wide and 13 m deep, with centrally positioned bathroom and toilet (the 'wet core') and kitchen areas, were turned into the basic type for Piraeus. [→ 06a–c]

There was a budget of 100,000 guilders per flat. At the time this was 10 per cent more than the norm – 10 per cent extra for the architecture! In the process of developing the dwelling types, however, ways of keeping construction costs down still had to be found. In order to stay within budget (a tight one, by Kollhoff's standards) the ratio of internal volume to façade area was adjusted. To achieve this, the flats were made 16 m deep. Their organization into three zones with the 'wet core' in the centre made this tricky. Curiously enough, the ceiling height of 2.8 m, exceptional for the time, was never questioned. Given the sizable depth of the flats, a little extra height is definitely a welcome deviation from the norm.

The design of the flats is predicated on tunnel-form construction. The basic type is based on a broad bay of 5.6 m and a narrow bay of 2.8 m. The 5.6 m bay was enough to accommodate a corridor, a bathroom and a central kitchen counter area with plenty of room to move about; in addition, it allowed two bedrooms to fit side by side. The 2.8 m bay afforded room in various configurations for an entrance vestibule and stairs; this bay also served as an 'interlock bay', a slotting element that made the required three- and four-room dwellings possible. A unique aspect of this basic type was the conservatory or winter room, an unheated room encased in single glazing that serves as a buffer between the inside and outside.

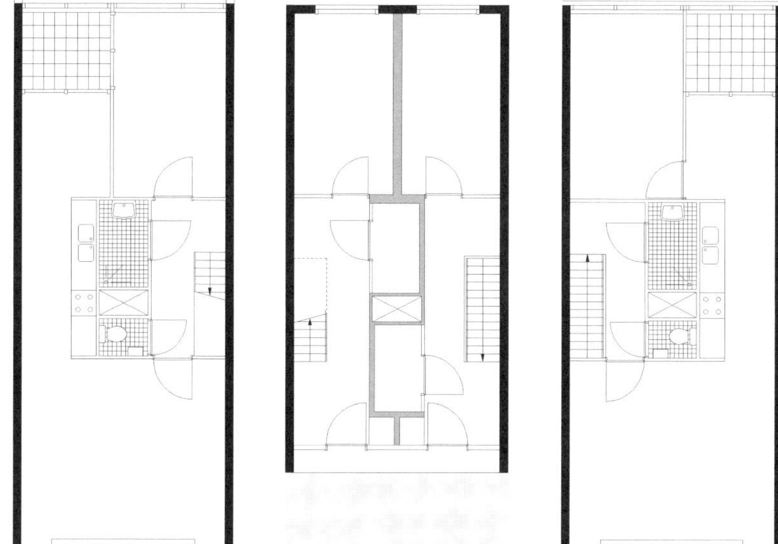

06a

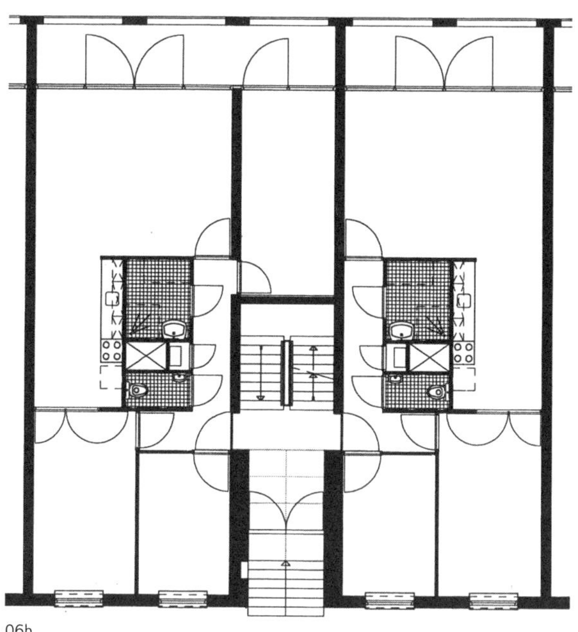

06b

06a DKV's building on the St. Janshaven harbour head served as a model.
06b Piraeus basic dwelling floor plan
07 Piraeus north façade with access staircases for the lower four storeys; on the left the glassed-in galleries and on the right the galleries carved out of the main body of the building.

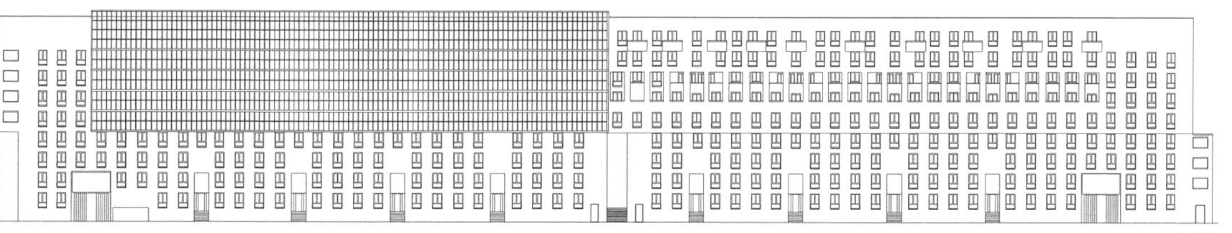

07

Kollhoff had previously used winter rooms in his housing project on the Luisenplatz in Berlin (1988). Dutch building regulations, however, require such rooms to be ventilated to such a degree that they lose their function as buffers – when it is freezing outside it is also freezing in the winter room. In order to provide the required ventilation, a slit for air was cut around the winter room's steel frame.

The Configuration of the Dwellings and the Building

As we noted, the form of the building took precedence over the development of the dwelling floor plan. In practice, this meant the designers 'filled' the pre-determined basic form of the block with dwellings based on a basic type. The filling of the block took place according to the applicable *rules of combination* for housing construction. These are rules (some unwritten, some stipulated in building ordinances) intended to produce the most efficient arrangement, stacking, linking of and access to dwellings possible.

Briefly summarized, the following rule applied in the early 1990s: provide access to as many housing units as possible with the least possible access space. This rule means that in residential buildings in which apartment doors are less than 10.8 m above ground level (the 'lift limit'), apartments are accessed by means of a central access staircase. As dwellings increase in size, the ratio of dwelling surface to access improves. In the case of narrow dwellings (5.4 m maximum), such as one- or two-room flats and maisonettes, a gallery access can be more efficient.

Above 10.8 m a lift was required. To minimize the number of lifts, designers opt for horizontal access at this height, such as corridors or galleries. Because horizontal access becomes more efficient the more dwellings per metre along its length, this is where narrow dwellings (maisonettes and one- or two-room flats) are situated. The efficiency of the gallery or corridor can also be increased by having it provide access to more than one storey. This can be achieved by means of stairs, as in projects like the Smithsons' Robin Hood Gardens in London (see page 192), J.P. Kloos's Dijkgraafplein in Amsterdam-Osdorp and Frans van Gool's Buikslotermeer in Amsterdam-Noord (see page 115).

It should be noted that different rules apply today. That said, it is generally true that the smaller the façade area, the more efficient the dwelling design. In general this produces deeper dwellings, as it did here. Equally out of economic considerations, situating maisonettes on a central entrance stairwell is not recommended: this results in double stairways, inside the dwelling as well as in the access staircase. Furthermore it is unpleasant to have to climb two flights of stairs to get to the next front door.

In concrete terms this meant that access for Piraeus was organized as follows: the lower four storeys are accessed through an entrence and stairs – this applies to the entire south façade as well as to the lower four storeys of the north, east and west façades and the two connecting sections lining the courtyards. A maximum number of standard three- and four-room flats are situated along these access staircases. The dwellings above are accessed through a gallery on the north side. The galleries are accessible by means of generously proportioned stairwells with lifts located at either end of the north façade of the block. From these same stairwells, galleries run along the courtyard side of the block to provide access to the dwellings via the short perpendicular sections. Up to this point the configuration is straightforward, but one glance at the cross section is enough to reveal that what we simply call 'filling with the basic type' is a great deal more complex in practice [→ 08]. Without going into too much detail we do want to highlight a few elements, in particular the different kinds of galleries, the space under the sloping roofs and finally the dwellings in the 'junctions' of the block.
In order to produce different dwelling types, different types of galleries were used: galleries along the façade and galleries that run immediately behind the line of the façade. These latter galleries are, in a manner of speaking, carved out of the volume of the block. This gallery type has an additional, unusual variant: two galleries, one above the other, with the top gallery set further back into the block (see cross section).

The galleries beyond the façade line are encased in an enormous glass box on the north façade. These galleries provide access to standard three- and four-room flats, comparable to the standard flats accessed by the entrances and stairs. Where the gallery cuts into the block, it no longer leaves space for two rooms side by side along the north façade. Consequently the dwellings on this gallery are smaller (two-room flats, or three-room flats with an 'interlock bay'). Maisonettes with entrance stairs leading down are also located here. The upper of these two galleries provides access via a staircase to unique maisonettes situated under the sloping roof. As a result, the two galleries, one above the other, together provide access to four and a half storeys. [→ 09]

Unique dwelling types are created not only under the angled roof, but also at the corners of the building – these often include studio space. The dwellings under the sloping roofs are unusually spacious, thanks to the added height and angled ceiling offered here. The dwellings at the angled corners are given a unique spatial development, with a bend inside the dwelling, as though they were flats in the old city centre. In the process of filling the block with

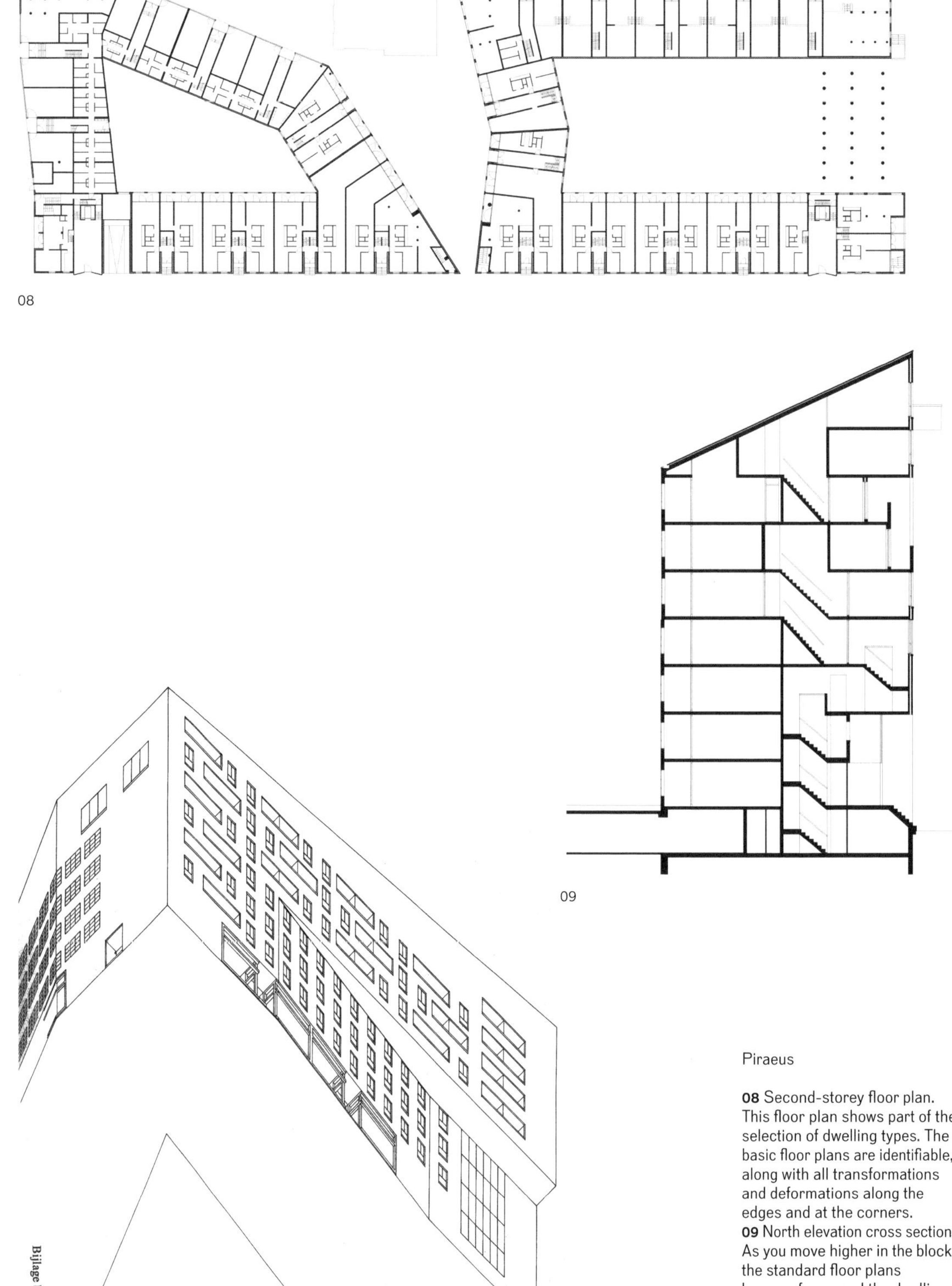

08

09

Piraeus

08 Second-storey floor plan. This floor plan shows part of the selection of dwelling types. The basic floor plans are identifiable, along with all transformations and deformations along the edges and at the corners.
09 North elevation cross section. As you move higher in the block, the standard floor plans become fewer and the dwellings become more complex.
10 Eastern end, axonometrics viewed from below, with incision into east façade

a

11b

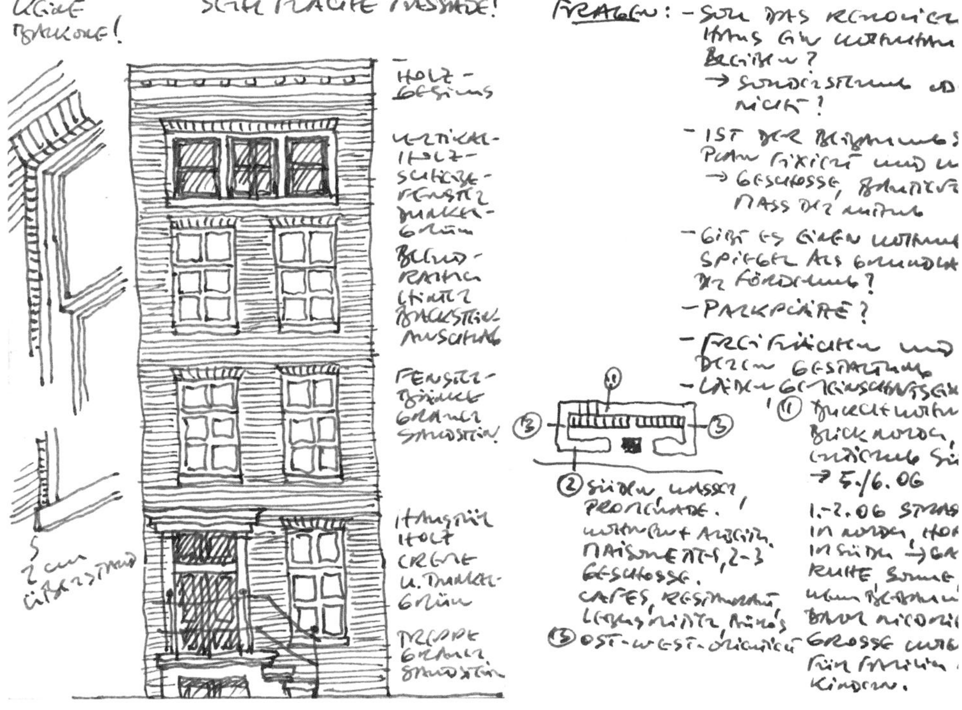

12

11a, 11b Span with Vierendeel truss
Portal with twice as many columns as necessary
12 Hans Kollhoff, sketch of Amsterdam canal façade, with comments

dwellings, the form of the block itself was further refined and its plasticity increased. An additional incision was made into the eastern end of the block, the galleries were suspended in a glass case on the north façade or carved out of the block, and the plasticity of the west façade was reinforced by the addition of projecting balconies.

Tectonics and Materiality Tectonics has always been a vital aspect of architecture for Kollhoff. Indeed, the introduction to the 'Tectonics' chapter makes a reference to one of his texts. In the Piraeus residential building his attention to tectonics comes to the fore in a variety of ways and is particularly discernible in the block's elaboration and detailing. The main load-bearing structure features two noteworthy elements that reveal a great deal about his attitude towards tectonics. The brief stipulated that the building was to be built using tunnel-form concrete construction, and it was largely designed accordingly. Oddly enough, it was the contractor who ultimately balked at the idea. The flats were apparently too deep for tunnel-form construction and presented too many deviations. Nevertheless, the building's floor plans still reveal the characteristic structure of tunnel-form construction.

Of much greater interest, however, are the deviations in the load-bearing structure and the way Kollhoff addressed them. First there is the huge wedge-shaped breach with a portal in the middle of the block. At this point, part of the block seems to flow effortlessly across the portal, supported by the two perpendicular blocks protruding under it. At the level of the façade this block spans five half-bays, or 14 m. It does not take much engineering insight to realize that the tunnel-form structure originally intended would have presented significant problems for this span, both in terms of the span itself and of its seating on top of the dwellings below. The solution was found in a load-bearing façade, which was constructed like a Vierendeel truss, that is to say a huge slab with holes cut out for windows. In order to anchor this truss, a column over half a metre in diameter was installed. This can be identified in the general floor plan as a large dot on the balcony of one of the flats. [← 08]

In Kollhoff's conception of tectonics the structure has to look self-evident and strong. Stacking one block on top of another seems solid, especially when they are built in sturdy dark brick. How the structure actually fits together is of lesser importance to him.

We find an even more significant example at the western end, where the little park designed by Mien Ruys flows into the courtyard. Here too there is a huge opening, in this case no less than four and half bays (about 25 m) wide. What we find here are not Vierendeel trusses but a forest of columns four storeys high, which makes the

portal feasible. A whole forest of columns: rows of three, every half bay, 24 in all–it definitely looks reassuring. Only half of them are actually positioned under a bearing wall, and that means that the other half are not supporting anything. They are there for the sake of tectonic expression, to impart the feeling that the load of the block on top of them is being kept securely in place.
When it came to the materiality of the building Kollhoff was inspired on the one hand by the industrial architecture of docklands and on the other by traditional Dutch housing architecture as found, for instance, along the canals in Amsterdam's city centre. The architect's sketches show that he was concerned about the materiality of the building at an early stage of the design process. Painstaking studies done by Kollhoff, with façade compositions and complementary details such as solidly proportioned wooden door and window frames, pavements of natural stone and carefully applied brickwork, are a testament to this. But it is also clear from his lecture at the symposium 'How Modern is Dutch Architecture?' in 1990,[1] in which Kollhoff argued that current Dutch modern housing architecture was sloppy in its detailing. He illustrated his argument with a series of slides of canal houses and Amsterdam School architecture contrasted with housing architecture details from the 1970s, such as thin wooden window frames and slap-dash lead flashings.

1
Symposium to mark the end of Rem Koolhaas's appointment as a visiting professor at the Faculty of Architecture of Delft University of Technology in 1990; see also B. Leupen, W. Deen and C. Grafe (intr. and ed.), *Hoe modern is de Nederlandse architectuur* (Rotterdam: 010 Publishers, 1990).

This argument also served as a guiding thread in the design of Piraeus. If you are going to make an entrance, then make it a true entrance. If you place a timber façade underneath masonry, make it good and solid, as though it could support the whole building. Where this façade reaches the ground, show that it is really resting on the ground, no fussing about with lead flashing, directly on natural stone. Even his choice of hard-fired North German brick fits in with this narrative. At the same time, it is this brick that gives the building its aura of vast scale and massive industry. This effect is further reinforced by the use of the slender steel frames, with their ingenious sliding-cantilever windows, that close off the conservatories or winter rooms on the south façade. In every instance there is craftsmanship in the detailing, which gives this mega-form a trustworthy appearance. [← 12, → 13–16]

13

14

Piraeus

13 Steel sliding-cantilever windows of the winter rooms
14 North façade, main entrance
15 Sketch and construction of the black timber fronts at the foot of the south façade for the commercial premises in the plinth course of the building

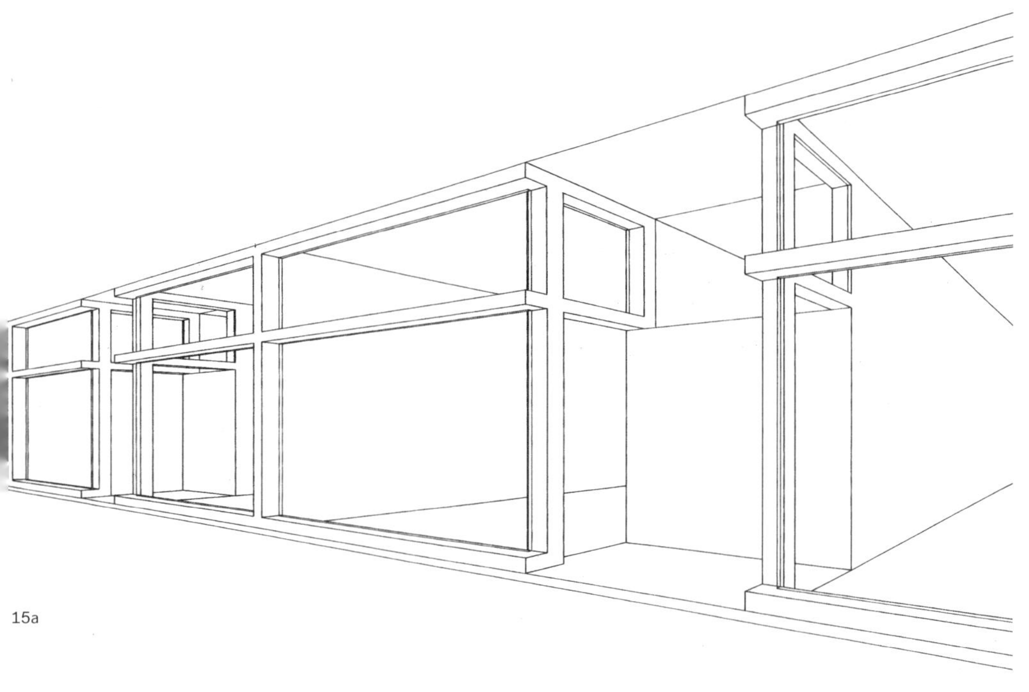
15a

15b

Logements PLUS, Badia Berger architectes (Paris, 2008)
(competition 2003 – completion 2008)
46 dwellings

Logements PLUS by the Badia Berger architecture practice is part of the Quartier Massena in Paris. Designed by French architect Christian de Portzamparc, this quarter is in turn part of the great urban transformation zone on the left bank of the Seine. This zone between the Seine and the railroad tracks, and in fact partly over these tracks, is famed among other things as the location of Dominique Perrault's Bibliothèque Nationale de France (1996).

Urban Design

The urban design is the realization of studies De Portzamparc conducted in the 1970s and 1980s. The focus is on the concept of the open block. This is a reaction to the perimeter block, which always entails problems of orientation and sun exposure for the dwellings. In contrast to the Modern Movement's response to the perimeter block, however, what De Portzamparc did is bring back the street. In the open block concept De Portzamparc combines two contradictory principles: on the one hand he uses the freedom of the free-standing block, on the other he recognizes the strictness of the form of the public space. An intelligent 'zoning' system that occasionally functions as a building line is meant to enable the quarter to effect an interaction among different architectures. De Portzamparc's objective was 'to open the city to fickleness, to variety, to the unknown, to the future'.[2] In the Quartier Massena, the urban space is defined neither by the form of the blocks nor by the design of the street, but by the articulation of the two. [→ 16–17]

2
B. Leupen, 'The Massena Quarter', *Time-based Architecture International* (June 2009), 53.

Rules and Freedom

The blocks are circumscribed by a system of rules based on the zoning envelope principle. In contrast to the *plan masse*, zoning stipulates a maximum allowable volume; the architect of the building, however, need not follow the contours of the envelope. In the Massena Quarter an additional rule was set: depending on the location of the block, 30 to 40 per cent open space is required. This ensures uninterrupted views and sun exposure. Badia Berger architectes used the freedom granted them by the urban design rules to create what they call 'an urban landscape . . . in which a successful balance between density and housing quality is achieved'. [→ 18–19]

The Design

The Logements PLUS are the result of a competition. Badia Berger's design is an implementation within the prescribed envelope and its attendant rules. In this implementation process the building masses were designed first, and the dwelling floor plans were worked out

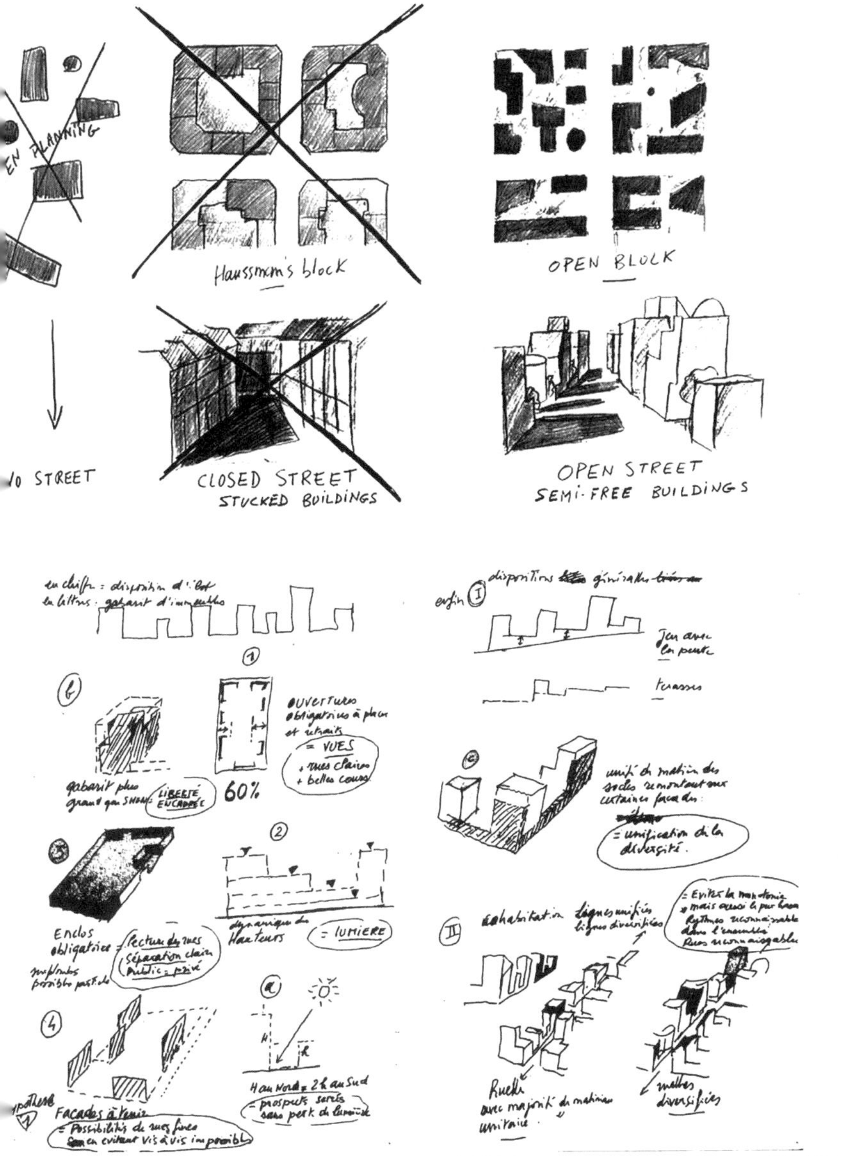

EN PLANNING

Haussmann's block

OPEN BLOCK

NO STREET

CLOSED STREET
STUCKED BUILDINGS

OPEN STREET
SEMI-FREE BUILDINGS

The rule made in 1995: simple and open principles rather than an overall block plan.

16

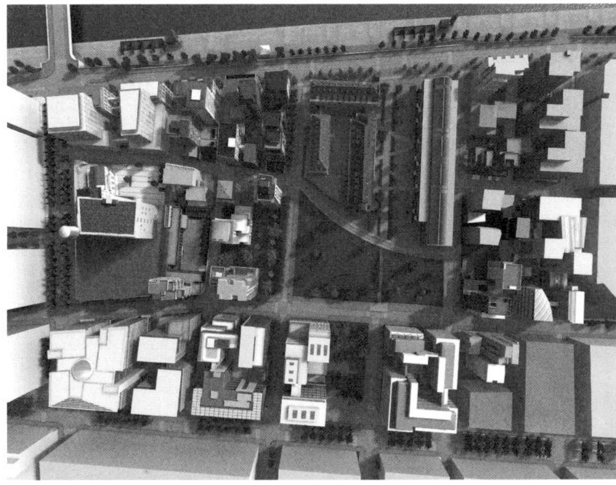

17

16 Christian de Portzamparc, studies into the open block and zoning rules
17 Christian de Portzamparc, Quartier Massena urban design

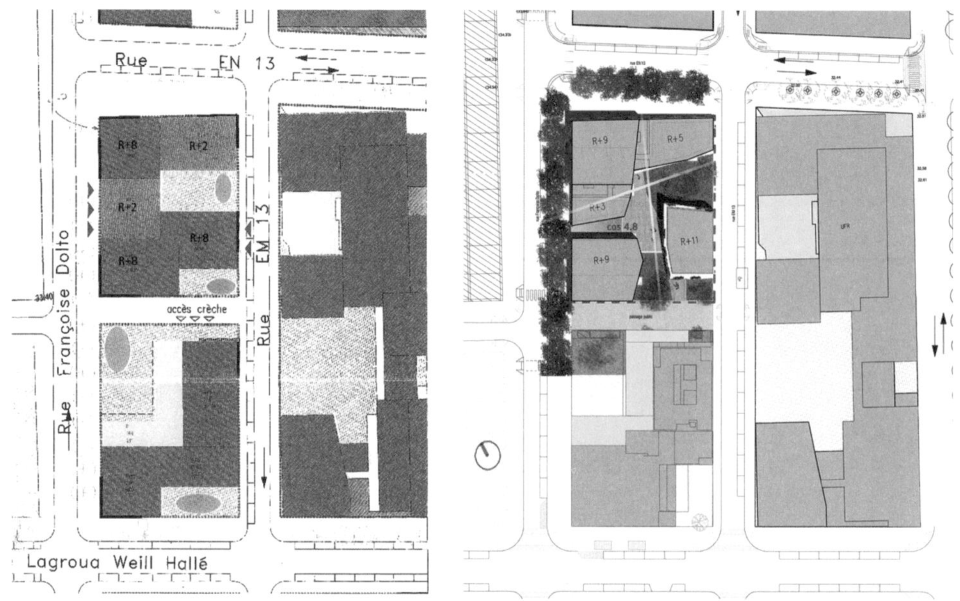
Rue EN 13
R+8
R+2
R+2
R+8
R+8
accès crèche
Rue Françoise Dolto
Rue EM 13
Lagroua Weill Hallé
R+9
R+5
R+3
cos 4,8
R+11
R+9

18

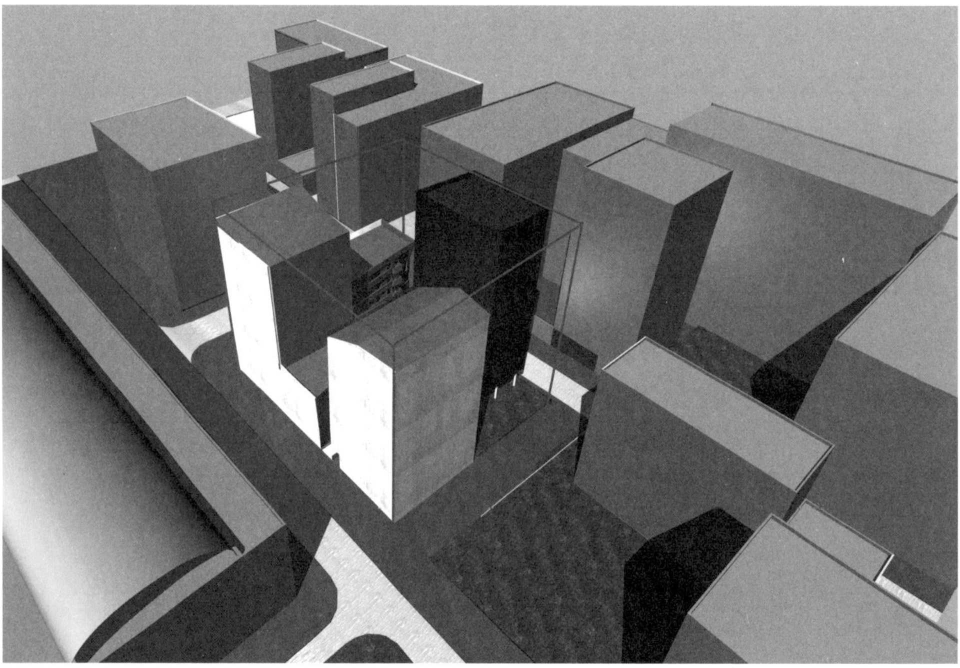

19a

19b

19c

19d

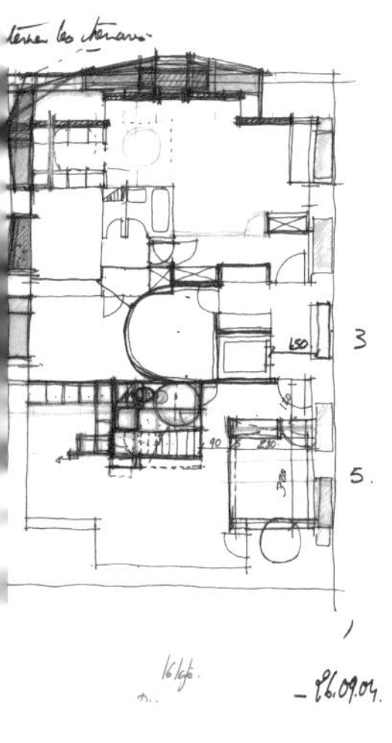

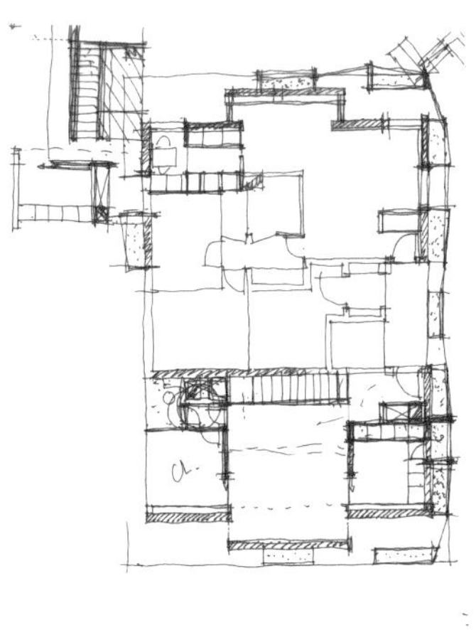

20a

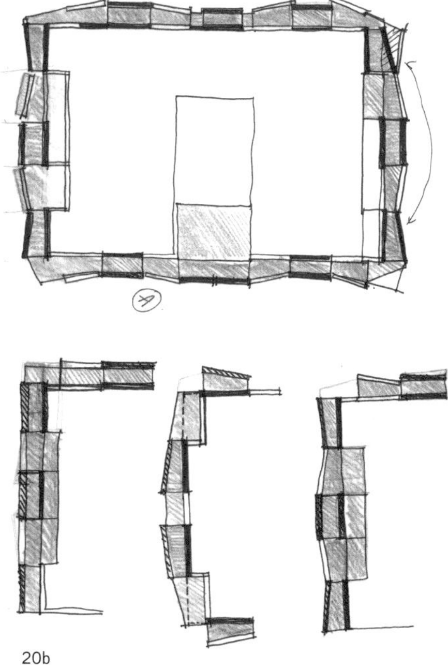

20b

Logements PLUS

18 Studies of the building mass within the prescribed envelope
19a, 19b, 19c, 19d Trial model
20a, 20b Study for the floor plan in relation to the façade

afterwards. The rules of the urban design were a determinant factor in the design of the building masses. These rules allowed a great deal of freedom, but they simultaneously placed the designers before a complex puzzle. In principle, the lot upon which Badia Berger were building was subject to a building coefficient factor of 4.8, which meant the allowable floor space was 4.8 times the land area. This implies a very high density, comparable to the highest densities in Paris.
In order to create the required open space needed for views and sun exposure, Badia Berger positioned the building volumes at the corners and along the edges of the site as much as possible. This creates walls along the street. Here we see that the rules naturally lead to the street being formed as a space, exactly as De Portzamparc envisioned. To maximize views and sun exposure the volumes were also made as slender and as tall as possible. [← 19] One limitation on this was the usual dwelling type applied in new constructions in Paris: access through a central stairwell and lift, to which two or three apartments are connected. The apartments were of the three- or four-room type. Within the rules of the land use plan and within the given land area this produced three little tower blocks of nine and 11 storeys. The two nine-storey towers are 'troikas' (three dwellings linked to one central access). At the top of the towers there are unique flats with extra-high ceilings under a sloping roof. The tallest and most slender tower has two flats per storey. The architects checked the sun exposure and the views both during the competition process and during the implementation.

The Apartments

As we said, the towers were filled with the usual Parisian dwelling types with central access. In the more block-like towers with 'troikas', the access is located in the middle and separate from the façade, something that is no longer permitted under current regulations for high-rise construction in the Netherlands. Thanks to the slender building volumes, the flats have two façades, and even three in the tallest tower. This double or triple orientation gives the apartments a lot of light and ample views. [← 20, → 21–23]
The apartments were designed to create a spatial continuity in relation to the façades. The spatial relationship between the kitchen and living room, especially, means there is sunlight in these rooms for the greater part of the day. The slender 11-storey tower benefited from extra attention during the process. Its situation across the narrow (11 m) street from the Faculty of Biology of the Université Paris Diderot is the least favourable. The orientation on three sides compensates for a lot, and the façade of this block was given a special treatment. A double façade zone creates more distance and privacy in relation to the faculty building. At the same time the little tower, through its double façade, also gives something back to the biologists.

The façade elements that define this double façade zone are graced by a special ornamentation inspired by ripe vines, designed by Elisabeth Guilhem. [→ 24]

The Courtyard and Private Garden

We find the urban landscape Badia and Berger aimed to create, as mentioned above, in things like the courtyards and private gardens within the block. The openings in the block let passers-by share in the enjoyment of the communal and private spaces in the block. The façades that look out onto the public space are white and flat, in contrast to the brightly coloured façades that line the inner courtyards. The open, green spaces are located not just on the ground, but at higher levels as well. A communal and a private roof terrace make the urban landscape complete. During the design process the effects of the block, with its open spaces, roof gardens and alternating façades, were continually tested as to their cohesion and interaction with the surroundings, using 1:100 test models.

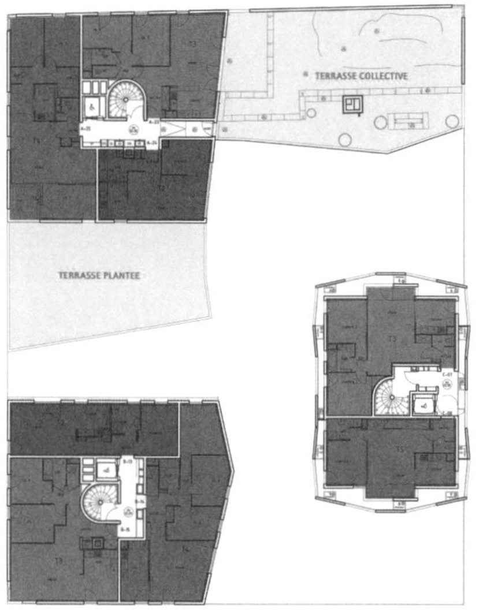

21

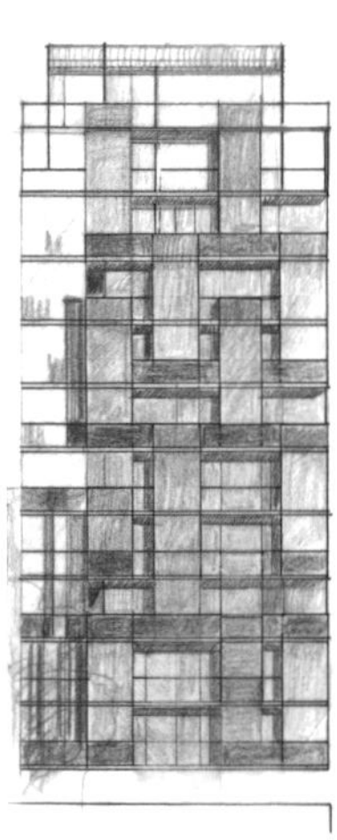

22a

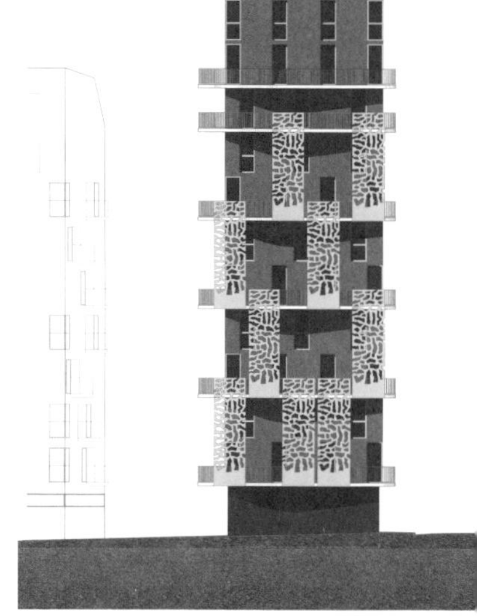

22b

23

Logements PLUS

21 Apartment floor plans
22a, 22b Façade studies
23 Street view
24 One of the towers
25 Tower façade studies

24

25

Le Medi, Geurst & Schulze (Rotterdam, 2008)

(design 2004–2006, implementation 2007–2008)
98 dwellings, including 18 with gardens

Initiative

In describing the design process of Le Medi we delve deeper into the run-up to the process. Unusually, at the start of this project there was as yet no client, programme, location or architect. There was only an enthusiastic Rotterdam businessman of Moroccan origin, Hassani Idrissi, with an idea. At the time Idrissi was running a successful restaurant on the Kop van Zuid and dreamt of a residential neighbourhood in which the influences of Rotterdam's various cultures would be perceptible.
At the end of a search for potential commissioning clients Idrissi found the housing corporation WoonbronMaasoevers (later shortened to Woonbron). A team was formed, including the corporation's director of innovation & strategic advice and its director of housing, as well as, among others, the Delfshaven sub-municipal council's alderman for public housing and an urban designer from the municipal administration. Their goal was 'to complete a project that would enable Rotterdam to demonstrate that diversity is also significant for the physical habitat'.[3] In late 2001 the parties decided to undertake a study trip to Morocco, which was organized by the architecture firms One Architecture from Amsterdam and XS_2N from Eindhoven.

3
Y. van Dael, *Le Medi. Een procesverslag. Van droom naar realiteit* (Rotterdam: Com Wonen, ERA Bouw and Woonbron, 2008).

Toolbox

On the way they came up with the idea of developing a 'toolbox', a set of methodological concepts to implement their ideas. [→ 27] The XS_2N and One Architecture practices drew this up. The initiative group wanted to find out which elements in Arab architecture and which modes of dwelling in Morocco were particularly noteworthy and might be applicable to the Dutch situation. The toolbox, which was given the working title 'Le Medi', is divided into architecture, urban design, management and use of materials. The constants highlighted during the trip were the following: rapport with the private and the public, growth potential of the dwellings, use of space, dimensions and materials. To give an impression of the toolbox, we quote a few passages from it below.[4]

4
XS_2N and One Architecture, *Le Medi, het beste van twee werelden*, Le Medi workshop results (Amsterdam, 2002).

Urban Design Toolbox
The Moroccan city is made up of a number of introverted, often walled elements . . . that incorporate the public space and are otherwise accessed internally through narrow alleys and cul-de-sacs, with a hierarchy from public to semi-public. Growth takes places from the inside out, through renovation, elevation and condensation . . .

Architecture Toolbox
A very clear difference between the Dutch and the Moroccan dwelling is the way it deals with the public and the private and its relationship with the climate . . . The dwelling is oriented inward towards the patio, where family life unfolds . . . Privacy (also) finds expression in the multiple use of dual traffic flows. The separation of traffic flows for family, friends and visitors or man/woman, parents/children, etcetera.

Management Toolbox
In Morocco we find many gradations of what we now call 'private commissions', both in the dwelling, collective private commissions, and in open sites. This form of management is also discernible in the Moroccan grid city. Clear differentiation between the public and the private is reflected in the separation between the public space and the building sites.

Materials Toolbox
One of the primary principles in Arab Islamic architecture is the ornamentation of buildings . . . The decorative themes and principles are not linked to a particular type of building or object: they are applicable to buildings and objects of all periods and types . . . The cooling features of certain materials such as mosaic, natural stone and water make their use, in relation to the hot climate, very appealing . . . The use of water symbolizes life.

In Search of a Location

Now that the idea of what the Le Medi project would look like was slowly beginning to take shape, there was still one problem: there was no location. From the outset the initiative group had set its sights on the Bospolder-Tussendijken area in Delfshaven. The city already had plans in 1999 to demolish 1,000 run-down dwellings in this area and replace them with 675 mainly owner-occupied homes with parking facilities. These plans were set down in a covenant the city had signed with the corporation De Combinatie, which was active in Bospolder-Tussendijken. The 'Schippersbuurt' neighbourhood seemed to present the best potential for a location. The city planned to invest mainly in the exterior environment, so the WoonbronMaasoevers housing corporation's Le Medi plan was a welcome positive impulse for the area. To give the whole project more clout, it was decided an experienced construction firm and developer should be involved even at this early stage. ERA Bouw was selected. So there were ultimately three commissioning clients involved in the development of Le Medi: the housing corporation WoonbronMaasoevers, the corporation De Combinatie and the construction firm ERA Bouw. By then, not only was a location planned, but it was also clear who the clients were. It was now time to develop a master plan for the area.

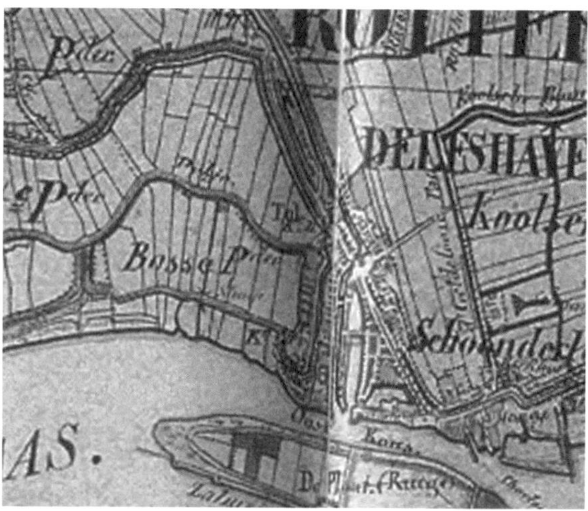

Bospolder rond 1850

Bospolder rond 1933

26

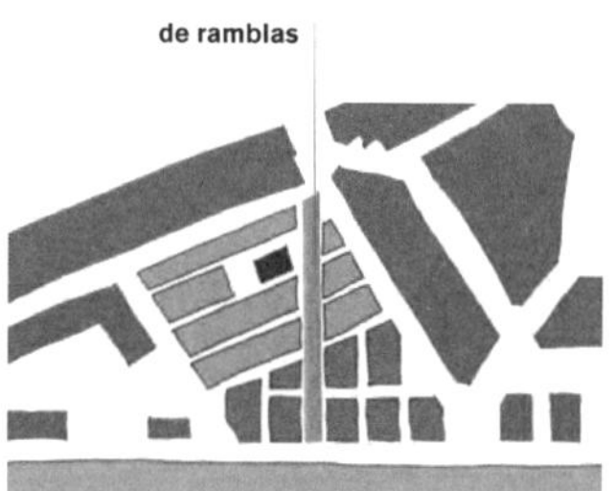

studie Le Medi - One Architecture

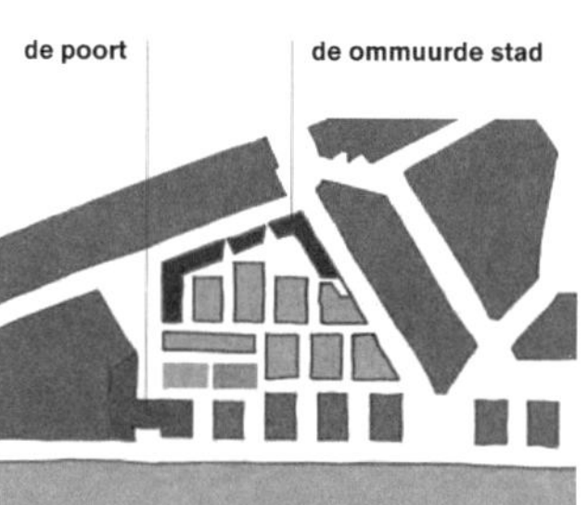

studie Le Medi - One Architecture

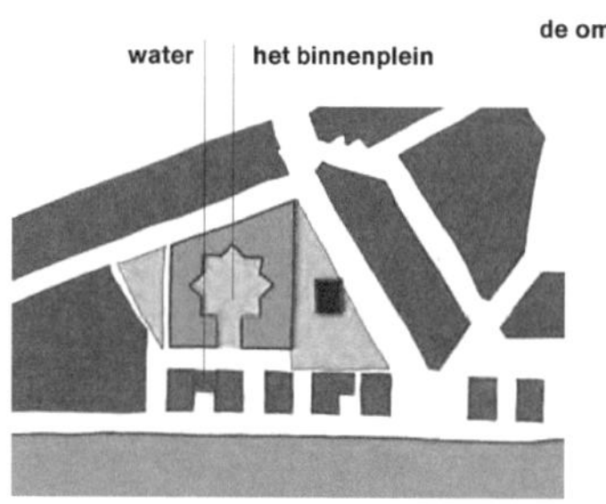

studie Le Medi - One Architecture

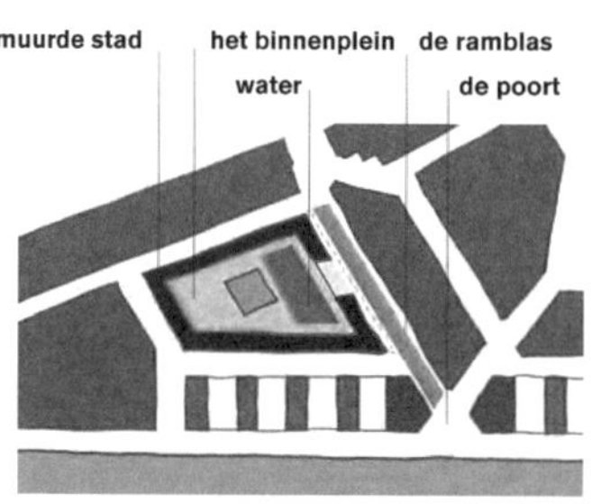

elementen "Le Medi" verwerkt in het Masterplan

27

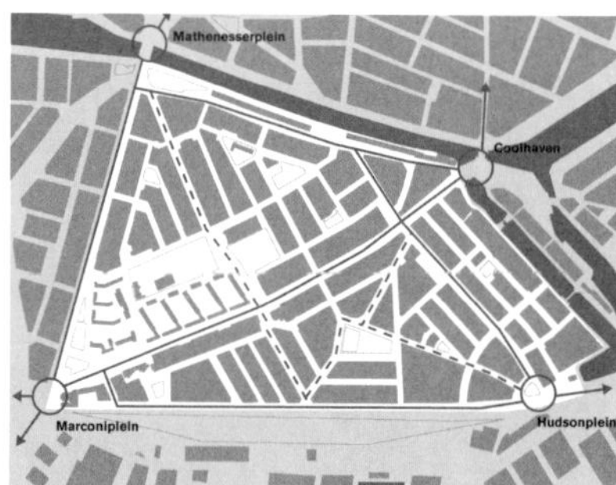

ontsluiting en entrees tot de wijk

28 openbare ruimtes

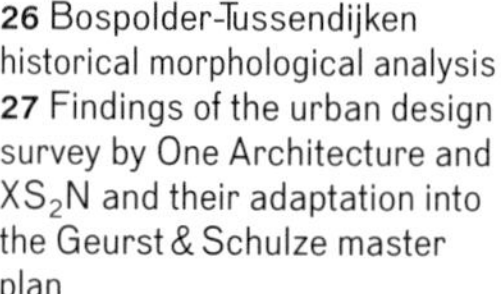
26 Bospolder-Tussendijken historical morphological analysis
27 Findings of the urban design survey by One Architecture and XS_2N and their adaptation into the Geurst & Schulze master plan
28 Bospolder-Tussendijken spatial organization analysis

Master Plan

WoonbronMaasoevers, De Combinatie and ERA Bouw decided to further develop Le Medi based on the toolbox. To begin with they asked One Architecture and XS_2N, the makers of the toolbox, to conduct an urban design survey. The findings of these surveys, however, did not entirely correspond with what the clients had envisioned for the area. As a result, and given the complex brief, the corporations and ERA Bouw decided to find an agency with more experience for the master plan. A selection process found the architecture practice Geurst & Schulze to be the best candidates. Geurst & Schulze would incorporate both the toolbox and the findings of the urban design survey in their plans. To be clear: what we are talking about here is not the selection of an architect for the design of Le Medi, but the selection of the designer and supervisor of the urban design, the master plan for the Schippersbuurt area. The context of the area had two primary aspects: on the one hand there was the physical context, the decaying nineteenth- and early twentieth-century district of Bospolder-Tussendijken, with its many dilapidated dwellings, cluttered spatial structure and sparse public space, and on the other hand there was the social and cultural context. This was not limited to the district – a socially and economically deprived area with a number of problems – the area was also part of a greater sociocultural system. This raised the underlying political question of how to deal with different cultures in the city. Simply put, the choice was either to adapt to Dutch culture (whatever that may be) or mix. At Le Medi, the choice was clearly for blending and cross-pollination of cultures as a concept for a regenerating metropolis. Following a historical morphological analysis and research into the spatial organization of Bospolder-Tussendijken, the outlining of the master plan could now begin. [← 26, 28]

The urban design surveys by XS_2N and One Architecture brought out four vital elements that were adopted by Geurst & Schulze. These included, to start with, the unique enclosed space, an inner plaza with water. The second element was the portal. This element was directly connected to the enclosed space. A third element was dubbed the Ramblas, a broad street with a lot of greenery that links the centre of Bospolder-Tussendijken with the park zone on the former railroad yard. Finally there was the repeated row of urban villas forming a transition between the area and the park zone.

All of these elements were given a place in the master plan. The Le Medi complex began to take shape as a walled city block, with two inner plazas and water features. Portals provided access to the inner world of the block. The 'Ramblas' was translated into the upgrading of one of the existing broader streets. In contrast to the Ramblas as outlined in the survey, this diagonal street connects better with the planned park entrance. Finally, the transition zone of urban villas was incorporated into the master plan. Everything fell into place: it seems so simple, and yet it took many rough drafts to arrive at this result, of which the One Architecture sketches shown here provide only a glimpse. [← 27]

Geurst & Schulze paid particular attention to the Le Medi block in the master plan. As evidenced by the detailed elaborations they produced, they found this unique element extremely appealing – not entirely without reason, as subsequent events would prove. Of particular interest in this regard are their proposals in which their idea of Le Medi is presented as an analysis of all the elements. Many of the themes from the toolbox found their way into this. We see the walled enclosure, the expansion options for the dwellings (growth), the special element with water features (inner world) and even an element that mediates the relationship between public and private (veranda). The series of proposals concludes with a representation of the entire block as they envisioned it at that time. Geurst & Schulze presented three additional variants for Le Medi. [→ 30]

Growth Potential of the Dwelling

One theme from the toolbox is the focus of special attention in the master plan: 'Growth takes places from the inside out, through renovation, elevation and condensation.' Inspired by Le Corbusier's famed Obus plan for Algiers (1930–1932) Geurst & Schulze outlined how the dwellings, starting from a basic element that serves to partly define the 'city wall', could expand backwards and upwards. The interesting aspect of this proposal is that it makes a statement both about typology and about style. [→ 31]

Architect Selection

Once the master plan was ready and the concept for Le Medi had been received positively by the press and the public, the issue of selecting an architect for Le Medi arose. The clients were looking for a 'practice with guts that would dare to use ornamentation and colour, but also a practice with a predilection for the sleek and modern'.[5] Based on these virtually irreconcilable requirements, Com Wonen (the former De Combinatie) and ERA Bouw opted – and how could they not – for Geurst & Schulze. Korteknie Stuhlmacher architecten were asked to help conceptualize variants in the dwelling types. In the end they produced seven alternative types for the plan, all recognizable by their centrally situated entrance and the bay window placed above it.

5 Van Dael, *Le Medi*, op. cit. (note 3), 22.

The Plan

Once Geurst & Schulze were assigned the commission, the urban design pre-conditions were determined by their own master plan. This master plan started by defining the public spaces. The urban

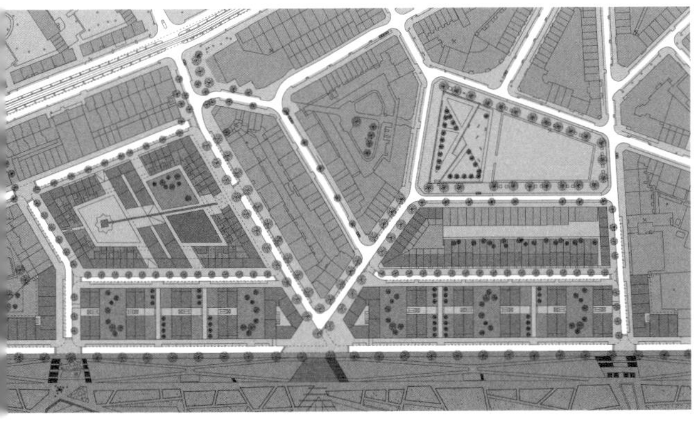

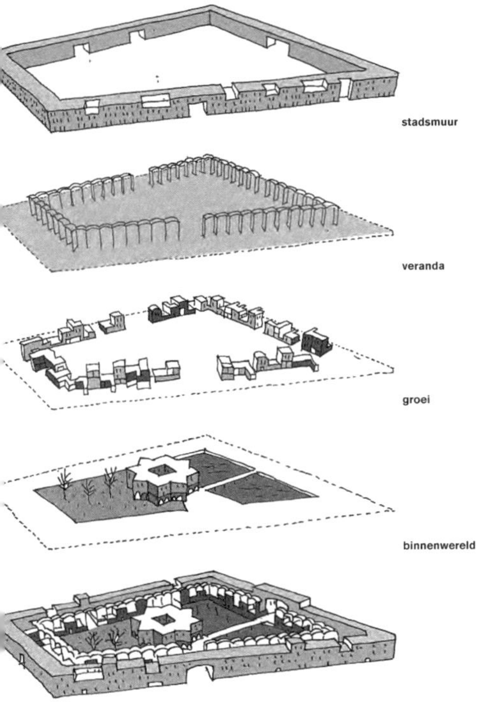
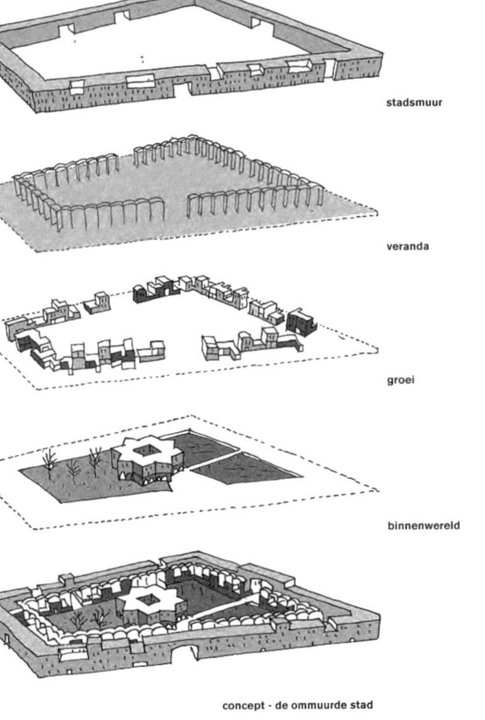

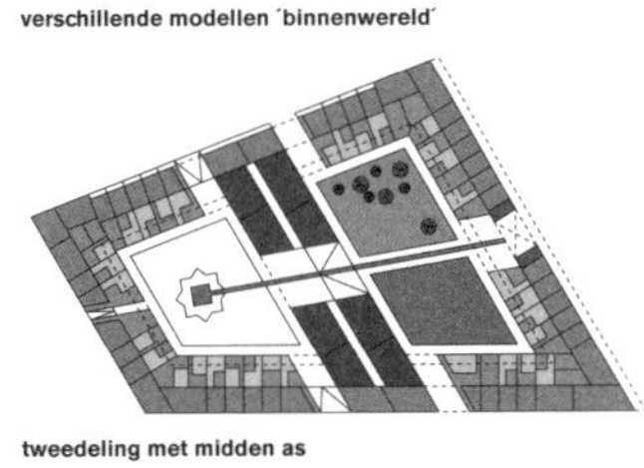

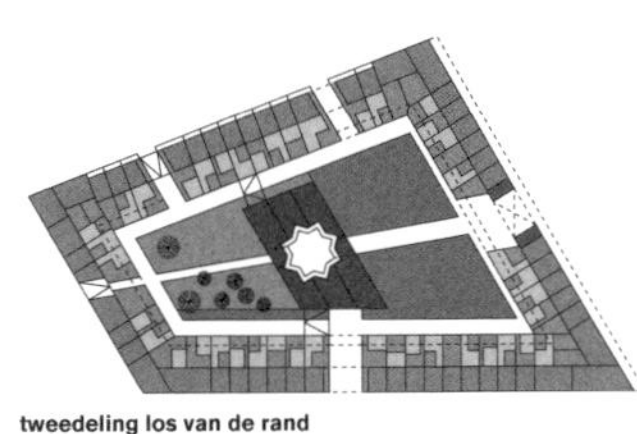

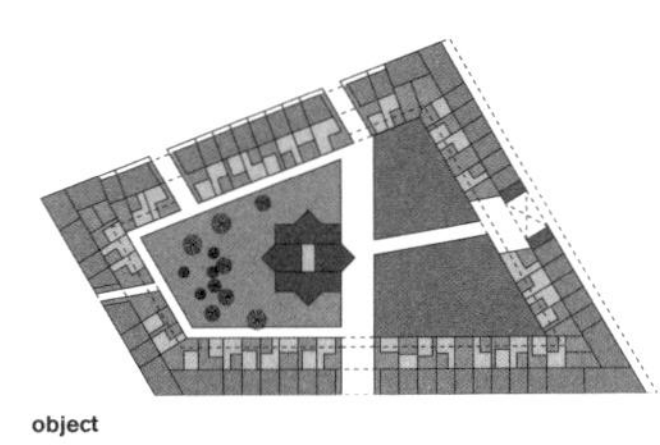

Le Medi

29 Bospolder-Tussendijken master plan, Schippersbuurt
30 Studies into variants for Le Medi block for the master plan
31 Studies into dwelling expansion possibilities for the master plan
32 Façade studies for Le Medi block for the master plan

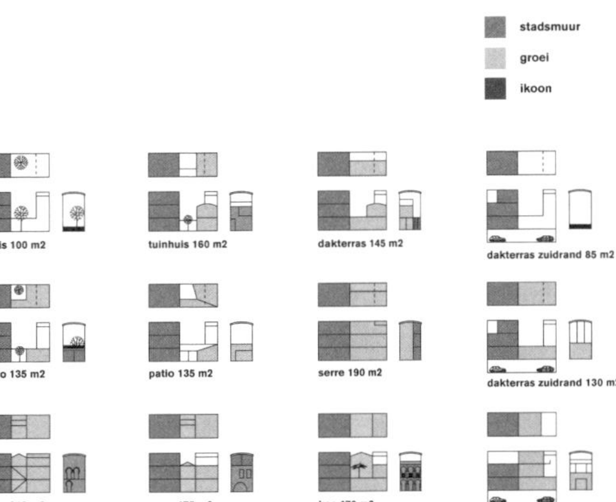

32

design instrument employed was thc building line. Building lines determined the location of the street walls, so that what was behind the line of building alignment had to meet a number of conditions, such as density, parking possibilities and dwelling type. In addition, the master plan served as an aesthetic quality plan, which incorporated suggestions about façades and agreements about visually distinctive elements. An urban design supervisor was appointed to ensure all of this would be implemented successfully. As previously noted, this role was filled by Geurst & Schulze as well. The contours of Le Medi were set as a building line; within these contours there was still a great deal to do.

As architects, Geurst & Schulze had to elaborate Le Medi within the framework that had been outlined. To this end they first went back one step in the design process. The initial proposals from the master plan only defined boundary structures and a special central area. In the studies, to increase density, an additional street was drawn across the block. One of the two courts created as a result was to become the special place with a water feature. The problem with this proposal was the mixing of front and rear sides. The informal rear sides of the dwellings opened out onto what was supposed to be a formal space. Moreover, this front-and-back issue also meant a mixing of public and private. The informal rear side, which was considered more private, bordered on the central public space with the water feature. An undesirable situation, from the point of view of privacy as well as of security. The veranda planned here did not sufficiently resolve these issues.

This is why Geurst & Schulze, in the initial phase of the final design process, went back to a city block subdivision with dimensions derived from the original street pattern. These subdivision studies featured open blocks with a clear division between private and public. But what remained of all those elements related to the toolbox, like the walled enclosure with portals and the space with special access? All three proposals did feature a space with an area marked in blue–water. In none of the three, however, did this produce a convincing picture. [→ 33] Yet the third proposal, with some expert refinement, proved adaptable into a design into which all of the elements were able to be included in equilibrium, simultaneously solving the issue of the public and the private. The great thing about design is that sometimes you get to a higher level via a detour or by taking a step back. That takes courage, the courage to abandon your beautiful ideas: 'kill your darlings'–darlings that stand in the way of a more beautiful and more successful plan. Sometimes, if you're lucky, as in this case, the beautiful discarded ideas can still find a place in the new composition–but don't count on that.

In the final design we see that all the elements have found their way back in. The small open blocks, for instance, are deftly demarcated

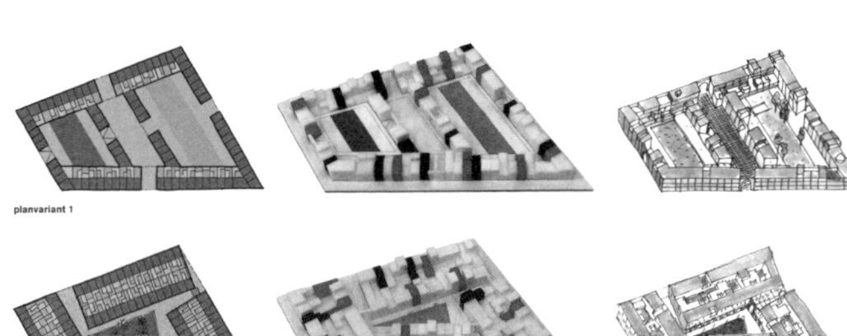

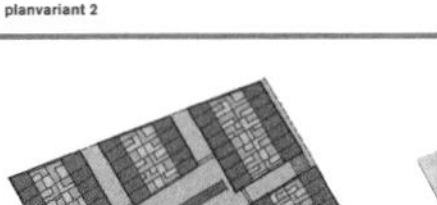

3

34

Le Medi

33 Variants for preliminary design
34 Inner world full of colour, central space with veranda and water feature
35 Analysis of preliminary design: all the elements find their way back in.
36, 37 preliminary design, maquette, plan and Alhambra projection

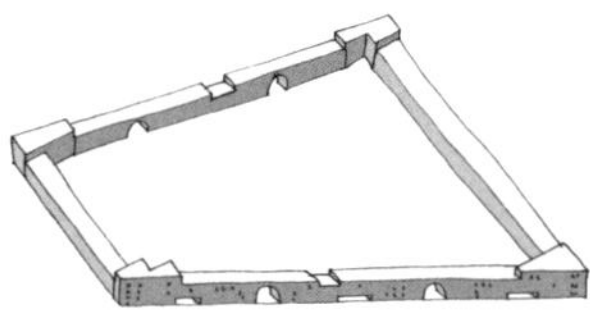

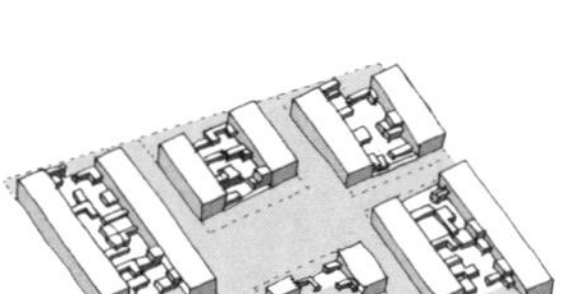

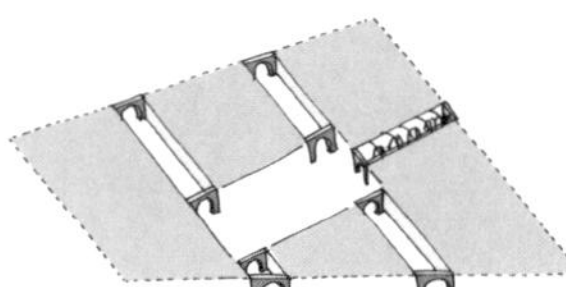

35

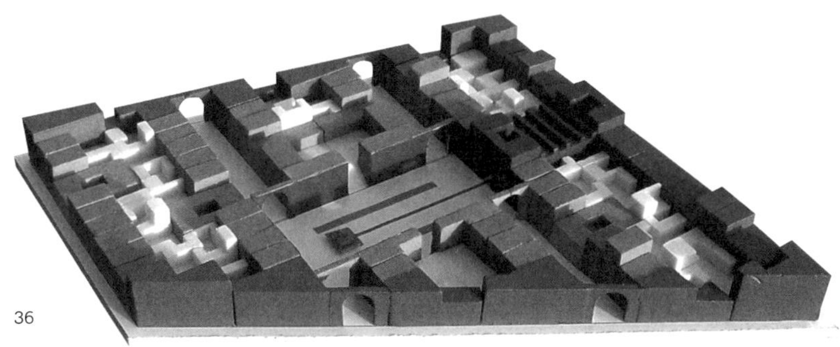

36

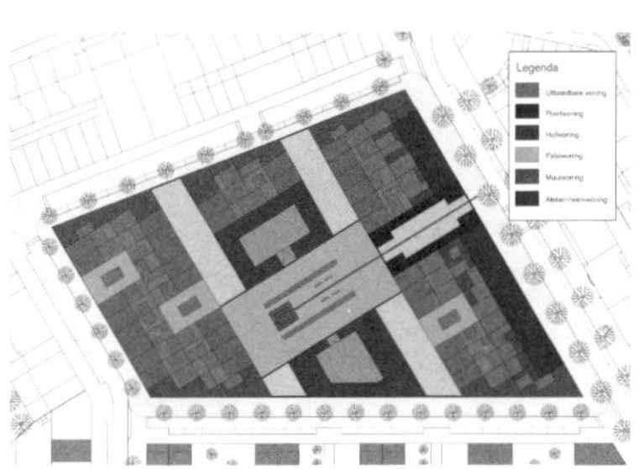

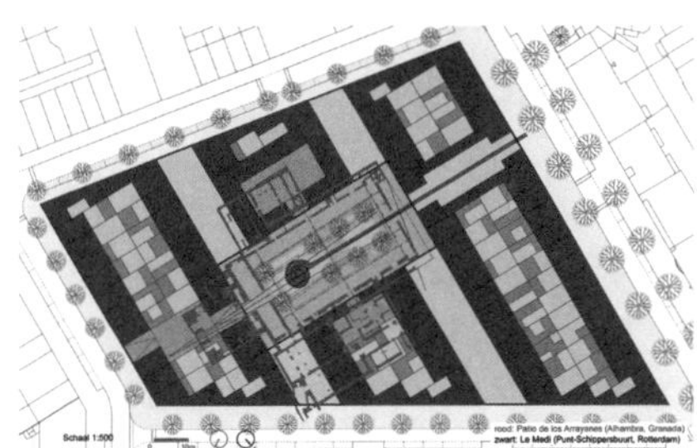

37

by boundary buildings filled with unique dwelling types. The passages incorporate portal-like elements, particularly articulated in the main entrance off the 'Ramblas'. The central inner space, graced by a small water feature, is positioned so that is almost touches the edge of the block, making it just possible to catch a glimpse of this inner world from the outside. The proportions of this space are inspired by one of the main courtyards of the Alhambra (see fig. 00). Even the veranda around the central space made it back into the final version of the project. Here it serves as a filter between the public life in the central space and the front sides of the dwellings that surround it. We discuss the expansion options for the dwellings in the section on the development of dwelling types. In Geurst & Schulze's analysis of their own plan, shown here, they once again demonstrate how all the elements have been given a place in the block. [→ 34–37]

Spatial Organization of the Dwelling

Le Medi is a clear example of a plan based on a conception of dwelling culture and public spaces. In such an approach, the design of the dwelling risks becoming the tail end of the process. Risks, because this is not inevitable. It is possible to work from the larger whole down to the details, as long as you have sufficient experience with these details, in this case the dwelling. If you know how large and particularly how deep the dwelling can be, you can get quite far by using the dwelling as raw material.

An important factor here is the city of Rotterdam's stipulation that in urban regeneration areas with limited on-street parking, new constructions must incorporate parking facilities. In practice this means that in low-rise, high-density buildings, parking has to be accommodated in garages under a large proportion of the inner premises and even partly under the dwellings themselves. Parking under the dwelling has incontrovertible implications for the dimensions of the dwelling. Put another way, the optimal width of the parking spaces dictates the dwelling's bay dimensions. This produces a familiar calculation: 2.7 by 2 m equals a dwelling bay size of 5.4 m. We see these dimensions come back with a vengeance into the dwelling proposals shown here. A size of 5.4 m is unwieldy for the dwelling once a staircase needs to be introduced.

If you want a staircase as well as a corridor or a landing, for privacy inside the dwelling for example, you are left with about 3.5 m for the living room. The living room can be extended across the whole dwelling width along the façade, but if you are not willing to access the upstairs through the living room, you need a small hallway or landing. The proposals shown here show various layout options – variants made possible by the application of the empty-shell principle. The home was conceived as an empty shell, which can be filled in many different ways as its occupants see fit. Future residents were able to communicate their

preferences by going to the website www.lemedi.nl and configuring their own variant within the allowable parameters. [→ 38–40]
In seven places we find a somewhat divergent dwelling type. These are the dwellings designed by the Korteknie Stuhlmacher practice. These dwellings were also developed using the 5.4 m bay size. The difference is mainly on the ground-floor level: whereas the dwellings by Geurst & Schulze are entered from the left or right side, Korteknie Stuhlmacher opted for a more formal arrangement, positioning the entrance in the middle. This asymmetrical approach makes it difficult to fit a room alongside the entrance; the central arrangement more or less locks down the plan: you enter via a large vestibule. This was a spatial organization that, in Korteknie Stuhlmacher's view, was more in keeping with Mediterranean dwelling culture, in which the house features a hierarchy of spaces, from more public to very private. In this dwelling the vestibule fills the role of a space for welcoming visitors. The ground floor also includes a bedroom and toilet, so that this level can serve as guest quarters. The stairs lead to the upper floor, reserved for the family. The living room located up here is extended across the entire width of the front façade and features a bay window. [→ 41]

Tectonics and Materiality

Geurst & Schulze began working on the external appearance of Le Medi when they were still developing the master plan. Even the toolbox was explicit about the façade and the material. In designing the façade, there was an effort to achieve a Mediterranean ornamentation on the one hand, and to find earthy materials on the other. There was also a clear distinction between the façades that form the boundaries of the block, and therefore must underscore the idea of a walled enclosure, and the façades that line the inner premises. The façades overlooking public spaces, in particular the outside of the block, are relatively closed, to vouchsafe the seclusion of the block and the privacy of its occupants. The façades that form the block's walled enclosure feature an earth-toned brick – comparable in colour to the dried bricks used in North Africa. The wall openings were given an additional articulation through the use of a white surround, as in Cino Zucchi's Mediterranean block on Guidecca, in Venice (see page 364). The top of the façades is crowned in the same band of white. Decorative patterns have been applied to the façades by having some of the bricks protrude a little. These patterns allude to Mediterranean masonry work as well. [→ 42–44]
The alleys display a great deal more colour. The façades here feature the same sort of frame around the openings, but the walls are painted in Mediterranean colours and the frames here are done in unrendered brick; the same material is used in many places to mark the edges of the façades. Where brick has been used in the façades of the internal alleys, there is again the decorative patterns of protruding

38

38 Screenshot of the website http://www.lemedi.nl/dewoningen/?page=woonplanner
39 Studies for the spatial organization of the dwellings
40 Dwelling, basic floor plan and cross section
41 Korteknie Stuhlmacher dwelling floor plans

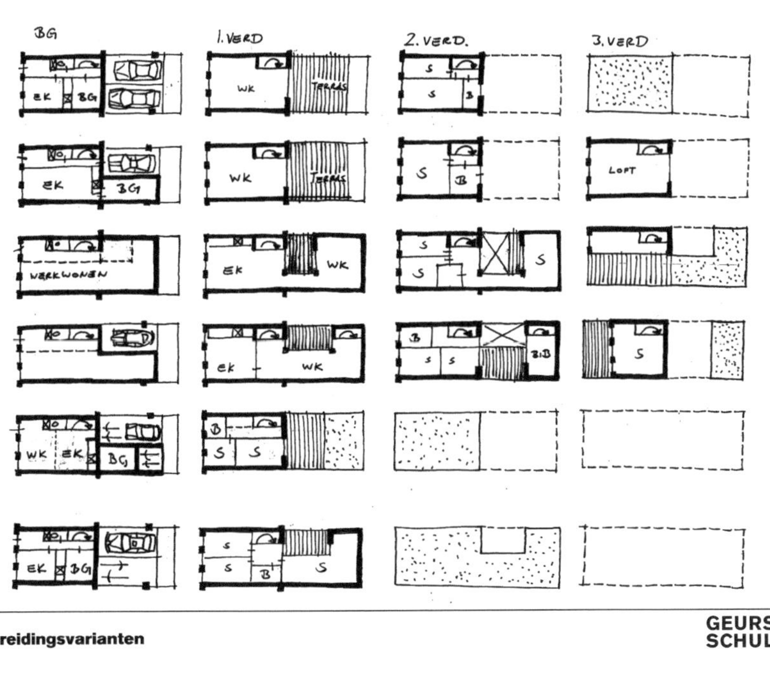

tbreidingsvarianten

GEURST&
SCHULZE

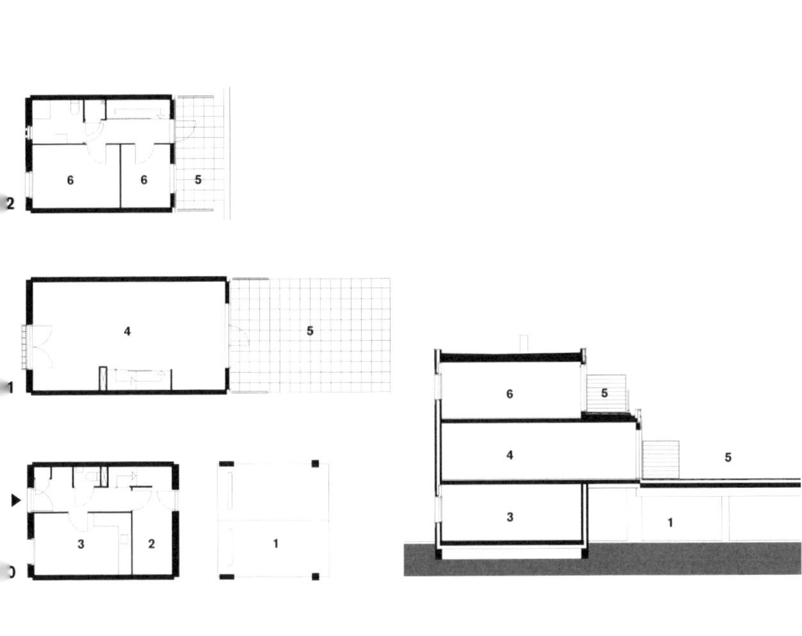

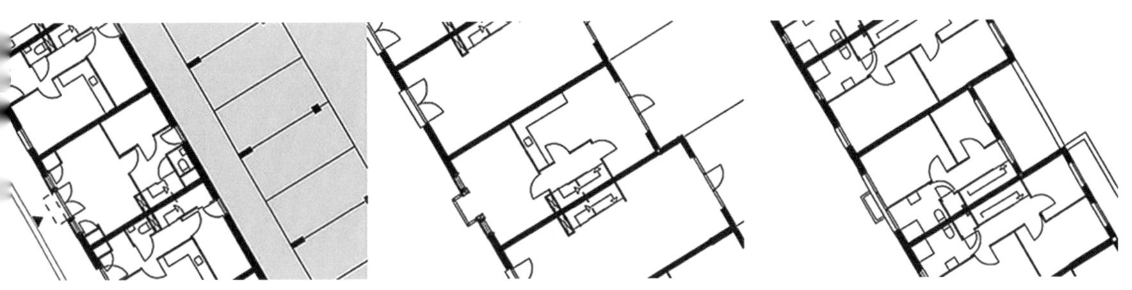

42

43

44

Le Medi

41 Reference image for masonry work
43 Street view
44 Entrance portal into the estate

bricks. The homes designed by Korteknie Stuhlmacher are distinguished not only by their central front door and bay window, but also by their façade finish. Brick is again the main material in these façades. The brick façade is framed on the left, right and top with a white trim. The bay window also has a white frame.
And finally the load-bearing structure: this consists simply of a concrete tunnel-form structure with a bay size of 5.4 m. The stairwell is set in a fixed spot, but otherwise this tunnel-form structure offers substantial freedom of layout within the confines of its reinforced concrete. The dwellings by Korteknie Stuhlmacher follow the same rhythm. Parking facilities are housed under a simple concrete structure one storey high, set on columns. This structure was calculated to support any extensions to the adjacent dwellings. Because of this and because of its striking architecture, the project has great potential for the future.

In Conclusion

The project discussions in this chapter are intended to give an idea of the process of housing design. It is not at all our intention, however, to furnish set guidelines for the design process. Every project is different, and the working methods of architecture practices differ widely as well. Indeed we have not come anywhere close to providing an exhaustive examination of the design process theme. Further and more extensive research is required in order to better understand the processes that lead to the final design.
The problem for this sort of research is that architecture practices are not often conscious of these processes. Most practices in fact do not keep their draft materials, except for a few like OMA, which from the outset was mindful of the value of every sketch and trial model to architecture history. The advent of the computer has meant fewer and fewer sketches are produced on paper; obsolete files are no longer readable with today's software, and little priority is usually given to saving older versions of computer-aided designs.

BIBLIOGRAPHY

Abrahamse, Jaap E., *De grote uitleg van Amsterdam: Stadsontwikkeling in de zeventiende eeuw* (Bussum: Thoth, 2010)
Alexander, Christopher, *Pattern Language* (New York: Oxford University Press, 1977)
Argan, Giulio Carlo, 'On the Typology of Architecture', *Architectural Design* (December 1963)

Back, Susanne, *Een woning met schuifdeuren* (Rotterdam: Housing Experiments Steering Group, 1991)
Balmond, Cecil, *Frontiers of Architecture 1* (Humlebæk: Louisiana Museum of Modern Art, 2007)
Banham, Reyner, *The Architecture of the Well-Tempered Environment* (Oxford: Architectural Press, 1969)
Benevolo, Leonardo, *Die Geschichte der Stadt* (Frankfurt: Campus, 1991)
Benjamin, Walter, *Kleine filosofie van het flaneren. Passages, Parijs, Baudelaire* (Amsterdam: SUA, 1992)
------, 'Die Wiederkehr des Flaneurs', quoted in: H. Heynen, *Architecture and Modernity: A Critique* (Cambridge, MA: MIT Press, 1999), 114–115
------, *The Arcades Project [Das Passagenwerk]*, transl. by Howard Eiland and Kevin McLaughlin (Cambridge, MA: Belknap Press of Harvard University Press, 1999)
Berman, Marshall, *All That Is Solid Melts Into Air: The Experience of Modernity* (New York: Penguin Books, 1982)
Bijlsma, Like and Jochem Groenland, *De tussenmaat. Een handboek voor het collectieve woongebouw* (Nijmegen: SUN, 2006)
Blundell Jones, Peter, *Hans Scharoun* (London: Phaidon, 1995)
Boesiger, Willy (ed.), *Oeuvre complète 1938–1946. Le Corbusier et Pierre Jeanneret [4]* (Zurich: Artemis, 1946)
------, *Oeuvre complète de 1946–1952. Le Corbusier et Pierre Jeanneret [5]* (Zurich: Artemis, 1953)
------, *Oeuvre complète de 1929–1934: Le Corbusier et Pierre Jeanneret, [2]* (Zurich: Artemis, 1964)
Bouwcentrum, *Functionele grondslagen van de woning. Algemene inleiding* (Rotterdam: 1958)
H.M. van den Brink, *On the Water* (translated by P. Vincent London: Faber and Faber, 2001; New York: Grove Press, 2002)
Broek, J.H. van den and J.B. Bakema, 'Woningbouw te Hengelo', *Bouwkundig Weekblad*, no. 20 (1960)
Brouwers, Ruud (ed.) *Architecture in the Netherlands. Yearbook 1990–1991* (Rotterdam: Publishers, 1991)
Calvino, Italo, *Invisible Cities [Le città invisibili]*, transl. by William Weaver (New York: Harcourt Brace Jovanovich, 1974)
Carr, Richard, 'Lawn Road Flats', *Studio International Yearbook* (New York: Studio Trust, 2004), 94–99
Castex, Jean, et al., *Lecture d'un ville: Versailles* (Paris: Moniteur, 1980)
Castex, Jean, Jean-Charles Depaule and Philippe Panerai, *Urban Forms: The Death and Life of the Urban Block* (Oxford: Architectural Press, 2004)
Chermayeff, Serge and Christopher Alexander, *Community and Privacy: Toward a New Architecture of Humanism* (Garden City, NY: Doubleday, 1963)
Cieraad, Irene (ed.), *At Home: An Anthropology of Domestic Space* (Syracuse: Syracuse University Press, 1999)
Christiaanse, Kees, et al., *Strip. 1,5 kilometer woningbouw in Den Haag* (Rotterdam: NAi Publishers, 2003)
Colomina, Beatriz, 'The Split Wall: Domestic Voyeurism', in: B. Colomina (ed.), *Sexuality & Space* (New York: Princeton Architectural Press, 1996)
Cornelissen, Hans, et al., *Denk-beelden van het wonen* (Delft: Publikatieburo Bouwkunde, 1996)
Cullen, Gordon, *The Concise Townscape* (London: Architectura Press, 1961/1973)

Dael, Y. van, *Le Medi. Een procesverslag. Van droom naar realiteit* (Rotterdam: Com Wonen, ERA Bouw and Woonbron, 2008)
Department of City Planning, *Zoning Handbook* (New York: Department of City Planning, 2006)
Deplazes, Andrea E., *Constructing Architecture: Materials, Processes, Structures: A Handbook [Architektur konstruieren. Vom Rohmaterial zum Bauwerk. Ein Handbuch]*, transl. by G.H. Söffker (Basel: Birkhäuser, 2005)
Deutscher Werkbund, *Bau und Wohnung. Die Bauten der Weißenhofsiedlung in Stuttgart, errichtet 1927 nach Vorschlägen des Deutschen Werkbundes im Auftrag der Stadt Stuttgart und im Rahmen d. Werkbundausstellung 'Die Wohnung'* (Stuttgart: Wedekind, 1927)
Dini, Massimo, *Renzo Piano* (Milan: Electa, 1983)
Duiker, Johannes, 'Ingezonden brief aan Collega Van der Steur', *Bouwkundig*

Weekblad Architectura, no.2 (1928), 63–64
Duin, Leen van, and Bernard Leupen, *Blok Architectuur Propadeuse inleiding* (Delft: Publicatiebureau Bouwkunde, 1982)
Duroy, Lionel, 'Nîmes le quartier Némausus', *L'Architecture d'Aujourd'hui*, no.252 (September 1987), 2–6
------, 'Liberté, de qui ?', *L'Architecture d'Aujourd'hui*, no. 252 (September 1987), 7–10

Engel, H., 'Veertig jaar Unité d'habitation een nieuwe formule voor stedelijkheid', *OASE*, no. 37/38 (1994), 32–67
Eyck, Aldo van, *Binnenhuiskunst*, lecture on 6 February 1961 in the building of the Royal Academy of Arts, The Hague, recorded as 'Interior Art' in: V. Ligtelijn (ed.), *Aldo van Eyck. Collected articles and other writings 1947–1998* (Bussum: Thoth, 1999), 295
------, 'There is a garden in her face', *Forum*, no.3 (1961) 107–117
------, 'The Medicine of Reciprocity Tentatively Illustrated', *Forum*, no.6–7 (1961), 205–206

Fraenkel, Francis F., *Het plan Amsterdam-Zuid van H.P.Berlage* (Alphen aan den Rijn: Canaletto, 1976)
Frampton, Kenneth, *Studies in Tectonic Culture* (Cambridge, MA: MIT Press, 1995)
Fuksas, Massimiliano, 'Îlot Candie-Saint-Bernard', *L'Architecture d'Aujourd'hui*, no.294 (1994)
Futagawa, Yukio, Bernard Bauchet, et al., *La Maison de Verre* (Tokyo: A.D.A. EDITA, 1988)

Gaillard, Karin, et al., *Berlage en Amsterdam-Zuid* (Rotterdam: 010 Publishers, 1992)
Gameren, Dick van and Hans Ibelings, *Revisions of Space: A Manual for Architecture* (Rotterdam: NAi Publishers, 2005)
Gameren, Dick van, 'Peterstorp 3', in: *De woningplattegrond, standaard en ideaal, Delft Architectural Studies on Housing*, no.4 (Rotterdam: NAi Publishers, 2010)
Gemeentelijke Dienst Volkshuisvesting, *Amsterdam Wonen 1900–1970* (Amsterdam: 1970)
Geurtsen, Rein, and L. Bos 'Kopenhagen, dubbelstad, een bewerkte reisindruk', *Wonen/TA-BK*, no.10–12 (1981), 14–51
Geurtsen, Rein, et al., *LAS werkboek* (Delft: Afdeling der Bouwkunde, Technische Hogeschool Delft, 1982)
Grinberg, Donald, *Housing in the Netherlands 1900–1940* (Delft: Delft University Press, 1977)

Haan, Jannes de, *Villaparken in Nederland. Een onderzoek aan de hand van het villapark Duin en Daal te Bloemendaal 1897–1940* (Haarlem: Schuyt & Co., 1986)
Habraken, N. John, *De dragers en de mensen. Het einde van de massawoningbouw* (Amsterdam: Scheltema & Holkema, 1961)
------, *Supports: An Alternative to Mass Housing [De Dragers en de Mensen, het einde van de massawoningbouw]*, transl. by B. Valkenburg (London: Architectural Press, 1972)
Hårde, Ulla, and Eric Sigfrid Persson, *Skånsk funktionalist, byggmästare och uppfinnare* (1986); new edition (Malmö: Holmbergs, 2008)
Hauptmann, D., 'Farnsworth House, 1946–1951, Plano, Illinois, VS', in: W. Wilms Floet (ed.), *Het ontwerp van het kleine woonhuis: een plan-documentatie* (Amsterdam: SUN Publishers, 2005), 114
Heeling, Jan, Han Meyer, and John Westrik, *Het ontwerp van de stadsplattegrond* (Amsterdam: SUN, 2002)
Heidegger, Martin, 'Building Dwelling Thinking' ['Bauen Wohnen Denken'], transl. by Albert Hofstadter, in: *Poetry, Language, Thought* (New York: Harper & Row, 1971), 143–161
Herbst, René, *25 Années U.A.M.* (Paris: Salondes arts ménager, 1955)
Hertzberger, Herman, 'Flexibility and Polyvalency', *Forum*, no.3 (1962)
Heuvel, Charles van den, '*De Huysbou'. A Reconstruction of an Unfinished Treatise on Architecture, Town Planning and Civil Engineering by Simon Stevin* (Amsterdam: KNAW, 2005)
Heynen, Hilde, *Architecture and Modernity. A Critique* (Cambridge, MA: MIT Press, 1999)
------, *Architectuur en kritiek van de moderniteit* (Nijmegen: SUN, 2001)
------, Hilde, and Gülsüm Baydar (eds.), *Negotiating Domesticity: Spatial Productions of Gender in Modern Architecture* (London/New York: Routledge, 2005)
Heyning, H.W.L., *Methodisch ontwerpen in het IBB-gietbouwsysteem* (Leiden/Eindhoven: IBB-SAR, 1969)

Hoeks, H., 'Wonen als grensverkeer', in: E. Wils, *Wonen in Indië* (The Hague: Tong Tong Foundation, 2001)
Holl, Steven, *Rural and Urban House Types in North America, Pamphlet Architecture 9* (New York: William Stout & Pamphlet Architecture Press, 1982)
Hoogewoning, Anne, et al., *Architecture in the Netherlands. Yearbook 2002–2003* (Rotterdam: NAi Publishers, 2003)
Houellebecq, Michel, *The Elementary Particles* [*Les particules élémentaires*], transl. by Frank Wynne (New York: Alfred A. Knopf, 2000)

Ibelings, Hans, *20th Century Urban Design in the Netherlands* (Rotterdam: NAi Publishers, 1999)

Joedicke, Jurgen, *Weissenhofsiedlung Stuttgart* (Stuttgart: Karl Krämer Verlag, 1989)

Kirsch, Karin, *Die Weissenhofsiedlung: Werkbund-Ausstellung 'Die Wohnung'. Stuttgart 1927* (Stuttgart: Deutsche Verlags-Anstalt, 1987)
Kaufmann, Emil, *Architecture in the Age of Reason* (Cambridge, MA: Harvard University Press, 1955)
Klaren, Maurits (ed.), *Piraeus. Een woongebouw van Kollhoff* (Rotterdam: NAi Publishers, 1994)
Kloos, Maarten and Dave Wendt, *Formats for Living*, ARCAM Pocket Series, no. 12 (Amsterdam: Architecture & Natura, 2000)
Koerse, Willem 'Over wonen, woning en privacy', in: *Architectuur als decor. Filosoferen over de gebouwde omgeving* (Amsterdam: Thoth, 1992)
Kollhoff, Hans (ed.), *Über Tektonik in der Baukunst* (Braunschweig: Vieweg, 1993)
Komossa, Susanne, et al., *Atlas of the Dutch Urban Block* (Bussum: Thoth, 2005)
Krausse, Joachim and Claude Lichtenstein (eds.), *Your Private Sky. R. Buckminster Fuller – The Art of Design Science* (Baden: Lars Müller Publishers, 1999)
Kruijt, Cornelis Simon, *De verstedelijking van Nederland* (Assen: Van Gorcum & Comp. NV, 1961)
Kuhnle, Jana, 'Tre edifici residenziali degli anni '20 e '30 a Roma di Mario De Renzi', in: M. Farina (ed.), *Studi sulla casa Urbana – sperimentazioni e temi di progetto* (Rome: Gangemi, 2009), 157–173

Leupen, Bernard, *IJ-plein. Een speurtocht naar nieuwe compositorische middelen. Rem Koolhaas/Office for Metropolitan Architecture* (Rotterdam: 010 Publishers, 1989)
------, 'Concept and Type', in: T.M. de Jong and D.J.M. van der Voordt (eds.), *Ways to Study and Research Urban Architectural and Technical Design* (Delft: Delft University Press, 2002)
------, *Frame and Generic Space: A Study into the Changeable Dwelling Proceeding from the Permanent* (Rotterdam: 010 Publishers, 2006)
------, 'Polyvalence, a concept for the sustainable dwelling', *Nordsk architekturforskning*, no. 3 (2006)
------, 'The Massena Quarter', *Time-based Architecture International* (June 2009)
Leupen, Bernard, et al., *Design and Analysis* (Rotterdam: 010 Publishers, 1997)
------, *Time-Based Architecture* (Rotterdam: 010 Publishers, 2005)
Leupen, Bernard, Wouter Deen and Christoph Grafe (eds.), *Hoe modern is de Nederlandse architectuur* (Rotterdam: 010 Publishers, 1990)
Ligtelijn, Vincent and Francis Strauven (eds.), *Aldo van Eyck: Collected Articles and Other Writings 1947–1998* (Amsterdam: SUN, 2008)
Linnaeus, Carl, *Classes Plantarum* (Leiden: 1739)
Loos, Adolf, 'Architecture' (1910), quoted in: R. Schezen, K. Frampton and J. Rosa, *Adolf Loos: Architecture 1903–1932* (New York: Monacelli Press, 1996)
------, 'The Priciple of Cladding', in: *Spoken into the Void: Collected Essays 1897–1900* (Cambridge, MA: Opposition Books, MIT Press, 1982), 66–69
Lootsma, Bart, *Cees Dam* (Rotterdam: 010 Publishers, 1989)
Lüchinger, Arnulf (ed.), *Herman Hertzberger. Buildings and Projects, 1959–1986* (The Hague: Arch-Edition, 1987)
Lynch, Kevin, *City Sense and City Design*, in: *The Writings and Projects of Kevin Lynch* (Cambridge, MA: MIT Press, 1990)
------, *The Image of the City* (Cambridge, MA: MIT Press, 1960)

Maas, Winy, Jacob van Rijs, and Richard Koek (eds.), *FARMAX. Excursions on Density* (Rotterdam: 010 Publishers, 1998)
Maretto, Paola, *La casa Veneziana nella storia della città* (Venice: Marsilio, 1986)

Margolis, Ivan, 'Villa Muller', *The Architectural Review* (November 2000)
Mateo, Jose Luis, *Herzog & de Meuron* (Barcelona: Gustavo Gili, 1989)
Menin, Sarah and Flora Samuel, *Nature and Space: Aalto and Le Corbusier* (London: Routledge, 2002)
Menzel, Peter, Charles C. Mann, and Paul Kennedy, *Material World. A Global Family Portrait* (San Francisco: Sierra Club Books, 1994)
Michel, Han, 'Moderne Beweging in de Dapperbuurt', in: R. Brouwers (ed.), *Architecture in the Netherlands Yearbook 88/89* (Rotterdam: NAi Publishers, 1989)
Miranda, A., 'Manuel de las Casas, Viviendas protección oficial en Alcobendas', *Tectonica* (1997), 22–31
Molema, Jan, *ir. J. Duiker*, Serie Architectuur, no. 4 (Rotterdam: 010 Publishers, 1989)
Mozas, Javier, and Aurora Fernandez Per, *Density. New Collective Housing* (Madrid: a+t ediciones, 2004)
------, *Dbook: Density, Data, Diagrams, Dwellings* (Madrid: a+t ediciones, 2007)
Müller, Werner and Gunther Vogel, *Sesam Atlas van de Bouwkunst* (Baarn: Bosch & Keuning, 1976)

Nakamura, Toshio, 'Renzo Piano Building Workshop 1964–1988', *A+U* (March 1989), 104–113
Netherlands Ministry of Housing and Spatial Planning, *Voorschriften en wenken voor het ontwerpen van woningen* (The Hague: 1965)
Neufert, Ernst and Peter Neufert, *Architects' Data [Bauentwurfslehre]*, third English-language edition (Ames, Iowa: Blackwell Publishing Professional, 2002)
Neumeyer, Fritz, 'Tektonik: Das Schauspiel der Objectivität und die Wahrheit der Architekturschauspiels', in: H. Kollhoff (ed.), *Über Tektonik in der Baukunst* (Braunschweig: Vieweg, 1993)
Neutelings, Jan Neutelings and Michiel Riedijk, *At Work, Neutelings Riedijk architecten* (Rotterdam: 010 Publishers, 2005)
Nieuwenhuizen, J. and Maarten M.J. Vissers, et al., *Jellema Hogere Bouwkunde. Deel 8: Woningbouw* (Delft: Waltman/Thieme Meulenhoff, 2000)
Nishihara, Kiyoyuki, *Japanese Houses: Patterns for Living* (Tokyo: Japan Publications, 1968)
Norberg-Schulz, Christian, *Genius Loci: Towards a Phenomenology of Architecture* (New York: Rizzoli, 1979)

Oliver, Paul, *Dwellings. The Vernacular House World-wide* (London: Phaidon Press, 2003)

Pallasmaa, Juhani, *The Eyes of the Skin* (London: Academy Editions, 1996)
Pallasmaa, Juhani (ed.), *Alvar Aalto, Architect. Vol. 6: The Aalto House 1935–36* (Helsinki: Alvar Aalto Academy, 2003)
Palmboom, Frits, *Doel en vermaak in het konstruktivisme. 8 projekten voor woning- en stedebouw–OSA–Sovjetunie 1926–1930* (Nijmegen: SUN, 1979)
Panerai, Philippe, 'Typologieën: een middel tot inzicht in de logica van ruimtelijke patronen', *Wonen-TA/BK*, no. 2 (1981), 7–21
Patijn, W., et al., *Prijsvraag Jongerenhuisvesting Kruisplein* (Rotterdam: DROS Volkshuisvesting, 1982)
Pevsner, Nikolaus, *A History of Building Types* (Princeton: Princeton University Press, 1976)
The Physical Planning Department - City of Amsterdam, *Oostelijk Havengebied Amsterdam* (Rotterdam: NAi Publishers, 2003)
The Physical Planning Department - City of Amsterdam, et al., *Stedenbouwkundig plan Haveneiland en Rieteilanden-West* (Amsterdam: The Physical Planning Department - City of Amsterdam, 2000)
Pommer, Richard and Christian F. Otto, *Weissenhoff 1927 and the Modern Movement in Architecture* (Chicago: University of Chicago Press, 1991)
Pouw, L., 'Voorwoord', in: *Victorieplein, niet aangepast inpassen* (Amsterdam: Woningbedrijf Amsterdam, 1990)

Quatremère de Quincy, Antoine Chrysostome, 'Type' (1825), in: K. Michael Hays (ed.), *The Oppositions Reader: Selected Readings from A Journal for Ideas and Criticism in Architecture 1973–1984* (Cambridge, MA, and London: MIT Press, 1998), 617–620
------, *De l'Architecture Égyptienne, considérée dans son origine, ses principes et son goût, et comparée sous les mêmes rapports à l'Architecture Grecque* (Paris: 1785)
Quatremère de Quincy, Antoine Chrysostome, *Encyclopédie méthodique: Architecture*, Vol. III (Paris: 1788)

Riegler, F., 'Is architecture no longer any use?', symposium on Time-Based Buildings (Delft: 2004)

Rietveld, Gerrit, 'Een nieuwe volkswoning', *de 8 en Opbouw*, no. 9 (1941), 122–127
Rijk, Timo de, *Het elektrische huis* (Rotterdam: 010 Publishers, 1998)
Risselada, Max (ed.), *Raumplan versus Plan Libre* (New York: Rizzoli, 1987)
Rowe, Colin, and Fred Koetter, *Collage City* (Cambridge, MA: MIT Press, 1984)
Rybczynski, Witold, *Home: A Short History of an Idea* (London: Penguin Books, 1986)

Schneider, Friederike (ed.), *Floor Plan Atlas: Housing* (Basel: Birkhäuser, 1994)
Sherwood, Roger, *Modern Housing Prototypes* (Cambridge, MA: Harvard University Press, 1978)
Sijmons, Dirk, *Landkaartmos en andere beschouwingen over landschap* (Rotterdam: 010 Publishers, 2002)
Smeets, Huub, et al., *La Fenêtre Den Haag* (Maastricht: Vesteda architectuur, 2007)
Smithson, Alison and Peter Smithson, 'Criteria for Mass Housing', *Architectural Design* (September 1967)
Spies, Paul and Koen Kleijn, et al. (eds.), *The Canals of Amsterdam* [*Het Grachtenboek*] transl. by Alan Miller (The Hague: SDU, 1991)
Stam, Mart, 'Scale–Right Scale–Minimum Scale' ['Das Mass, das richtige Mass, das Minimum-Mass'], transl. by C. van Amerongen, in: *Mart Stam: A Documentation of His Work, 1920–1965* (London: Royal Institute of British Architects, 1970)
------, 'M-Art' ['M-Kunst'], transl. by **C. van Amerongen**, in: *Mart Stam: A Documentation of His Work, 1920–1965* (London: Royal Institute of British Architects, 1970)
Sting, Hellmuth, *Grundriss Wohnungsbau* (Stuttgart: Verlagsanstalt Alexander Koch, 1975)

Terwen, Johannes Leonardus, *Het koningrijk der Nederlanden–voorgesteld in eene reeks van naar de natuur geteekende schilderachtige gezigten, en beschreven door J.L. Terwen* (Gouda: 1858; reprint: [Groningen: Foresta BV, 1979])
Tijen, Willem van, 'Hoogbouw aan de Kralingsche Plas Rotterdam', *de 8 en Opbouw*, no. 11 (1938), 101
------, 'Woningbouw 1948–1953', *Forum*, no. 8 (1954), 305–340
------, 'Het onderzoek naar de ruimtebehoeften in en om de gezinswoning', in: *De ruimtebehoeften in en om de Nederlandse volkswoning* (thesis proposal) (Zandvoort: 1966)

Ungers, O.M., H.F. Kollhoff and A.A. Ovaska, 'The Urban Villa–A Multi-Family Dwelling Type', *Cornell Summer Academy 77*, Berlin series (Cologne: Studio Press for Architecture, 1977)
Ursprung, Philip (ed.), *Herzog & de Meuron, Natural History* (Montreal: Canadian centre for architecture/Lars Müller Publishers, 2005)

Venturi, Robert, and Denise Scott Brown, *Learning from Las Vegas* (Cambridge, MA: MIT Press, 1977)
Vitruvius, *The Ten Books on Architecture*, transl. by Morris Hicky Morgan (Mineolo, New York: Dover Publications, 1960)
Vreeze, Noud de, *Woningbouw, inspiratie & ambities* (Almere: Nationale woningraad, 1993)
Vriend, J.J., *Bouwen deel 1* (Amsterdam: Kosmos, 1961)
Vroom, P. de, 'Australië-Boston Amsterdam', *TBA International*, no. 2 (2008)

Wal, L. van der, et al., *Beter wonen 1913–1938. Gedenkboek* (Amsterdam: Arbeiderspers, 1938)
Weitz, Ewald and Jürgen Friedenberg (eds.), *Interbau Berlin 1957* (Berlin: Internationale Bauausstellung, 1957)
Wilms Floet, Willemijn (ed.), *Het ontwerp van het kleine woonhuis. Een plandocumentatie* (Amsterdam: SUN, 2005)
Wortmann, Arthur, 'De zegeningen van de woningdifferentiatie. Drie projecten van Neutelings Riedijk architecten', *Archis*, no.8 (1997), 8–17

Zantkuijl, H.J., *Bouwen in Amsterdam. Het woonhuis in de stad* (Amsterdam: Architectura & Natura, 1993)
Zwol, Jasper van, *Het ontwerp van het woongebouw. Plannenmap* (Delft: Publicatiebureau Bouwkunde, 1993)
------, *Het woongebouw* (Amsterdam: SUN, 2009)

XS²N and One Architecture, *Le Medi, het beste van twee werelden*, Le Medi workshop results (Amsterdam: 2002)

Publications on Dwelling Typology

Countless books have been published on dwelling typology. Most provide a historical introduction on the evolution of mass housing, guiding the reader along a series of its milestones. This is followed by a more or less dated collection of projects, selected by the authors. Some publications include detailed figures (number of dwellings, housing density, etc.) for each project. These publications do not usually rise above the level of a collection of plans as examples. In their composition these books are reminiscent of old architecture treatises. Any typological classification is absent from these examples of housing plans, however, or else it lies in the selection of the plans as a whole, as evidenced by titles like '*Wohnhochhäuser*', 'Row Houses', 'Cluster Houses' and 'Apartments'.
Beyond this, two groups of publications on dwelling typology merit closer attention: publications based on Italian and French research into typology and urban morphology and German and American publications that aim to provide an overview of dwelling typology in an encyclopaedic fashion.
The former category consists of concrete analyses of residential buildings in conjunction with the urban tissue. In these analyses, the emphasis is on the development of the city in relation to the types used, but there is no attempt to construct a comprehensive dwelling typology. In these typological analyses the focus is instead on the way types are applied in a concrete situation. Multiple analytical drawings show how a particular section of the city has been composed of residential edifices and how the types applied were transformed and deformed. The examples in these analyses are always specific, but the method has a general applicability. This method is primarily crucial for the analysis of existing projects and locations (see also Chapter 7, 'Context'). One of the finest publications in this vein is *La casa Veneziana nella storia della città*. This book, naturally, is a product of the Venetian school.[1]

1
Paola Maretto, *La casa Veneziana nella storia della città* (Venice: Marsilio, 1986). A fine Dutch example in this genre is Susanne Komossa et al.,*Atlas of the Dutch Urban Block* (Bussum: Thoth, 2005).

Grundriss Wohnungsbau (1975)

In contrast to the publications just discussed, the emphasis in Hellmuth Sting's *Grundriss Wohnungsbau (Housing Floor Plan)* is much more on the construction of a classification system. Sting opens with a general introduction in which he sets out his method and goes on to provide examples of residential buildings. These examples are divided into categories with great precision and detail. He employs a categorization based on dwelling access. According to Sting, access to the dwelling is the linchpin of stacked housing. Dwelling access has an impact on the dwelling floor plan on the one hand and on the stacking and linking of the dwellings on the other.
Sting attempts to construct a conclusive and universal system that can accommodate any conceivable property. The complexity and

versatility of today's housing production would seem to doom such an approach to failure. While Category 1.1 is still clearly expounded in Sting's typology, he is compelled to resort to stranger and stranger concepts in order to group all sorts of divergent dwelling floor plans into one category. Sting tries to compile a 'flora à la Linnaeus' for residential buildings. It just so happens that, unlike living nature, buildings – and therefore dwellings – do not reproduce. There are no genetic lines progressing according to Mendel's laws. New buildings and dwellings are 'born' almost every day, but new residential buildings are created through the intervention of the deliberate actions of an architect.
Designers interpret experiences and existing types according to their views on architecture and housing and adapt existing types according their interpretations of the programme and the situation. Precisely because new kinds of buildings and dwellings are added to the existing repertoire every day, a classification of buildings can never be exhaustive: it has to be an adaptable system capable of continually absorbing new and unforeseen properties. [→ 01]

Modern Housing Prototypes (1978)

In the introduction to his beautifully illustrated *Modern Housing Prototypes*, Roger Sherwood sets out what he sees as the purpose of dwelling typology. Alluding to the debate waged by Alan Colquhoun with the first generation of computer-aided-design architects, Sherwood affirms the necessity of a typology for design: 'Various writers have suggested that it is never possible to state all the dimensions of a problem, that "truly quantifiable criteria always leave choices for the designer to make." In the absence of clear design determinants, and to avoid purely intuitive guessing, it has been argued that analogous reference might give design insight . . . that during the period when many of the variables are unknown, a "typology of forms" might be used as a simulative technique to clarify the problem'.[2]

2
Roger Sherwood, *Modern Housing Prototypes* (Cambridge, MA: Harvard University Press, 1978), p. 1.

Sherwood's introduction also includes a framework for a typology of dwelling. He relies to a significant degree on Sting's categories, but applies them more loosely, sometimes even carelessly.
Sherwood proposes a typology based on the placement of a dwelling within the block ('single-orientation unit' and 'double-orientation unit') and a typology based on dwelling access. The second part of the book contains a series of international projects for which Sherwood employs a typology based on characteristics at the level of the urban ensemble (from 'detached and semi-detached housing' to 'towers'). In contrast with Sting, Sherwood draws clear divisions among typological levels, summarized as follows:

Level 1: Unit Types
—Single-orientation unit
—Double-orientation unit
—Double-orientation unit, open-ended

Level 2: Building Types: The Private Access
—Corridor buildings
—Single-loaded corridor system
—Double-loaded corridor systems
—Double-loaded split-level systems

Level 3: Detached and semi-detached housing (described using a number of 'prototypes')
—Row housing
—Party-wall housing
—Block housing
—Slabs
—Towers

The appeal of this book lies in its presentation of the prototype projects. In addition to photographs and floor plans, every project features beautiful axonometrics showing the structure of the building in relation to the dwelling and the access.

Grundrissatlas/Floor Plan Atlas (1994)
A more recent publication of significance is Friederike Schneider's *Grundrissatlas/Floor Plan Atlas*. The book opens with an introduction by Hellmuth Sting in which the typology used by both authors is explained, followed by an extensive section featuring plans as examples. These plans are arranged in three categories according to the stacking and organization of the dwellings.
—Multi-storey housing
—Single-family housing
—High-density, low-rise

Each category is subdivided according to position in the configuration of the urban design. For 'multi-storey housing' this is as follows:
—Block-defining structures
—Urban infill
—Corner buildings
—Firewall buildings
—Urban villas
—Freestanding structures
—Residential towers
—Terrace houses
—Space-enclosing structures

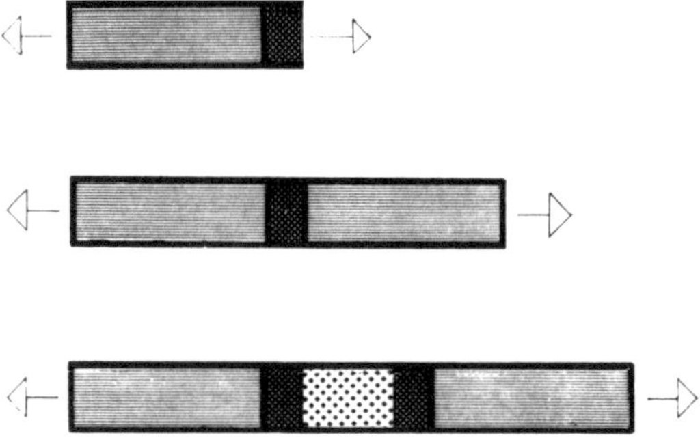

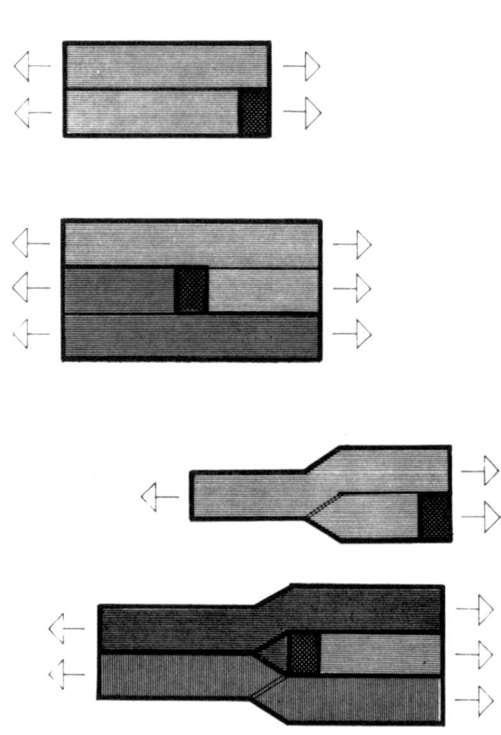

The projects are extensively documented, often with drawings produced especially for the book. The projects are all essentially represented on the same scale, which simplifies comparison. A nice detail is the ruler included to measure the plans. The latest edition features a sizable reference sheet listing all the typological characteristics of the plans. This makes the book a useful tool during the design process.

Het woongebouw (2009)

In *Het woongebouw (The Residential Building)*, J. van Zwol presents over 70 residential edifices. Classics like Johannes Duiker's Nirwana Building as well as more recent plans are discussed. Classic examples often serve as sources for new developments. They are transformed and referenced. The plans are classified according to block form and cross section. There is a group of plans featuring a complex cross section, for instance, and towers, perforated blocks and ensembles are discussed. In each chapter, plans from different periods are set side by side, revealing the connections between the old and new plans. Sometimes new plans are painstaking adaptations of never-built projects of the past, like the perforated blocks with stacked exterior spaces, as in MVRDV's Mirador residential building (2005) in Madrid-Sanchinarro, which can be seen as the realization of Le Corbusier's *lotissement à alvéoles* ('honeycomb housing', 1925). Another example of transformation is Denys Lasdun's project for clustered towers in Bethnal Green (1955) and Mecanoo's towers in Stuttgart (1993). The grouping of the plans, distributed across eight chapters differentiated by the form of the block and a group with complex cross sections, is as follows:

— Perimeter blocks
— Slabs and walls
— Towers
— Perforated blocks
— Ensembles
— Stepped blocks
— Groundscrapers and 'mat' plans
— Classic and recent designs
— Urban villas
— Blocks with a complex cross section

The book uses icons for the block form and for the access type, such as access staircase or gallery access. All the plans are listed in a matrix at the back of the book, displaying a number of aspects. The icons representing the block form, the grouping method and access were developed in conjunction with *Housing Design* and *Dwellingbase*, the housing project database.

Dwellingbase (2008)
The Chair of Architecture and Dwelling programme of the Faculty of Architecture at Delft University of Technology has developed a digital database for housing projects. *Dwellingbase* collects recent and less recent international residential buildings and makes them easily accessible via a specially designed website. In addition to high-quality drawings of floor plans, cross sections and elevations, photographs and schematics, the database contains details on locations, architects, building and individual dwelling dimensions, typological characteristics and materials used in structures and façades.
A smart search engine enables the user to navigate the projects using multiple pathways. A particular building, for instance, can be found using the name of the architect, the location or the project, while a search for a specific typology or dwelling size generates a selection of projects matching the search criteria. The systematization of the database follows the same distribution of typological levels and categories as used in this book.

DWELLING
01 Oliver 2003, p. 21
02 Oliver 2003, p. 56
03 Oliver 2003, p. 56
04 Oliver 2003, p. 62
05 Oliver 2003, p. 73
06 Oliver 2003, p. 73
07 J.J. Luna. The Prado, London 2002, p. 182
08 Heynen 2005, p. 200
09 Heynen 2005, p. 130
10 Heynen 2005, p. 130
11 Leupen 2002, p. 76

TYPOLOGY
01 C. Linnaeus
02 Holl 1982, p. 11
03 OMA
06 Pevsner 1976, p. 87
07 photo: B. Leupen
09 Pevsner 1976, p. 75
10a Zantkuijl 1993, p. 706
10b Zantkuijl 1993, p. 726
11 Maretto 1986, p. 23
12a photo: B. Leupen
12b Lüchinger 1987, p. 260
13a photo: B. Leupen
13b Wortmann 1997
13c–e Wortmann 1997
14a Boesiger 1964, p. 23
14b photo: B.Leupen
15a-b Dok architects
15c Leupen 2002, p. 193
16 Sting 1975, p. 11–12

DWELLINGS
01 Smithson 1994
02 Nishihara 1968
03 Nishihara 1968
04 Benevolo 1991
05 Menzel 1994
06 Menzel 1994
07 Woonkeur 2007
08 Sherwood 1979
09 Vreeze 1993, p. 297
10 Das Neue Frankfurt 1926–1927
11 Das Neue Frankfurt 1926–1927
12 Priemus 1970, p. 17
13 Smithson 1967
14 Alexander 1997 p. 622–626
15 Ligtelijn 1999 p. 98
16 Ligtelijn 1999 p. 166
17 Heyning 1969
18 Lüchinger 1987 p. 84
19 Leupen 2002 p. 172
20 Leupen 2006
21 Back 1991
22 Michel 1989, p. 75
23 Leupen 2006
24 Leupen 2006
25 Leupen et al. 2005, p. 143
26 Leupen, 2006, p. 30
27 DKV Architects
28 DKV Architects
29 Shigeru Ban
31a, b Mozas 2007, p. 193
32a, b Mozas 2007, p. 181
33a photo: H. Mooij
33b Van Duin and Leupen 1982, p. 48
34a photo: H. Mooij
34b, c Leupen 1989, p. 96
35a–c Herzog & de Meuron Architects
36a, b Chermayeff 1963
37a, b Architectural Review 1934, nr. 2
38a, b Gemeentelijke Dienst Volkshuisvesting 1970, p. 26
39a, b El Croquis 1998, nr. 92
40a photo: H.Mooij
40b Kloos 2000
41a, b Mozas 2007
42a, b Mozas 2007
43a photo: B.Leupen
43b Van Tijen 1938
44a, b ADP Architects Amsterdam
45a Photografische Dienst Faculty Architecture, TU Delft
b Leupen 1989, p. 97
46a–c de Architekten Cie.
47 Leupen et al. 2005, p. 143
48 Weald & Downland Open Air Museum, Sussex (GB)
50 Van den Heuvel 2005, p. 325
51 Leupen 1993, p. 34
52a–c Leupen 2002, p. 191
53a, b Klaren 1994
53c photo: H. Mooij
54a, b Mozas 2007
55a photo: B. Leupen
55b Photografische Dienst Faculty Architecture, TU Delft
55c Gemeentelijke Dienst Volkshuisvesting 1970, p. 42
56a, c Leupen 2002, p. 192
b photo: H. Mooij
57a–c Weitz en Friedenberg 1957
58a photo: H.Mooij
58b Kloos 2000
59a–d Ontwerpgroep MYJ, The Hague
60a photo: H. Mooij
60b photo: B. Leupen
60c Boesiger 1953, p. 207
61a-d Persson Collection city archive Malmö
62a–c Van Zwol 1993
63a, b Rietveld 1941
64a, b Van den Broek en Bakema 1960
65a, b Dok Architecten
66a Mozas 2007
66b drawings: M.A.Sedighi and A. van Zweeden
66c PLOT
67a Villa Müller Museum, Prague
67b, c Risselada 1991
68a photo: J. Leupen
68b Wilms Floet 2005
69a, b Blundell Jones 1995
70a, b Pallasmaa 2003
71a–c Brouwers 1991
72a–e Pommer en Otto 1991
73a, b, d dRO Amsterdam 2003
73c photo: H. Mooij
74a, b Molema 1989
75a photo: S.Burggraaf
75b Gemeentelijke Dienst Volkshuisvesting 1970

RESIDENTIAL BUILDING
01a–d Mozas 2004
02a–d Grosfeld van der Velde architecten
03a–d Dick van Gameren Architects
04a, c Van Zwol 1993
04b photo: S. Kaal
05a photo: H. Kawano
05b–f Van Zwol 1993
06a photo: H. Mooij
06b Mozas 2004
07a–e Leupen 2002
08a Van Zwol 1993
08b Stedenbouwkundige Dienst Rotterdam
08c dRO Amsterdam
09a photo: B. Leupen
09b–f Christiaanse 2003
10a–c Van Zwol 1993
11a–c Mozas 2007, p. 18
12a–e Dick van Gameren Architects
13a–e Domus nr. 900, February 2007
14 Komossa 2002
15a, b photo: H. Mooij
15c Komossa 2002
16a Grinberg 1977, p. 32
16b Zantkuijl 1993, p. 690
17a Wal 1938, p. 94
17b Komossa 2002
18a, b Grinberg 1977
19a, c photo: H. Mooij
19b Van Zwol 1993
20a–d Leupen et.al. 2005
21a Photografische Dienst Faculty Architecture, TU Delft
21b photo: H. Mooij
21c, d Leupen 1989, p. 97
22 drawings: J. Zondag
23a, b dRO Amsterdam 2003
24a, b Benevolo 1991, p. 810
25a, b Grinberg 1977, p. 75–76
26a, b Grinberg 1977, p. 125
27 drawings: J. Zondag
28 drawings: J. Zondag
29a–c Palmboom 1979
30a, d, e Van Zwol 1993
30b photo: B. Leupen
30c drawings: M.A. Sedighi and A. van Zweeden
31a–d Van Zwol 1993
31e drawings: M.A. Sedighi and A. van Zweeden
32a Leupen 2002
32b, c, e Van Zwol 1993
32d drawings: M.A. Sedighi and A. van Zweeden
33 CA 1927, nr. 4/5
34 drawings: J. Zondag
35a photo: H. Mooij
35b drawings: M.A. Sedighi and A. van Zweeden
35c, d Van Zwol 1993
36a Sherwood 1978
36b–e Van Zwol 1993
36f drawings: M.A. Sedighi en A. van Zweeden
37a Mozas 2007
37b photo: B. Leupen
37c drawings: M.A. Sedighi en A. van Zweeden
38a–d drawings: M.A. Sedighi and A. van Zweeden
39a–c drawings: M.A. Sedighi and A. van Zweeden

URBAN ENSEMBLE
01 Noord-Hollands Archief
02 Bijlsma en Groenland 2006

03a-c Springer Collectie, Wageningen UR Library, special collections
04a,b VLUG & Partners
05a-b DS Landschaps-architecten
05c Gemeente Bloemendaal
06 photo: M. Klijmij
07a, b BAM Vastgoed
08a, b Bijlsma en Groenland 2006
08c,d Komossa 2011, p.22
08e Ibelings 1999
09 Abrahamse 2010
10a Dorte Mandrup Arkitekter
10b, c photo: Tom Avermaete/ Eva Storgaard
11a-c Van Zwol 2009
12a photo: H. Mooij
12b,c de Architekten Cie.
13a Das Neue Frankfurt
13b drawings: B. Leupen
14a Das Neue Frankfurt
14b photo: H. Mooij
14c Das Neue Frankfurt
16a, b Bijlsma en Groenland 2006
16c drawings: B. Leupen
17a-c Das Neue Frankfurt
18a,b Ibelings 1999
19 Van Zwol 1993
20a, b Mozas 2004
21a-c Van Zwol 1993
22 KCAP
23a Grinberg 1977, p.75
23b Grinberg 1977, p.2
24a-d Van Zwol 2009
25a-c Kuhnle 2009

TECTONICS
03 Ursprung 2005, p.218
04 Müller en Vogel 1976, p.38
05a photo: R. 't Hart
05b DKV Architects
06a Miranda 1997, p.29
06b Miranda 1997, p.23
07 Nieuwenhuizen et al., 2000, p.156
08 Dienst Ruimtelijke Ordening Amsterdam
09a photo: B. Leupen
09c R. Uytenhaak Architecten
10 de Architecten CIE.
11a Neutelings en Riedijk 2004, p.193
11c Neutelings en Riedijk 2004, p.192
15a-c Dini 1983, p.113, 105, 106
16a,b Priemus 1970
17 Zantkuijl 1993, p.204
18a Risselada 1987, p.109
18b Leupen et al. 1993, 2005, p.115
19 Boesiger 1964, p.23
20 Frampton 1995, p.122
21a photo: Y. Cuperus
21b Leupen et al. 2005, p.178
22a photo: B. Leupen
22b XDGA
23 Müller and Vogel 1976, p.58
26a photo: B. Leupen
26b Herbst 1955
27 a-d Rudy Uytenhaak Architecten
28a photo: B. Leupen
28b, c Mateo 1989, p.47
30 photo: H. Mooij
31a Wingårdh architechts
31b photo: B. Leupen
32a, b Vandkunsten
33a photo: B. Leupen
33b Mecanoo Architects
34a-c photo: B. Leupen
34d, e Herzog & de Meuron Architects
35a photo: R. 't Hart
35b DKV Architects
36 photo: B. Leupen
37 Vriend 1961, p.294
38 photo: B. Leupen
41a Dok Architects
41b photo: B. Leupen
41c Dok Architects
42a, b S333 Architecture +Urbanism
44a Fuksas 1994
44b photo: B. Leupen
45 photo: B. Leupen
46a photo: B. Leupen
46b MVRDV
47a photo: B. Leupen
47b Diener&Diener Spies et al.1991, p.130
51 photo: Photografische Dienst, Faculty Architecture, TU Delft
53 Van Tijen 1954
54 photo: B. Leupen
57 photo: R. Uytenhaak
58 Krausse 1999, p.207
59 Duroy 1987
60 photo: B. Leupen
61 Futagawa et al. 1988, p.119
62 Huber en Steinegger 1971 p.59
63 CPZED
64 Yves Lion
65 DKV
66 a-d L'Architettura, cronache e storia, 1965 #8 p.500, 507 and 512

CONTEXT
01 right: Leupen et al. 1993, 2005, p.157 left: Heeling et al. 2002
02 photo: S. Momen
03 photo: S. Momen
04 analysis drawing B. Leupen
05 photo B. Leupen
06 photo B. Leupen
07 photo B. Leupen
08 Geurtsen et al. 1982
09 Geurtsen et al. 1982
10 Heeling, Meyer and Westrik 2002, p.61
11 Geurtsen et al. 1982, p.87
13 Geurtsen en Bos 1981, p.48
14 Rowe and Koetter 1984, p.63
15 Rowe and Koetter 1984, p.62
16 Cullen 1961, 1973, p.17
17 Lynch 1960, p.33
19 Venturi and Scott Brown 1977, p.5
21 Maas, Rijs and Koek 1998, p.501
23a,b photo: B. Leupen
23c-e Cino Zucchi
24a S333 Architecture+ Urbanism
24b photo: J. Bitter
25 Lootsma 1989, p.101
26a photo: B. Leupen
26b, c Department of City Planning 2006, p.63
27 Mecanoo Architetcs
28a photo: B. Leupen
28b, c BIG Architects
d Københavns Kommunes Planorientering, Lokalplan nr. 309
29a DKV Architects
29b Pouw 1990, p.10-11
30a photo: B. Leupen
30b Dienst Ruimtelijke Ordening Amsterdam
30c Dick van Gameren Architects
31a OMA
31b photo: B. Leupen

THE DESIGN PROCESS
01 l'Architecture D'Aujoud'hui 1992, p 14
02 photo: B. Leupen
03 Jo Coenen
04 photo: B. Leupen
05a-c Kollhoff Berlin
06a DKV Architecten
06b Kollhoff Berlin
07 Kollhoff Berlin
08 Kollhoff Berlin
09 Kollhoff Berlin
10 Kollhoff Berlin
11a,b photo: B. Leupen
12 Kollhoff Berlin
13 photo: B. Leupen
14 photo: B. Leupen
15a Kollhoff Berlin
15b photo: B. Leupen
16 Christian de Portzamparc
17 Christian de Portzamparc
18 Badia Berger
19a-d Badia Berger
20 a,b Badia Berger
21 Badia Berger
22a,b Badia Berger
23 photo: B. Leupen
24 photo: B. Leupen
25 Badia Berger
26 Badia Berger
27 Geurst & Schulze
28 Geurst & Schulze
29 Geurst & Schulze
30 Geurst & Schulze
31 Geurst & Schulze
32 Geurst & Schulze
33 Geurst & Schulze
34 photo: Geurst & Schulze
35 Geurst & Schulze
36 Geurst & Schulze
37 Geurst & Schulze
38 www.lemedi.nl
39 Geurst & Schulze
40 Geurst & Schulze
41 Korteknie en Stuhlmacher
42 photo: B. Leupen
43 photo: B. Leupen
44 photo: B. Leupen

This book was made possible in part by the generous support of The Netherlands Architecture Fund, the Department of Architecture, Faculty of Architecture, Delft University of Technology and the Open Access Fund of the Delft University of Technology.

Authors: Bernard Leupen and Harald Mooij
With the cooperation of:
Birgit Jürgenhake, Robert Nottrot, Rudy Uytenhaak and John Zondag
Academic Reference: JIA Beisi, Sigrid Loch and Roger Sherwood
Drawings: Mohamad Ali Sedighi and Alexander van Zweeden

Copy editing: D'Laine Camp
Translation: Pierre Bouvier and Laura Vroomen
Design: Studio Joost Grootens (Joost Grootens, Annemarie van den Berg, Tine van Wel and Josh Finklea)
Lithography and Printing: Drukkerij Slinger, Alkmaar
Publisher: Marcel Witvoet, NAi Publishers

NAi Publishers is an internationally orientated publisher specialized in developing, producing and distributing books on architecture, visual arts and related disciplines.
www.naipublishers.nl

Available in North, South and Central America through Artbook | D.A.P., 155 Sixth Avenue 2nd Floor, New York, NY 10013-1507, tel +1 212 627 1999, fax +1 212 627 9484, dap@dapinc.com

Available in the United Kingdom and Ireland through Art Data, 12 Bell Industrial Estate, 50 Cunnington Street, London W4 5HB, tel +44 208 747 1061, fax +44 208 742 2319, orders@artdata.co.uk

Printed and bound in the Netherlands

ISBN 978-90-5662-826-0

Bernard Leupen was a professor with the Faculty of Architecture at the Delft University of Technology, Architecture Department, until 2008, and from 2006 to 2007 he was a visiting professor at the Royal Danish Academy of Fine Arts, Schools of Architecture, in Copenhagen. He is also the author of the book *IJ-plein, een speurtocht naar nieuwe compositorische middelen* ('IJ-plein: A Search for New Compositional Methods', with a summary in English, 1989) and *Frame and Generic Space* (2006), both published by 010 Publishers.
He was the organizer of the symposia 'Whether Europe' and 'How Modern is Dutch Architecture', and editor of the book *Hoe modern is de Nederlandse architectuur* ('How Modern is Dutch Architecture', 010 Publishers, 1990). In addition, he was the coordinating editor of the journal *Time-based Architecture International* from 2006 to 2010.

Harald Mooij is an architect in Amsterdam and serves as a professor and researcher in the Architecture Department, Chair of Housing Design, at the Faculty of Architecture of the Delft University of Technology. He is the co-editor of the publication series *DASH (Delft Architectural Studies on Housing)* and writes regularly for professional journals in the Netherlands and abroad.

Aalto 117

Aalto 134

Aalto 316

Aarons & Gelauff 103

AART a/s 94

Aillaud, Émile 232

Broek & Bakema, Van den 126

Broek & Bakema, Van den 198

Broek & Bakema, Van den 221

Bruijn, De 190

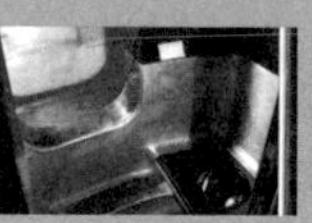
Buckminster Fuller 317

Casas, De las 248

DKV Architects 246

DKV Architects 292

DKV Architects 374

DKV Architects 327

Domus Architecter 114

Dongen, Van 102

Fink+Jocher 93

Fuksas 303

Gameren, Van 150

Gameren, Van 166

Gameren, Van 376

Gazeau 158

Herzog & de Meuron 280

Herzog & de Meuron 290

Ingwersen en De Geus 142

Juul & Frost 313

KBnG 119

KCAP 185

Le Corbusier 196

Le Corbusier 322

Lion & Leclercq 326

Loos 130

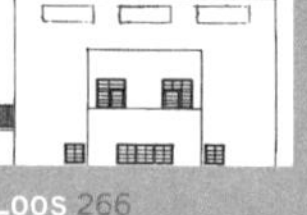
Loos 266

Loos 311

Mulleners & Mulleners 215

MVRDV en JJW arkitekter 104

MVRDV 164

MVRDV 231

MVRDV 306

Neutelings Riedijk Architects 174

OMA 378

Oud 136

Pesman 135

Piano 260

PLOT (BIG + JDS) 128, 372

PLOT (BIG + JDS) 200

Rietveld, J 100

Riewe, Riegler 109

Safdie 262

Scharoun 133

Sejima 101

ShoP Architects 368

Uytenhaak 252

Vandkunsten 288

Vlug & Partners 210

Weeber 95

Wiersema, Erik 106

Wingårdh 287